Actors In Action

How Our Favorite Action Stars
Became Their Characters

By Jason Norman

Actors in Action: How Our Favorite Action Stars Became Their Characters
© 2018. Jason Norman. All rights reserved.

All illustrations are copyright of their respective owners, and are also reproduced here in the spirit of publicity. Whilst we have made every effort to acknowledge specific credits whenever possible, we apologize for any omissions, and will undertake every effort to make any appropriate changes in future editions of this book if necessary.

No part of this book may be reproduced in any form or by any means, electronic, mechanical, digital, photocopying or recording, except for the inclusion in a review, without permission in writing from the publisher.

Published in the USA by:
BearManor Media
P O Box 71426
Albany, Georgia 31708
www.bearmanormedia.com

Printed in the United States of America

ISBN   978-1-62933-203-1 (paperback)

Book & cover design and layout by Darlene Swanson • www.van-garde.com

Praise for Jason Norman's previous works

Actors in Action...
"I really enjoy your writing how you so eloquently can change my ramblings into a wonderful piece of work. It was an honor to read your words."
~ Stephanie Finochio, *Jesse*, pro wrestling star Trinity

"You really can write, be factual, and entertain all at the same time."
~ Patrick Reynolds, *Mandroid*

"It is so beautifully written!! I will be honored to have your book on my bookshelf someday."
~ Christian Pitre, *Bounty Killer*

Before the Camera Rolled...
"You are thoughtful, keenly insightful, and clearly very studied in the world of film and TV. I applaud your work and highly recommend the book to fans and students of the art form."
~ longtime character actor Erick Avari

"I am humbled and in awe of your talent as a writer."
~ Mark Holton, *Pee Wee's Big Adventure* and *Teen Wolf*

Behind the Screams
"Thank you for including me in your book. What an honor! And a very accurate analysis as well."
~ Sarah Butler, *I Spit on Your Grave* series

"Thanks so much for reminding me of such a great experience I had. You are a wonderful writer."
~ Tonya Crowe, *Dark Night of the Scarecrow*

Welcome to our Nightmares
"As soon as I turned the first page, you hooked me with a fun read that re-introduced me to fabulous actors. Cover to cover, word for word, picture to picture, thank you for an awesome behind the scene adventure."
~ Dyanne Thorne, *Ilsa* films

"I love your writing! It is perfect!"
~ Lisa Wilcox, *Nightmare on Elm Street* films

Contents

Foreword vii
Introduction ix
Vitali Baganov: *The Sopranos* 1
Brigitte Bako: *Strange Days* 4
Macon Blair: *Blue Ruin* 10
Janus Blythe: *The Hills Have Eyes* 13
Tiffany Bolling: *Bonnie's Kids* 21
Kevin Breznahan: *Alive* 24
Natalie Burn: *Awaken* 28
Corina Calderon: *All She Can* 32
Delphine Chaneac: *Splice* 44
Alain Chanoine: *Suicide Squad* 47
Lana Clarkson 49
Frank Cullotta/Carl Ciarfalio: *Casino* 54
Brad Davis: *Midnight Express* 64
They Made *Death Wish* Come True 71
Larry Drake: *Darkman* films 81
Samantha Esteban: *Training Day* 84
Krisha Fairchild: *Krisha* 88
Chelsea Field: *Masters of the Universe* 94
Stephanie Finochio: *Jesse* 100
Dennis Franz, Gordon Clapp, Bill Brochtrup: *NYPD Blue* 106
Aaron Gaffey: *Dust Up* 115
Meet the *Gladiators* 118
Walton Goggins/Catherine Dent: *The Shield* 124
Carlena Gower: *Towering Inferno* 131
Lance Guest: *The Last Starfighter* 135
Megan Hayes: *Hunger Games: Catching Fire* 138
Dana Hee: *Mortal Kombat*/Stunts 150
Season Hubley: *Hardcore* 156
Sam Jones: *Flash Gordon* 161
Michelle Joyner: *Cliffhanger* 164
Anna Katarina: *Death of the Incredible Hulk/Blood of Heroes* 168
Andre Keuck: *Zero Day* 172

Richard Kiel 180
Martin Kove: *Karate Kid* 185
Jeroen Krabbe: *The Fugitive* 189
Hiep Thi Le: *Heaven & Earth* 193
Bruce Lee 198
Hudson Leick: *Xena: Warrior Princess*. 203
Blake Lindsley: *Starship Troopers* 206
Robert Maillet: *300/Sherlock Holmes* 212
Helena Mattsson: *Guns, Girls, and Gambling* 214
Alex McArthur: *Rampage* 217
Chris McGinn: *Kidnap* 220
Graham McGinnis: *Deepwater Horizon*. 224
Monnae Michaell, Brennan Elliott: *Flight 93* 227
Matthew Modine: *Full Metal Jacket* 231
Kent Moran: *The Challenger*. 254
Joel Murray: *God Bless America*. 258
Some *Natural* Women 263
Haing Ngor: *Killing Fields* 282
Long Nguyen/Linda Bright Clay: *Seven Psychopaths*. 293
Ólafur Darri Ólafsson: *The Deep*. 298
Josh Pais/Michelan Sisti/Francois Chau: *Teenage Mutant Ninja Turtles* 301
Bobbie Phillips: *Chameleon* films. 306
Lionel Pina: *Dog Day Afternoon*. 310
Christian Pitre: *Bounty Killer*. 313
Allene Quincy/Rebecca Marshall: *Raze* 319
Patrick Reynolds: *Eliminators*. 332
Eli Roth: *Inglorious Basterds* 336
Mickey Rourke: *The Wrestler*. 346
Jennie Russo: *She Kills* 353
Bob Sapp: *Elektra/Conan the Barbarian* 358
Scott Schutzman/Julie Cohen: *Once Upon a Time in America* 363
Arnold Schwarzenegger: *Terminator* films 369
Christopher Serrone: *Goodfellas* 377
Lauren Mae Shafer: *The Dark Below* 384
Aleisa Shirley: *Sweet 16* 387
Geno Silva: *Scarface* 391

They Who Played the Slimer! 395
Star Wars' Darth Vader(s) 399
The First Men of *Superman* 431
Jenni Tooley: *Arlington Road* 446
Marco Treviño: *The 33* 451
Raoul Trujillo: *Apocalypto* 454
Apollonia Vanova: *Watchmen* 460
Patricia Velasquez: *The Mummy* films 464
Paul Walker: *Fast and Furious/Hours* 467
John Wayne: *Sands of Iwo Jima/True Grit* 473
Sigourney Weaver: *Alien* films 483
Dreya Weber: *A Marine Story* 513
Epilogue 519
References 521
index 533

Years after he and the rest of the action/horror film fan world witnessed Camille Keaton's legendary work in 1978's *I Spit on Your Grave*, author Jason Norman was lucky enough to cheer Keaton on face to face at a Virginia Beach film convention in 2012.

Foreword . . .

I GET ASKED A lot of questions at conventions, and I just answer them the best way I know how. It's a lot of fun, meeting the people that come to the shows, being recognized for the movie that took so long to be released. I'm very complimented and very flattered.

In April 2012, I met Jason Norman at a convention in Virginia Beach. About two years later, he put me in his first book, *Welcome to our Nightmares*. Now I'm writing the foreword for his new one.

It's totally amazing. Who would have thought that when I was making *I Spit on Your Grave*, that it would be around for this long, and probably even long after I'm gone? It was a shocking film for a lot of people to see. People have a hard time with the first part, but the second part, when I get revenge, that was pretty cool. They're fine with second part—they can't wait to get to it.

In 2010, *I Spit on Your Grave* was remade, and I was happy with the way they filmed it. It was wonderful to see how Sarah Butler did the part of Jennifer Hills. It's a compliment that someone would want to remake it.

I Spit on Your Grave has been written about many times before, and Jason did a marvelous job of writing about it. Reading his words gave me a sense of pride; he was very true to everything I said. It was put out there in a way that was just so true to form. At the same time, he showed a lot of respect for the film.

I think readers will get a true insight to the films that he writes about, which is very important! His objectivity, and the way he writes, puts it out there in a way that's enjoyable to read. I've seen a lot of things written about the movies and myself. I've taken some flak (not very much, though!), and Jason's appreciation of the movies comes through. I highly recommend this to people who want to get more insight in the movies.

I want to tell all of his fans that he's a majorly good writer, and to read his books! I'm proud that he asked me to write the foreword for his book.

—**Camille Keaton**, star of 1978's *I Spit on Your Grave*

Introduction . . .

SOME SAY THAT ACTION films are a fine way to let off aggression; sitting there, watching someone else kick the hell out of a bunch of bad guys, and probably imagining ourselves doing it to our own personal "villains" can be a very healthy way to burn the stress right off.

Inspirational? Not a word typically associated with the genre, but these flicks usually have the goodies winning over odds that are greater than the lottery—and if they always escape and usually save some people in the process, then just maybe our hopes and dreams will come true. And maybe in the course thereof, we might just be the hero who goes up against insurmountable and potentially fatal odds, odds that have stopped so many and made others too afraid to even try . . . and win! Defeat those that specialize in antagonism, whose sole purpose of existence was to shut down all the good people! We've paved the way for justice, and screw any tempering of mercy! We probably even saved a few damsels (or dams—ever wonder what the male form of that word would be?) in distress, and now their hearts belong to us forever!

OK, so there's the appeal to those in the seats. What about the ones looking to do the entertaining? What have others done so well in this genre, and how can we learn from them? As a performer, there's the challenge aspect: up against special effects and scripts pounded with one-liners, it might be tough to stand out, to put a human spin on such a piece (the *Terminator* films—well, at least the first two—were strong examples of how this can work if done right).

Whatever the reason, it's an important part of American viewership. So let's meet some who have emerged past the explosions, beyond the gunfire, ahead of the death and everything else to stand out in action moviemaking. Let's learn more from them, what they went through, and how hard they worked for us. We loved watching them. Let's read about them.

And you never know: maybe something else will come out of this as well. Perhaps reading these stories, hearing so much about those who somehow found a way inside an area more jammed than a sardine can will get readers to search for their opening.

I don't have to tell you (although I will repeatedly here, and did in my other books!) that the odds for success are always well against an actor, even the experienced. But it can be done, and has been, by more and more people every year. I guarantee, you make it somewhere in the acting world and you'll look back at all the effort as absolutely worth it, regardless of what genre.

I hope you enjoy *Action*, and if reading's all you're here to do, that's fine. Read it, analyze it, argue about it, maybe use it in a research piece (with proper citation! The battle cry of the English instructor). Or if it gives you just a bit of enticement to go out and try it yourself, to follow those profiled below straight into the profession, hey . . . it's OK to be afraid. Many things have been accomplished out of fear, many wonderful things.

Like I said, action heroes tend to get the girl and vanquish the villain in the end. Proving the critics just as wrong can be equally satisfying.

Valery (Vitali Baganov) preps to haul into the snowy woods in the *Sopranos* Christmas season of 2001, and straight into TV mystery history.

Vitali Baganov: *The Sopranos*

As AVID TV VIEWERS, we're very well aware of what we'll never know. Like whether *Lost* was all a dream or who beat up Dr. Greene on *ER* or what the hell was up with those eggs we saw hatching in Buffy Summers' high school at the end of her first year of vampire slaughter.

Missing people? There's enough from TV history to fill a season of *Unsolved Mysteries*. Perhaps there's a lost island somewhere in time and space, magically reaching out to abduct helpless victims of producers or audiences, those who just up and suddenly vanished from their respective shows. Somewhere out there, Judy Winslow from *Family Matters*, Mr. Turner of *Boy Meets World*, *Grey's Anatomy* gal Erica Hahn, just about every supporting character who appeared on *Six Feet Under*, and others try to wonder where they are, and why.

Unless, of course, they happen to run afoul of another resident, a guy who's used to thriving in the worst of situations.

Oh yes—every time a *Sopranos* fan brings up the mystery of the Russian in the snowy woods, that's where someone always has to go.

"Oh, that Valery guy? Did they ever find out what happened to him?"

No, they didn't. We didn't. Even with six more years of the show to come, the fate of the mob man from Commieville was never revealed.

And it never will be. We'll never know. So let's not worry about it anymore. Let's learn something new about Valery.

Not about the character, the one that had killed many back at wartime in Russia, the one who managed to survive a beatdown from Chris Moltisanti and Paulie Walnuts and a later bullet in the head, only to get up and keep running.

How about Vitali Baganov, the man who acted out what no one knew would end up one of the most controversially unanswered questions in TV history?

Baganov's past wasn't too far from Valery's, minus the murder and war, of course.

"I couldn't breathe over there anymore," recalls the Leningrad native. "Nobody in the USSR believed in Communism, but pretended that they believed. Whatever I predicted, many things happened that I am not happy about." After acting on screens and stages across his Motherland (and teaching others to do so), Baganov crossed the Pacific just as the USSR collapsed on Christmas 1991.

"I just realized I had to switch my life," he says. "I didn't think I'd make it over there, and I didn't want to wind up in jail or a cemetery. The Soviets had a set of rules: you can't pay them, you can't ignore them. The people were living a double life."

He wouldn't show up on television until 2000, and that was as a bartender in an episode of *Law and Order: SVU*. The next year, however, came something special.

"I was playing my accordion in a cafe," he says. "I was singing, mostly in Russian, and then I switched to English. A guy walking through was a Russian director. We had a bottle of beer, and we talked. He told me that if I jumped into the business without the language, I'd get kicked out."

The fellow introduced him to a manager, who discussed a show that had blasted through HBO's ratings for the past year. Baganov hadn't seen it, but over the next few years, such a mindset would be considered unthinkable.

"My manager told me to go audition for *The Sopranos*," he says. "The character was for someone twenty-one or twenty-two years old. I was forty-seven, so I wasn't interested. But I went to the audition, and [series creator] David Chase decided it would be me."

Christmas came early for the Soprano family in 2001, the family celebrating in the "To Save Us All From Satan's Power" episode in April (the title comes from the legendary carol "God Rest Ye Merry Gentlemen"). Haunted by memories of his killing of former pal Big Pussy, patriarch Tony tries to focus on his family's upcoming holidays.

Here's where we meet Valery the man, enjoying his newfound American lifestyle with all the conveniences. But he's also got a nose powder issue, and owes some green to Tony's solider Silvio Dante.

"To me, it's about the product," Baganov says. "It was hard to switch the language. Key number one is that if you're capable of doing that, you have a chance. If you can make the illusion, they'll use you."

The next week, "Pine Barrens" became both the episode title and setting. Visiting Valery for a payment, a brawl erupts (didn't see that coming, right?) between him and the henchmen, who think they've come out on top after crushing his throat with a lamp.

Arriving at the Barrens, they find they were wrong. Valery's forced to dig his own grave, but instead whacks them with a shovel and hauls ass. Paulie shoots him in the noggin, but he gets right up and runs. Soon they're lost in the woods, their vehicle gone (did he steal it? That's a popular theory), and Tony has to go out and get them.

"I did what I would do under the circumstances," Baganov says. "About 99.9 percent of movie roles, each person could play. Whatever comes out, it comes out."

Everyone thought that Valery would return, even during the last two weeks of the third season. But he never did. We never found out whether he made his way back to New York, hopped on a plane to Russia, got eaten by a grizzly bear, whatever.

Maybe Valery was hiding in the restaurant, ready to spring on Tony mere seconds after the series finale cut away that mysterious day in June 2007. Perhaps he'd have shown up in the film version of the series that will never be made, the world robbed of it with James Gandolfini's tragic passing in the summer of 2013.

No one can say. Not Chase, nor the rest of the show's creators or writers. Not Steve Buscemi, who directed the episode.

And not even Baganov himself.

"It's a special chapter," he admits. "There was super secrecy on the set. I just don't know."

A desperate Iris (Brigitte Bako) tries to convince Lenny Nero (Ralph Fiennes) that they're both in the worst kind of trouble in 1995's *Strange Days*.

Brigitte Bako: *Strange Days*

IN ACTING, AS WITH many other professions, sometimes all the hardest work in the world doesn't get the payoff or the credit it deserves. Sometimes—far too often, actually—the crew, the cast, everyone unites, busts their tails, does everything they can and sometimes even more than that, and then . . . not enough, if anything at all. Things can go all kinds of ways in the performing profession—sometimes people will throw together something just to get it done, only to see it become a box-office smash, while other films will come in with everything a blockbuster should need, and audiences hardly glance at it. A flick can be made with all kinds of ammunition (big stars, big budget, strong plot) and full-blown teamwork from all behind the scenes and . . . nothing.

That's how things went with *Strange Days*. The investors that poured millions into it, the big-name stars (three of whom had scored Oscar nominations in the preceding few years) that signed onto it, the writers who put together a strong script with some great ideas, all had every reason to believe they had a smash at the ready. But film audiences, always the most unpredictable group outside of election voters or trial jurors, simply didn't visit the 1995 flick.

Even still, there's always something to take away. Something to remember. Something to learn, and carry on from the experience all the way into the future. Whether it's acting techniques, preparation methods, new career choices, every film can be an instructional capability for those involved, even if it's learning what *not* to do.

It's what one of the too-little-seen starlets of the too-little-seen story got during the *Strange* times, and why it helped her move in a direction she hardly expected, even decades later.

"I was bludgeoned and raped and killed in about forty movies," Brigitte Bako recalls, "and I went, fuck this, I want to be in a comedy. Everyone thought it was funny, because I was a dramatic actress, and I wanted to make my own comedy. The inception of starting to write happened about ten years before I actually sat down to write."

That would have been right around the time she did *Days*—and by that point, Bako had already seen some of the toughest parts of acting, her big entrance into entertainment in the pilot of the erotic *Red Shoe Diaries*.

About a year before, Bako had nearly snared the lead in the even-more-sensual *Wild Orchid* (1989). Zalman King, behind both its script and camera, had wanted to see her again.

"He said he was sorry it hadn't worked out, but he'd hire me again," Bako remembers. "People say that all the time in Hollywood, but it doesn't really happen. But he is one of the few people in Hollywood that kept his word." In the kickoff for King's small-screen creation, one of TV's most controversial shows (at the time—seems pretty tame compared to what's out there today), she played Alex, the wild jezebel ex of David Duchovny's Jake, a lady who ends up dead by her own hand, frustrated by her life's neverending instability.

"My saving grace was that David Duchovny was one of the nicest and most supportive guys," recalls Bako, who reunited with the *X-Files* star on a 2007 episode of his HBO show *Californication*. "We are friends to this day. But it was not easy. I was in tears most of the time. Then I got typecast, and everybody wanted to see me naked on page three. If you're pretty and sexy in Hollywood, if the script makes sense or not, somehow you're naked on page three." Alex would be flashbacked to in several episodes of the series.

Soon enough, though, it was time for a film that most probably thought would yank in the audiences. After playing pure evil in *Schindler's List* just two years before, Ralph Fiennes would become main *Days* man Lenny Nero, a disgraced cop now making green on the black market, selling a device that's planted directly into the brain of users, allowing them to record past experiences to re-live (sensory details included) later on, both their own and of others. It's a device that many probably hoped *would* be invented by New Year's Eve 1999, the story's setting.

In tape viewing mode, the film spends quite a bit of time in the self-filmed practice that horror would beat into the ground in the early 2000s.

For her biggest big-screen role (to that point), Bako worked up to become Iris, a call girl that, in true Hollywood fashion, is quite a bit easier on the eyes that the real-life walkers of the streets (it is, after all, a movie).

"There was nudity and I was trying to get away from that," Bako admits, "but I felt [the nakedness] was important to the script . . . and I had a crush on Ralph Fiennes! He had just finished *Schindler's List*, and he was one of the main stars on the planet. I was *mad* for him. I just got laser focused. I knew this was my part."

There's no buildup to Bako's gal in the film. As soon as we see her, she's already in hysterical overdrive, being chased by two crazed cops (one is longtime character legend Vincent D'Onofrio, Pvt. Pyle from 1987's *Full Metal Jacket*) who clearly show this is not just business. They rip off her wig, charging through a subway at high speed, then try to shoot her in the back in public. Obviously, she knows much more than she should.

With Iris, Bako says, "I felt that I could really show my chops. She was complicated, messed up, and I've never played a drug person. I loved the script. The icing on the cake was back in my 20s, I used to pick movies based on where they were shooting—this girl loves to travel the world!—and who are my co-stars?" Fiennes' Nero can't keep his ex Faith (Juliette Lewis) out of his heart and head, not realizing that his gorgeous gal pal Mace (Angela Bassett, ten times more intimidating than she'd made Tina Turner in 1993 for *What's Love Got to do With it?*) wouldn't mind moving from platonic to romantic.

The escaped Iris frantically calls Lenny, but he's nanoseconds late to pick up the phone. Then the nation learns that a famous rapper and bodyguard have been executed, and we start to catch on. Just a few years after the Rodney King incident whipped Los Angeles into chaos, *Strange Days* was being filmed in the City of Angels during the O.J. Simpson trial.

"It was a very surreal summer," Bako recalls. "We did five months of night shoots for a movie that takes place over the course of two nights! Shooting all night, it was nuts. I was upside down for five months. We were working nights and sleeping days, and you can get a little crazy when you change your clock like that and stay on that all summer because you never knew when you were shooting. It was in and out, in and out."

Still, that hadn't been as hard as what she'd done before shooting even started. Iris might have been lovelier than call girls come, but Bako still had to show the effects of Iris' powder-snorting practice.

"I had to get *really* emaciated," she says. "I worked with a personal trainer. I had to run six miles a day and get into this really crazy, sinewy shape. I had to get really healthy to look like a drug addict!"

A different type of training gave her an even closer look—Bako visited several Alcoholics/Narcotics Anonymous meetings to hear real-life tales of the danger of addiction.

"I can remember sitting with drug addicts, sitting with people who were detoxing, seeing what that looked like, what that energy was like," she says. "I saw people who were three days, ten days off drugs, and what that was like. I was living in (Iris') shoes for months. I am not a drug person or a drinker, the total opposite of Iris. I visited the seedier side of our society to pick up on that angst that people have."

She also wrote her way into Iris' mentality.

"I was writing a journal for my character," Bako says. "How did she get there? What brought her there? She's got to be a three-dimensional person, and I tried to get into her head for months. I had changed everything: my eating habits, everything."

Iris drops her recording in Lenny's car, but it's towed before he can see it. Eventually, another tape arrives from seemingly nowhere, and Lenny relaxes in the back of Mace's car, perhaps expecting to see some X-rated pleasure romps.

He's wrong. It's someone stalking Iris outside a motel room. The voyeur makes his way indoors, and straps the shocked woman down. Her desperate pleas unheard, he violates her again and again, then strangles her into the afterlife, her wide-open eyes left with nothing to see.

"I wanted to retire after that," Bako says. "I didn't enjoy that anymore. It was hell. I felt exploited as an actor, I felt exploited as a character. My death scene took three days to shoot. In another movie, we would have shot that before lunch. People don't understand what you actually have to go through to play these things truthfully, and they're taxing. It better be for something you really love and believe in. We really went through the ringer."

Iris is dead, but she's not finished in the film. As Mace views the first tape of her life, the film's toughest scene roars forward. . . .

Action in the acting sense has never been easy for American women to break into; the thought of a lady behind the camera for such a film is just about unthinkable.

Until Kathryn Bigelow showed up. Four years after rocking the box office with *Point Break*, Bigelow sat down to do *Strange Days* (her ex-husband James Cameron helped with the screenplay).

"She was really interested in the action of the film and the technical side of the stuff," Bako says. "For the emotional side, you were kind of left on your own. She didn't come to you and talk to you about your character. She would say things like, 'You have to cry. Cry from your left eye, and when that explosion goes off, hit that mark.'"

Fiennes sat her down for a quick chat.

"Ralph said that when you're a professional actor, you're expected to be totally prepared for all that," Bako explains. "Directors think you can give them what they want, and that they don't need to get you there. You had to have your emotional life already prepared."

Along with us, Mace sees Iris and a friend partying in a car with the rapper and his bodyguard, and the fact that the men are already dead (storyline-wise!) shows us that something really horrible is going to happen.

Eventually, the car is pulled over, and who should appear, but the cops who were chasing Iris earlier. Arguments ensue, bullets fly, and men die. Iris, the impromptu filmer, frantically runs off, nearly getting taken out by a train in the process.

"The emotional level that I had to stay at was a freaked-out, paranoid state for most of that movie, to pump myself up," Bako says. "You could be sitting in your trailer for twelve hours, and have to be ready as soon as they call you. You have to learn to not completely blow your emotional wad until shooting. As a young actor, I sometimes used to peak before that. You could be brilliant in your rehearsal, crying in your rehearsal, and then you're out of it by the time they do it."

For takes and takes, she and the rest of the crew had to stay in overdrive for about fifteen minutes straight. Iris blindly bolts into the subway station we saw her in earlier, dodging the cops, avoiding everyone until she finally escapes, the same scene from a different angle we saw at the start.

"It was a real lesson in harnessing that crazy energy that she had, because she was in such a state for that whole movie," Bako says. "It was a real lesson in discipline in harnessing that emotional experience and laying it out when it needed to come out."

Ironically, it actually isn't the cops who ended up killing Iris, but Lenny's supposed friend Max (Tom Sizemore), murdering her and framing Lenny for it to save Faith and run away with her. But Lenny and Faith manage to take him out, and the cops' doings are revealed (one gives himself the death penalty), leaving Mace and Lenny to celebrate the new year together.

"I took off a few months after that movie," remembers Bako, who sadly was severely hurt in a car accident shortly thereafter (she eventually recovered). "I didn't know if I could go to these places anymore. That was probably the inception of when I just wanted to laugh and write comedy. I'd rather make people laugh. Even if you deal with tough subject matter and you get into laughter it takes you deeper, rather than people accosting you over the head with stuff that's so much you can't take it in."

Indeed, the film flopped at the box office. But in hindsight, no one got hurt too badly, professionally if not financially. Fiennes, Bassett, and Lewis are still household names in the acting world, and Bigelow made history by scoring the first-ever Best Director Oscar for a lady with 2009's *Hurt Locker* (beating out Cameron's *Avatar*). About a decade later, Bako's career took a new turn with the stroke of a pen.

One day in the midst of TV work, "I was bored out of my mind," she remembers. "I had nice hair in the role, but not much to do."

She sat down to write an autobiography in script form.

"I wrote one script, and showed it to all my trusted producer friends," she says. "They said 'This is too good! It's a fluke, you couldn't have written this. Write another one.' I felt that was kind of a backhanded compliment." She wrote another one, and got the same reaction.

Soon enough, *G-Spot* came (Wow, could I have said that better?!) to tell the story of Gigi, an actress who'd seen her career backslide after far too much soft-core eroticism, now looking for a way to get back to stardom in the midst of Los Angeles. A few months later, Bako was Gigi, acting out her own words.

"I have writer friends that have been struggling for fifteen years," she says. "This one got on in six months. At the time I was writing it, I didn't understand that my new calling was to be a writer, for it to be a vehicle for myself."

In the same vein as *Sex and the City* did here in the U.S. of A (*G-Spot*'s title was even more unapologetic!), the adult comedy roared across Canada for the next few years.

"I had thought my calling was to be an actress for twenty-something years," Bako says. "When I became a writer, a creator, a show-runner, I found that that was truly my passion. My favorite part was writing it and being in the editing room, when you kind of rewrite the show. The actual doing of the show, I don't love as much as the before and after. Don't get me wrong, I really miss people doing my hair and makeup and giving me free clothes, but the real joy was sitting in a room by myself and creating it."

Gigi told Bako's life tale, with, in true acting style, a few dramatic improvements along the way.

"[Gigi] had a better attitude about me," she explains. "I can get down and blue about some stuff, but she always bounced right back up. It was very freeing and fun. My sense of humor is that I love to kick the piss out of myself. I like to make fun of myself, so basically it's about everything at the time I thought was so tragic and awful about my career and life. The great thing about comedy is that it's alchemy; you give it a little bit of time, and the worst shit that's ever happened to you ends up being funny."

One of the series' top moments came just a few episodes into its original run in 2004 (it ran until 2009). Ironically, the episode was itself called "HBO" (some places have it listed as "Gigi Gets a Job"). With Gigi nearly zonked on anti-depressants, her agent calls her in for an acting tryout. As with the rest of the series, Bako looked back to her past.

"I was parodying the time I was in this movie in the Philippines about poisonous sea snakes, one of the worst movies ever made," she recalls (it was 1994's *Dark Tide*, as Bako and her husband, played by Chris Sarandon, battled eels and gang members in the tropics). "I had to get into a bathtub without noticing that a snake was in there until it slithered up my breast. I remember thinking that I had arrived at rock bottom in movieland."

Perhaps, but it would take her to the tops of her writing career; the episode was nominated for several awards, including a Genie (sort of like the American Golden Globes).

"Even with time and perspective, it became one of my finest episodes," Bako says. "It was all a very amazing experience, because I don't take anything that seriously anymore."

Dwight Evans (Macon Blair) contemplates his shot at revenge in the closing moments of *Blue Ruin* (2015).

Macon Blair: *Blue Ruin*

A GUY WITH ONLY one thing to go for, one finish line in his life, he'll do anything to get to it and get it done. He's on his own, a complete unknown, with one direction home, not unlike a rolling stone.

That's how we saw the main man in 2015's *Blue Ruin*. To a lesser extent, it represented all those who'd been waiting behind the scenes and the acting spotlight for, felt they, far too long.

Ruin was, explains protagonist Macon Blair, "a film we saw as our last-ditch attempt to get a foothold in the filmmaking business after years of trying. We've been making movies together our entire life, so I would play anything Jeremy [Saulnier] asked of me." Like most in today's film world, the two were the cameramen, crew, screenwriters, directors, and actors for much of their early career—along with being just about the full viewing audience.

In 2007, they'd finally gotten at least some traction on the outside levels of the horror mainstream, knocking out *Murder Party*, again with some serious multitasking.

With so many options arriving on a nearly hourly basis, however, the horror film world isn't much for remembering. Like many such flicks, *Murder Party* came about, won awards, sold some tickets, got some attention . . . and faded away.

The two got started on something else. Something real, sadly enough. A piece that took a hard look and drew a hard line between right and wrong, justification and fallacy. The story of a guy who'd had everything stolen and never really tried to get anything back.

Until a reason ran up and belted him across the weary face.

A madman had taken his parents and his life. A home with four wheels, meals and money far away, there was nowhere and nothing for Dwight Evans.

Then a friendly cop lets him know that the man who stole so much is about to get the chance to do it again, helped along by the gullibility of a parole board.

"I truly loved the character [Saulnier] came up with for me to play," Blair recalls. "I loved Dwight's single-mindedness and the friction between that and his utter incompetence at fulfilling his goal."

Said objective seems the epitome of easier spoken than performed: kill the SOB! But it's always easier for audiences, who are allowed to take such liberties with direction and see villainous characters die violently and cheer about it. Doing it ourselves might be another thing, no matter how much they deserve it.

Again, though, it's all Dwight has. Showing more emotion in two minutes than he has all film, he gets the guy alone in a restroom and ensures only one leaves. However, we've got nearly a full movie of time left, so there's obviously more to happen. The bad guy had a family that wants the same revenge Dwight did. We often look past the flaws of those we love, even if murder happens to be one of them. And hey, they might just be in the same boat as Dwight; nothing to do until now, and suddenly a finish line just a few paces away.

Now they're after him, but not just Dwight; he's got a sister named Sam and she's got kids. Kids that only a complete scumbag or nutcase out of his mind would ever hurt. Someone just like the new pursuers.

"The scene in the diner with Amy Hargreaves [as Sam] sticks out in my mind," Blair says. "She was so powerful, sitting across from me. It was terrifying and exhilarating to keep up with her." The family can't, as she's out of town fast. This is going to end just one way.

You have a certain amount of hope. You get the optimistic possibility that the drive, the inspiration Dwight finds within to finish this job might just inspire him to find some desire to search out something else in his life, something better.

Because you remember that, even though this is a movie, it's been pretty real to this point. Dwight doesn't get inspired because he doesn't care to. It's not about giving oneself a happy ending, a new start in life. It's about getting this done, no matter what—meaning that he might die. Probably will. Probably wants to, or at least doesn't mind it.

"Dwight doesn't talk much, so it would have to be a largely physical performance, which I really enjoy," Blair says. "I grew a big nasty beard and I lost weight and I learned my lines backwards and forwards. I drew on some experiences working with the homeless community in New York, but mostly the preparation, such as it was, had to do with a year's worth on conversations with Jeremy about the character as he was still writing the script."

The revenge part gets even more jumbled on everyone's end. A relative of the killer claims the killing wasn't entirely cold blooded, just revenge for an affair Dwight's dad had with his wife.

Maybe it's true. It's not like anyone (including Dwight) has much in the credibility department here. But Sam's life is on the line now, and there are just a few things left to do.

Like killing the rest of the killer's family (the guy's mom Kris is Eve Plumb, and you can't possibly associate the former Jan Brady that Plumb was with Kris!), and he does. Still, one of them gets Dwight good and done. We'll see if anything happens next in the story.

It didn't take long for the next chapter to fall in Blair and Saulnier's tale: with Saulnier back in the directing chair, filming his own script, *Green Room* arrived in the spring of 2015.

Trapped in a club in the grunge-land of Oregon, the punk band Ain't Rights, led by late great Anton Yelchin, battle a group of skinheads desperate to promote the whole white supremacy thing.

Blair played Gabe, a baldie more talk than action. Far from the group's leader Darcy Banker – himself none other than Patrick Stewart, on the opposite side of Jean-Luc Picard!

"He's a guy surrounded by tough and violent men who is not especially tough or violent himself and is doing his best to keep up, all for the approval of a kind of father figure," Blair remembers. "I researched white supremacist culture a great deal and cut my hair short and leaned my lines backwards and forwards. I guess I focus on the lines and the hair."

The only member of her family to show an iota of humanity, Ruby (Janus Blythe) sadly sees the brother she helped defeat get his justice, payback in 1977's *The Hills Have Eyes*.

Janus Blythe: *The Hills Have Eyes*

NOT ANOTHER AUDITION. NOT a costume fitting.

The crew didn't have any more money for that, any more time, nothing. It was time to put up or get out.

Or rather, to pick them up and lay them down—hard and fast.

"They took us outside and said they wanted to see us run," Janus Blythe remembers. "It was a very physical role." That would be an understatement for whoever got the part she was going for.

The Hills Have Eyes (1977) would have an easy time of creating an action-jammed, horrifying atmosphere; the crew would all be working deep out in the California deserts, sweltering during the day and below freezing at night.

Of course, it was different from Blythe's typical surroundings: but not by *that* much.

"I was a dancer, and I'd run three to six miles every morning," she says, "so I could run up and down mountains without getting out of breath."

But the race's starting line didn't represent the beginning of her climb of the *Hills*.

"I heard they were casting some horror movie down on Sunset Boulevard, and I crashed the interview," she recalls. "They liked me, and gave me the script."

Hills might be a true story, or maybe not, at least not all the way. Short of a time machine invention, we'll never know. We might label it "unlikely but possible" early on—we'll see the story of a family of mongoloid, near-feral cannibals that patrol the Golden State desert, surviving on who or whatever happens to be the next unlucky visitor.

But Ruby, the sole young lady of the clan, doesn't seem quite as rough as her brethren. First off, she looks sort of normal. Second, she shows a bit of compassion for the cuisine, not just seeing her next meal. Maybe she's not one after all. Maybe she just happened to stumble in, and they saw something about her that made her worth keeping breathing instead of buffet.

In any case, the story's supposed to be based on the Bean clan, a family that inbred itself into the dozens over a few centuries in Scotland, eventually being blamed for killing about a thousand people and eating many of them.

Or so legend says. Many think it's just a piece of folklore.

"They had someone else to play Ruby," Blythe says. "I said I liked it." Whatever or however she spoke, it worked, and she was in the running.

Eventually, literally so. It was time to race.

"They said 'Go!' and I just stood there," Blythe remembers. She looked at the director. Five years before, the fellow had foot-stamped his name on Hollywood with *Last House on the Left*, and now he was blending reality with supernatural.

Wes Craven told Blythe to get going.

"I took off, passed everybody, came back," she says. "He said, 'You got the role.'"

Off to the mountains and deserts that make up America's version of the Sahara.

"Standing there in the dirt and rocks," Blythe says, "I just got into character."

The Carter family, looking for a fun California vacation, happens to get snared by one of the family's traps. Soon, brothers (and possibly cousins and/or in-laws as well) Mars, Mercury, and Jupiter attack, killing some and stealing the family baby, who Ruby tries to protect.

"If I was real, if you didn't believe me," Blythe says, "those kinds of movies would fail badly. For me, my acting challenge was to throw myself into it. What's going to become of it? Roll the dice." She'd have a run-in with a cactus during filming, and had to corral a poisonous snake that got loose. The snake that Ruby uses to distract Mars long enough for him to get stabbed to death, however, was actually frozen.

The finish was a bit iffy, as DVD viewers can attest. In one ending, Ruby goes off to join the Carters; in another, she doesn't. But in any case, when Craven brought her back for the sequel in 1984, her name was Rachel and she was married to one of the Carters, now the prey of Michael Berryman's Jupiter.

"A great ending leaves you stunned," Blythe says. "Wes was open to suggestions, that I should walk up and Brenda and Bobby should accept me."

When the story came back in remake mode in 2006, Ruby was in Laura Ortiz's body, and her ending was much clearer, sadder, and more heroic, as Ruby fatally tackles her brother off a cliff to keep him from shooting a Carter.

"What I didn't like [about the remake] was that Ruby was almost non-existent," Blythe says. "You can't get back the magic."

While we're dancing on the line between action and horror, let's cross it for a moment to pay a bit of tribute to one I didn't quite get into 2015's *Behind the Screams*, a fellow BearManor Media publication! Like much of those outlined in my books, this performance didn't get the praise it should have on first release. Let's give Imogen Boorman a bit now.

Her character was trapped on the edge of Hell. Boorman hoped she'd never escape.

Yes, her Tiffany, the eventual focal point of *Hellraiser II: Hellbound* (1988) might have been the only one blocking the door from Hell to Earth. She'd been traumatized into near-catatonia. She'd been turned into an unwitting (she'd have been unwilling had she known) pawn in her doctor's experiments, work more deranged than every human and animal experiment combined times infinity.

Traumatized into near-catatonia, Tiffany looks within and out to save the planet from the Underworld in *Hellraiser II* (1988).

And at the end of the day, or the shoot, Boorman didn't really want to leave Tiffany or her whole new world behind. Because while Tiffany was certainly a painful character in a terrifying world, she would always, unfortunately, be just that: a character. Not real. Not someone who lived in Boorman's real world, the one she'd been glad to leave long enough for a casting. Someone who Boorman couldn't become for nearly long enough. Sometimes, she thought forever would be OK.

Though barely old enough for high school, she'd been through just about as much as Tiffany had, and while these experiences had certainly been useful (though far from welcome) to become the young lady, Boorman could only wish all she had to do was act.

"Having been sent away to boarding school at the age of nine years," Boorman recalls, "I could remember the shock and strange discombobulated confusion of suddenly being taken away from everything that was comforting and familiar. So I knew those memories would be useful to bring to Tiffany's tragic circumstances, having been kidnapped and hidden away in Dr. Channard's institution." Just one year after the infamous Cenobites had stepped up from the Underworld to reality in the original, the Hippocratic Oath-ignoring doctor had trapped their original prey Kirsty Cotton (Ashley Laurence) in his establishment, looking for a way to resurrect them.

She'd been on to him quickly enough, but Kirsty's fellow patient (she and we would probably go with "cellmate"), well . . . there was really no way to tell what Tiffany knew or what she wanted. She hadn't spoken since her mom was killed months before. Now she just sat around, working her way through Rubiks cube-type puzzles with a speed and skill no one could comprehend.

Boorman wasn't fully performing. Sadly.

"Tiffany had an obsession with solving puzzles, again my memories of boarding school and being shunned and isolated by other girls, in trying desperately to fit in," she remembers. "To please my parents I stopped eating, thinking I was too fat, or that being thinner or depriving myself of food would make me more acceptable."

And then there was the pain. From the body or the mind, whatever, wherever, she'd found it within to bring it to Tiffany, and Boorman hadn't had to search all that much.

"When I was eight or nine, my father had left the family home," she says. "My beloved Uncle John suddenly died. My poor pony, Popcorn, broke his leg while I'd been riding him, and he was shot dead there and then. Just like Tiffany, I hardly spoke after such events happening so suddenly and without warning, and took comfort in sucking my thumb, and for the most part silently nodded or shook my head when having to communicate."

As the Cenobites, led by Kirsty's stepmother Julia (Clare Higgins) start to emerge, stealing blood, skins, and lives from others for resurrection, Tiffany again becomes a weapon secret to herself; she's been tricked into opening the box that releases them.

"Tiffany couldn't stop herself playing with her puzzle toys," Boorman explains, "needing to fix that similar need, to feel better, desperately trying to make sense of reality, to ease the hideous fear of powerlessness. Powerlessness and obsession, in shock and uncommunicative, being alone and somewhere strange and uncomfortable were all things I knew about, vividly remembered, and found natural to bring into the portrayal of Tiffany." Still, head Cenobite himself Pinhead, always one of the more fair and rational as horror movie villains go, stops his colleagues from killing her, knowing that Channard is their true target.

But the only way for Kirsty to send everyone back where they belong is to go there herself, and she and Tiffany are soon in Hades as Channard is turned into his own new Cenobite.

"A little caffeine, nicotine, and hunger were what I used to get into an obsessed trance-like state that was my preparation for playing Tiffany," Boorman remembers. "Hunger was the bitter. Happiness was the sweet. I spent hours and hours, days and days just absorbed in my own thoughts, allowing the details in the script to infiltrate my daydreams and almost, trance-like, so deep in meditation, picturing in my head all the wonderful imagery [creator] Clive Barker's creations put there."

By now, the terror outside is starting to break through Tiffany's trauma, and who the hell could be surprised? This isn't exactly a medical miracle, although we certainly wish the mentally challenged could be frightened back to coherence. She's talking, she's running, she's reacting. Now she's about ready to take on Julia and the 'Bites, and Kirsty can only watch helplessly and hope. By now, Boorman had begun to visit a bit of suffering upon herself outside of the cameras.

"I practiced that state, thinking Tiffany must have been hungry, beyond hungry," she says. "I didn't eat much while at Pinewood, fruit salads and tuna buns. When obsession takes hold, when it is indulged, a natural high occurs as the brain produces chemicals designed to help you endure and survive a crisis and I could remember that well. There was no food or eating scenes in Clive Barker's hell. Food was the temptation I knew about; the other adult stuff, I concluded, was just like satisfying a terrible hunger."

With all the other Cenobites dead by his snake-blasting hands (apparently lacking the loyalty that Pinhead's pals showed to him!), Channard goes for Tiffany one more time, but, just as she figures out the final puzzle, it's Julia that saves her.

Except it isn't. Showing that two can certainly play *that* game, Kirsty's stolen Stepmom's skin and hidden inside to rescue her friend. Though neither lady will ever be back to normal again, it's time for them to step out of the hospital and back to the safety of realism (it would take four years for part three to arrive, and neither Laurence nor Boorman would be back, though Laurence would re-become Kirsty a few films later). But for the last time, Boorman wasn't really looking forward to the final cut.

"I could not wait to get to get to Pinewood and start shooting," she says. "Just thinking about it now is giving me goosebumps and tingles, 'trance-like.' Still, even the longest days in the studio were better than being at boarding school."

Then she and the rest of the cast sat down at the premiere to see their own bloody work. For the first time in a long time, Boorman could feel all the agony she'd been through, her own and Tiffany's. But now, it didn't seem so bad. Just for a short while, it had been worth it. She had never expected a reason to feel, to remember it, to use it, and absolutely not to be proud of it, but right there on the screen, there it was in Tiffany's form, now for everyone to be impressed by.

"Exhilarating," she remember of her first viewing. "Spellbinding. Empowering. I couldn't take my eyes away from the screen. Even when my mother, who'd insisted on being there, was muffling screams and had to run out of the auditorium to throw up, I couldn't move, my heart pumping with genuine fear and pride, as it was all so much better than I'd imagined. I knew at that moment what it felt like to be successful . . . and it felt good!"

In the world of small-screen acting, the whole "spinoff" term is fairly commonplace. A character shows up to do some supporting work, and somehow manages to steal the show, or at least a few episodes, so much so that he or she manages to finagle a new TV tome, becoming a brand new main man (or woman).

This happens all the time in television. Movies, though, are another story. To grab one's entirely own flick, to go from a few minutes on screen to convincing someone we're worth handing an entire film to carry, well, that's one of an actor's toughest tasks, especially for one without many resume entries.

Now we learn from someone who did, a lady whose work shows the up-and-coming world a new inspirational reason to really go for it when those lucky auditions arrive, no matter the genre, screen time, or anything else.

Early on in 2012's anthological *V/H/S*, viewers saw the tale "Amateur Night," the tragic story of lovely young Lily. Robbed of her heart by a college guy who couldn't deal with who she was within, the heartbroken lass truly showed her darkly wild side, transforming into the film world's most smoking succubus and turning him to prey.

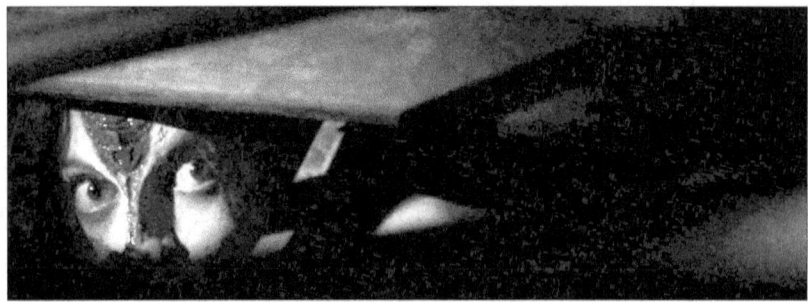

After wowing the cinematic world with her short turn as the lovely succubus Lily in 2012's *V/H/S*, Hannah Fierman got to tell Lily's full-length life tale four years later in *Siren*.

"I was shocked that we made such an impact," remembers Hannah Fierman, the lady behind Lily. "We had no idea it would take off the way it did, and surprised that people liked it enough to make a feature out of it."

Almost from the time Lily's bloody work was first seen, ramblings rolled through the cinematic universe that she might get another, much longer try at the camera. At the film's premiere, screenwriting newcomer Ben Collins informed Fierman of his hopes to turn Lily's biopic into his first full-length flick.

"That was a rumor early on," Fierman says, "but it was never certain whether I was going to be cast or not." A *V/H/S* sequel arrived in 2013, another the very next year, but still, nothing showed up much for Lily. Meanwhile, Fierman kept adding to her arsenal with TV movies and shorts, soon making her way to the lead of 2014's vampiric tale *The Unwanted*.

Then, in 2016, it finally happened.

After waiting nearly five years for another shot at Lily, a call came for Fierman to be her again, the center of a full-blown trek—and sooner than she could have guessed.

"I don't think I even had weeks [to prepare]," she remembers. "We had to jump right into it."

Siren would show us Lily's true beginnings, as a young girl stolen by a sadistic scumbag who'd made her into the personal sex toy of anyone he wanted. But though she'd never been able to summon enough strength to show it, Lily was actually from far below, and far more deadly than anyone (well, except those lucky enough to see *V/H/S*) could have guessed.

Along with stunt doubling for Fierman in *V/H/S*, Elizabeth Davidovich had done the same job on three *Hunger Games* films, several seasons of *The Walking Dead*, and a host of other flicks. Fierman knew just whom to ask for a literal crash course in going back to action.

"We had to jump right into it," Fierman remembers. "We went to the gym, and she stretched me out. She taught me how to use a little muscle if I needed to." She also sharpened up her song skills—it is, after all, how sirens lure their catch!

The story started out much like *V/H/S* had—a group of fellows out for a wild night with liquid and smoked encouragement and women in liberal attire. Lily's captor offers them an even better time . . . but all it'll cost is their lives.

By now, we'd seen Lily's sad backstory of how she ended up here. Here, Fierman had moved from student to actress, all the way to teacher herself. Herself new to the acting world, Ava Atwood would become Lily's younger self.

"She was really great," Fierman explains. "I told her to imagine herself as a feral cat, the kind that's wild and doesn't want to be petted. She picked it up really well."

Per Lily's luck, the most decent guy in the group, the one who shows her just a little respect, just *happens* to be the one who's getting married soon. For a demon, though, she seems to have a tad bit of warmth, finally finding the power to take out the bad guys as he escapes.

But maybe it was all just a ploy to take a bit of control, for her first time ever. Weeks later, he and his new wife start to enjoy their honeymoon together. This sort of film can't possibly end this way.

Lily's there, and on the attack against the one woman standing between her and love. The guy sacrifices himself to save his wife, but Lily's got him now, and, again as we saw in the closing moments of her *V/H/S* tale, carries him off into the ominous night.

Will her spin-off get its own part two? Many certainly hope so, and Fierman sees some possibilities.

"There's a lot of story that they haven't really explored," she says. "You still don't know where Lily comes from. I think they could go further and show an underworld where there's lots of Lilys."

A lady with a very large gun—a welcome sight to viewers, but not so much to her prey, as Tiffany Bolling showed us in 1972's *Bonnie's Kids*.

Tiffany Bolling: *Bonnie's Kids*

BUTCH CASSIDY AND HIS sundancing pal did it.

Bonnie and Clyde pulled it off.

Sonny Corleone finished up that way, as did Tony Montana.

They'd done too much to keep going, gone too far to come back. Now they were trapped, out of space, out of options.

But damned if they were going to just stand there and make it easy. It was going to take a hail of bullets to put them down—and who had the backbone to fire them?

It's certainly not the kind of equality the feminism movement of the 70s was looking for, but Bonnie Parker had shown that women could be just as murderous in the spree area as men, including her mostly worse half Clyde Barrow. Five years before, Faye Dunaway had shown Parker's cinematic story.

Now Tiffany Bolling had a shot, and not just the type from the firearms we'd see early on in *Bonnie's Kids* (1972)—and, trust me here, the title character's name is *far* from coincidence.

One has to bend pretty far to accept these kinds of hypotheticals, themselves pretty rare in the action world. It's a rarely spoken fact that Parker was a teenage bride, but *not* to Barrow. Her husband was a local stud who didn't believe much in marital *or* legal fidelity, off philandering, boozing, and, yes, even robbing before and after his young wife found new love (it appears that delinquency was high on Parker's list of attractive traits!), in jail for robbery when she and Clyde met their lawmakers.

But what if she hadn't gone down on that May 1934 morning in Shreveport? What if she'd made it through, had kids (she didn't, not that has ever been proven), got re-married, and *then* purchased the farm?

Would her daughters have turned out like her? Headstrong, assertive, but still lacking judgment of male character? *Bonnie's Kids* showed us what might have been.

"I was tired of playing the lovely yet subservient characters that chauvinistic society had women trapped in," remembers Bolling. "I loved the fact I could be a front runner of hell-bent-for-leather women." She's Ellie, struggling to make it in 1970s California with no mom, little education, a dead-end job, and a stepdad whose friends keep reminding him just how nice it might be to get disgustingly close to his stepdaughters.

You'd think a guy his age might be too old for peer pressure. You'd wish to be right.

"An important element to prepare for a role is simple," Bolling explains. "Use what, where, why, when, and how to define your character. The role of Ellie was simple to me; she's a small town girl, but street smart."

And stoic as well. Ellie arrives home to find dear old stepdad trying to have his way with her sister.

Most people, on and off the film screens, might have flipped out. Perhaps gone into screaming hysterics, pounding, hitting, kicking, throwing things, in full-blown animalistic mode until someone was unconscious or worse.

Not her. Not Bonnie's baby. She gets a gun as big as her, and gives an order she won't repeat.

"This is an iconic scene in the film," Bolling says, "so I wanted to not do what people would think, and downplayed her action, making the scene more dramatic. Ellie is fed up with him; he's probably been sexually hounding and slapping her around since she was a kid."

He's done, in every single sense. He takes the last steps of his life toward her. She wastes him.

It's off to Los Angeles to live with an uncle, but he's only a bit better, enveloping his own family in a money scam. Ellie's resourcefulness comes in handy for a while, stealing the money and running south for El Paso. Still, as we find out throughout the film, she's about the only person with a set of brains and vertebrae, her chickenshit boyfriend cowering behind a car as the uncle's hitmen move in on the desert. Time for Ellie to be just like her mommy.

She roars out, mouth and guns blazing at high speed. But it's tough to aim a weapon while running and in hysterics' grasp, and there's more opponents than bullets. She gets the same lead-based treatment as Parker in reality, a death undoubtedly preferable to what a bunch of sex-crazed idiot gangsters would have done to a young beauty.

"My doing stunt work back in Miami paid off," says Bolling, in that area of performance employment since her late teenage years. "The only special effects were gunshot wounds, which I wore well in the end. Ellie was a badass, a very strong character. She was totally out of the box."

If Ellie had forced Bolling to tiptoe around the gray area between good and evil, she got to blast hell out of both areas the very next year. *Wicked, Wicked* had her as Lisa, an upcoming singer who finds herself in the path of a bloodthirsty nutcase.

"Playing the role as a singer was right up my alley," says Bolling, who released an album in 1970. "It was a campy horror movie with tons of blood and gore and great character actors. What fun I had on that set as Lisa, shooting it all at the beautiful Hotel Del Coronado in San Diego."

The Candy Snatchers, however, had her in a different role. A different world. A different genre. One that let her play that type of the character that America eventually saw Parker as, one reason why public opinion went slam against her and Darrow in their last months.

Her Jessie and male pal Eddy kidnap a teenage girl, burying her alive and giving her a pipe to breathe through. But their ransom demands aren't met, and her partner takes it out on Jessie in the worst of ways.

"The rape scene was particularly tough," Bolling admits. "I turned victimized fear into a true power-shift to show her strength and an 'I could care less' attitude, not letting Eddy get the upper hand. Always in control was her name of the game."

It looks like the victim's stepdad is just as malevolent as Elle's, ready to keep the ransom for himself. A gun in his face changes his mind *fast*, but he's able to get free and blast Jessie to eternity.

"This role was insane," Bolling says. "Jessie was nuts, at the end of her rope when everything backfires on her. Although Jessie was very evil, she was also very strong, a natural born leader. I really let it rip. *Candy Snatchers* was extremely cathartic. My personal life was a mess at the time, so I used that deeply in her character to give her the edginess you see on screen. This made her quite over the top, which I hope it conveys." Almost as much as when Bolling went to the mat with some of society's most terrifying creatures in 1977's *Kingdom of the Spiders*—almost!

"There's a great rush in accomplishing what I set out to do, which was get the job and do it well," says Bolling. "Doing extra and stand-in work is a really great way to break into the business. And truly as wonderful as show business is, it is the greatest test of character. None of this is easy. It's long hours. It's hard work, and 'waiting' gets longer as you become well known. And always remember my favorite line from Sir Laurence Olivier: 'To just be delighted.'"

Kevin Breznahan (right) played Roy Harley in *Alive*, the 1993 film that told the story of a South American rugby team who fought off Mother Nature after a plane crash in the Andes in 1972.

Kevin Breznahan: *Alive*

ONE DAY BACK IN the early 1980s, a group of junior high-aged New Yorkers found a book that just *had* to be fiction.

People living for months with hardly any food or water—in the midst of the Andes? Even for a rugby team, these were the same moutains so often covered in snow and ice, victimized by blizzards and avalanches, so far from, well, *anything*? This had forced these people to resort to *what* before they were rescued?

Never happened. Couldn't be factual, even if the 1974 work's title was *Alive: The True Story of the Andes Survivors*. Boys at that age know everything anyway, and they knew that author Piers Paul Read (what a great name for a writer!) and the ones interviewed in the book were just reaching over their eyes and yanking down the wool.

"The book was taboo," remembers Kevin Breznahan, one such student of the time. "It had cannibalism in it, so we were told we shouldn't read that." About a decade later, Read's story came charging right back into the now-struggling actor's career. It was indeed based in truth, and now someone was looking to show the story that had shocked the world in the last months of 1972.

"When I was first told I had an audition," Breznahan remembers. "I first thought, how am I going to play a South American rugby player? Then I did some research, and I found that I actually looked like some of the guys on the team, especially Roy." That would be Roy Harley, one of those lucky enough to make it home from the crash.

"I spoke with Roy, but mainly I relied on the screenplay," says Breznahan. Five years before, John Patrick Shanley had won an Oscar for writing the script for *Moonstruck* (1988), and now he'd adapted Read's words for *Alive*.

"There was so much to play in his words, what he created," remembers Breznahan. "Then I found out that Frank Marshall was directing it. I was working with the top of the food chain, in a sense. People with a wealth of knowledge created an environment when it was like a family doing this, in this world."

Marshall and the rest of the crew decided to shoot *Alive* in sequence—as in, the film was filmed in the same order that audiences would see it. That's rare in the film world, but there was certainly some justification behind it: we'd see people spending weeks, then months in the mountains. No restaurants, no gyms, nothing at all. Couldn't have people gaining weight, muscle or otherwise, their hair lengths and skin tones jumping around as the film progressed.

"I gained some weight before the film," says Breznahan. "I started off at about 170 pounds, and I was about 142 at the end. We went on some restrictive diets. I read the book." As the flick starts on the plane, filming began in a Vancouver studio, in an actual plane fuselage. The crash happens just moments into the film, so it would be the first—and arguably most graphic—part of *Alive*, both what they filmed and what we saw.

Misjudging both the headwind they're up against and their distance above the mountains, the pilots realize that they're going down too fast, and the passengers pick up on things, the cliffs outside far too close.

Some pray—the team is, after all, from a Catholic school. Others grasp each other, hoping to stay aloft, and alive, for just a few more moments.

"Filming that took two or three weeks," Breznahan says. "They had the fuselage of a plane up on two contraptions, rotating the fuselage up and down, like in a plane going through turbulence. It was a little scary at times."

One cliff smashes the back of the plane, and some are sucked out. Panic ensues. It smashes to the ground. Some die on impact, others crushed under seats and fellow passengers. Thirteen people die then and there, and two more pass on the first night.

"When the plane comes down, and the tail gets ripped out, the seats right behind my character go," he continues. "It was easy to act in that sense, so provocative, so much adrenalin." The crew moved to Western Canada to film on the top of a glacier.

"You didn't have to recreate in your mind being up on a mountain—you were there!" remembers Breznahan. "I felt a real responsibility to have as much integrity as I could. All of them are heroes in a way, because they survived." A plane flies by, inspiring the survivors that they'll be rescued soon, but days later, a message comes over the radio that the search is cancelled. Nando Perrado (Ethan Hawke), whose mom and sister are killed, is knocked into a coma by the crash, and assisted by some medical students.

Waking up, he soon convinces the group that the only way to survive will be human consumption. They indulge—but if that wasn't enough on them inside and out, eight more people die in an avalanche a few days later.

Small groups continue to venture out, finding wreckage here and there. Roy, said to be into electronics, is consulted for help on the radio, but he's not exactly optimistic.

"The main hero is Ethan," explains Breznahan (the real Parrado was an advisor on the film). "My character is sort of the antitheses of that, very emotional. Roy is not afraid to admit that he's scared, and the real Roy Harley was concerned about that." Several actual survivors flew up to meet with the crew, but Harley had never stepped back on a plane after the crash, and he wasn't making even this exception.

"I spoke to him on the phone, and I told him what I believed," says Breznahan, "that it takes a lot of courage to process your feeling and let them out. Everyone else *wanted* to cry all the time, but my character had the guts to do it, to express his fears."

Nando and Roberto Canessa (Josh Hamilton) head off on one last trek. Somehow, they manage to stagger for nearly two weeks. Then they find a plantation just outside the valleys. Soon the rescuers are on their way, and Roy and the rest find the strength to celebrate.

The real Harley, "seemed pleased with it," Breznahan says. "It was one of the most provocative moments of my life, the beginning of a lot of different things for me."

He played two roles in the midst of one of Hollywood's most diverse casts of 1999 in *Magnolia*, and had a small role alongside Daniel Day-Lewis' Oscar-winning work of *There Will Be Blood* (2007). Three years later, he'd help form the launching pad of one of the fastest shots to stardom in acting history.

For the first few years of the new millennium, not many were aware of a young actress named Jennifer Lawrence. Some TV shows, a few small film roles, little at the upper level.

Then, in 2010, someone decided to hand her the lead in *Winter's Bone*.

In a situation only a bit more hopeful than we'd seen in *Alive*, she was teenaged Ree, leading her family, with her dad in the drug trade and her mom down by her own inner demons. With her dad about to go on trial for drug charges, the family house will be gone unless he shows up. There's nothing to do but find him, and the cost might be what little she has left, including her life.

"It's about a female who supersedes her age," Breznahan explains. "It's amazing what she does to survive and take care of her young siblings in such a bleak situation, with these families trying to survive in a meth area. It's an epidemic in that region." During her search, Ree meets Little Arthur, a meth-dealing colleague of her father.

Filming took place in the same type of southwestern Missouri town we see in the storyline. Breznahan had headed down early to find some impromptu role models.

"I based my character on a guy I met down there," Breznahan remembers. "I spoke with this man, who actually wound up in film. I met a lot of people who had issues."

Little Arthur is certainly one of many dirtbags in the film; denying he's seen Ree's dad, he kicks her out of his place when she says no to drugs. But Daniel Woodrell's 2006 novelization of the story had given him a much darker outlook; it's revealed he raped Ree.

Lawrence scored her first Oscar nomination for the film (some, like me, still call it her finest performance, even after her win for *Silver Linings Playbook* two years later). The next year, *X-Men* launched her career into the stratosphere. 2012 brought the first *Hunger Games*, which put the final touches on her rank of phenomenon.

"Filmmaking is such a collaborative experience," Breznahan explains. "There's so many people working at once to pull it together, so much technical stuff involved. It's very complex, and you're one element in it, in a way."

Awaken (2015) gave Natalie Burn the chance to be the next one to fight her way to the top of the action film ranks.

Natalie Burn: *Awaken*

THE TOUGHEST OPPONENT IN Natalie Burn's film career just can't leave her well enough alone.

Set to set, film to film, crew to crew, it just keeps showing up, and always to be an enormous pain in the area that her characters so often kick!

It can't be written out of the script, left on the cutting room floor, or even removed from the final product, perhaps hoping to cameo in a "Deleted Scenes" section on a DVD.

Neither Burn nor anyone else can control this enemy, although many characters throughout action film history have tried, usually for villainous purposes.

It's the weather. Mother Nature in her pissiest mood.

Burn wasn't able to crush this adversary as she would if it were one of the many that have attacked her characters and come out worse, if at all. But if she couldn't beat it, she didn't decide to join it: only to make it work for her.

Moving a few countries over from her Ukrainian homeland, Burn stepped into Croatia, strapped up a rifle, and targeted the worst in human history, backing up Natassia Malthe's title character in 2011's *Bloodrayne: The Third Reich*. The Reich in titled question is the same group that terrorized the world and darkened Germany's name forever in history, and Rayne was out to stop them from finding the same secret to unstoppable undead-ness that had allowed her to battle evil for eternity (Kristanna Loken had started the series in 2006, with Malthe stepping in for the first sequel the next year, and now again).

Ready to show her sniping skills from behind a trigger, Burn felt the opposite of her last name (though she actually went by Natalia Guslistaya until meeting American audiences as Mel Gibson's trophy wife in 2014's *The Expendables 3*). Croatia's not known for low temperatures, but, again, lack of climactic luck would become a sad staple of Burn's early career.

"It was freezing outside, and unfortunately we were outside for the majority of the shoot," she remembers, "[but] the environment helped me shape a tough badass assassin that I played. The wardrobe helped to make me feel more like the character and gave me a boyish behavior than preparing for the role beforehand without nature and the outfit." That same year, Burn spoofed her role in *Blubberella*, this time with Lindsay Hollister's plus-sized babe battling back both Hitler's army and her own sweet tooth.

In *Awaken* (2015), Burn's battles got just a bit more realistic. But there's quite a bit more story to tell to set this one up.

Anyone who has ever made it in Hollywood—hell, anyone who has ever put forth any kind of effort to do so!—will tell you in all kinds of detail that success isn't something that anyone's going to hand you, or that you're going to stumble upon. It's about going out to grab it, and then going out and grabbing it again. Getting one or two big roles lasts until the next big film comes out; it won't assure you of anything.

Since she was in elementary school, Burn looked all over the world for success on the ballet stages, and found it. Hoping to get somewhere in the action film's high (or even moderate) ranks shoved her over to Los Angeles, learning to take those same fitness skills and putting a new aggressive spin all over them. So did forming 7Heaven Productions to put a business' name next to hers in the hitmaking ranks.

"You have to be in shape and be able to be original and come up with interesting things to catch people's attention," she explains. "Be unique, be bold, and someone will notice you. If the opportunity doesn't come up for you, then make your own opportunity. Have a good attitude that your dream can become a reality and stay working towards what you want."

A year after putting out the award-winning short *Fallen Angel*, 7Heaven looked to the full-length ranks.

"We all came up with the idea that audiences now are more interested in a female lead," she explains, "so I knew from the start Billie had to be a powerful woman, but someone that is relateable to."

The lady in casting question would find herself one day on an island right out in nowhere, with no clue how she got there or who these people around her are or what they want. But there are a few things she does know, and they'll launch some twists right into the plot.

It was the same plot that Burn had helped script out, along with Mark Atkins (and others), who'd soon direct the film. It would be one of the few credits that wouldn't have Burn's moniker listed.

Credits like casting the film. Like helping to produce it. Like putting together and belting out the flick's lead soundtrack tune. And, of course, leading the way in the main actress ranks.

"It was hard and tough since I was wearing many hats during this film," she remembers, "and, at times, pretty exhausting, but it was all worth it in the end. I've learned a great deal from doing the film. I realized how much really goes into making a movie. I salute people that actually get movies made, let alone make good films! That's even tougher."

After all of that, even Burn might have needed a bit of help with her final, and perhaps toughest, role in *Awaken*: becoming Billie herself. She went to the same place and person that had helped kick off (all puns intended!) her Hollywood career to begin with, spending over a month refining the kickboxing and brawling skills she'd honed years before, sharpening the skills Billie'd use throughout.

And when we'd see flashbacks of the young lady learning it all from her dad, well, that was a bit on the inside of the joke spectrum; fight pioneer Benny Urquidez, known so much better as Benny The Jet (not the slightest bit related to the kid from *Sandlot*!), portrayed him, after prepping Burn to act out his little girl.

"The process of coming up with Billie helped me to mold the two of us together," Burn says, "making sure I was in shape for the role and being able to pull off the action moves we wrote. I based Billie off of a girl that loves her family, even though she is a badass. Also, she is a character that I always wanted to play, so from the start to finish, it was a process of seeing what worked and what didn't and fitting it together to make a whole story."

Making her way across the new strange land, Billie soon realizes what happened to her sister: yes, Kat's living in a gorgeous house and rolling in dough, but it's all from the worst ways.

The island's a breeding ground, a stockyard for those in great shape to get greater—so their organs can get harvested and sold to some seriously high bidders. And it just so happens that one has just arrived.

It's Daryl Hannah's Mao, along with her bodyguards and the true reason everyone's here: her daughter Violet, who needs a new liver to see her next birthday. Kat (Christa Campbell) isn't the queen of this organization, but she's one hell of a henchwoman, and there's several others just like her, there for the money they get for forcing their captives to hand over their organs.

So Billie and her fellow "prisoners" will have to fight their way to her and back again, and there's no rules, of mercy or otherwise, in this brawl. And just as it had back in Croatia, nature became Burn's unwelcome and out of control co-star.

"Since the weather was gloomy and rainy, it was hard to shoot," she admits, "but looked amazing on camera. I tried to make the movie as close to reality as possible."

With her new, although stolen addition, Violet looks to be OK. But things go awry there, and Mao takes it out on a few who failed her. Meanwhile, those on both sides take their final bloody bows as Billie gets closer and closer to her sister. We see her training with her dad, learning just what she uses here. Her friends die, and Mao gets the jump on her.

But with just a bit more compassion than she showed as Ellie in the *Kill Bill* flicks, she realizes that this wasn't Billie's fault, and walks away, leaving Billie to go for her final revenge.

She doesn't get it, not the way she hoped; realizing it's what she deserves, Kat takes herself out so Billie can slaughter her boss, then walk away, us hoping she'll at least find some kind of purpose, with this quest over.

"A lot of the stunt scenes were hard to pull off when time was restricted or the weather didn't help us out," she admits. "There were a few injuries, but in the end we got the shots we needed. Time was tight and with having the names we did in the movie and making sure we got the shots in we needed without going over budget was a challenge. The fight scenes didn't have many special effects added, besides a few stabs here or gunshots, but it look awesome to see the final product come together."

Powerlifting isn't one of women's most popular sports just yet, but Corina Calderon's Luz found out how wonderfully challenging it can be in 2011's *All She Can*.

Corina Calderon: *All She Can*

CERTAIN WORDS, SEVERAL STRONG pieces of advice, could apply to several professions.

"People will try to break you down," she says, "and *will* if you allow it. Not everyone is going to like you. Some might even say you're not good enough . . . but don't ever give up on something you love and know in your heart is your passion! The right opportunity will show up and you just have to be sure you're ready. Do great work always that they won't be able to overlook you and your talent and hard work."

Pessimistic parasites like the ones described in that quote have used words like that to speak down to many with a dream. A guarantee: everyone who has ever been a success in many fields has heard such naysaying. Everyone who has ever made it to the big leagues of any pro sport. Anyone who's ever done anything significant in any aspect of the entertainment business.

We've all heard it to one degree or another. Long before she tore it up in 2011's *All She Can*, Corina Calderon (the speaker from the above quote) had gotten more than her fill of that garbage. So had the lovely Luz that would become a biggest role of her career.

As tough as it is for men to make to the top in any sport, female athletes are up against odds as strong as winning the lottery—and even those that make it don't get much past the levels of "squat" when it comes to pay or respect. Our male soccer teams get crushed in the World Cup and Olympics and lead off *Sportscenter*, while our women win the damn things and it's hardly an afterthought. The NBA finals put America on hold; the WNBA is considered almost satirical (the same could be said for gals' NCAA b-ball). Comparing the number of lady athletes who land endorsement deals to the guys, it's not even close.

It's fitting that I started writing this piece just as the 2016 Summer Olympics were starting off. Men have been lifting for gold ever since the first Games back in Athens; women only began in 2000, although two "local" ladies medaled at the Sydney Olympics, and Sarah Robles brought America a bronze at the most recent Games (no American male won anything).

So yes, it's still an underrated, underappreciated game, by everyone except its partakers. The Luz Garcia that Calderon became would find some serious respect—fast.

And it wasn't too hard. Because it was all she had. In a Texas town that few would ever hear of, there wasn't much for local high school girls like her to look forward to. The outside world didn't exactly give off an aura of optimism, but her only way there was out of the gym.

"I too have grown up in a small Texas town where I spent most of my summers with my grandparents in Uvalde," Calderon recalls. (Uvalde is the birthplace of a Hollywood fellow named McConaughey.) "The lifestyle, culture, and the area is so familiar, I immediately connected and understood the character from her family life to everyday life struggles, such as wanting to see what else is out there beyond the small Texas town life, to struggling with the lack of money and support from my family who I felt just didn't understand my dreams, but tried to because they love me so much and we're so close."

Luz was in the same position. It's tough to imagine our sisters, our daughters, our nieces walking up to us and announcing a desire to hit it big in the lifting world. But all we could do is stay positive and see where things go, and Luz's family does, even when things get tough for her in and out of school.

"I've always loved very physical roles, roles that push me to see my true physical strength and potential," Calderon explains. "Playing a powerlifter was truly a dream role for me. I've always been pretty athletic and powerlifting is a sport that will push you to your limits and beyond, physically and mentally." Some crew members put her to work with a few local high school teams.

"I was working out and lifting every day," she says. "It took a couple months to prepare and really become a powerlifter, to learn the technique and that way of life to make it work and come off on screen." Legal issues, school issues, job issues, family issues, the same thing that victimize so many other feel-good sports heroes and heroines just as the main event approaches, sneak up on Luz as well. Interestingly, *All She Can* doesn't use the typical sports movie ending—the main character just makes it into final competition, then somehow sets record and wins everything to thunderous applause and rising music!

No, it actually finishes up before Luz's high school career does. Her life goes right off track, and a school official and some family members start to help her get it back on, her lifting career just starting back up at the finale. Maybe it's more realistic that way; life doesn't always have a happy ending or answer every question. We don't actually get the spoon-feeding of Luz's dreams coming true, but we have a pretty good feeling.

"I learned how powerful and strong our bodies really are," Calderon explains, "and that a lot of time, it's just all in our heads: the limits we put on ourselves." With the same strength she gave Luz through the arts of deadlifts and bench presses, Calderon tries to hang on to that mindset as her career moves forward (in a double irony to writing this piece on the first weekend of August 2016, *Suicide Squad* just opened at the box-office, with her playing the wife of Jay Hernandez's demonic pyrokinetic El Diablo).

"This business can be absolutely brutal and unpredictable that you really have to develop a strong sense of self and confidence and self-worth," she says, "and remember why you are acting constantly, and hold on to that love you have for the craft as an artist."

OK, so maybe our women haven't been quite the picture of dominance in Olympic weightlifting. Gymnastics, on the other hand, has long established such a dynasty. Just as they did in 2012 and 1996, our ladies scored an overall team gold in 2016, their nine total medals setting a new sport record for Old Glory (our men won three, including Danell Leyva's pair of silvers).

Notwithstanding Melissa Rauch's jaw-droppingly hysterical guilty pleasure *The Bronze* (2015), gymnastics is just about as tough as powerlifting to find in film. That's sad—and, if for just a moment, audiences could step inside the mind and heart of the ladies lucky enough to be on the floor, vault, or balance beam, it might not always be the case, asserts Tarah Paige.

Tricia Skilken (Tarah Paige) learned that gymnastics' benefits go far beyond physicality in 2006's *Stick It*.

"Performing is a huge part of the sport," says the Phoenix native. "Getting up in front of a crowd, doing your routine for an audience, and being able to tap into a crowd's emotions and get them going." She experienced it for over a decade, winning national championships as a kid and coming *that* close to the 2000 Olympics.

"Having my skills as a gymnast, as well as being a natural performer, really helped me to feel completely comfortable in the film and television industry," she explains, "and also gave me a lot of bonus skills to fulfill roles in commercials, television, and film that required this sort of athletic ability. In addition to acting and gymnastics, I'm also a dancer and a singer, so having multiple skills really helped me to get my start in the business, as I had more to offer even beyond just my theatrics." She'd start showing that sort of thing right around 2005, but let's talk about acting for now: the type that allowed Paige, and others, to cartwheel and backflip all over the line between competing and performing.

"Being part of this film would mean combining the two loves of my creative life: gymnastics and acting," she says of Disney's *Stick It* (2006). "Once I was selected, of course, I went immediately to work preparing for the role, which not only included my acting training but also getting back into the gym to get back in competition shape for my role as a top-notch competitive world champion gymnast. I spent many months getting back into my competition shape so that I could help make the movie as realistic as possible."

Along with the rest of America's finest in the sport, Tricia Skilken had done it all and given up even more to make it to the world championships of gymnastics, ready to send a strong sense of Americanistic sportsmanship right across the globe. But on the eve of winning it all, her teammate Haley Graham had walked out on her girls, rooking over all those that had stood with her and cheered her on, from the teammates to the coaches to the fans just hoping to follow in her role modeled footsteps someday.

Stick It told a new chapter in the life of Haley (Missy Peregrym), now just as close to juvie as she ever was to stardom. Gymnastics gives her a chance at some community service, but it's literally her against the world; those she cheated, directly or otherwise, aren't reaching for her olive branch.

Like Tricia, about ready to make a new run at the nationals, who rebuffs her ex-friend back and forth. And the judges, who keep rooking Haley's scores. The whole "underdog wins over disbelieving fans" trope is nothing new in the sports film world, but this is one of the few instances where everyone has a damn good right to be ticked at her.

"*Stick It* really pays great tribute to the gymnastics world and community by showing how mentally and physically tough and strong you must be to be a high level competitive gymnast," Paige says. "I don't think everyone really knew or appreciated how many hours of work it took every girl in the gym to accomplish such great feats, but to have *Stick It* immortalize gymnasts in such a wonderful way on film is such a huge step forward and an accomplishment for the sport in general."

Gymnastics, as with any sport in which one's performance is judged by opinion alone—figure skating, dance, etc.—will always be undercut beneath the surface by bias accusations, valid or otherwise. That's a strong plot point in *Stick It*, and how big an issue it is in reality is a question that can't be answered in books like this.

That's where things end up coming together in the final meet. Faced with the possibility that judges might just pick whoever they want or like, performances secondary, Haley and Co. decide to pick the victors themselves, forfeiting ("scratching" in sport lingo) so the true champ wins (Nastia Liukin, the film's uneven bar champ, won the all-around gold two years later at the Beijing Olympics).

Tricia's not into it at first, roaring past the competition her own way to take the balance beam title. But when Haley gives the floor routine of a lifetime, Tricia finally realizes something else about her sport: that you don't always need the highest score to be a winner, and sometimes losing is all there's rightly to do.

"Seeing the culmination of all our efforts on film in the final edit with music and sound effects and editing was just a dream come true," Paige remembers. "The movie came together really well and I was very happy to see the final product in all its glory."

There's a reason why Paige was one of few *Stick It*-ers to work without a stunt double. Actually, more than one; her ability, of course, but also because stunt work has become her other foray into performing since her career began. She stunted for Mia Wasikowski in *Alice in Wonderland* (2010), for Reese Witherspoon a few times, in two *Transformers* movies, and on an ever-increasing resume of other films, TV shows, and even the XBOX's 2013 innovative update of *Tomb Raider*.

"Every project I work on is a new adventure," she remarks, "and I always love seeing what my 'day at the office' will look like. I feel extremely fortunate to be able to use my gymnastics background in such a cool field of the entertainment industry, and I hope to entertain audiences on the big screen for years to come."

Before carving out his legendary career in the NCAA basketball coaching ranks, one that would lead all the way to the Hall of Fame, Don Haskins, as most do, spent a few years bouncing around the small-town high school levels in Texas in the 1950s. His name wouldn't become echelon worthy until he reached the University of Texas at El Paso (called Texas Western College when he began), but Haskins first sharpened his skills leading both boys' and girls' court battles back when "women's basketball" was all but an oxymoron.

"I've had boys quit on me," Haskins once remarked, "but I never had a girl quit. Not once." If one were to survey many who've helped both genders in the board-crashing arts, such a memory would be a pretty common answer.

Ability, drive, desire, teamwork . . . some of these things can be coached, some not so much. But toughness? Within and out, female athletes are *far* ahead in that department. *Believe in Me* ended up as one of 2006's most feel-great films, and still ranks among the top ever in women's sports focus, but it was a sad story for a time.

A small team from a tiny school in a miniscule town in the drought-whomped state of Oklahoma, the Lady Cyclones have almost no one to believe in them. Their school hasn't cheered them on. Their town doesn't care. Their new coach didn't want to be here. The girls don't really even work much as a squad.

And their opponents? Forget it. No respect here. Winning's not enough for these players; pushing the Cyclone-ettes around is an added incentive, just dark fun.

She's defending her heart out, but Frances, one of the court's smallest players, is taking about as much punishment as the hardwoood, and more than the rules allow.

OK, enough already. He'd hoped to lead the guys, but Clay Driscoll's going to make the best of this toughness. One timeout and pep talk later, his girls are enticed not to take it anymore.

One more cheap shot against Frances is just too many. Seconds later, fists are flying, bodies are falling, and the Cyclones are more together than before—*ever* before!

"That was one of my favorite scenes," remembers Alicia Lagano, the actress behind Frances. "We kept losing, and losing, and one team was bullying us. Our coach told us to stop taking crap from these girls, to go out and stand up. Frances kind of snaps, and it turns into this huge brawl. I'm jumping on people's backs."

How often have we heard this sort of statement in real-life sports? Two teams get into a big brawl, smack it out for a few minutes, and somebody gets ejected, maybe fined. Then you hear someone at a press conference saying, "We were out there as a team, and this put us all on the same page! That's how teammates stand up for each other!"

Often just hyperbole, but it comes true in *Believe in Me*. Here's where the Lady Cyclones become a single twister ready to tear through the state.

"I really think that that's where the team became a team," Lagano explains. "Frances had all these other girls who she thought never really liked her stick up for her. She became a part of them."

She'd had quite a few reasons to become a part of the film.

"You always look at any audition as a chance to *not* be a struggling actor," Lagano says. "The fact that it was based on a true story got me excited. It was about girls playing basketball in high school, and that was my sport." Born in Brooklyn, she'd moved to Oregon in time to play high school basketball.

Driscoll and his squad were based on the doings of Jim Keith, whose girls won over 600 games at five different schools in nearly four decades of coaching. Now Lagano and her co-stars could act out of the beginnings of a team that inspired their state, and ultimately the nation.

Alicia Lagano and the rest of 2006's *Believe in Me* showed that their squad could make it to number one if they just had enough people who believed in them.

"You want to do it right," she says, "because there is a real person out there, and it feels more important. We knew that we would be meeting some of these women and their real coach, and you want to do their story right."

Lagano gave herself the chance to do that back on the courts she hadn't seen for nearly a decade.

"I called a bunch of friends," she says. "Let's get some people! We were playing basketball, and I threw myself out on the basketball court. I picked it up again pretty fast." A few weeks and auditions later, she won a roster spot, and things got a bit more real and difficult.

"They flew us out of New Mexico," she says, "and for two or three weeks, we practiced for seven or eight hours a day. We had playbooks to learn. I felt like I was back in high school."

As her squad starts to win more and more, Frances starts to experience the benefits basketball offers, far past physicality.

"Frances was a sweet, shy, odd teenager," Lagano describes. "Her strict religious upbringing had a tough side. She found through basketball how to be part of a team. That was different from me at that time, and I was drawn to it."

But remember, this is 1960s Oklahoma, and female basketball players aren't supposed to really care. It's not about winning, just about having something to do between classes and motherhood preparation. Driscoll's not supposed to *coach* or anything, just be a body, a mannequin, a talking head.

So when he actually asks his players to try, they're OK with it, per usual for girls. But their folks aren't, and Frances' yank her off the team. But they didn't expect her to stand up for herself, to run away, to get pregnant. That's what happens when parents push their daughters too hard for too long.

"There was a lot I had to come up with on my own," Lagano says. "(Director Robert Collector and) I came up with a backstory for her and what she went through, growing up in a religious family and a strict background. You have to trust in the words on the page sometimes."

Believe in Me's script, whose words had first drawn Lagano to the storyline like a magnet, gave her plenty to jump from. But she and the rest of the crew got an extra boost from those who had been there and played that: the cast met with the people they'd be portraying.

"They told us story after story," she remembers. "Back in the 1960s, women playing basketball weren't taken very seriously. We heard their stories about who they became."

As they practiced, the performing Lady Cyclones got some help from the fellow whose life story begat their cinematic quest; Keith coached them through a few practices.

"We got some one-on-one time with him," she says. "We were all asking him questions."

Frances was based on a real person, to an extent; in the film, Frances leaves the team, gets pregnant, becomes a mom, then comes back to the squad just in time. In reality, Frances' role model did leave, but didn't return.

Still, we the audience would see a bit more, realistic or otherwise. Frances and her fellows become so close to Driscoll that she actually asks him to be there for the birth, another scene probably sprung from a screenwriter's imagination—and anyone who sees a lady go through that, not to mention the nine-month preamble, has no business even debating who the stronger sex truly is!

The morning of filming, Lagano remembers, she was lucky enough to find an unexpected role model: a mom in wardrobe.

"She had given natural birth," Lagano remembers. "I told her, you're in the room with me, to walk me through this. She taught me about the sounds I was going to be making, the pains I should be feeling. I had her by my side the whole time." She comes back, and the team keeps winning.

Believe in Me is nothing like a conventional film; ergo, no one need be surprised that it doesn't take the usual way out with the conclusion. The Lady Cyclones win the state title: huge comeback, last-second desperation shot, and hugging galore (of course, Frances and her coach share an embrace), and most flicks would have ended on that high note.

Not this movie. Bruce Dern's superintendent Ellis Brawley, in the typical jerkweed mode that educational higher-ups usually play in such films, still wants Driscoll gone, and he's going to use Francis' pregnancy and school leave not just to get the coach fired, but the title forfeited. With connections all over town, Brawley's quite used to getting his way.

"Bruce Dern is an interesting man to work with," Lagano says. "He stays with his character. He's pretty intense; he scared the crap out of us. This turned out to be a really intense scene." Driscoll steps into Brawley's office.

But it's not just him. The parents, finally behind him, are standing with him. The school administrators are there too. And the players come to back him one last time. Finally, the state school group sides with Driscoll, against Brawley, in favor of those who worked so hard, and, in Keith's case, stood behind him for nearly forty years (Keith died in 2011).

I've always been too cheap to be a gambling man, but I'd be willing to bet that if some experienced boxers learned about what Hilary Swank did to get ready to act like one of them for just a few months, they'd probably say, "Wow, I never even trained that hard for any of my fights!"

Try about five hours of training a day (in the gym and the weight room), six days a week. Needing nine hours of snooze time a night, but having to break it up in order to awaken and down a protein shake. Downing enough eggs whites to cause exhaustion in a henhouse, a few schools' worth of raw fish, and gallons of flax oil.

Hilary Swank trained harder than many actual boxers to
grab her second Oscar in 2004 for *Million Dollar Baby*.

"The biggest thing I learned in making this movie were the obstacles I set for myself," Swank recalls of her marathon regime for *Million Dollar Baby* (2004), as hard hitting in the emotions as in the jaw. "I will tell you that as my body started physically getting stronger, I felt so powerful, but not in an 'I'll kick your ass' type of way. You realize that your body's a machine. When you see that people, a long time ago, were running to hunt their food, you realize that our bodies can conform and adapt to what we need." She was working on becoming Maggie Fitzgerald, a streetwise, upbeat young lady who never found her spot in life until the first time she stepped between the ropes. Behind the camera in the directing chair, Clint Eastwood stood before it as Frankie, a trainer battling his own inner demons until this new beam of light comes from nowhere.

Over a decade later, Maggie's toughness stays in Swank. Sure, the actress freely admits, she had a bit of shoulder trouble. A couple of bloodings and bruisings across her face. Nothing too far out of the ordinary for someone who needed to get used to spending time inside a boxing ring.

Oh, except for that little staph infection that just about took her foot and leg, and could have been more if nothing had been done in time. Swank shrugs it off like nothing but a glorified splinter.

"I got a blister the size of my palm on my right foot from pivoting," she explains, "and it was really swollen, and I couldn't train and walk on it. So I popped it myself, and it got infected." Soon after, she woke up one morning with a streak running up her leg.

"When I got to my doctor, he said, 'Put your foot down. Stand up,'" she remembers. "He said, 'This is very serious. You have to stop boxing immediately, and you are going to stay right here.' He drew a line on my leg, so it wouldn't go above that, because if that gets to your heart, you die. If that infection makes it up to your heart, that's it. So obviously, it was devastating news to me that I wasn't going to be able to box.

"I said, 'I need to box. Will it be over in two days?' and he said, 'Listen to me. You have to stop. This is life threatening. You have to stop. Just stop. Get your infection until it's gone, and then you can go training again.'"

Her work ethic inadvertently violated, Swank sat down and waited for the potentially fatal pest to run its course. And while she back-kicked, she may have just sat back and remembered. Perhaps she thought about how lucky she'd been to tell another tragic tale five years earlier in *Boys Don't Cry*, beating out hundreds of other performers for the lead of Brandon Teena, whose rape and eventual murder forced America to acknowledge anti-gay violence for one of the first times. She could have recalled how she'd carried it all the way to her first Oscar, something millions of others only dream of. Swank had beaten much bigger odds than any staph infection could offer; this was just above nothing at all.

And eventually, she and Maggie would be taking chances far, far bigger than it. But that would only be part of a movie.

"When I felt like the line was gone and it wasn't red anymore, I couldn't box still because I couldn't pivot on it, but I was still doing weight training," she says. "My trainer would piggyback me to the gym, and I'd do everything I could where I wasn't standing on it. I was doing all my upper body and my sit-ups, and then he'd piggyback me back to my place." Nearly twenty pounds of toned muscle found their way onto her frame.

But it wasn't all physical for her, as with any boxer. It's easy to label boxing just a brutal brawl-a-thon, a whoever-hits-hardest-wins, mindless sport, but anyone who has stepped into the ring for a time (as in, a long career, not just a few fights) can attest to the mental tenacity that goes right along with hooks and jabs.

That's something that Swank had to implant in Maggie as well. From the stands, she watched over her real-life colleagues, looking past the physical strength they displayed, all the way to the mind games that boxers utilize, the true mentality of the sport.

"It's like a great game of chess," she explains, "and I say that because when you're in the ring, you're one with this person. Everything goes silent and it's you and that person. You hear your breath. You hear the other person. And as you try to figure out your [opponent's] strength and weakness, you're learning about your own. And each person that you spar with, their strength and weakness brings out new strength and weakness in yourself. And the second you think, 'I have this person,' and you get cocky, you're going to get beat."

Swank never let Maggie cross such a line; Maggie's skills take her further than about any actual lady boxer has ever gone, but her ego never reaches that point. But just as she gets there, it all crashes down in every sense of the expression; a cheap shot from an opponent renders her a quadriplegic, faced with losing the only thing that meant anything to her.

Off camera, Swank's preparation didn't stop when her role changed. She stopped hitting the gym and the ring—couldn't have Maggie getting buffer from a hospital bed. But this new plight gave Swank a chance to show yet another side of herself as a performer, different than anything she'd done on the screen before.

"More than anything, it was a reminder," she explains, "after all those days when I complained about getting up to use my body—of the position I could have been in, or anyone can be in, where all of a sudden there's a big shift, and you're not able to use your body, and how easily we take our health for granted . . . Every time I got to get up out of that bed and realize that I hadn't broken my neck and I could still utilize my body was also a wonderful reminder to me to not take my health for granted and to use it."

It's a lesson that Maggie herself seems to learn as well; in her hospital bed, she's unable to stop looking back, and can't bear to forget where she once was. There may be nothing left, but she got what she needed, and it's enough for her, and eventually Frankie, who Maggie convinces to give her a lethal dose of adrenalin.

Swank—and the film—didn't make Maggie necessarily heroic, only human. The inspirational, Disney-type ending would be to have her decide to be the best she could, even with her physical ailments, or, by some miracle, overcome them. But Eastwood films have never gone for the sappy, feel-good ending; just like with *Mystic River* the year before and later in 2008 with *Gran Torino*, *Million Dollar Baby* went out the realistic way, not necessarily the pleasurable one.

And it worked to perfection; Swank got her Best Actress, Eastwood his Best Director and Best Picture, and Morgan Freeman, long considered to be one of the most underrated performers in the game, took the Best Supporting nod he'd deserved for years.

But even after scoring her second Oscar, Swank still appears to moving toward the main events of her acting career—at least nowhere near the farewell match. There's never enough to learn, to do, and to work hard for. She's one who showed that putting hard work above luck and connections can push a person to stardom and keep them there.

"The reason I became an actress is that I love people and love people's stories and every person has a story," she explains. "It's my job to tell those stories. Whether I agree with the story or believe in it or believe in that way of life, it's important for movies to entertain, or to discover, or to escape. And that's my job. I believe in showing all different ways of life whether I live in it or not. The great thing about [this job] is that I get to learn a lot about life. And it constantly helps me discover what I believe and what I don't believe. That stuff is ever changing because we're growing all the time."

We found out once again that science can be our worst enemy in 2009's *Splice*, even if the end result is as lovely as Delphine Chaneac's Dren.

Delphine Chaneac: *Splice*

DIDN'T WE LEARN ANYTHING from Mary Shelley?

Don't we know by now, centuries after she wrote the book on it (literally!), and nearly a century after her story first hit the big screen, haven't we understood that humanity is the best that it can be?

Stories about scientists trying to take what people had to offer and making it just a little bit better, only to see it blow up in their faces, pardon the pun, tend to turn out the same, for all sorts of reasons. Somehow or other, things appear to start out wonderfully, as Shelley's doctor and his colleague Moreau showed us. But eventually, these new creations, for love, evil, insanity, or any other reason, end up turning against them and causing all sorts of death and destruction.

Films like this don't just show the danger of upsetting the balance between man and nature, and that of allowing egotism to turn into a Higher complex. They show a true but rarely mentioned threat to humanity that science can cause, if we allow it. Eventually, the project we create might become better, smarter, and more evil than us, and in sci-fi films, it often does. But beyond that, the thing we create might even become a bit more pure, more caring, more loving. In other words, it might end up being a more ideal version of humanity than we ourselves.

For her first big role in America, Delphine Chaneac had to bring said human-esque variation to life, albeit not quite human life.

"For Dren, I have to feel (rather than say) everything, to communicate with the audience and the people," recalls Chaneac, as she prepared to become Dren, the creation of scientists

Adrien Brody and Sarah Polley in 2009's *Splice*. "At the beginning, when I read the script, I was a bit frustrated, because I didn't speak. But after one week of rehearsal, I felt much better."

Brody and Polley are Clive and Elsa, a pair of genetic scientists in and out of the lab. Frustrated by their bosses' nervousness to go to the bigger and better levels of blending human DNA with other animals' for hybrid experiments, the pair are on their own, not letting little things like laws and ethics get anywhere near them.

Their new creation? Thy name be Dren (Nerd spelled backward, not exactly an inside joke).

Over in her French homeland, Chaneac was acting her way through a scene in a previous work when a casting director came by.

"She said I had a lot of muscle," says Chaneac, an eight-year karate aficionada. "She said it was nice because a Canadian guy was coming to France looking for someone to do a physical role."

The flick would be the next creation of Vincenzo Natali, who'd creeped out American audience in 1997 with his directorial debut *Cube*, the *Saw*-like story of a few strangers trapped in a deadly maze.

"I thought Vincenzo was crazy," Chaneac says, "but [*Cube*] was an amazing movie." The description of her next tryout, however, probably didn't improve her assessment of the director's stability.

"He told me I had to play a bird mixed with a girl," she says. "I was like, 'What?'" Then she found out that Natali had been working all millennium to bring his vision to reality. That, combined with the chance to spread her name across a new continent, gave her some new reasons to go for it at full force.

Then she learned even more about what becoming Dren would allow her to do—or, in this case, not do at all. As in, no speaking, no life skills, no idea of how to interact with others. In this case, the whole child-trapped-in-an-adult's-body term didn't mean that she was immature.

"She's instinctive," she says of Dren. "I put everything into my eyes, my skin, my nose, my mouth, to say different kinds of feelings."

Indeed, physicality was going to make up the overwhelming majority of the character. Fortunately, her background gave Chaneac a head (and high-kicking) start.

"[Karate] helped me because it helps you to control your body more when you practice something like this," says Chaneac, who stepped up her avid running getting ready for the flick. "I think you have more control on your feet, on your arms and maybe on your mind. It helps you to focus on just one thing . . . I think karate is very good, whether for women or men or children or adults, because you are more focused, you can separate your mind—one part is for acting and one part is for how you move your body." It wasn't until much later, however, that she realized just what kind of physical study Dren had, perhaps inadvertently, become.

She shaved her head, and makeup widened and added scars around her naturally bright eyes to make them just a bit more inquisitive. Prosthetic hands and feet gave her the ability to improvise as a bird. She also gave Dren a series of curious gestures and grunts, the true nature of a newborn trying to find a place in the whole new world, and listened to music from The Cure to get into character.

"I didn't use anything specific and just used my imagination," she says. "[Dren is] new in this world, so I have no reference. I tried to forget everything I know about the world . . . [Dren] doesn't know anything."

It wasn't her looks that made Dren so memorable; although Chaneac has them to spare (she's like a cross between Mila Jovovich and Angelina Jolie, and that's one hell of a combo), she didn't get to show them off. Not her physical gifts, but they were there too. It was quite simply that Dren started out as a kind, decent creation of innocence, and lost it not because of choice, or anything she could control, but by society itself. It's the same qualities that made Dr. Frank's monster such a frightening but lovable character.

Eventually, Elsa takes on a maternal nature towards Dren (it's insinuated in the plot that she previously miscarried, or lost a child otherwise), while Clive can't seem to figure out exactly what he feels. Eventually, he and Dren get a bit too close during a dance scene—Brody and Chaneac both called it one of their favorites of the film—and end up making love, only to be caught by Elsa and sending Dren over the edge of sanity.

"At the beginning [of filming]," Chaneac says of her co-stars, "I didn't know that much English, so I was shy and was afraid to say stupid things. It made a wall between us, but a good one. I think I put it up and put some distance there. I wanted to be a bit of an outsider."

Shocked, confused, and terrified, even trapped in her own body, Dren appears to commit suicide. But it turns out she was just in a coma, and the evolution that caused her to grow from a fetus to an adult in a few days continues, turning her into a crazed guy (that's quite a plot hole, isn't it? A woman *evolves*, ergo *improves*, into a man? Pretty good way to alienate your female viewers!) that manages to kill Clive and rape—and, as we learn in the last scene, impregnate—Elsa before Elsa manages to kill her, or him, or it, depending on one's opinion.

A few months later, Chaneac, along with millions of viewers, checked out her Old Glory debut. When she showed up on screen, no one was quite sure exactly what they were looking at, including her.

For the viewers, that was because Dren was an only part-human scientific creation born light years away from nature. For Chaneac, it was because she honestly didn't realize just how far her physicality had gone.

"[Watching the film] the first time was very strange," she says, "because I couldn't recognize myself. Not because they changed my body a lot, or because they changed my face, but just because the work was so hard physically that my body was completely not the same. My shoulder was doubled, my legs were doubled, my neck was big, with a bald head. It wasn't the same girl. But I didn't feel that when I was on set, because I was working and didn't pay attention to my body, to me. I was working for Dren."

The Incubus' power and strength, in the persona of Alain Chanoine, turned him into one of the *Suicide Squad*'s toughest opponents in the 2016 film.

Alain Chanoine: *Suicide Squad*

ONCE A DEMON GETS inside of you, well, there's no telling what the hell it might bring. It might make you babble all kinds of high-speed obscenity, toss others around like toys, even kill them, just because it can.

Gerard Davis, like all of those who become the inadvertent habitats of these critters, never knew about it, never expected it, certainly didn't want it. He just happened to be in the wrong subway station at the wrong time.

"It's a little hard to approach," admits Alain Chanoine of the man/monster he became in 2016's *Suicide Squad*. "How does a demon think?"

There's a ton of options to try, and if we find one that *might* work, that *could* be correct, that's enough for fans; after all, no one can ever truly answer that question. People in Chanoine's position just have to give it up to their all and more.

The incentive had been there for him, and effort had followed soon after. "My agent had told me that there was a huge project, and I met with [director and writer] David Ayer," Chanoine remembers. "I was a big fan, so I was interested at first more because of the director than the movie at the time." Then he found out he'd get to battle some folk he'd been reading about for decades.

"I'd been a fan of the comics since I was a little kid," says Chanoine. "I read *X-Men* all the time." He'd been part of the stunt crew of *X-Men: Days of Future Past* in 2014.

"This was going to be the biggest movie I'd ever worked on," he continues. "Knowing I'd get to work with Jared Leto, Will Smith, and Cara Delevingne, I was in love with the whole experience. The fact that it was DC Comics, with such a big budget, the people I was going to work with, it was a no-brainer."

After years of modeling, Delevingne was looking for her own break in a new business, starting off *Squad* as June Moore, a fellow innocent carrier of evil. The succubus Enchantress steps inside her, and goes looking for a partner.

She and Chanoine had worked things out with a "chemistry read" early in filming. "We got along right away," he remembers. "Once we got on set, we knew we had that vibe. We're supposed to be brother and sister, so we can't be acting like strangers."

The demoness happens on Davis, and jams her sibling's spirit into him. Soon he's the giant Incubus, destroying subways, buses, and all those unlucky enough to be around.

"An Incubus, originally, is a sexual demon, who in medieval times would impregnate women in their sleep," Chanoine explains. "I read all about demons, their backgrounds. What are my familiar traits with the character? With his ego size, how do I like power? Who do I like having power over? This incubus and succubus have power over the world. I focused on these traits, some I have, some I don't have, and how I could get in character from there." Though death and destruction are normalcy for the Incubus (a very small part of the Squad's battles on the pages, which first launched in 1988) early on, but there's still the potential for good, as he heals Sis's wounds after a battle, showing traces of the makeup that won the film an Academy Award.

"It was challenging, because we had to learn a language called Moonspeak that our demons speak," Chanoine says. "David Ayer was very flexible, letting us make up the language. He knew that I speak French and Creole, and he asked me to make it sound like me, but nothing like anything but Moonspeak. We were speaking this language that no one else could understand."

He whomps an attacking military force, and nearly takes out Squad man El Diablo (Jay Hernandez). But a military guy shoves a bomb under both of them, and it takes out himself and both metahumans.

"I was ten feet tall in the movies, except when I am [Davis]," Chanoine says. "It was unreal, everything I'd done on green screens, all the effects, I can't describe it. There's just certain times in your career when you think, 'This is it! This is one of the biggest movies I've ever been in!'"

Tragically and unfairly, Lana Clarkson's tragic murder in 2003 won her more recognition than decades of being one of the hardest-working ladies in the action film world.

Lana Clarkson

WHAT IF LANA CLARKSON had just had the night off?

Why couldn't she have missed the strange-looking man in the House of Blues restaurant? If only she'd decided not to go to his home.

Just how far would she have gone in the acting world? Would she have snared the superstardom that always seemed to loom just out of her reach? Would she be able to break through the glass ceiling of acting roles and work that sadly typecasted her because of her height, and on to those that would really push her straight to the upper echelon of stardom?

Because of the bullet that fallen music legend Phil Spector fired that dark February 2003 night, we'll never know. Now all we can do is look back at the person she was, the actress she hoped to become . . . and wonder.

Clarkson was a bright light that didn't get to shine long enough—not just because of her gorgeous smile and physical being, but because of who she was off the screen.

A devoted performer who went full force into every piece of work she did (how many have made such as splash with a one-word performance as Clarkson's walk-on as Mr. Vargas' bombshell wife in 1982's *Fast Times at Ridgemont High*?)—and not just in acting; Clarkson volunteered in programs that delivered food to Los Angeles HIV/AIDS patients. The uncommon devotion she showed her fans at sci-fi and comic book conventions across the Golden State, thanking those who formed her a cult following from her roles in *Amazon Women on the Moon* (1987) and the *Barbarian Queen* films, was all but legendary.

"She was an awesome beauty," says Edward Lozzi, Clarkson's publicist. "She loved to be on the sets, loved to get her lines right, loved the preparation of it. She could turn herself into anyone. She was a chameleon; she had a knack for becoming a role. They knew that if they needed a particular type, that she would be the person for that."

After short roles in *Fast Times* (a performance originally intended to be much more diverse, but strapped by time constraints, according to Lozzi) and *Scarface* the next year, Clarkson appeared in dozens of television shows, ranging from *A-Team* to *The Jeffersons* to *Who's the Boss*.

"She was lovely and terrific to work with," recalls Tom Holland, who directed Clarkson in a 1986 episode of Steven Spielberg's fantasy TV series *Amazing Stories*. "Miscalculation" was the tale of a young nerd (Jon Cryer, in a role not unlike the one he'd undertake about over a decade later as neurotic Alan on *Two and a Half Men*!) who invents a potion that brings magazine photos to life. Clarkson was his first model project, emerging as an angry giantess and tearing apart the student's apartment after he pours too much of the potion on her picture. In the darkest of ironies, the episode also starred Rebecca Schaeffer, whose 1989 murder at the hands of a stalker would lead to new laws protecting celebrities' privacy (the killer had obtained her address and other person information from the DMV).

"[Clarkson] was also taller than me and statuesque as they sat," remembers Holland, whose name continued to pop up in the horror flick world for the next few decades, as he directed and/or wrote *Child's Play* (1988) and *Fright Night* (1985), as well as the Stephen King novel adaptations *The Langoliers* (1995) and *Thinner* (1996).

Clarkson's film cult following started to take off in 1985, playing the main role of Amethea, the sword-wielding heroine of the over-the-top (fitting for her!) action flick *Barbarian Queen* (a tall, athletic, martial-arts-gifted blonde, it's easy to imagine Clarkson playing many of Uma Thurman's roles, especially the Bride). Clarkson, her trademark devotion showing, worked hard with saber handling and martial arts—her lifelong love of horseback riding also came into play—getting ready for the role, in which she led a group of women to a Roman city to free their former villagers, who'd been kidnapped and forced into slavery.

Two years later, her training would come back around when she reprised the role in *Barbarian Queen II: The Empress Strikes Back*. This time, Clarkson's character would be terrorized by an evil king and his daughter Tamis.

"Lana Clarkson was a really nice girl," says Cecilia Tijerina, just a teenager when she portrayed the cold princess. "I didn't know she was a big, huge icon. She was very down to earth. She didn't behave like a star."

Clarkson helped the youngster get ready to be evil, including a scene where Tamis places a huge tarantula on the warrior's arm.

"I was surprised that I wasn't afraid of [the spider]," says Tijerina, still a common sight on Spanish screens big and small. "[Clarkson] gave me several suggestions on how to do the scenes, and even invited me out for cocktails. I told her I was too young to drink."

At about the same time Clarkson was trying to break into the film world, people like Michael Worth were working their way in. After making his film debut in the 1992 kung fu flick *Final Impact*, Worth, a black belt in karate and lifelong film fan, did stunt work for 1995's *Batman Forever*.

One day, he was stretching on the stairs outside an independent film studio when a familiar lady strolled over and inquired of his athletic background. Worth knew he'd seen the woman before, but he didn't know where.

Then, in the midst of a conversation about the commercial she was making, Clarkson offhandedly mentioned her own film background.

"My first impression was how tall she was," he remembers. "She had striking features and really stood out in a crowd, with a lot of energy. She was not shy or introverted to be sure." (Note: with virtually everyone mentioning her height, it's easy to see Clarkson as some kind of fairytale-esque giantess or something; in actuality, she was just under six feet).

"Lana wanted to just try and improve her skills to help push her into a more legitimate area for film," Worth recalls. "There were a lot of female action heroes coming out and she knew with her size and personality, it was a skill she could use. She was athletic, so she was an easy person to assimilate the training. She had long legs and was flexible so I helped her use that to her advantage. Those high kicks would be impressive on film, and she was getting pretty proficient with them."

Learning about editing to diversify his own filmmaking career, Worth put together a demo reel of her career. Clarkson asked him to include some footage of her and John Ritter during her short appearance on *Three's Company*.

"I was explaining to her that, since she was concerned with her age and getting the prime roles, that including the clip would date her, even though she was very young at the time she did it," he explains. "It's a silly part of the ageism battle performers go through, particularly women, but she was always very positive about her future and certainly never showed a despondent or futile attitude about her career."

Just before Christmas 2001, Clarkson fell and broke some ribs while dancing with some youngsters at a holiday party. She'd be on the acting sidelines with rehabilitation for much of the next year, and take on the House of Blues job until her career kicked back up (Lozzi called the restaurant job "a very good source of income" for Clarkson).

Displaying the upbeat attitude that made her a favorite to all, Clarkson worked hard to get back in shape, even putting together *Lana Unleashed*, a comedy tour in which she'd personify a crazed nun, a psychotic real estate agent, and a post-plastic surgery Little Richard.

In late 2002, Worth was signing autographs at a Pasadena convention. Suddenly, a familiar voice rang out.

"Lana was at a big table with a group of other celebrities, signing pictures from her films," Worth recalls. "She was talking about some new auditions she had felt good about and was wanting to get together and grab something to eat sometime soon."

But he'd never get the chance—and before Clarkson would be able to show the public a new side of Lana, tragedy struck.

No one will ever know the full story of what happened that fateful night of February 2, 2003. Suffice it to say that Clarkson and Spector, known of one of the music world's most innovative producers during the 1960s and a member of the Rock 'N Roll Hall of Fame, ran into each other at the eatery and ended up back at his apartment. Before the sun came up, Clarkson was dead, a bullet in her head.

Driving around the city that night, Worth heard on the radio that a "low budget film actress" had been killed. He hoped it wasn't who he suspected.

"Both times I heard about this anonymous starlet," he remembers, "I was immediately thinking of Lana, as I think in one case they mentioned she had done some sword and sandal type films, but shrugged it off, as the coincidence seemed too great."

Later that night, the sad truth came. Laying in bed, Worth heard his old friend's name come across the news.

"I immediately sat straight up," he says. "The moment was so surreal to me. I don't know, maybe I somehow felt that life force of hers burn out that night, but I'll never forget it."

Spector, who had a history of drug and alcohol problems, claimed that a depressed Clarkson—herself experienced with guns—had turned the firearm on herself.

Problem was, that statement flew into a lifetime of counterclaims, as anyone who'd known Clarkson could attest, and many, including Lozzi, did so on television and in the media.

"The defense was that was she was a down-and-out actress, who was suicidal because she'd turned 40," says Lozzi, who claims that Clarkson contacted him as late as December 2002 for help promoting her comedy tour. "Give me a break."

Spector must have convinced some; he remained free for over four years. His first trial ended in a mistrial. But on April 13, 2009, he was convicted of second-degree murder. A month later, he was sentenced to nineteen years to life in prison.

Sadly, Clarkson's name became more well known than ever because of how she died. But in her career, she personified exactly the qualities that can make a performer successful: a never-give-up attitude, a passion for her work, and a first-class attitude all the way around. Like many in her profession, Clarkson was never too concerned about world-famous superstardom, about seeing her name written in huge letters on a billboard or marquee. She acted because acting was what she liked to do (among other things, obviously), and no one who ever made a success in the profession did it just because it was a business. Add that in to the fact that Clarkson took the time to pay her own tribute to the people that appreciated her, and we have a role model for performers.

"I take the responsibility of carrying a picture very seriously," she said in the early 90s. "You have to believe in the moment. There's a fine line you have to walk. I don't mind being typecast in fantasy, but I also don't mind making fun of my own persona."

Millions of people know how Lana Clarkson died—let us now remember how she lived.

No one knew the inside connection that Frank Cullotta (right) held to the events of 1995's *Casino*.

Frank Cullotta/Carl Ciarfalio: *Casino*

NO MATTER HOW HIGH you get, no matter how many people you scare, no matter how intimidating you believe you are, no one's ever safe in the mob. Loyalty simply doesn't exist. In fact, your closest associates (friends? Don't even use the term) are the most likely to backstab you, and that's in every sense of the term. The ones that spend the most time next to you are the ones that end up turning on you, and even the untouchable are rendered human.

Even with the name of Martin Scorsese heading up the credits, the same mind that dumped endless blood and gore into *Raging Bull* (1980) and *Goodfellas* (1990), many were surprised at how violent *Casino* (1995) was. It's just what happens when things go wrong within the mafia.

Many in the life don't live to tell the tale. Those that do, though, may end up in the movies.

"I'd been on the inside," Frank Cullotta remembers. "I'd seen it all. They knew I was the only survivor of that crew."

The crew in terminology was the "Hole in the Wall Gang." Not quite the most intimidating mob name, but you wouldn't say that to their faces.

For a few of the late 1970s and early 1980s, Tony Spilotro headed up the group, which started out in Chicago and headed to Las Vegas. Cullotta, who deemed himself "The Las Vegas Boss," took things over in Nevada.

Here's the film connection: Scorsese turned Spilotro into Santoro. Nicky Santoro. The same guy that Joe Pesci made into just as rough a mob man as he had Tommy DeVito in *Goodfellas*. Cullotta was Frank Marino, now in Frank Vincent's body. Unlike his former boss, though, Cullotta was around to speak his past.

"I found out about *Casino* in 1993," recalls Cullotta. Nicholas Pileggi, whose *Wiseguy* tome had helped *Goodfellas* to the screen, was heading behind the dangerous scenes again to write about the rise and fall of mafia involvement in Vegas of the 1970s and 80s.

The two talked for a while, and Cullotta, perhaps not intentionally, discussed what became the film's most infamous scene. Not too long after, Cullotta, who'd done time behind bars and in Witness Protection, got a notice from Scorsese.

"I didn't know who he was," Cullotta says. "I don't follow movie stars or directors. He wanted to make a movie about cheating in the casinos." Eventually, Pileggi and Scorsese uncovered sufficient information to put *Casino* on the pages and the screen.

"I kept meeting with De Niro, meeting with Pesci," Cullotta says. "Finally, they had enough ammunition." Talk about a rough way to say it.

He watched De Niro (yes, Robert, like you didn't know!) become Sam "Ace" Rothstein, who Cullotta had known as Frank "Lefty" Rosenthal. Pesci was Santoro, the same longtime friend of Rothstein that Spilotro had been of Rosenthal. Just as Rosenthal did, Rothstein heads up a casino in Vegas. Just as Spilotro did, Santoro represents the mob muscle behind it.

Just as Cullotta was, Marino's one of Santoro's right-hand men.

"Frank Vincent followed me around, to see my eyes, my slang, how I spoke, my demeanor, to learn how to portray me," Cullotta says. "Sometimes he used New York terms, and I straightened that out." At the time, Cullotta was representing the gap between his real life and the film's fictionalized one as a consultant.

Not enough.

"I told them I wanted to be in the movie, to do some hits," he says. "I got more money. They said sure. It was very easy." Very easy. Frighteningly easy. Unthinkable to many, except those who'd been where he had.

A bit past halfway through, Santoro's group starts to collapse under its own weight, and, pushed along by backstabbing, adultery, drugs, and everything else that can drag down the most illegitimate of businesses, everyone loses it all—and those that still have their lives are the only lucky ones.

Here's where all the violence we discussed comes around. People get whacked just for seeing or knowing a few wrong things. They're killed, buried, hidden away forever, just because they *might* say something wrong. These guys shoot first and don't worry about asking questions later.

In one of the film's saddest scenes, Alan King's Andy Stone, one of the few who'd tried to do right even amongst the mafia, steps through a courthouse parking lot.

Suddenly, a far from inconspicuous fellow steps behind him, and calmly puts a bullet through his head. Another follows suit. The two walk away, as stoic as if this were an everyday thing.

It might not have been *that* common for Cullotta, who'd played the first man. But he was ready for it, and another.

Fleeing the country, one of Santoro's other former colleagues holes up in Costa Rica. But then we land outside his condo. We see him desperately run down the breezeway, already carrying a bullet. He smashes a window to get back inside, but a pursuer follows. More gunshots roll, and the man staggers outside, falling to his knees. Then another man, the same one that shot Stone, comes up behind him and plants a bullet straight through his head.

It's hardly the film's roughest scene. But it just might have been the most factual.

In the fall of 1979, the Hole men learned that a man named Sherwin Lisner was telling the cops about them. With Spilotro's blessing, Cullotta and another fellow paid Lisner a visit on October 10. By the end of the night, Cullotta had put three bullets in Lisner's head.

"It was just my life," he says. "You don't think of those things. If you do, you'll wind up in the nuthouse."

Ironically enough, after all that, Cullotta's character's toughest scenes are two the man himself wasn't even present for. The first happens about halfway through, and we'll go into all kinds of down and dirty detail later. This one is one of the film's finales.

Santoro's gone too far. Too much violence, too much heat, too little control. Back near the Windy City homeland, he goes to meet with some pals out in a cornfield. His friend Marino's right there with him—with a baseball bat that he puts into Santoro's back. The others have them too. Santoro and his brother get a taste of the medicine they'd been handing out all film. Bashed nearly unrecognizable, the two are buried alive.

Oh, it happened, all right; Spilotro and his brother were found buried in an Indiana cornfield in June 1986. But Cullotta, who'd already had dangerous issues with Spilotro, was under government protection at the time.

"I brought that up," he remembers. "I said, 'Marty, I didn't kill this guy.' He said he was trying to show that it's usually your best friend that sets you up to be killed. I didn't like it, but it's part of Hollywood." You never know—after Pesci beat up Vincent in *Raging Bull* and killed him in *Goodfellas*, maybe Scorsese just wanted Vincent to get some payback. *Note: Sadly, Vincent passed away on Sept. 13, 2017, just days before this book went to press.*

"I've seen so much violence in my lifetime that it didn't bother me," Cullotta says of seeing the film. "It was just the way I used to live."

Now let's talk about the scene that introduces us to just how far the mob is willing to go in the wrong directions, one that we only wished had been made up.

Cullotta admits he wasn't present during the "incident," but he swore to Pileggi that it happened, when Spilotro and two other guys trapped a fellow named Billy McCarthy, who'd made an unauthorized triple murder, in a workshop.

They'd punched, kicked, and beaten him forever, but the SOB just held on. Finally, Tony was forced to do what we saw.

Ask anyone lucky enough to check out the epic to name the flick's most memorable scene, and chance are it won't take long to find someone who says, "Oh, man, that part with the vice was friggin' crazy!" or some variation thereof.

Yes—we're going there, led by a man so many had seen before *Casino*, but few would recognize offhand.

"What keeps me in stunt work is the same challenge that keeps everyone in it," explains Carl Ciarfalio. "We're a different breed, even on the sets. On the sets, the best, the funnest place to hang out is with us, with the stuntmen. We're pretty much all full of life—and a lot of us are full of ourselves—but we have a mutual respect with each other, or what we do. Whether you'll ever eat dinner with a man or not, if you're there on set, you're there for him. If you're a team player, that's the place to be."

Over the past few decades, he's been a member of more such teams than the NFL and NBA combined.

"I studied acting since I was twenty years old," he remembers. "I went to acting classes once or twice a week, and still do. I was fortunate enough to be working in my field performing live shows at amusement parks." Visitors to Knott's Berry Farm and/or Universal Studios saw him do his thing at the parks' live stunt shows.

"I thought I could be a professional ballplayer or something, and was never big enough or good enough, but I still wanted the challenge," he says. "Stunts afforded me the challenge. I could put myself in a situation where I would have to confront the situation itself, and it also gave me an opportunity to be an actor. It helped me channel that. I was thirty-two years old before I found out I had a career; my first ten years or so, I was just having fun. [Stunt people] are those personalities that want a challenge."

After starting off in the film stunt business in the late 1970s, Ciarfalio stepped—or in this case, fell—into the public eye with his turn in the 1984 action/crime drama *Against All Odds*. Doubling for NFL legend Alex Karras, he dropped sixty feet off a cliff into water.

"It made the people think two things," he says. "One, that I was an idiot, and, two, that I had a real heart and wanted to work. That was one of those opportunities that I got away from all right."

He did stunt work in dozens of films throughout the 80s and 90s, everything from *Beetlejuice* (1988) to *Wayne's World* (1992) to *In the Line of Fire* (1993).

Then came *Casino*.

Near the middle of the film, a rival boss decides to make a statement against Santoro's fellows. In typical mob fashion, he skips the phone and greeting cards and goes straight to the carbine.

We briefly see henchman Tony Dogs leading a trio into a restaurant, and suddenly turning it into a human target range. Shots are fired. Innocent people die. It's the in-out-type job that the pros specialize in.

And it's the sort of role in which Ciarfalio is at his best.

When he went to audition for the title of Tony, he recalls, "The casting director told me, 'I want you to call me every type of F-word that you can. Can you do that?'" Trying not to crack up, Ciarfalio assured her that he could.

"She said, 'Pretend I'm going to kill you, and I've got you tied down with your head in a vice, and you're yelling.' We had a 'Fuck-You Fest.' I guessed I had the best 'Fuck You's,' because I got the part."

While he was getting ready for the role, Ciarfalio visited a special effects house.

"They made a mold of my head," he says. "They altered it to the shape that would have me squeezed in the vice, with my eye popping out. They didn't know if they wanted me or the head to be squeezed." Imagine being given such a premonition of one's own demise.

The torturous slaughter of Tony Dogs (Carl Ciarfalio) won *Casino* an instant place in cinematic infamy in 1995.

Back on the screen, Santoro and his colleagues (including Marino, again only in the film) are out for revenge; no one's going to shoot up their place and not suffer for it. Only moments after we see him in full cock-of-the-walk mode, idly blasting away human lives like most people do with clay pigeons, Tony's on the other end. He's dragged through a warehouse, one eye basically enucleated, as a voiceover from Santoro describes the torture Tony endured in the time between the scenes ("We even stuck ice picks in his balls!" he exclaims, almost reverently). But Tony's still not ready to rat.

"I think Pesci screamed in my face for about an hour [beforehand]!" Ciarfalio laughs. "It was a real comfortable situation."

For the mobsters, there's only one choice left to get the name of the shooting mastermind. They toss Tony onto a table and plant his head between two large pieces of a vice.

"The first time the two guys are dragging me into the warehouse, and throw me on the table, I tried to sit up," Ciarfalio says. "I came off too strong. Scorsese said, 'No, no, you've been down for three days.'" He stayed down, hardly able to speak.

"Don't make me do this, Tony," Santoro almost pleads. "We go way back." (Remember what we said about doing this to an old friend?!) "Don't make me be a bad guy."

Recalling the words that won him the part, Ciarfalio only gets Tony to blurt a very weak, "Fuck . . . you."

The audience is shocked, and Santoro feels the same way.

"Two fucking days and nights!" he rages. "Fuck me? That's what you fucking tell me?" He turns the crank, and one of Tony's eyes starts to pop out of his face, though he can hardly scream in pain.

Tony's associates can't even watch—how grotesque does something have to be if *mob hitmen* are turning away in disgust?

"Charlie M!" Tony finally admits.

"Charlie M?" Santoro snorts, in a new kind of disbelief. "Charlie M?! You made me pop your eye out of your fuckin' head to protect *that piece of shit*?!"

"Kill me," Tony demands, weaker by the millisecond. In a final act of "mercy," his wish is granted.

Now, guess what? The scene was actually intended to be worse.

"The first cut was rated NC-17, because my eye came out and onto my cheek," Ciarfalio says. "Scorsese went back and edited it out, so my eye just starts to pop out. When I saw it, I wasn't so much watching myself as I was watching the scene." Perhaps that's why Scorsese chose to make the scene one of his film's most (in)famous—it's the climactic moment for the flick. Moments later in the film, Santoro and Ace start to lose control of their empire, and it's almost all downhill from there. It's Dogs' death that starts the downturn.

Shows that truth is more brutal than fiction, isn't it?

Audiences kept getting brief looks at Ciarfalio: he played a nameless criminal in *Con Air* (1997), and was the first murder victim of the Oscar-winning *Traffic* (2000). In 1999, he had another one-shot deal as a bodyguard in *Fight Club*.

A fellow named Lou (Peter Iacangelo) owns a bar, and he's just found out that a group of ruffians are using its basement to work out their differences with fisticuffs. Apparently, someone broke both the first and second rules of the club: "You do NOT talk about Fight Club."

Lou, with bodyguard Ciarfalio on his shoulder, storms down into the basement to straighten things out with ringleader Tyler Durden (Brad Pitt, although film fans know there's a twist to that one!). That was actually the toughest part of the scene, Ciarfalio says.

"I remember we did go up and down the stairs about forty-two times," he says. "Three hours turned into days, turned into weeks. [Director David] Fincher shoots a lot of takes until he gets some incredible stuff."

With ever-so-non-PC language, Lou orders everyone out. But Tyler can't seem to understand, until Lou plants a fist into his stomach.

"I didn't get it, Lou," Tyler groans, receiving a punch to the face.

"Still not getting it." One more blow seems to convince him.

"Ok, ok, I got it," Tyler admits. "Shit . . . I lost it."

Lou proceeds to beat the left side of hell out of Tyler, as the bodyguard keeps Tyler's friends away with a gun. As Tyler eggs him on, Lou proceeds to lay down a beating that few outside the worlds of boxing and ultimate fighting ever got in their lives.

Then Tyler springs at him, rubbing his broken, bloody face into Lou's body, just near the camera. Who is he? *What* is he? Tyler Durden is something other than human, past the experience of pain, not to be trifled with.

"You don't know where I've been, Lou!" he roars through clenched teeth. "You don't know *where* I've been." Lou, the bodyguard, and the viewers are freaking out.

"Fucking use the basement!" Lou fearfully concedes.

"Thanks, Lou," says the calming Durden. Then he points at the bodyguard.

"You too, buddy," he says. "See you next week!"

"Brad was a dream to work with," Ciarfalio says. "There was no ego. I took direction well, and knew what my job was. I knew where to stand, work, and jump in."

He was quickly back on the job, stunting in *Daddy Day Care* (2003), *Bruce Almighty* (2003), *Mission Impossible III* (2006), and other films.

For a guy who makes a living falling off or getting blown up in buildings, crashing cars and motorcycles, and getting shot, stabbed, beaten down, etc., Ciarfalio considers himself one of the more fortunate of his profession.

"Injuries? Yeah, I've been hurt," he says. "But when you sign up for it, it's just like football, and it's going to be pounding. You take all the precautions you can take, and if you don't, you're not going to last long. I had a double-hip replacement ten years ago, and I've been going strong ever since. I never had back or neck surgery, and those are the things that really hobble you up."

When he gives seminars to up-and-coming stunters, Ciarfalio lets them know that there's a few schools more important than those that teach him and his colleagues.

"Most [stunt workers] have a physical or highly athletic background," he says, "and I would tell [upcoming workers] that they can't do anything without a high school diploma, and that college matters. The business will always be here.

"Practice what you want to do. If you're a great motorcycle rider and that's what you want to do, that's great. But also learn gymnastics. Learn about stunt driving and fire. Go to a school, and learn how to choose stunts wise, because you can't live on just one ability; you can't be the guy that just does one thing. Knowledge is power. Knowing the cause and effect, how to set these stunts up, is a wealth of knowledge for people who are going to be skeptical. You can't be a one-hit wonder. You can't live in this industry with blinders on hoping to get noticed. You have to find a niche and make a conscious decision to be unique inside that niche—and then expand yourself."

There's respect out there that needs a bit of earning, and some dues that are paid with things other than bills and coins. It's all part of the starting line in the business.

Four decades ago, Martin Scorsese and Robert De Niro were part of the crowd that even then was already enlarging at high speed, swarming all over Hollywood's inner circle, gazing at that ominous arc. Might be tough to believe of the two now, but it's where most begin.

It's also where most creativity takes its roots. The film that launched a pair linked forever in cinema started off back in Scorsese's beginnings back in the Italian neighborhoods of New York. The rough lands of Queens he'd trekked through were the *Mean Streets* that De Niro, Harvey Keitel, and the rest of the cast would travel into one of 1973's most unexpected success stories . . . and, ultimately, more than a little bit more for all.

With filming taking place in Los Angeles, far from New York's storyline location, Richard Romanus didn't have much time to transform himself into a Big Apple mobster.

"My biggest hurdle was the New York accent," explains the Vermont native, "so I spent the whole rehearsal and shoot working on the accent by speaking with and listening to people in Little Italy." Such learnings would carry into animation in 1981 as Romanus voiced Harry Canyon, the death ray-firing cabbie of *Heavy Metal*.

Just like any other career path (like acting!), everyone who starts hopes to move towards the top, or at least near it. Even those considered, well, a bit short of enviable.

Keitel's Charlie Cappa dreams of truly making it as a made man. A Don. A Boss. Whatever means a higher-up in the most prestigious, affluent, and dangerous of businesses.

Loyalty can be one of the most dangerous qualities to practice in the mob, which is why it's so rare. It's partially why Charlie's stuck at the number running ranks; he just can't (or won't) get rid of his friend Johnny Boy. Like a crazy nerd who's managed to attach himself to the popular jockish big man on campus, Johnny's fast-talked and BS'ed his way into serious debt with too many wrong people, like the sharks far more predatory than their gill-gasping namesakes.

A few years later in *Goodfellas* (1990), De Niro would hold the position Charlie desires, but back then, being on the bottom rung of the acting world had De Niro, and Johnny, at the same mob rank in the *Streets*.

"My philosophy of life has always been the things you say yes to lead somewhere while the things you say no to lead nowhere," recalls Romanus, reaching for the role of debt "collector" Michael

Longo. "Michael was a New York character with great style. Also, my house was in foreclosure."

Sounds tough. Still, those pissing off the mob tend to end up losing far more than materialistics.

That, however, always happens to others. Not to Johnny. He's too slick to catch—and if his mouth doesn't get him out of trouble, his fists and friends will, as Charlie and others stand and fall aside him in bar brawls galore.

But Charlie's not going to do this forever. The mob doesn't leave well enough alone so well. If it's him or Johnny, he'd rather make it out alive.

It might be too late to save Johnny; people like Michael have seen his manipulation types before, and walked right over them. With Johnny's gun in his face, Michael shows just how much talk he knows this loudmouth is.

Martin Scorsese (right) might have been behind the camera, but it was Richard Romanus' Michael Longo (left) showing the dark(est) side of mafia handiwork in 1973's *Mean Streets*.

"I thought he was silly and funny and had to laugh," Romanus remembers. "De Niro thought it made his character look ridiculous and wanted me to appear frightened. We both spoke to Scorsese about it until I finally had to say to Marty 'Who's the director here, you or him?'" The director went with Romanus, and ended up with one of the film's top scenes.

Longo leaves, but this can't end like this. Even as Charlie and Johnny drive away, audiences can feel the tension building all film just about to boil over.

Then it does. Michael drives up next to them, and his underling Jimmy starts blasting away. It's Scorsese himself.

He's a good shot, but not a great one; Charlie's hit in the hand and wrecks the car, and Johnny gets one in the neck, but cops and docs arrive just in time—an ending De Niro and Scorsese recycled three years later, in a *far* different context, for *Taxi Driver*.

In 1980, Scorsese directed De Niro to his second Oscar in *Raging Bull*. The two went back to mob world in *Goodfellas* and again in *Casino* five years later, but De Niro sadly wasn't before the cameras of the 2006 mafia epic *The Departed*, which finally brought Scorsese his own statuette.

Romanus showed up all over screens big and small for the next three decades, including a recurring arc on *The Sopranos* as Richard La Penna. The estranged husband of Lorraine Bracco's Dr. Jennifer Melfi, La Penna's ironically a member of the Italian Anti-Defamation League, fighting those jerks in the media that keep showing Italians as little more than mad mean mobsters.

"Film is film," Romanus explains. "Whether it's a feature or television, the prep is the same: learn your lines so well as to be able to recite them without thinking."

Billy Hayes (Brad Davis) stares out into a future to nowhere in 1978's *Midnight Express*.

Brad Davis: *Midnight Express*

"IF THERE WAS EVER a chance to go back,
  Closer to my home,
  Closer to what I had once loved
  And still do
  To see Susan again,
  To hear her voice."

It's the opening moments of 1978's *Midnight Express*, which kicked off the career of future Oscar-winning director Oliver Stone (he wrote the script), and should have been the first step toward a lasting stardom for an acting career that everyone hoped and believed would last a few decades.

Trying to hide sheer nervousness under his typical carefree attitude (which isn't all he's trying to hide), Billy Hayes steps onto a subway in Turkey with his lady friend Susan.

"You never take anything seriously, do you?" she quips, obviously used to this sort of behavior.

"No!" he flippantly and proudly responds.

It's that attitude that almost costs Hayes his life; moments later, he's yanked from boarding a plane by some guards, who notice the packets of drugs taped under his shirt and send him off to a descent into hell—the film tells the story of his torturous daily life at a Turkish prison.

But what no one knew at the time was that Hayes' portrayer might not have been acting in this scene—the same attitude applied for him as well.

Whether he was in front of the camera, on the stage, or out in everyday life, Brad Davis always went all out. And in the end, all it cost him was his life. Drugs, alcohol, sex, acting—for too much of Davis' life, it was one full-blown addiction after another. But in the sort of ending that audiences go to the movies to escape, the actor missed his "Happily Ever After" conclusion, getting everything straightened out just before learning that he was HIV-positive.

Success almost never comes easy for an actor, and Davis was no exception—it took him years to catch the break that *Midnight* provided, and he never got anywhere near that type of recognition, even in death, for the remainder of his life. (His first step in the direction was watching *Pinocchio* in elementary school and telling his mother, "I could play the puppet better than that cartoon.") But for the man born Bobby, and forced to change his name after the local acting union already had a Bobby Davis, it's tough to find a point where much came easy.

Growing up with a mentally ill mother who allegedly sexually abused him. Working as a street hustler early in his acting career. Drugs and alcohol to the extremes, often used to deal with the mind-wracking frustration and depression that many actors go through looking for a break. To become a drug user who suffers for years in jail, Davis, like many others in this book, called upon a great deal of his past to become Billy Hayes.

Arrested in October 1970 for carrying two kilos of drugs at an airport in Istanbul, the New York native was handed a four-and-a-half-year sentence at Sagmalcilar prison. Soon after, the Turkish government raised his sentence to life after the Nixon administration attempted to stop drug farming. But after five years of hell in Turkey, Hayes escaped in October 1975.

In June 1977 (the weekend before *Star Wars* opened), Davis went to pick up his new wife, Susan Bluestein, as she arrived at a Los Angeles airport. They'd met when she was a casting agent in New York and he was looking for work (it was Susan that thought of Davis' new first name, monikering him after a cousin), and married, perhaps impulsively, just after Christmas 1976. She'd stayed in New York while he went to Hollywood and honed parts of his craft on stage, then with small roles in TV movies like the Emmy-winning *Sybil* (1976) and the trend-setting *Roots* (1977). Now she was coming across the country for a new job, and he didn't exactly welcome her with open arms.

The whole way home, Davis treated his car's steering wheel like a punching bag.

"I blew it," he groused. "I fucking blew it."

He'd gone out to audition for the story of an American caught up in drug trafficking overseas, a role Davis may not have truly understood until it was too late. Showing up for the acting tryout under the influence of adult beverages without even having read the script, he'd been shown the door.

Storming through the door to his home, Davis called his agent, pleading to ask for another shot. Then the agent called—he might get a second chance.

He and Susan hauled back to the casting offices, and Davis, like always, gave his all. But fellows like John Travolta and Richard Gere—a former acting school classmate of Davis'—appeared to have the upper hand, and the crew was heading to New York for even more auditions.

Long before he had the first assurance of becoming Hayes, Davis went into transformation mode around the house.

"He was obsessed with the idea of playing Billy Hayes," Bluestein recalls, "because the whole story, the drugs, the violence, the antiauthoritarian attitude, appealed to Brad." Davis turned his bedroom into his own reformatory for the majority of the summer, reading, re-reading, and re-re-re-re-reading copies of Hayes' book and Stone's script, underlining line after line and writing out his own guides for scenes. He even scribbled the prison's name on one page, and drew dripping blood on it.

Finally, it came down to Davis, Dennis Quaid, and John Savage (Gere was out of the running after differences with Director Alan Parker). In early August, the three were screen-tested for the role. Soon after, Davis got the call he'd longed for.

"Brad Davis/Billy Hayes," he wrote in his copy of *Midnight Express*. "Sept. 12, 1977: Start/Yes." On that day, he flew off to Malta, a small archipelago in southern Europe, for filming.

Once there, he found kindred spirits in Quaid's brother Randy, playing a fellow inmate (seriously, go watch the film right now and see how long it takes to recognize him in that role), and in fellow debuting performer Norbert Weisser, who'd play the streetwise Erich that becomes a bit more than platonic with Hayes. He started spouting the Turkish saying Hayes had used throughout the book of *"Gecmis olsun,"* meaning "May it pass quickly."

Studio executives whined about Hayes' homosexual encounters and the time where Hayes bites off the tongue of a prison official, but Davis found a different scene to be far more difficult: the one in which his reluctant wife (Irene Miracle) flashes Hayes during a visit, spurring the emotional wreck Hayes had become to some accelerated self-pleasure. Feeling the pressure of carrying a film so early in his career, after teetotalling through most of production, Davis got drunk to film the scene. In hindsight, Bluestein was one of many who considered it one of the finest of his career.

One day during filming, Hayes signed Davis' copy of *Midnight Express*.

"I feel a contact, a connection with you," he wrote. "Stay on, stay strong."

When the film came out, critics didn't really take to it. But audiences did—Davis would receive fan mail and get asked about the film for the rest of his life. Off screen, though, things started to come apart, as he sank into the dark worlds of drugs and alcohol, once ripping off his shirt at a party and roaring, "Who's got the drugs?" while a director grumbled, "Well, there goes THAT career."

"I'd achieved my greatest ambition and I was still only 28," Davis said. "How did I follow that success? I got high and stayed high. What did I want to do next? Well, there wasn't anything I wanted to do. Not a thing." He was in talks to star in 1982's *First Blood*, which launched the Rambo series, but it didn't happen. He turned down a role in *Alien* (1979), which would start off one of the biggest sci-fi series in film history. In January 1979, Davis won a Golden Globe for his work as Hayes, but, surprisingly, wasn't even nominated for an Oscar (the film grabbed six nomination, including Best Picture).

He'd make a quarter-million for starring in *Small Circle of Friends* afterward, and spend just about all of it on nose candy. He spent three days in a detox facility, and was high again less than an hour after release. He appeared in the next year's Best Picture, *Chariots of Fire*, but the role was so small that it was totally overshadowed.

"After *Midnight Express*," Davis recalled, "I went from 'Brad who?' to 'Look, it's Brad Davis, and I think he's drunk.'"

Eventually, he realized that, as jammed with people on the brink of stardom as Hollywood has always been, he wouldn't be around in a career capacity if he kept giving people reasons *not* to want to take a shot with him. In late 1980, spurred on by problems with his wife and friends and a silent phone, Davis tried for sobriety.

In the summer of 1981, working with Helen Mirren—already a household name in Britain, but not yet to the same levels she'd reach in Old Glory—on a film in France, Davis had one last binge, resulting in a car accident with his co-star. That August, he'd stop drinking forever.

In April 1983, Bluestein gave birth to their daughter Alexandra. Davis went back to the stage, and then to TV, turning in a critically acclaimed performance in the title role of a miniseries about Robert F. Kennedy. But then, in December 1985, Bluestein—in the midst of casting the *Cosby Show* spinoff *A Different World*—got a letter from a medical facility that Davis had recently visited.

He was HIV-positive. No one will ever truly know how this occurred, though a dirty drug needle seems the most likely scenario. Bluestein and Alexandra would test negative, although Bluestein would fight and defeat thyroid cancer a few years later.

Remembering the firestorm that ignited during Rock Hudson's public admission of his AIDS status and subsequent death, the family tried to keep his status secret. Davis kept working, turning in a fine performance as Captain Queeg in a TV version of *The Caine Mutiny* (1988). But around Hollywood, the ignorance of humanity when it comes to HIV/AIDS began to show itself as word about the disease got around.

"If I had not died,
Would I still be with her?

And my dear sweet child
Where is she?
My Alex had been so small,
So small.
Her hair so long and bright.
Has she grown?
Would she be taller than me?

Bluestein found out for herself just how far people would go to avoid being associated with AIDS as she tried to cast a Hudson biopic in 1989. No one, even those yet to make their mark on the acting world, wanted the lead.

"I got pass after pass after pass," she recalls. "And not just from stars, but total unknowns." She'd eventually end up picking Thomas Ian Griffith, known for martial arts films above anything else, for the part.

One night in the summer of 1989, she arrived back to the family home, and suddenly smelled smoke.

"Then I saw it," she recalls. "This huge pot, my cooking pot, sitting on the lawn, blackened as if it had been in a fire." Davis had burned all of his *Midnight* memorabilia, down to the clothes he'd worn to become Hayes.

"Like some witch in *Macbeth* trying to alter the fates," Bluestein says, "he'd gone out in his black cashmere coat and burnt his past in a caldron, sent it up in a cloud of ashes."

Davis kept working here and there, and Bluestein became a common name in casting around the world of television—she'd win an Emmy in 1994 for helping put together *NYPD Blue*. But eventually, the disease wore Davis down, and he died September 8, 1991: not from the disease, but from assisted suicide, using some drugs from someone—not Bluestein—whose identity has never been revealed.

Sadly, people like Brad Davis become targets for the self-righteous, the Monday-morning quarterbacks of the world, the people who only look at the mistakes and wrongdoing and choose to climb up on their self-constructed pedestals and glare down. Brad Davis lived to excess, and just as he emerged from winning one battle, he found himself enveloped in another, one that no one, not yet, has ever won. The fear of AIDS is rampant, and while AIDS may be accepted openly—as in, people with the courage to fight it are praised in public, but feared in private—those not in the know all too quickly jump to the know-it-all mode. It's sad, but it's true; Davis (and, through him, Susan and Alex) had to find this out on his own.

Think about this: just two months after Davis died, Magic Johnson announced that he was forced to retire from the NBA after testing HIV-positive, amid a ton of negative publicity, mainly from people who had no clue what the hell they were talking about. The acting world has been touched by HIV several times since, perhaps most notably in November 2015, when longtime star Charlie Sheen announced he'd been infected.

"I'm an actor and I died of AIDS," Davis said in the first pages of *After Midnight*, the biography that Bluestein would finish after his death. "But I also worked for six years (with HIV) and whether you liked me or not or whether or not you agreed with my decision to keep on working, you hired me . . . I'm writing this because there are so many others like me, so many HIV-positive actors who are healthy and working, but who live lives of paranoia and fear because they can't tell the truth. Now I'm telling it."

Davis tried to teach America, or at least Hollywood, how not to fear AIDS, and they didn't listen. Even now, two decades after his passing, AIDS is still a curse word in every sense in moviemaking city, just as it is in so many other spots. But until we find a cure for AIDS, it's something we need to live with, to learn more about. Ignoring it or pushing it aside isn't going to solve anything, and painting those with the misfortune to get it as enemies doesn't work either.

It's often ignorance that leads to hate and fear, but it's acceptance and knowledge that push these negative emotions aside. Davis, Hudson, Johnson, Arthur Ashe (what a horrible tragedy that was), and many others have shown us that AIDS doesn't discriminate by age, race, creed, gender, or anything else. It's out there, and hopefully it will be destroyed someday, but if we aren't going to try to cure it ourselves, we've got to do what we can to bridge the gap between AIDS ignorance and acceptance.

And if we open our minds just a little bit, it shouldn't be too hard. It's tough to make things anymore black and white, but, despite what dramatic TV shows and the like would have us believe, AIDS is not a plague out there, just waiting to snatch up its unsuspecting victims. The people who have it don't deserve to be treated like a modern-day Typhoid Mary; AIDS isn't spread by handshakes, hugging, kissing, sharing water bottles, breathing the same air, or anything else that the conclusion-jumpers of America want to believe.

Stopping AIDS from spreading is up to the doctors of the world, and the people of the world, through awareness and common sense—as in, don't stick strange needles into your arms, have unprotected sex, or wade through someone else's blood. But looking down on those who have it, trying to pretend they don't exist, or doing anything else hurtful to them, intentionally or otherwise, isn't going to make the disease go away. It's education, awareness, and common sense that eventually solve the problems of the world, and they can solve AIDS discrimination.

"That is, if we allow them.
Can AIDS be cured?
Or is it still a terror, a mystery?
If I could see them once again,
It would make me so happy,
Just once.
Could they hear me?
Could they see?
Would they understand
I would always be with them,
In the heart,
If they believed."
—"Brad" by Alexandra Davis, 10

Even after three decades in the business, Charles Bronson became a new action icon through five chapters of vigilante justice in the *Death Wish* series.

They Made *Death Wish* Come True

REVENGE-TYPE ACTION FLICKS, VIGILANTE gigs, man(woman)-as-a-person-against-evil movies, well, they're pretty common today. Have been for a while. It's a story we've seen and read about in comic books, video games, and, of course, movies.

They tend to have at least one thing in common, to a degree: criticism. There's always going to be someone who whines and moans about how things like this are leading our society straight down the path to ruin, a world built on anarchy, a sign of things to come, perhaps even the apocalypse being brought about here. Some label that a prime example of the slippery slope fallacy: take one step down, and you won't be able to stop tumbling to the bottom. It's right up next to "If we legalize marijuana, cocaine will be next!" or "Same-sex marriage today, polygamy tomorrow!" or some other ludicrous statement.

Still, they keep coming. Like many films we've read about in these pages, *Death Wish*, certainly unexpectedly and unintentionally (though many will always consider it a fortunate coincidence) helped set the tone for so many more aspects of this entertainment genre, though it's made to look about G-rated compared to today's offerings.

"It gave people a feeling that there's an opportunity to fight back," explains Hank Garrett, who helped kick-start the series back in its 1974 opener. "You don't have to be a complete victim."

When we analyze the *Death Wish* films, it's not a political thing, it's not a conservative-liberal thing—labels like that are usually placed by outsiders on a quest to offend. It's more of an Occam's Razor issue here. The simplest ideas work the best. There's a man, he's pissed, he's pissed for a reason, and he's taking it out on those that deserve to have things taken out upon them. That's not self-righteous; it's a blatant fact.

Like he did for almost all of his career, Charles Bronson made the tough everyman look so easy. Paul Kersey didn't make his livelihood; Bronson had been in the business for almost thirty years when the first edition arrived in 1974. He was already arguably (how many ways can *this* be defined?) the biggest movie star on the planet. At five foot nine, Bronson wasn't exactly the most physically intimidating guy you'd meet, but he had arms like tree trunks and a face that gave you the impression he'd sharpened some brawling skills through trial and error on the streets—and he certainly *had*, as Bronson had done time for assault and battery before his performing career got rolling, then turned around and won a Purple Heart during the Second World War. Yeah, this guy could kick John Wayne's ass without sweating.

So, yes, it was pretty tough to imagine him as a corporate man and anti-gun war objector, which Kersey began as in the first film. Money, a lovely wife, a wonderful daughter who seems about ready to add a generation to the Kersey clan, all's about going his way.

Per usual for life itself, although certainly not to this degree, there comes a big flip. A group of dirtbags sneak to his home, murder his wife, and rape his daughter, leaving her permanently damaged in and out. How in the hell does *anyone* move forward from this? How could we *not* do what Kersey does?

More importantly, who could ever criticize him for doing so, or the film world for depicting anything else? Yes, some badmouthed *Death Wish*, even boycotting it or fighting its release. Audiences looked at those people and basically told them to get off the pedestal and step down into reality. Realizing they were hopelessly outnumbered, the naysayers shut up and found something else to whine about.

The seeds of Kersey's journey are sown in an impromptu meeting with client Ames Jainchill, a dinner turned into a target lesson at the local gun club. For a guy who swore off guns after losing his dad in a hunting accident (again, how was he even able to make it this far?), Paul's quite the marksman.

"I did a little bit of work on the accent that I wanted to do," explains Stuart Margolin of getting ready for Ames. "I got to spend a few days in Tucson." Wowed by his pal, Ames gifts Kersey with a gold-plated gun, and Kersey doesn't get rid of it. Things will happened soon.

"I'm the guy who falls from the sky and hands the protagonist an instrument that he uses to destroy," says Margolin, who'd later win Emmys in 1979 and 1980 for playing Jim Rockford's pal Angel on TV's *The Rockford Files*. "I worked hard for the scene where I handled the pistol, finding the confidence I tried to exude so [Kersey] would feel confident in taking it and doing what he needed to do."

That doesn't appear to be the case at first. Back home in the Big Apple, Kersey's luck keeps going wrong, accosted by a punk with some conservative views of the second amendment. But he's got the drop here, blasting the SOB straight down.

Forgetting that he is, after all, being played by the two-fisted legend named Bronson, Kersey goes home and reintroduces his dinner down the toilet. The next night, however, he's back on the prowl, searching alleys for some prey. Three abusers of the elderly meet his integrity. Four more follow over the next few nights.

Hooked on the thrill of the gun? That's an easy assumption, and there's a certain degree of factual root. But let's be optimistic to cockeyed levels—nothing but justice, and a thirst for it, with nothing else to more forward to! Yeah, that's heroic!

With the media hot on the trail of the self-made avenger, crime's starting to drop in the nearby areas—crooks, particularly the violent kind, don't enjoy playing on a level field. But more and more citizens are starting to stand up to the bad guys. As he and his construction colleagues happen to happen upon a mugger, Andrew McCabe and the guys . . . restrain him, or so he (sort of) explains to a reporter.

A former pro wrestler and comic, Garrett was used to dancing on the line between violence and entertainment.

"Comedy was a matter of saving myself from gangs," remembers Garrett. "I started doing really stupid and silly things to save myself from being beaten by gangs. I was the only white kid on the streets of Harlem. I lived in an area that was Puerto Rican, African American, and, further east, Italian. I was the only Jewish kid in the area." His humor skills won Garrett a spot as Ed Nicholson in the cop comedy *Car 54, Where are You?* (1961) and some other shows and films.

One day, Garrett met a fellow managing the career of a youngster named Pacino. The man soon called, asking if Garrett wanted a new shot before the big screen. Soon after, he was next to Al himself in *Serpico* (1973).

Then came a shot at *Death*.

"I auditioned and met the casting people," he remembers. "They asked if I could play a New York character, a hardhat from Brooklyn. I said, 'Yeah, I can do dat!' I could do improv."

McCabe, he continues, "was the kind of character I was on the streets. At one point, I slept in cardboard boxes. I was the son of fruit and vegetable peddlers, and they didn't always have time for me. I talked like that on the streets with the other guys."

Kersey's reign continues, and we get the feeling that he might just say the hell with everything and go nuts. But a blessing arrives in disguise when he's shot, and ends up in the hospital. The cops let him off if he leaves town (an action that had the self-righteous critics of the film world going psycho), and it's an extended vacation to Chicago.

He doesn't happen to find the cretins that started this whole matter, as that would be contrived even for this type of film. But the last frame has Kersey pointing at the camera and forming his hand into a gun—not doing the whole Norman Bates-evil grin sort of thing, as he's angry, not crazy—showing that he's not done. The film's gross blasting past its budget gave him a chance.

It wouldn't take as long today (and if it did, the film would probably flop, what with the short attention spans of today's audiences), but *Death Wish 2* wouldn't come about until 1982. Now on the other side of the nation, Kersey's dating reporter Geri Nichols (Bronson's real-life bombshell wife Jill Ireland, with whom he'd made fourteen films), with his daughter moving up.

Then his pocket is picked by a bunch of guys who don't know who they're dealing with; now, were the Net around back then, things might have gone differently.

Their leader was named Nirvana. Talk about a self-contradiction.

Born in the infamously tough town of Newark, Thomas Duffy went to Ohio to study law and help bring Ohio University a conference hockey championship in 1979, helping him win a spot in the 1981 TV movie *Miracle on Ice*, playing a member of the squad that had shocked Russia the year before at the Lake Placid Olympics.

"I didn't think I'd do acting," Duffy admits. "I broke my wrist playing football, and stumbled into acting." Not far from training to be a courtroom enforcer of the law, he'd now have to act out some horrible shit, things that help us justify Kersey's actions. Fresh off starring next to Sylvester Stallone in *Paradise Alley* (1978) and *Rocky II* (1979), Stuart K. Robinson was stepping onto the other side of the law along with him.

"Opportunities were few and far between for actors of color," Robinson remembers. "I was never the prototypical inner-city youth. The roles I was always being offered at the time were this gang member or that gang member, saved from a life of crime by a hero. Then I realized that those roles would be fewer and farther between, so I had to get some experience playing bad guys too. I really wanted to prove that I could play all characters, and do it well, good guys, bad guys, and the in-between."

There'd be no question at all as to where the guy named Jiver that Robinson became would fall, as the performer found long before his role found him.

"It was the most unusual audition I've ever been on," he says. "We never read any script. We never saw the script prior to the scene. We had a meeting with the director [Michael Winner, who'd also done the first film], who just wanted to talk, to see what we were made of, and how much depth we had."

Winner called group after group back into a small room. Eventually, Robinson had a chance.

"I want you," Winner explained to the triers-out, "to come back and rape my office." Want to read that a few more times?

How could anyone know just what to do with such a direction? Robinson hesitated.

"I went another way," he says. "I was the guy who liked to watch. So I would just hang back and enjoy the mayhem to the Nth degree during that little improv, and I guess that caught their eye."

Duffy had his way with an ottoman.

"I had to make believe that this was a woman," he says. The two, along with Laurence Fishburne's Cutter and some others, went into mental gang formation mode. They rode buses through downtown Los Angeles, occasionally getting out to walk the streets and hang in the nightclubs. They slept on rooftops. They stepped into detention centers to meet some who'd made such roles their lives. Filming was occasionally interrupted by nearby gunfire.

"It was just to get the feel of being street kids, to be authentically bringing it," Robinson explains. "By the time we got to the set, we were pretty much almost a gang. At lunch time on the set, we'd cut to the front of the line. We had no regard for rules. I think it helped."

With Kersey's license and address, the group visits his house. But the maid happens to be in the wrong place at the worst time, and Rosario (Silvana Gallardo) becomes the most innocent of victims.

"Doing the rape scene was pretty intense," Duffy recalls. "Poor Silvana. There was no physical contact, but mentally, I think she almost felt that she'd gotten raped." The gang stayed away from their supposed victims during filming, he continues.

"The rape scenes were really difficult for any sensible human being," says Robinson, who became violently ill after nearly every take. "You're legitimately putting yourself in a position of taking away a woman's dignity. It went against my principles as a human. It was humiliation and it was abuse, and you could feel that there was a spirit that was being dominated. It was pretty brutal, and I had a really hard time with that." Beating Kersey unconscious, as they did when he arrived home, might have actually been a step up in comfort. The maid is killed, the daughter kidnapped and abused as much. She escapes through a window, but lands on a railing below, to her death.

Back on his feet, Kersey starts taking off the gangsters one by one, gunning down Jiver in the midst of another mugging. He soon corners Nirvana, but the main boss has a special weapon within.

"I watched films of guys on PCP," Duffy says. "I'd never seen anything like PCP before. I talked to some cops, and one told me about a guy on PCP who'd broken his arms while in handcuffs to get away. No cop was going to take [Nirvana]." But they do, and he's off to a very, very special home.

Not good enough. Kersey steals a doctor's ID, and the two finally have a showdown. Nirvana gets the upper hand with a scalpel's help, but inadvertently slugs an electroshock machine, allowing Kersey to dish out his own capital punishment.

"When [Bronson] had me on the ground, kicking me, they did over 100 kicks," Duffy says. "Finally, he said, 'He's had enough.' Bronson was a great guy." A lanky upcomer named Jeff Goldblum had played one of the muggers who'd killed Kersey's wife in the first film. Two decades later, Duffy would back him up in *Jurassic Park: The Lost World* (1997). The long-haired outcast that would have been right at home at Woodstock or following the Grateful Dead across the country, Duffy's Dr. Robert Burke did all he could to save the overgrown lizards, only to get trapped under a waterfall and eventually chomped by an ungrateful T-Rex.

Ironically, Geri, upon finding out she's dating a vigilante, leaves Kersey at the end. Ireland and Bronson would be married for over thirty years before her sad passing from breast cancer in May 1990 (she wrote a book about her fight called *Life Wish*). In 1995, Bronson starred in the TV movie *Family of Cops* alongside Kim Weeks. The two would appear in the sequel in 1997, marry the next year, and add a third chapter to the tale in January 1999. It would be Bronson's own farewell, his last role before his August 2003 passing.

Winner and Bronson got back together in 1985 for the third flick, which had Kersey back in New York, unfairly jailed for the beating death of his friend. Soon after, he's on the hunt for the gang that actually did it, and finishes up by disintegrating the leader with a rocket launcher, becoming a local hero in the process.

Even in films like the *Death Wish* series, there's a place to send a message. And hey, don't get smart by spewing out something like, "Yeah, don't fuck with Charles Bronson!" No, more of a sadder, scarier something else, like terrifying version of the "Just Say No" message that blasted across America in the late 80s and 90s, there to show kids just how dangerous the drug world can be. She'd have a small role in *Death Wish 4* (1987), but Dana Barron saw a shot to scare viewers straight from a new, deadly force in the drug world.

"A lot of my career has had to do with issues and things to bring to the forefront of people's awareness," says Barron, who'd win an Emmy in 1989 for her performance as a rape victim in an *Afterschool Special*. "In film, you can reach a larger audience, and say, 'This is dangerous, this is what can happen, so don't do it.'"

"It" was crack cocaine, the drug world's then-newfound goldmine.

Kersey's back in Los Angeles, dating Karen Sheldon (Kay Lenz). Barron was Karen's daughter Erica, finding herself falling too far in with the "cool" crowd.

"I'm not into the vigilante type of filmmaking," admits Barron, who said she'd never seen any of the other *Death Wish* films, "but this was a legendary film, especially with the actors involved." As so many young women are, Erica's all too eager to score points with the guys, even if it means trying out some new substances.

"I went to rehab centers," Barron says of getting ready. "I talked to a young girl at one to find out what crack was all about. At that time, it was becoming an epidemic."

And she's a victim. Erica takes too much of the stuff, and Karen and Kersey can only watch helplessly as doctors can't shock her back to life.

"I had done a lot of death scenes," Barron says, "but this was a little more drawn out. I showed the movie to my parents and my father went out of the room crying. I didn't even think about that. That was the strongest part of how it affected me."

Now after those that took Erica—and others—away, Kersey's helped by Nathan White (John P. Ryan), who lost his own daughter to drugs. Dozens die, including Karen, but Kersey makes it away once again.

With the avalanche of remakes that have rolled through Hollywood over the past few decades, it's surprising that a new *Death Wish* hadn't come around as of 2017, although a few have started and stopped; Sylvester Stallone was involved in one attempt. For now, the last *Wish* came to light in 1994, with Kersey protecting his lady companion from her mobster ex Tommy (Michael Parks, later as Texas Ranger man Earl McGraw in three Quentin Tarantino movies). **Note: Just before this book went to press, it was announced that Bruce Willis would become the next Kersey in the new *Death Wish* of November 2017.**

It doesn't work; she's quickly trapped in a bathroom, her face smashed through a mirror by her husband's pal Freddie, who eventually shoots her dead. A year after acting out Stephen King's words in *The Dark Half* and a decade after being Madonna's boyfriend in *Desperately Seeking Susan* (1985), Robert Joy was Freddie.

"He was a fascinating character," Joy says, "eccentric enough to have some humor, but also to be incredibly menacing. I'd admired Charles Bronson from way back when." Shooting in the Canadian homeland of Joy (and many others) saved the film a ton of tax money.

"I absorbed the screenplay and learned my lines," Joy remembers. "Things occur to you when that sort of thing happens. When you get into a script, you see a lot of opportunities in there. A lot of the preparation happens in your own home. Then the circumstances of the shoot brought up some other ideas." Like, say, Freddie dressing in drag to follow the lady into the restroom.

"Freddie was having a wonderful time, dressed up as a woman in charge," Joy says. "When I bashed her head into a mirror, I had my hand in her hair, and it had to be coordinated precisely with the person with the hammer behind mirror, breaking it."

On the other hand, Claire Rankin was making her cinema debut as Maxine, the mobster's gal (or *moll*, to spin the jargon wheel), after years acting out Shakespeare's work on the stages. Like Barron a film before, she said no to getting into the altogether.

"When they agreed to take [the nudity] out of the script," she recalls, "I accepted the role." It's sad that we notice these things, but the fifth film in the series is the only one *without* a rape scene.

She did get a whomping from Tommy's tossing of the cannoli (gangster movie trademark alert!) "Those things stung and left marks!" she says. "I really thought about Maxine in the context of a gangster's moll, in the most traditional sense: young, naive, uneducated, and using her body and femininity to find her place in the world. I have high hopes that after Tommy's demise she gets herself out of that world."

Nearly thirty years before, Bronson had been part of the legendary war epic *The Dirty Dozen* (1967). Heading back to his hotel after filming, he'd sometimes toss a few coins in the guitar case of a fellow performing outside.

That person's name was Saul Rubinek. Two years before *Death Wish V*, he'd scored a small part next to Clint Eastwood in 1992's Best Picture *Unforgiven*. Now he'd be Brian Hoyle, one of the few attorneys that Tommy hasn't been able to bribe off.

Or so we think.

"I wanted to work with Charles Bronson," Rubinek remembers. "That, and the fact that we all have bills to pay." Hoyle's indeed in with Tommy, but relents when he realizes who he's friends with—and that Kersey isn't someone you'd exactly want to piss off.

"I was working with a great actor, trying to make the scenes work," says Rubinek. "It was just like any other good experience, working with people who cared about their work. One of the things I learned as an actor is that you can overdo preparation if the writing doesn't earn it. What happens is, you tend to come off pretentious or, it looks like you're trying to work way too hard. What's important in a situation like that is to let the story and the plot carry you, and to be as spontaneous as possible to be able to do the scenes without any fuss or too much work."

Now in his 70s, Bronson could only muster up *seven* killings in his final theatrical film, Kersey's lowest total of the saga. But they were certainly some of his most imaginative; Kersey blasts Freddie away with a bomb disguised as a soccer ball, tosses another baddie into a wood chipper, and takes out Tommy by knocking him into a pool of acid. For the first time since the first film, though, he still has someone to care for, taking away his girlfriend's daughter for the final cut.

Even if Bronson were alive and in perfect health today, I doubt he'd had held forth for this book as much as his co-stars. Not that he was angry or difficult as a person; those with that attitude don't stay in the business for half a century. Just that Bronson, like so many action heroes of yesterday, wasn't one to talk about himself, at least not from the acting sense. Without the Internet there to put one's words in public before the speaker's next breath ends, or paparazzi cameras in someone's face twenty-four hours a day, people tended to keep to themselves.

And based on what little he did say about Kersey, there might not have been much detail to explore, in the preparatory sense we've seen throughout *Actors in Action*. Kersey was someone he could just become. The few chats he had about the *Death Wish* hero showed that he might have had enough in common with Kersey that there was little work to do.

"He's an average guy, an average New Yorker," Bronson explained around the time the first film came about. "His whole approach to life is gentle, and he has raised his daughter that way. Now he has second thoughts, and he becomes a killer."

"To play him I draw upon my own feelings. I do believe I could perform this way myself."

Something else that set *Death Wish* apart was its substance. Violent, gory, painful, yes, but with a bit of humanity all the way through, and not just on Kersey's part. Small things like that can go a ways toward lifting an action flick from everyday to special.

For his first lead way down under, Peter Marshall hoped to find something similar in 2008's *The Horseman*.

"I auditioned because it was violent," Marshall admits, "but beautiful, sad. It had a lot of emotional scope." He looked to become Christian Forteski, who'd just been through a loss sadly not far from Kersey's. Drugs had stolen his lovely young lady, and a person in that situation has no one to ask why.

But he can sure as hell get some kind of revenge.

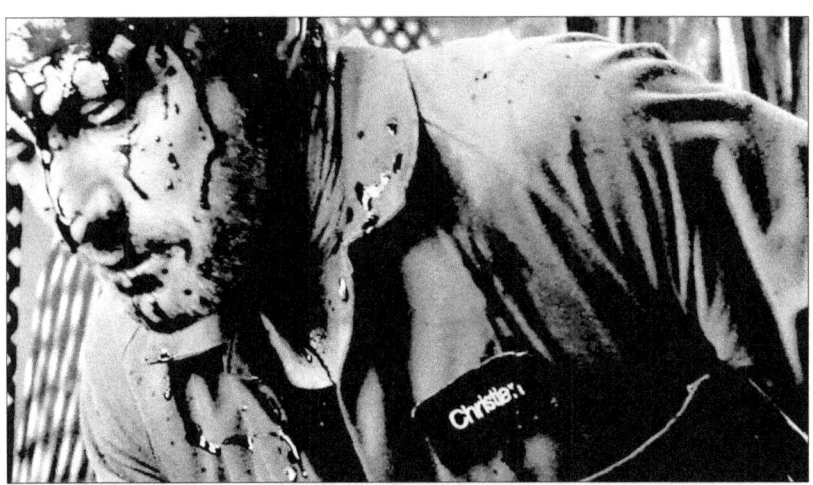

A man out to avenge a loved one's death will shed his own blood in the bargain, as Peter Marshall showed us in 2008's *The Horseman*.

Like, say, on the nimrods who made and sent him a porno tape of his daughter getting abused in every form. He kills the distributor. He kills the director. He kills again and again, a crowbar becoming Christian's best friend.

"All the fighting scenes were extremely difficult," he remembers, "as it was usually around 40 degrees Celsius [104 Fahrenheit], in an Australian summer or raining!"

But he also picks up a young girl named Alice, herself near to motherhood, hoping to find at least one place for her direction to lead.

"My favorite scene is in the van with the young actor [Caroline Marohasy]," Marshall says, "where I talk about what it's like to be a father. I was allowed to improvise this, as I was [a father]."

He soon gets to the main offenders, whomping one after another, fighting back in ways only someone with very powerful reasons can. But Alice has already been made a victim, fatally tortured by the same people who helped take Christian's daughter. This one won't have *Death*'s happy (well, happy-ish) endings.

"To prepare for the role was just a case of remaining totally open to emotion and violence and love," Marshall claims. "Before each extreme scene, the director would get us to push, shove, and beat each other and then call action! It got everyone hyped, to say the least."

Darkman villain Robert Durant (Larry Drake) came face to terrifying, terrified face with himself in the 1990 film.

Larry Drake: *Darkman* films

WE CAN'T BE COLDHEARTED if we don't have a heart to begin with. We can't ignore our conscience if it doesn't exist. We don't worry about our spirit's final destination if we can't send it anywhere. We also don't worry about taking down anyone, anywhere, any way . . . because they can't matter to people who don't know how to give a damn.

That's how Larry Drake approached Robert Durant, the villain (well, to those of us with a sense of decency, clearly not to himself) in 1990's *Darkman*. It's why Durant was successful enough—if not in his personal plight—to bring back for the title role in a sequel.

And that's a pretty good reason why the same audiences that ended up hating Durant enough to want a second shot at reprisal couldn't believe their eyes when they saw just who was playing him.

You see, up to that point, Drake's biggest work had been on the other side of caring. For years both before and after, TV audiences saw him open some pretty heavy doors as Benny Stulwicz on *L.A. Law*. From when he showed up in 1987 for his first of seven years on the show, Benny became something of an impromptu motivator for those he clerked for at the firm of McKenzie, Brackman, Chaney, and Kuzak. Playing one of the first developmentally disabled characters in mainstream TV history, Benny, as many afflicted in the same manner do in reality, always tried to do right because he didn't know anything else to do, inspiring not just the men and women of local law and not even just audiences, but voters that handed Drake a pair of Emmys in 1988 and 1989.

Still, right in the midst of being Benny on a weekly basis, Drake stepped all the way to the opposite spectrum.

"I just considered [Durant] a soulless man," Drake recalls. "He was very basic and primitive and crude. I considered him a degenerate, irredeemable human being. What it boils down to is the acting choices you make—whatever is appropriate to the character and the script. It sort of just happens."

He had to make quite a bit happen in the opening moments of Sam Raimi's first action flick, following several jaunts at horror. Moments in, Durant coldly witnesses one of his men removing the hand digits of a fellow who's going to tell the mob boss and his colleagues exactly what they want to know.

"That's what I love about acting," Drake explains. "Not so much the hiding in it, but the exploring of another angle on the world within the character I'm doing. Getting to explore, in a controlled context, what it might feel like to pull a gun on somebody, to chop off somebody's fingers, to do whatever I need to do in film."

Liam Neeson's scientist Peyton Westlake was in the title role, but not for a while; as Westlake dances on the edge of success at finding synthetic skin to help burn victims, his girlfriend Julie (Frances McDormand) is doing a bit *too* well at her reporting job, finding info that a local developer is working behind the scenes to take down several parts of the city.

Then Durant, a secret partner in the deal, shows up at Westlake's lab with some of his employees, kills his assistant, and burns him with fire and acid. It would probably be better for Westlake to die, but he's sadly still alive, blown up and into a river and hospitalized, comatose. But soon, with a new lab in an old building, he finds some ways to improve the "skin," and to turn himself into a makeshift clone of others: to become Darkman.

The new technique sends confusion straight through the local marauders. Durant's not sure what's going on. How is his man standing right *there* . . . and still over *there*? What's going on here?

Then, in the midst of a scouring chase at a carnival, Durant, in earth-shatteringly innovative special effects action for the year, comes face to shocked visage with himself. Ironically, it was that very scene with which Drake had so impressed Raimi at his tryout.

"They handed me the scene when I'm seeing myself," he recalls. "It would be a split screen, and I was on both sides of the door. All I was trying to do was make a distinction between the two. I was jumping back and forth. It amused Sam, and it showed how far I was willing to go for the role."

More and more, for the first time all film, Durant's façade is starting to crack. Stoicism is one of a mob boss' biggest assets, but he's only (mostly!) human. Westlake's got weaponry that not even he's run up against before.

"My general plan was to make him as cold as ice until Darkman got to him a little bit," Drake explains. "That's the character arc: that Darkman gets to this guy. He gets mad, because there's something he can't control."

He's got one chance left, and it's Julie, an unknowing piece of bait that leads the group straight to Westlake's hideout. But Darkman's disguises help him escape again, and he's soon hanging from a chopper that Durant's piloting. The boss' rationale now further gone than ever before, he plays right into Darkman's scarred and gloved hands; the hero hooks the chopper to a trailer, and, in the type of physics defiance we all but expect in action films, the copter's yanked straight down into a bridge, blowing it and Durant to bits.

Well, we thought so. Keep reading this.

"How often in your real life have you met someone that you'd call a good guy, or a real bad guy, a real mess, completely unredeemable?" Drake ponders. "What [actors] do is exaggerate certain stereotypes and assumptions. We feel like the odd man out. Acting is acting. Actors are never who they play. It's a character."

Once again, reality isn't much of a component in the action world, and, just as Westlake's survival and recovery went right past the line of believability, Durant somehow managed to make it back for part II in 1995, honored by calling the flick *The Return of Durant*. With Raimi doing production, Bradford May behind the directing camera, and Arnold Vosloo as the new Westlake, Durant, aided by the old reliable "He was in a coma forever, but happened to wake up good as new!" film cliché, goes back on the attack. Westlake, however, has an old trick or two straight up his sleeve as well, using the same impersonation techniques to take out Durant's gang, and enlisting a car bomb to put a second end to the antagonist.

May, Raimi, and Vosloo reprised their cast and crew roles the next year for *Die, Darkman, Die*, but Drake sat this one out, with Jeff Fahey stepping in to play the bad guy.

Actors, Drake explains, "are lucky when [our work] turns out really well and might be considered art, when we get those opportunities to enlighten others. Enlightenment comes from being disturbed, from going to somewhere new and learning something new. Ultimately, movies teach you a level of morality and behavior that can set the tone for your whole life. It's so nice when you get a variety of different aspects of a human being, with more dimensions than the obvious, the predictable. Everybody has different aspects of all of humanity in them, and as actors, we're supposed to reach in and touch that, shape it, and make it serve the story we're telling, and that's the blessed skill we have."

Note: The acting world suffered another tremendous loss on March 17, 2016, when Drake passed away. We will never forget him.

Stepping away from the malevolence that won Denzel Washington his second Oscar, supercop Alonzo Harris consoles a frightened Letty (**Samantha Esteban**) early in 2001's *Training Day*.

Samantha Esteban: *Training Day*

WHAT WOULD IT BE like to hold someone's life in your hands or on your lips, and not even know it? Knowing not now, maybe not ever, that a few words could make the difference between a person you may not even know lives or dies, even in the most agonizing of ways?

Mere hours after finding herself in another unthinkable situation, a young woman named Letty stepped into this one, and a young actress was there to help her do so.

"I just loved her because she was feisty," Samantha Esteban recalls of Letty. "Even though she was a victim, she was right back to her feisty, firecracker self. I completely identified with the character. I immersed myself to really be in that situation. Acting comes from a place of truth, to find a person you can identify with, to find out how you would identify with it, or how the character would react."

Ideally, Letty's first situation would be something no woman would ever have to react to at all. We're not too far into 2001's *Training Day*, and it's tough to really comprehend much just yet. There's a young and pure—well, as pure as a cop can be—officer, looking to finally step into the dark and dangerous world of the detective, and one overly seasoned veteran there to train him.

We're learning about Alonzo Harris, the man who Jake Hoyt (Ethan Hawke) may find himself just like, and he's not sure he wants to be there anymore. Being in this line of work often forces detectives to do things they'd never dream of, and smoking things far past nicotine is one, even if Harris's gun to Jake's head ended up being the final persuasion. Harris is truly a bad guy who decided to use his powers for good, and that's tough to pull off, on or off the screen.

We in the audience aren't sure how to react either—after all, this was *Denzel Washington*, and he didn't play those types of roles! Sure, he'd already won an Oscar a few years before in *Glory* (1989), but that character had been someone we'd all cheer for. Harris might have seemed cool on the outside—both in the social and emotional sense—but we'd run like hell if we knew he was even in the real-life area code. Both in reality and in fiction, there's often a fine line between cop and criminal, and this guy seems to land of whatever side is convenient to him.

Things are going to get worse for Harris, but let's get back to this piece's subject. Spurting down the street, Hoyt's evolving eye notices a guy in an alley atop a young woman, and her consent was far from the guy's concern. Impressed for the first time, Harris watches Hoyt dish out some legal justice to both the scumbag and his partner.

Then, with another new emotion in the form of compassion, he comforts the young woman, trying to recover from one of the world's worst situations. Gasping out that she's Letty, playing hooky from school, the lady's allowed to leave. But her wallet was knocked out, and Hoyt scoops it up to return later. We have no clue how important that will eventually become.

Things go back and forth for the cops for the rest of the day. Loads of money are stolen and people die, and it hardly seems to affect Harris at all. But when he drops Hoyt off with some "friends," it's clear just how ominous this fellow is.

Realizing too late that the men, led by a gangster with the ironic title of Smiley, are there to take him out, Hoyt's dragged to a bathtub with a shotgun between his eyes. But Smiley's pal happens to reach into Hoyt's pocket, and finds that lost wallet.

And in true Hollywood irony, Letty just *happens* to be Smiley's cousin. As Hoyt gasps out the truth in the scene many credit for Hawke's Supporting Actor nomination (Jim Broadbent won for *Iris*), Smiley gives Letty a call—and while the truth may set him free, she's not sure she wants to reveal it.

"I think we've all been in that kind of situation with a parent, an elder, an older sibling," Esteban says. "We just try to stay out of trouble, even if we have to fib a little bit. My cousin knew I was up to no good, trying to get to the bottom of a serious situation." Indeed, Letty sticks to her falsehood—she'd gone straight to *every single class* that day. But getting information out of unwilling witnesses is what this guy does, and Smiley eventually gets her to own up.

Hoyt is let go in thanks, but Harris isn't so lucky; having pissed off too many people, he's gunned down just before the credits roll. Still, Washington could take serious solace in his second Oscar.

"It was very real film," Esteban says. "Very real surprises, real things going on. It can be tough to get to a certain place mentally, but if you're willing to work, it's possible for success."

Three years later, Esteban's power in networking came through. After banging out the *Training Day* script, David Ayer was doing double duty as both screenwriter and director for

Harsh Times. Back in the same sad section of Los Angeles Harris and Hoyt had inhabited, it was time for a different story with a familiar actress.

With an uncommon but ironically familiar name—Esteban's *Harsh* character was also monikered Letty.

"Maybe one of [Ayer's] most favorite people growing up was Letty!" Esteban jokingly theorizes. "But not to my knowledge, the two aren't related. It's two completely different stories."

Just a year removed from Bruce Wayne in *Batman Begins*, Christian Bale was Jim Davis, battling PTSD from his turn as a U.S. Army Ranger. With his gorgeous girlfriend Marta (Tammy Trull) down in her Mexican homeland, he's back home in L.A., looking for a job.

But PTSD can make a man do some unthinkable stuff, and Jim goes to see an object of his past affection, looking to bring it back to the present. Thy name be Letty.

"I grew up in a part of town where that was the culture," Esteban recalls. "It was very mixed, but I was very immersed in that culture, the street culture. It was very easy for me to connect with that character. My preparation was putting myself in the head of the character. It's definitely the knowledge of the character, who she is, her backstory, the chemistry between her and Christian Bale's character."

However, when Letty's boyfriend and his colleagues suddenly show their true selves, just as Harris did, Jim decides to fight fire with fire, knocking them down and robbing them. But also like Harris, Jim's past quickly catches up, as he's soon killed after a fight with the guys he robbed.

Perhaps the toughest pain to act out is that which is all too possible, and Esteban had been through that more than once. For her next television role, however, reality and the supernatural would meet.

A decade and a half after directing *From Dusk Till Dawn* on the big screen, Robert Rodriguez decided to shrink the screen and stretch out the storyline into one of the first series for his new El Ray Network channel. Following the story of bank-robbing brothers Richie and Seth Gecko, the 1996 film started out as a typical brutal crime drama before ending in a war between the Geckos, their hostages, and a group of vampires in a bar near the Mexican border.

But even with the battle against the bloodsuckers, many felt that the toughest scene of the film was Richie's early brutal rape and murder of the Gecko brothers' bank teller hostage Gloria (Brenda Hillhouse), which enrages even Seth. Trying out for the role reprisal in the TV series—D.J. Cotrona and Zane Holtz, *much* easier to accept as brothers than George Clooney and Quentin Tarantino had been in the flick, were the Geckos—Esteban got ready.

"I was very excited just to go on audition alone, because I loved the movie," she says. "Robert Rodriguez was someone I'd dreamed about working with for my lifetime." Still, she didn't get a response for some time, and figured someone else would be the lady, now named Monica.

Then one day, the phone rang, and it was the signal for the best news.

"I was in shock," Esteban remembers. "I couldn't cry, couldn't laugh, couldn't scream. I just let it sink in." That very day, she headed out towards the set, perusing the holy hell out of the material.

"It was a very emotional character," she says of Monica. "She was taken hostage. There was a lot of fear, high-intensity emotions." Just as with the pair of Lettys, she looked back to a part of her life that should never occur to anyone, although it has, to far too many.

"I chatted it up and laughed with the cast members," Esteban says, "and then they say 'Action!' and I jump right into crying, fearing for my life, to separate myself and mentally and emotionally get into that space. It has to happen very quickly." Monica would have a bit better luck than Gloria had, hanging on for several episodes. *Terminator 2* (1991) villain Robert Patrick showed up as a preacher, Don Johnson as a ranger who gets killed fast, and Wilmer Valderrama, light years from his work on *That 70s Show*, as a powerful mob boss and supernatural villain.

"I put myself in that place as that character," Esteban says. "The character had children and a husband. I have children and people I care about, so it wasn't very difficult for me to put myself in her shoes. That allowed me to focus and portray that character and how she was feeling."

Those are two tools that she hopes to continue on for quite some time in a tough business.

"We're interpreting the story through our skills and our craft, helping people get some impression and emotion from watching it," she says, to herself and the audience. "If it's something you can watch and you believe, and you're pulled into the film, I feel like I've done my job."

Hiding off in the darkness, peeking out into normalcy is the sad life of too many addicts, as Krisha Fairchild sadly showed us all in 2016's *Krisha*.

Krisha Fairchild: *Krisha*

SHE WORE THE RING that had been on her mom's hand before graduation; one of many memories that booze and dementia had teamed up to steal from the woman's mind.

Acting out a solo bathroom scene, her dad's ashes sat near her; he was another family member victimized by addiction.

Through her performance, Krisha Fairchild carried a lockbox full of medicine that had belonged to her niece, before the young lady died of an overdose.

These and other family issues had inspired Trey Shults to write and direct *Krisha* (2016). His aunt and others from the clan were performing them, acting out the past and present of reality, and a future that we all hope won't happen.

But we know it will, to someone, somewhere.

"It was written as a mélange of people from our family," Fairchild explains. "Based on our impressions and memories of them, not anything they confessed to us, we climbed inside them and tried to make sense of their lives."

Is there truly one in every family? The oddball, the dark (or even *black*) sheep, the crazy one that makes everyone else wish for a millisecond that the whole "holiday gathering" concept hadn't been thought of?

Basically, the one who makes us glad we're just so goddamned healthy. So straight. So normal. Lonely on the pedestal sometimes, isn't it?

Films usually take the comedic route with this sort of thing. Real life tells a different story. That's where we have to remember just how flawed this world can be. In the movies, parents always care for their kids, no matter how old. Families get through all their issues before dessert.

But it's not actually that way. Not here. We live in a place where parents might not love their children, and that might be a mutual feeling. Sometimes we use up all our chances with others, no matter how many we have. Families don't always give a flip about each other, and sometimes they have good reason not to.

Substance abuse is one of the most infective of such cancers. It can be treated, but never really cured. We have only so much control over how long its remission lasts, assuming it starts at all. And the suffering might be treated as contagious; spending time with them might cause us to catch the same affliction, or so we fear.

Fairchild and Shults had seen this, felt it themselves. Their fellow family members had as well. With other family members playing themselves, or at least fictionalized versions thereof, the story hits almost unthinkably hard.

"This was a fiction I created of her, based on the fiction Trey created with his script," Fairchild asserts, "because nobody is inside an addict, and nobody is inside a hero. So even if they are based on a real person, it is the job of the artist to create their own version of loser or winner, and bring that."

It's Thanksgiving, and Fairchild, in the title role, hoped her folk would grant just one more "last" chance. Her addiction and some of their issues had built a brick wall between her and the family and outlined it with explosives. She'd been choosing poisonous pals like booze and drugs over them for far too long, and no one stays in second place forever.

"I begin from the inside, feelings, and work outward," Fairchild explains of her prep work. "Then I find a prop or a style or a piece of music or an idiosyncrasy that anchors me to the character. And from that point on, I use my senses to reconnect to that thing, and step inside the character's insides." Sadly, as we saw back at the start, there was far too much there for Fairchild to choose from.

"The books and catalogs she packed, her clothes, and her lighter," she remembers, "all of those things were touchstones for me: I handled or wore them, and I was *there*, in the moment with the character as I envisioned her."

As Krisha goes about cooking up a huge turkey, some of her family members err on the side of optimism, hoping she's finally come out on top. Others keep keeping their distance, being realistic instead of hopeful.

One is Shults himself, his character also named Trey. He's playing Krisha's son. One is Krisha's sister Robyn, who raised Trey. Fairchild's sister Robyn, Shults' real-life mom, is in the role. The film was shot in her actual house.

Krisha and Robyn's mother is there as well. This might be her last Thanksgiving. This might not be a negative, as we see a sad lady, confused by an enemy heartless enough to torment those too old and weak to fight it off, her own demons of the past showing back up to support it.

She was the Fairchilds' actual mom Billie. We wish her amazing "performance" had been only that.

"Any scene with her," Fairchild says, "was actual heartbreak for me as an actress."

The magnetism of addiction will never be understood to those who haven't been through it. Alcohol, street drugs, even legal drugs . . . everyone, including (even especially) the sufferer, is well aware of the effects they can and often do have. Why do we torture ourselves? Why do we constantly keep putting ourselves through pain that keeps worsening? Some medical treatments hurt to undergo, but end up with a positive outcome. That never happens to those up against opponents within.

Others don't understand. They can't understand. So they make an effort *not* to understand. It's why frustration becomes a larger and larger part of an addict's sad life. We thought they loved us, but the only place we can find any kind of peace is a world without a happy ending.

So Krisha looks for it, and our hearts start to break, but not in surprise. As she guzzles an adult beverage, warm, relaxing music plays. The type of tunes we'd expect to hear as the credits rolled in a rom-com, a newly reunited couple dancing out their love in the background. That's the feeling addicts somehow get from this.

"I do not know how they got it to happen," Fairchild says of the soundtrack, "but it is genius how it creates a home for the visuals and marries the tension to the action."

She was doing so well, and now she's fucking it all up. She's fucked.

"Fuck me," she sighs, waking up from a booze-fueled nap. She doesn't need any help with that.

"My preparation was a mix of research and memory," Fairchild explains. "[My niece] was bipolar, so I researched how her meds would cause her to act if mixed with wine and pills. I studied the symptoms for bipolar, and for addiction, and the various ways families deal with both."

In the bathroom, surrounded by her dad's ashes, memories of past and present and fear of the future starting to envelope her mind like a tornado, Krisha slowly starts to relapse, hoping she can hide it, that she can do just enough to take her pain away without her folks, like her son, noticing.

"[I wanted] to unsquash her a bit, loosen her up, let her laugh, let her hope, let her try harder to please," Fairchild says. "So then, when her demons moved in, my own joyous soul was beaten down by them much more clearly."

Her high too high, Krisha can't serve the turkey right. That music flowing, we see a river of drippings fall to the floor, followed by the bird itself. This beautiful meal will never be sampled.

Her family comes back to reality, her lies revealed, her sobriety a facade. Krisha does too, back upstairs to hide her pain under her medicinal menaces.

Does she want to die? Regardless of that, does her family care if she does? Robyn comes up and lets her sister know she's not welcome. She probably will never be again. Maybe she will. It's hard to tell which would be a sadder outcome.

"I remembered family gatherings through the years, what was said and what was held in," recalls Fairchild, who called the scenes with Robyn some of her toughest. "Feelings and facts. Secrets and suspicions. How it feels when someone you love, who loves you back, looks into your eyes and lies. That was huge for me. All of these were the insides."

Frustration. Desperate grip to pride. Denial that she's only one still allowing. These things force Krisha back downstairs once more. There's nothing, no one left. Her sister rejects her. Her son lets her know she'll never be his mom. Krisha's in attack mode. Some fight her back. Others are too deflated to give a damn anymore.

Then one last closeup of Krisha's face. Breathe in, breathe out. Slump back.

Is she dead? Is that better?

"The one thing I think none of us expected, was how moved people would be by the film," Fairchild remarks. "How much catharsis we would cause in how many lives. For me, that is the real takeaway with *Krisha*: how it moved people to feel empathy for a loser.

"And maybe they'll transfer that to their worldview a bit.

"Maybe.

"Hopefully."

Prison isn't the only place for one to get institutionalized.

If a certain world is all we've ever known, we just make the best of it, as there's nothing else to do, nothing else to know. Others might look at it and run, but we don't even know who they are, or really that there's anyone but us. If we never had much to start with, we don't really have the means to develop a sense of loss.

Honestly, that might not sound so bad, or even that unusual. To an extent, it probably happens to us all. It's our surroundings that cause this. They mold us. We just hope that their final creation learns enough to live outside its own natural habitat—culture shock is everything but a legitimate medical epidemic.

Without a single explosion, death, or even a gunshot, a film can go straight into the genre of action . . . just from a different perspective. Sometimes the action that goes on within, things that happen far inside the darkness of a character's mind and past, can be just as and even more destructive than a few Michael Bay films put together. What we can't see and have to create and experience within our own psyche sometimes stays there for much longer than we might want or hope.

Krisha was one such flick, but a few years before, *Dogtooth* had charged out of Greece and jumped the Atlantic over here, jam-packed with action of the hidden kind. We'd only see its outer effects, a fraction of the agony of those forced to find it for portrayal purposes—and we were impressed enough to make it just the fifth Greek film in history to snare a Best Foreign Language film nomination (Denmark's *In a Better World* came out on top).

Fairchild had shown us a sort of pain she'd found by *living* it, far from her life as an actress. *Dogtooth*'s stars had to search it out on their own for the 2009 flick. Of course, they couldn't wait to act out the aches.

"It was a huge pleasure for me," remembers Angeliki Papoulia. "It was the first time in my life that I've read such an amazing and brilliant script."

She'd never had a chance. She'd never had a name. Her character was the eldest daughter of a family of five, hidden away forever in a fenced compound by her folks. Along with her brother and sister, she had no clue that *anything* was on the other side of the walls.

Forced under her parents' will, physically and mentally, for so much of 2009's *Dogtooth*, Angeliki Papoulia finally attempted to realize a painful way out of imprisonment.

For a while, that had been all right. We can't fear or even find interest in what doesn't exist, even in our imaginations. But this is humanity, and people get curious. They want to think, to learn. And those in control—like Mommy and Daddy—want to squash that bothersome independent thought. When people know too much, or even want to, the show-runners' stroke falls into peril.

"We rehearsed for about a month," Papoulia says. "We basically had rehearsals with the siblings and the parents. We improvised a lot on what they would do in their spare time in the house, what kind of games they were playing, and how they would spend time with their parents."

Puberty may not strengthen us in the mental sense, but it sure as hell smartens up our mouths, makes us question probably just a bit more than necessary, and fires our libido up for the first time. As the dad brings home a young lady to satisfy the brother, for the right price, the lady seems to want to try it her own way—with Papoulia's girl. With no concept as to why people enjoy this sex stuff, or with whom to try it, the gal goes along for the riding.

She likes it. Then her sister gets in on it too. Soon the brother joins. On the outside, in the audience, we look at this stuff, this incest, and call it sick, but these people don't know the difference.

Remember, Papoulia's character hadn't had the chance to really develop at all. That's tough to keep in mind, when we see her experimenting with her own siblings, at Daddy's own whim. She'd never had much to do at all. So, away from all the rehearsing and improv drills, Papoulia spent some serious time doing nothing. Withholding from herself, and ultimately from us, the life her character never led.

"I was prepared for the role in the sense that I practiced on not expressing a lot," she recalls, "and trying not to act at all, and also trying to leave an open space for the unknown."

As it always does with sexual awakening, emotion follows along, and often goes up at high volume. As we learn the lessons of adulthood, we sometimes get quarrelsome. Angry. Quick to hit fury. Tormented by her brother, Papoulia gives him a beating, then knifes him in the arm. Not surprisingly, she gets all the blame, her mom turning her into a punching bag.

"It was tough to film the cutting scene," she recalls. "We couldn't do it very easily because it was a matter of synchronization, and we had to shoot it many times in order to achieve it."

In typical Hollywood, she'd make it out, away from the evils at home, and charge into society, ready to become its newest and biggest asset. But this isn't Hollywood. It's not even America. That's not how things work. Not all audiences are lucky to get the happily-ever-after mess that we're spoiled with.

The daughter stows away in the back of her dad's car, but when it parks, she doesn't emerge. Maybe she can't. (Tragically, Mary Tsoni, who plays Papoulia's younger sister, suddenly passed away in May 2017, at just thirty years old).

"When I watched the film, it wasn't about the special effects," Papoulia remembers. "I was surprised and thrilled and couldn't believe it."

In 1987, Chelsea Field and the rest of the cast of *Masters of the Universe* humanized those who'd defended Castle Grayskull in the cartoons for years.

Chelsea Field: *Masters of the Universe*

IT WAS A SWITCH that no performer in the world had ever faced. Changing from the stage to the screen, from comedy to drama, or, as the eventual subject of this piece did, from dancing to acting, nothing comes close to this alteration.

For about four years, the residents of Eternia had been locked inside the animated world, more than enough of their time taken up by the most uncivil of wars raging around the planet. On one side, there was the legendary warrior He-Man and his pals at Castle Grayskull, battling off one attack after another by Skeletor, Evil-Lyn (she really needed that hyphen to stand out as a bad girl!), Beastman, and everyone else who felt that the fellow with the skulled face had his act together—that, more than He-Man, he deserved to be the *Master of the Universe*! But right up next to He-Man was Teela, the champion swordswoman there to back up her daddy, Man-at-Arms himself.

On either side of the battle, the Eternians (or, to be fair, those that drew them) had more than enough of fighting their war in the cartoons. Still, in 1987, they were forced to get real. He-Man, Skeletor, and everyone that followed either of them had to jump from animation to humanity when their story hit the big screen. Now Teela, just like everyone else, was transitioning in a way that no one, not even the lady who'd inherit her persona, had ever faced.

From just about the start of her entertainment career, Chelsea Field got used to putting out all kinds of effort with no sure reward in sight.

Just as with the acting world, and maybe even more so, those hoping to make it in dance are left to do all they can to make it, with many knowing from the start that things will be all for naught. Trying to make a mark in this sort of field will undoubtedly cost all kinds of time, and all too often, people will have every reason to see it as time *not* well spent if the part goes to another.

"Having the background of being a dancer and that kind of discipline, just training and training and training," Field recalls, "you do a million things, and there's not a payoff. You just try to do better. It's an art form. It's different than being a celebrity or having stardom."

For about a decade, she'd been dancing across the world, the occasional singing gig stepping in every now and again, her finale being a year on *Solid Gold*, the *Soul Train*- or *American Bandstand*-type series (albeit a bit more risqué, at least for the early 80s) that featured Field and so many others like her getting down to the tunes of the times.

"I realized that my days as a dancer were numbered, and it was better to start looking for something else," Field recalls. "I didn't type, I didn't do anything else. So I started taking acting classes, and I felt like a bird out of a cage. I had a teacher that was very disciplined in the way he taught and spoke to me, and it was like the way I had been trained as a dancer in ballet and all that type of discipline. It felt like a whole new world of freedom to be expressed through a different name than dancing or singing."

Just as it's almost always the case in any genre, Field's action career got started slowly. Between commercials, she showed up on the small screen for an episode of *Airwolf* and the big one, aside a guy named Schwarzenegger, in *Commando*, both in 1985.

Then another role came calling. Though it's become commonplace for quite some time in today's film world, taking a cartoon from the small to big screen—animated or in live-action mode—was a task very few had dared to even embark upon back in the mid-1980s. Perhaps that's part of the reason why the crew went beneath the A-list for its cast.

"It was a leap of faith by producers," Field recalls. "I didn't have a track record. Most people have ten years of work by the time they're 28, but I didn't." She hadn't been a big fan of Teela's small-screen work, but there was much more to worry about, at least at first.

"I still had the mentality of staying there and doing work and work until I achieved it," Field recalls. "Just like if I was working on a double pirouette or doing a split, I just keep working at it until I achieve it. Also in those days, there weren't many professional dancers that crossed over into acting. It was the intestinal fortitude and strength. I didn't have a backup. I didn't finish college. I didn't have a four-year degree. There wasn't anything else for me to do. There was no safety net while I was on the high wire."

Fortunately, not literally. But over the exceptional period of time it took for her to even try for the role (she was in the audition process for what seemed like months) the feeling of being up there was quite relatable. Tryout after tryout, Field couldn't know if the next one would be the end—and if it were, whether someone might just suddenly say, "Thanks, but we're going in a new direction!"

"Most of the acting was through body language, very physical," she remembers. "You see these actresses today with amazing bodies. But back then, a lot of actresses weren't physical, so I had a bit of an edge. I must have been in to audition seven times, jumping over couches, pretending I had a laser gun. Originally, Teela was going to do broadsword, so I was pretending I had one, fighting off Skeletor."

It worked. Not nearly soon enough, she won the Teela contest.

"When I found out I got it, I felt I had won the Super Bowl at the last second," Field recalls. "It was the greatest feeling ever." After attempting to destroy Americanism with his gloved fists in 1985's *Rocky IV*, Dolph Lundgren undertook He-Man's masterpiece of patriotism, with Frank Langella on the other side as the skulled man. Jon Cypher was Teela's pappy.

Hard at battle over on Eternia, He-Man and his forces try to break through Skeletor's minions to grab a Cosmic Key that can take anyone anywhere at any time. As the evil army breaks through, the good guys are forced to use the Key, and find themselves on a strange planet called Earth. Skeletor sends some of his friends too, with Evil-Lyn (Meg Foster) leading the way.

Field had been checking over Teela's drawn escapades by now.

"We had a rehearsal period, which was very nice," she says. "They ended up not having us use the broadsword; we had laser guns."

A couple of teenagers—one of whom was a young up-and-comer named Courtney Cox, far from *Scream* (1996) or even *Friends*—find the key and attempt to incorporate it into their fledgling music career. It doesn't work; soon enough, Skeletor's down there and the key is destroyed. Even He-Man's about ready to give up, surrendering to save his friends. The rising moon gives Skeletor all the power in the universe, and, just as it so often did during the cartoons, it looks like the goodies are done for.

"In the scenes where Skeletor's landing on the roof," Field remembers, "we're looking at a crane, and Frank Langella's on a crane, and we have to imagine that he's in a spaceship. It was my first big job, so I applied everything I had in my acting classes."

And, of course, as they always did on the show, He-Man's friends find a way to win. A new key transports everyone, including the weird-looking creatures called Earthlings, back to Eternia, where Evil-Lyn and everyone else, ticked that Skeletor took *all* the power, leave him to his own. He's got no chance against He-Man one on one, and the warrior prince blasts him straight into a pit, with Teela and everyone else left to celebrate.

"Six weeks of night shoots was very bonding for the cast," Field says. "There's this feeling like you're the only people in the world, especially in Los Angeles."

Skeletor's galpal Evil-Lyn hid malevolence behind Meg Foster's beauty in 1987's *Masters of the Universe*.

On the other side, Foster ate up Evil-Lyn's malevolence like chicken chow mein.

"I wanted to do something for children," she remembers. "I interpreted Evil-Lyn in the wardrobe. It was quite fun. It came naturally in a way, once everybody was in costume." The sinful seductress originally had locks flowing out of her helmet; Foster convinced the crew to shorten her hair.

"Something happens inside of me," she says of performing. "There's a freedom I remember. Sometimes it is to not be afraid, which is important. You're edgy, and when they say cut, you can laugh. It's fascinating, and you have to be prepared for anything. All of a sudden, I think I know where I'm going, and then all of a sudden, it goes somewhere totally different. That's really strange and wonderful."

1991 brought a double shot for Field. Some saw her as Virginia Slim (the cigarette moniker resemblance was intentional), the ex of Don Johnson's title character, the second name in *Harley Davidson and the Marlboro Man*. In the action flick that later found a home in the cult classic section, the Man and his friend (Mickey Rourke) get caught up in the dark double whammy of bank robbery and drug dealing as they try to save a friend's bar.

Field spent time with a policewoman to get ready for Virginia, who resists the Man's urges to get back with him.

"That role was more about looking at a scene," she remembers. "For a lot of the scenes, the writing was challenging. I remember trying to make each individual scene work, making sense of my character."

One of her toughest scenes came when Slim and Harley hang out in a coffee shop.

"Here's some info that's good to know for readers: you never know what you're going to get in a scene," Field says. "At the coffee shop, they did a close-up of me, and then they turned around and did something totally different. It was so out of the box that my reactions were clear, and I played the scene really different."

The same year, she'd play Bruce Willis' adulterous wife in *The Last Boy Scout*, which would require an even bigger switch near the end. After establishing himself from behind the cameras of *Top Gun* (1986) and *Days of Thunder* (1990), Tony Scott turned Willis into a broken-down drunk private eye who happens to stumble into a conspiracy that could destroy pro football.

"Tony was a fan of doing stuff that wasn't rehearsed," Field says. "There was never any talk about what was the intention of the scene, what does the director want to get out of it. He wasn't particularly verbal. That was kind of a challenge. You have to answer your own questions and be your own director."

Home for the first time in far too long, Willis' Joe Hallenbeck catches his wife Sarah in the aftermath of a mattress romp with his best friend. Moments later, the friend, and almost Joe as well, get taken out in a car bomb.

"They shot so many takes of every scene," Field says. "There was so much money in the studios that people weren't worrying about saving anything. There was not a lot of rehearsal. You have to acclimate to who your director is, who your acting partners are, who you're in the scene with. Those are some of the hardest jobs, because you're in and out. It's like being a guest on some TV shows, because [guest stars] come in and they have sometimes the hardest work, and yet they're kind of the odd men out, because they're not regular."

She finished up, and headed down to Africa for a few months to do *Dust Devil* (1992). Then Field learned that Sarah hadn't made enough reparation.

Scout's original ending had Joe just hugging her and the two walking off together. Test audiences felt that that wasn't enough; she had to get heavy on the groveling. Months after wrapping *Scout*, Field had to come back and have Sarah beg Joe to start caring again. "I'll buy a dog!" she tearfully weeps.

"They had a new ending where I apologize," she says. "'You're perfect and I suck, it was all my fault that I slept with him!' I was angry that I had to do that. I understand it more now."

Devil had her playing Wendy, on the run from a horrible marriage, chased around the Namibian desert by an evil spirit who gains power by sucking up human blood, culminating in her blasting his ass to hell with a shotgun.

"There was a lot of energy around me," she says of the role, for which she prepared by forming a South African accent. "The woman had to get out, and she doesn't know what's going to happen. Very little was told to me during the beginning. You have to make up your own background in that situation, and that part of the movies is interesting to me."

It became something of a springboard toward so many other self-taught aspects of the profession, she continues.

"I always base everything on the evidence," Field says. "I've got to read the script many, many times. There's little things in the stage direction, and you stage everything on your evidence. I can start adding in background information of things that have happened to me. Even though I'm making it up, I can feel like it's coming from outside of me, a little bit like the creative process when you're not in it alone. I'm one who commits to that. Sometimes, there are things going on in my life that I can look at and say, wow, that's very close to that, or if I heard a story from a friend, if maybe that could be applied some way to the character I'm playing."

Those are technique that she continues to use today—and much like the start of her career before the camera, Field's still bridging a gap, this one between performing and reality. It's something that not all of her colleagues try.

"Emotional work is clearly the hardest," she explains. "I might be doing a scene where I'm bawling. I'll go in and they'll tell me to do a scene where my son just died. It's so hard to do that kind of work. It can wipe me out for an entire day. I can't fake it; I'm not that kind of actress. I have to muster up to make myself cry."

She calls a scene in 1993's *Extreme Justice* when a man commits suicide in front of Field's news reporter still one of the toughest of her career.

"It's hard to talk about," she says. "It's not real, you're acting, but the feelings are real. We have these emotional bodies that go through this preparation, in scenes and auditions, but our emotional body doesn't know we're acting."

Deadlier than she ever was as Trinity in the world of pro wrestling, Stephanie Finochio became a woman of the law in the title role of 2011's *Jesse*.

Stephanie Finochio: *Jesse*

AT PRETTY MUCH EVERY stage, any aspect of an acting career, one thing will be few and far between for a performer: control. The parts you grab, the scenes you do, the ones that don't get cut, these things will quite often come down to the luck of the draw (or the choice of the crew).

Still, there's something to be said, in high praise, for those who can function quite well without the benefit of stability, not being able to even remotely predict what's happening next.

That's been an asset to more than one side of Stephanie Finochio's performance resume.

It helped quite a bit in about the biggest role of her acting career, in and out of character. It's a big part of the reason why she made it so far in the heavily improvised world of pro wrestling. And it's why, after over two decades in the least controllable and most dangerous occupation in the acting business, the lady from Long Island is still going pretty strong.

"I actually feel I was born to be a stunt woman," Finochio theorizes. "I was such a dramatic theatrical kid. I have an amazing imagination and was always playing make-believe and dress-up." Trading in femininity for physicality, however, opened up her eyes, hopes, and a hell of a lot of career possibilities.

"I played almost every sport throughout my school years and ventured into more extreme sports outside of school," she recalls. "I grew up on motorcycles, motocross, ATVs, and horses. I grew up in the water: scuba diving, boating, racing jet skis, water skiing, and surfing, which led to snow skiing and snowboarding."

In hindsight, it's tough to see her doing anything else. But even those who make it in entertainment will tell you that education should be everyone's starting point and fallback, and Finochio took all kinds of care there with a trio of college degrees from Long Island's Dowling College, ending up with a Master's in Education (sadly, Dowling closed in August 2016).

It wouldn't be the last time the number three would be a staple in her life. We'll be there soon.

"A friend of the family said, 'You should be a stunt woman!'" she says. "The bells went off in my head, and I set off for Hollywood to fulfill my destiny."

In so many ways our minds go straight to the action world when thinking of stunt work, and Finochio spent quite a bit of time there, starting with her film debut in 1997's *Anaconda*. But diversity is as important in acting as in any other field, and Finochio's resume grew through drama (1997's *U-Turn*) into biopics (*Pollock* of 2000) and even to family fare (*Stuart Little 2* of 2002)!

"I really love all stunts, and I love that I am able to do most anything I set my mind to," she asserts. "I've been fortunate to perform so many stunts, from stair falls, fights, high falls, fire burns, car stunts, motorcycle stunts, horse stunts, water stunts on jet skis, wire work, just to name a few! I love fire! I love anything that has to do with fire, being on fire is an amazing challenge. Explosions too!"

In the early 2000s, she started training for a different type of entertainment—one with "sports" and a hyphen in front of it. For five years, Finochio's lead role was the far-from-holy Trinity, her top stunt being a moonsault off the top rope onto one hapless opponent (male or female) after another in both TNA and WWE rings.

"Growing up, I was the only girl on a street with all boys," she explains, "which helped in making me the tomboy I am today. As the only girl on my block, I constantly had to prove myself to get to play and be included. Sometimes I even had to fight. This made me grow up always trying everything and playing everything and pushing myself to be the best at everything and be able to do everything."

Finochio hung up her tights in 2007 to head back to stunt work full time, though she'd kept up with the business between Trinity trysts, like in *Eternal Sunshine of the Spotless Mind* (2004) and *World Trade Center* (2004).

"I'm very proud of all the stunts I have performed in my career, safely and professionally," she says. "I think I'm most proud to have had this career for twenty-three years and counting. I'm proud of the stunt person I have become in all my years, the learning and growing and the awareness. There is so much more to this work than the stunt itself."

What Finochio's fans see may be what we get, but she and her colleagues often get a hell of a lot more than they ever bargained for on the job.

"New people come into our business, so they think they can do stunts," she says. "Yes, sliding cars in a parking lot or in the neighborhood might be fun and easy for some, but on a set there is so much more to think about: the location itself, the pros and cons, the obstacles, the safety involved. Then you add the crew, the actors, the equipment, the extras. Then there are more obstacles and safety to think about. Now you have the director's vision and how the stunt coordinator envisions the stunt and how the actor wants you to portray them in the stunt. Then there is putting it all together and being *aware*."

Finally, in 2011, came a new chance and challenge for Finochio to lead the way, in both the character and physical sense. She grabbed the title role in *Jesse*, the story of a lady just about ready to quit on everything before a reason to move forward gets all but forced down her throat.

"When I was presented with the role of Jesse, I was well into my stunt career and had expanded my skills in acting and special effects," Finochio says. "I felt more comfortable with portraying the character of Jesse because she was similar to me in some ways: a strong female. I feel I'm always playing this role in life—dealing with problems, having to be tough, having flaws in many ways, and dealing with it all in the best way you know how."

Well, we all do that. Unfortunately, for too many, the best way, the only way, is found in the world of addiction, which rarely has a Hollywood ending. That's how things look for Finochio's girl early on. Her law enforcement job heading nowhere, her kids living with her jerkweed ex, her mother and brother just taking up space; there's little for her to look forward to.

Until her bro, mixed up with the wrong people, appears to die a painful death at their hands. That could have been Jesse's knockout punch, but it instead becomes an overdue turnaround. With him, and her little ones, to stand up for, she grabs for that thing that few actors, or cops, ever experience, the tidbit we mentioned back at the start.

A control that allows her to go at the mob with guns blazing in every sense. It pushes her back into top condition. It gives her the fortitude to give a deserved death sentence to some scumbags who try to rob her. And she's out to avenge with a vengeance.

"I feel in real life, I have to cover up the flaws and hide the pain and put on a front and make believe to go out in the world," Finochio says. "I'm still me most of the time, but it's life; you have to suck it up. But in this world, this role, this experience, you dig down and let out the things you hide, the flaws you have, the problems you are dealing with, the feelings you experience. You let it out, you exploit it and become the character you can freely express in this world."

Things get even more jumbled for Jesse in the closing act, including a discovery that there might have been much less to her brother and his action than she theorized, not to mention some hardcore brawling and gunfights. But as anyone who's spent much time around cops and criminals—voluntarily or otherwise!—can attest, the line between the two can be all but impossible to find, often coming down to a choice here or there. And just as a cop can be drawn out of line sometimes (much less than the media would have us believe), once in a while a crook can go right, as long as there's a benefit involved. *Jesse*'s happy ending comes from the most unexpected spot, but it's still as upbeat of one as such a film could grab.

"I'm most comfortable with the stunts and effects, because that comes more natural to me: the tough strong badass!" Finochio jokes. "The deep emotional parts are harder, but that's the challenge. That's the acting, or is it? It's the stuff you are afraid to let loose because then it's out there. I love the challenge and the thrill and the control and being somewhat out of control."

Hey, maybe that's it. Sure, we're lucky if we have any control at all over much in our acting careers. But perhaps one way to establish some is to figure out what tactical techniques might just come in handy for the next job we're lucky enough to grab, and shove them straight to the forefront.

"Awareness!" exclaims Finochio. "I feel that is such an important key in being a stunt person: awareness of your surroundings, awareness of everything that is going on, where everything is and everyone is and where they will be, and movement. Awareness in anticipation what can and might go wrong and being ready to avoid it or handle it when it happens, if it happens. I believe this only comes with experience and a certain type of person. I definitely take pride in my awareness and alertness and being an overall skilled stunt woman."

You can get in great physical shape, you can study, you can watch videos, you can do all sorts of things to get ready for a stunting job, even one in which you might be covered by a costume or specially effected out in the final product.

Unfortunately, and this is going to be a shocking revelation . . . there's no preparatory act to grow hair all over one's body, suddenly double- (and even quadruple, we might think when we're watching them) joint all of one's limbs, quickly alter one's DNA a few degrees, and develop a voracious hunger for leaf-chomping and limb-swinging!

In any case, that's all pretty unfortunate for John Alexander; such practices would have not only won him perhaps a Nobel Prize in science, but made his acting career *quite* a bit simpler. Seven times, the Scotland native has stepped onto the big screen, but all we audiences saw was one of the tree-swinging species.

Alexander's first step toward animalism was in his film debut in 1984's *Greystoke: The Legend of Tarzan, Lord of the Apes*. He'd be prime primate White Eyes (perhaps an homage to Bright Eyes, the name the new rulers gave to Charlton Heston's Taylor back in 1968's *Planet of the Apes*?).

"I studied a lot of chimpanzees at all ages," Alexander remembers. "We studied their behavior for a very long time." One of the makeup men was Rick Baker, three years past his first Oscar for *An American Werewolf in London*. Over the next few years, the pair's names would be seen side by side more and more. It's a shame they didn't meet sooner; Alexander might have gotten to be the main movie monkey of all time in 1976's *King Kong* (Baker himself donned the suit for that one).

"In stunt work, one thing often leads to another," says Alexander, whose past as a gymnast got him in stunting shape at high speed. "You get a lot of people saying, 'He did good there, so he'd do a good job in this.'"

Alexander's next work would take him even closer to the gorilla world, perhaps closer than he'd intended or hoped. As Sigourney Weaver acted out the work of legendary naturalist Dian Fossey and her work protecting the mountain gorillas of Rwanda in 1988's *Gorillas in the Mist*, a job that nearly won Weaver an Oscar, she filmed a ton of footage alongside real animals on location in Kenya. The filming gave Alexander a new study guide to act out Digit, one of Fossey's favorites.

While Sigourney Weaver rolled toward an Oscar nomination for playing naturalist Dian Fossey in 1988's *Gorillas in the Mist*, John Alexander (left) played Fossey's furry friend Digit, one of many primate-based portrayals in his career.

"We watched the footage and copied their movements," Alexander recalls. "You can't direct a real gorilla, and it was a really challenging role to be matched up with real gorillas." Tragically, Digit and Fossey would be forever linked by tragedy; his brutal slaughter by poachers pushing her to wage war against the hunters, culminating in her still-unsolved murder in December 1985. The two still lay next to each other, along with many of Digit's primate pals, in the same cemetery.

Alexander played a friendly gorilla in *Baby's Day Out* in 1994 and one not so nice the next year in *Congo*. Then, in 1997, a newfound action/buddy comedy/sci-fi flick arrived, one that would spawn (at least!) two sequels and countless conspiracy theories.

Were these people, and those they protected us from, truly real? Had we seen them in the past and not realized it until now? And how could we become a member of their ranks?

As *Men in Black* kicked off in the summer of 1997, we met a critter named Mikey, a weird-looking fellow that the title characters had seen before. But a curious policeman steps too close to the action, panicking Mikey to predatory rage and forcing Tommy Lee Jones' Kay to blast him to liquidity, then erase everyone's memory with the trade's trusty . . . flashy thing.

We'd never know it, but Alexander had been Mikey. We didn't know it yet, but Baker's work on the flick would bring him another Academy Award.

"I was running around on leg extensions," he recalls of acting out the alien's rough movements. "When it came time to putting the head on, it made me blind. You couldn't know where you were." He'd show up again in the 2002 sequel, playing Jarra, ready to visit all kinds of delightful torment on Will Smith's J.

Alexander's final (for now!) appearance(s) as a simian relative came as two separate creatures (and a side mark as a human servant) in Tim Burton's *Planet of the Apes* remake of 2001. He showed a bit of animalistic diversity the next year as one of the title characters in *The Country Bears*.

1998, however, brought his biggest, in every sense of the word, creation to date.

Nearly half a century after the story of *Mighty Joe Young* had amazed and thrilled audiences of the late 40s, the story came back. Technology was well past the stop-action and animation that the crew of the original had been forced to use, but not quite as much as they'd hoped.

"They wanted to do a lot of CGI, but it wasn't working," Alexander remembers. But who else could be so ready to be a primate?

"It was the Rolls-Royce of gorilla suits," he remembers of the title character's outfit. "People were like, 'You're just a little guy. How are you playing this nine-foot gorilla?'"

Yes, Joe lived up to and past his Mighty moniker, towering above his caregiving galpal Jill (Charlize Theron, showing that even apes recognize great tastes in ladies).

"Most of the stuff I did was with miniature objects, like Humvees and jeeps," he remembers. "Anything I worked with was about forty percent reduced." Like the King of all monkeys, Joe heads to America to be a big star, only to get hunted down by a poacher who killed both his mom and Jill's a few decades before. But unlike the Kong man, Joe has a happy ending, escaping back to Africa to live out in freedom.

Dennis Franz (right) and Gordon Clapp (second from right) were the only two characters to appear on all twelve seasons of *NYPD Blue* from 1993 to 2005, with Franz winning four Emmys and Clapp one. From left, Henry Simmons, Bill Brochtrup, and James McDaniel helped the series take top honors at both the Emmys and Golden Globes.

Dennis Franz, Gordon Clapp, Bill Brochtrup: *NYPD Blue*

A BIT OVER TWO decades ago, a veteran actor in Hollywood was approached by two familiar producers. Just as he had on a previous show of theirs, they asked if he'd mind playing a policeman.

At first, the fellow balked. With good reason—he'd played nearly thirty roles in the characters of law enforcement, and now he wanted something new. Not only that, but the man he was to play was a drunk, a womanizer, a bigot, a selfish vitriol container that no one in their right mind would want to get anywhere near.

But Steven Bochco and David Milch kept asking their *Hill Street Blues* (1983) alumnus—and fortunately for all, Dennis Franz changed his mind, took on the role of *NYPD Blue* detective Andy Sipowicz. He ended up as one of the most well-known (and shockingly, beloved) television characters of the 1990s and early 2000s.

"For once in my career, I made a correct decision!" jokes Franz. "It was the most rewarding, invigorating creative experience I've ever had. It was twelve years of wonderful-ness."

The twelve years, which began in 1993 amid a sea of controversy over the show's use of language and nudity—charges that seem comical by today's television standards—kicked off with a half year of deep deliberation for Franz.

"It took a long time to think about this," he recalled. "I had about six months of thinking about this character. Then I saw a script, and realized the complexity of Andy Sipowicz. How was I going to make him likeable, or have anybody give a hoot about him? Everything that could be wrong with someone was wrong with him."

His problems multiplied about a millionfold in the very first episode, when Sipowicz was gunned down by Alfonse Giardella (Robert Costanzo, who, in what was either a simple coincidence or one hell of an in-joke, played Franz's brother in 1990's *Die Hard 2*). The two would be at each others' throats until Giardella met a similar end a few episodes later; by that point, Sipowicz had made what the show's doctor referred to as an "amazing" recovery.

"Whether the audience was going to jump on board and like me or care about me remained to be seen," Franz said. "We had meetings, and I said, 'How am I going to get anybody to care about him?' David said, 'You will, because it's inside you.'

"I said, 'Thank you very much for the compliment, but I don't know how I'm going to go about doing this!' So I went about thinking, how can I make the audience care and believe that this was a good man, a good husband, a good father, a good provider, a good human being?"

First, he made Sipowicz human—flawed, but human. He made him an alcoholic who wasn't quite all bad, a person who'd given up on much of human contact, let alone love, but allowed it to creep its way back when he started to fall for bombshell DA Sylvia Costas (Sharon Lawrence). He recovered from the gunshot wounds, but ended up relapsing into alcohol and turned angry again. With the help of Alcoholics Anonymous, he tried to get back with Costas as the season ended.

But she wouldn't be the only one he'd charmed so quickly; after just one year on the job, Franz brought home the first of four Emmys he'd win for playing Sipowicz.

"The very first time that you hear your name announced, it truly is an out-of-body experience," he says. "You hear about Academy Awards, Emmy Awards, Grammy Awards, they go to other people. Suddenly, you're in the mix, and that's hard to accept. To just be a part of that was so foreign, and so exciting. To watch all these other actors, and the live ceremony, and knowing your name is going to be announced as a nominee is really heart-pumping.

"When they announced my name, I didn't hear 'Dennis Franz.' I heard 'Deeeeennnnnnnisssss Fraaaa.' It goes on for an hour and a half in your head, and goes blank. It was not a realization that I was prepared for. I didn't know what to say. I was tremendously flattered and grateful. The ones that came after that still had tremendous impact—something I never prepared for. When they came, they were equally appreciated. I didn't think it was going to mean that much to me. The work is the work, but when you get patted on the back that way, it's very rewarding." And as an added bonus, Sipowicz wouldn't be the last cop Franz would portray, to an extent; he voiced a police horse in Eddie Murphy's 1998 comedy *Dr. Dolittle*.

"That's what the intent of the show was," he explains, "to show the livelihood of the men and women that do this work. To focus on their good qualities, their not-so-good qualities, their flaws, everything that makes up a human being. These human beings, who I definitely think of as our heroes, are special people, and to focus on what makes them was the intent of the show."

In just about every season, the writers put Sipowicz through one trauma after another. Some were major, like the Giardella shooting or the other violence he encountered (stay tuned for more on that), and some were of his own doing, like his standoffish nature when original partner John Kelly (David Caruso) was forced out in the second season, and Bobby Simone (Jimmy Smits) showed up to replace him, leading to this classic, hilarious exchange between Sipowicz and his boss, Lt. Arthur Fancy (James McDaniel):

Sipowicz: "I met the new guy, and it's not going to work out; his attitude's all wrong."
Fancy: "What do you mean?"
Sipowicz: "Ooh, don't get me started—this 'Hi-how-you-doing?' stuff."
Fancy: "He asked you how you were doing?"
Sipowicz: "Yeah!"

"Like life, we make new friends and new acquaintances on a daily basis, and with each new one, we don't adjust our personalities, but we work out that relationship," Franz says. "The same thing happens with these characters. They come into your life, and they lead you in a new direction. So with each new character that came on board, it was kind of exciting to establish the new rapport, whatever the new relationship was going to be. How it affected my character was that it was another challenge and interest to show whatever sides I had left—how it affected Sipowicz and how he related to these new people in his life."

Fortunately, it didn't take long for his opinion of Simone to change.

"I had it in my mind that John Kelly was going to be my last partner," Franz remembers. "Nobody was going to replace John Kelly; Jesus Christ himself wasn't going to replace John Kelly. It wasn't going to work out. Then along comes Bobby Simone, and I wasn't going to accept this guy, but he showed his colors, and what type of man he was from the very first episode that

Bobby was introduced (in his first five minutes in the squad, Simone helped Sipowicz foil an in-house shooting). How could I not start to love this man, and accept him as a partner, and more importantly as a replacement for a guy that I thought was irreplaceable?

"That relationship turned into a marriage of sorts. It was a real deep relationship, man to man. It was a wonderful, equal relationship." Tragically, a heart infection would befall Simone in season six, though Franz called the few episodes leading up to his passing some of the best of the show's entire tenure (Simone showed back up for a heartfelt cameo in one of the series' last episodes).

A new partner arrived in the character of Danny Sorensen, and grownup child star Rick Shroeder.

"It was smart on Steven and David's part to not look for a replacement for Jimmy, but to go in an entirely new direction," Franz says, "with a young guy that Andy accepted as a father-son relationship. He didn't always like that, neither Danny Sorenson or Rick Schroeder always liked that, but that was the mindset that I had."

Sorensen was murdered, as was Sylvia—"Anybody who came on the set," Franz jokingly remembers, "I told them, 'Don't get too close to me if you want to keep your job.'"—and fellow former young star Mark-Paul Gossaleer showed up as John Clark, a second-generation cop with growing skeletons of alcoholism and women trouble in his own closet.

"I saw in him a young [Sipowicz]," Franz says. "As our relationship evolved, and his character developed, I saw him becoming a young, beginning-to-be-troubled, innocent voice."

Another of Franz's favorite works—for the quality of the acting, obviously not the upbeat nature of the storyline—came in the third season, when Sipowicz's estranged son Andy Jr. (Michael DeLuise) was murdered, pushing his father back into the dark depths of alcoholism he'd worked so hard to climb from.

"That haunted me for a while," he recalls. "I had to get the impact of actually seeing my son dead on a gurney, out of the blue. I had to do some soul-searching—where could I go to get that emotional? I tried to think of the very worst that I had experienced in my life, and how it impacted me."

Franz imagined the death of his parents. He thought about what life would be like if he lost his wife Joanie (who, thankfully, is still alive in real life).

"I imagined that, all those things," he says. "That was something that stayed with me for a while."

He also enjoyed the love-hate relationship that Sipowicz shared with his boss Fancy, as Sipowicz wasn't always good at taking orders, let alone from a minority person.

"I was begging my entire run on that show for Sipowicz to have a black wife or a black girlfriend," he says. "We can't pick and choose who we fall in love with, but to try to cope with the feelings of denying who you are would have been a wonderful storyline. [For Andy] to fall for people he had hard feelings about and not being able to deny his heart would have made for wonderful drama. It's the same thing that I felt about the relationship between John Irvin and Sipowicz—two different worlds that turned into a very warm relationship." Irvin, one of television's first mainstream gay characters, helped Sipowicz get over his homophobia.

Like many characters in the final seasons, Sipowicz's standing in the law enforcement world changed—he was promoted to sergeant. The scene, a few episodes from the end, where he went downstairs in the squad, only to find everyone saluting him, is perhaps the season's most lasting individual image. As the series ended, he'd take over the squad.

"The biggest question was how would Andy and the 15th precinct leave the audience feeling after the final season," Franz said. "I loved the end of *The Sopranos*—nobody could have guessed that one." The longtime HBO series ended in 2007 with a stoppage, rather than a conclusion, as the Soprano family sat together at a restaurant, with the show halting in mid-dialogue.

"Steve Bochco had a plan, and it was to leave the show on the feeling that life was going to continue in the world of the 1-5," Franz says, "and it represented an awful lot of realizing and accepting that Andy was not the same person he was when he started."

The intimidation that Sipowicz so often displayed to get suspects to speak their mind—by choice or otherwise—sometimes carried over into the actor himself, recalls Gordon Clapp, who played Greg Medavoy, the socially-challenged detective so often used as a verbal punching bag by other characters.

"I knew that Dennis Franz was a fairly intimidating type," says Clapp, "so I just went into the thing on a whim. I decided to put all my eggs in the Medavoy basket because the guy actually had a desk in the squad room. I thought it would be a guest character or potentially recurring."

Medavoy's social awkwardness came out long before the character hit the script, Clapp recalls.

"They were bringing in different characters, hoping to eventually hit on somebody who worked," he said of his audition. "I had about half an hour with the material, and I introduced a stutter, saying everything twice. It was a nervous stammer. I got on set, and I was so jazzed, like I got shot out of a cannon. I was a little too hyper on the first few takes; I had to go calm down."

It worked—a recurring role in the first season evolved into a regular in the second, and Medavoy and Sipowicz ended up being the only characters to appear in every season of the show.

"Bill Clark was our guy on the set," Clapp says of one of the show's storyline creators (Clark is a former detective himself). "He was a real deal, a New York detective. By the middle of the second season, he was there all the time, writing and casting. He was the go-to guy in terms of who we would consult about police work, the approach, and the way of thinking. It got to the point where we thought we might be able to handle ourselves in a real situation."

Life outside the squad was never too easy for Medavoy. He went through a rough divorce, and his relationship with his daughters suffered. His partner and friend, James Martinez, graduated to sergeant, though newcomer Baldwin Jones would show some surprising chemistry with Medavoy in an opposites-who-somehow-get-along sort of way. He also had a tendency to put his foot in his mouth—Baldwin once tricked him into saying Medavoy might have sex with a little person; Medavoy also considered becoming a dog breeder, only to find that he'd have to extract the canines' reproductive material by hand—literally.

"The writers loved writing for Medavoy. One of David's favorite things was to send Medavoy over a cliff, and then find some way to reel him back. Medavoy was always going full speed into a situation he hadn't really thought about."

That situation came to a strong head in the sixth season, when Sipowicz tricked Medavoy into thinking he was under investigation for receiving free Chinese food from a shop owner Medavoy had assisted. Medavoy spent much of the episode digging through the trash, then went verbally off on a clueless investigator, only to find he'd been played.

"That was exactly the type of thing that David liked doing with the character," Clapp says. "He always tried to maintain or resurrect his dignity. He was always trying to test the limits."

In 1998, an episode entitled "Twin Petes" forced Medavoy to try to solve a case in which a man reported that his twin brother was threatening his girlfriend. It was up to Medavoy to decide whether the twin existed to begin with.

"There was one episode where I had a really difficult monologue about the twins, Peter and Paul," Clapp recalls. "I asked David to give me two full days to learn it. I rehearsed it, and it was letter perfect.

Then the script supervisor told him that changes had been made.

"We changed Paul to Patrick," he says. "Standards and Practices didn't want Peter and Paul. I had twenty minutes to go to my trailer and rehearse this thing. But that's what it was about: just rolling with the punches. Just being there, being ready, and being open to what another character is doing." His work that season, which included Medavoy's helping a lesbian friend get pregnant through artificial insemination and later aiding her when her lover is murdered, won Clapp an Emmy.

"The big thing for us is that we sometimes didn't have scripts in advance," he says. "We never knew what was going to happen from one day to the next, let alone from one episode to the next. When I broke up with Donna [Abandando, played by Gail O'Grady, with whom Medavoy had an affair], they told me, 'There might be a little bump in the road with you and Donna,' and the next thing, I know, we're broken up."

During the final season, Medavoy moved on—not just to a new partner, a new relationship, but a new career; in the second-to-last episode, he and the rest of the squad celebrated his retirement from the force on his way to a real estate occupation.

But it wasn't his final scene—that came, all too briefly, in the final episode.

Reading over the script, Clapp recalls, "I got to page 32 or something, and I was thinking, 'Oh man, I can't believe they're not putting me in!' Then I saw one scene where Medavoy comes into the squad room."

His final lines came in a scene when Medavoy briefly entered the squad during a busy day, when everyone nodded to him and rushed out, leaving him alone to kill time with John Irvin.

"I said, 'When you're gone, you're gone,' and that was the end of Medavoy," Clapp says. "I was devastated—we had an eight-day shoot, and I was only going to be there one day! But then I calmed down, and I realized that this was a beautiful way to go out. I got over it, and really was a great scene for him."

That's because, while Sipowicz, and Kelly before him, may have been the main attraction, it was supporting characters like Medavoy (and Jones, Martinez, Fancy, and the rest of the *Blue* boys and girls) that held him up as the foundation.

"Medavoy was a decent guy who'd been through so much, and never had the easiest job," Clapp said. "We would go to New York, and meet a lot of cops. The cops would come up to us and the most consistent comment that I got was, 'You're the real guy! You're the working stiff. Not every squad has a Sipowicz, but we've got quite a bit of Medavoys.' Guys would come up and say that there were a couple of Medavoys of their squad. The guy who's in the second marriage, the guy who has the nightmare commute, the guy who was trying to put two kids through school. Medavoy was the everyman. Sipowicz was more of a hero; he was the guy that everyone wanted to be, but Medavoy was the guy that everybody was."

After O'Grady set the trend for the importance of the squad's receptionist, Bill Brochtrup followed in her footsteps—after showing up recurrently for the first six seasons, his character of John Irvin went full-time.

To Brochtrup, Irvin represented the silver lining in the all-too-often dark clouds of police station work.

"I always wanted John to have this sunny outlook, a real positive outlook on the world," he says. "I thought that would be a good contrast to the gritty darkness that was pervasive in the squad room."

That showed from his audition.

"I had done a play in Los Angeles, playing a character with a sunny nature that lets things roll off his back. For auditioning, you only have a couple pages of dialogue, and you don't know where the character's going to go. I tried to be the same way I had been in that character. The character was based on a guy I knew in high school, who was a cheerleader. I tried to think about him and way he would react to things."

Like Clapp, Brochtrup didn't expect his character to become a household face and name—at first, he was hired for a few episodes.

"[The character] was originally only supposed to be a revolving character, to replace Donna. I thought it was great insight, the way they molded the character and made him more real, so he didn't turn into a joke.

"I think they were looking for somebody who was a little funnier and a little more over the top, and that's how I went in, really flamboyant. It made me a little nervous when I got the job. On our first day, I remember them taking me aside and telling me that John was a very real person, a very strong person who can handle himself well in the squad room. He had a type of self-awareness. His whole reason for being there was to protect the guys in the squad room. I thought that was such a simple, clear type of explanation. I thought, 'Wow, we may be in business.'"

At first, the business didn't appear to be a long-term investment.

"I finished the first episode, and they told me, 'OK, the next time, you're going to do this and this.' They were talking all kinds of storylines to me, and I was like, 'Wait a minute, I was only hired to do two episodes!' It was a huge surprise."

In between his part-time stints as John, Brochtrup left the show to act in a few of Bochco's series, *Public Morals* in 1996 and the next year's *Total Security* (John's absence was written off as a foray into computer graphics business). When those shows went down, John and Brochtrup came back to *Blue* work.

"It was a short conversation," he says of his return. "They asked if I wanted to come home. I said, 'Yes!' It was a big surprise, but a happy one."

Over the years, John watched his good friend Delores Mayo die of a drug overdose, and tried to save Sipowicz's wife Sylvia from Mayo's gun-toting vigilante father, who inadvertently shot her while aiming for the man he blamed for his daughter's death. He became a minister, a controversial step for one of television's few non-comedic homosexual characters.

More than almost anything else, however, John helped Sipowicz overcome the homophobia that had clouded his life all through the series (aided, of course, by alcoholism, a murdered father, and occasional racism). John became a babysitter to Sipowicz's son, and officiated at Sipowicz's third wedding.

"I was very pleased with [the character's changes throughout the show]," he says. "I think it's always a little bit difficult for the writers to include you when you're playing the receptionist: someone who's not a cop, who can't go out into the streets, who can't go into the pokey [interrogation room] and get too involved in the cases. I think it was difficult for the writers to figure out what to do with my character, but they did a fantastic job of picking things out for John to do.

"It was kind of like a Greek chorus, with John sitting there as a gatekeeper to the squad room. All the perps had to pass by him. His reaction to all of the people coming in might be seen as a reaction to how the audience might feel about the people coming in. The character became an emotional center for the show, in some ways."

When the series ended with Sipowicz as squad commander, John was one of the last characters to say goodnight during the series' final moments.

"Ending a series that's been on for twelve years is not easy, and people expect some kind of huge thing, but what I thought was so fantastic was that the ending was pure; they didn't try to sensationalize it in any way," Brochtrup says with a laugh. "Life went on in the squad. Andy got promoted, but it was just another day at work. The feeling was that you would see more cases come on, just as with before in the show. It was certainly hard to play, because as I was saying goodbye to Andy and walking out the door, I was walking out on an amazing time in my life. For John, it was just going home for the day, ready to come back tomorrow, but it was very difficult to do that last scene. It was very true."

It's a truth he hopes to see continue as more gay characters show up on television.

"I thought it was a stroke of genius for them to go that route, and I was surprised that they did it," he says. "The past few years, there's been a lot more gay and lesbian characters on television; the nice thing is that there's no one character trying to represent the gay and lesbian characters of the world."

The writers never tried to make John into a role model for gays and lesbians, he said.

"In some ways, John was a breakthrough character, but there were so many other shows that did the same kind of thing, like *Will and Grace* and *Queer As Folk* that were more about gay people and relationships."

Aaron Gaffey's war vet Jack leads his impromptu troop into battle in 2012's *Dust Up*.

Aaron Gaffey: *Dust Up*

A PERSON HOME FROM combat has much he (or she) would like to leave behind: gunfire, death, blood, destruction, almost everything.

Yes, almost. There are some things that soldiers never get rid of. Things they shouldn't forget. Like doing what's right, just because. That's something our men and women of the armed forces spend years—usually far longer than anyone should have to—sharpening, developing, maintaining their skills at giving, giving, and . . . oh yeah, *giving*, all the while getting somewhere between "jack" and "squat" in return.

He'd heard these stories before. We all had. Aaron Gaffey though, had a different objective in following them, a new role to play. It was the lead in *Dust Up* (2012).

"I interviewed a few of my friends that had and continue to serve our country in the Marines," Gaffey recalls. "It was eye opening. I am thankful for them for their service. I am sorry they have had to endure war the way none of us civilians will understand, so, I carried their stories, as best as I could, as well as search for peace."

He was far from civilization, far from everything at all, but the same mental and physical issues that, to an extent, have followed millions back from battle had latched onto Jack like leeches from hell, keeping him from anywhere near the person he might have been or tried to be. But then came another chance to move in that very direction, though no one would have wanted anything like it to occur.

Back in 2006, Gaffey acted next to Ward Roberts in the horror flick *Joshua*, with Travis Betz behind the camera. A few years later, Roberts was looking to take his own turn in the directing chair, looking to get by with a little help from his friends.

"He said he wanted to do a western, write and direct one," Gaffey remembers, "and that he thought I needed to be in a western. I was absolutely on board." As was Betz, playing Jack's friend Herman.

"I was always set to play Jack, the stoic man of few words," says Gaffey. "I am very attracted to those types of characters. I love the silence in between dialogue. I love reactions without words. Jack embodies all of that." And quite more, we will see.

In a past full of bad drugs and worse men, Ella (Amber Benson) has little left to move forward, even with someone to lead there: her baby daughter Lucy. Now Lucy's idiot father is in heavy bar tab debt to local barman Buzz (Jeremiah Birkett), who isn't someone anyone would want to tick off, mainly because his perception of reality is, well, far from that of most of us—something we're quite glad for.

In typical action-film-coincidence, Jack happens to get called into action. It would be so easy to say no, to walk away, to not get into something that has little to do with him and might get him hurt or worse, up against people who have a hell of a lot less regard for human life than Jack and those he fought next to.

Once again, very few vets ever fully rid themselves of the unwelcome passengers they carry back from battle. Jack had found something quite rare amongst his colleagues, but surprisingly effective.

"I really got into yoga," Gaffey says of his role model's newfound practice. "I had done it on occasion, but, never as a dedicated practice, which is what it became for me. I had never felt more centered and at peace."

He hadn't made it all back in one; like the revenge-film trendsetter Rooster Cogburn that got John Wayne an Oscar and nearly brought one home to Jeff Bridges, Jack left an eye in battle, and a flashback scene shows us his loss.

"During filming I was in a constant state of recalling something horrible and then trying to find some peace around that," Gaffey says. "Working with Ward, Travis, and Amber made it easy: they were my safe and peaceful place. While Jeremiah, the antagonist Buzz, loud and brash, was the off-center place. We all fit together so very well."

Some people just have motives that make sense only to them. We see such folk quite often in the movies, especially in the action and horror genres. Buzz and his pals kidnap the good guys, even putting a gun to Lucy's head (Roberts' own daughter played Lucy. Interesting to think about her responses to watching *Dust Up* right around 2033).

"The scenes with Buzz were emotionally draining," Gaffey says, "as well as the scene when we let Ella know that Buzz has Lucy and we are going to get her back. Those were the scenes where Jack had to embrace his past in a very raw way, not just meditate it away."

Herman, always good with the bow and tomahawk, takes out most of the evil, decapitations and impalements galore. Lucy's dad sacrifices himself for her, maybe the first decent thing he's ever done for someone else.

Jack's brawling skills brought him home alive, and now they help him out with Buzz. But it's Ella that ends things once and for all there, putting a bullet through the villain's forehead.

Films like *Dust Up*, Gaffey explains, "are most fun. More often than not, they do not take themselves seriously, but are very serious about doing the best work that they can do. You have to love doing this to stick with it. It is absolutely exhausting, disheartening, and yet the most fulfilling job that you can hope to be employed doing."

The cast of *American Gladiators* gave millions of kids (and kids at heart) many an enjoyable Saturday from 1989 to 1996.

Meet the *Gladiators*

Watching *American Gladiators* in the 80s and 90s, kids always felt that they were seeing something special (I know, as I was one such avid viewer). Not quite the cartoons that the show often followed on Saturday mornings, but something you couldn't just walk outside and find either. With these title characters, hardly able to be labeled people, we had a reason to cheer for them that was tough to find, partly because kids of that age typically don't have the attention span to care much about pro sports.

Yes, they were athletes, but a different sport. Giving them names like Gemini, Blaze, Nitro, and Ice was so much more effective than having them use their real monikers. They weren't your common everyday human; they were *Gladiators*! These guys were superhuman—and the show's multiple female competitors opened the door to a young lady audience that few of the time even looked for.

"Putting seven hot girls and seven good-looking guys in great shape, in tight lyrca/spandex, made them into almost superheroes and you have a recipe for great family entertainment," asserts show veteran Daz Crawford. "Something for the moms, something for the dads, and something for the children. It couldn't fail." It didn't; the show ran from 1989 to 1996, racking up three Emmy nominations along the way. Dozens of visitors showed up to do battle with the title characters, but we didn't really want them to win.

Putting it on Saturday mornings was a hell of a risk, but it worked. Taking these people and their opponents and making it a living-action cartoon took some doing, but it ended up the right way to go. During the show, you'd see audience members of all ages cheering for and reaching out to high-five and hug their heroes. Afterward, autograph rushes got as crazy as the events.

"Every show was great because of the kids," remembered Lee Reherman, who spent four years as Hawk. "I never got over that. They'd come running up to you. When you're taping a *Gladiator* show, and those kids are there, some of them having come from all parts of the country, and it is the highlight of their life. To see the looks on their faces, there's nothing like it—*nothing* like it. You were bringing so much to that moment for them."

They weren't like the superheroes you saw in comics and cartoons, but a special kind of human, folks above us. That's what made you feel a new connection to them. You looked at them and saw something above most, but possible. Reachable. Get in the gym, start working out, and you could be just like them, and then you'd feel their power and probably never have any problems. Be the same kind of superhero they were, and superheroes always win.

That wasn't how it was, of course. Off the stage and away from the cameras, the people were, unfortunately, quite similar to those who iconized them, lacking the superhuman powers that was all part of a persona they were *acting* out. The show itself doesn't really carry the same enjoyable memories as it once did, and its competitors aren't always so highly remembered—those of them that are still around.

There's a couple of reasons why the show's 2008 revival lasted less than a year. First off, by then, the superhero aura was gone. People were well aware of the unnatural sides, i.e., the dark and too often deadly sides, of bodybuilding (and wrestling, of course), and we consider (perhaps in a stigmatized, stereotyped way) these people not as heroes, but more as freakish. Secondly, the show went to prime time and towards an older audience. That hadn't been the appeal of the original show, and it didn't work this time. Back then, kids were too young to take it too seriously. Today's audiences don't have that naiveté.

Shortly after showing up next to John Ritter in *Skin Deep* (1989), Raye Hollitt heard from a fellow named Johnny Ferraro, himself looking to put together a show based on people who put, well, more than a little extra time into their physical look.

"I am fortunate enough that I live in Southern California," remembers Hollitt, a champion competitive bodybuilder at the time, "and trained at the mecca of bodybuilding: Gold's. Santa Monica has beach rings which I practiced on and got really good at."

Over the next few years, Hollitt (or rather, her character Zap) set all kinds of trends for female Gladiators and the show's huge female audience, her trademark long blonde hair flowing down all over her strapping arms and shoulders—the same ones that allowed her to knock and drag unlucky competitors off the rings in Hanging Tough, whack them off platforms with padded bo sticks during Jousts, and anchor them to the ground in rounds of Powerball.

"I fit right into the role of Zap," Hollitt says. "'Strikes like lightning, causes a lot of damage, and gets out fast' was the description for that character at the time." By the time the show ended, she'd done more episodes than any other Gladiator except Jim Starr's Laser.

The show's hosts came straight from their own kind of Gladiator-ship, with NFL vets Joe Theismann and Mike Adamle heading things up at the start and Todd Christensen and Hall-of-Famer Larry Csonka showing up later. Several Gladiators had started there as well, as Starr and Dan "Nitro" Clark spent time on the pro gridiron.

Years on the fields of Big Eight college ball and three seasons in the NFL had sharpened some *Gladiator*-like skills for Lynn Williams; ironically, the same injury that ended his NFL career helped start his role as Sabre.

"I'd broken two bones in my back with the Chargers in 1988," recalls Williams, who also played with both Los Angeles squads. "I was working out all the time." Three years later, Williams was working for a health firm when his wife called.

"She said [*Gladiators*] was having tryouts, and it was tomorrow," he remembers. "I didn't have any time to prepare. When I got there, the line was wrapped around the block."

He smoked some fellow triers-out in a forty-yard dash, did fifty-five one-handed pushups in a minute, and charged up a rope like Tarzan on fast forward.

Then came tryouts on the Joust, one of the show's longest-running events. Up against a guy a few (dozen) pounds heavier than him, Williams heard his opponent tell a cameraman that Williams was going down in pain.

"That inspired me," he asserts. "I was on a spiritual quest. In my mind, I was going to stick the front end of my stick through his facemask." He didn't go that far, but he came out well ahead.

Next came Powerball, the perfect event for a former running back. One competitor darts around a course, trying to drop large balls into cans. Another tries to prevent this.

Out for revenge, Williams' former Joust opponent knocked the ball from his hands on the first try. That would be it.

"I juked left, juked right, and ran him over," remembers Williams. "The only reason we finished was because we ran out of balls." Now he'd be playing defense.

"He elbowed me in the mouth, and blood shot out of my mouth," he says. "I said I was OK." The man came again. Williams was ready.

"I'd bench-pressed 545 pounds, no steroids, no acids, no protein powders," he says. "I exploded. I've never hit a man that hard in my life. I must have hit him with a thousand pounds of force."

His physicality had convinced the crew. But the *American* team was looking for more than just muscles. Without a way to connect to their heroes on a personal level, audiences might not keep tuning in.

Making it to the top of college ball and the NFL had been tougher than most people could handle. But Williams had also found a way off a much tougher, sadder squad, overcoming a "tenure" in Los Angeles gangs to find his own success.

When an interviewer asked why he should become a Gladiator, Williams had a response at the ready.

"I said there were a lot of inner-city youths watching, and they needed to have somebody they could identify with," he says. "I'm that person."

He first became Panther. After a few weeks of being a "backup" Gladiator, there in case a main man got hurt ("I did Powerball from New York to California and back to New Jersey, every night across the country!" he claims), Williams became Sabre, and eventually one of the show's most popular competitors.

Reherman, only a few apperances behind Zap and Laser for most on the show, had followed a similar path to the show.

"I really fell into it by accident," he recalled. "I played football at Cornell, and played for the Dolphins for a half a cup of coffee." He headed to UCLA for an MBA, then started on a PhD.

Nearby one day, a certain show was holding its own kind of "auditions."

"They asked me if I would try out," he says. "I told them they were off their rocker. I'd seen the show and thought it was clever, but I was sucking wind just trying to compete with the best business grad students in the world. I wasn't about to go out there and slug away with a bunch of big meatheads. But my competitive side and my curiosity got the best of me, so I decided to go ahead and try it out."

A group of tryouts and some high-class beatings later, his phone rang.

"They beat the living snot out of me," he remembers. "Then I got a call saying, 'All right, you're the Hawk!'"

For the next few years, "we'd do twenty-four shows in five weeks. It was a three-day on, four off kind of thing. It was grueling." He'd never get the PhD., but Reherman still taught grad school economics.

Along with Powerball, Reherman called Breakthrough and Conquer his favorite event. Breakthrough allowed him to flash back to his gridiron days; contenders had to score a touchdown from fifteen yards away, with helmets their only extra protection, while gladiators waited to plant them into the ground, or at least out of bounds. Conquer was closer to freestyle wrestling, as contenders and gladiators would square off in a small ring, each competitor trying to shove his/her opponent outside it.

"I like those and Joust," he says. "Anything that I could keep my feet on the ground and hit you."

Williams Conquered even more unlucky contestants, once winning sixty matches in a single sitting. "In five years, I might have lost five or six times," he proclaims. Today, Sabre's jersey hangs in Los Angeles' Planet Hollywood.

Crawford carried a different kind of athletic background to the show; he spent over a decade in the Air Force, making it to the top ten worldwide rankings in boxing and the 1988 Olympic team, along with a brown belt in kung fu and a ton of other athletics.

"I guess my previous life had prepared me for *Gladiators*," he says. "I was approached by a talent agent who asked me if I would be interested in becoming a Gladiator, and of course I said yes. She set up an interview and fitness test with the producers." From 1993 to 1996, he'd be Diesel.

"The longevity came from some simple components to make up the show," he says. "I had no preparation techniques; to me, each contender was the same as boxing an opponent. We had such good laughs during the shows; I got a buzz out of it. It was a doorway for me into entertainment, something I thoroughly enjoyed." He'd soon show up next to Pierce Brosnan's James Bond in *The World is Not Enough* (1999), then with Wesley Snipes in *Blade II* (2002).

"We never stop learning in life," he says. "This is the same in acting. All your experiences will come in handy: put them in your pocket and remember them. Even if you don't get your 'big break,' enjoy it all. When you book that first job, you will then realize why it's all worth it."

That's how many of his Gladiator colleagues still feel about their time searching for competitors in the Maze, yanking them off the legendary Wall (the show's credited with launching the appeal of indoor wall-climbing, still a popular fitness event today), and, of course, doing all they could to personify the event called The Eliminator.

"There was nothing fantastical about our show," remembers Hollitt, who cameoed as Zap in 1993's *Hot Shots: Part Deux*. "It wasn't staged. It was pure competition where middle America could say 'Hey, I can be on that show!'"

Hey, maybe I overshot back at the back of this profile. Of course, there was so much more good about the show than bad. So many more great memories. We have rights and reasons to see Hollitt and her co-stars as heroes. Because being a hero doesn't mean you're perfect, just human. Decent. And that there's something about you that makes others want to say something like, "I want to be like her, in *this* way."

Maybe I'm just upset on a personal level. Upset because I was so into this show, and then found myself disappointed at all the steroid scandal accusations that were made against its people. Some of them were probably true, but big deal. Like I said, you can admire someone while acknowledging their flaws.

In 2008, before I even started this book, *Gladiators* fans lost Shelley Beattie to her own hand. Far past her accomplishments as Siren, Beattie gave us so many more reasons to admire her. Like overcoming deafness to make it in bodybuilding, then as a star on the show, and doing all kinds of work to counsel troubled kids and inspire those with hearing trouble that being different doesn't make them any less.

When I interviewed Reherman back on St. Patrick's Day of 2011, he told me something I'll never forget.

"To this day," he said, "I'll have a kid, except now in his 20's, come up to me and say, 'Hey, I was in California and my parents brought me down to see your show. I never forgot it. You signed something for me!' I still get a kick out of this."

I wished I'd been one such kid. I hoped I might still be someday, maybe meeting him at a convention or *Gladiators* reunion or something. Then, on Feb. 29, 2016, just as I was getting started on the finals of *Actors in Action*, I found out that Reherman had passed away.

How? It's never been made public, but men who haven't even reached fifty, especially after a lifetime of fitness, tend not to naturally just drop. Maybe Reherman did, and you feel like an asshole for even hoping so.

Note: As it turned out, he did, to an extent; after hip replacement surgery, Reherman developed an infection. Perhaps not realizing how serious it was, he didn't seek medical help, and it maneuvered into a clot that went to his heart and caused cardiac arrest.

But even putting aside the truth, we still have to acknowledge that a fellow who made us cheer and feel inspired and entertained for years is just, well, gone. When stuff like this happens, when possibilities just suddenly disappear, you're left with memories, and you try hard to focus on the good ones.

Remembering how much they outnumber the negatives certainly helps there.

Even with one of the toughest jobs in law enforcement, Shane Vandrell (Walton Goggins) kept things together until the very end of *The Shield* in 2008.

Walton Goggins/Catherine Dent: *The Shield*

TOO MANY LIES HAD been told, too many backs stabbed, too many, too much ... of everything. Everyone was coming, and he had no way out.

Shane Vandrell was going down, and he knew it. His co-workers had abandoned him, with reason. Gang members were screaming, and aiming, for his head. His attempts to straighten out the crooked cop he'd always been had fallen short, and now there were only seconds left.

Vic Mackey knew. Everyone knew. Even the ones who'd started out liking Shane or not knowing him were aiming for him. He had no one and nothing left, and he had two innocent people that were too entangled in his web to ever find their way out—or so he believed.

But as the team burst through the door to his hideout, a shot rang out....

Depicting the black and white on the small screen has always been, well, pretty black and white. With TV, the cops have always been the heroes, walking the beat right down the straight and narrow, with the criminals out for themselves, just ready to dish out some needless, selfish, unfair harm to others and society. Sure, we got the occasional dramatic aspect, seeing the backgrounds of those behind the badge and the hellish lifestyle that so many who wear it are forced through, but never so much that we could stop believing in and cheering for the police we saw in TV—where, again, they're typically your modern moral masterpiece.

Like, say, *The Commish*, the dramedy that spent four years showing us the wild and wacky (and, yes, once in a great while, painful) ways of running the local PD, led by Michael Chiklis' Tony Scali, who everyone could trust to get all the bad guys and set some examples by the end credits.

A fairytale. An act. That's *not* the way things work for cops, and it never has been. The members of our law enforcement community sometimes live in something not unlike hell. Working for poverty wages, getting treated like garbage by the people they swear to protect, they enforce the law the best they can . . . but sometimes that means breaking it themselves. And why not? Criminals don't care about the law, so cops shouldn't always either. It's not like criminals are going to say, "Well, those cops are doing right, so I'd better change my life to be more like them!"

That's how it's always been in real life, and shows like *The Shield* finally had the balls to admit and depict it. From the moment it premiered on FX in 2002, the show took things to a new level (not necessarily a better one, only a new one). The Strike Team bent the rules, made their own laws, and then broke through them to break down local evildoers. The line between cop and villain wasn't blurred or even broken; it was trampled into oblivion. Viewers responded; when the show went off the air in 2008, it was *FX*'s longest-running series.

In the lead was Chiklis' Mackey—to call this guy the opposite of Scali wouldn't come anywhere near adequate. A few years before, HBO had engineered the perfect model of an antihero as the main character in the form of a certain mob boss. But Tony Soprano's own family got as much camera time as his Mafioso one; Vic Mackey was at home on the dirty job.

Along with quite a few others.

"To see a vigilante cop was very unusual," explains Catherine Dent. "The portrayal of the humanity of those characters was groundbreaking. You saw these people as alcoholics, in troubled marriages. You saw a cop shooting another cop and then breaking down himself, and that had never been done before."

The series made its impression from a trigger. The March 12, 2002, pilot episode (helpfully titled "Pilot") showed that Mackey's Strike Team might be on its way out already, a member plotting with new Captain David Acevedo (Benito Martinez) to get a case made against Mackey and his men. Near the show's end, the group raids a drug dealer's place, taking his life in the process. But before the informant can celebrate, Mackey plants a bullet right between his eyes, Shane and the rest of the squad stoically looking on, all the way in on it. There's no place for outside loyalty and secrecy on this team.

The episode won Chiklis an Emmy. The storyline would weave its way in and out of the show for its entire run.

"It became about asking ourselves as a society, what we were willing to accept from law enforcement for the pursuit of our own security," Goggins recalls of the show's beginning. "It became a question for our nation, subsequently. It was a blissful ambiguity."

Along with Shane, we'd already met Danielle Sofer, a fellow officer who went by Danny; her given name was a bit too feminine to be taken seriously by those she'd be next to and occasionally against. One of several ladies in the district stuck in the sadly neverending battle to reach female equality in law enforcement, Danny just wanted a few chances, and it had long since stopped mattering from whence they emerged.

Danny Sofer (Catherine Dent) emerged as perhaps *The Shield*'s toughest member during the show's years on FX.

"It was important to me to be believable as a cop," Dent recalls. "I wanted [Danny] to be a total badass professional, and I had to look that way." When Dent went looking for guidance from some gals on the beat, however, their ideas seemed quite different in the cosmetic sense.

"You'd think they would be tough, badass women," she explains, "but it surprised me what girly girls they were. A lot of them had painted nails and lots of makeup."

It might be tough for viewers to swallow that an officer who went so far past gung ho levels as Danny did had so much trouble with a firearm, but that's just part of Dent's talent in the performance biz.

"I hate guns," she admits. "I'm terrified of them. The first time I picked up a gun, I cried, I was terrified I would shoot my toe off." Early in the second season, Sofer's gun usage would go straight to the *Shield* forefront, but not yet.

Goggins also got to know those who lived Shane's, Danny's, and even Vic's lives without cameras, scripts, or stunt doubles.

"I had played police officers before, and I had been on a fair amount of ride-alongs," Goggins says of his preparation (on a ride-along, a non-cop takes a beat ride with police officers to get a feel for their everyday—and night—lives). "Technically I felt like I had a pretty good grasp. What I didn't feel like I had a pretty good grasp on was the culture of Los Angeles, in respects to this particular community, a community in an urban area. I came from a bucolic upbringing, and I hadn't spent a lot of time in downtown Los Angeles."

The show takes place in the fictional Los Angeles village of Farmington, built to resemble just about every gang-dominated inner city.

"When the show came about, I spent a lot of time down in East L.A. and in Compton," Goggins says. "I drove around, met people, went to swap meets. A wonderful part of Los Angeles revealed itself to me in a way that helped me understand the world that I was about to play in. I had lived all over the city, but never lived in Compton. It was a place I really wanted to see and experience. That was a big part of my early exploration of Shane."

Another part of Shane's early development came from within; Goggins thought about what his character had been up to since long before wearing his first badge.

"I thought about Shane, and his high probability of not having a strong male figure in his life as a teacher," says Goggins. "How he looked up to Vic Mackey, how he respected Vic Makey and understood the perverted philosophy that sometimes people have to do bad things to help the greater good."

As the show filmed through the summer of 2001 (that same year, Goggins won an Oscar for starring in and producing the short film *The Accountant*), everyone looked forward to setting new network trends, possibly advancing on those that *NYPD Blue* (1994) and other shows had put down in the decade before.

Then the September 11 attacks occurred, and nearly kept the squad off the air entirely.

"The fact that we even made it to air, a show that was kind of vilifying police officers after that incredible sacrifice by our nation's finest, was unbelievable to me," Goggins admits. "The disparity between those two realities was a great opportunity."

Despite Goggins' past experience at playing those in law enforcement, FX had been on the iffy side about letting him become Shane. Fortunately, a couple of believers rewrote and moved around early episodes like "Our Gang," and "The Spread," to give Goggins a bit of extra character developmental time, and by the time the ironically named "Pay With Pain," episode came about a few weeks later, everyone knew that Goggins was the man.

Like *Blue*, along with every version of *Law & Order*, *The Shield* reached out and yanked reality into its storylines, but this was no dramatization. Right off the start of season two, the terrorists were still fresh in everyone's mind.

Shield threw it straight into their faces, with Danny explaining to a troublemaker that, "You're a suspect because nineteen guys who look like your twin brother killed 3,000 Americans." Rough, but no blacker than the rest of the humor we'd come to all but demand from the group.

Maybe that's why the show went even farther; later on in the episode, Danny's called back to the guy's house, and now he's got a gun. She blasts him to the world of seventy-two virgins.

"That was a really difficult thing to wrap my brain around as a character and an actor," Dent says. "I asked the writers, 'Should Dani be a little more savvy?' They said, 'Nope, you shoot him.' It's what would happen under those circumstances, and it made me very aware and very serious about the kind of role I was playing and the message." Danny got harassed about the matter for the rest of the season, and it still flared up here and there for the show's full run.

But the series' darkness would shine even brighter in the third season episode, "Mum," in which Aceveda is orally raped by gang members.

As a television audience, Goggins says, "We're anesthetized to women being raped. We see a woman being raped on television, and we don't think anything of it. It's only when a man gets raped that we're reminded of how violating it is. [Martinez] did a great job in that episode."

Throughout the show, Danny mentored fellow officer Julien Lowe (Michael Jace), whose religious nature, self-righteous attitude, and repressed homosexuality kept him on the squad's outer levels throughout. Right around season five, Danny learned she was expecting, enticing the entire office to openly pool on just who the baby's daddy was (it was never made clear, although Vic, who dallied with Danny throughout, was the prime suspect).

Dent had some practice; she'd had a child a few seasons before. At around the same time she'd become expecting, Michael's wife April was pregnant as well.

"We went through it together," Dent remembers. "We compared pregnancy notes. April was wonderful."

Years after the show end, tragedy moved from drama to reality, in the saddest of way. On

May 19, 2014, April, a world champion track and field runner, was murdered by her husband. Two years later, he was sentenced to forty years to life.

"I was very fond of Michael, but he was certainly a complicated man," Dent says. "He had a full life going on. What happened was horrific and tragic, the worst of what life rips out of us. I felt for April's family from the depth of my core."

As the show went on, the Strike Team broke up and got back together in and out of the precinct, and Shane grew further and further from the shrinking violet he'd earlier appeared to be. He tried to extort gang leader Antwone Mitchell (Anthony Anderson), only to have Mitchell turn the tables and turn Shane into his messenger. Afraid that fellow member Curtis "Lem" Lemanski (Kenny Johnson) would sell the group out, Shane killed him with a grenade. Shane even got in trouble with the Armenian Mob, which forced him to confess to the Strike team's heist of money from a train.

"The opportunity to be on television is built upon the year that came before it and the two or three years that came before it," says Goggins, who called Shane's murder of Lem and confession to Vic in the next season some of his personal series highlights.

"My preparation didn't change; I just lived in my imagination, and I think that my job and our job as actors was made very easy by the writers who did such a good job of writing the characters so three-dimensionally. It was up to us to get what they wrote right."

Finally, as the last season wound down, Shane tried unsuccessfully to have fellow squad member Ronnie killed. It didn't work.

And as the series ended with "Family Meeting" in November 2008, all his choices ran out. Cornered in his home, Shane poisoned his wife and son, then shot himself.

"I don't know that one can fully prepare for something like that," Goggins says of the final episode. "You just have to approach it with as much love as you possibly can and as much humanity as you possibly can. People understand that there was no option left. It wasn't malicious or mean; this was coming from a man who was at the end of his rope, and doing what he thought was best for his family. As perverted and strange as that may be, that's what I tried to do: to make it about love."

And just as he had before ever stepping into Shane's persona, Goggins tried to make himself all about Shane. Just as he felt Shane would have responded to a situation by calling up his longtime past, Goggins used Shane's personality to develop him throughout the show, in the present and even near future.

"I don't think that [series creator] Shawn [Ryan] or any of the writers on the show made the decisions that they made based on gratuitousness or for shock's shake," he says. "It was rooted in authenticity to how the characters might react. So much of it was based on information and access to information, which translates into power. To have Shane go out on his own was just how this person would react to certain information. That's what the writers did such a good job on, kind of painting these people in a way to make them authentic and three-dimensional."

But Shane's words gave him a strange, sad sort of justification; his suicide note confessed to everything he and Vic had done, and how Vic had ruined him and so many others. The immunity deal Vic had been promised didn't seem so attractive now—his own family had abandoned him, his new work sitting in an office, studying gangs, far from the streets that had become his home.

As Danny, who'd found new love with her longtime friend/colleague Dutch (Jay Kames), led the street troops out to battle some robbers, Vic could only forlornly watch from his high-rise office, knowing he'd never be back.

Or will he? Perhaps *The Shield* will hit the big screen someday.

"Vic lived in a blaze of glory," Dent explains, "He wasn't going out in a blaze of glory. Life is so ambiguous anyway. Life humbles us. A lot of great people end up lonely, eating dinner by themselves in their mansions. There's no real get-out-of-jail-free card for any of us. I thought it was sad and pathetic and perfect."

The fiery terror of *Towering Inferno* (1974) becomes more and more real for Angela Albright (Carlena Gower) as her mom (Carol McEvoy) reassures Angela—and herself—that they'll make it out alive.

Carlena Gower: *Towering Inferno*

FINALLY, BACK ON SOLID ground. Finally, she was in celebratory territory.

"I danced with Fred Astaire," Carlena Gower remembers of the finale of her first feature flick. "Steve McQueen twirled me around, and that was amazing."

This was a bit more than the typical post-wrap party. It was more than deserved. More like absolutely necessary. One of the biggest crews in Hollywood history (a mark it still holds today) had just put together a cinematic creation of a battle, centuries before, decades later, and certainly long after this profile's publication, we still fight and usually lose to.

A collective breath of comfort and relief could finally be taken; after where the *Towering Inferno* (1974) cast had spent some serious recent time, such an act would literally have been impossible.

In the early 70s, while the story was making its way onto the pages of the two novels that would eventually become the *Inferno* screenplay, someone far too young to read such words had more to worry about.

"I was in a local beauty pageant," recalls the then-elementary schooler. "Back then, pageants were about poise, modeling, talent, and personality, not about makeup and fancy dresses." As Gower was winning both that local contest and another a few months later against all of California for the state title, one of the judges saw a potential future star.

The lady's name was Leigh Snowden, who'd compiled quite a resume on screens big and small throughout the 1960s. "Leigh spoke to my parents," Gower remembers, "and said they should really consider putting their daughter in the acting business."

They did. Soon after, the family was farther south in the Golden State, and the first-grader went out to become the smallest aspects of the flick, but only in the physical sense.

"They sent me straight to [Producer] Irwin Allen," she remembers. "I spent about forty-five minutes with him, and he signed me that day. I had to cry for him and show fear, and I guess we hit it off." Allen, along with John Guillermin in the directing chair, could only pray for similar fortuitousness from the cast—it's tough to fit so many big names on a marquee, let alone an entire set.

McQueen was there, with fellow headliner Paul Newman. Established star William Holden was around, along with Faye Dunaway, though it's doubtful that *Inferno* fans could have predicted what the two would do two years later in *Network*. Oscar winner Jennifer Jones made the final casting cut, as did Astaire and Richard Chamberlain, and Gower's had been one of millions of hearts he'd set aflutter as Dr. James Kildare on TV!

"I had a crush on Richard Chamberlain," she recalls. "I followed him around as much as I could." By the film's end, viewers wouldn't feel nearly as strongly about the man Chamberlain played.

Yes, it's time to get serious. San Francisco partied the night away at its new addition, the Glass Tower hotel: at 138 stories, there's no bigger one on Earth (today, it wouldn't even be the tallest in America). Newman's Doug Roberts can only hope his architectural dream comes true.

It doesn't; *Inferno* gets things going fast even for an action flick, a short circuit flaming eighty floors in the air. Soon, the whole "spreading like wildfire" saying jumps from analogy to reality, the flames bursting out windows, trapping guests, collapsing floors (outer shots used a model for filming). As high up as eighty floors can seem under normal circumstances, imagine looking down from the distance and seeing a firewall between us and the precious, beautiful solid ground.

Jones' Lisolette manages to tear herself away from the conniving charms of Astaire's Harlee Claiborne, and she, Roberts, and, ahem, *someone* else roaring up to rescue Mrs. Albright and her son and daughter.

Gower was daughter Angela. Just after wrapping up five years as the youngest male in *The Brady Bunch*, Mike Lookinland became her older bro Phillip.

"He was the coolest kid!" Gower recalls. "He was Bobby Brady, for heaven's sake, and I was his little sister. I hung out with him all the time." In her own film debut, Carol McEvoy played their mom. After years of translating words to signs on TV, McEvoy was a hearing-impaired single mom.

"I remember her teaching me sign language," Gower says. "I worked hard on my script and my lines."

But physicality would be an even bigger issue. Perhaps McQueen's playful dance floor volleys of the youngster were done to make up for all the time Angela spent in Roberts' arms, him carrying her up and down stairs, over holes, everywhere the fire had been and could return to at any time.

And, OK, let's get this out of the way. Along with Roberts, security man Harry Jernigan had put on a heroic show, helping save Ms. Albright early.

Who played him? Just some cretin named O.J. Simpson, who, as we'd all find out far too late, did a more convincing job of *playing* a decent (*cough, cough,* worthless-heartless-murdering-lying-wife-beating-piece-of-shit) folk than we could ever predict we'd seen.

"I'm sure I met him," Gower admits of the future double-killer himself, "but I have zero memory of him."

Even on the set, the danger was there, though Gower was far too young to realize it. The fire was controlled, but, hey, it's *fire*—there's only so much we can do. The greatest fire marshals on the planet can't just snap their fingers, flip a switch, and turn off the flames if they get crazy. The special effects and CGI stuff that would be used today weren't around yet, just another sad example of how quick we can be to forget films like *Inferno* and the trends they set for today's flicks to jump from.

"I didn't grasp the enormity of it," Gower recalls, "but I understood all the people working with me, that the fire was very real. There were three firemen assigned to me, two for my hair and one for my body."

And nothing's solved here; the group makes its way upstairs, surviving a pair of explosions along the way, only to find their way back into the main building blocked by spilled cement. Basically, if it's not one thing, it's another, and if it's not that, it's something else entirely!

As McQueen's fire chief O'Halloran tries to figure out what to do (we find out the whole thing's the fault of head engineer Roger Simmons, giving us a reason to cheer when one last explosion knocks Chamberlain's character to a new source of fiery eternity), the fire's captives get one more carrot-dangling temptation of fate, as the chopper sent to rescue them crashes. They make it to an elevator, but another explosion blasts Lisolette out of its door and to her death—it's sad that this would be Jones' screen finale, as she stopped acting until her December 2009 passing.

The blasts would ultimately be the toughest part of Gower's work. "Any time we did explosions, I heavily anticipated having to do the scenes," she remembers. "It was loud, and I was really trying to plug my ears."

But, c'mon, this was the 70s, and kids can't die in action movies, right? Hell, people were still hesitant about killing them off in *horror*! O'Halloran and the rest of a chopper crew lift the elevator from the building and lower it to the ground.

Then he, Roberts, and others blast the million-gallon water tanks on the roof to knock out the remaining flames. There's still a sad shot of Roberts glancing over some bodybags on the ground, and the final determination that nearly 200 lives were lost in the fire—far fewer than were present, but enough to put it in the top five deadliest American fires.

The Godfather II was the broom at the next year's Oscars, taking six statuettes, including edging *Inferno* for Best Picture and Robert De Niro slipping past Astaire for the Best Supporting Actor honor. But the film still pulled in tops in cinematography and editing, along with its "We May Never Love Like This Again" scoring the main song prize (Maureen McGovern added the tune to the soundtrack and cameoed to sing it in the film). Four decades later, *Inferno* still stands stories high in the annals of disaster flicks.

"I think it had the biggest Hollywood star power in one film of all time," Gower explains. "Nowadays, they may have these films with more actors in number, but to me, that was the greatest cast ever assembled. It was so real, so ahead of its time."

Alex Rogan (Lance Guest), a young man with a penchant for video games, found himself launched into a battle for the universe in 1984's *The Last Starfighter*.

Lance Guest: *The Last Starfighter*

BEING EDUCATED IN AN arcade?!

Sounds like the dream of every kid who ever wandered into the worlds of *Space Invaders*, *Pac-Man*, and all their friends in the lands of electronics of the 70s and 80s, doesn't it? Well, for a few fellows near the top of the video game age crowd, it came a little truer.

Stepping away from the horror worlds that had started their careers—one had played Michael Myers, the other had run from him—two fellows did their best to blend into the backgrounds of the arcade world, watching the impromptu role models for their next cinematic adventure.

"Nick Castle and I went to a video arcade and looked at the glazed-eyed fourteen-year-olds bumping and tilting their electronic consoles until their quarters ran out," remembers Lance Guest. "I had grown up on pinball, so I was fairly unacquainted with arcade-style video games. I never really got that into it, but I knew that 100-mile gaze." As any video game addict of the past (and many of the parents of those fighting the joyful battle today!) can attest, staring at the screens for long enough can cause one's mind to degenerate right inside, until either the quarters fall extinct or one's annoying younger sibling *accidentally* kicks the cord from the wall!

Guest might not have been a video game fan, but to become *The Last Starfighter* (1984), he'd certainly have to act like one. It would be quite a switch from his role in *Halloween 2* (1981), although not as big as Castle's jump—after being the first man to play Myers back in 1978, he'd be behind the *Starfighter* directing chair.

"Nick and I went through the script and found the pace for every scene weeks before we actually started shooting," Guest says, "which saved a lot of time and was a great help to me. . . . The important thing about film acting is to always track which scene immediately precedes the one you're doing, because that scene may not be shot for weeks, since a film is not usually shot in order." For this role, he'd have to alternate between two characters—and two galaxies.

He was Alex Rogan, a young man whose prowess at the *Starfighter* video game had made him a hero around the local trailer park. One evening, Alex gets a visit from a strange fellow who claims to be the mind behind the game.

But nothing's what it seems: the fellow's not a person, and his car isn't a car. He's from the planet Rylos (didn't see that one in the planetariums, did we?) and he and his shocked passenger head back to the creature's home. Because *Starfighter*, as fun as it was, wasn't just a game; it was an involuntary training program for upcoming spacecraft pilots in Rylos' war against the invading Ko-Dan—because if the Ko-Dan takes that planet, Earth might very well be next.

And we thought Luke Skywalker had it tough in his first Millennium Falcon ride.

"Alex was not a movie hero," Guest explains of the role's appeal. "He was just a regular kid, a disadvantaged kid definitely, and this stuff was really happening. There's kind of a different tone to the heroic action movie that presupposes that the hero has this huge reservoir of courage, which most people don't actually have, that enables them to do all that really over-the-top stuff that action heroes do. So I liked that Alex was very unsure about what was a very weird situation."

All the while, back on his planetary homeland, Alex's place was taken by his Beta android form, and Alex's neighbors, family, and bombshell girlfriend Maggie (Catherine Mary Stewart) can't fathom where Alex's emotions and personality went—perhaps that 100-mile stare that Guest had seen during his prep time had gotten a bit too far inside Alex!

"I figured Beta should be as naive, arrogant, and stupid as comically possible," says Guest, who based his duplicate work on a fellow comic friend. "It's maybe not the best call to torment your director and fellow actors with acting-class angst if you are doing a lightweight, fun parody."

Such a scene would be a piece of cake and take about ten minutes today, but when Alex comes face to circuited countenance with himself, it became one of the film's toughest jobs.

"In those days they covered up half the camera lens with a piece of gaffers' tape and shot the scene with me as Alex on the right side," Guest recalls. "Then they switched the piece of tape to cover the other half of the lens and shot me as Beta on the left side. Then they spliced the film strips together vertically."

Alex's mentor sacrifices himself for his protégé—well, it appears so—and his new intergalactic pals rush him through training. As it turned out, Guest's work would be just as tough there as Alex's.

You see, there was a new technology stepping cautiously through the film world, one that might just save filmmakers a ton of time and travel if it caught on. Computer-generated imagery, soon to be broken down to CGI, would allow actors and film crews to travel around the world and throughout the universe, not just toss a cheesy graphic across the screen. As Alex learned *Starfighter*'s techniques in so much more living color, Guest and the crew were working around strange effects that no one would see until filming ended.

"Everyone wanted to know how the effects would look," Guest recalls. "The producers really went out on a limb for this. No one on the set had any idea what they would look like, so we had to use our imaginations, which shouldn't be hard if you're an actor."

The Ko-Dan attacks, and just about everything and everyone there to defend Rylos is destroyed. But there's one last Starfighter and one last Gunstar ship for him to pilot right back at an unsuspecting army.

"The hardest line I had to say, at the time, was 'Maybe there IS a Starfighter left,' since it sounded movie-hero like," Guest says. "However, I see it now as totally necessary.... Most acting is making contrived dialogue sound natural. If the writing is good, the acting is easy. You have to have a solid overall sense of the arc of your role, and to be very specific about how your character changes from scene to scene, and why, especially in a film where there is a surprise around every corner."

Alex was about the only surprise Rylos needed, as he and the Gunstar hammer the Ko-Dan's mothership from one side to the other. And the same techniques that won him stardom back on Earth now save the planet, as the craft's secret Death Blossom weapon just about throws a knockout punch to the invaders.

"They didn't look like models because they weren't," Guest says of the technology. "They were somewhat as limited as models in the early phases of this technology, but they really paved the way to the incredible stuff they do today. None of it would've been possible without the painstaking work that our guys did in writing the code and creating the process that would become the foundation of the technology we have today."

Rylos is safe again, but just for now—the Ko-Dan's first attack effects linger, and some of its alumni are around. But so is Alex's original instructor, who just went off to heal himself. A quick trip back tells Alex's fellow Earthlings the story of his heroism, and Maggie accompanies him on his new quest to make his Ryland homeland impenetrable.

"Action movies depend on the actor's ability to suspend belief, and make what you are doing seem believable, even though it's usually outrageous," Guest tells hopeful action stars. "Try to establish trust and chemistry with your fellow actors. It helps also to be in shape and physically agile. Learn how to do fights and stunts. If you don't know already, learn how to run so you don't look like a dork, and look for the laughs, always."

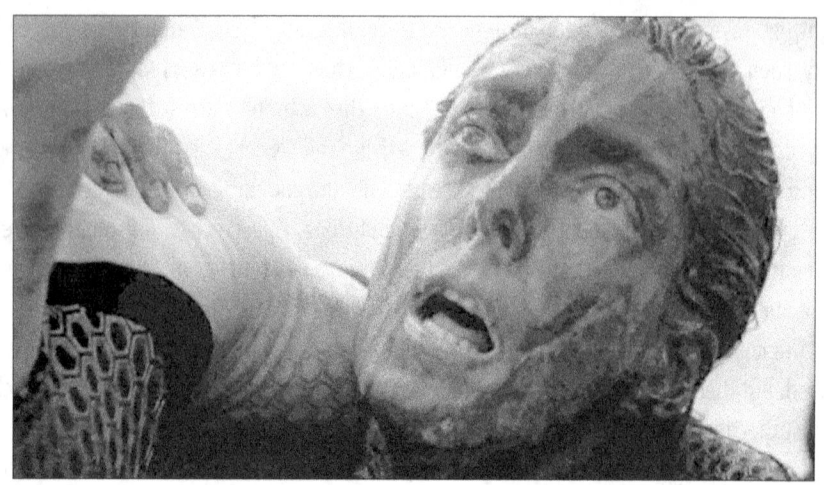

Megan Hayes played the Morphling lady that gave her life for a fellow competitor in *Hunger Games: Catching Fire* in 2013.

Megan Hayes: *Hunger Games: Catching Fire*

WHILE THE *H*UNGER *G*AMES series couldn't be classified as any kind of horror work, it's actually terrifying in a prophetic sort of way.

Because it won't be long before it comes true. Somewhere in the un-distant future (probably before the late 2000s depicted in the District tales of terror), there will come a time when such a reality show arrives in American pop culture. Today, people turn on competitive shows like *Big Brother* or *Survivor* and hope that their favorite people don't get kicked out of the house or off the island; someday, human life will be at stake on those things. Someday, shows based near flicks like *Hunger Games* (and the 1987 Schwarzenegger throwback *The Running Man*, which will be touched upon soon), where human life is the prey and prize, will be handed to the American culture.

Sadly and frighteningly enough, there's a good chance it'll be embraced: viewers glued to the TV to see who dies next, and celebrating when those we bet against go down forever.

No use praying that it won't happen; if nothing else, we can just hope it's involving adults instead of youths like Katniss and Peeta and Gale and Rue and everyone else who gave their young lives and freedom, warring all over the Panem's Capitol, desperately looking for a way to save themselves and their Districts.

"As a woman, I love how appealing it is, because it's so rare for the protagonist in an action movie to be a female," Megan Hayes reflects of the opinion of millions entertained by the saga. Four years after Suzanne Collins' words told the first literary tale in 2008, Jennifer Lawrence turned main lady Katniss Everdeen from a literary heroine into a film one for young gals (and, of course, fellows) across the globe. Katniss fought her way to victory with her friend Peeta Mellark (Josh Hutcherson), while still maintaining the inside morality that combat too often knocks right out of those in battle.

"I love that she's not just having boy problems," Hayes reflects. "She's strong willed, trying to protect her family and start a revolution. She had a bad attitude, which is kind of fun." Expectedly, the film did to its box-office competitors what Katniss did to hers, ensuring that we'd see a new chapter the next year, the series living all the way up to and past its *Catching Fire* subtitle.

This time, a bit of history came to the 75th annual Games, and so did those that had made it. We'd met Woody Harrelson's past winner Haymitch Abernathy (think names like the ones Collins made up will be commonplace in the future?) in the first flick, and here came some ladies whose footsteps Katniss hoped to fall into, some who had established some gender-equal *Games* grounds long ago by coming out on top.

Like former champ Seeder, ready to give things another go.

"She resonated with my own life," Maria Howell explains of her character, "a strong leader, yet a nurturer. Fortunately, I just tapped into what my natural outlook on life is, to prepare for the role. I was slightly familiar with the books before I began working on the film, but did quite a bit of research and completely fell in love with the characters."

She takes on something of a maternal role toward Katniss, but it turns quickly to heartbreak, as Seeder is felled by Stephanie Leigh Schlund's smarmy Cashmere, spearing Seeder straight through the windpipe.

"I think what made the series so endearing is because the human spirit was so strong," Harris explains. "People defending each other, yet at the other end of the spectrum, having to look out for themselves. There was always a question of who to trust, and that struggle occurs constantly in our daily lives."

Just over a decade beforehand, this guy Gloss had emerged from the Camelot-esque District One and won. The next year, his sister Cashmere copied the accomplishment, her knifing skills as flashy as the fabric she's named for. For the *Fire* games, the two were teamed up . . . but would they end up having to take each other out?

"I trained for four months before filming and had an extremely strict high protein diet," remembers Schlund, playing the sister to Alan Ritchson's Gloss. "It was a lot of hard work, but I became stronger as a person from it. The training center was challenging because it put all of my knife skills I had been taught to the test."

Gloss (Alan Ritchson) and his sister Cashmere (Stephanie Leigh Schlund) explain to Caesar Flickerman (Stanley Tucci) just how they plan to win his *Hunger Games* for the second time.

Players from the first District were long known for their looks, but these two had some serious tenacity to back things up. Unfortunately, morality didn't always follow. Early on the second day of battle, Wiress (Amanda Plummer), her mind already whomped by something or other, slips away from her group. Gloss goes for ease over honor, slitting the throat of a lady twice his age and half his size.

He won't get to celebrate; with one slash, the chain reaction begins. Katniss puts an arrow through his chest, and Cashmere roars forward, now out for revenge over victory. Then Johanna (Jena Malone) buries her trusty axe in the older gal's chest, reuniting the siblings before Gloss could ever adjust to the afterlife.

"I have always found playing characters completely unlike myself intriguing," Schlund explains. "I love masking myself in a deeply character-driven role. The fact that Cashmere was viciously competitive, trained from birth to kill anything that got in her way, and had a ruthless caress for life, were all things that I found appealing to her."

Fame and fortune are so often labeled synonymous by those still hoping to obtain them, but many who do so find themselves wishing they'd been more careful what they wished for. Winning a battle had made them Games legends and heroes, idols of the people. On the inside, sadly a common story for today's soldiers after the last deployment call, the war never ends. Few in battle, on either side of the final result, are ever totally healed up.

We'd already seen Abernathy turn to the bottle after roaring to the top of Gamesmanship; others had used similar and just as painful manners to face this issue (possibly a cause of Wiress' mental deterioration?).

Years before the first Games we read about or saw, a young woman had triumphed above all others to make her District 6 proud with a title. But said pride couldn't make her whole again; as so many veterans of every battle have and still do in modern society, she'd gone elsewhere and found her own type of fixing.

It was called morphling. The drug's name came from Collins' mind, but its effects were just like so many, so sadly real. Burning a user's mind nearly to incoherence. Shrinking the body down to skin and bone.

In a fourth-world, war-torn land like Panem, it's a safe and very sad bet that this sort of thing was rampant. We'd see it in Hayes' heartbreaking form, her champion felled by the drug, so much so that her proud name was overtaken simply by its own.

"Usually when a role comes along, and I'm scared of her, it turns into me wanting to play her," she explains of the Morphling lady. "At first, I thought it was terrifying, and then I was like, I really have to play this." Collins' book, which Hayes carried throughout filming, wouldn't be her only study guide for the role.

"I did a lot of research on heroin and morphine addiction, any drugs that were similar to the Morphling's," Hayes says. "I had to lose about twelve pounds so I'd be underweight, looking malnourished. I had journals, a very vivid picture in my head of whatever I was fighting or being attacked by."

The innovations of CGI might look great to those with the luxury of seeing the completed project, but it's tough for those forced to use their imagination to act against things that aren't really there. For her tryout, Hayes had had to go hand to claw with a pretend primate and not win.

"It wasn't that much of a leap to go to that world," she recalls. "You have to trust that it's going to look amazing. You just do the best you can in that moment, that take, and you trust that the CGI is going to look amazing, and it totally did."

With about half their competitors gone, Katniss and Peeta search for a way through one of the many dense forests that helps make up their playing field. His mind on her, Peeta's within milliseconds of being taken out forever by mankind's nearest genetic relative.

But perhaps feeling that, though her mind and life are about gone, she can still leave a bright spot on her legacy, the Morphling leaps out and saves him, giving her life for someone she hardly knew at all. With no idea how to thank such an act and little time to make a decision at all, Peeta carries her to the beach and asks her to focus on the lovely sky as she slips away.

"She navigates the games in a non-aggressive way," Hayes says. "She put Peeta before herself, but also the idea of her being this struggling drug addict, this combination was very interesting to play. So wounded, so sad, so tragic. There was a lot of room for me to bring my own creativity of the character to the role. You bring something of yours, and bring someone else's vision to life." Right around Thanksgiving 2013, filmgoers paid more green to experience the vision than they had for any November release in American history. It eventually became the highest grossing of all the *Games* films, in the top twenty of all time (surprisingly, it didn't get any Oscar noms, even for special effects).

"It was overwhelming and exciting and exhilarating to see everything come together,"

Hayes remembers. "Hundreds of people put work into it, and it was amazing. You have to put so much faith into something and don't know what the outcome's going to be, and when you see the outcome, it's better than I ever imagined. The reason I became an actress to begin with was because I wanted to be a storyteller, and it's the best. Maybe winning an Oscar would be better than that, but that's it!"

Like most of Hollywood, and audiences around the world, Maria Conchita Alonso was realizing at high speed that a fellow from far away might be the action film world's new *thing*. Halfway through the 80s, millions had seen him on both sides of battle, and they kept coming back. There was something about the Austrian muscleman that went a bit below his mesomorphic outside, something that can't be learned or taught, but just *is*.

"It was him that made me want to be in the project," Alonso recalls of the then-still-rising star of Schwarzenegger, "besides really liking the script. I always wanted to be in a futuristic film and this was it; it was so ahead of its time." Sadly, *The Running Man*'s time appears to be drawing nearer every day, or at least every TV season. It takes place in 2017, and comes across with some seriously sad soothsaying ability to today's readers, with the year having arrived.

Like *Hunger Games*, *Running Man* (1987) began on a book's pages, knocked out in 1982 by some former English teacher named Stephen King—who, mystery of mysteries, allowed a guy named Richard Bachman to steal his thunder.

Alonso admits she hadn't read the novella ahead of time, and it's doubtful she'd have gotten much if she had; one is pressed to find a film that delves further from its literary blastoff.

First off, while the Bachman ("Bachman") work had Ben Richards in the same time and setting, he's not a wronged solider forced into the competition, but a husband and father who enters to land some green for his suffering wife and daughter. Next, while the film's title show takes place over one night, the book stretches out for days. The movie is only in quake-crushed California; the book goes all over the nation, including King's Maine homeland. In the film, those after the contestants are called Stalkers (and there's several of them, considered national heroes and the movie's good guys), while the book has them as Hunters, and just one is named.

Alonso's character is hardly necessary in the book; the literary Richards carjacks a lady named Amelia Williams and uses her as a hostage, but she doesn't do much, and him being already married kills the romance the film needed.

And the ending . . . Christ almighty, the ending?! Suffice to say that *Running Man*'s separate finishes perfectly showed how something so effective on the books wouldn't possibly work in films, and vice versa. Had the film concluded as the book had, audiences would have been furious and really depressed, calling it all kinds of anti-climactic—likewise, had the story taken the "happily ever after" sap-athon the film used, it would have been far less interesting and emotional, as situations like it can't work without us being able to see, hear, and really feel the action.

Actors in Action

Amber Mendez (Maria Conchita Alonso) finds herself an unwilling contestant in a literal fight to the televised death in 1987's *The Running Man*—and after so long as the warm-hearted persona of *Family Fued*, Richard Dawson (right) went to the deplorable extreme as *Man* host Damon Killian.

Nonetheless, the film gave us Richard Dawson's evilly hysterical performance as *Man* host Damon Killian. So friendly and funny before the cameras, Killian was comic book-level villainy backstage, one of the most notable bad guys of Schwarzenegger's career.

Much of *Running Man*'s target audience may not have been aware of Dawson's pre-*Family Feud* acting career, highlighted by six years of tasteless TV "comedy" on *Hogan's Heroes*, but, talent aside, the part would not have worked nearly as well without the inside joke/self-deprecation aspect Dawson's presence gave it.

Wow, if *Running Man* were remade today (and judging from American cinema's "In With the Old" attitude of the past decade, chances are it soon will be), would we have Pat Sajak, Alex Trebek, or even current *Family Feud* host Steve Harvey in the role? Can you imagine one of them randomly cussing out a janitor or staff member, or casually saying of the country's justice department, "Tell them to go fuck themselves"?

The cinematized *Man* had Richards—single and framed for mass murder—kidnapping young beauty Amber Mendez, who happens to work for the show's network, which blackmails him onto the show; it's hilarious to see how innovatively impossible the film's pseudo-Big Brother technology seemed when the *Man* came out, considering how far behind it is to today's actual tech-obsessed society, with cameras putting us on the Internet in seconds, and so many sacrificing their privacy for a few seconds of Youtube fame.

This being an 80s action film and all, Mendez coincidentally starts to believe that this guy might be innocent, and that it's worth taking on the dictatorial authorities and risking her career, and her life, to find out. Of course, she gets thrown into battle and vilified, and falls in love with her captor throughout death and bloodshed as he goes from society's most hated to a global hero in a matter of hours!

"I have always done a lot of exercise, so I was more than ready for a physical role," Alonso remembers. "I didn't do exercise while shooting the movie. Our schedule most of the time was at night; our call time was around 4 p.m., and we went to sleep when the sun came out, so I did not feel like exercising, but Arnold did every day!" Seeing her in the film makes this next statement tough to believe, but Hollywood performers, fictional characters in manufactured worlds, often get shoved to higher standards than us common folk.

"My agent got a phone call from production . . . that I had to stop eating," Alonso claims. "I had put on maybe a pound or two, [and] I was going to gain weight and it was going to show in that very tight outfit I had. Now I laugh, but back then, it was not funny."

The contestants—"runners," the film labeled them—had only their wits, muscles, and whatever happened to be laying around to take on their stalkers, as well as an audience that cheered for and wagered on those sent out to kill. But all the while, Richards' friends are hacking into the show's tech background, looking to expose Killian and the rest as the coldhearts they are.

Again, in true 80s action tradition, the scrappy rebellion brainiacs just happen to topple Big Brother just as Richards and Amber vanquish their last few opponents—on national TV, of course, we have to let the world see what's going on—and Richards and Killian are finally left alone.

"Many times, the media," Alonso says, "without generalizing, uses the TV and or press to brainwash people, kind of like propaganda." Killian basically admits as much, but Richards has had about enough, making the former host an unwilling contestant. While hoping that Killian wasn't representative of the persona behind him (Dawson's sad passing in June 2012 kept me from asking him directly), you really have to give Dawson some serious props for allowing his villain to get such hardcore comeuppance, why critics have been acclaiming his work in the film for three decades.

Still, while we, and the *Running Man* audience, get some strong satisfaction at his fiery demise, it's just one more reminder of just how violent they (and, today, we) as a society are. Some rooted for Killian like crazy, probably for years in *Man*'s fictional timeline. Then he pissed us off, now he's violently dead, and we still go straight to ecstasy. No shocked silences; we're programmed to love this stuff, even if two seconds ago this guy was our best friend. Clapping, jumping up and down . . . it's how we respond to pain and death, as long as these people have done *anything* to piss us off. Just one more indication that *Man* might be a preview of coming attractions in 2017 America.

"I loved it!" asserts Alonso, whose gal got a quick makeout session with Richards before walking off into the credits. "After watching the film with the special effects. I said, 'Wow! I am finally in one of those movies I always wanted to be in!'"

Only months before raging futuristic battle, Arnold had taken it on in the supernatural sense, up against a giant extraterrestrial killing machine in Central American jungles in *Predator*. Three years later, the title character's colleagues came to America and the generous human hunting grounds of Los Angeles drug dealers and armed cops.

Arnie survived the first film, but he didn't go Dutch in part two (ironically, Kevin Peter Hall, whose title character had died in part one, came back to become a different such alien). This edition's hero is Lt. Harrigan (Danny Glover), who realizes that even armed men on the nose powder might not be the police's most dangerous enemy. Even so, it gets personal fast, for both him and Alonso's Leona.

Whatever the opposition, it just took out Harrigan's friend Danny, leaving Danny's wife and fellow officer Leona a sudden widow. But she'll soon find the silver lining in pitch-black night.

"I really liked the first *Predator*, so it was a must for me to be in the second one, and it was another futuristic film," Alonso says. "I did practice a few times with real cops so I would look credible when holding and using a gun."

The first film established that our visitors, unwelcome though they may be, are hunting with honor, not malice. Anxious to test his skills against heavily armed military men, the creature could have had an easy kill on a defenseless lady, but he didn't. That's not a predator's way.

These things only attack someone who could put up a fight. You've got to respect that.

Caught in subway warfare with gangsters and a few other conservative Second Amendment believers, Cantrell and her colleague Jerry Lambert suddenly get some shocking, unintentional assistance as a predator racks up some serious prey quota marks. Even Lambert falls short and falls forever, cementing late great Bill Paxton as the only person killed by a terminator, an alien, and now a predator (no, Lance Henriksen doesn't count—he was a friggin' *robot* in 1986's *Aliens*, out of the running of humanity!).

Looks like Cantrell will be just another number on its hit list. But when the predator literally holds her life in its hands, the same infra-red vision that allows it to sneak around undetected reveals a new life within her.

But, again, even non-Earthlings have a code. Cantrell's free, leaving Harrigan as a weird sort of worthy prey.

"Believe in yourself," Alonso asserts to performing upcomers. "Believe that there is *nothing* you cannot do."

Based on her acting work body alone, that advice would be credible enough. But it means just a bit more when we remember what else runs through Alonso's resume.

Like, say, winning the Miss Teen World pageant of 1971, and finishing in the top ten in

1975's "older" version. And recording a platinum-selling album and four gold ones, nearly grabbing a Grammy.

The mindset's worked for her on several levels. It can work for us all.

"Be ready for anything that could come your way," she continues, "because *anything* can come your way! So be prepared for that—don't wait until the last minute."

Movies like these, and the worlds they depict, just get closer and closer. More and more realistic. More and more possible.

A world on the brink of utter chaos, run by people who openly couldn't care less about the commonfolk. A society thrilled and gratified by mindless violence, as long as it's up close and dying, right in front of them. A population that will follow its leaders off a cliff, as long as someone's in fact leading them around.

And all of it plastered right in front of everyday society, slightly easier to see than to be a part of.

Some say that's where America is headed. Some say we're already there. Maybe it's all just wishful thinking, a sad realization that some things just can't be saved.

With the *Death Race* films, we see a sad crossover from satire to reality. *Death Race 2020* opened the saga almost half a century ago, introducing a world we could still look at and feel safe from (along with Sylvester Stallone). Now we're into new territory, one we're not sure how to classify and don't really want to try.

When the first flick came out, we cheered, we laughed, we did everything but worry. People cheering as racers mowed them down to score points, jumping before (and under!) the cars themselves to help out their heroes, a welcome release from the war-like barren land of poverty their Old Glory had become.

A bit frightening and sickening, yes, but we could enjoy it because it was safely caught in fiction. Not possible.

Can't say that today. As *Death Race 2050* made its way into cinematic lore in 2017, it looks prophetic, a soothsaying of things to come—perhaps sooner than we will have time to prepare for.

Generations of cult fans have labeled Roger Corman something resembling royalty for decades, before and after the first *Death Race* became one of the hundreds of flicks with his name attached. Producing the new chapter of the anthology might have elevated him to near-clairvoyance. His name alone, though, was plenty to entice one proud member of the Corman Aficionado Regime to race toward death.

"What an honor!" Anessa Ramsey exclaims of working with one of the few filmmakers with his own breed of fanatics. "Are you kidding me? Any excuse to further stretch my range is a good one, so I suited up and dove right in!" After pondering all over the original *Race* (Corman also produced the 2008 Jason Statham prequel), Ramsey headed in to strike a new blow for female athletes everywhere.

To its credit, the first Race had been ahead of the times in sports, in a sense; it came out the year before Janet Guthrie became the first gal to race on a superspeedway, burning through Charlotte in the 1976 World 600 (finishing ahead of a youngster named Earnhardt!). Two women had taken the first *Death Race*, and Ryan hoped to follow in their overdrives. At first, though, she and the crew seemed a bit far apart.

She'd be Tammy, a pint-sized fireplug all too anxious—as we'd soon learn!—to strike some serious death blows. But who *was* the character in question? The answer was unclear.

"I went in to the audition room prepared to just be a tough badass chick," she says, "black tank top, torn skinny jeans, tattoos a-blazing!" A pleasant sight to be certain, but not quite what they were looking for. We'd see something else.

Yes, in 2050, there are too many people and not enough jobs. Left to their own everyday lives, too many find it depressing, probably frightening. But when race time draws near, the stadium's jam-packed with screaming, chanting fans. When we have nowhere to go, we'll go anywhere and do anything as long as someone's there to show us how, and a schedule that gives us some sense of stability. It's where many live today. Reality can scare the hell out of us sometimes.

Her enthusiasm as strong as the accelerator in her car, Annessa Ramsey's Tammy roared into deadly—for her and others!—battle in 2017's *Death Race 2050*.

And of course, nearby, they can hear the comforting words of the Chairman (not the President, that's too diplomatic) of the United Corporations of America (Malcolm McDowell). Clearly, business has overtaken politics at the top of the nation, and this guy's got about 98 percent of the nation's budget in his pocket, his followers dumb enough to think he might just share a drop or two with them . . . someday.

Yeah, a really rich ruler full of himself to the forehead, itself decorated with an ugly fake-ass comb-over: wanna guess what leader *he's* spoofing? (hint—he was inaugurated three days after *Race* came out!).

Then the racers arrive, and Tammy's in the lead. But as her lovely, albeit boisterous countenance flashes onto the screen, her attire's a bit far from Ramsey's impression.

"Boy, was I surprised when I was handed the equivalent of a *Toddlers in Tiaras* costume!" she recalls. "I seriously thought there had been some sort of mistake!" Tammy's attired in a layered bathing suit-type runway model outfit, complete with stocking and shoulder-length gloves.

That had shoved Ramsey down a whole new preparatory road. "The southern accent got *way* thicker," she explains, "and I drastically changed my posture from the tough chick to the flamboyant Tammy you see on screen." Exuding a seductive side of innocence, Tammy's got a special surprise for those that hope to see some death soon.

"I also took a lot of time scribbling alternative celebrities to idolize in the margins of my script, and pages of other notes or ideas that came out as possible improvisations or actions," Ramsey explains. "I find that the more homework you do, both physically and mentally, the more the character comes to life. After all of that, Tammy just kind of . . . happened to me." Tammy proclaims that she's only here to spread the Word of Someone special—and starts by sending a few in attendance His way.

There's a partner of hers in the stands, and the box he's holding blasts himself and some stadium neighbors straight to eternity.

Tammy points. She cackles madly.

And the crowd follows in kind. Tammy's just racked up a new load of fans. That's how you do it in a place like this. This is what people like. Public murder is OK, as long as it's entertaining.

Again, we can see it happening in reality.

Watching the scene, "I gotta admit, I giggled a little," Ramsey says. "It set the tone for the rest of the movie for sure. Going into this film knowing that the Corman-esque style was intentionally humorous and kind of cheesy gave me a sense of odd security." With the race on, Tammy looks for some numerical safety of her own, mowing down one group of those eager to die one after another to hop out to an early advantage.

About that stuff about people following certain others anywhere? Religion has proved that time and again since the start of time. War, murder, mass suicide, Higher Powers have gotten us mere mortals to do just about anything.

Tammy's about to follow. Those preachings she mentioned have already reached others. There's a huge group of cultists ready to sacrifice themselves for their leader, going out in a blaze of dirt and rubber (not as sad as an earlier scene in which some teachers try to place some crippled kids in death's way!). But another rider slips in and wipes out Tammy's clan, setting the two up for a showdown.

Tammy wins that one, but there's one participant immune to her evangelization; the one run by artificial intelligence. He (well, actually, It!) slams her against a wall and blasts both of them to bits, leaving her to take her chances with the afterlife.

"This role is *so* different than *anything* I've ever done before!" Ramsey remarks. "It was a joy to watch! And it wasn't just different because it was Roger Corman's extra sticky bubble gum candy flavor that we all love: it was also the character herself. Tammy is such . . . a *cartoon*! What a dream come true for a physical character-driven actor like myself."

After her martial arts skills brought Dana Hee an Olympic gold medal, action and stunting became her new work, with sai-wielding Mileena was one of many roles Hee played in 1997's *Mortal Kombat: Annihilation*.

Dana Hee: *Mortal Kombat*/Stunts

THINK MAKING IT BIG in acting is hard? Try getting to the top of a sport that only awards three titles every four years!

That's been the two big parts of Dana Hee's life. But it wasn't always that way for her.

Looking for a way out of a family not just broken, but nearly shattered by abuse, alcoholism, and poverty, the young woman's home life carried all the stability of uphill ice skating. Abandoned at the age of three, shelters, street life, halfway and foster homes became the closest thing she'd ever have to a home.

But even with all that going on around her, Hee managed to find and zero in on a newfound talent during her high school years. Deciding to give the combination of track and field a try, she suddenly found her own natural high: the high jump.

Day after day, meet after meet, she soared higher and higher. A college scholarship was right in front of her, and a coach at Stanford was ready to help her right out as she finished high school. Even the Olympic Games started to come into view.

For one of the first times in her life, Hee had found something to make her feel special. Something that made her feel like someone she'd never been before.

But just as she was about to take some of the last steps (or jumps) toward the top of the sport, everything just . . . stopped.

She didn't suffer some kind of serious injury or illness, or have some kind of personal tragedy. Hee just called it quits far too early. The dread that so many had beaten into her crept up, took over, and pulled her right back into the darkness.

"I started getting into my head a fear," she explains wistfully, "a fear of failure. I was psyching myself out. Finally, after a tournament at which I totally blew it, I just gave it up. There's a saying that the further up the ladder you climb, the farther you have to fall. I was climbing up that ladder for the first time in my life, and then I started thinking about what it would be like to fall. Instead of pushing myself, I just walked away. I didn't even say goodbye to my coach, or thank you."

Back into directionlessness, Hee didn't know if such an opportunity, or anything like it, would ever get anywhere near her again. This had been her first or perhaps only chance at success, and these sort of things rarely happen once, let alone more than once.

"For the first time in my life, I actually realized what I was doing," she says. "Why was I such a coward? Why was I running away from everything? I let it sit in my mind, and then it grew into a feeling a self-disgust. I realized that I needed to stop running from my fears and 'step up' in life, but I didn't know how."

Then another shot came around. Right around the time she stepped off of track and field, Hee had gotten interested in the martial arts.

"I was really intrigued with it, and I really needed something to fill the gap after I'd lost the high jump," she says. "It's very cool to watch the classes, and see their strength, their power, and their movement. At the same time, there were the Bruce Lee movies that I'd watched growing up, and I was thinking, 'Wow, it would be cool to jump into a tree!'"

Taking up a few classes at her junior college, Hee's new taekwondo hobby grew into a passion. Then it became her new life direction.

"Of all the sports I had done, the martial arts were different," she recalls. "It seemed that the more I put into my efforts the more I got out for myself. With each step I took in the martial arts, I began feeling better about myself. My self-esteem got better and I began learning how to focus and overcome difficult things."

Working her way up America's ranks in the full-contact department, Hee took second in her first national competition. That's when she learned that the Seoul Olympics would be the first chance for women to compete in her newfound sport.

"It was my second chance to have my dream come true," she remembers. "I was determined to take my dream and really go toward it 100 percent. No matter what I would not give up. Even if I failed, I'd need to know that I'd given 100 percent. It was very difficult. I'd had self-confidence issues, self-esteem issues, and I was given a second chance at my Olympic dream. So I gathered up what little courage I could find and took that first tiny step towards my long-standing dream of Olympic gold."

Even with years to go before the event, Hee jumped—and kicked and punched—straight into training, up to eight hours a day. When the games finally neared, she made it through the Olympic trials to get on the team. But as tough as everything had been up to that point, life had at least one more roadblock to toss in front of her dream.

At the Olympic trainings in Colorado, a nagging back injury suddenly flared into a brushfire for Hee.

"Training was mandatory," says Hee, whose asthma and rapid heartbeat didn't help her endurance much either, "so I didn't have time to let the injury heal. We tried all these remedies, from modern sports medicine to holistic medicines and treatments, but it kept getting worse and worse. By the time we got to Seoul, two weeks before the games, I tried to do a high kick, and it brought me to my knees. I was in tears and agony."

Doctors told her that the only way to end the pain was to stop training. Hee knew she was too close to halt.

"I was debating, how could I tell my teammates and my coach that I wouldn't be able to compete, much less win?" she says. "I'd sacrificed so much and made it to this point that I couldn't just give up. Then I realized that there was an alternative: I realized that I could train in my mind."

For the next two weeks, as her teammates put on their finishing physical touches, Hee sat on the sidelines and meditated, watching herself succeeding, doing techniques and winning her matches all in her mind.

"I would find a place to sit and put myself in a zone," she says. "I would visualize practicing my moves. I would see myself doing everything perfectly. My back got some much-needed rest, along with acupressure and acupuncture. By the morning of competition, my back was better. I felt ready. I'd been doing all the training in my mind."

It worked; she became one of the first ladies to take home a taekwondo gold. Still, victory wasn't quite everything for Hee.

"[Winning] is a high," she says. "It's a dream come true. But the real victory for me wasn't winning the gold medal. It was the fact that I'd finally drawn a line in the sand and said that I was willing to fight for what I want. The real victory was that I knew that I was no longer a failure. It made me aware of how much is truly possible. From then on, I started using what I'd learned from the Olympics to apply to other things."

One of the first things was the film world. Writing for a martial arts magazine in the San Francisco area, Hee got a call that someone was looking for a stuntwoman for the Dennis Quaid/Kathleen Turner 1993 action/comedy flick *Undercover Blues*.

"I did two weeks of work on *Undercover Blues*," she says. "I was like 'Hell, yes!' I just had a blast! It was the same thing of pushing myself [as with taekwondo]. It was the realization of seeing what I could do if I really tried." She kept trying, doubling for Sandra Bullock in *Demolition Man* the same year, and soon for Nicole Kidman in *Batman Forever* (1995)

"The good thing is that when you're stunt doubling for an actress and you do a good job," Hee explains, "the next time the actress works, they'll say, 'OK, let's see who has doubled for this actress before.' Referral from one job to the next is the key to a life in the dismissive business of film, so it's also important to conduct yourself in a professional, cooperative, and humble manner."

The next time she'd stand up for Kidman, however, things didn't go too well. Working on the 1997 action film *Peacemaker* with the actress and George Clooney, Hee had one of her most memorable moments in film, and not in a safe way.

"In the scene where we jump out a window in a church during an explosion," she recalls, "there were a lot of complications with the pyrotechnics, building set, and a stained glass paint on the tempered glass we needed to jump through. The bomb went off too soon and blew out the entire back wall of the scene. As a result, we were engulfed in the explosions. I thought I was dead." Second- and third-degree burns and severe cuts from the broken window glass sent her to the hospital.

Hee came back for Kidman in *Practical Magic* (1998) and *Moulin Rouge* (2001), and worked for Uma Thurman in *Batman and Robin* (1997)

As Thurman's cartoonish Poison Ivy plots to launch her natural wrath upon an unsuspecting public during a large party scene, she wows the crowd atop a platform, boogieing in a gorilla suit. Adorned in the costume and not-quite-matching stiletto heels, Hee dropped her furry getup and collapsed into a group of fellows below.

"I fell backwards and down into the arms of six bare-chested, golden-sprayed hunks!" she says. "The fall was actually twenty feet, but on screen it looked like only two! But to land in the arms of six handsome strong men was pretty cool."

She kept working, helping out Kristanna Loken in *Terminator 3* (2003), and showing up in *Terminator: Salvation* (2009), *Spiderman 2* (2004), and some others. She even won a World Stunt Award ("the Olympic gold medal of Hollywood!" Hee proclaims) for her work in *Charlie's Angels* (2000)

"I am not an adrenalin junkie," she asserts. "I don't like jumping out of buildings and putting myself at risk. The simple truth is that I like to prove to myself that I can do whatever I want to do, regardless of my fears. In order to be successful with whatever you do, it is important to remember the power of the mind and use it to succeed."

As with any aspect of acting, stunt work doesn't come with a manual detailing the surefire way to get ready for every role. But Hee's still discovered a little common ground that runs through just about every job.

One short television role had her playing a security guard at a movie studio. As a car careens out of control near her, Hee had to toss herself onto a fire hydrant, then use it for a springboard to the top of the car. On the first take, she hesitated for an extra millisecond and jumped too late, ending up on the back of the car and then crashing to the ground.

"I realized that I could not allow any element of doubt into my mind," she says. "The odd thing was that on camera, it seemed so easy and inconsequential. Considering that I could've been run over if I messed up, this was really disappointing!" Her doubt disappeared, and she nailed it on the next shot. It marked a new rush of confidence that's stayed with her throughout her career.

"In my preparation for any of the stuff that I do," Hee explains, "a lot of it is physical, but it's also mental, what I call realization. I visualize what I'm going to do beforehand. When they say 'action,' I'm thinking about where I'm going to be at each moment in time, and that helps to prevent fear. Preparing 100 percent gives you the confidence to do what you need to do, when it is needed. In front of camera, whether as an actor, or stunt doubling an actor, I need to BE that character! That means I need to read the script, understand the storyline and character, and most of all, study the actress I am doubling! I need to imitate their actions. I need to 'feel' their motives and allow the camera to see this."

Once in a while, Hee got a shot at creating her own character. Natasha Henstridge might have gotten the credit for becoming the human/alien combo Sil in the sci-fi production *Species* (1995), but Hee did some serious dirty work, spending hours inside a costume to play Sil's creature form.

"I was in a rubber suit," she says. "It took three people and half an hour to get me into it. If I tried to raise my arm, it was like there was a force pulling it back down. Working in the water, crossing pipes, jumping and climbing about like an athletic and graceful creature was truly difficult."

After working in stunts on the first *Mortal Kombat* (1995), Hee did quintuple duty on the film's 1997 sequel *Annihilation*, doubling for four other actresses while playing the sai-slicing Mileena.

"Training with the sai was the biggest challenge for that role," she recalls. "It was the best of both worlds to be able to act in a film where I got to do martial arts and still double for everyone else. Seeing and working in the temples and cliffs of the amazing historical site of Petra, Jordan was a dream come true, and although difficult, the icing on the cake was fighting [good girl] Sonya Blade in a hurricane in Wales and then working in the beautiful spiritual temples in Thailand."

Now, Hee acts in yet another role. Though she still works in films, she's also an international public speaker, discussing her past in growing up, heading to the Olympics, and making it in Hollywood. Too much of her life was spent running away from difficulties and fears—it's time to focus on overcoming them, and helping others do so as well.

"In my mind," Hee says, echoing the opinions of quite a few others, "I know that I am no longer a failure!"

Season Hubley got seriously and sadly *Hardcore*, showing the dark, dangerous world of pornography and prostitution in the 1978 film.

Season Hubley: *Hardcore*

IN THE BACK ROOMS of the massage parlor, neither knew what exactly would happen. She was brand new to the job. He was light years out of practice.

Sounds like the start of so many raunchy comedies.

With the greatest set of options to choose from, the fellow had chosen his new favorite gal, one he just knew would give him a great time. Now they had some privacy, and he had a plan.

OK, now this is angling toward thriller territory, even of the erotic type.

"I was Niki," the lady remembers. "I was doing a nude wrap session, so I undressed."

The man was just back in the states, from nearly a year in sailing service. After endless months of not even seeing a member of the opposite sex (this was before women played much of a militaristic role), he was in the perfect place to, well, make up for all that time.

Again, this was a few decades ago. Back then, massage parlors were far more common and much less monitored. Back then, clients could ask for more than just a relaxing rubdown if they knew where to go.

Not him. Not with Niki.

"He just wanted to talk," she remembers. "He hadn't seen a woman in all that time. He asked me a lot of questions. It made me feel good that this guy really wanted to talk. I was his sounding board for about a half hour." The fellow even paid for another half hour, just for a conversation.

In the cinematic sense, her "venture" ended up closer to the awkward world of romantic dramedy. Soon after, though, a much larger audience would see Niki in a much tougher area of the erotic workplace – and, sadly, one that's more dangerous, more common, and more real.

1979's *Hardcore* lived up to its title throughout, in a more graphic way than many films even express today. As she became Niki for the flick that Paul Schrader had already written and would now direct, Season Hubley had visited the lands of sex entertainment. Before the Internet, or even cable television, the porn industry was quite different. Back then, satiating one's erotic individualism typically involved leaving the home. The parlor would be just one place she'd visit, and soon portray.

Niki wouldn't show up until quite a ways into the flick (although she'd make one hell of a first impression). *Hardcore* began far from sleaze in every sense, a Calvinist family celebrating Christmas back home in Michigan – minus TV, of course, per their beliefs. Soon, young daughter Kristen is off on a church trip to California.

She doesn't come back. Then her dad Jake (George C. Scott) gets some news he can't possibly fathom. The daughter who this widower worked so hard to place a fear of Someone inside has somehow gotten caught up in a profession marked by the X-rating.

She had to have been kidnapped or forced. There's no way Kristen would have ever done this by choice. Good little pure girls don't do this sort of thing.

Soon he's off to the Golden State…but where does such a search begin?

Meanwhile, just as was reality for many porn flicks of the time, we see one being shot in the confines of a sleazy motel. Niki's there, although she's forced to dress down with a wig bigger than Mozart's.

You know, as awkward as sex can be when alone with one other person, imagine trying to get the hormones going with a camera crew in the room, and a director shouting instructions the whole time. Fortunately, Hubley's co-stars (and bedmates) in the scene had been there many times before.

"The other woman was a real porno star," she explains. "I had gone to see her strip in New York, and she was fascinating. The other guy was a real porn star too, and then there was me. It was a little odd, but Paul was very comforting."

Writing the *Hardcore* screenplay and seeing others act it out, Schrader might have been looking back to his own past. Like Kristen, he'd been raised in a staunch religious home where pop culture was all but the eighth deadly sin. Just as the typical adolescent boy ventures into secret agent mode to get a glance at Dad's girlie magazines or even -- gasp! -- a glance at X-rated cinematic extravaganza, Schrader had long mastered the art of sneaking around to see any kind of flick at all, not knowing he was witnessing the start of a legendary career. Hardcore took us even deeper (tsk, tsk!) into a business long built around secrecy.

"(Schrader) has some strange things about him," Hubley says, "but don't we all? The reason he felt so strongly about making this film was that he grew up in a time and place when he wasn't allowed to see movies. I found it interesting that he had really lived that and knew that feeling. He had that secretive side."

Apparently she'd imagined some of her own upbringings in Niki as well.

"I left home when I was fifteen, in New York City and Manhattan," she says. "I lived on the streets in the 60s. There were a lot of crash pads. I've always been very independent and in charge of my life, but inside, I wasn't really like that. I was a lot more fragile, and I saw that in her."

She'd seen it throughout her pre-filming transformative work. Along with the massage parlor, she'd been to the strip clubs, the peep shows, everywhere that Jake visits on his search.

"The lives of those girls is really, really sad," Hubley admits. "Maybe not really sad for all of them, but some are, with the drugs and everything." In his infiltrations, Jake finds Niki, recognizes her as one of Kristen's colleagues, and hopes she can become his link inside the mysterious world, and hopefully to his daughter.

A bond forms. We start to see the woman behind Niki, and we're not just talking about the actress here. We see strippers, porn actresses, we might even run across a prostitute once in a while – look, but don't touch, people!

In any case, we think what we see is all they ever are or will be. Their reasons for getting into the business, and/or staying in it. Their original hopes for their lives and their careers. The dreams they might still realize one day.

These are things we don't really take the time to think about, mainly because the sex industry – even if it's "just" the stripping aspect, as clean as sleazy can be – is about the last place in the world where deep thought could ever come in handy.

Maybe we should consider it. Maybe there are some things we could learn, or at least some stories that might be worth hearing. Of course, there's more to these women than the eye can ascertain, we just don't feel like looking for it. Hubley had looked for Niki inside some of the character's colleagues, and found a few things.

"We started hanging out, and I experienced their lives for a week or two, and it was great," she says. "One girl was putting herself through college. Everybody makes up their own names. There were a lot of dead ends, girls who would not come out of it. They had a lot of fantasies, living in fantasy lands. 'Someday I'm going to be rich and famous!' It made them ignore what they were doing. It was interesting that they could put blinders on and not have the reality really sink in."

As Jake and Niki's quest nears its end, Jake promises he won't forget her. Maybe he'll even take her home and try to create a new Biblical protégé.

Then reality truly sinks in for all of them. He finds Kristen in the back of a sex show, and she doesn't want to come home. Love and acceptance, in her own preferred form, are here in ways she never got back home, and Jake doesn't know what to do.

If this were typically Hollywood fare, he would certainly take both ladies back with him, probably punctuating things with a group hug. That had been the flick's intended ending. But *Hardcore* has been real since it began, and it's not going for sentiment now.

Jake and Kristen are heading home, and Niki's left back where she was.

"He just says goodbye," Hubley says. "She was just expected to walk off and be fine. I don't think she really was." Rumors spread across the film world that she'd gotten close to an Oscar nomination (this was the year that *Kramer vs. Kramer* swept up with five statuettes, including Meryl Streep's second straight supporting actress nod.

Kristen would be Ilah Davis' only film role; tragically, she succumbed to multiple sclerosis at just age 51 in Sept. 2007.

Less than two years after a man called the King lost his life in one of music's most heart-breakingly infamous moments, Kurt Russell led the way through *Elvis* on the small screen in Feb. 1979, with Hubley as Presley's ex Priscilla (Russell's real father Bing played Elvis' dad Vernon in the film).

The next month, Hubley and Russell wed. Not long after, Russell made his way through the fourth-world nation that many thought New York would actually become by 1997. An ominous eyepatch hiding his face and a wealth of weaponry at his hands, his Snake Plisskin looked for a way out of the prison that Manhattan had become in John Carpenter's 1981 directed vision. He hoped to get away from the Crazies (gang patrollers of the area) and everyone else. If he could only... *Escape from New York*.

About out of time and space, Plisskin refuges inside an old coffee shop. There's someone else with him, and, this being the "future" and all, co-ed prison life is commonplace.

"You're a cop!" she accuses, clearly having been here before.

"I'm an asshole," he sadly asserts.

Will she comfort him? Take him away from his task? Toss the whole film right off the reels? Who better to do so than Russell's own wife? What better place to toss in an inside joke?

"That character was a hoot to do!" recalls Hubley, compensated for her one-night role with the gift of a new alarm system for her home (sadly, she and Russell divorced in 1983). "People wondered about her, was she a gang leader? I said no, she was a crime groupie." The Mr. Hyde version of the followers of musical acts like the Grateful Dead and Phish, such people are known to trail criminals, finding a dark enjoyment in those who've done the worst of the worst.

Virtually every well-known criminal of every time has had such "fanfare," and one like Plisskin would be a magnet for gals like Hubley's New York-er.

"I felt that her old man was put in New York, and she sliced up some girl's face to be with him," she explains of the character's backstory. "I'd grown up in New York, and the Bronx was a place you didn't go in that time."

Even if a lovely lady was there to lead you. When the two move toward affection, viewers might see a serious plot twist in the gal.

"The kiss was going to happen, and then something more," Hubley says. "Was she going to seduce him into not doing what he was supposed to do?" But the Crazies show and live up to their label, yanking her away and sending Snake on his journey.

Sam Jones turned *Flash Gordon* into an everyman that saved the planet in 1980.

Sam Jones: *Flash Gordon*

FIRST OFF, LET'S GET a misconception re-conceived (that may or may not be the right way to say that, but you get the idea).

Flash Gordon was hardly *any* kind of box office bomb. Not by any stretch; the 1980 film made more than its budget, went nuts on ticket sales just about everywhere else on the globe, and tore it up and down when it hit home video, elevating it to the cult classic status it still enjoys. People like to badmouth *Flash* because it got monetarily creamed by the first two *Star Wars* movies of about the same time, but, hell … what didn't?

Perhaps most notable, at least to today's audiences, would be the impression Sam Jones' title titan made upon a certain elementary school student at the time way back when.

Before filming even began, the production had gone through enough turmoil to become its own disaster movie. Director after director (including a fellow named George Lucas) had attempted to make the flick, but it didn't work. Dino De Laurentiis had already seen too many try it out before finally deciding to himself make the story of which he'd long since owned the rights, with Mike Hodges doing the filming.

Then came a new kind of tryout. Kurt Russell was a contender. So was some bodybuilder with the odd moniker of Schwarzenegger.

"The audition process went on for seven or eight months," Jones remembers. "I'd spent thirty days in London. We were doing the old-fashioned Hollywood screen tests—they'd put you on film, hair, makeup, and wardrobe. You'd rehearse, they'd shoot, they'd critique it."

After half a year of narrowing his field, De Laurentiis stepped up to the impromptu victor.

"He said, 'You are Flash Gordon!'" Jones recalls. "Tomorrow morning, we shoot!"

OK, so it might not have been *that* short of a notice; Jones admits for a bit of dramatic embellishment when convention audiences and interviews are involved. But the fact remained that, in just the second role of his career (he'd been the envy of American men as bombshell Bo Derek's husband the year before in *10*), Jones would be leading the way in a role that would have him seen in just about every scene.

"I just focused on my task at hand, what I needed to do," he explains. "I can't be like the original. They hired me because it's me, so I'll just give them pieces of me playing this character. The job at hand was enormous." The "original" in question was Buster Krabbe, who'd played Flash in three films from 1936 to 1940. Jones didn't meet Krabbe, who passed in 1983, until after filming.

Instead, he glanced over the old *Gordon* comics that had first showed up in 1934 (it's credited as inspiring the *Superman* drawings that arrived five years later). The physical prowess that had scored Jones a spot in the marine core beforehand came back to bear; after all, Flash starts out as an NFL quarterback before getting caught in an inter-planet war.

"That's Flash Gordon anyway," Jones says. "He's one of the few superheroes who does not have a superpower. He relies on his athleticism and his wit."

Trapped on the planet Mongo—is that the one that stole the rings from Saturn?—Flash is the new prey of Max von Sydow's gleeful Ming the Merciless, just one more extermination on the way to taking Earth slam out.

Of course, he escapes, with the help of Ming's smoking hot daughter Aura (Ornella Muti) and Dr. Hans Zarkov (Topol, who couldn't possibly be further from playing Tevye in 1971's *Fiddler on the Roof*). Then it's open season on creatures, Ming's soldiers, and, ultimately, the no-mercy man himself.

Jones had been prepping all the while.

"I was in everything," he says. "They'd pull me away, and I'd go rehearse a fight scene. They'd pull me away, and I'd go outdoors and work with a bullwhip artist. It didn't stop. It was a whole lot of 'Keep your mouth shut, hit your mark, and get your line out before the explosion goes off!'"

It's clear that everyone thought, and certainly intended, for there to be a part two at some point (the last scene is Ming's ring getting snatched up by a hand whose owner we wish we could see), but the film's lack of blockbuster-ship kept that from ever happening, even with the help of Queen's legendary theme, which even made it to the band's *Greatest Hits* album of 1981 (it did become a short-lived Sci-Fi channel series in 2007, with Eric Johnson in the lead and Jones cameoing on one episode).

But in 2012, audiences saw what an impact it had made on someone who could show off his appreciation in an unusual way.

The animated entertainment world was well aware of the name Seth MacFarlane; he'd been the driving force behind *American Dad*, *The Cleveland Show*, and . . . oh yeah, *FAMILY GUY*! Now he was directing real people, like Mila Kunis, one of the biggest reasons why audiences demanded *Family Guy* back in 2005 after Fox kicked it off two years before. She, MacFarlane, and Mark Wahlberg stepped forward to tell the R-rated, F-bomb-jammed story of a man, his love, and the teddy bear that can't stay the f*** out of their way.

Ted it would forever be.

We hear early on of the characters' hero worship for Flash, and it soon gets too good to be true; in Hollywood coincidental form, Jones just happens to show up at a local party, complete with Queen's theme and lots of booze!

"Seth MacFarlane called me a year before *Ted*," Jones remembers. "He said, 'When I was eight, (Flash Gordon) changed my life. I knew walking out of the theater that I was going to be a creative guy!'" The flick would gross more than any other R-rated comedy in history. Jones ended up marrying Wahlberg and Kunis at the end, but they'd be done by the time the sequel arrived in 2015. Jones showed up there too, and rumors were already on the Internet about a third go-round, which hadn't arrived as of the spring of 2017.

The tragic death of Sarah (Michelle Joyner) kicked off the 1993 mountain-jammed thriller *Cliffhanger*.

Michelle Joyner: *Cliffhanger*

As captivating as Michelle Joyner's performance appeared in the opening sequence of 1993's *Cliffhanger*, it seems easy to get the wrong impression.

"After all," we might think, "all she had to do was act really scared while she was dangling from a broken harness—and Sylvester Stallone's arm—on a line between two mountains, thousands of feet above the ground. In that setting, how hard would it be to appear terrified out of our mind?"

But that would be far too assumptive on the part of us, the audience outsiders. We can't know all of what went into Joyner's work, and just how far she came during the process, as an actress and a person.

"At the time I auditioned for the film, I was very excited to get the chance to be in an action movie with Sylvester Stallone," Joyner says. "That's appealing to anybody. I was trying to get a break in features, as I had been doing a lot of television at that point. But when I got involved, I thought it was a fun part because of the impact that it can make; it was such an exciting scene, with [Sarah's] vulnerability and her bravery. I thought it was a great little part when I went to the audition."

And while all acting requires a certain degree of imagination and subjectivity, Joyner's audition went to a brand new level; standing in the midst of a casting director's office, she'd have to pantomime being suspended near the top of a mountain line.

"There's an old adage that I like to follow: 'Assume the position,'" she says. "A lot of times, if you assume the position of terror, joy, or whatever extreme emotion you're trying to do in a particular scene, even if you're not feeling it, you can kind of trick your body into following what your mind is setting up. Your body doesn't necessarily know that you're pretending."

In the weeks leading up to her tryout, Joyner put herself in Sarah's flailing boots, trying desperately to hang on to the line—and her life.

"I practiced a lot at home, just trying to get to the point physically," she says. "When you're physically scared like that, your body goes through some changes; you're shaking, you're terrified, and I was able to get to that place in the audition. I really, really tried to put myself in the position that the character is in, pretending that I wasn't in an office with the phone ringing and noises outside.

"I was really, really focused on reading with the casting director and trying to imagine stepping out onto the line and pulling myself across the line. It was a difficult audition, because you're in somebody's casting office on a couch, and you're pretending that you're falling off a mountain to your death! It was challenging, but I pulled it off."

After the cast and crew headed to Italy's Dolomites to film—filming was repeatedly held up because of snow and wind—Joyner put the finishing touches on her switch to Sarah.

"Once I was there, I started working with the stunt climbers, the best climbers in the world," she says. "They would take me out on the line, in a cage. It made me really nervous; there was nothing I could grab on to if something were to happen. But I got used to being out there on the wire, and going out in the climbing harness."

So much so that she started climbing out to the midst of the rope to hang out—literally—as other scenes were being filmed. Matter of fact that, by the time it came to shoot the scene, she had to do more acting for the role than anyone could have guessed.

"I had to really act scared, because I wasn't anymore," she says. "I'd felt terror once upon a time, but not at the time that we were actually shooting, because I'd been up there so much. I just had to pretend and let my body feel the way it did in the audition, assuming the position of terror in the film."

As the movie opens, the audience is treated to a wondrous pan shot of some gorgeous snow-covered mountains.

"[Director] Renny Harlin had this idea, and it was very effective, to do one long opening shot through the credit sequence," she says. "It was clear, there were no cuts, to show that we were actually on the mountain. We were lowered from a helicopter onto the peak where we were stranded. We were about 4000 feet off the ground. That made me a little nervous. I'm not bad with heights, but that would be an uncomfortable place for just about anybody."

Except, of course, for veteran climbers Hal (Michael Rooker), Gabe (Stallone), and Jessie (Janine Turner), in their everyday environment and ready to slide across a line between two mountains, a very small starting hurdle in their journey to a day of fun. But a nervous Sarah, Hal's lady friend and a climbing newcomer, can't seem to get a feel for the action.

"When you see all the dialogue with me and Stallone and Michael Rooker, that was all done on a sound stage," Joyner says. "As soon as [I get hooked in] and step out onto the wire, no nets. I was 4000 feet off the ground."

Hal and Jessie try to show her just how easy it is, quickly yanking their way across. It's Sarah's turn, and Gabe casually helps her get rolling.

"We're having dinner tonight, right?" she gasps to Gabe, who grins back an affirmation.

"It was like I was saying that just having him tell me that would make it come true, that we'd be having dinner and laughing about it later," Joyner says. "I was striving for normalcy I think playing against the fear, and playing more for covering the fear, was something that made it relatable. It's easy to play something on the nose; it's harder to play against something. People have a visceral experience of watching it, as opposed to you the actor having to do it. It gives them more room to be involved."

Pulling herself hand over hand, Sarah tries to keep her worried nature beneath her facial features, spurred on by Gabe's jovial encouragement. But as she nears the middle, everything goes tragically wrong.

Her harness suddenly breaks, and Sarah desperately claws at the cloth beneath it. Trapped in freezing, windy weather, hanging onto a sheer piece of material, she's thousands of feet in the air, but only milliseconds from a far-too-soon ending.

Overriding Hal's panicked suggestion to send Hal's harness to Sarah, Gabe hurriedly makes his way to the terrified climber.

Sarah is literally inches from death. She's panicked. She's on the edge in every sense of the phrase.

Gabe hangs on to her, with panic pushing everyone's voice up a few more octaves. But the audience gets a close-up view of Sarah's glove slipping off, and it's far too easy for us experienced action movie-watchers to guess what happens next. But that doesn't make it any easier to see.

Sarah falls, and a cavalcade of scenes follow.

We see her dropping in slow motion, perhaps the most realistically heartbreaking part of the sequence. We see Gabe screaming, and everyone joining in on a chorus from Hell. We see a closeup of Sarah, the background hurtling upward past her. We see her from far away, and that's the last time.

"The whole sequence was done it a lot of different shots," she says. "I think it really served the movie, because it made it a little more seamless. It was memorable, because everybody watching it felt so moved, because everybody can identify with being in such a horrifying situation, both from [Gabe's] point of view and from [Sarah's]."

During the scenes from above Gabe's point of view, a remote control camera was used. But for the shot of the harness breaking, the terror that Joyner thought she'd left behind came roaring back.

"When the harness broke, I had another real harness inside my costume. They had to intertwine the wire and lower me down. I was at the end of a tether, and that was really, really scary. In fact, that was probably the worst aspect of doing the scene for me.

"When you're out on that wire, you have this illusion that if something went wrong, you could save yourself, but realistically you probably couldn't. You could try to grab the wire and hang on until someone got out there to save you, but when you're out at the very end, you know that there's nothing you can grab, and you're a goner. That part, I actually wished later that I hadn't done."

In the scenes of her glove slipping down, Joyner says, she was a few feet off the ground on a sound stage. When Sarah looks up and falls backward, she was actually falling 30 feet onto an air bag. The close-up of Sarah falling was filmed with a movie running behind her, as she was held over a huge wind machine.

The last scene, the faraway shot, was the only one Joyner didn't do herself; a stuntwoman fell over 300 feet for the sight.

"Everybody came out to watch that stunt," she says of the last scene. "That was incredible."

In hindsight, she admits, "I look at the movie, and I think to myself that I probably didn't have to do all that. I didn't need to be up there and put myself at such risk, since they had the means, with computers and everything, to make it look like I was up there. But I don't regret it, because it was a very challenging and exciting experience. I don't think the average person has the chance to do something that outrageous."

It sparked her talents as both an actress and an athlete; not only did Joyner develop an interest in climbing after filming the movie, she used many of the same techniques for a short performance in the 1995 Dustin Hoffman thriller *Outbreak*, the story of a pandemic that envelopes the nation. Joyner plays a young mother and victim of the virus who gets ripped away from her family and taken away to die.

"I really tried to think to myself, 'How can I make this memorable? How can I take a small part and really do something with it?' I felt terror in both [roles]. I was striving for normalcy again. I was striving to pretend that everything was normal, even though it wasn't. I was trying to put a brave face on the situation for the sake of my children, who I was leaving and would never see again."

Millions of people, on the other hand, have seen Sarah's fall over the years; aside from grossing over $80 million in the United States and passing a quarter-billion around the globe, *Cliffhanger* is still a common sight on television. Recently, the film gained a new pair of critics: Joyner's twin sons.

"My kids hate watching it," she admits. "It's so hard to watch me go through that. I still have a hard time watching the film, especially with my family, my friends, my kids. It definitely still has an impact."

She's not doing well here, but Cimber (Anna Katarina) and her squad managed to come out on top in 1989's *The Blood of Heroes*.

Anna Katarina: *Death of the Incredible Hulk/Blood of Heroes*

THE LEADER, THE MAESTRO, the Absorbing Man, and even the Abomination couldn't get it done in decades of comic pages.

Military agents, societal outcasts, even typical good guys like cops and scientists failed on a weekly basis for nearly five full years of TV shows.

Through four big screen appearances in this millennium alone, no one can boast of the accomplishment.

Just one person can. Someone without a single superpower, who'd hardly heard of the target in question before battling him, who'd never so much as held a gun before using an oversized type to finish out one of the impossibilities of Marvel comic action.

"I killed the Hulk!" crows Anna Katarina. Take *that*, General Ross!

Before the days of CGI, tons of muscle and enough makeup to, well, coat the massive mesomorph were all producers had to make the Incredible One, and Lou Ferrigno fit the bill (although not the clothes!) from 1977 to 1982 on *The Incredible Hulk* TV show. But the series ended with just a normal episode, rather than a conclusive period, so few were much satisfied.

Not to worry; Ferrigno and Bill Bixby as his human starting point David Banner (maybe *he* was the *Hulk*'s alter ego here—perhaps Banner was just a puny human the Hulk de-morphed into when he had the nerve to relax!) brought the man of green back in extended small screen feature form in *The Incredible Hulk Returns* in 1988 and *The Trial of the Incredible Hulk*, featuring a cameo by comic god Stan Lee, the next year.

That was about the same time that Katarina's career started to take off. "I had acted since I was a child in Switzerland," she remembers. "I love the craft, to transform and morph into somebody else. To become something else, to explore other characters, other circumstances, and relationships was an endlessly fascinating, never-ending process." Her big-screen vocation began in 1989 with *The Blood of Heroes*, a tale we'll return to in a few paragraphs.

For now, let's go back to the Hulk. As *The Death of the Incredible Hulk* arrived in February 1990, his fans hoped the title wasn't true. Bixby's Banner, still looking for a cure for his illness (albeit one that many would probably not mind being infected with!) falls in love with Russian bombshell Jasmin (Elizabeth Gracen), herself bullied into one more job by her boss, who's holding her sister Bella captive. Katarina was the hostage.

"I think a lot of humans have big secrets," she explains. "As you learn the lines, you go deeper into the psyche of the character, and you answer any questions for yourself. I ask myself questions as the character: what's my relationship to my sister, to the Hulk? Where do I come from? What am I fighting for? What are the events?" Just about all of those answers would become clear, but not in the way superhero movies usually do.

Bella was behind the whole thing all along, and she and her right-hand man look about to fly to freedom. His strength and speed and his effectiveness, the Hulk chases down the plane and breaks in as liftoff commences.

Unfortunately, Bella's as prepared as a villainess can be; she blasts the shit out of him with a huge gun, a slightly miniaturized AK-47 sort of thing. He manages to blow up the plane, but smashes into the concrete below. Back in Banner mode, he gasps out a near-sigh of relief to Jasmin, his journey at an end.

"Bill Bixby was a dream," Katarina remembers (sadly, Bixby died of cancer three years later, at just age 59). "It was unique to play a terrorist. I had to find a vulnerability, then struggle for hardness that overcomes that feeling of being human."

That act alone would be enough to warrant Katarina's inclusion in any kind of action actressing debate, but she'd gotten further down and a hell of a lot dirtier in *Heroes*. Down in that her Big Cimber lady was stuck in the stereotypical post-war world that so many in the genre are forced to venture through. Dirty in her being a very willing participant in the impromptu battle royals that become their only form of real entertainment.

It's called The Game. Simple, and yet so dangerous. Attired in all kinds of makeshift armor and brandishing clubs that can hurt somebody five different ways in one swing, teams from each village whoop ass on each other, all the while trying to "score" by placing a dog skull on the opposing team's marker.

And we thought rugby was confusing and dangerous.

"You can find so much in every part, even if you don't see it right off the bat," says Katarina. "The fact that I was a woman, fighting for survival with scars on my face, there was a lot I could play and find. I was lucky to be alive, wandering through these villages that had died out."

Cimber's the squad's main gal, until a young lady named Kidda (Joan Chen) shows up, leaving bodies in her trail. It's the spark the team needs to make it to the Nine Cities, who hang on to the world's only remaining riches and don't plan to let go.

"They gave us personal trainers to get strong physically," says Katarina, teamed with Delroy Lindo, Rutger Hauer, Vincent D'Onofrio, and others on the team. "We were trained very severely every day. We started a month before we traveled [filming was in Australia], and we trained there too. There was a lot of conditioning and strength training to familiarize ourselves with these weird weapons, wearing clothes made from tires. They'd been the only thing that didn't burn in the catastrophe."

Her squad makes it to the Cities, surrounded by a huge crowd, cheering its heart out, probably betting on the outcome. Two years before, we'd seen a similar tale in *The Running Man*; today's audiences would probably equate it as a darker form of *The Hunger Games*.

In the final battle, up against a guy twice her height and width, Cimber takes about the worse beating of the squad, but her opponent will know he's been in a brawl for a long time as well.

"My main opponent was a former wrestler," she remembers. "He went to town, and I had to go to town. He forgot that I am a woman. That was a little challenging. I was a little worried about that. But we had a very good stunt coordinator." She's on the sidelines for the final battle, but her team comes out ahead, and, just as boxers, UFC brawlers, and even members of underground fight clubs can nearly kill each other and still hug it out afterward, the film's credits roll amid cheers and congratulations.

And surprisingly enough, that's still reality. The sport commonly labeled Jugger has become a college league sport in Germany, and it's spread up and down Europe—and, not surprisingly, its Australian birthplace—occasionally breaking into the United States (*Heroes*' teams are called Juggs, and the film was released as *The Salute of the Jugger* elsewhere in the world). International tournaments have been going on since 2006, including Colorado's Mile

High Tournament in 2015. Rules tend to vary by country, but most games stick pretty closely to *Heroes*—minus the blood, of course!

Katarina can't explain it. Probably no one can.

"It's fascinating," she says. "Maybe because you have to put a lot of your own strengths and strategies into it, or maybe because it's so very original. Maybe it's that people like to put themselves in the minds of folks that live in the future."

In April 1999, two seemingly normal teenagers murdered over a dozen people and broke America's heart in the Columbine High massacre. Four years later, Andre Keuck (left) and Cal Robertson dramatized the months leading up to the attack in *Zero Day*.

Andre Keuck: *Zero Day*

As HIS SCHOOL YEAR rolled toward an end in April 1999, Andre Keuck piled up the top priorities of any eighth-grader.

Like escaping from the rigors of middle school. Then plotting out a high-class summer. Soon, ensuring that the high school he'd venture into that fall would never know what hit it.

"I had to go to a high school earlier that day," he recalls. "I did this every day. When I got back, I would normally check in at the administrator's office and then just walk back to class."

But something was different this time. Something was wrong.

"A teacher escorted me," Keuck says. "That had never happened before. I asked why she had to walk me to my class, and she was very mum."

A similar mood had overtaken his classmates. No one knew much yet, but it was clear that something very big, very bad, and very sad had happened. Something that would ruin countless lives and break America's heart—and, even more tragically, not for close to the last time.

Earlier that day, two students had walked into Colorado's Columbine High School, ready to launch the kind of attack that takes all kinds of time to plan, and, unfortunately, doesn't only happen in nightmares. With distractive explosive devices and the types of guns one needs special permits to purchase, Eric Harris and Dylan Klebold had murdered thirteen people and hurt over twenty more before taking their own lives. It was the deadliest school shooting in the nation's history, a mark that would sadly be broken.

"Everyone was terrified that it was going to happen at their school," Keuck says. In the two decades since, more students have walked into school and never left. More administrators have helplessly watched as their kids and teachers were used for target practice. More parents have said a morning goodbye to their children, never knowing that it would be for the last time.

In the midst of his own high school career, Keuck went the common route for budding performers, doing Shakespeare in Connecticut. Flipping through *Backstage Magazine*, something of a biblical periodical for those in his profession, he noticed a basic ad that carried so much more meaning between its lines.

"It talked about auditions for a coming-of-age film," Keuck claims. "I e-mailed my information. I didn't think much of it."

Some time later, he and classmate Cal Robertson heard the welcome word of callback. But auditions would get going within days, and the film's protagonists would be doing their thing with very much of little: time, camera work, special effects. It's all part of the excruciatingly tough "induction" process for those new to the business.

But every young performer gets used to that. The toughest part of *Zero Day*'s storyline would be telling it, showing it, and finding out the whole story about everything that led up to that horrible Colorado tragedy.

Keuck and Robertson would become the dramatized (probably not by much) versions of Harris and Klebold. We'd see, and they'd tell, with most of the 2003 movie in self-filmed mode, just how and why the massacre came off. Their names would only slightly be altered (both went by their real first names, only the last monikers manipulated), but that's about all.

In as matter-of-fact and laid back a manner as if they were prepping for an exam, Andre's Andre and Cal's Cal spend nearly a year plotting out the attack. Casually deciding what guns to use, and how to snare them. Who and when and where to kill. Chatting about when to do it for maximum effect, and what should be done afterward. Harris and Klebold did the same thing, all on tape, in the months before the massacre.

"I just worked off the script and went more from the standpoint of *telling* a character," Keuck explains. "To a degree, he had to be sort of a likeable character, normal, fundamentally, in almost every other way. If you play it as some kind of caricature, you're doing a disservice to everyone involved. I didn't want to make him grim or morbid."

Whether such was the common mindset of Harris and Klebold depends on who is telling the story. Still, this is high school. It's the teenage years, where instability is commonplace and mindsets and intentions shift with the wind. The typical student doesn't really exist. Sometimes the most popular, smartest kids in class have dark secrets that come straight to light.

Sometimes the most carefree, likeable people on campus get too overwhelmed with demons attacking from the inside.

And, as students at Columbine, Virginia Tech, Sandy Hook, and everywhere else that the wrong student(s) have gotten hold of the wrong weaponry keep finding out, that person that they sit next to every day and might have eaten lunch with that afternoon might just become the next person to write a new name in the dark pages of history.

When things like this happen, everyone always turns into a Monday morning quarterback. After the Columbine tragedies occurred, so many people just had to have something, someone still around, to blame.

It had to be because they played violent video games, like *Doom*, or some other first-person shooter. It must have been because they watched those movies that show the bad guys getting violently killed. It was all Marilyn Manson's fault, wasn't it?

Zero Day told another story. Take away the drama, even much from the outside at all, and you have the worst display of Occam's Razor.

"The thing that I remember most was that they didn't try to give any reason or excuses for the way things were," Keuck says. "There are allusions to videos games and movies and pop culture, but the point of this movie was not about why it happened or how to stop it, but the way that you can glimpse at their lives. It was honest in the sense that it wasn't some 26-year-old film school grad trying to say, 'Hey, this is how it is.'"

The way these kids talk, the way they plan it all out, there doesn't seem to be any real justification for their act, other than they feel like it's just the right thing to do. That, yes, people will die, but it's OK for some reason. They talk in a way that military troops might discuss going into battle; the less we know about the enemies, or at least the opposition, the easier they will be to kill.

Not much doubt to it, no second thoughts. Just the mentality that everyone is here for a purpose, with a goal, and this just happens to be the two of theirs.

"We decide who lives and who dies," Andre (the character) calmly explains. "Their puny little lives will have meaning, and they're going to thank us. We're not trying to waste anybody's life, just to show that their lives have value. It's the most respectful, most loving thing we could ever do." A heartbreaking scene shows him directly spelling out which guns to use for this specific purpose—which one would give him the most shots before a brave soul takes him down, for example.

There's talk about bullying to an extent, but schools aren't Utopia, and never have been. These guys have something else in mind, something as moral as mass murder can be.

The cretins who shot up Columbine that sad day might just have had that mindset. They might even be right. Not because they caused the school survivors to find some zest for life, at least not to any measureable extent, but more because the names of Eric Harris and Dylan Klebold were the ones that everyone crowed, and still do, far before anyone else who never walked out. We remember the killers before the killed.

Finally, it came time to reenact that horrific day. We see the two heading up to the school, stepping out of their car, and heading in, packing for tragedy. Now the home videos end.

"We'd spent an entire summer shooting this casual movie," Keuck explains, "and then that day comes along, and there's a dozen or two dozen crew members, and all these other actors. It became a much bigger deal very quickly. We weren't really aware of the gravity of what we were building towards, but then you start to think about the real implications of what you're filming, and it becomes very overwhelming."

There are far too many web sites today that allow anyone who can type to see the real massacre up close, the school security cameras telling the terrifying story of so many students launched into a world of terror by two young men and several guns. Keuck and Robertson, along with the rest of *Day*'s crew, acted out the same steps the Columbine shooters had taken, strolling through the cafeteria and library, picking off those who just happened to be in the wrong place. It looks like everything's going about to plan for them, as it did in 1999. Having a gun in your hand tends to override your sanity with savagery, and we hear Cal screaming a bit, but, again, this is just what needs happening, in their eyes. Soon it's just them, and a few bodies.

"You're amped up on all this adrenalin, screaming, with all the people, these normal kids, it's very jarring," Keuck remembers of filming. "After the first hour, everybody just kind of fell into this very strange acceptance of what we're doing and recording. A lot of that emotion fell away, and you're in a bubble for the rest of the day."

Knowing all along that this would be how it would end, Andre and Cal have another sadly stoic debate as to the right way to follow the same path they'd just sent so many ("Should we count to three, and *then* shoot?"). Following in the shooters' steps one last time, the two spend their last bullets on themselves.

"Even harder than shooting it was having to show it to my parents for the first time," remembers Keuck, whose parents Gerhard and Johanne played Andre's folks in the movie. "As a parent, you're watching this, and it looks just like what you saw on the news recently. To watch them go through that, even knowing that it's fake, seeing their kid behave in such a manner, it has an effect."

As a teacher, you're looked to for example. Guidance through times to which you have no clue how to respond. Answers to questions no one should have to ask.

Your students look to you for these things every day, and when you can't provide them, you just feel like one more failure in a society full of them.

Years before Columbine, teachers across America experienced just that, and have too many times afterward. We'd already felt it in March of 1998, when two students, including an *eleven-year-old*, killed five people and injured ten at Arkansas' Westside Middle School. Less than two months later, an Oregon teenager killed his parents and went to Thurston High School, where he murdered two more and wounded twenty-three.

And it didn't stop with Columbine. In March 2005, in Red Lake, Minnesota, a teenager killed his grandfather, a family friend, a teacher, a security guard, and five of his classmates at Red Lake Senior High School. Then there was the Sandy Hook tragedy. People who should be worried about driver's licenses and prom dates continue to demonstrate the worst humanity has.

Again and again, students keep coming to us and asking why, and we can't answer. They look for comfort, and we can't even find it ourselves. It's a hard thing to look a student in the eye and admit that you don't know.

"I'll go on my killing spree against anyone I want. More crazy, deeper in the spiral, lost highway repeating, dwelling on the beautiful past.... All people I ever might have loved have abandoned me. My parents piss me off and hate me ... [they] want me to have fuckin ambition! How can I when I get screwed and destroyed by everything?"

In the near-two decades since the Columbine Massacre, millions have read those words all over the Internet. Long before social networking entered the mainstream, online blogs and journals were all over the web, giving the mind a place to empty itself, something that would listen when no person would.

An avid user of such rant landings, Klebold blasted his thoughts into the 'Net—and the paragraph above was written a *full year and a half* before he and Harris turned a dark fantasy to reality.

"I remembered seeing pictures of these guys, and thinking that they kind of looked like me and my friends," recalls Kett Turton, also in high school at the time of the tragedy. "We were in a high school clique, with the black jackets and the punk rock influence, holding a certain position in the social pecking order."

We wish we could have read those words, and the ones Harris put out, and have seen something coming. But we can't. A search engine can find hundreds, even millions such entries all over the web—written, acted out in videos, whatever. Sometimes they're much worse than that. These writings, the eerily detailed report on Charles Manson that Klebold turned in early in the year, his creative writing assignment about a man on a shooting spree that brought his family in for a conference ... signs, yes, but far from certain, and no one should feel guilty about "missing" them.

Like the Second Amendment, which comes into debate every time these shootings occur, there have been instances where we wonder if our right to freedom of speech is really worth it. But we can't just point to one entry and say, "Hey, that person's planning a real spree!"

What we *can* do, though, is learn, to make something positive out of the worst of situations. Yes, lessons like this sometimes can only be learned from tragedy, but they might prevent another. In 2002, Turton saw a chance to tell a side of the story that we as people often try very hard to ignore.

"We needed to understand why someone would do something like that," he explains. "There's so much ugliness in our society, and we like to separate ourselves from that, but we need to take a look at why these things happen and why we do these things to ourselves." With this in mind, he got set to become a dramatized form of Harris and Klebold (albeit not to the extent of *Zero Day*) in *Heart of America*, a sadly ironic title if one there ever was.

"I say kill mankind," Harris scribbled in the summer of 1998. "No one should survive. We all live in lies. The human race isn't worth fighting for, only worth killing." Turton found these vitriolic spewings and so many others on the net.

"I read as much of that as I could," he remembers. "You find bits of experiences from the character, what moves you. It's an imagination game, where you collect pieces of material and see where your brain takes you."

With just a few hours left in the school year at Riverside High, the sad but sadly common happenings are all on the attendance sheet. Teachers losing it on students and parents who can't be bothered to care, drugs finding their way in, broken hearts aflutter, and, of course, the ever-present cancer of bullying.

It was as everyday to Turton's Daniel Lynn as gym class and study hall. It was a sad flashback to reality for the performer himself.

"It was nothing like in the film," he quickly asserts (Daniel's abused by both the school douchebags and his idiot father), "but it was there. I was a bit of a geek, not an athlete or anything." With nowhere to turn and nothing to try, Daniel's only worried about taking some local scum down with him.

Just as Harris had been.

"I have a goal to destroy as much as possible," he wrote early in the 1998-9 school year, "so I must not be sidetracked by my feelings of sympathy, mercy, or any of that, so I will force myself to believe that everyone is just another monster . . . so it's either me or them. I have to turn off my feelings. Keep this in mind: I want to burn the world."

We'd seen Daniel going through the same preparation methods the self-deemed Trenchcoat Mafia had used. Filming in an abandoned mental hospital fixed into Riverside, Turton's fellow followed one of his main enemies into a restroom, ready to settle the score forever.

But he couldn't, not right away. Neither could Turton, himself armed with a real, albeit doctored, firearm.

"With a real gun, even filed down and broken down," he claims, "holding one made me very nervous. It has an effect on you. You can't do that without clicking into the scene."

Actors in Action

Daniel Lynn (Kett Turton) took the worst kind of final revenge against his classmate bullies in 2002's *Heart of America*.

"This is pathetic!" Daniel blares. "And this is your fault! How weak am I now?"

But he doesn't shoot, not yet. Instead, Daniel starts with an impromptu veterinary lesson.

"What happens when you kick a dog one too many times?" he inquires. He starts to shake, what little control he has starting to disappear.

Was this all for nothing? Is the target, himself starting to grin, going to escape? Even Treton wasn't certain during warmups.

"With that monologue, I couldn't figure out why he would stand there with a gun," he explains, "because someone could walk in. He had to get up the nerve to pull the trigger."

Finally Daniel gives his canine puzzle's answer.

"They bite!" he snarls. The gun goes off, and even he seems surprised. His prey falls.

The first time's the hardest with this. Storming down the hall, Daniel meets some of his adversary's colleagues.

No words this time. No hesitation. Just enough lead to send them six feet down.

One-bettering wasn't the objective here, but that's all the killing Daniel's here to do (remember, this wasn't as much of a Columbine dramatization as *Zero Day* had been).

Except for himself. Just as Harris, Klebold, and so many others ended, his final theft is of his own life.

"High school can be miserable," Turton says. "I felt like it was an important thing, to tell the story from the point of view of this kid who doesn't know anything. He's sort of awkward, naïve, the sort of person you wouldn't think twice about, who felt he had to go out and do these horrible things. When someone commits violence, it's because they feel they're threatened, and this applies to the bullies themselves—in the movie at least, though I feel this hold true in real life. Daniel is in the same boat as his aggressors, he just can't see this because they keep beating him up."

Ironically, while bullying is commonly cited as a reason for these shootings, and rightfully so, it didn't seem to be the case at Columbine. Assuming, of course, that Harris' word means a damn thing.

"Do not blame anybody else besides me and [Klebold] for this," reads his journal entry from April 1998, nearly a year before the shooting. "Don't blame my family. They had no clue and there is nothing they could have done. They brought me up just fucking fine . . . don't blame the school." Ironically enough, the same entry discussed his hopes to crash a plane into New York City, which some other group of cretins would act out in Sept. 2001.

"Just because we went on a killing spree doesn't mean everyone else will . . . if there is any way in this fucked up universe we can come back as ghosts or what the fuck ever, we will haunt the life out of anyone who blames anyone besides me and [Klebold]."

He'd start off evil and stay there for a film and a half, but Richard Kiel's Jaws ended up as James Bond's ally in 1979's *Moonraker*.

Richard Kiel

As I sit here at my living room coffee table writing this (September 10, 2014), I read that Richard Kiel has passed away. Just days before his 75th birthday, just days before appearing at a film convention, and just a week after doing a radio show with his on-screen nemesis and eventual pal Roger Moore, one of the film world's most gentle giants is suddenly gone forever. Let's put everything else on hold for a moment and give this fellow the credit he deserves (as, just hours after his death, tons of others already are all over social media doing so).

James Bond's legendary battles with Jaws carried the superspy through two movies—well, one and a half, as the big man was a good guy by the end of the second one—but even though Jaws was still a strong, stoic, and silent villain (must have been tough to talk with those huge, metal teeth), people already were cheering for him. Walking out of Jaws' first appearance in 1977's *The Spy Who Loved Me*, filmmaker Lewis Gilbert's grandson turned to him.

"Grandpa, I like Jaws!" the youngster said. "Why does he have to be such a bad guy? Why can't he be a goodie?" The kid was one of many—this guy would be the rare anti-hero that loses the term's prefix; much like a pro wrestler that the fans happen to cheer, he'd switch sides.

The Bond film franchise is one of the most well known in cinema lore, not just action. For nearly half a century, actors from Sean Connery to Moore to Pierce Brosnan to Daniel Craig—and that's just as of this writing; the future will undoubtedly bring others—have brought the secret agent to the big screen, and audiences can almost always be counted on to respond favorably at the box-office.

But since no hero can truly earn his title without someone on the other side, the series would never have worked had it not been for those on the other side: the villains, the baddies, the slick geniuses who Bond, often with help, always finds a way to foil just before the ending credits roll.

And to that regard, one in particular stands out—in more than a few ways.

Between battles with Gene Wilder on a train one day in the 1976 action-comedy *Silver Streak* (the evil killer is a common role for those over seven feet tall and 300 pounds, as acromegaly sufferers tend to reach all too quickly), Kiel got a call saying that a fellow named Cubby Broccoli wanted to have a bite with him the next day.

"I said, 'Cubby who?'" Kiel recalled. "[The assistant director] replied, 'Cubby Broccoli, the James Bond producer.'" Kiel may not have recognized the first name, but the longtime Bond fan certainly nailed the second (Broccoli, whose first name was actually Alfred, produced fourteen Bond pictures, ending with 1995's *Goldeneye*).

Still, hearing Broccoli's pitch, the actor wasn't quite sure what to think. He heard about Jaws, a silent character with steel teeth that could become deadly weapons with the slightest chomp. The giant henchman would be Bonds' new tormentor, picking up where Odd Job, Francisco Scaramanga, and Dr. Kananga left off in *The Spy Who Loved Me*.

Kiel almost said no. Just in time, he stayed quiet.

"For a moment," he admitted, "I thought, 'Here I am, working in a major motion picture, playing a killer on a train who talks and has scenes with Gene Wilder. Why consider playing a monster role?'"

Then he took a moment. After all, Jaws had to be better than portraying Bigfoot in *National Geographic* specials and having to wear thick contact lenses and have his entire body painted green to play the Incredible Hulk, both of which Kiel had done in the past (he'd been the original choice to play the comic book superhero before being replaced by the legendary Lou Ferrigno).

Though Kiel had been a frequent sight on television and the movies—his hilarious crying scene in the 1974 Burt Reynolds football dramedy *The Longest Yard* being a particular scene-stealer—the starring spotlight hadn't quite shined on him.

"Before I said anything, another thought passed through my mind," Kiel said. "This is a James Bond movie. Why not try and make the best of it?" Eventually, he agreed, heading off to London for the fitting of Jaws' infamous teeth, then to Cairo for the filming. As a footnote, many credit—or blame—the Jaws oral decoration for the "bling" gold and silver tooth designs known as "grills" so common in the rap music and urban world of today.

As Jaws, Kiel found himself shoved out of a train, had a building fall on him, got in a car crash, was electrocuted, and just about everything else that Bond usually does to those who get in his way of saving the world—all still without ever wrinkling his suit, and always with enough left over to bed the gorgeous gal just before the closing credits role.

Long before the film hit screens across America, the entertainment world's insiders gathered at MGM Studios to check out the premiere. Sitting in the audience—probably in the back, not entirely fair but commonplace for the seven-foot-plus population—Kiel wasn't sure what would happen.

"The Jaws character even scared me when [Bond love interest] Barbara Bach opened up the closet in the compartment on her train and I was in there," he remembered. "They threw in a loud train-whistle blast at the same moment they . . . cut to Jaws' mouth filled with those ghastly teeth, and I jumped out of my seat like everyone else."

But what Kiel especially wanted to know was whether he'd see himself live or die. Bond villains rarely made it through to the next film, but studio execs had predicted that Jaws might have something never really seen, or felt, before in the Bond franchise.

Near the end, Jaws is dropped into shark-infested water, which has already claimed one victim during the film—think it was intentional to have a guy named Jaws go toe-to-fin with a shark in the finale? Kiel had filmed himself chewing on the shark to beat it at its own game, then a scene of his escape, as Jaws pops out of the water and comes to shore. But even as the film rolled, Kiel didn't know if the producers would bring him back. He watched Bond and Anya (Bach) escape as explosions blast, and everyone waited for the credits to pass before them.

Then Kiel, and the rest of the crowd, saw Jaws do something that no anti-Bond man had ever done: survive. The giant strolled out of the water, hardly the worse for wear and ready for a sequel and Jackie Chan in the top two roles, and the main villain now Yu Rongguang's Master Li.

"The audience cheers and applauds, and I was absolutely dumbstruck by the reaction of the crowd," Kiel said. "After seventeen years of struggling as a working actor, I was suddenly an overnight success. I knew at that moment that I had finally made it big in the movies."

So everyone knew that Jaws would be back for another shot at Bond. But no one, at least not until the first script reading, knew what direction the character would take. Hundreds, even thousands, followed in the aforementioned grandson's thought process, as letters poured into the studio offices, asking for a chance to really cheer the man who'd set out to be hated.

Two years later, Moore, Kiel, and the rest of the cast set out to make *Moonraker*, the next addition to the Bond franchise. It was the story of Bond's battle with Hugo Drax (Michael Lonsdale), who steals a nuclear warhead and prepares to wipe out Bond and the rest of the Earth's population—except, of course, for his chosen few, those that, in a plot eerily reminiscent of Hitler's Aryan fascination, represent the best in looks and intellect. Like Kanaga before him, Drax enlists Jaws' help to carry out the plan.

Oh, Jaws starts out up to his old tricks, tossing Bond out of a plane without a parachute, only to have Bond steal Jaws' chute—realism has never been a key component with the 007 franchise—and send Jaws toppling through a conveniently placed circus tent and into a net. Later, Jaws chomps through a cable car's steel rope (really made of licorice), leaving Bond and, in a name that probably wouldn't make it into a screenplay today (well, maybe it would—there *was* a lady named Pussy Galore in 1964's *Goldfinger*), Dr. Holly Goodhead teetering on the side of death.

"Hang on!" Goodhead (Lois Chiles) shouts to Bond.

"The thought had occurred to me," he responds, in one of the hilarious one-liners that made the Bond character such a hit with pop culture. Not surprisingly, the two manage to escape, and Jaws is buried under a crushed building.

This time, however, he doesn't have to make it out alone—and here's where one of the most controversial issues of the film came to light.

Kiel knew that he'd have a love interest in the film, but he wasn't sure who it would be. Sitting down with the producers, Kiel learned that Jaws' girl would be able to look him in the eye.

"In my early years, everyone was always trying to fix me up with the tallest girl they knew," he recalls. "I had nothing against tall girls, but I didn't like the idea that I had to date only the tallest girls in town." Kiel's wife Diane is just over five feet.

The giantess would pull Jaws out of the cable car wreckage and win his heart, and that part was fine. But it was later that things wouldn't work, as far as Kiel could see.

After Jaws captures Bond and Goodhead and traps them in Drax's spaceship, Drax discusses his plan to eliminate the imperfections of humanity from the earth, preserving a master race. Jaws suddenly realizes that his new girl will be one of the exterminated.

"A 7'4" woman who could yank him out of the wreckage didn't need Jaws' help," Kiel says. "She could save herself." Kiel suggested a shorter gal, using his wife as proof that the match could work. French star Blanche Ravelec won the part, and even more than that.

Her Dolly saves Jaws from the mess, and his eyes and smile widen in a way that filmmakers hadn't seen before. Under his dark persona, and about five feet below his iron incisors, Jaws had a heart of gold. In the climactic fight seen, Jaws teams up with Bond to destroy Drax and his operation, and, as the space station disintegrates around them, Jaws and Dolly sit down for what may be their last moments together.

In the end, love managed to get Jaws to do the one thing he hadn't yet accomplished in nearly two films' worth of screen time: speak.

"Well, here's to us!" he warmly quotes, as the two clink together some champagne. But this Bond film, like all the others, has a very happy ending, as the module holding the two floats away from the station, and everyone is rescued.

And Kiel would get to be a goodie again over a decade later, playing Adam Sandler's protective former boss in the 1996 dark golf comedy *Happy Gilmore*, then spoofing Jaws as a metal-mouthed fellow the same year in *Inspector Gadget* and voicing a warm-hearted thug in 2010's *Tangled* (he nearly got the role of the giant Fezzik in 1987's *The Princess Bride* that Andre the Giant made immortal).

Many don't have a high opinion of the media and the way it allows us to barge into others' privacy, the up-to-the-second coverage it carries. But if there's one benefit we can take advantage of, it's the high-speed ability of we the readers to log onto social networks like Facebook, Twitter, and other sites and pay our own tributes to people like Kiel (just as we had in the past month alone, as the losses of Joan Rivers, Lauren Bacall, and Robin Williams had already rocked us recently—and, in the saddest type of irony, Moore himself passed away in May 2017, just before this piece went to press). Looking over the countless tributes that immediately piled in for him, just as they did for them, it's something that we can take pride in.

And, something just wants to tell me, that somewhere else, maybe better, Kiel's a proud man too.

John Kreese (Martin Kove, left) became a bully to everyone he'd meet through three *Karate Kid* films.

Martin Kove: *Karate Kid*

FAILURE WAS A PIECE of foreign language. Not even a choice.

In years of one of the toughest sports around, he'd never felt it. He'd been the best around in high school and college. Karate doesn't have much in the way of pro ranks, at least on NFL and NBA levels, but he'd just have to find the same success with similar skills elsewhere.

Like maybe across the globe. In both World Wars and many others, hundreds of thousands of young men had charged straight into battle, roaring and bleeding patriotism, and John Kreese would be next, he and his American brothers ready to go to Vietnam and beat down the Vietcong and Communism, both enemies to his home of the free and the brave.

But it hadn't happened for Kreese. It hadn't happened for his country. America had started right in 'Nam, cheered on by Kreese's countrymen and welcomed by our allies. But as years went by and so many didn't come home alive or at all, we'd turned against the war. By the time the last troops left in the summer of 1973, the winners, the losers, and even the goal were all too cloudy to recognize. It will forever be considered one of the darkest spots of American history.

Kreese had made it back, but something brand new had followed him, and it wasn't letting go: defeat. What it means to lose. He'd never felt it before, and after so long a buildup, it was too large for even someone so strong (physically, at least) to get rid of.

"Our boys weren't successful in Vietnam," explains Martin Kove. "It was the wrong war. He suffered from that, and when he came back, he vowed that he would never lose again, ever."

We've just read the backstory that Kove wrote for the man he'd elevate to sports film villainy. This might sound strange to karate's unacquainted, but the sport's not about fighting and never has been. Self-development, physical fitness, concentration, all of these come far before combative objectives.

But not for Kreese, and, ultimately, not for his students. It was all he had left, and he'd use it for whatever reason he wanted.

And it worked: long before Daniel Larusso and his mom arrived in the *Karate Kid* (1984) timeline, Kreese had turned the local Cobra Kai class into one of San Francisco's top attractions for young men.

"He taught the Cobrai Kai, 'You must be triumphant, no matter what goes on in your life,'" Kove says. "'There's no excuse for losing, under any circumstances.' That's why he seemed to be such a dark character: not evil, just a man with a destiny never to surrender, to lose any battle, what he experienced in Vietnam." For the first chunk of *The Karate Kid*, it appears his methods will keep working, even after Daniel hooks up with mysterious maintenance man Mr. Miyagi, carrying a few secrets of his own; Pat Morita's performance there was beyond legendary—as great as Haing Ngor was in *The Killing Fields*, who edged Morita for the Oscar, Miyagi was one of those characters that will *never* be forgotton.

By the time *Kid* came about, Kove had been in the midst of small-screen action on *Cagney and Lacey* for a few years. "I thought the script was good," Kove recalls, "but I thought [Kreese] was just another heavy." Still, even heavies take time to prepare for, as Kove had found playing a shambling cop in *Last House on the Left* (1972) and a crazed driver three years later in *Death Race 2000*.

He wouldn't have said luxury here. Told he had a few days to get ready, Kove prepped to epitomize badness and badassedness in once high kick.

The next day, his agent called. "She said they wanted to see me that day at noon, and it was now or never!" Kove remembers. "I was so pissed off, and my then-wife told me to use that." He imagined storming up and down Kreese's dojo, treating the Kai in a way that would make drill sergeants say, "Wow, he's *harsh*!"

Then he rolled in and got ready to explain a few things. About a decade before, John Avildsen had turned the story of a Philadelphia club fighter into film legend. Now he looked for Daniel-San to have the same effect in a different sport.

"I went right in with veteran's energy," Kove says. "I screamed at John Avildsen: 'You know, we wait for years to meet directors of your caliber! We fire our agents, we fire our managers, and all that stuff!'

"'And you're a real asshole, John!' He was cool with being called an asshole. I got all worked up, and he liked my audacity."

Over the next few weeks, Kreese, Morita, and Daniel-in-training Ralph Macchio worked with Pat Johnson, himself a black belt under Chuck Norris.

"It was three different entities," Kove recalls. "I copied his *kiai* strikes." Kiai is the term for that vocal boost that karate participants give to their strikes, often stereotyped as "Hi-yah!"

But Kreese's lines would push the character from just a jerk to outward cold-heartedness. They'd intimidate Johnny Lawrence, Dutch, Bobby, and the rest of the Kai into top-notch, even dangerous performance.

"We do not train to be merciful here," he asserts. "Mercy is for the weak. A man confronts you, he is the enemy. An enemy deserves no mercy."

The script, Kove says, "was written so well that I always condescended to [the Kai]. I was always a bully to them, always very offensive to anyone who asked a question. They were all very submissive. The chemistry worked. They always had a huge respect for both Martin Kove and John Kreese, and it helped me maintain character at all times."

Right down next to "No mercy," Kreese's order to Lawrence to "Sweep the leg," during his final match against Daniel became one of the most frighteningly memorable moments of the 80s. But Kove calls a later one his personal top choice.

Just before Daniel's crane kick conclusion, Kreese shouts once more to his protégé.

"Finish him!" he calls. Hey, maybe that's where the makers of *Mortal Kombat* got their game's infamous line!

"'No mercy' and 'Sweep the leg' are the most classic lines that I repeat," Kove says. "I sign them on autographs, and people always love it. But 'Finish him!' was my favorite line. I was doing it on the sound stage because it needed to be louder. I loved the intention of what was going on there at the height of the battle. All those moments worked."

The next year, Kove played another 'Nam vet, acting out Ericson in *Rambo: First Blood Part II*. Then Kreese came back.

Karate Kid II (1986) took two years to make it back to theaters. In terms of timeline, it starts moments after the first one.

In a scene originally written to end the original, Kreese confronts Miyagi in the parking lot outside, and age beats attitude. Kreese's fists lose the battle against some car windows, and Miyagi wins against him.

"We were waiting to shoot that back in 1984, and then they decided not to shoot it, wanting to end the movie in the tournament," he remembers. "Years later, in the same parking lot, I blasted my hands through real glass. I had shards sticking in my wrists and everything. I taped it up and dealt with it." With Miyagi and Daniel in Japan for much of the second film, Kreese wouldn't be there for long. In Part 3 of 1989, however, he'd return with assistance.

Not the Kai; he'd lost everything there after the first film. It was local dollar-hound Terry

Silver (a debuting Thomas Ian Griffith), home from 'Nam because Kreese had allowed it. With Kreese's skills and Silver's green, the two had one last chance to take down the kid who'd destroyed Kreese.

"*Karate Kid 3* was a drag," Kove admits. "I was doing the show *Hard Time on Planet Earth*, so I couldn't do the movie the way it was written." In a show that lasted half a season (ironically ending less than two weeks before *Kid 3*'s premiere), Kreese's military officer was up against forces across the galaxy, forcing the film crew to create a new villain.

"A new guy came in, and they put me on vacation," he says. "You can't take Darth Vader out of *Star Wars*." Audiences agreed, as the film was, well, short of successful.

"I did an interview for the film's 25th anniversary," Kove recalls, "and the interviewer said, 'If you were not so dark, the light on Miyagai and Ralph would not burn so brightly.' I thought that was very astute."

Morita and Miyagi came back in 1994 for *The Next Karate Kid* (Johnson did as well, choreographing all four *Karate Kid* films and the first few *Teenage Mutant Ninja Turtles* movies), which, per usual for any part four film, was repped as a decent enough film with no legitimate reason to be made. It did, however, help launch a career that lifted Hilary Swank to a pair of Oscars.

And speaking of "good but unnecessary," the original was remade in 2010, with Jaden Smith and Jackie Chan in the top two roles, and the main villain now Yu Rongguang's Master Li.

"At all the different panels, the autograph shows, the things I do," Kove explains, "I find that people identify with the movie because it's so well structured and written. The movie was written so well that people identified with the movie like you would a song. You have a high school sweetheart and you loved her, so whenever you hear *your* song, you make identifications. The movie was so identifiable. Adults take their kids, they watch it on video, it's endless, very exciting."

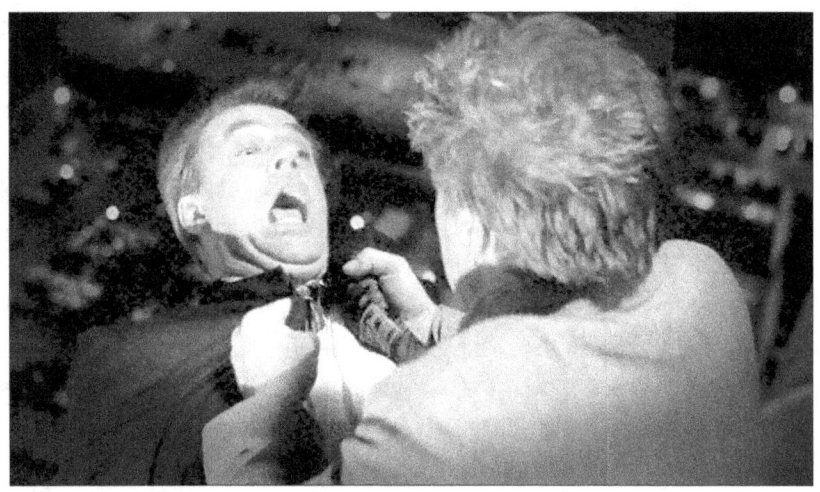

Harrison Ford's Richard Kimble (right) goes for revenge against his former friend Charles Nichols (Jeroen Krabbe) in the climactic moments of *The Fugitive* (1993).

Jeroen Krabbe: *The Fugitive*

AS HE STUMBLED AROUND, searching for the phone, Jeroen Krabbe feared the worst.

"No one calls you up at 3 a.m. in Holland," he recalls. "I thought, was something happening with my children? It was quite confusing."

Finally, he located the ringer and grabbed it up. Seconds later, he was breathing a sigh of relief.

Then he tensed up again.

The relief came because it was "only" his agent, offering him a role in a blockbuster film. The apprehension was because it entailed a trip to Chicago—the next day.

Over in America, Harrison Ford, Tommy Lee Jones, and Director Andrew Davis (not to mention Julianne Moore, who was just starting to break into the acting mainstream) were putting together a 1993 film version of the 1960s TV show *The Fugitive*, the story of Dr. Richard Kimble, wrongfully convicted in the murder of his wife, who escapes from prison and searches for the one-armed man that killed her.

Longtime actor Richard Jordan had been playing Kimble's friend Dr. Charles Nichols, who's secretly behind the entire crime, and filming was just about done. But before Nichols' final scenes could be made, Jordan had become ill with the brain tumor that would sadly take his life the next year, and a replacement needed to be found.

"My family was planning an Easter vacation to Italy," Krabbe says sadly, "and I had to inform them I was going away to Chicago."

Still, after decades in the theater and quite a bit of time on screen, even so little time can be enough for the seasoned performer, he continues.

"Being in drama school, and being on stage every bloody night for 25 years," he says, "that is where you really learn your craft. When you're confronted with something like this, when you have to jump right into it, it gives you a sense of security; you can think, 'No problem.'"

As he flew across the ocean, Krabbe checked over the screenplay, and recalled watching David Janssen play the role of Dr. Richard Kimble in the series. For four years, Janssen eluded Barry Morse's Lt. Phillip Gerard (whose rank was changed to a U.S. Marshal and first name to Samuel when Jones took the role) and the rest of law enforcement across the United States—twelve-year-old Kurt Russell played Gerard's son in one episode. The series' two-part finale in August 1967, was then the highest-rated episode in television history until eleven years later, when millions couldn't wait to learn who actually had pulled the trigger on J.R. Ewing.

"I remembered a lot of the show," Krabbe says. "When I was 16 or 17, it aired in Holland. I knew of the show, but was not really aware of the role I was to play. When I grabbed the script, I remembered everything."

Rushing off the plane, Krabbe headed straight to the film's makeup and wardrobe section. Then he bolted into action—that day, he and Ford filmed the scene where the title character meets his "friend" in a parking garage (remember, this is long before Kimble finds the truth).

"It was like jumping into a pool and not knowing how to swim," says Krabbe. "When I came on the set that day, I was very nervous. They had been filming for six months, and then I came on. They had done all the scenes with [Jordan], and now they had to do everything again. It must have been boring when I came on."

Then Ford, who according to Krabbe had requested him as Jordan's specific replacement, stepped forward and slipped a comforting arm around the man who'd become his best "friend."

"I'm going to help you," Ford said. "Don't worry." It was advice that Krabbe himself would never forget.

Fortunately, he quickly got a few days off to get into character.

"I had to wait for four or five days," Krabbe says. "I could really get into the script. I started thinking about role and preparing for the role.

"I thought, 'You should play the opposite, because it's much more surprising. You should play Harrison Ford's best friend, until the very end, in which everything shifts, and you find out what his real role is.' You should never play what's on the pages; always look for something hidden behind lines. That's what makes it interesting to watch."

Nichols keeps the audience, and Jones' obsessed lawman (in an Oscar-winning performance), in suspense throughout, refusing to help the authorities find his friend, while keeping his own secrets hidden.

"I had two confrontations with Tommy Lee Jones, and I could go either way," he says. "I could have played it with a question mark—is he lying? I thought I should play it completely honest; he's my best friend, and I just saw him, speaking with my eyes open." Nichols assures the detective that Kimble's an innocent man who'll never be found, subliminally letting them know that he wouldn't tell them if he knew.

"Is he as smart as you?" Gerard asks, in a tongue-in-cheek manner.

Nichols hesitates. Then his eyes burn straight ahead, intensity blaring from his face and voice.

"Smarter," he vows. The pair's next meeting won't be nearly as cordial.

As Kimble avoids Gerard's deadly mousetraps throughout the town, he comes closer and closer to the truth, and names start falling from the list of suspects. With Gerard only a few steps behind (literally, in a few cases, such as when Kimble narrowly avoids his gunfire and escapes through a parade), Kimble investigates the doings of the missing-limbs community, searching for the real killer.

Unlike in the TV series, Kimble finds the murderer, Sykes, (the late Andreas Katsulas) on a subway, rather than atop a tower. Also, while the one-armed man is shot dead by Gerard in the television series, the film's version has him getting beaten up and left for the cops by Kimble.

It's time for their final confrontation, which takes them through the doors of the conference, down a corridor, outside to the rook, and back inside—a sightseeing tour with a few right crosses here and there—as Gerard, now fully aware that he was chasing an innocent man, desperately tries to save the life he repeatedly almost took. But just as Gerard reveals himself as Kimble's new ally, there's a twist to the TV ending—just as Nichols is about to eliminate the only other person aware of his guilt, it's Kimble that saves the marshal's life.

During the week of nights it took to shoot the scene at Chicago's Hilton, Krabbe's stuntman—who'd spent the week watching the actor, learning his own physical mannerisms, he says—did most of the work.

"I wasn't allowed to do ninety percent of the fighting," Krabbe says. "I wasn't allowed to do the dangerous stuff. Insurance doesn't allow you to do the dangerous stuff; if you so much as break one of your fingers, you might not be able to go on. But I said, 'I'd like to try some of it myself.'"

Once again, Ford stepped forward.

"Harrison was an incredible help. He does almost all of his own stunts. He said, 'Just do it. Throw me to the floor. Throw me on the wall, kick my ass, and I'll react. Trust me, just do it as fine as you're able to do it.'" Krabbe did—and his double was so impressed that he awarded Krabbe an honorary membership into the Stunt Association of America.

"When you see the result, it's amazing that it was so well done," Krabbe says, "especially when [Kimble and Nichols] fell through the glass roof [done by stuntmen]. It inspires when you see these guys working; the way they work is a class in its own."

About the same time he was finishing up *The Fugitive*, Krabbe snared a role in Steven Soderbergh's 1993 Great Depression drama *King of the Hill* (no relation to the Fox TV show!). Krabbe was Mr. Kurlander, whose son Aaron (Jesse Bradford) is forced to make it on his own after his mother is committed and his father takes a traveling salesman job.

One day, Krabbe noticed a young actor still in the early throes of uncertainty about his career, and his role. He remembered what Ford and *The Fugitive* cast had done for him.

As an experienced performer, Krabbe explains, "You should be open to people who are nervous and scared. I had that attitude toward him."

The two talked about their respective backgrounds (obviously, one's was a bit more diverse). They talked about listening to, and watching others. They discussed using and testing one's instincts as an actor and a performer.

Nine years later, the young man would take home an Oscar, as Adrien Brody's work in *The Pianist* was named the best of 2002.

"I rely on my experience and what I've done," says Krabbe. "I tell new people to just use their intuition. Do what they feel is all right. Talk about the preparation in a general way. If the scene doesn't go well, they'll get it right."

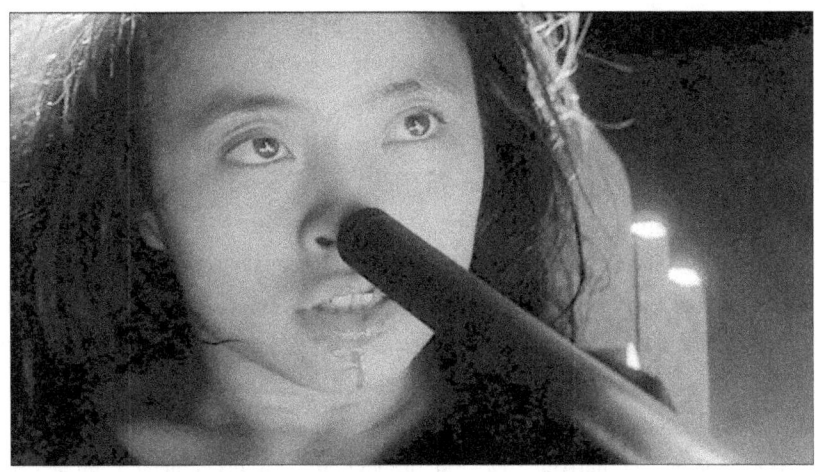

With acting newcomer Hiep Thi Le leading the way, 1993's *Heaven & Earth* told a bit of the Vietnam War story from the view of those America battled.

Hiep Thi Le: *Heaven & Earth*

NOW IT WAS TIME to switch sides. He'd gone over and fought, and, unlike far too many, made it back in one piece, at least on the outside. Then he'd told their tales—not from behind an M-16, but a camera.

A veteran himself, Oliver Stone had used *Platoon* (1986) for the story of men in the midst of the frightening and deadly jungles of Vietnam. *Born on the Fourth of July* (1989) had focused more on the war's aftermath; men home from combat, but now forced to handle obstacles even tougher than any VCs. For the third piece of his (not exactly intentional) trilogy, Stone took a different route, one that he'd probably been smart to hold off until the end.

Far too often in war films (including, in all fairness, much of *Platoon* and 1987's *Full Metal Jacket*, both seen as landmarks in the genre) those on the other side from America are little more than living props. The *bad* guys. The ones that want to kill us, and we just *know* that their reasons don't have the slightest bit of justification, not nearly to the levels that ours hold.

Their stories don't get told much, at least not over here. We don't want to know, to even consider, the parents who lost children, the children who lost parents, the friends who lost friends, the suffering that those who fought us went through, and probably still do. We make films, we build memorials, we praise those who came back to us and remember those that didn't. Let those in opposing countries worry about solving their own problems in those regards.

No, spending time and money hasn't been much of priority for American audiences when it came to learning of our "enemies." Fortunately, by the time Stone put together *Heaven & Earth* in 1993, a few perks to our interest came right about.

Like the Oscars for Best Director he'd won for his first two war outings. And the value his name carried, not just for those flicks, but *JFK* (1991) and some others. Once reaching a certain level, a director can attract auditioners through name magnetism by itself.

But not alone. He needed a powerful subject, and the people to act out the story.

Stone's first problem was solved on autobiographical pages, themselves delving even further into the subtopic world. The writings *When Heaven and Earth Changed Places* and *Child of War, Woman of Peace* told Le Ly Hayslip's tales of herself as a young girl growing up in Vietnam, the arrival of the South Vietnamese, who rape her and too many others, her illegitimate pregnancy as a teenager, her marriage to an American and move to his homeland, and her triumphant return home with her sons.

A war movie in America about a non-American. A war movie with a *woman* as the center protagonist? Armless boxers have it easier!

But that was for Stone to worry about, at least at first. Filling up the cast went to the other side of difficulty, as over 15,000 tried to get to *Heaven*. At least one hadn't really done so on purpose.

Like Hayslip, Hiep Thi Le had been born in Vietnam, and lived in Da Nang, where Stone and so many other Americans had served. Before adulthood, she'd made it over to the Golden State, and studied physiology at the University of California in Davis.

One day, she took a study break for a quick shopping jaunt with a friend.

"I was heading for the flea market," Le recalls. "I hitched a ride with a kid who decided to take a detour. We ended on an open call on a college arena instead of a flea market."

Finding out what was going on, she was excited that a part of her country's story would be told. But by someone else, Le assumed.

"I was over the hill with celebration at the knowledge that my people's voice was given a chance to be heard!" she says. "[But] I believed Oliver Stone was looking for a seasoned professional."

Reasonable assumption. But then a casting director handed her a copy of Hayslip's words. Hours later, Le'd learned more about her homeland and its time during the war than she, like many here and there, had ever dreamed existed. What Vietnam had been put through, and by whom, and how the country, then and still today, struggles for stability.

"I read it in one sitting and was profoundly shaken by the voice and history of my people," she remembers. Could she make it? Might a lady with no acting training somehow find a way into the spotlight of one of the biggest films of the year?

Well, nothing right away. It would take six months to whittle down the tryout list to become Le. Over and over, she kept reading up on Hayslip, learning more and more about a woman whose plight should have been so much more important to others. She thought back to her upbringing in the land ruled by Ho Chi Minh, who America had blamed for trying to jam Communism, the same basis for our Cold War with Russia, down the throats of our allies in Asia.

And perhaps Stone was remembering too.

A decade before, his colleague Roland Joffe had put together 1984's *The Killing Fields*, which had opened millions of American eyes to the genocide that had ravaged Cambodia, a land few could even identify on a map, let alone tell its story.

One of Joffe's biggest assets had been Dr. Haing Ngor, who'd portrayed news correspondent Dith Pran in the film. Like Le, Ngor had never thought of a career in acting. He hadn't even wanted the part when he was offered it.

But eventually he'd realize that the story he'd been through during years in Cambodia deserved to be told around the globe. Seeing people tortured and killed by the Khmer Rouge terrorist group. Losing his wife and child. Feeling the pain they'd so gleefully caused him as a person, nearly losing his life in the process.

Ngor had decided to take a chance. It had paid off. He'd won a place in film history by becoming the first Asian to win an Oscar.

Stone didn't have to look far to remember Ngor's work; Ngor was there to play Hayslip's dad.

That, Le's effort, Stone's personal preferences . . . whatever came together was enough. Le's film debut would be the center of a biopic.

And acting would be just one burden to carry.

"Since I was not from the industry, I was given a tour to all the departments, pre- and post-production as well," she remembers of meeting some of the most underrated aspects of filmmaking. "I was blown away to see how sound effects were added in a sound booth by manipulation of unrelated objects, and how an editor studied each frame thousands of times in order to match angles to assure lighting was compatible. I take my hat off to the post-production team!"

Now it came time to become Hayslip, thirty years' worth of her life, from Vietnam and back again. Le kept learning from the lady's words—then she heard even more firsthand.

"I met up with the real Le Ly, met her kids, and asked her everything I needed to fill in the blanks," Le explains, "i.e., her philosophy on 'the ends justify the means' vs. karma. Most importantly, I wanted to feel her passion and dilemma on Ho Chi Minh and his movement. She believed Ho Chi Minh was a nationalist, hence [she] became a nationalist." Nationalists put an extremely high priority on tradition, called patriotic by some and oppressive by others.

Le could relate herself. Like many in Vietnam still feel about Ho Chi Minh, she felt he had a tough job with rough means, done for the right reasons.

"My family believes in the means justifying the end," she says. "Hence, Ho Chi Minh was another mean. [Hayslip and I] spent 48 hours together. I pretty much asked everything and she answered. She believes in the ends justifying the means and you just deal with the consequences."

Early on in the film, Hayslip's village is overrun by the same soldiers America went over to fight. In full McCarthyism mode, she's falsely accused of being a traitor, and raped. As it would be were it Le's first or hundredth role, it was one of her toughest scenes.

"Guess it was inevitable as a human being to be violated against your will that way," she says, "to have felt helplessness and ripped of life's hope."

Soon she moves to Saigon as a housekeeper, and has a son by her employer. But he has a wife who really runs the show, and Hayslip's out. However, she soon meets Steve Butler (Tommy Lee Jones, the same year he won an Oscar for *The Fugitive*), a marine who treats her right and takes her back to his American home.

Almost every day, or at least it seems so sometimes, we check over the news, or sometimes hear it from our friends and family, the stories of soldiers coming home from Iraq, Afghanistan, and other places of battle unable to leave their experiences behind. Their minds damaged, if not ruined entirely, they can't relate to work, their loved ones, even their military friends. At an average of almost every day, we hear of a solider ending things permanently for themselves, and sometimes others, from the stress that stayed around.

Such situations affecting soldiers from our past wars don't get as much attention as the ones we're in today, but this is nothing new, and *Heaven & Earth* showed it. Butler's anger and depression followed him home like an epidemic, and, as cureless as PTSD is today, it was foreign a half century ago.

It ended up as one more trauma for Hayslip and her sons (she had three by this point), as her husband, named Dennis in real life, assaulted her. Soon after, he, as Butler does, committed suicide.

Years later, Le took Hayslip back home. One of her sons saw his birthplace, the others her old home. For the first time that any of them could remember, they walked across the same grounds, saw the same places, met the same people, or at least their descendants, that their mom and grandparents had known in a life that seemed much farther before than she could ever know.

Sadly, Le's work didn't garner as much acclaim as Ngor's. The film didn't hit as hard as Stone's usually do. But she could be proud of something that few in the profession ever get a chance to try, let alone in their debut.

"I concluded it was not a story of a Vietnamese woman," she explains. "It was a story of a nation's desperate action for justice."

A few years later, 2001's *Green Dragon* gave her another chance to tell a similar story. Just after the war, a group of Vietnamese refugees tries to adjust to life in America. Le played Thuy Hoa, whose father had led a troop of Vietnamese. The character represented the country she (Hayslip, Le, and Hoa) came from, remembers the actress.

"Thuy Hoa was a symbol of knowledge," she recalls. "She was well read, world knowing, came from Catholic mother and Buddhist father. Her life had perspective. Yet, as she remained firm footed to shelter her younger sister from a bleak future, to find justice for her disillusioned father, she was losing grip on herself [aka, she *was* Vietnam]."

While his friends try to find a place in this strange new world, Tai Tran (Don Duong) translates for them, looking after the children of his late sister. But there's one eternal language that we can't translate, because we feel it, long before we speak it. It's one of the strongest marks of purity, of decency, of doing what's right.

Love. The same love, the same cure that Tai and Thuy eventually find with each other.

"Thuy Hoa took more character development on my end as there was no book," Le remembers. "I had to understand her background, her baggage, her cause, and her femininity. Every scene of hers had to be purposeful in order to create intrigue and a desire to learn more about her. Thuy Hoa had to represent the force of Vietnam: optimistic, vulnerable, yet determined."

Bruce Lee's sad, mysterious death robbed him (and us) of the long life and career he should have had, but the impact the martial arts master made across so many worlds will live forever.

Bruce Lee

IF BRUCE LEE HAD never lived, or had decided never to pursue martial arts, it's interesting to converse on what might have happened . . . or *not* happened.

If the man born with the female moniker of Sai Fon ("Small Phoenix") Li, whose name was shortly changed to Jun Fan ("Return Again") and eventually nicknamed Bruce by one of the doctors who oversaw his Nov. 27, 1940, delivery in the Chinatown section of San Francisco, hadn't done what he did, how much of a loss would it have meant for the entire world?

Perhaps martial arts films would never have taken off, and scored their own genre in filmmaking. Maybe American audiences would never have realized and appreciated the talent of Asian performing. Possibly, millions of children across the globe would never have wanted, or even gotten the chance, to learn and hone their skills at karate, kung fu, and other martial arts in schools worldwide, many of whom still carry Lee's name and likeness.

Is Lee personally responsible for all those things? That's probably an overstatement. But you know, it's really not too big of one. Lee's star still shines across America today, with martial arts performers and directors from Chuck Norris to Jean-Claude Van Damme to John Woo naming him as their inspirations. Professional fighters like Tito Ortiz and Randy Couture turned to Lee's teachings on their own journeys to stardom in the ultimate brawling worlds.

His high intelligence often overshadowed by rambunctiousness in his early years, Lee got interested in kung fu as a child, practicing his kicks on trees after school every day. Though he still used his skills for the wrong reasons in street fights—one such brawl took place between Lee's gang and another one on a rooftop, *West Side Story*-style (1961) before the film was even out—back in Hong Kong, Lee returned to San Francisco in 1959 and kept up his training. The energy that had been his enemy for his entire life suddenly transformed into a stream of intensity that would power Atlantic City, pouring all his energy into the martial art.

In 1964, Lee, now a teacher, was doing a demonstration at the Long Beach International Karate Tournament. A Hollywood producer in the audience checked him out.

The next day, Lee got a phone call. The TV version of *Batman* was ruling the airwaves, and someone was looking to convert another comic book to the small screen in *The Green Hornet*. Always a fan of the movies, Lee snared the role of Kato, the bodyguard to Van Williams' title character.

"I'll tell you why I got the *Green Hornet* job," he recalled, "because the hero's name was Britt Reid, and I was the only Chinese in all of California that could pronounce Britt Reid!" During filming, Lee had to actually slow down his moves so the camera could get everything.

Lee's star quickly soared past Williams' in the fan adoration ranks, but the series lasted just one season. Lee starred alongside his student James Garner on the big screen in *Marlowe* (1969), then got a guest role on the series *Longstreet*. Soon, he took a jaunt back to Hong Kong, and met a fellow named Raymond Chow, who'd just kicked off the Golden Harvest production company.

Recognizing a career with momentum, Chow offered Lee the lead in *The Big Boss*, the 1971 story of a peaceful man driven to violence against the overlords that kill his family. Lee went to see some similar films from the past.

He didn't like them.

"I prepared by going to see a bunch of Mandarin movies," Lee recalled. "They were awful. For one thing, everybody fights all the time, and what really bothered me was the fact that they all fought exactly the same way. Nobody's really like that! When you get into a fight, everybody reacts differently. And it is possible to act *and* fight at the same time." Soon enough, he'd make these films just a bit more realistic.

In *Big Boss*, he said, "The character I played was a very simple, straightforward guy. Like, if you told this guy something, he'd believe you. Then, when he finally figures out he's been had, he goes animal. This isn't a bad character, but I don't want to play him all the time. I'd prefer somebody with a little more depth."

With the arrival of *The Big Boss*, as America already had in the *Green Hornet*, Hong Kong met a new superhuman of the cinema. The term "superhuman" is used here for a reason, as Lee's character didn't have the mythical or magic powers that good guys in the movies and comic books typically come equipped with, which that added to the mystique that still surrounds Lee today.

"The word 'superstar' really turns me off, and I'll tell you why," he explained. "Because the word 'star' is an illusion; it is something that the public calls you. You should look upon [yourself] as an actor. I mean, you would be pleased if somebody said, 'Hey man, you're a super actor!' It is much better than 'superstar.'"

The Lee acting persona was quite simply that, while he was light-years above many mere mortals in terms of physical fitness and intensity, he was just as realistic, as much as one can be in these types of movies. He wasn't glorified, not even always the hero of the piece. He was just a hardcore hyperactive fellow who made throwdowns a favorite pastime. *Big Boss* rocked audiences with the strength of Lee himself, rolling through Asia and its box-office records.

Soon after would come arguably the most famous martial-arts film (albeit not really for the right reasons) of all time.

Originally called *Blood and Steel*, the flick showcased Lee as, ironically enough, Lee, an author and martial arts champ who takes part in a martial arts tournament to infiltrate a drug lord's rings.

"I tried to present a sort of spiritual and physical expression of a dedicated artistic athlete," Lee said, "who in this case [happens to be] a Chinese martial artist, as set apart from the ordinary, because he can 'deliver' and communicates with the audience and is capable to get across to the audience that which is considered the ultimate value of a martial artist."

As the film was eventually and very fortunately renamed *Enter the Dragon* (1973), Lee started to solve some of the problems he'd seen in earlier films, helping stage some of the fights to show the differential in the arts of street fighting. Sometimes he'd have to take on over ten guys at once, jumping everywhere, punching, chopping, kicking everything in sight, sometimes for over a dozen takes at a time—and no stuntmen for Lee. No one else could do this. No one else could come close.

In an impact so far beyond anything he ever did on screens big or small, Lee brought a new light to American audiences about a culture that we may never have gotten or wanted to take the chance to learn more about: the area that Lee always felt both a personal and professional obligation to educate others about—and fulfilled in both objectives.

"There were no role models for young Asians growing up to see within the context of Hollywood and the star system that Hollywood represented," says Andre Morgan, a producer on *Dragon*. "So one of [Lee's] goals was to achieve that kind of status, a role model for young people and example for other people, inspiring minority actors all over the world who were trying to break into Hollywood."

In *Dragon*, as with every film he ever made or hoped to make, Lee's goal was never only to show his skills as a martial artist, but to break through any stereotype anyone in America may have had about the Chinese in general. Too many people tend to dislike things or groups that they don't understand or take the time to know, and such an attitude was far too prevalent toward Asians at the time. People like Lee did a much harder job than they ever should have had to to show us otherwise.

"I have a hell of a responsibility because Americans really do not have firsthand information on the Chinese," he said of the film. "*Enter the Dragon* should make it—this is the movie that I'm proud of because it has been made for the American audience as well as for the European and the Oriental." Sadly, *Dragon* still lives on today more because of Lee's shocking end in its midst, not as much because of its amazing quality as an individual film.

Acting, Lee said, "is my way of expressing myself. . . . I have this intensity in me that the audience believes in what I do because *I* believe in what I do. The intensity is there, and I have to act in such a way as to border my action somewhere between reality and fantasy."

It's far too easy for those who make their first stance in the martial arts film genre to get stuck there, and it becomes a double whammy; not only does the demanding physicality of the roles typically shorten their careers, but they get typecast into the film genus and don't get a fair chance to even try out others. Chuck Norris (who Lee killed in 1972's *Return of the Dragon*), Jet Li . . . these people might be outstanding on the dramatic sense, but hardly ever get a fair shot. Instead they're unable to get a screenplay that doesn't involve at least one dropkick. If he'd gotten a few more years of shots, Lee, who spent time working with dramatic coaches, might have been able to shatter another myth, and he certainly hoped to.

"An actor is a dedicated being who works very hard—so damn hard—that his level of understanding makes him a qualified artist in self-expression, physically, psychologically, as well as spiritually," he said. "An actor, a good actor, not the cliché type, is in reality a 'competent deliverer,' one who is not just ready to artistically harmonize this invisible duality of business and art into a successful appropriate unity. To settle down to train a 'competent' actor mentally and physically is not an easy task. . . . To me, an actor is the sum total of all that he is—his high level of understanding of life, his appropriate good taste, his experience of happiness and adversity, his intensity, his educational background, and much, much more—like I said, the sum total of all that he is."

Lee's death shook the fight film industry, and nearly destroyed it. It wasn't only that a famous performer had died; it was also that Lee, one of the healthiest humans that ever lived, could suddenly pass away out of nowhere, at age 32. The official verdict was a strong reaction to painkiller medication, but Lee's death is still a favorite discussion in conspiracy theory circles, with as many theories abounding as the Kennedy assassinations. People around the world—not just in Lee's Asian homeland—nearly stopped watching action films, taking martial arts lessons, everything. It wasn't for over a decade that Jackie Chan's work in the 1995 surprise hit *Rumble in the Bronx* re-ignited our interest in American martial arts films, a fire that he turned into an inferno with the *Kung-Fu Panda* (2008, 2011, 2016) and the *Rush Hour* (1998, 2001, 2007) movies.

Is he, or Norris, or Li, or anyone else, as good as Lee was? That's an argument that no one can possibly win. Let's focus not on comparison, but on glorification of the work done by an individual. With originality so lacking in the filmmaking world, it's more important to see what new things so many people, like Chan, Li, and everyone else, have to offer, rather than spending so much effort trying to look back where we *might* have seen it before.

Perhaps, in that regard, we can look to just one more of Lee's lasting legacies.

"Bruce believed that the individual represents the whole of mankind, whether he lives in the Orient or elsewhere," Linda Lee recalls of her late husband. "He believed that man struggles to find a life outside himself, not realizing that the life he seeks is within him."

Repetition works, but only for so long. Eventually, we need to try new things, to look new places, to independently consider what we might find, what we could embrace and enjoy. Bruce Lee did more than enough with his life, and there's no reasons left to try to recapture lightning in a bottle, which would in all probability be much easier than taking Lee in a brawl. Lee kept showing us, or telling us, that finding something new and exciting might be much easier than we ever thought, and the so many others making their own marks in martial arts deserve their own recognition, without the shadow that Lee never intended to cast still hanging over them.

"Even though I, Bruce Lee, may die someday without fulfilling all of my ambitions, I feel no sorrow," Lee once said in a sad prophecy. "I did what I wanted to do. What I've done, I've done with sincerity and to the best of my ability. You can't expect much more from life."

Lucy Lawless' legendary Xena finds herself in an unfamiliar defensive position against Callisto (Hudson Leick), one of the Warrior Princess' toughest opponents in her show's history.

Hudson Leick: *Xena: Warrior Princess*

LIKE MOST ACTORS PROBABLY do after the latest tryout, Hudson Leick strolled around the block, her body and mind feeling that deserved breath of fresh air. A time of reflection, and of hope.

What she had done, and how well. That she might just get the job. And most importantly, where it would take her.

"I was thinking I really wanted this part because I wanted to go to New Zealand," Leick remembers, "and not having a clue where New Zealand was. I loved travelling." The Cincinnati native had modeled in Japan and France before switching to acting.

After a season on *Melrose Place* in 1995, Leick was out for something a bit different. Well, much more than a bit.

"My job as an actress is not just to act," she explains. "It's to prepare, to get the script, and to go to the audition. That's a huge part of your job, even if you're not paid for it. You can audition for tons of things before you get anything, because there's no rhyme or reason. There's no reason why you get something or why somebody else gets something." Trying out for this new show—an action/fantasy tale with a lady in the lead, itself rarely explored territory—she hoped to give its crew a reason to want something a bit different.

In March 1995, a brash brunette named Xena had shown up alongside the title character of *Hercules: The Legendary Journeys*, and audiences had flipped out with the ferocity the amazon laid on her unlucky opponents. Six months later, Lucy Lawless' Warrior Princess had spun off into her own show.

"I thought that *Hercules* had been pretty lame," admits Leick, "with the women in it, and how they were dressed and acted." She walked into the audition showing off as little skin as possible, but still ready to roll.

"They asked me if I could do a kick, because she was a very physical character," Leick says of her role goal. "They asked if I could pretend to throw a chakram." Like the Frisbee's evil cousin, a chakram is a circular weapon with sharpened edges, perfect for drawing blood at thirty feet. Xena fans saw her use the tool throughout the series, and Leick's lady would as well.

From the show's opening, *Xena* made clear that its lead's brilliant battle skills had been sharpened by drawing all kinds of blood for the wrong reasons. Murder, even massacre, destruction, all of it had been commonplace in her path to join the warlord ranks.

Was it too late to atone? Even if not, how would she, in this land with so little left? She could only try, but there were plenty of people out for revenge on her, and it was hard not to sympathize with some.

Like the role Leick landed. As the first season neared its end in May 1996, Xena is felled and nearly killed by a poison dart, only to (you'll never guess!) just *happen* to wake up and whomp everyone *just* as the situation seemed hopeless! *Sure*, this *never* occurs in the action entertainment world, *right*?

The next week, though, we'd meet the infamous dart shooter, and Xena would see her toughest opponent yet, some might say of the entire series.

Debuting in an episode carrying her name, Callisto was the woman Xena had once been, raging from one village to another, her makeshift army taking everything it could, including lives. Soon enough, she and Xena are waging all-out battle. Then we find out why.

"It's karma," Leick says. "What we put out into the world, we manifest something back. Xena had done horrible things in her past, and some of the things she did were so damaging that they touched other people and created its own mess. That's where I got born, out of somebody else's rage and hate. It ignited Callisto's rage and hate." Long before the series, Xena had attacked Callisto's Cirra homeland, burning it to the ground. Callisto's parents and sister hadn't escaped the flames.

"I didn't have to prepare for being angry or traumatized; I already had that in me," says Leick, who learned a bit of kung fu for her role. "It was so brilliant and true. I may not be a killer inside me, but suppose you kill my mother? In a rage, I want to kill something that you love. It's a really despicable part of humanity, but it's part of humanity. It's what we tend to do. We have a choice in it, but sometimes it doesn't feel like we have a choice in it."

Long before this point, *Xena*'s top-level ratings had convinced everyone at the network that a second season was the only thing to do (it crushed *Hercules* in Nielsen numbers and fanship). The new arrival, however, though a certainly nightmare for the characters, sent her own surge through the fanbase, and Leick's role grew past an episode.

"It was something so childlike and horrific at the same time," Leick says. "She wasn't just filled with rage, but filled with insane delight. She was delighted with some of the things she did, which I thought was hilarious and fun to play."

Five weeks into season two, we saw "Return of Callisto," as the villainess left a line of slaughtered guards in her escape from prison, then kills the hubby of Xena's friend Gabrielle in one of the series' saddest moments. Xena and Callisto pick up the battle we saw in *Ben-Hur* with a chariot war, but Callisto crashes into quicksand, and is sucked underneath forever.

Or at least two weeks. Down in the Underworld, Callisto sneaks into Xena's body, now wreaking her havoc from within. By the end of the episode, however, Xena's forced to live inside Callisto, giving Leick a chance to play her own enemy.

"That was very confining," she says, "like being in a prison, mimicking somebody else, just doing what you can to mimic the other person. I find that very boring." It didn't last, as Xena would have her own body back the next week.

Callisto would be back and forth on the show over the next few years, even getting the chance to show up on *Hercules* to kick the piss out of its main man. She'd end up back in hell after being killed by Xena once again, only to have Xena purge out both of their pain by taking her place and sending her to heaven. In Callisto's last appearance in early 2000, the cleansed murderess reincarnates herself as the baby Xena carries, drawing tears from the princess for one of the few times in the series.

"Even though *Xena* was a comic book story," Leick says, "the stories underneath were incredible, potent, deeply spiritual stories that everybody can relate to. Being a part of that and playing the dark part of that, I was honored. It's against the dark that you see the light. I have dark in me, we all do. I'm a human being. Being able to express myself in such a ridiculous and incredible way and being empowered to do almost anything I wanted and not be punished for it felt freeing."

Will she return to the screens someday? Time will tell. But Leick has another outlet for her love of travel; a yoga instructor for over twenty years, she's taught at retreats all the over the country and throughout Europe and Australia (http://www.hudsonleick.com).

"Yoga is about finding oneself and finding kindness within oneself," she says. "I started practicing yoga at a time when I needed to find peace and centeredness. I didn't go looking for it, but when I found it I never stopped, and I even started teaching. It brings me clarity and joy, reminds me to be more present and to have gratitude for having a body and being healthy. Yoga is very much like a prayer, a physical prayer: a prayer to the body."

Boot camp can never fully prepare a solider from battle with the actual enemy, as Katrina (Blake Lindsley) found out in *Starship Troopers* (1997).

Blake Lindsley: *Starship Troopers*

WAR, AND FAR FROM the civil type! And none of that man-against-man shit that's so depressing in the various cinematic realistic depictions of battles of America's (and the world's) past! This isn't one of the World Wars, Korea, Vietnam, or any of the others that are guaranteed to be a downer!

No, with sci-fi in the equation, it's man (and woman, remember that this is futuristic!) against *bug*! The two-legged vs. the eight-legged! Huge guns, bloody battles, all against those with no name, no mechanic weaponry, but *far* higher in the numbers!

It certainly sounds awfully tough to make *that* sound lackluster! Certainly not stained with political subtleties. But, long before anyone *saw* the story's title characters in action, that's what many labeled *Starship Troopers*.

Pretty fair assessment, actually.

Indeed, Robert Heinlein's 1959 novel—yes, the story was in print decades before it hit the screen—is certainly about a war that's over territory elsewhere in the universe, against bugs (sort of like spiders and centipedes on steroids from hell). But the navy vet claimed his tale wasn't so much to put him near Ray Bradbury in the authoring ranks, but to express his fear that the military of the time would do away with the nuclear testing that he, and several others, saw as a necessity to survival.

Why the "BOOOO-RIIIIIIING!" complaints, you ask? Well, the book spends quite a bit of time in flashback mode, so it's not the easiest story to follow. Not only that, but huge swaths of the writing are of classroom dialogue, of the political type: mainly, that war and violence are usually the best and sometimes the only way to fix something, and that individual sacrifice, even of the ultimate kind, might just be required for the greater good of the many. Democracy might be a nice-sounding term to utter, but in practice, it gets lost in the shuffle of effective governing choices.

Still, regardless of the stigmas (there were others that we'll see soon here) that darkened some of the book's luster—not much amongst the general public, as it sold strong for decades and still has some heavy influence on other culture-popping areas—its 1997 cinematic adaptation could hardly be called tedious, equipped with *much* more action and death than the literary version. Seeing war up close and personal, even not the slightest bit realistic, all but forces us to feel the stabbing rush of emotion.

"When I did *Starship*, I would have probably done anything that anyone had asked me to, short of a porno or something," remembers Blake Lindsley, "but I was immensely lucky to get a gig in a huge action film. I would have taken any job acting, but it happened to be in a massive action film by a great writer [Edward Neumeier moved Heinlein's words to the screenplay] and great producers; it's a highlight of my career."

Just as with the book, the tale's main character is Casper Van Dien's John Rico (an Americanized version of the book's protagonist of Juan), making his way through high school, between full-contact, pads-less arena rugby battles, to break through to graduation—which, in this land, means service.

There's certainly a need here—Rico's Buenos Aires hometown has been overrun with rich Americans, everyone still scared that the bugs so violently trying to destroy us might find a way here. Earth's goals of global unity have been realized, but arachnids from the far-off planet Klendathu, which WE want, are a whole new danger.

Just as with the book, nearly all of Rico's instructors have been through battle themselves, which the film really goes the extra mile to show. One is blind, and several others are missing limbs.

And of course, the force and violence debates are here. As an author, Heinlein could be a bit more one sided in his views; mainstream films are forced to ride the fence when it comes to opinions like this. Yes, the instructors are there to preach war—it's history's most successful problem-solver, according to one citizen—but it can't go as far as the book.

This was another issue many had with the film; it didn't stay close enough to the book. Some, however, considered this a positive.

Stepping his uncertain way through boot camp, Rico becomes an unwilling participant in the most impromptu of discussion sites: modesty is a thing of the past, as co-ed showering is the new norm, and it's time to crash-course everyone's background. If we didn't know her much before, here's where Lindsley's Katrina grabs her first spotlight step.

Why is everyone here? It's Katrina's motives, and those of many of her colleague, that reveal the realities of their world. Of course, there are some who just can't wait to see their uniforms stained with the weird-colored blood of the arachnids. Some want to be there to the end of the war, and maybe longer. But some are there for other reasons—some extra, very special rights that come with service and citizenship.

Just as with many today that glance toward the GI Bill, some are looking to get an education on the government's dime. One is headed all the way to the top of the political field—can't vote if you don't serve.

Katrina? The young beauty wants a baby. In this time and place, one's service gives them a special shot at that licensing.

That's right—in the future, we *earn* the right to reproduce. What would happen if some American politician tried to get *that* through Congress?

"In that militaristic society, everyone pretty much has to serve," Lindsley explains. "You could compare it to Israel, where everybody has to serve in the military to be citizens—otherwise, you don't have the ability to have a child. In this society, you need a license to have a child. I'm sure there are a lot of people that would argue for that in today's society. My character was not that different from me: no interest in the military, but wanted to get married and have a family." In real life, Lindsley eventually did so.

One must certainly look *far* beneath the surface here, but that quote not only solidifies Katrina's character, but really shows a side of the *Troopers* theme that cause the book—and, to a lesser extent, the film—to still be debated today.

As for Katrina, it's a perfect way to show the diversity of the military itself. The stereotypical soldier—like Rico begins as ("I say KILL 'EM ALL!") —is overflowing with patriotism, his red blood tinged with blue and white, there to destroy those who dared to screw with us and laugh and cheer over the corpses. Little in his life but to slaughter for all the right reasons.

But now we see that there's more to military existence than that. More to this society than that. In America, military service brings one all kinds of opportunities that stick with us long after our discharge. But in the *Troopers* world, you *have* to give before you *get*. Whether we're at war or not—being in conflict has always caused a temporary rise in enlistment numbers—those who serve are entitled to more than those who don't.

Many people raised in a democratic environment certainly wouldn't agree, and Lindsley felt the same way after making her way through Heinlein's words.

"The novel was a Fascist manifesto," she exclaims. "It takes itself very seriously. The movie was more about poking fun at itself." Her assessment was commonplace from the moment the book hit shelves—and, in all fairness, *Starship* director Paul Verhoeven (himself never one to avoid controversy!) didn't help much by costuming his soldiers in uniforms similar to those seen in Nazi Germany.

But before anyone gets to put those on, there's some heavy training to fill, and even in the performing arts, it wasn't easy for anyone.

After scoring her role in early 1996, Lindsley grabbed her last chances to get in shape ahead of time; studying at Yale, as she was at that point, doesn't leave much personal freedom for anyone, let alone an upcoming actress.

"We didn't start shooting until late May," she remembers. "I started working out at the gym in my apartment, running on the treadmill and lifting weights." As shooting drew nearer, and even after it began, she and the rest of the cast worked with several trainers, with tae-bo guru Billy Blanks showing up for a few lessons.

"I'm someone who likes to get as much information as possible and then go with my gut in the moment," Lindsley says. "What they were really going for was finding actors who were just themselves. Paul really wanted to find a group of beautiful young people, innocent people at the peak of their physical prowess—so that he could exploit, in a nice way, them in this film, and then get them torn to shreds by insects, victim of this overbearing society, a patriarchal government that wants to go to war with other planets at a cost. He didn't want us to prepare that much—to just be sweet young girls and boys, then grow in this environment of horror and see what happens."

And once again, the terrifying times were both on and off the screen for Lindsley, van Dien, and so many others. Just as he'd done with the casts of the (slightly) more violent *Natural Born Killers* (1994) and *Platoon* (1986), ex-marine Dale Dye led the campers to combat—and what better place to do that than the land named Hell's Half-Acre?

Winding their way through the 300-plus acres of the Wyoming land (other filming took place in North Dakota and Orange County), stumbling through ravines and charging through rock that would make cement feel like a down mattress, the group figured that real combat could hardly be worse.

Knives were tossed with deadly accuracy. Machine guns were hoisted and toted about. Live flares were fired off.

"The night shoots were hard," Lindsley recalls, "being up all night, wearing heavy gear, running out of spaceships, lots of difficult things, but very exciting and interesting. It was half an hour to a toilet and taking off the gear if you had to go."

Finally, it came time to shoot the human-bug war, on the creature's home turf of Klendathu. After all their training, the humans are ready to stroll in and walk right through. After all, how tough can a group of unarmed arachnids without even the sense to reason be?

Disastrously so. These things are bigger, stronger, and more explosive than anyone could have dreamed. The humans' weaponry is turned against them. More bullets are needed on the creatures than anyone ever thought necessary. People are stabbed and torn apart in milliseconds. Hundreds are killed.

And for all her training and hopes for her life, Katrina's the first lady to fall, literally. As the ground gives out beneath her, a bug drags her into a cave for its friends to feast upon. All her hard work vanquished in seconds.

"They built a set for me called 'Katrina's Hole,'" Lindsley remembers. "I did all the stunts myself. Every shot that involved one of the insects was tough, because you had to imagine they were there. In some shots, they had puppets, but for the most part, when the bugs were moving, we had to imagine it. For the most part, it was all CGI. Not only am I reacting to seeing this bug in a hole, but they had to strap me to a sort of sled and pull me out of the shot on the sled, which took some maneuvering. I was black and blue for days after that!"

Even by the end of the film, the humans haven't won, perhaps a subtle message that we'd see sequels (we did, a pair of them). But by the end of the film, the ones that are still alive have clearly changed. Rico and his friends are no longer than laid-back group we saw in the opening moments. War has indeed hardened them, as it has so many before and since in real life. On of Rico's friends is killed near the end, but he proclaims her citizenship as more important than their personal relationship.

Still, the film can't go too far on either side of the "Are force and violence ever the best?" debate, not like the book could.

What's the answer? No one can really know.

Some might have said that Heinlein created the bugs to eliminate the issue of political ideology, or at least its anti-American side. Until the end of time, free-thinkers in our political world will defend both sides of the Civil War, the Korean War, all the World Wars, and every other one that we've stepped into long since Heinlein wrote his final words. Heinlein removes our ability to argue for the Bugs; they're against us, and why really isn't the issue. We can't defend them, no one can, because we don't know their reasoning. The novel forces us to look only at us—us, in this case, being the residents not of America, not of democracy, but of humanity in general. In this book, it's not a question of why we as individuals are right and our enemies are wrong, but of whether or not the way of thought amongst Rico and his colleagues is truly the way to success.

Many said—some in praise, some in criticism—that *Troopers* indeed glorified war. But after all this time and on until forever, war is a mystery without a solution. Some will always preach for it, others against it, still others will switch sides. Maybe that's what Heinlein—and, through him, Verhoeven—really wanted us to do after all: to think for ourselves.

So let those debates continue!

Just as he did for years in pro wrestling rings, Robert Maillet towers above his upcoming victims, as the Giant in *300*, Dredger in *Sherlock Holmes*, or anything else on screens big and small.

Robert Maillet: *300/Sherlock Holmes*

When you're upwards of seven feet tall, it's pretty easy to get noticed. Being at least a foot taller than someone who themselves would be considered above average, one tends to stand out in a crowd.

And, yes, not necessarily in a good way. It's easy to come across as threatening, even when not intending to be.

So yes, it may be easy, even accidentally natural, to overawe others when one is nearly tall enough to, as NBA center Artis Gilmore once said, "wash giraffe ears."

But what about the person who's toughest to intimidate? What about the one who's used to seeing all that height and strength up close and personal?

What about . . . yourself?

That accomplishment marked Robert Maillet's first jaunt into acting. Preparing to become the Uber Immortal giant in the 2006 special effects action-packed *300*, the former pro wrestler knew that the first person he'd have to convince would be one of the few he can't look down on.

"Because of my physical attributes, being seven feet and 320 pounds, I knew I could play the giant troll," he says. "I approached the role the same as my character in the [World Wrestling Entertainment], trying to be scary and loud and intimidating. My goal was if I could scare myself, then the audience would feel the same way."

It was a show he put on for years before audiences that could see, hear, and interact with Maillet on a much larger scale than any in a theater—he spent years portraying Kurrgan, one of the most recognizable faces in the WWE. After starting his WWE career as a heel (bad guy that fans love to hate), Maillet turned his character into a fun-loving, dancing hippie that often had fans shucking and jiving in the aisles.

"I was fascinated by the pro wrestling world and taught I would have a better chance making a career out of it than being an actor," he recalls (Maillet appeared next to fellow longtime mat man Dwayne "The Rock" Johnson in 2014's *Hercules*). "But I was concentrating on learning my skills as a wrestler. I realized over time that filmmaking and the wrestling world had a lot in common: playing characters, memorizing matches, telling a story and making magic, creating an illusion. Our job in wrestling was to entertain and suspend disbelief."

A lifelong fan of the motion picture, Maillet actually learned of *300* from a wrestling promoter.

"I dreamed of being in movies, but thought it was out of my reach," he says. "After I got the role, I felt very comfortable on set with the crew, lights, and camera pointing towards me. Being a wrestler helped a lot. I always loved the fantasy genre, especially about Greek mythology."

So while Maillet was used to heading into battle against those looking to take him down, it's safe to say that no battle royal was ever quite like the wars between Sparta and Persia that ravaged in the B.C. centuries. And no wrestling match, be it at a house show, on television, or even pay-per-view had the end result that his Immortal meets in battle.

"It was very cool to see it all put together with the background, the editing, and the special effects, especially when I saw my head getting chopped off!" he says. "My friends and family applauded my demise. Every shot was a work of art!"

His next big role would hit just as close to home; as the French henchman Dredger, Maillet took on the world's greatest detective, a villain to the cause of one Sherlock Holmes in the 2009 film of the same name.

"I read the script and thought it was a great part," says Maillet, whose natural French background came to the forefront as he and Robert Downey Jr.'s detective fired one-liners back and forth during their fight scene in a shipbuilding factor. "My role was more important in the story when they realized I was French. They added dialogue between me and Downey." In one shot, the acting crossed over to reality a bit painfully for Hollywood's newest Holmes, as Maillet inadvertently decked him during a fight scene.

"They took [Downey] to the hospital after we finished for the night," Maillet says. "He had five stitches in his mouth, nothing broken. They were more worried about the swelling of his lip. The next day he gave me a nice bottle of champagne and a note on a card to say 'You're the best and let's get through this week!' He had a lot of class."

Not that things were always easy for the former matster himself, left to do his own stunts for the film.

"There's a scene where I had to jump out of a two-story building that I wasn't sure about," he says. "I trusted the stunt team to get through it!"

That's because, just as the physical skills that made him a success in the wrestling world have carried over into his new career, Maillet knows that his height will always be an issue; it just doesn't have to be a negative.

"The more roles I get for being big and tall, the better," he says. "I want to take advantage of my attributes. I know I will never get the Tom Cruise roles, but I'd rather be the bad giant who fights him. I know how to play that type!"

Up against guns, robbers, and leering eyes, Helena Mattsson's Blonde never lost control of anything in 2012's *Guns, Girls, and Gambling*.

Helena Mattsson: *Guns, Girls, and Gambling*

IF ONLY WE COULD live one day, even just one hour, like she lives every single day of her life.

A lady who can just walk into a room and grab it all. Take over everything, just by stepping forward. Exuding an aura stronger than all the magnets in the universe put together, all over everyone, including those that might know her and those that don't. Just one glance at her, they're shocked, they're scared, they're intimidated, everything they knew would happen is gone in a second, along with any semblance of control they only thought they possessed.

People like her are tough to locate in everyday society. It's one more reason why such characters are so popular in the movies—and not only for those in the audience watching.

Her name? We'd never know, and we'd even feel like we didn't deserve to. She was just that strong, that special. We'd see her strength, outside, inside, always ruling whatever situation she entered, no matter who she went up against, no matter what danger loomed here and there.

She was just The Blonde, the true focal point of *Guns, Girls, and Gambling* (2012). Before she'd get to realize a dream character, Helena Mattsson felt the seductress' power herself.

"She is such a cold badass with so much swagger," Mattsson says. "Pretty far from who I am! But I really enjoyed that about it. It's always fun to portray someone who is nothing like you, because you really have to prepare and figure out who they are."

The ability to show some serious power inside and out had come in handy for Mattsson before, and, ironically, so had her blondeness. After Natasha Henstridge had gotten the *Species* series started in the 1990s, Mattsson (who bears perhaps a distant cousin-type physical resemblance to Henstridge) carried the lead in 2007's *Species: The Awakening*.

While Henstridge's characters had spent three films trying to carry on the alien race by mating, Mattson's Miranda was a bit further along, a college professor with a memory every student envies. Then she finds out some sad, heartbreaking truths: that she's just an experiment combining human and alien genetics, one that won't live much longer.

Like her predecessor, Miranda goes into murderous alien form when things get rough (clearly lacking The Blonde's self-controlling power). Like her predecessor, Mattsson spent quite a bit of time in cosmetics to show her animalistic side.

"It took long hours applying the special effects makeup for some parts of the film," recalls the actress, who used Henstridge's work as her own starting point. "But I enjoyed watching the process. It gave me some time to get into the character." After a walk-on bombshell role in *Iron Man 2* (2010), she learned of The Blonde.

"I was immediately drawn to the role," she says, "although a lot of the approach was about fully committing to the rather absurd circumstances and having fun with it! Action films are fun because they are so physical—lots of running, shooting, and fighting."

Just the last two would come in handy as The Blonde. She could shoot and fight, and we'd see both in abundance. But not running. That would imply that she had to get somewhere fast, faster than she'd intended or expected. Perhaps on someone else's time.

Not this lady. She was where she wanted, and everyone else had damn well better accept it. And if they didn't, it meant their lives.

It takes some time, but the *Guns* storyline gist comes around about a missing mask, passed down through generations of Indians (or Native Americans—as the flick repeatedly points out, the Indian word is as slur-ish as anything starting with N or K or W). It's worth a cool million, so she's not the only one on the hunt.

Doesn't matter. As Christian Slater's John Smith tries to figure out why everyone thinks he's the thief, she kills three Elvis impersonators and a bus driver. As cool hit(wo)men so often do in the action film world, she just has to punctuate her violence with some soothsayings, the words of a man who wrote about happenings far sadder that what we see.

Mainly "The Raven," which is everything but constitutionally required to read at least three or four times, and "Annabel Lee," also right up there on the ranks of Poe's top works. Of course there's a connection between her and the writing legend, but this is one of the most surreal—yet realistic—action films of the millennium.

"It was trickier than I thought to make the poetry sound right and fit into the scenes," Mattson admits. "Actually, there wasn't a huge amount of special effects in the film. I did all my own stunts and all the guns going off are actual 'fake' bullets."

Eventually, everyone winds up at a secluded house armed with two briefcases with a million each inside, with the mask (so they think!) inside with her. After methodically kicking the hell out of a giant Native American (shit, the guy's name was "The Indian," just like hers was "The Blonde"!) without gasping, she has the crowd outside all but spellbound.

"I had to do several weeks of stunt and weapons training to prepare for the fights and action scenes, which was really fun and challenging," Mattson says. "I did taekwondo and hapkido."

As she and John get alone, we find out they were once an item before she ditched him for another lady. But she still gives him a briefcase, scares everyone into staying away from him, and runs off with her girlfriend and some money.

And the mask? He gives it to the lady whose family it was stolen from, and wanders off.

"I have always been fascinated by the magic of making movies," recalls Mattsson, who ironically would play "The Blonde Lady" in *Seven Psychopaths* that same year, and had been a gal nicknamed the Blonde next to Bruce Willis in 2009's *Surrogates*. "I was pretty shy growing up, but I was always brave and confident being on stage. So I decided pretty early on to pursue it and give it my all. I really enjoy doing a variety of genres."

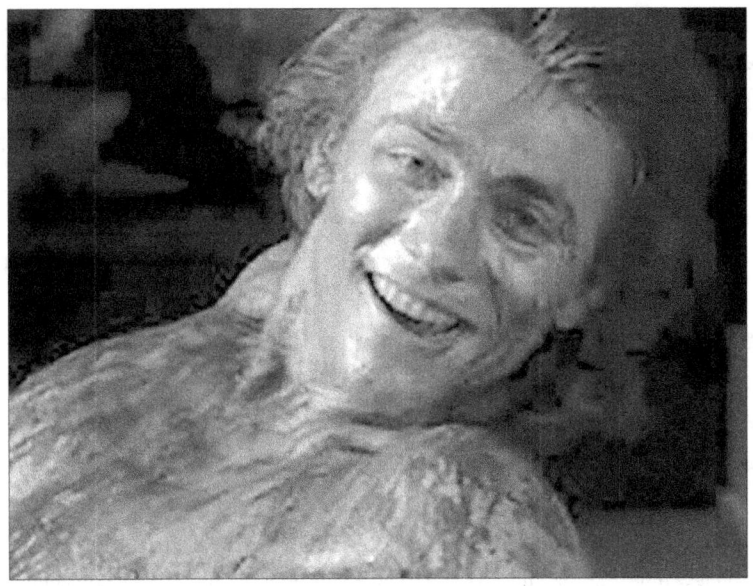

Insanity can get anyone, and makes us do all kinds of horrible things. It's left to the legal system to sort things out, as Alex McArthur's Charles Reece found in 1992's *Rampage*.

Alex McArthur: *Rampage*

ON ITS FACE, THE insanity defense might look pretty solid.

After all, who can say that a sane person will drown her own kids, which Susan Smith and Andrea Yates did? Kill people, chop them up, and hang out with their body parts, like Jeffrey Dahmer and Ed Gein? Shoot a president to impress an actress, as was the John Hinckley Jr. case?

But there's another argument to be made from the other side: if we go too far with insanity, we're basically saying that committing an unthinkably horrible, barbaric crime becomes in and of itself the excuse for not being punished for the act.

It all boils down to who jurors believe, which shrinks tell the best story. Unfortunately, when one of directing's greatest names tried to take us a step further into the argument, very few got to see it. Even today, a quarter-century later, not nearly enough have checked out arguably William Friedkin's most underrated work. It's a sad example of how much work can be wasted when politics and bad financial decisions get involved in the filmmaking business—and Friedkin's not the only one who got shafted on 1992's *Rampage* (not the 1963 Robert Mitchum vehicle of the same name, the 2009 Uwe Boll flick, nor even the guilty pleasure video game series in which players get to be Godzilla or King Kong!).

"A lot of time people think you get to pick and choose in this business," Alex McArthur explains, "but the rest of us are thankful to get an offer of any time. A lot of times, you get an offer and it's something that you don't want to do, but it's not like you're really picking and choosing. You have to make a living, and unless there's something *really* repulsive about the part they're offering, you take it."

Of course, the director's name would alone be more than enough to attract any upcoming performer, with one Oscar for *The French Connection* (1971) and almost another (and certainly even more box-office success) two years later for *The Exorcist*. It was all McArthur needed, even to play this kind of role.

Becoming a serial killer. One that, like many do, did his work for reasons far past personal—as in, nothing against the individuals being harmed, but for some higher, even "greater," motive that the world's greatest group of brainpeekers couldn't explain.

"As a young actor, Charles Reece was my dream role," McArthur says. "I had the opportunity to create something pretty much from scratch, and play it with Friedkin's guidance, any way I wanted."

Here's a great coincidence—guess how Friedkin had come across the young performer? Not for the few roles that had just started to fill his resume, nothing that came anywhere *near* Reece. Something that it takes a special kind of microscopic intuition to see.

"I had done a video with Madonna," explains McArthur, who'd played the songstress' boyfriend as she showed "Papa Don't Preach," which helped launch both her iconic career and a then-still-blossoming network called MTV. "That's why [Friedkin] wanted to hire me as a serial killer: he told me that he thought I had an innocent vulnerability, and that's what he wanted." Wow. Just . . . wow.

Like many serial killers, Reece wouldn't be the physically intimidating type—who in hell could have possibly been intimidated by Charlie Manson's pip-squeakish 5'2" form?

"I was really muscular at that time, and they thought that was really inappropriate," McArthur says. "I lost a lot of weight on a real strict carbohydrate diet. It affects your mind when you cut out protein. Staying within the boundaries of nutrients can affect the way your brain is working. It's hard talking to a doctor about that; they look at you cross-eyed. It helped me reach the state of mind I wanted to achieve."

And, *man*, would any actor, even putting experience and talent aside, need some serious assistance here. Reece is the first person we see, and he blasts an old lady's brains out, then knocks off her husband and daughter. Soon after, a woman and child are dead too, all so he can drink their blood.

But it's not even a Dracula complex here. He does it not to live forever, like the fanged folk, but to purify himself. Yeah, when it comes to derangement, we could argue these motives up there with Hinckley, Dahmer, or that piece of shit Mark David Chapman, the John Lennon assassin who they should have fried about two seconds after he was convicted.

McArthur and Friedkin read up on many such mass killers and more, including Richard Chase, who killed (at least!) six people, including two kids and a pregnant lady, in December 1977 and January 1978 in the Sacramento area. Reece followed in Chase's blood-drinking ways, but fortunately not in his necrophilia!

"I met with psychiatrists several times," McArthur says. "They told me I shouldn't practice schizophrenia too much because I could start developing schizophrenic symptoms, and that's exactly what I did. There was a lot of religion involved too; my character was into religion, feeling like [his victims] were physically affecting him."

It's tough to believe, but Reece's actions aren't really the focal point of *Rampage*, instead more of a setup. It's more about Michael Biehn's prosecutor Anthony Fraser's battle with himself as to whether the death penalty is appropriate for even *these* acts (he used to be against it). Reece is convicted and sentenced to die, full of remorse that we'll never know is real or not, then declared nuts after a brain scan. But here's where things got really complicated off the screen.

Originally, the film ended with Reece dead after OD'ing on pills he'd smuggled into his cell (as had been Chase's fate). The film was literally days away from release in the fall of 1987; the *Los Angeles Times* gave a great review, and some European audiences got a look.

Then De Laurentiis Entertainment Group, founded by the legendary producer Dino himself, which had knocked out the similar *Manhunter* the year before, went belly up after several of its flicks failed at the box office. Some, like *Bill and Ted's Excellent Adventure* (1989), were distributed elsewhere, but *Rampage* wasn't picked up until Miramax grabbed it in 1992.

By then, there was a new ending; Reece didn't die, but was institutionalized and up for parole. But it was too late; the virtually ignored film lost millions. Today, it's hardly an afterthought in the career of Friedkin, who took an even closer look at the uncomfortable world of jury duty with his own 1997 TV remake of the legendary *12 Angry Men*.

"Everybody's hard work went right down the drain," McArthur admits. "Six years later, nobody gave a shit. Too much time had passed. It was just bad luck, just unfortunate."

He hit the action world hard in 1997, showing up next to Mel Gibson and Julia Roberts in *Conspiracy Theory*, then coming *this* close to playing serial slaughtering detective Nick Ruskin in *Kiss the Girls* before Cary Elwes grabbed the role. McArthur ended up as Ruskin's law-abiding colleague Davey Sikes—strangely, though, his prep methods would be even more realistic to get on the good side of the law.

Filming down in the Durham area where the story itself took place, he connected with the local police department.

"They got a call for a homicide," he remembers. "I left my hotel and jumped into a cab to get to the scene. They told me what had happened, and walked me through it. They were so organized, nothing like the way they're portrayed in the movies."

Over half a century after helping make horror history as a kidnap victim in 1991's *Silence of the Lambs*, Chris McGinn played a villainess who snared Halle Berry's kid in *Kidnap* (2017).

Chris McGinn: *Kidnap*

IT WAS TIME TO give them a taste of her own medicine!

Nearly two decades before, she'd been kidnapped (well, her character had). Tortured. Her life stolen. Her body preserved only to be shown off, a trophy her captor and killer used to laugh in the face of the hapless law enforcers he knew would never catch him.

Now Chris McGinn was on the blackened offense. It was her turn to play the kind of cretin partaking in one of the worst crimes ever.

"It's strange for me too," she says of 2017's Kidnap. "It's kind of crazy to see me as the bad guy!"

Her as the evil Margo, and Lew Temple as Margo's husband (read: sidekick) Terry. Their abductee Frankie (Sage Correa), just the next in a line of victims. Karla, Frankie's mom, out to do whatever it took and even more to save him. That would be Halle Berry, her status as one of Hollywood's top workhorses translating once again into heroine mode, just as it had for her in four *X-Men* films and elsewhere.

Everyone had gone to the extreme before and behind the camera. But for years, it wasn't likely that any of it would be seen by anyone. Per usual for such an occurrence in the business, it was far past anyone in the group's control.

"The waiting for the movie to come out could be its own movie," McGinn sadly admits. "It was pretty miserable, the ups and downs and craziness of what happened before it actually was released."

A year before in *The Call*, Berry'd been a 911 operator yanked into action to save a kidnapped young lady from a sadist, past and present meeting in typical action mode for Berry's gal. This time, her connection was clearer and sadder, now up against several opponents instead of one in a film she'd produced.

"It's good to have some female representation in action," McGinn says. "Halle wanted there to be a female villain."

Margo was scripted as a Southern belle on the larger side, far from the shrinking violet that so many ladies from below the Mason-Dixon line are raised to become.

"It fit me pretty well," McGinn remembers. "I audition for whatever's offered if I believe in the project."

Across the country from the Kidnap crew, she fired up a Skype camera and monitor to morph into Margo.

"They asked if I could self-tape, meaning have someone tape me doing scenes," McGinn says. "They sent notes and told me I was in the running." Face to face on opposite coasts, she explained to Luis Prieto why she could lead the antagonist ranks in his next directing foray.

"We talked for about forty minutes," says McGinn. "He said he wanted to talk to me to see if I was a nice person. I was so much like Margo in the videos that he wanted to make sure I wasn't really like her."

Two days later, her phone rang. The good news was, she didn't have to hop on a plane and fly all the way to Los Angeles for another conversation – the role was hers.

If the bad news was worth it: four days from then, she'd have to land down in New Orleans, and expect to stay for over a month.

But of course!

Kidnap gets right to acting out its title; early on, Margo's hauled Frankie out of his pleasant carnival day and into a car, leading Karla into panicked action.

"By the time I got the part, I felt pretty comfortable with who she was," McGinn says. "In my taping, I had dressed in a tight T-shirt, worn yoga paints, with my hair all greasy and messed up, and they ended up dressing Margo like I dressed in the audition." Eventually, Terry's got Frankie in his car, with Karla forced to follow, Margo giving her orders from the backseat.

"They made sure that Sage was comfortable with me," McGinn says. "We made sure he knew it was a game. He was new to (acting), and we wanted him to always feel that he was safe. He could always say to stop if he felt something was wrong. He wasn't afraid to go to some places that would scare me or piss me off as a character."

Just six years old at the time, the youngster had been a ways away when McGinn's biggest (or most seen) role had come about. Her experiences there would be a different kind of starting point for Margo's mindset.

In 1991, she'd played a kidnapping/murder victim in a flick that raced to the ranks of legend. Stretched across an autopsy table, her body inadvertently provides a huge clue to a serial killer haunting police all over the Southeast.

There's a very rare moth down her throat. It pushes cops and FBI agents toward Buffalo Bill. One's a young lady named Clarice Starling, herself locked in an inadvertent mind war with a (temporarily) captured killer the press gleefully monikered Hannibal the Cannibal.

It was *Silence of the Lambs*. McGinn's memories of Anthony Hopkins' Oscar-winning work as the flesh-chomping shrink helped her locate Margo.

"I think that (Hopkins') villain is so genius because he isn't the obvious villain," she says. "You're charmed by him. I used to jokingly say that he was kind of like a man who just happened to eat people's faces. I felt like the darkness of Margo needed to have that kindness, to not be afraid to go to that place, to do whatever it takes to get what she needs. But as things go on, they happen to make her even more angry, more crazy, more volatile."

Fighting off Margo for now, Karla soon kills Terry, her possible links to Frankie vanishing faster and faster. A quick glance over a "Missing Kids" collage at the local police station shows her that these people have been at this trade for far too long. Arriving at their house, she finds Frankie, but Margo's back for one last brawl.

"I felt that Margo was misunderstood," McGinn explains. "My subtext is, and was, that this was gonna be their last kidnapping, the last big thing. It was going to give them enough money and security to get out of this business, and instead everything went haywire and wrong. That's why I connected with her: because she's trying to get by the best she can. Obviously, morally, stealing kids is not the way to go, but I could commit to being really, really bad."

It's commonplace to have one last chase scene and bloody brawl in the closing moments of this type of cinematic pack. Two women acting it out, however, is quite a bit newer. Just one more rule to which Kidnap became an exception. Spilling off a boat nearby, Karla and Margo engage in the day's main event, Margo's own weight and Karla's adrenalin holding the jezebel underwater for a bit too long.

"Everyone was worried that I was going to hurt her, because I'm a big girl," McGinn says. "There was a lot of 'Halle, be careful!' I was always careful and aware. I would make sure that we felt safe with each other."

After filming wrapped, everyone felt safe. Their work had been done, and now it was the public relations group's responsibility to spread the word, and hopefully the audience's job to respond. Then, for reasons no one on the *Kidnap* crew could predict, control, or repair, things nearly vanished.

You see, everything described thus far in this profile happened in the last months of 2014. Before *Kidnap* could come out, its production company, Relativity Media, filed for bankruptcy the next summer. For over three years, the film sat in the annals of lack-of-distributorship, looking more and more like a wasted effort.

"It was pretty miserable," McGinn says. "Here I am, in a movie that I think is going to come out the next year, and then, because of event after event after event, it keeps getting put on hold." Finally, in 2017, a new group called Aviron Pictures picked up *Kidnap* and released it that August.

"It was really exhilarating for all of us," remembers McGinn of the flick's overdue arrival. "We were all hugging and laughing at the premiere, we had kept in touch, been rooting for it for so many years, knowing it was finally going to come to pass was a really exciting experience. It felt complete by then."

Coast Guard member Graham McGinnis recalled the shock that he, as much of America, felt when learning of the Deepwater Horizon disaster as he acted out the Guard's real-life duties in the 2016 film version.

Graham McGinnis: *Deepwater Horizon*

It's TOUGH TO BELIEVE that the sudden, tragic loss of humanity could become a secondary part of a worldwide news tale, but that's pretty much what happened in the Gulf of Mexico on April 20, 2010.

That was the sad day the Deepwater Horizon, in the midst of drilling for oil, exploded, caught fire, and sank. Hundreds of millions of gallons of the thick, dark liquid would pour into the ocean like a slowly erupting volcano for the next five months.

The eleven people from the rig that still today rest in their watery graves off the coast of Louisiana were treated as an almost afterthought, as were the seventeen that were injured. The focal point, quite literally, became the ocean's poisoning. Broadcast around the clock on TV and the Internet, the leak wasn't sealed for nearly five months, plenty of time to give the horror its infamous place way down next to the Exxon Valdez in the ranks of America's worst oil spills.

Stationed in New Jersey at the time, Graham McGinnis and the rest of the Garden State's Coast Guard wing cheered on their colleagues down south.

"Most of the people from the rig had already been picked up by offshore vessels," he remembers (over a hundred workers had been on the rig at the time). "We picked up a lot of the really injured guys and took them back to New Orleans. What really captured the nation's attention was how bad the oil spill was."

What exactly happened? How did the explosion and spill occur? More importantly (well, eventually), who were the people that were lost? Not until the fall of 2016 were these questions answered when the Horizon became its own title character at the movies.

By that point, McGinnis was a veteran in the Guard rescue swimming program, helping out those in trouble far from the land—but, like over half of his colleagues, he'd needed a second try to make it through an initiation that many would call harder than Marine boot camp.

"It was really tough, not making it the first time," recalls McGinnis, who finally passed the test in 2014, taking a few years to muster up a comeback. "It was hard to get the gumption to go a second time, knowing what's in store for you. I always say that the two proudest moments in my life were the day I got married and the day I passed. There's no other job that I would see fit to go back for a second try."

Working in the Big Easy, the same one that found out how tragically flood-prone it was during Hurricane Katrina in 2005, McGinnis and his colleagues got an e-mail asking them to do their thing before the cameras.

"We all made videos and sent them in," remembers the trouper of high school and college drama. "I always liked acting, always had a performer's personality. I just never knew it would happen that randomly."

Three years after *Lone Survivor*, Peter Berg and Mark Walhberg were showing another real-life visual tale. With Wahlberg in the lead as rig fire fighter Mike Williams (whose actual voice would open and close the film), we'd see just what happened before the strongest lasting image of the oil leak occurred.

Like the issues with the rig's drill pipe that not enough people took seriously enough. The explosions of mud that blew it apart. The gases that built up more and more until it was too late to stop them.

That's what really would set *Deepwater* apart from most other such flicks—not necessarily *improve* it, just differentiate it: how long it takes for things to get going. The blast doesn't happen until over halfway through the flick. The people whose stories hadn't been told, whether they were around to see it or not, were shown instead.

The film didn't go for the cheap clichés; there's no guy saying, "I just got engaged, and we're gonna have the biggest wedding in history!" or somebody else that's all, "I'm going to meet my kid for the first time as soon as we get back home!" or other sorts of things that show us right off who'll make it and who won't. Cop-out drama doesn't happen here, because it didn't happen there. This isn't a place for the sappiness/cheese combo.

As Williams and the others try to fight back the fire raging on the rig, one of the largest self-made movie props in film history, the Guard is alerted, albeit too late for too many.

Just weeks after snaring the role, McGinnis and his colleagues were acting out their work.

"Peter Berg came in and looked around the room, saying 'How would you do this? How would you answer the phone?'" he recalls. "He wanted it to be as real as possible. It transitioned into me and another guy who didn't expect to have any lines getting a more principal role."

As word of the Horizon finally comes over, we see McGinnis' lieutenant calling his impromptu troops to action, letting them know that it's time to go to the same kind of work we see in every branch of the Armed Forces, always ready to go anywhere and do anything to save people they'd never even heard of, just because it's right.

"I was very comfortable with managing a communications room like that," explains McGinnis, who'd reviewed some qualification manuals and stood in for some of his instructors to get ready to perform. "One of my first jobs was monitoring radio transmissions, when search and rescue missions would happen. I've been in a room when it's crazy like that."

Again, showing some tragic aspects of which not enough of America was aware, the film has Williams and his friends, with help from the Guard, making it back home, mourning their loss and trying to figure out where to go and what to think, or even how. Many who escaped with their lives never ventured into the water again, but *Horizon* pays a special, well-overdue tribute to those gone forever, along with the ones that made it and folks (like McGinnis' co-workers) who were the reason they did so.

"What you see on the screen is a job I had performed in my career," he remembers. "Having the experience already in my life was preparation for the role."

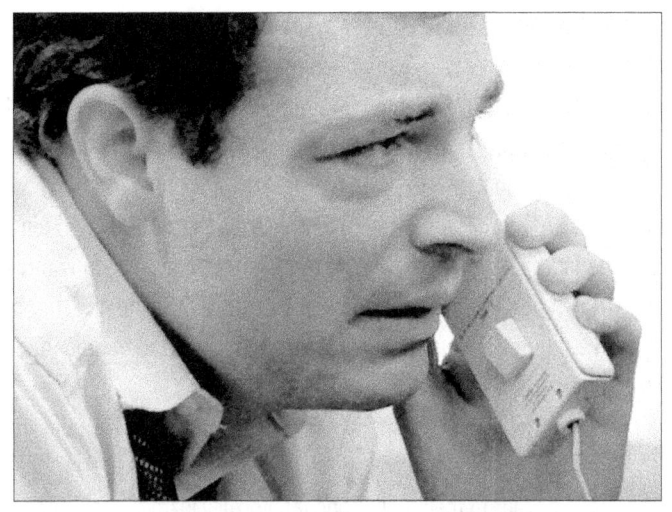

Brennan Elliott and Monnae Michaell portrayed the conversation that Lisa Joyner and Todd Beamer shared on the infamous morning of Sept. 11 in 2006's *Flight 93*.

Monnae Michaell, Brennan Elliott: *Flight 93*

LIKE MILLIONS OF OTHER Americans, Monnae Michaell found her world turned upside down on a September morning that will never seem very long ago to those that were around.

"I was going to the first day of a spiritual class in Los Angeles," she recalls. "That morning, I got a phone call from a girlfriend. I went to the television, and tried not to panic."

The New York native prayed that her sister, who worked in the World Trade Center, would make it out all right. She did, but a family member lost a cousin in the attack.

For the next few years, America went through a recovery it may never completely finish. Then, slowly, unavoidably, the film world started to form its own depictions of an American tragedy.

Michael Moore was first on the scene, with his 2004 Oscar-winning documentary/editorial/comedy/all-out-attack-on-Republicans *Fahrenheit 9/11*. Two years later, Oliver Stone put out the character study *World Trade Center*, which focused on the aftermath of the New York attack.

That same year, two films stepped aboard an infamous plane, the one that put a human face on the attack; the one that millions could rally behind, as it had more names, faces, and, through two people, voices.

While two planes hit New York and another smashed Washington D.C., passengers aboard United Flight 93 watched in horror as terrorists killed several pilots and others, and took control of the plane. Making frantic calls to their friends and family, they learned of the other attacks, and guessed that they were aboard a guided missile, perhaps to destroy the Capitol Building or the White House. Herded to the back of the plane, the passengers said their last goodbyes to their families.

We'll never really know what happened—everything that was said or done. But there was one conversation that truly brought to light the heroism of the American spirit in a group of people who should never have had to show it.

A married father of two, with another on the way, New Jersey native Todd Beamer called the GTE Customer Center in Oakbrook, Illinois. Seconds later, supervisor Lisa Jefferson was with him in the inadvertent spotlight.

Beamer, whose wife was also named Lisa, said that he didn't think the hostages would make it. Jefferson tried to comfort him, and two recited the Lord's Prayer together.

Then Jefferson heard Beamer say the immortal words: "Are you guys ready? OK, let's roll." Moments later, the plane crashed in western Pennsylvania—and America won the last round.

For Fox's 2006 television depiction, *Flight 93*, Michaell was asked to become Jefferson, while Brennan Elliott won Beamer's role.

"I wasn't familiar with her beforehand," Michaell says of her character. "I tried to find stories about her, read everything that I could. I pieced together some things, and the rest I made up."

She did so by calling upon her own memories of the moment, and trying to guess what she might do in such a situation.

"There's a certain methodology to what we do," she says, "and there's a certain amount of creativity that happens that we don't know how to put into Step One, Step Two, Step Three. I knew how [September 11] had impacted me, and I went to that place. I realized that all the character and emotions were completely accessible."

To play Todd Beamer, Elliott looked for words that could tell the story like no other.

"I went on the Internet, and I got *Let's Roll*," he said, referring to the 2002 book by Beamer's widow Lisa (Elliott said that Beamer herself declined to actually get involved in his preparation).

"I was playing somebody who was a part of something worldly famous," he says. "I want to let the material affect me—feeling images, impressions, whatever comes out of my instrument, my soul, I play it. The impressions become choices that I can use on screen. I had material that was about an experience that no one should have to experience. While I was reading [the book], I felt incredible amounts of fear, and the need for justice. These were just feelings, emotions coming out."

Elliott explored Todd Beamer's Christian faith and devotion to his family. He thought back to the dark, manipulative people Elliott himself had the bad luck to encounter from time to time.

"There were times in my life when I had been unjustly attacked," he says. "I recreated those experiences on set, with people, places, smells, everything, to make them real for me and unlock the emotion."

Michaell didn't have far to do so, either.

"I imagined how I would feel out of the blue: having no warning on the news that anything was happening, I get a call," she says. "Is it a prank call, or is it real? Then I turn on the news, and I see this happening. I'm in total shock, yet I have to keep my cool."

But as the audience saw, sometimes a cool can't be fully kept. As Jefferson gets the closest unpresent view of the tragedy, Michaell brings her emotions straight forward. She's nearly shaking, tears streaming down her face, but she manages to keep focused.

"It was a deep well of compassion and love that I felt [Lisa] had to have," Michaell says. "She had to be present for [Beamer], and she had to contain all that, because he wanted her to relay messages to his family from him, since his wife was named Lisa as well. How would I feel if the world was coming to an end? He was in shock; let me be there for him."

As the scene winds down, the two share the special prayer.

"That scene showed me where to start. I decided that [Lisa] was already, in some way, shape, or form, religious, so she knew the Lord's Prayer," Michaell says. "She had some connection between her and God. It was as if that scene, that moment in the scene, made the rest of the scene for me.

"When I got to the part, 'Thy will be done,' it was like, they were going to their deaths. I had no idea what was going on on this earth right now."

Watching the film later—it was nominated for six Emmys and took home the award for Best Editing—Michaell went back once again.

"I was pleased that it wasn't done in a sensational way, but it was difficult to watch because it was still very personal," she says. "I cried, and I felt very honored to be a part of the storytelling and the history. I was honored to play a role in which someone had to totally put themselves aside and be there for somebody else." Later, she says, Jefferson even called and congratulated her on her performance.

Author's note: The widespread 2006 cinema release, United 93, *which didn't spend as much time on the Beamer-Jefferson conversation, used several people who were actually on the ground when the plane was coming down, and family members of the flight members helped in making the film. The film scored two Oscar nominations and raised over a million dollars for a memorial to the flight near the Pennsylvania town where the plane crashed.*

Pvt. Joker (Matthew Modine) went from boot camp to battle in Stanley Kubrick's 1987 Vietnam masterpiece *Full Metal Jacket*.

Matthew Modine: *Full Metal Jacket*

OF STANLEY KUBRICK'S MULTITUDE of skills as a director, one of his finest was creating an atmosphere that his performers slowly became a part of. Often without realizing it, Kubrick-ian performers would find themselves stepping into a world of his creation, one that subconsciously switched their existence. If they weren't outwardly aware of the change they would undergo, their subconscious mind certainly was.

Kubrick wasn't one to spend individual time with his performers, talking them through the job he was looking for; he created a new existence, and let nature take its course. With *The Shining* (1980), Kubrick didn't sit down with Jack Nicholson and Shelley Duvall and explain to them just how crazy he wanted them to portray. He simply made the Overlook hotel the terrifying mind-altering location it would become, and watched his main stars cross the line from realism to fiction without realizing it until the final scene was shot.

Time and space played huge roles in Kubrick's films, and with *Full Metal Jacket* (1987), the same thing happened with Matthew Modine. Too young to have served in the Vietnam War, although certainly old enough to recall it, the man who'd become Private Joker found himself in a new overtaking . . . and never truly realized that it was as much in control of his performance as the actor himself.

As Kubrick subtly and gleefully pulled his puppet strings, Modine changed. Walking across the fields and streets of England that Kubrick had molded into the Ho Chi Minh Trail, the actor became the character, a much watered-down Jekyll to Hyde. His mind became that of so many who went through Vietnam—the one that long kept them from returning to normal function back home after the war.

It's how he started to speak with Joker's voice. Think with Joker's mind. Act with Joker's emotions. Transform into the man who openly admits that he joined the marine core strictly to become a killer, then feels himself shatter when his dream was forced to come true. . . .

Modine has been here before, though not to this extent, playing a Vietnam veteran in 1984's *Birdy*. But he hasn't worked for a while.

"I haven't found the script that I want," he recalls. "I want a film that has some balls. And I know something good is coming. I'm afraid that if I take one of these pictures that are just so-so, I'll be working on that when the great opportunity comes, and I won't be available."

Then he hears about Stanley Kubrick, a director that performers on any roster from the A- to Z-lists would hand over three paychecks to work for. Kubrick's supposedly got a screenplay based on the 1979 novel *The Short-Timers*, about a troop in the land of Saigon and Hanoi. With two brothers and a sister in the military, Modine can relate . . . sort of.

"I was probably interested in the role from having grown up with it," he says. "I just watched the war on television. Listening to the body count—listening to the score. Who was winning. It was like a baseball game. We got ten casualties. They got a hundred. Oh, we had a good day."

He gets a script draft, but he's a bit puzzled. There's terms like "crazy tough" and "phony brave" to disguise the characters, but not much more. The film's not editorialistic about the rightness or wrongness of the war—Kubrick was always among the greatest when it came to leaving his films open to public interpretation—just a story about men in a series of situations that can't be understood without being experienced.

But working with Kubrick is, after all, working with Kubrick. Modine's ready to roll.

He's just not sure who he's there to become. Maybe he'll find out from the master himself.

Outside Kubrick's England estate—in which Modine claims to have seen rooms filled with thousands of rejected audition tapes—Modine notices a watermelon separated from its colleagues, seeded and seedless. Kubrick asks him if he'd like to take a shot.

Not with the click of a camera. With the trigger of a shotgun.

"It's called a street-sweeper," Kubrick instructs. "When you fire, the drum turns automatically. It's a semi-automatic, short-range weapon."

Suddenly feeling like a perpetrator of the St. Valentine's Day Massacre, Modine levels the weapon against his side.

"I fire at the hapless watermelon," he recalls. "I see why Stanley set the melon aside. Not being familiar with the weapon, I could have easily destroyed his entire vegetable garden. . . . After a couple of tries, I finally connect, sending the red pulp and green flesh of watermelon all about the garden." After all, this is where the film's title emerges: "full metal jacket" refers to a lead bullet inside a copper jacket.

He'll be Private Joker. For the role of tormented colleague Pvt. Gomer Pyle (like Joker, clearly an antagonistically ascribed moniker), Modine mentions his pal Vincent D'Onofrio, a fellow acting student working as a bar bouncer between theater jobs. He, like everyone else, has no idea what D'Onofrio's going to do with this.

But Modine's not worried about that now. He's got to go further with Joker than with any other role before in his career (or since, many familiar with his work would argue).

"Trying to understand Joker is like trying to understand the Vietnam War," he realizes. "Why did we get involved? Why do young soldiers get sent to fight in wars that they don't know anything about?"

There's a very fine line between patriotism and fanaticism, between devotion to one's country and jamming said piety down someone's throat, or endangering oneself in the process. Many discovered this just after Pearl Harbor. Many felt it right after 9/11. And many found themselves just a bit too caught up in the jingoistic fervor that gripped America just after her entry into Vietnam, only to find it tapering off and then becoming reversed as the war wouldn't come to a satisfying conclusion.

Trying to understand his character and country's involvement in the battle, Modine keeps setting off on new paths, only to find out he's been travelling in a circle.

"It seems like the Americans were just fighting to prove something," he says. "Like a big bully constantly trying to prove his strength."

Despite the popular depiction, Vietnam wasn't all shooting and killing. That happened, and far too often, but much of it was sitting around, wondering when, where, or even if the next battle would be fought. Caught up in the perfectionist style of endless do-overs and other details that Kubrick's style always exemplified, Modine can feel his interest starting to wander off as everyone gets ready to shoot an interaction with a woman of the streets. More and more, this is really starting to feel like Vietnam, on a duty tour.

Like the journalist Joker is, Modine finds himself scribbling away in a notebook as the others toss out slurs—indiscriminately based on race and gender—towards the women in the scene, particularly the hooker. It's not Joker's act, and it's not Modine's either.

"We may be in a world of shit," he thinks (ironically so, as a later scene would prove), "but I don't want to be a turd in the toilet." Several days and dozens of takes later, they're finally done.

How could Kubrick look through so many takes of the same sequence and decide that one in particular stood out? It's impossible to know. Maybe he was just trying to make the first full-length film in history without a single continuity error (didn't happen, if only because people who pick that sort of thing out have far too much time on their hands).

"If he wants to do 50, so what?" Modine reasons. "I've seen his films and the performance of the actors. . . . Maybe he doesn't know what he wants and is trying to find or discover it. . . . The director has a vision of what he imagines a scene to be. What he imagines his film to be. If he doesn't see that happening, does he have to create a situation, an environment that will mold his actors into the form he has imagined?"

The actor has no idea what a prophet he truly is. Caught up in a new world and far out of his own control, Modine starts to see reality as a mixed bag, a jumble of emotions where the line between sense and nonsense is broken like one of the bombed buildings littering the set.

"Am I here? In London? In Beckton? The Fall?" he asks. "Aggression and xenophobia on the one hand and altruism and cooperation on the other. Sir." He doesn't say, "Sir, yes, sir." Not yet.

Unsure of what to do next, he even starts avoiding Kubrick, to whom he's become pretty close. Modine says he's not sure where to go with the character. Kubrick asks he only be himself.

That's one of those things that always sounds so simple in theory and impossible in execution. How can we be anyone else? How can we know what one of us, which side, will work? When are we ever truly ourselves? Obviously, we're different people when we're interviewing for a potentially high-paying job, as opposed to being out with our friends at a bar, having Crown Royale-shot throw-back contests. So which "himself" should Modine bring to bear?

"The important part was [Kubrick's] choice of words, how he interpreted my situation," Modine remarks. "There's a tremendous different between 'play' and 'be.'" At a boot camp, those in charge don't spoon-feed anyone; they put charges in a situation and make them find their way out. Joker hasn't been to camp yet (few films are filmed even remotely close to sequence), but Modine's finding a new respect for how they feel.

And then he, like a private on the verge of graduation and maybe even promotion somewhere in the future, finds something in himself.

"As of today, I am Joker," he declares, two months into filming. "I'm not playing . . . I am bringing my life and my experiences to this role. Not someone else's." He remembered reading about the war and watching it on TV. He looked back to the books he'd read, particularly *The Short-Timers*. One of the things that attracted him to Joker was that *Jacket* neither glorified nor vilified the war, only displayed it.

"I now reject the traditional movies about war and its nobility," Modine asserts. "I honor the stories about soldiers' dedication toward each other, but I question the motivation of the governments that send young men to battle. I confirm my choice not to work on films that glorify war and perpetuate lies about other countries and cultures." Like *Platoon* (1986), *Born on the 4th of July* (1989), and *Good Morning Vietnam* (1987) in the same days, *Jacket* didn't really show the Vietcong as the enemies, just people who cared about their cause and their country and standing up for each other.

"I'm going to make you feel the horror of death, the sickness of brutality," his mind coldly informs him. "I want to demonize the violence that I have grown up with. The violence that is so deeply a part of my consciousness. I need to purge it from my blood.

"And I want this to be the greatest war movie ever made."

He's a soldier in Kubrick's army now; the general has helped the private move up in ranks, again in character and as a person.

But he's not the only one. As he and his colleagues feast on food left over from the real Vietnam War, Modine can feel a new sense of camaraderie rushing through the troop.

"The environment of this film, while not 'real,'" he says, "evokes a mood or war. I am not alone in this belief. Others feel it too. I see the confusion. The sense of loss. Hopelessness . . . We are clearly out of our environment. We are being altered."

However, the ending still must be filmed. But as of November, it still wasn't finalized. So while we wait, let's skip ahead to the boot camp scenes that toned the entire film.

Not until January 1986 do the first audience-seen scenes commence. R. Lee Ermey has a legendary role in his grasp, and he's not about to let it slip away. The familiarity is there, as he's a former drill sergeant playing a drill sergeant, but he and Kubrick have prepared with a fervor.

His lines, Modine remarks, have been "learned to the point that they become unconscious thought. Organic. Learned to the point that they are a surprise even to the person saying them. Learned to the point that there is nothing more appropriate to say than the written lines—even the use of a 'reach-around.'"

Ermey accidentally slaps Modine during filming. Kubrick says to do it again. Modine isn't happy. D'Onofrio, now dozens of pounds heavier than when we last saw his name (he'll pay for that later when the overstressed ligaments in his knee give way), asks Ermey to whack him for real. Ermey is happy. Kubrick is happy. The scene is filmed at warp speed, by Kubrick-ian standards.

Modine and D'Onofrio aren't getting along—the tension that builds up between Joker and Pyle throughout the first part of the film now spills over to the set. For days, the two film together without speaking. Modine hopes that D'Onofrio's just staying in character, driving others away just as Pyle did. It's why, as Pyle's punishment scene at the hands of his troop (the toweled-soap whipping scene, which is description enough for any *Jacket* fan) draws near to filming, Modine hopes not to get too goddamned real.

"We've been at odds for weeks now," he says. "I do want to kick his ass for being such a fucking dickhead, but I take no pleasure in this towel beating. . . . What pleasure is there in beating the defenseless?"

Vincent D'Onofrio's Pvt. Gomer Pyle felt the terrors of war inside and out.

Still, once the scene gets through, Modine realizes what he doesn't feel anymore: the tension. The anger. The aura of emotion that's been almost visible between the two lately.

"I'm finished being angry with Vince," he says. "It's stupid. A waste of life."

But just when they're about done with the boot camp scenes, Ermey's in a car wreck, and knocks everything to the sidelines for a few months. During that time, the Chernobyl explosion stuns the world. It's as if Kubrick and fate are tag-teaming to keep Modine on edge until Joker takes his final march.

How he'll do so is up for grabs. A few months ago, several endings were kicked about. The first had Joker being gunned down by enemies with a machine gun, then flashing back to childhood as he talked his way to heaven. Elsewhere, he was shot and things went black, only to have him wake up in a hospital. There was the idea of him coming back home in the grasp of post-traumatic stress, then running into a fellow war buddy. Finally, thought up was the vision of troops marching through fields, singing the Mickey Mouse Club song, as a prologue informed viewers that Joker made it home, only, as so many vets did after Vietnam—and many wars before and since—to take his own life.

The final print would keep the song but leave out the suicide, and it's something that few other than Kubrick could have made audiences take seriously. It would have been so easy for viewers to look at a group of soldiers walking through hell in the midst of a kids-based chorus and laugh hysterically, but no one ever would.

Still, that's anti-climactic compared to the scene where Joker finally rises to the occasion he couldn't stop looking forward to and never really wanted to arrive.

Modine and his colleagues have made it through the scene where the troop tries to make its way across a clearing littered with burned and bombed buildings. A few brave souls venture out into the open, but a sniper cuts them down, including Joker's longtime friend Cowboy (Arliss Howard). Still, Joker and the rest have snuck into the killer's hideout and stolen the advantage of surprise. Joker's wish to kill hasn't come true yet, but as he squeezes the trigger upon his target, fruition appears to arrive.

Then he sees who he just shot. A girl who might have been enjoying her sophomore year of high school had the war not broken out. This sort of thing happened over there.

Yes, a moment ago, this child was trying to kill him and his friends, and succeeded—not a chance it was the first time for the character. Yes, if she had that gun that's about as big as her, she'd add a few more notches to her body count, and maybe blink as she did so. Maybe.

But this is a woman. It's not even a woman, but a young girl. Children die at war, and those who cause it often spew out garbage like "collateral damage," or the terminology used earlier by Joker's friend, who gleefully picked off women and kids from his trusty chopper. But thinking about it, hearing about it, practicing for it, even seeing others do it . . . well, none of that truly prepares us for what Joker's going through. In all fairness, absolutely nothing can.

"It is agonizing for me to imagine standing over another human being and deciding their fate," Modine says. "The scene makes me sick to my stomach. I have to go there. I look at the ground. I have to do this."

He's scared. He's angry. He's scared again. It's right. It's wrong. It's for the best. It can never be good. It's vengeance. Vengeance brings us down to the level of our targets.

He makes Joker's gun go off. It's the only one-shot take in the film—the girl who played the sniper isn't going back. Modine's much happier that way.

"The others speak to me," he says of his set-mates, "but I do not understand. I am changed. I have climbed the wall and fallen to the other side. There's no going back. I've drunk from the well of human blood and am poisoned."

He couldn't get out of Joker if he tried. It will be a long time before he's Modine again, and maybe he never fully will be. Kubrick's tactics worked, and no one will ever criticize his methods. On a Kubrick film, performers knew what they were in for. Job had to walk through hell to get to heaven. Joker waded through a world of shit, but he was alive.

Yes. He was alive. But he wasn't a hero. *Jacket* had the guts to go a bit farther than the simple blacks and whites of good guy and bad guy. The protagonist of a film doesn't always have to be the one who always does the morally right, and Modine could always feel Joker tottering on the line between good and evil.

"Joker doesn't have a name in the film," he says, pointing out a fact that's so easy for film fans to overlook. "He's Private Joker from the get-go; he could be any soldier in any war. He has so many contradictions . . . you want to live in a world of peace, but if you scrape the veneer a little bit and get into man's psyche, he becomes an animal; there's a beast just beneath this thin façade of power."

Kubrick, he continues, "doesn't try to create some sympathy for somebody because it's a film, because he wants to win the audience over. It's not pleasant to see somebody killed. And it's not pleasant to die. Why try to make something romantic when it's not?"

War is a sad, depressing thing, but it's also a complex thing. People don't go to war just because they get angry and decided to go on shooting sprees (*individuals* may do that, but countries don't). They do it because they feel there's no other choice, and that losing some lives and ruining others is worth it for the greater good. And while many say that falling in battle is the greatest honor a soldier can achieve, and as wonderful as it may seem when the enemy surrenders (remember the "Soldier Kissing Nurse" photo from after World War II?), Kubrick was one of the first not to glorify war or those that fight it, but simply to show it. Not as good, not as bad, only as human.

And decades later, critics and fans everywhere still hail *Full Metal Jacket* as the best war film (not just Vietnam film) of all time. Some even go so far as to call it Kubrick's best movie, though no one will ever fully win that debate.

It's fun to toss around the expression, "It's my/her/his/their world; we're just living in it." Modine found out firsthand just how real Kubrick could make that cliché.

"To the military, the world is chaos," he explains. "The military recognizes this and imposes conformity. There is only one way, one god, one country. You do not belong to yourself. You are part of a machine. Theirs.

"Directors are the same way."

While we're here, let's take a minute to review the preparation of the pair that inadvertently takes center stage during the first half of the film. D'Onofrio and Ermey had taken different paths to wear the *Jacket*, but it's a performance that they would be forever remembered for.

Doing Hartman's role had been a breeze for Ermey; a former drill sergeant and Vietnam vet himself whose wounds knocked him out of the war far too early in 1971, he'd wowed Kubrick with a single audition, one that defined the term "impromptu."

The technical advisor on 1979's *Apocalypse Now* and other such films, Ermey had asked to try out for the character of Hartman. Kubrick wasn't sure he could be mean enough.

This causes sudden flashbacks to the 1984 NBA draft, when Portland decided to take Sam Bowie over Michael Jordan, or the NFL in 1991, when 32 picks came before Brett Favre (who spent all of a season in Atlanta before being shipped to Green Bay). Unlike those unlucky choosers, however, Kubrick gets another eager look from his new protégé.

Actors in Action

R. Lee Ermey's drill sergeant performance shot straight to iconic ranks.

As Kubrick interviews British soldiers for roles in the flick, Ermey suddenly morphs over, verbally giving them a beating that would cause an intensive care visit were it physical.

"Lee lined them up like recruits who had just come off the bus into Parris Island," Kubrick said, "and let go with the barrage of intimidation and insults which the occasion always brings."

D'Onofrio, on the other hand, must face lottery ticket odds for his own win of the role.

He'd hunted down a speech that had been given to new members of the law enforcement community, and altered it a bit to give it a military edge. Then he'd put on some fatigues and a military hat, located a barracks-type stairway, and taped himself giving the speech. With thousands to pick from, Kubrick notices something special in the tryout.

Meanwhile, Ermey was writing most of Hartman's dialogue, especially in the opening boot camp scene when the two meet for the first time, and the foreshadowing commences. If it looks especially genuine, that's because it is; Ermey was never allowed around the rest of the crew during rehearsals—if his costars saw him as an actor instead of a character, he and Kubrick figured, their acting talent wouldn't be enough to reach the levels of intimidation, even terror, that the director wanted.

"My objective was intimidation," Ermey explains. "No one had ever entered their private space. No one had ever put his head close to them." His tactics worked; the first time Hartman and Pyle interact, D'Onofrio needed a few takes to simply say, "Sir, yes, sir," and "Sir, no, sir."

"There's a rhyme and reason for damn near everything a drill instructor does," Ermey says. "The new privates arrive and it's immediate jaw-flexing, yelling, screaming, jumping up and down intimidation for the first week. The reason for that is to put the private in the capable palm of the drill instructor's hand. Back in those days intimidation was the greatest tool the drill instructor had. Without that tool, he would not have had control. The drill instructor must have total and complete control. Mindless obedience is what he's after."

Still, during rehearsals, Ermey's pushed back to his own trainee days for the time being. In a large room, a crew member fires fruit and tennis balls at him as he practices his rants.

"I had to catch the ball and throw it back . . . as fast as possible and say the lines as fast as possible," he says. "If I were to slur a word, drop a word, or slow down, I had to start over. I had to do it 20 times without a mistake."

Pyle becomes both Hartman's target and project. Military service will never be for the physically and/or emotionally iffy, and Hartman was faced with overcoming both or neither, convinced that this kid could be a physically explosive killing machine if he could just reach up his ass and pull out his head. Tragically, he turns out to be right.

"Because of the weight and the fact that he was totally out of his element," D'Onofrio recalls, "[Pyle's] mind became weak. He was slow to start, a country bumpkin, but I don't think he was insane." Well, not at first. But just as Dr. Frankenstein's creation eventually turned against him, Pyle slips to a place he can't get back from and takes Hartman with him.

Pyle makes a progressive step here and there, but eventually falls back to where he started off, and perhaps a bit further back than that. We get the feeling that he might be suffering from a slight form of mental disability—more of the autistic type, not schizophrenia or something similar. We also guess that this isn't the first time he's encountered bullying in his life. As tough as it is to diagnose today, mental disability was all but unknown as recently as a few short decades ago. Carrying around a few extra pounds can make a person a target for tormentors of any age.

Even after filming, D'Onofrio recalls, "Women didn't look at me; most of the time I was looking at their backs as they were running away. People used to say things to me twice, because they thought I was stupid." That's both a compliment to his performance and a dark side of society that, even years later in the 2010s, still creeps across America.

And in the infamous bathroom shooting scene, Pyle's character becomes the next in line to display the dark, demonic grin that no one with an ounce of sanity could see as friendly. Just as Jack Torrance stared at us and his family in the "Here's Johnny!" *Shining* scene, just as Alex DeLarge bore holes through the audience at the opening of 1971's *Clockwork Orange*, it's Pyle's turn to show the dark side of a smile.

Looks like Modine wasn't the only one who fell under the Kubrickian spell.

Before we step away from the *Jacket* men, there's another few stories worth telling about the tale and those behind it, and, for some other actors, it all started back even before the actual dark and dangerous jungles of Vietnam itself.

Just out of high school, one young man was looking to be the newest addition to the armed forces—which particular arm, however, was yet to be determined.

"They told me that the Army and Marines both had two-year shifts," **Tim Colceri** recalls. "I looked at the posters. The one for the Army had a guy in a tree with a gun. The one for the Marines had a guy in a tree with a gun too, but he had greasy stuff on his face. You could hardly see his eyes."

In the threatening countenance, Colceri saw his future, one that would end up including thirteen months in the Da Nang bushes.

Tim Colceri's work as a door gunner was called a film highlight by many veterans lucky enough to see *Full Metal Jacket*.

"I was a normal guy," he says—as with most vets of any wars, Colceri doesn't seem too thrilled to revisit the service. "I wanted to do my time, get it over with, and come home. It's how I learned I wasn't afraid to jump in the fire and get burned. If I got burned, I jumped out."

It's tough to imagine a wider set of career extremes: from dodging and firing bullets, Colceri stepped into the world of the flight attendant. One day, he went with a friend to an acting class.

"I said I could do that," he remembers. "I've been doing it ever since." Then, not long into his acting career, he heard the K-word, the name of the director that most actors would put themselves through torture worse than boot camp to work with.

"A friend of mine found out that Kubrick was doing a story about the Marine Corps," Colceri recalls. "I had written a screenplay about my experiences in boot camp and Vietnam."

A friend filmed him putting on an impromptu drill sergeant show, and Colceri dropped the tape in the mail. A full three years later, his phone rang.

Colceri's agent told him someone from London wanted to talk with him. It turned out to be Leon Vitali, Kubrick's longtime associate. Having acted for Kubrick in *Barry Lyndon* and helped him produce *The Shining*, Vitali was now casting Kubrick's most action-packed film (he'd later do the same job on 1999's *Eyes Wide Shut*).

The actor charged into Hartman's persona. Like the troops he attempted to awe into submission, the *Jacket* crew was blown away.

"I got a call from Warner Brothers, saying they wanted me to be the drill instructor," he says. "I'd done three or four commercials and one film [1986's action flick *Never Too Young To Die*, aside the motley crew of John Stamos, Robert Englund, and Gene Simmons] and now here I am with this big role."

After that, however, things got a bit choppy.

While Modine and others spent a few months filming combat, Colceri stayed home and rehearsed. At this point, Ermey was only the film's technical advisor. Then it finally came time for the boot camp scenes.

That's when Kubrick noticed Ermey handing out the dressing-downs to some recruits. As gently as possible, he told Colceri he'd been switched.

But not removed—the sad performer would still get to play the door gunner later on, and *Jacket* fans know where we're headed here.

"I had more time to think about this character," Colceri says, "and the ironic thing was that as the drill instructor, I had read the rest of the script, and when I read [the gunner role], I thought, whoever gets that role is going to have a ball! I never thought it would be me." Even such future household names Bruce Willis and Val Kilmer had wanted to do it, he continues.

He had one short shot to make a difference in the film, and it was even harder than it looked—because to viewers, looks would be deceiving.

Heading to a new post in 'Nam, Joker and his colleague Rafterman (Kevin Major Howard) try to keep their composure intact and lunch down, crowded into the back of a helicopter.

And the door is wide open—that's because it's filled with a gleeful marine with a huge gun, blasting away those on the ground.

In other words, Colceri's gunner.

Before we go further into his character's background, check this out—Modine and Howard had already filmed their part of the scene (notice that viewers only see them from behind, their faces never in the same shot). Colceri was actually on the chopper without them, talking to people he had to pretend were there.

"I spent a week memorizing their dialogue, talking to them in a scene that they weren't even in!" he says. "It was extras doing dialogue. I spent a week with Stanley. Every day, I'd come to his house. There was a helicopter in his backyard. I thought, 'No one will ever believe this!'"

Moving into his preparation, let's touch on a few of the most memorable dialogues of the flick. With seemingly enough enthusiasm to power the chopper itself, the gunner can't wait to share his own statistics of lowering the Vietnamese population, a number in the hundreds that we just saw him add to.

"Anyone who runs is a VC!" he blares. "Anyone who stands still, is a *well-disciplined VC!*"

"How can you shoot women and children?" Joker asks, almost wistfully, looking for a way to find at least some shred of humanity in the fellow. We can tell he expects (hopes!) to hear something like, "Well, you know, it's tough, but you know what you're going in for and all with this job and . . ."

Oh, HELL no. Not this guy. This is his life's work, and he's anxious to share the tricks of the trade.

"Easy!" he bellows, prouder than a kid whose homer won his little league game. "You just don't lead 'em so much! Ain't war hell?!" He's almost cackling with pitch-black boasting.

By the way, in non-military layman jargon, he means that shooters aim more directly at the slow-moving targets, rather than ahead of them ("leading them"). Fact is scarier and one hell of a lot more painful than fiction in this case.

Much like Ermey did for much of Hartman's dialogue, Colceri added to the ad-libs for the gunner; the line was originally the more redundant, "I just like to shoot people!"

"Dialogue is a blueprint, and it's my job to make it magical," Colceri says. "It's how I play all my roles: no matter how bad a killer you are, if you play it as likeable, the audience will like you. As far as my character, the way it was written, to me he was having fun doing what he was doing. It was smart the way they got it in there, and didn't make it so serious."

Early one morning the first day of shooting, he strolled around the helicopter before lift-off, looking through his mind for the gunner's persona. Some people are right at home in the middle of bloody battle, and Colceri hadn't been, but his character certainly was.

"I played him like a happy-go-lucky guy," he says. "He was crazy, but he was a happy, smiling guy."

Kubrick asked him to do it a different way, perhaps trying to instill in Colceri the same characteristics he'd helped Modine locate for Joker. About thirteen takes later, Colceri's work was done.

Someone else was having too good a time in the midst of battle himself. Just as Joker arrives overseas, he and his pals find their reacquaintance interrupted by a matter soon known all too deadly well as the Tet Offensive, the Viet Cong's largest attack of the war.

During a lull in the fighting back, the men grab some precious moments of relaxation in front of a visiting news crew. That's when a guy named Crazy Earl lives up to his name.

Calling the crew over, the squad leader invites them in for a look at his "friend," apparently napping with a huge hat for an eyeshade. As he removes the hat, we see that it's not a pal at all, but a VC who's fought his last battle. Earl sits there and discusses the situation.

"In the book, Crazy Earl is this colorful anarchic character—untamed," says **Kieron Jecchins**. "I found that attractive." In the book, the fellow's mentally off, but he's frailer and underhealthed, quite physically different from the man Jecchins made him.

Getting ready to become Earl, Jecchins checked over some books and flicks about the war. He met a fellow who'd been there.

The nuttiness of *Crazy Earl* (Kieron Jecchins) was clear on the outside during a break in the action.

In the first speaking role of his career, Jecchins had one of the toughest speeches in the movie. Sitting next to his "pal" in a scene reminiscent of the Abu Ghraib photos that scared America during the Iraq conflict of the early 2000s, he mentions what a fine time he's truly having, and all in a voice that adds a bit of pride to a monotone.

"These people we wasted here today are the finest human beings we will ever know," he admits. "After we rotate back to the world, we're gonna miss not having anyone around that's worth shooting." Sadly, or maybe fortunately in his own mind, Earl doesn't get the chance to return; leading the troop through the battle that will end in a sniper war, he finds a huge stuffed rabbit. Pulling it triggers the land mine that it's attached to, quickly ending his life and pushing Cowboy through to leader, a term that will also be quite short.

"My first monologue in *Full Metal* was a challenge because it was the first time I'd ever spoken on film, so I was pretty scared," Jecchins recalls. "We did thirty takes on that. I think we got something good out of that."

It would still be another year before anyone would see *Jacket* in the theaters. Fittingly enough, one of the first audiences was a group of Vietnam vets in London.

The studio called Colceri one last time.

"Every single one of the vets had said that the best guy was the door gunner," he recalls (the scene lasts less than two minutes). "I've talked to many, many door gunners and they told me that he was exactly like they were." Two decades later, he'd get an ironic shot at playing a drill sergeant on *Weeds*.

"I thought [Kubrick] was going to make me a better actor," he says. "I like to think I made him a better director. I look back [at *Jacket*] as a movie that'll play for a long time after I'm gone, and everybody will remember that character."

They do. But watching *Jacket*, they also get a sense of when American culture was a bit simpler, more straightforward. When military men spoke their minds to each other, and that was it. Things were said, and then put away. Not forgotten, but not an issue, mainly because avoiding the blasting off of one's head was a bit higher on the priority list.

The flick's pitch-black humor shows this right off the bat, as Hartman vows that, "I do not look down on niggers, kikes, wops, or greasers. Here, you are all equally worthless!" Were a sergeant to get caught saying that today, he'd probably end up on YouTube in two seconds, then court-martialed out and vilified by society, with his colleagues on a newscast crying that, "That sort of talk has *no* place in society! I'm just so ashamed to be associated with him."

Not then. Back then, it was just boot camp stuff. Red-blooded shit. People said things, but were tough enough to have them bounce off. Back then, men were concerned about fighting the enemy, and the only enemy was the one wearing a different uniform, not a different skin tone.

Before the *Jacket* events were even thought of, Paul Kersey had worn the red, white, and blue as a combat medic in Korea, and the shooting skills he'd learned over there had made him into a hero of vigilantism in the first two *Death Wish* films. As the third one got rolling in 1985, some guy called the Giggler gave Charles Bronson's cinematic creation an impromptu practice round with his trusty .475 Magnum Widley, the same piece he'd use to take care of much of East New York's gang activity later on.

Taking a break from his Giggling gig, **Kirk Taylor** heard that Kubrick was casting *Jacket*.

"I said, 'No, he's not,'" Taylor recalls. "I'd sent him a tape over a year ago. How could he still be casting?" Just as some of his eventual colleagues were learning about then, Taylor found that Kubrick had indeed *not* finalized the *Full* draft.

"I called Kubrick's office," he remembers. "I was doing a British accent, impersonating my own agent, asking if I could show up for an audition." He did, meeting Vitali.

"They put the camera on me, and I asked if I could tell Mr. Kubrick a story," Taylor says. Confused but intrigued, the crew agreed.

"I told a story about Little Johnny in school," he says. "Little Johnny was at show and tell, and he said, 'I had a brother who went to Vietnam, and got shot in the ass!'

"The teacher said, 'Oh, no, Johnny, we don't say that. Please say rectum.' Johnny said, 'Wrecked him? Shit, it killed him!'" The joke had the same effect on the crew. It looked like Taylor would become 8-Ball.

Equipped with these technological miracles called FAX machines, the crew sent Taylor a few scenes to do 8-Ball's thing. Not much compared to the trek he was about to set for himself

"It was huge," he says. "I was meeting with guys from New Orleans to get the accent down. I met with a *lot* of vets." He trained with a fellow who'd instructed others in 'Nam on proper gun usage in battle.

"One guy took me out into the woods to help me understand what they'd gone through," he says. "Some people thought the war was about having John Wayne War Syndrome, when you're fighting standing up, yelling at the enemies. The Vietnamese would bait soldiers into following them and set traps along the way. Many guys died that way."

His role model went a step further, telling him tales that, if they'd made it into the public—on the movie screens or the news ones—could have turned America against the war long before we did.

"They took guys to the top of a hill and buried them up to their neck," Taylor recalls hearing. "They slathered their faces with a pineapple K-ration, and stood there and watched while these guys were eaten up by fire ants. Stories like that really got into my psyche. I started having nightmares about Vietnam."

Then, in the span of a phone call, it all came crashing down. Almost.

"Leon Vitali called me, and said that Kubrick didn't think I was black enough for the role," Taylor says. "With the [script's] words like jungle bunny, spearchucker, jigaboo, I wasn't dark enough." After all that work, someone else would be 8-Ball.

Dorian Harewood's performance there would be a film highlight, but that wasn't much consolation for Taylor.

"I collapsed in my apartment," he says. "About fifteen minutes later, I got up and said, 'Not without a fight!' I prayed. I made some calls. I prayed some more."

It worked. He learned that Kubrick had appointed him as Sgt. Payback, Joker's fellow John Wayne fan, a sad expert on the infamous thousand-yard stare that would become the soldier's stereotypical caricature.

And the racism he wasn't racial enough to play came back around. Early on in his 'Nam venture, Joker's hanging out with his barrack buddies, like Payback.

Kirk Taylor worked as hard as his character would to snare the role of Payback.

Someone tells a stupid joke about black men and a basketball. Today, again, such a slur would probably get a guy discharged without honor and plastered all over social media as a dredge on society; Payback, as many did at the time, just invites him to shut the fuck up, and everyone laughs.

Seconds later, they're under attack, and it's all in the past. All that matters now is backing each other up. The guys that just met, the guys that acted like idiots, whoever—they're Americans, they're soldiers, they're teammates, and there's a job to do when Charlie attacks.

"It was very exciting and a big responsibility," Taylor says. "You knew that you were part of something very special, something that people really liked, a message that needed to be heard." Ironically, his research would come back in hand just two years later in the midst of *Jackknife*. As fellow returned vets Megs (Robert De Niro) and Dave (Ed Harris) try to help each other deal with the PTSD that wasn't really named, let alone studied for at least another decade, they're suddenly tossed into the same sort of flashback that sneaks up on veterans long after the last bullet flies.

Taylor's a gunner, alongside whom Dave saw his friend die.

"When roles come along, and you've done the work already," he says, "it's like it's meant to be."

Quick! Name all the women you remember from *Jacket*!

Took you about three seconds, didn't it? That's about all anyone needed. They just were hardly in the film, although no one would ever forget the sniper we discussed. For completely opposite reasons, the one we're about to meet is pretty easy to recall as well.

Would that every actor could get so much mileage out of two simple, seemingly innocuous sayings!

"I wish I'd patented those lines," admits **Papillon Soo Soo**. "I still get ribbed by some friends with those lines, especially when I heard that those lines were used in two songs which were hits."

The axioms in question? Oh, just "Me so horny, baby!" and "Me love you long time!"

Indeed, Soo Soo was the Da Nang hooker who ushered in the second half of *Jacket*. Fresh out of a hellish boot camp that ended in tragedy, Joker and a colleague are relaxing between rounds—of combat, of course!—when Soo shows up to strut. "These Boots Are Made For Walkin'" is playing in the background the whole time, adding to the darkly (OK, pitch-coal-midnight-black wouldn't even come close to describing it) comic tone of the film.

A member of the world's oldest profession, Papillon Soo Soo's gal tried to woo her way into the hearts and wallets of a few vulnerable Americans.

"Sorry to be such a rude gal," she jokes, "[but] working on *FMJ* was like a 24-hour orgasm! Only because I was working with the late great Stanley Kubrick and the very talented Matthew Modine."

Those were the qualities she took away from her film debut a year before, joining the infamous legions of drop-dead gorgeous ladies who show up to seduce, and usually attempt to murder, the world's most famous Super Agent.

"Good chi and more chi!" she explains of her karmic victory of the villainous Pan Ho role in 1985's 007 flick *A View To A Kill*. "I believe everything you have in life comes from a greater source." Grace Jones played the murderous May Day, working with evil gazillionaire Max Zorin (Christopher Walken) in a plot to blow up mines under the Hayward and San Andreas Faults, flooding them and eventually causing an earthquake bigger than the one that devastated San

Francisco in 1906, all in the name of destroying Silicon Valley to control all the world's microchips. Ho became one of Day's henchwomen.

A short time later, the seeds for two of the most famous lines from 80s cinema were sown when Soo Soo took the rough, tough, excruciating task of . . . walking down the street!

"Fate!" she exclaims of the role. "It can't be a coincidence. I walk outside my front door and walk straight into one of the actors from the Bond film who had played Roger Moore's stand-in who just was passing by. He told me that they were looking for girls for a new Stanley Kubrick film on the Vietnam War."

Her agent called the *Jacket* casting crew, and Soo headed in for a meeting with the man himself. "They videoed a scene I had learnt," she says, "and that was it."

With all the subtlety of a chainsaw, the film is split into two halves, jumping from black to black (no, not a misprint there) in separate settings. The first deals with the forced stoicism that every marine recruit—well, every effective one—finds within in boot camp, as Modine is one of a group of men physically and emotionally forced straight into solider mode as Vietnam rages overseas.

"I think *FMJ* is current for what is happening in Iraq," Soo said in 2004. "You get boys and girls who were all sweetness turning into monsters torturing and abusing prisoners."

For Joker, things at camp finished off with a horrifying bang, as Pvt. Pyle, far over the wrong line to sanity, blasts his drill sergeant into eternity before taking his own life. Years later, however, Joker seems to have recovered, chilling on a street side when a representative of the world's oldest profession shows up to make a quick few bucks, demonstrating some blockbusting sales(wo)manship along the way.

It actually worked, although viewers didn't get to see it.

"I did a nude scene with Matthew Modine that was cut out," she says, "so now you know what happened after I picked up the two GIs for $10; I wasn't too beaucoup then! I think the scene didn't meld with what [Kubrick] wanted to get across in the film: that war is mean and look what happens to people involved in the war machine."

Kubrick, Soo recalls, "actually said very little to me on the set. [Now where have we heard *that* before?] It was a very Zen experience in the sense that he was so silent, but it was a silent understanding as I believed I knew what he was after in the frames he was shooting. . . . Film work is hard as you have to be up very early and I'm not too good in the mornings, and you work very long hours. But, hey, spare a thought to the nurses who work in dirty wards for long hours for which they are under-remunerated, or try to be a dustman or work in McDonald's for a day."

But no one could have predicted how far into pop culture two lines would take her. Sir Mix-A-Lot used them in the 1992 perennial hit "Baby Got Back." 2 Live Crew's "Me So Horny" became America's top rap hit of 1989, pushing the album *As Nasty As They Wanna Be* past the three-million sales mark.

The next year, a judge declared that the album was obscene, and the band was prosecuted. The case became a landmark First Amendment issue, going all the way to the Supreme Court before the group was exonerated on free speech grounds. Shows like *South Park* and *American Dad* worked the lines onto the air, and Jim Carrey spoofed it in *Bruce Almighty* (2003).

"I think we all have the possibility to go above time, space, and motion," says Soo Soo, explaining her personal philosophy, not her status from the lines. "I hope that doesn't sound ethereal. I mean just to do something extraordinary with our life; to be original, to be a flame of light for more than just oneself." Her lines made the words true.

Just as some performers from *Jacket and Platoon* had at around the same time, Daniel O'Shea met with some who'd never have the luxury of leaving Vietnam.

Decades after the war and thousands of miles from its fields and jungles, too many would never get completely away, in a small sense.

"I met tons of guys who were veterans," he recalls. "It was a life-changing, life-defining experience. They'd been home for twenty-five, thirty-five years after the conflict, and were still there, kind of. It was a very powerful thing." He'd just been handed one hell of a burden for any young actor, and now had a load of other reasons to carry it high.

Fresh off the boxing dramas *Streets of Gold* (1986) and *Heart* (1987), O'Shea was handed a script much more emotionally violent in every sense.

At first, he admits, "I wasn't enthralled with the whole project. I thought it would take me out of the country for thirteen weeks. My agent convinced me that it would be a good thing, and I acquiesced to that." Unlike most Vietnam tales past and present, *Hamburger Hill* (1986) wasn't a years-long epic of a group of young men and the hardness dumped on them inside and out by a war so few back home even understand, let alone respect, today.

The title location, near the Laotian border, was called Hill 937, is named for its height in meters. Officially titled Dong Ap Bia, its new nickname came after a ten-day period in May 1969, as it chewed up soldiers like meat, one man after another dying in a fight over a huge plot of land. Over seventy Americans died in the combat; the Vietnamese lost nearly ten times that number.

Again and again, O'Shea read over the screenplay. Then he delved into the volumes of research written on the war, plentiful even just over a decade after our last troops left.

"I read all the stuff available about the conflicts of Southeast Asia, from the Tet Offensive onward," he remembers. Perhaps the largest and certainly most well-known campaign of the war, Tet drove over 80,000 North Vietnam troops into over a hundred South Vietnam towns from January to March 1968. Two more similar, albeit smaller, attacks later in the year (one of which occurred during the battle depicted in *Hill*) raised the casualty total to nearly 50,000. Cities and lives were destroyed forever, and the world found out—or was reminded—just how strong the Vietcong could be.

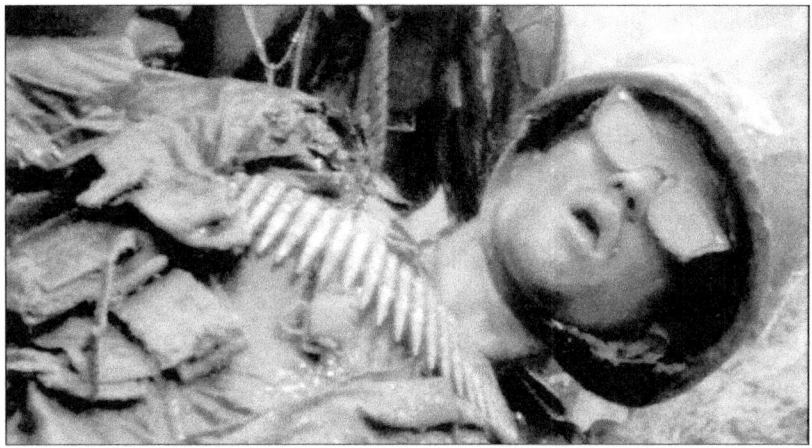

Daniel O'Shea helped *Hamburger Hill* (1986) tell the (unfortunately) true story of a battle that took too many lives on both sides of the Vietnam War in May 1969.

Meanwhile, back in America, well, we were all about love. The Summer of Love had rolled across Old Glory in 1967 (mainly in San Francisco), with thousands spreading their passion for art, music, poetry, and all kinds of inhaled relaxation, while sneering at the Establishment and the government that had us in Hanoi. Two years later came a concert called Woodstock.

"How [Tet] played out in relationship to the whole culture at large," O'Shea remembers, "it was two completely contrasting things going on at same time. What was happening here and abroad, the zeitgeist, the feelings, the culture, it was interesting."

Like Oliver Stone, who'd directed two Vietnam films all the way to Oscars, Jim Carabatsos had been in 'Nam (the year before, Clint Eastwood had acted out his words in *Heartbreak Ridge*, the story of a man who didn't exactly miss his time as a marine). Some of Carabatsos' friends—far too many—with everything to live for and so much waiting for them back at home, never returned (over 60,000) or, decades later, are still unaccounted for (over 1,600); his screenplay pays them a quick tribute with some shots of the Vietnam Veterans Memorial in DC, which should be legally required for every American to visit. John Irvin, who'd made some documentaries on the war during the actual conflict, was directing.

In a casting search that had taken the *Hill* crew across the country, O'Shea had found a spot in the 187th Infantry Regiment. He'd be the gunner Gaigin, who seems to wish that his poor eyesight had won him a 4-F in the draft ranks.

To his colleagues, though, the combat rookie would just be another FNG: Fuckin' New Guy.

O'Shea and the rest of the crew studied like college kids cramming for a history exam. Handed a reading list from the crew, they ripped through one tome after another. The 1976 work *What Really Happened to the Class of '65*, which told of the futures of a Los Angeles high school's graduating class (many such stories revolved around the war) was one of the biggest helps, he claims.

Newspapers and magazines of the time, textbooks of then and today, and, eventually, the Internet, would forever carry the visual displays of the war, some of which are considered the finest in American history. Schoolkids of any age (well, those that were taught right!) can recall the heartbreaking photo of children fleeing a nuclear blast, as well as the one of a police chief executing a VC officer.

The *Hill* crew looked over those and many more. They helped O'Shea bring Gaigin into focus.

"There were tons and tons and tons of photographs," he remembers. "They had so many during the Vietnam War, and I developed the character out of that."

Finally, it was off to film in the Philippines, where *Platoon* had just been made. The *Hill* crew trained with some marines and veterans. Then came filming, and everyone could feel the same fear, the same hopelessness that had enveloped and ultimately killed far too many not too long before

"They put us out in the jungle," O'Shea says. "In the Philippines, it's exponentially worse than being in a forest. Northeast, southeast, you don't know where anything is. Everything in the jungle looks the same. There's no points of reference, just vines and trees and leaves and stuff."

Like the other films we've gone over, *Hill* didn't come close to glorifying the Vietnam War. In all fairness, it didn't even really dramatize it. Drama implies manipulation of emotion, and *Hill* doesn't do that, as even its heartbreak is real. There's self-created racial segregation. One solider tells of a visit back home, being harassed and insulted by those who only *thought* they knew what was going on. Another fellow gets a letter from his beloved back home, saying she's ending things because of his cause.

And, yes, men die, some just after arriving at the Hill. That's what happened to too many on either side of the war, at the Hill and elsewhere.

Up against the hellish geography of the hill, the godawful weather, and an enemy just as determined to win and get home alive, more and more of the troops fall. O'Shea kept remembering those whose stories he'd heard while becoming Gaigin.

"That's always in the back of your mind," he says. "The presence is not there, yet always there at the same time. It's always in the air when you do acting. In the world of art, when you're creating everything, there's no mistakes. Things just happen."

But just as the Cong appears through, a chopper gunship shows up, and starts blasting the Americans to eternity.

It was one of their own. Our own. A U.S. group whose orders got screwed up. A catastrophic example of what the military disgustingly refers to as "friendly fire."

What a ridiculous term. And what a disgrace that this happened thousands of times during the actual war. Sadly, tragedy extended over to realism during filming, as an electrician was electrocuted during a scene.

Gaigin is killed soon after, face down in the muck. So is almost everyone else before the Hill is taken on May 20. Actually, to call it "taken" gives too much credit: once the Cong left, the Americans did as well, abandoning it less than three weeks later. Soon after, President Nixon began taking troops out of 'Nam.

The film taught America something new about a war we'd never fully understand. It showed what people, on either side of the war, would do for their country. O'Shea and his colleagues saw just how different the responses to war can be, from those in its midst to those back at home, things we still see today as our countrymen fight and die in Iraq, Afghanistan, and other conflicts.

"These politicians launch these wars," he says, "but war is not kids playing Cowboys and Indians. Acting isn't real life; you can't take yourself too seriously, but I really respect the people protecting us. When I see things like people burning the American flag, I can't tell you what that does to me. It's so sad and infuriating, I'm almost crying talking about it now. I have tremendous respect for those young men and women and the sacrifices they've made for my freedom."

If writing and directing *The Challenger* hadn't been enough, Kent Moran (left) became the main character in the 2015 boxing flick, helped along in and out of character by late great acting veteran Michael Clarke Duncan (right).

Kent Moran: *The Challenger*

NO SPORT HAS GRACED our silver screens more often than boxing, and, hey, why not? Underdogs without a chance in hell can somehow, often suddenly, come out on top. Other guys who should have quit long ago may find it within to reach out and blast their opponent into the ground and themselves right back to glory. It's a sport where names in the newspapers and high-level paychecks (while welcome!) come so rarely that they don't matter much. They can't. Not when a person steps into a ring he or she might not leave alive or intact—and, maybe worse, neither will the opponent.

Boxing films have jumped through about every genre since the beginning of film. With 2015's *The Challenger*, Kent Moran became the next to climb through the ropes to hopeful stardom, and countless more will continue to do so until long after his great-great-grandkids have grandkids.

Like many such films do, Moran's creation began in reality, inspired by a great-uncle who threw gloves in the Bronx about a century ago.

"He even fought some of the greats of his time and had several big fights at Madison Square Garden and other great venues," Moran recalls. "Hearing stories of him as a kid was one of my inspirations behind Jaden's character in *The Challenger*. Jaden is a guy who cares deeply about his family and helping his mother, yet is struggling to find his own calling."

His calling might have been education, earning a degree from a school and heading to stardom.

Then a hot temper and the brawls it led to put him down and about out, into a shitty job with nowhere to go but down. But the same qualities that tossed a roadblock before Jaden might help him find a way around it, as the gym across the street just happens to be a place for wannabe punchers.

Moran hadn't lost as much as Jaden, or much at all. More to the point, what he had wasn't what he'd hoped for. Like many dreaming of the business, he'd taken the safe way out instead, scoring a degree and Wall Street job.

"That's when I was met face to face with the fact that it wasn't what I wanted to do with my life," he remembers. "I wanted to be an actor. So on my first day, I quit my nice salary and new Wall Street job to move into New York City with no real plan, no connections, and no income, to become a struggling actor." A rough ambition, but an unavoidable one for any before that big opportunity happens to come knocking.

This upcomer decided to build it a door. Everything that Jaden had gone through or would, he'd go through himself. Moran would write Jaden's story. He'd direct it.

And he'd become him. That's the kind of ethic that the higher-ups in the film world tend to recognize.

"At first, I was worried about taking on both directing and starring at the same time," he admits. "Acting, like life, is about challenging yourself and sometimes doing things that scare you. In fact, my biggest accomplishments or successes in life have always been things that initially scared me. And so I decided to go for it. I wanted to explore what it actually might be like to make it today as a new boxer, especially with boxing's fight for ratings at the height of MMA."

With the help of a trainer we'll meet in a moment, Jaden cautiously steps into boxing shape. Moran was learning at the same time and speed.

"We follow him from day one of his training to the end," says the actor, "so I wanted to document my training as a new boxer in that way. I trained for eight months to play Jaden." Six of those months were at a Los Angeles gym, then another two back in the Big Apple with one of his great-uncle's colleagues.

"I kept training throughout the shoot," he says proudly, "starting off my day running five miles a day, directing and acting for twelve hours, and the same thing the next day. I learned a ton and I wrote many of my training sessions directly into the script. It was so much work, but so much fun." In typical Hollywood mode, he's quickly in the ring, and opponents start to fall. Soon, he starts to get the same sort of attention Moran himself hoped to attract with the film itself. The media shows up, snaring a story about a local rookie with a shot at rags to riches. There's a champ looking for a new challenge, a new meal for his ego, and Jaden becomes just one more dreamer for him to uppercut down to reality.

Think this stuff's without precedence? Wrong. Remember the day after Valentine's Day of 1978 when a guy named Leon Spinks, eight fights into his pro career, defeated—and *outlasted*—the greatest of all time, Ali himself? The infamous Tokyo afternoon in the spring of 1990 when a journeyman called Douglas knocked the sports world and the Mike Tyson mystique into oblivion? How about when George Foreman and Bernard Hopkins, both at young grandpa age, somehow won world titles?

And, hey, sometimes even the guy who doesn't win can score an upset, a moral victory that will always overshadow the loss column. That's what we saw on March 24, 1975, when Chuck Wepner stood up until the end with Ali. If he hadn't, we might never have met Rocky Balboa.

And these are just the ones we know of. At tiny gyms, small shows with a few hundred people in the stands, without fanfare or riches, sometimes upsets happen, titles switch, dreams come true.

This happens in boxing. It spawns far fewer successful competitors than almost any other sport, so when we see someone who makes it to the top or even near it, it reminds us that somewhere, somehow, things might just go right for us.

"Movies like *Rocky* and *Cinderella Man*, stories of underdogs coming up from nothing and making something out of their lives, against all odds, also inspired me a lot," Moran explains. "I wanted to make a movie that could touch people today in a similar way, except for a modern audience. How could a newcomer boxer realistically get a shot at the title in today's reality TV culture?" The same type of reality show that Moran's life becomes, spreading his name, face, and life across nationwide screens until the main event night arrives.

With all of his, and Moran's, training finally coming together, Jaden finally goes up against the man that no man has beat before. Over two days at Albany's Times Union Center, with the help of a real-life fight card and room full of fans, the *Challenger* group finished off some of the last few scenes.

"The crowd watched the real fights and then, without interruption, we filmed our fight right after," explains Moran. "Since shooting a movie is usually a lot of waiting around, in order to keep the crowd's attention and keep them there, we decided to shoot the whole fight scene like a real fight, which meant we had *one* chance to shoot everything: us walking out into the ring, each of the twelve rounds, etc. It was amazing. The crowd had great raw energy and it felt like we were really in a championship fight."

He felt it. Jaden felt it, getting stronger as the match went on. And it's just enough, with him taking the fight with only a few moments left to spare, the trainer, the crowds, and everyone else going as nuts for him as they did on the screens for Rocky Balboa, James Braddock, Billy Flynn, and so many others.

But even the most upbeat feel-good films can cause a type of heartbreak, and we're not talking about the sad death of a character, one whose portrayer can get up the next day and make a new film. This one's is a bit more real.

The trainer we've been reading about was Duane Taylor, a disgraced former manager with a hidden connection to Jaden.

He was portrayed by Michael Clarke Duncan, whose far-too-soon death a full three years before had robbed Hollywood of one of its greatest talents. In one of *Challenger*'s final scenes, as Duane looks back at his empty gym and turns off the lights as he leaves, it's tough to feel the feel-good sentiment the film wanted.

"Working with Michael was an honor," Moran recalls. "I learned a lot from him both as an actor and as a person. I remember being impressed that he just brought it every take. He never needed time to build into it: his performance always came out right away. I respected that about him. He gave it his all every time. And he also improvised a lot. He could go on for minutes and it was all great. We had a lot to play with in the edit. I really miss him. He was a great actor, man, and friend. I was lucky to have known him, even if for only a short time."

Even so long after finishing up the script, the training, and finally the film, Moran still hadn't felt the final connection between himself and the character he'd created. Not until *The Challenger* started winning awards and showing up at festivals. Not until his name began to spread faster than ever before.

"It was my journey to finding myself and my purpose," he remarks, "and that's what Jaden's journey in *The Challenger* really is all about: fighting for who you are."

Frank Murdoch and Roxy (Joel Murray and Tara Lynne Barr) spent *God Bless America* attempting to kill off the deterioration of American culture before falling to it in the 2011 film.

Joel Murray: *God Bless America*

TO REALLY APPRECIATE, OR even want to understand, some of Bobcat Goldthwait's directorial work, there's quite a bit of work to do ourselves, and even before we hit play on the DVD remote. It's a burden to really accept some of the director's soothsayings about who we are and how we act.

In our society, deep conversations are out the door, as many see them as just not worth the time. Front porches are no longer on houses. One-liners and sound bites have become American culture as a whole, not just its pop culture. Things that should matter to most, especially in a shitty economy, such as working, getting a meal, or finding a place to sleep, are thrown by the wayside, as we obsess about celebrities' adultery, their speeding tickets, and special treatment. We know more about the lives of cartoon characters than our neighbors. Walking past a camera is enough to quantify oneself as a celebrity. We buy their books and watch their shows, then whine when we find out how much dough they rake in. Too many people would rather be hated than unknown—as long as we watch them.

Intelligence and creativity are stigmatized. Independent thought is feared. As cell phones started the trend, or at least accelerated it, social networking has made face-to-face chat not just unnecessary, but obsolete, even awkward and frightening.

Indeed, "America has become a cruel and vicious place. We reward the shallowest, the dumbest, the meanest and the loudest. We no longer have any common sense of decency. No sense of shame. There is no right and wrong. The worst qualities in people are looked up to and celebrated. Lying and spreading fear is fine as long as you make money doing it. We've become a nation of slogan-saying, bile-spewing hatemongers. We've lost our kindness. We've lost our soul."

Most of these things are, quite sadly, the stone cold truth, and it brings to mind the proverb that he who tells the truth is ultimately chased from several villages. American livelihood and the society in which it's lived can be sad, somber places to exist, and the endings are rarely all that happy. Goldthwait's work goes about showing and/or reminding us of that; it just tries to put some humor, midnight-black though it often is, around the situation (in 2006's *Sleeping Dogs Lie*, he asked us to find bestiality funny and sort of understandable. Do the math here). Basically, we have to accept some knee-deep flaws about ourselves before we can get the full message he's sending.

The seeds for 2011's *God Bless America*—as with Goldthwait's *World's Greatest Dad* (2009), the sarcasm began with the title—were sown in 1993's *Falling Down*, when Michael Douglas, in what many call his best or at least their favorite performance, played a man at war with society, strolling around Los Angeles wreaking havoc—only, of course, on the guilty.

Placement of *God Bless America* in a selection on action films might be confusing to some—looking over it, as opposed to some of the other entries in this category, might call up many more differences than likenesses.

But on the other hand, putting it under a different label isn't the easiest thing either. Sure, it's funny at times, but there's much more violence than you see in most comedies—hell, one of the first scenes is *a baby getting gunned down*! Yes, it's a dream sequence, but we see it. Blood, gore, violence, gun rampages; there's quite a bit here that we shouldn't find funny.

Drama? Well, maybe; there's some pretty deep human issues with this film—terminal illness, divorce, social concerns, but, again with the violence. Too much killing, too much shooting, and the fact that a huge chunk of it is done by a female minor just pushes it further into this classification.

Now that that's out of the way, let's have some fun here; after all, that's what Goldthwait usually intends with these films, if we can get over our too-often-self-imposed-uber-seriousness for a few hours. *God Bless America* tells us the tale of a man out to cleanse society of its own faults, and, as we all know, there's no better purification than pain.

Like Douglas' Bill Foster, more fondly nicknamed D-Fens, Frank Murdoch is just about out of reasons to give a good goddamn about anything—including himself. His ex is with another man, both of them being bossed around by Frank's spoiled little brat of a daughter. His shitty apartment is tormented by neighbors with a screaming baby. He's just been canned from his job, an attempt at friendliness interpreted as sexual harassment.

And those migraines that the roaring dervish from next door has exacerbated to hell? They're actually from a brain tumor, the news delivered by a doctor who clearly has other, better things on his mind.

But nobody cares—they're too busy modeling themselves after reality TV stars whose main claim to fame is their artificial smile or catfighting ability, or crying after getting yelled at by a judge on a singing tryout show.

It's not that Frank has become a tornado of uncontrollable rage, or not *just* that. More like he just wants to share his own pain, and that there are those out there who deserve it. Not because of what they've done to him personally, but because they're a part of the virus that's spread through humanity, which he just hopes isn't terminal. Neither he nor the film tries to make him out to be some paragon of virtue—suicide's on his mind early—but there's no reason not to leave a mark before he goes, even one painted with plasma.

Of course Joel Murray didn't prepare for the character by going on a killing spree. Of *course* he didn't practice—as Frank does early in his introductory spree—by stalking women (tragically, he did remember the pain he'd felt at losing a friend to suicide).

Still, he, as it seems (hopefully!) that more and more people are, isn't thrilled with the direction that his country's heading when it comes to where we look for entertainment, and what we accept as it. His family had been dishing out a more wholesome, or at least deeper, rounds of comedy and drama for decades (his brothers are fellow performers Bill and Brian Doyle Murray, with whom he turned down a chance to star alongside of in 1980's *Caddyshack*), and maybe he and Frank could start to show people the error of their ways. Well, maybe.

"I don't understand why people spend a lot of time watching other people do their jobs or live their lives or hang out with their family," says Joel, "as opposed to being with their own or doing their own job better with more élan or more verve."

Aside from his role in the 2011 Best-Picture-winning *The Artist*, Joel tore up the 60s ad agency show *Mad Men* as Freddy Rumsen, who won a battle with alcoholism.

"Has [the pop culture] gotten worse, or is it just under the magnifying glass because there's so much media attention?" he asks, a bit rhetorically. "[There are] these talk shows on and the guy has slept with the sister and the sister's daughter and it's just, 'Why are you on TV saying this?' Like when Chris Farley died, there was a girl on the cover of the *Enquirer* saying, 'I'm a whore.' I mean, when did prostitutes start yelling that? Nobody has any shame anymore because, 'I'm getting my fame,' you know. 'Who cares if my father has a heart attack or dies a sad man because I got to be on the cover of some horrible magazine.'"

Frank, for his part, is tired of channel-changing and web surfing when something he doesn't like appears. With nothing left and nothing left to lose, he's headed out for as many revenges as a common man can snare before someone finally takes him out . . . which is what he wants anyway.

So yes, there were some ingredients of *Falling Down* tossed into *God Bless America*. The country's fixation with the trashiness of TV dropped in some elements of 1976's *Network* as well (lord, how sadly prophetic *that* film ended up becoming!). But mixing up *The Professional* (1994), or maybe a little *Natural Born Killers* (1994), wouldn't hurt too much either.

Typical male, Frank's not really smart enough to think this thing out, or at least pull it all off on his own. Some lady intuition does the trick, and it comes in the form of a female feeling force-fed up with some of American pop culture herself.

"Girls my age, we audition for the hot cheerleader, the goth girl, the really generic characters," she says. "This girl was so different, and it excited me so much." Her Roxy wasn't that different from Frank, albeit quite a bit younger. Like him, she was tired of underserved glorification, and she'd had a much closer look than him—one of Roxy's own classmates was a spoiled little reality TV star princess that America got to see piss and moan at those who didn't fight to get their lips on her ass, her family being the most guilty.

It wasn't ludicrously far from Tara Lynne Barr's own views of reality TV—or "reality" TV, as she and many others label it.

"It bugs me to no end," she says. "It's just that they don't seem like nice, genuine people. It's all an act. Oh, we just happened to catch them getting in a catfight? It's scripted, not real actors."

In American school halls today, not being seduced by this sort of thing, looking to delve past the most superficial levels of independent thought and communication all too quickly gets one labeled an outcast, a nerd, and whatever else.

"[Roxy is] invisible in high school," Barr says, "but not because she's a mean person or because she's weird, but because she is smart and because she's not like the rest of her classmates. She's not vapid, and she doesn't just talk about reality television and pop politics and stuff like that. She has an opinion, and she listens to offbeat music like Alice Cooper, and she pays attention to politics and what's going on in the world, unlike her classmates." When the jezebel we badmouthed a moment ago becomes Frank's first victim, Roxy can't wait to become the Bonnie to his Clyde.

In her first big film role, Barr, a Nickelodeon TV veteran, had to take a big step towards adulthood.

"I guess I have an offbeat personality like Roxy," Barr says. "I don't swear like her, but I would say my personality is definitely offbeat—as with her hobbies and stuff, and her interests. I'm not a psychopath. There's a difference there."

Barr checked out Goldthwait's infamous voice, which she'd been hearing since childhood in 1997 in Disney's *Hercules*, on the standup stages.

"I was like, 'Oh my God, this callback is gonna be so stressful. He's just going to be yelling at me the whole time.' But it was such the opposite. When I went into the callback room, it was him and the casting directors, and he was so low key.... It's just like, 'Whoa, is this the same person?'"

Less than two weeks after snaring the role, Barr was alongside Joel on cinema's newest fun killing spree, helped along by an afternoon of practice at a shooting range. The whole killing thing is awkward for Frank at first, but Roxy can't wait for the serial murder auditions. She stabs the spoiled princess' mother to death. She takes target practice, imagining she's shooting at other celebrities she doesn't like.

The two kill religious protestors. Rude drivers. A Bill O'Reilly-type conservative-slave talk-show host. Some moronic people in a theater, and an idiot videotaping the act (a scene done *long* before the horrific movie theater shooting in Colorado). But they never take their relationship to the darkly romantic levels of Bonnie and Clyde or Mickey and Mallory Knox, as Frank makes clear that to do so would be much more despicable than mass murder.

"It's great, because you have two generations, and they're both angry, each with their own reasons," Joel says.

Things culminate in one last mass work, as the two storm an *American Idol*-type show, and Frank lets all of America know exactly what they're doing wrong. That quoted speech you read back at the start of this profile? He says all that.

With nothing left to live for but to physically show the country the dangers of falling too far, the two slaughter a contestant, the judges, and the audience before, just as Parker and Barrow did, falling under their own hail of lead, dying live in living color, something that was undoubtedly on *YouTube* before the bodies were removed.

Uplifting music plays, morons die, and through it all, we're not sure if we should feel sympathy for anyone. The people that perpetuate the myths Frank preached, or those that don't have the guts to stop those very people? Neither, really. Some call it murder. By this point, we might not see it as all that different from lighting off an insect bomb in a garage to take out a cockroach invasion.

In a sense, it's not that different from *Network*'s legendary climax, as protagonist Howard Beale is blasted away on live TV. He'd been exploited by the people he was making rich and famous, and when there was no more blood to suck out of the stone, he was murdered in living color. Frank and Roxy, in their own demented way, are the last gasps of human morality that America carries, only to become its final victims.

That's when we find the last and biggest reason this film could never be in the comedic genre. They shoot, they kill, they die, we laugh, we cheer. And as the two take their final bow in the only way the film could end, we realize that they've become not the victims of themselves, but sad examples of what they hate, what they've been rebelling against.

And as their fans in the audience, so have we. We've been demonstrating it all film long, and now it's time for sad acknowledgement and the hopes that someday, an American generation will start to learn from its mistakes—although considering who we elected president in 2016, it's up for debate as to whether we did.

Like *World's Greatest Dad*, there's no happy ending here (again a reason for its inclusion in action). Just one last sad look at where we are, and why we need to start changing as a society.

"It's a very violent film," Joel summarizes, "about the need for kindness."

Mallory Knox (Juliette Lewis) shows the technique that made her one of the title characters of Oliver Stone's 1994 masterpiece *Natural Born Killers*.

Some *Natural* Women

WHEN IT COMES TO public figures, we can be rather stupidly optimistic.

Americans, quite simply enough, just don't like to be sad. We as a nation will basically snare any chance in the world to see any bright side, to overlook any flaw (though senseless, brutal murder can hardly be labeled a simple *flaw*) to cheer, to like, to be fans of those we see on TV. We don't enjoy anger or depression, or, as is so easy to find throughout American culture today, frustration. We use all kinds of defense mechanisms to justify our actions—half-wits who assured Chris Brown that he'd feel better soon after the mental torment caused him by beating the hell out of Rhianna, morons who wrote love letters to serial killers Ted Bundy and Richard Ramirez, goddamned fools who stood atop highway overpasses cheering O.J. Simpson on during his Bronco chase, and even more who wildly celebrated when he got away with double murder.

Many of us, far too many, will do just anything to like them, to deny, ignore, or forget the horrible things that they've done. Sure, we could and perhaps should feel anger, even hate for those who commit these horrible acts . . . but it would just take too much of a toll on our own psyche. Let's cheer for 'em instead!

That ended up being the focal point of 1994's *Natural Born Killers*. It's not all about violence, and it certainly doesn't glorify it. What it does is showcase our reaction to these things, us being the American public. Our desperation to look through the darkest clouds to be the first to find any kind of silver lining.

We certainly can be superficial and ignorant, and that's bad. But hey, at least it doesn't hurt, right? At least it doesn't put us in a bad mood. Life's just easier that way. It's the simple way out. It's not worth the effort to get upset, to worry about things we really can't control—like, say, how many people the cretin we're cheering on mercilessly slaughtered. Yes, more problems might get solved, more progress might be made, more serious issues—like unemployment, crime, etc.—might be faced and even overcome, but, hey . . . life's too short to worry.

It's not all the blood. Or the gore. Or the death. Or the murders, or anything else about *Natural Born Killers* that we see.

What's scariest about *NBK* isn't its violence. More specifically, it's not so much what the film shows, but *how* it shows it. It's the truth that it tells. We see a couple brutally killing tons of innocent people, ending lives, destroying families . . . and getting cheered for it. Worldwide, they become heroes. And before we label it overblown or unrealistic, look at the examples above—chances are, you'll be able to think of many more.

Violent movies, video games, TV shows, and/or the Internet have long been blamed for stunting our compassion towards our fellow person, for making us so desensitized to violence that it makes us like it . . . to want it.

To say that showing something alone glorifies and encourages it is incredibly superficial. But superficiality, a lack of attempting to think very hard, to pry open the surface and look beneath it, is all too common in society today. Maybe more than the blood, the guns, the gore, the rape in *NBK*, is the realization that it might not be who we are, but it's what we *like*. And through that, we can learn from it.

It's why, as the final credits rolled, and we looked beneath the excitement, the fear, the adrenaline, the multitude of combinations therein that the film inspired in us, we might find, *feel*, something unexpected. It might take a while, but we could locate the lesson it sends, the uplifting (yes, I said *uplifting*) message we might just carry with us—if we're strong enough.

Don't impersonate it. Learn from it. Don't cheer for it, at least not what it depicts. Look at it and see what we shouldn't be, what we shouldn't do or think.

Few directors could have pulled off such a feat. Maybe Quentin Tarantino, who banged out the original script and then disowned it, might have been able to make *NBK* work—his *Pulp Fiction* (1994) and *Reservoir Dogs* (1992) were very challenging films to do right, let alone to live on in cult lore as they have. Oliver Stone's skill in the chair wasn't a matter of debate; two directing Oscars and a Best Picture was more than enough to solidify that. But to make a couple of serial killers the good guys, or at least the main characters, and make it deep enough to understand *why* they could ever become so would be all but excruciating.

Still, Stone's films are his own way, his own viewpoint, with no holds barred and no questions unasked or areas unexplored—winning awards gives a guy the stroke to dare anyone to question his opinion. Aside from telling Jim Morrison's dirty stories in 1991 for *The Doors* (Val Kilmer's non-Oscar nomination for that film was ludicrous) and getting half of Hollywood to help him give his view of American history's biggest conspiracy the same year in *JFK*, Stone gives us what he wants. Usually we like it, but if we don't, well, tough shit.

So it was time for his thoughts on our desperation to *like* each other, even if the others involved are killers, whatever. If they're on TV or in the tabloids, someone will go out of their way to cheer for them, to show up outside their trial with signs, to buy their books, whatever. *NBK* had to get our attention with shock value and make us pay enough attention to get its message.

It's tough to ascertain how Stone could have looked at Woody Harrelson's past acting work and seen a guy who'd do a great job playing a serial killer—millions had seen the fellow as lovable goof Woody on *Cheers*, and in comedy in *White Men Can't Jump* (1992), and *Indecent Proposal* (1993) had allowed Harrelson to show off some dramatic skill, but nothing anywhere near Mickey Knox.

Stone wasn't looking at Harrelson's professional past. He saw his mind. He saw something that few people knew much of, at least until the Internet and warp-speed news worlds of tabloid cable TV came about—the dark heart that had beat out Harrelson's genetics.

His father Charles, a figure in organized crime who died in prison in 2007, was convicted of two murders and alleged to have been involved in the JFK assassination.

Stone saw, "the violence in [Harrelson's] eyes." It was enough.

Mickey's gal, on the other hand, took a bit more time to locate. A big part of the tryout process was showing off Mallory's dance moves, a true focal point of the character. Some wouldn't do it; others just weren't up to her level.

Then came Juliette Lewis. An 1991 Oscar nomination for *Cape Fear* and some high marks from *What's Eating Gilbert Grape* (1993) were already on her resume, but still . . . how does one convince another that she'd be successful at joyful murder, particularly since, Aileen Wuornos and Bonnie Parker notwithstanding, the concept of women performing such an act is still tough for America to comprehend?

Lewis had her own way, and grooving had nothing to do with it. She took Stone by the collar.

"If you think that any of these other actresses could physically kill you, like I could," she snarled, "then hire them." Still in her last year of teenagery, Lewis had the part.

While Harrelson looked over speeches of Charles Manson (whom Mickey refers to as "The King," in the film), Lewis studied the words of Wuornos and Richard Kuklinski, whose career of over a hundred confessed contract killings earned him the nickname of "Iceman."

"I'm more of a loose cannon," Lewis admits. "Even though the movie looks like a feast for the eyes, we all did our homework as to what we were drawing from. . . . I based Mallory more in the animal kingdom. She's more of a hyena. But I did research human beings who'd been cut off from their civil humanities. . . . I had my own pain going on. It's a big thing going in this world, of cinema or the arts, of being female, because oftentimes you are the girlfriend, the thing of desire. This is a multi-faceted creature. I really loved the idea of shedding vanity, being connected to animalistic, raw emotion, and that's all that Mallory is."

Still, Lewis' wouldn't be the first female face *NBK* fans would see. We start things out in a truck stop, slow music playing, travelers just looking for a breath of fresh air. Mickey and Mallory are there, but we don't know them yet, and neither does Mabel, the lovely redhead just hoping to grab a few dollars in tips.

Playing a waitress was old hat to **O-Lan Jones** by the time *NBK* came about—two years earlier, she'd been one in the "Bubble Boy," episode of *Seinfeld*, and would do so again in the 1998 Jim Carrey flick *The Truman Show*—playing Mabel put her in the worst position a person can be in, but one of the best for a performer with a small role.

O-Lan Jones cast a scared but enthralled glimpse as deadly action unfolds before her Mabel, the waitress in the opening of *Natural Born Killers*.

"For the first few days on the set, everyone was joking around and playful," recalls Jones (her name comes from the Pearl Buck novel *The Good Earth*, of which her mother was a fan, and is Chinese for "profound wildflower," or "profound orchid"). "But by the end, once the FX people brought out the splattered brains and chopped-off fingers, people had started messing around more—pretending to hit each other and shoot each other. That atmosphere was already right there. We didn't have to go too far to find that kind of hysteria. It had permeated the whole crew and the cast."

Mabel and Mickey discuss his cuisine choice, then the scene immediately changes to a black-and-white dream sequence in which she flirtily asks the same question, showing that there's going to be much more to this film that the eye and mind could ever truly comprehend. Stone's taking us inside the mentality of Mickey's evil.

"Especially with waitress roles, it's about interacting with the other characters," Jones said. "Like with any role, it's about knowing your lines and being available."

As Mabel goes to fetch Mickey's key lime pie and nonfat milk (looks like Mickey's as much as health nut as Harrelson himself!), Mallory strolls over the jukebox and puts on some tunes. A slow, sensuous treat of a dance routine ensues.

She's soon joined by another customer, a trucker trying to put the moves on her. Then, seconds later, everything changes. The music, the bright colors . . . every single thing.

Mallory, roughly half her impromptu dance partner's size, blasts him upside the face with a bottle, then pops him with a jab. The scene, and the entire film, doesn't just do a 180. It does a 360, goes back with a 180, then swings another 600 degrees until all levels of comprehension have been destroyed.

The man tries to fight back. He has no idea. He throws a desperate left to her jaw, but it barely causes a blink. A punch, a knee from her, he's cowering in pain. This isn't just some comical "Oooh, a girl beat up a guy!" mess. It's something else. Something stronger. Something much, much worse. More real.

"That fight sequence, to me, was like a dance," recalls Lewis, who trained in street fighting to become Mallory. "It was jab, jab, and then I did a knee, and I take a hit. Knee, right cross, and then he's down. I went into this animalistic realm . . . it's really rare as a female that you get full, involved fight sequences. It went dark real fast. Oliver's toeing the line, and we are, 'Yeah!' in the dipshit-ness of it."

For one quick second, we see Mabel casting a look toward the action—a look that conveys a ten-foot deep well of emotions.

There's fear in her face that's quickly heading toward terror, but we can also see a kind of morbid interest, the kind that makes people slow down on the freeway if there's a crackup on the other side, or go to a bullfight specifically hoping to see a matador get gored. In this seconds-long shot with one quick facial expression, Mabel's eyes open the door to her personality. Maybe she's the type of person that pushes down the brake pedal driving by an accident. Maybe she was one of the students that inconspicuously made her way through the crowd in high school toward the two students who were having it out. Not one of the people that chanted, "Fight, fight, fight!" as that wasn't her style. But someone who wasn't exactly repulsed by the sight of violence . . . even death.

"My intent was always to be completely immersed in the scene," Jones recalls. "It really is a response to what's going on. I knew I'm supposed to be seeing this ghastly array of stuff. It's all connected to violence. There's something about the frequency, the vibrational frequency of violence. Even if it's all pretend, it's so close to the real thing that it agitates everybody on a personal level."

Mickey slashes the man's friend with a knife, then blasts the head off the cook, who was charging forward with a meat cleaver. Her opponent unconscious, Mallory's not content with just winning, stomping him into the ground and breaking his neck. She's hardly breathing heavy. As Mickey robs the register, we know this is commonplace for the twosome. Soon everyone's dead but Mabel and another trucker.

"How sexy am I now?!" Mallory roars triumphantly in lines Lewis improvised. "How sexy am I now, flirty boy? Why are they always fucking with me?"

As the Knoxes work their black magic, Mabel doesn't know what to do. What *is* there to do when a spree murder happens before our eyes? We may like to think that we'd turn into Chuck Norris, whoop ass on all the bad guys, and save everyone (maybe even winning the heart of the damsel in distress that just happens to be there at that exact moment), but when things go to hell right in front of us, there's no real script to follow—something that both Mabel and Jones found out. We see her widening eyes and mouth again: panic, fear, but still a bit of curiosity about what's going to happen next (unfortunately, she can't whip out a gun and blast a demon to hell like Jones did at the start of 2016's *Miss Peregrine's Home for Peculiar Children*!)

As happens many times throughout the film, things revert to a line between childlike humor and utter demonism. With only two possible victims left, Mallory, her gleeful eyes three feet wide in an utter euphoric madness that she can't possibly get enough of, splits into a wicked game of "Eeny, meenie, miney, moe," trying to decide who should get the last bullet—after all, Mickey and Mallory's trademark is to always leave one victim alive to tell their nightmarish fairytale.

For a moment, there's a lost glimmer of hope in Mabel's eyes. Maybe she'll make it out. Maybe the other bystander might be the final corpse. At this point, it's every man and woman for themselves, and Mabel just might be lucky enough to watch one other person die, instead of herself.

But perhaps Mallory saw the burst of optimism. Maybe her evil comes straight to the forefront. Maybe anything. Because coming down to the last line, she cheats.

"My mother told me to pick the best one," she says, waving back and forth on each word. Then she spends a few words on the trucker.

"And you are it!" she declares, suddenly switching back to Mabel. The gamesmaster has changed the rules, and Mabel, suddenly caught in the crosshairs (much of the scene is filmed from behind Mickey's gun barrel, like the first-person shooter video games that weren't *quite* mainstream yet), goes down.

"As I was getting shot again and again," Jones says, "at a certain point, it took me a matter of time to calm down and get back in character, to play these very deep emotions. That was technically difficult, because there had to be a moment where I thought I was saved. I had to have that on the back burner. I was fighting for my life, and the character had to feel a moment of relief before the end."

As filming ended, Lewis and Jones heard a tremendous cheer go up from the women on the set. Stone sat off to the side, stunned into silence.

The scene took a week to shoot, and Jones needed some time to recover. But she'd done even more than she'd originally anticipated; the film's original script called for a weeping Mabel to just be shot—artistically, through a coffee pot she was holding; after she auditioned, Jones got to do just a little more—a definite bonus to making a one-scene deal truly belong to the people playing it.

"The next day, after I was done shooting, I felt like I was convalescing from an illness, because it uses up so much adrenaline," she said. "It's a fabulous scene. It's kind of exciting to watch it all put together. I thought it was super filmmaking."

After that, nothing about the film stayed the same for more than seconds. Animation, color tricks, cinematography, everything spinning like a crazed merry-go-round. Soon enough, we hit just about the most controversial scene of the flick, which says something.

Complete with a title card and intro music, things change to a sitcom. It's *I Love Mallory*, and the title character, looking much more young and innocent (well, except for her black fishnet stockings!) than the lady that just beat a guy to death, nervously smiling at we the audience. Then we see her mom and dad, Ed—and he's played by . . . Rodney Dangerfield?!

Was that a continuity flub? Did he wander onto the wrong set? Is this actually a comedy? Dangerfield was never politically correct, but what the hell was he doing in this type of film?

As things progress, we can't believe more and more. Ed spews out profanity like it's going out of style. Domestic violence shows up. And all along, the cussing comes along with not only corny sitcom music, but a laugh track.

Then we find out that Ed's even worse than we thought—he's doing things to Mallory that no real man does to any woman, let alone his goddamned daughter! But just in time, a delivery boy named Mickey arrives (applause included!), and we see the beginning of the Knoxes.

The sounds, the laugh track, the audience laughed at this sort of thing. And it's not unrealistic to believe that, helped along by the subconsciousness that laugh tracks are supposed to explore and the feeling they're intended to entice from us the viewers, that many of us might not have been able to stop ourselves from snickering right along with it, immediately trying to catch ourselves as pass the giggle off as a cough or sneeze.

Many critics and fans called this a highlight of the film, if nothing else than for crediting the crew for having the brass to go this far into bad taste to push it all the way back through to fruition, while others, perhaps still hung up on *Cheers*, badmouthed it for Harrelson's work on the darkest kind of sitcom spoofs. Though he created a few of his lines, Dangerfield was uncomfortable during filming (for Christsake, who wouldn't be, playing a guy who molests his daughter, especially after so many years of comedy?!).

"I wanted to root Mallory not just as a superhero killer, but in some kind of humanity," Lewis says, "and there's not a serial killer woman alive that didn't have a horrible upbringing [Wuornos claimed she was raped and beaten as a child]. Maybe with men, it varies. In the audience, [Stone is] giving you this information, that this is her home life, and at the same time, it's Americana and [everyone is laughing]. He's flipping everything on its ear, because that's the existence of America; you have the front of a chipper family, the churchgoing family, and you have this evil that lurks behind closed doors. [Stone] was using the medium of a sitcom, which I felt was really, really brilliant, as strange as it was."

Indeed, Mallory's humanity shows up. A bit later on, she and Mickey brutally slaughter her parents, enjoying every minute of it. But when her younger brother Kevin (played by Stone's son Sean) walks out, she stops Mickey from harming him.

"You don't often get to play psychopathic, or these dark colors, what I call the Tasmanian Devil," Lewis recalls. "I use my entire body when I act, and *NBK* is the perfect example of a very physical role with a lot of complexities. With *NBK*, the main emotions are apathy, rage, and despair, or torment. That's the concrete of that character."

By the way, the sappy Brady Bunch-type tune we heard during the sitcom scene? It shows up again and again. When Mickey blasts Ed upside the head with a tire iron, we hear comical birdie noises. We'll hear it again shortly, but first it's time to meet the guy who truly personifies the media's fixation with celebrities, whether their reasons for being so are right or wrong.

His name's Wayne Gale, and we can tell early on that he's a fame addict. Probably a wannabe actor who never went anywhere, he's content to yell into a microphone, searching for the scandal that will rock America so deeply it tears the Constitution in half, looking to be a hero while catching the bad guys on his show *American Maniacs*, then sitting down and chatting with them in exclusive interviews.

The role had nearly gone to Geraldo Rivera, and we can see a great deal of him in the part. Then Robert Downey Jr. showed up, and followed Stone and the rest of the cast straight over the top.

Downey had hung out with Steve Dunleavy, the longtime host of the tabloid show *A Current Affair* and columnist for the *New York Post* to prepare for the role. When he returned with Dunleavy's natural Australian accent, Stone and he decided to leave it with Gale all the way through filming. Downey also met John Wayne Gacy to get ready to meet with a fake serial killer, as Gale and Mickey converse later on.

It's Gale that represents, or at least introduces us to, the national sensation that the Knoxes have become. They're on magazine covers. There's crowds cheering for them, dressing like them. People around the world sing their praises.

And for what? Because they're good at what they do, even if what they do is murder? What exactly makes them *cool*? Nothing ... other than they're well known. As has been commonplace for decades and is much more true today, if we see a person's face and hear their name enough, some of us, too many of us, start to like them, or at least say we do.

"It's a social commentary film," Lewis says, "but because of the brilliance that is Oliver Stone, he makes you the audience start rooting for Mickey and Mallory a little bit, and that's exactly what he's commenting on: the media's ability to make rock stars out of serial killers. He does it in a really exaggerated way. It's a very complex, layered movie in the mixed media, intellectually. In script form, you knew it was a risk—are you rooting for these terrorists? But you knew the script was something different."

Channeling the spirit of Stanley Kubrick, Stone created a new world for his performers to evolve into their characters, an atmosphere that would subconsciously entice them to live in, to become a part of their new world. To all but force his characters to step into the mindsets of serial murders and the lives affected by it, the film was shot in chronological order. As filming went on, Lewis was found off set, crying secretly, perhaps fearing that Mallory was taking too much control of her.

The Knoxes' psychosis starts to take over even further. They see things that aren't there. The control they executed during the diner scenes starts to slip away. Demons of the dark karma that they've been toying with start to creep up, and pass the line from possible to visible.

"There were so many things in this move that worked for me," Lewis says. "It was like acting boot camp, like a workshop. With Oliver Stone, anything goes. You can write scenes and show them to him, and he'll be, 'Yeah, yeah, yeah.' With this movie, there were no rules, visually. As actors, we had setups where we had to imagine there were demons running by, because there was surrealism in the movie as well. It's a collision of pseudo-reality and humanity and all the shades in between."

With music blaring around her and air blasting in her face, Jane Hamsher dressed for a role in the film she'd worked hard to produce.

"My teeth were covered in black stain, and I had lipstick smeared all around my lips, my eyebrows drawn up like flames across my brow," she recalls of getting ready to become one of the Knoxes' demonic tormentors. Putting on a black leather jacket backward to resemble bondage wear, Hamsher grabbed a long sword to wave around, frightening those on and off the screen.

The pain that Mickey and Mallory cause others starts to reach inside them, and with no one else around, they're left to take it out on each other. After one big spat, Mallory storms off in the middle of the night, looking to find her sex appeal appreciation from another....

It's often speculated that stepping into a prison or hanging out with cops for very long will make one appreciate the very thin line between law enforcement and those they protect us from, that a different decision here or there could have switched prisoners' and guards' positions on the sides of the bars. That, and the ludicrous amount of pain, stress, and even hate that police undergo every day from both those they protect and those from whom they protect us (not to mention the poverty-level paychecks they receive) can play hell with a cop's psyche.

It was those sorts of things, along with the murder of his mother before his own eyes by Charles Whitman, known (and, terrifyingly, admired by too many) as America's first mass shooter, that pushed detective Jack Scagnetti out of stability and straight into madness, even obsession. A mania with taking down Mickey and Mallory, not so much to solidify his name next to Hoover in law enforcement legend, but to get a piece of Mallory's gorgeous ass. Like many men with a mother fixation (such as Hoover), he's into powerful ladies, and one who's stolen so many lives would be tough to beat. He's spent much of his career trying to put away her kind, but this guy's got his own dark fascinations once in a while.

Months of chatting with, hanging with, and reading about cops and detectives and the oft-pitch-black world in which they work had attuned Tom Sizemore to Scagnetti's life, so far from any type of normalcy. He'd read up on serial killers and the worlds they create for themselves, the worlds in which they reign supreme, where they decide what happens. For so many of them, it's the only semblance they've ever had of such a world.

From Scagnetti's first appearance, there's a foreshadowing of his own similar existence. It's a gas station, and a man lies dead. Angered and hormonally charged after a fight with her love, Mallory was on a late-night hunt for satisfaction, reassurance of her feminine wiles, and a station attendant appeared to have hit the libido lottery, a beautiful woman showing up to give it up.

As energized as Lewis had been acting out one brutal murder after another up to now, this one was tough; perhaps Stone's chronological experiment of the Knoxes' crimes was starting to wear on her. Maybe she felt Mallory taking over inside, taking a bit much. Maybe the lifelong fear of guns she'd attempted to fight off with some pre-film obstacle course firearm training (glocks, machine guns, the whole arsenal) was creeping through her.

Or maybe she just thought it weird to blast a guy who was going down on her. Whatever the reason, Lewis had some difficulty with the scene—mentally here, as the physical side would come later on. The aftermath, on the other hand, put Scagnetti in his element.

For a detective, he doesn't seem the slightest bit concerned about finding the perpetrator, of bringing justice to the loved ones who just suffered a tragic, violent loss. For him, it's a step closer to the woman of his fixations. We can tell he's been here too long. Mallory isn't an object of his affection; this is stalking. With flashbacks to Ted Bundy, we get the feeling that this stuff is about power over women, and corralling this little princess would be the ultimate prize.

And just as thirty innocent women (that we know of! Billions to one says it's many, many more) learned through Bundy's misogynistic brutality, one—and we can tell it wasn't his first time—finds something similar in Scagnetti, now alone and unclothed (not a GQ moment!) with a lady of the dark nights.

As is typically the case in the entertainment world, the beauty's far lovelier than most real-life walkers of the street. Watchers around the globe had seen it in a different medium.

"I was in Australia to clear my head," **Lorraine Farris** recalls. "I was bicycling, and some photographers took my picture." More and more people saw it; modeling took Farris across Europe and Asia, and eventually back to New York, where it helped fund her original goal of acting.

"You get comfortable in front of the camera," she explains, "being aware of the camera." Still, up to her *Killers* role, Farris hadn't yet stepped in front of a filmer.

"They told me, 'This is not a Tennessee Williams play!'" she recalls. "I said, 'All right!'" As she'd turn into a custom as her career continued, Farris sat down and wrote out a biography of her character's life.

The lovely Pinky (Lorraine Farris) inadvertently readies to become the next victim in *Natural Born Killers*.

"Any character I play, I write about her," she explains. "I write her backstory, so there's a full history of who she is and where she came from, so you have an understanding, a personal view of who she is. I wrote about who her parents were, where she lived, what had taken place in her life." Stone, always known for being open minded with his crew during filming, let her use some of the new story in the film.

Her Pinky nickname came from her brother (hey, a little personal info helps at this! Lots of times the johns are uncomfortable knowing you), and she's not the most experienced as this prostitution thing; her customer is sitting there *admitting* he's a cop! What call girl worth her trade would so casually let herself be stung?

Perhaps recognizing her inexperience, "Oliver created a really safe set for me," Harris recalls. "He created a situation that I felt free to explore."

It certainly wasn't the most welcoming from a visual sense; the dark motel room lit up by images that only viewers can see (including *Scarface*, another film that showed the dark but popular side to violence), the young lady climbs atop her new patron. He asks her to gyrate in the way we saw Mallory doing back at the beginning. We know who's in his mind.

Then he strangles her. Just a bit.

He assures her it's just his dark sense of humor, but there's still more than apprehension, perhaps even more than fear in her eyes.

And, heartbreakingly, it wasn't all an act.

"I had been working through some victim things in my life," Farris says, "and that experience helped me worked through them. It was a deep experience for me. It brought up a lot for me, but it was a very healing experience, playing some of that stuff out in a safe place."

Perhaps having been here before in her trade, she sinks onto Scagnetti again.

His hands go back around her neck. This time, they don't let go.

They topple onto the floor, him now on top. He keeps asserting he's just kidding, but there's nothing she can do. After a while, she can't struggle anymore.

Now atop his own rush, Scagnetti vows Mallory will be next. Doubtless he forgets Pinky's name within seconds.

"If you really press and you know who this person is, you're free," Farris says. "You're not set and hooked into one idea, but you already have this person embodied, so everything you do is within her. It's what I always hope to do." Sizemore, who'd already been around violence in *Point Break* (1991), *True Romance* (1993), and *Born on the Fourth of July* (1989), called it the toughest scene to that point in his career.

Lost in the desert, the Knoxes find some random compassion—rather than the sleazy lust from the diner guys—for the first real time all film, taken in by a Navajo who sees straight into their souls and doesn't like the sight. As they sleep, he tries to go even further, reaching in to pull the darkness from Mickey's mind and heart. But doing so brings the killer's agonizing past to the top of his subconscious.

Not every person we see in films, even the biggest blockbusters, is a Hollywood star. Many of them aren't even from Hollywood. People like **Sally Jackson** help some literal outsiders find work, and save the highers-up some money in the bargain.

"I'm in location casting, which means I go to the location where they're filming," explains Jackson, who'd already done such work in the west for *City Slickers* (1991), the *Young Guns* films

(1988/1990), *Indiana Jones and the Last Crusade* (1989), and others. "I hold auditions and hire actors on location so they don't have to bring everyone in from LA." Hanging out in Gallup, New Mexico (right near the Four Corners where the state meets Colorado, Arizona, and Utah), she'd already helped put together the diner scene and tons of photos of the couple's victims.

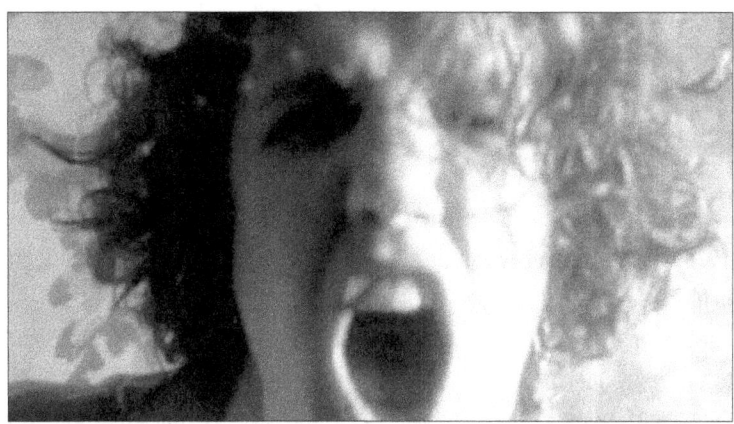

Sally Jackson instantly became one of the worst moms in movie history in *Natural Born Killers*, roaring profanities at her single-digit-age son Mickey Knox.

That had already caused a serious issue with the locals. Sitting in her office, Jackson waited for the pictures to come back from a local development store. Then she got the most surprising and ominous of visitors.

"A bunch of cops came in, pretty scary, to my office," she remembers. The developer, seeing out of context, hadn't known what he was looking at and called the local fuzz.

"I had to explain that those were actors, extras," she says. "It was not real, it was a movie, Oliver Stone was directing it." Even lawmen get starstruck once in a while; the cops departed. It wouldn't be Jackson's last surprise of the shoot.

Pulling up to the set one morning, she was nabbed by a crew member.

"She came running up and said, 'Did you know you're going to be Mickey's mom?'" Jackson remembers. "I didn't, but I thought it was just going to be a photograph on a mantel." She'd already hired a set of twin boys to play the little Mickey, but wasn't looking for a role herself.

"I would never go for a part in a movie I'm casting," she says. "You just don't do that. But Oliver is crazy, as everybody knows, and the movie was in his head, not on paper. He was coming up with stuff at the last minute."

Then she learned she'd have to actually act it out. The night before, the character hadn't existed to her. Now Jackson was becoming her.

In the midst of his impromptu ceremony, the Navajo tries to chant out the demons that run roughshod through Mickey. Now we see them as well, not far from Mallory's roots. Perhaps he wasn't naturally a mass murderer.

Ominous dark colors and shadows abounding, we see him as a kid, even younger than Mallory was. We see his parents. We hear them arguing, inciting each other, getting physical. We see his younger form, staring at them with wide eyes, sadly used to this.

Jackson looked inside, for something no woman should ever become.

"[The crew member] said, 'Just think of the worst thing you could possibly think of to say to a child that would cause them to grow up to be a serial killer!'" she remembers. Just as Lewis had, she got right in the director's face.

"Oliver was there, and I stood about three inches from his face," Jackson says, "and I screamed in his face, 'I hate you, you little motherfucker! I wish I'd never had you!' I screamed it, and spit in his face." He was impressed.

"I ended up there all day in the weirdest outfit you can imagine," Jackson says. "I had on this bra top with my boobs hanging out and my fat hanging out over these 1970 bellbottom jeans with four-inch shoes, just yelling." With her as the wicked mother, film stunt coordinator Phil Neilson became the dad.

"He beat me up all day long," Jackson remembers. "I never had so much fun in my life!"

Well, perhaps not the whole time. Inexperienced at the whole acting out action thing (*Killers* was her film debut), Jackson wasn't reacting fast enough, particularly playing a lady who was used to violence.

"I finally went to Oliver and just said, [Neilson would] have to hit me," she says. "I wasn't worried about getting hit. He was actually connecting with my face and my body, and that was great, because then I could roll with the punches, so to say." With his dad elsewhere (his suicide, also before his son, comes later), Mickey becomes mom's anger recipient.

The shaman's still looking for evil, but we also see clips of him cackling mockingly. Like much of this film, it's tough to tell the real from the surreal. Then Mickey's mom screams in his face, straight into ours.

"I hate you, you little asshole!" Jackson's creation roars at her elementary-school-age son. If we were sympathetic to her plight before, she quickly becomes one of the film's biggest villains.

"We did it all day long," she remembers. "I yelled and screamed at those poor little boys. One was crying in a corner, and I was crying, saying I didn't want to devastate him. But the other one got it. He's the one you see on film, looking up with the shadows."

It all explodes. Not even all the way conscious, Mickey grabs a nearby gun and blasts away, accidentally killing one of the few people that ever showed him an ounce of care, the Navajo dying before their and his grandson's eyes. Mallory's upset too, for the first time feeling remorse for their actions.

Now it's finally time for some comeuppance. Perhaps out for revenge, their host's slithering friends set upon his killers, looking to share their venomous tastes. They escape, but not for long. . . .

Scagnetti finally gets his prey outside a supermarket one night; the weakened couple finally gets tracked down, with the detective at the lead. With triumphant music playing in the background and Mallory already under locks, Mickey gets a taste of what his wife put the trucker through back at the diner, as world kickboxing champ Kathy Long plays a cop who, quite literally, kicks the living shit out of him.

"All artistic mediums, to me, deal with energy and communication. So when you're dealing with emotion, emotion has different frequencies, in the way you carry your body, in the way your voice changes, depending on if you're feeling vulnerable, scared, angry, lustful, all these qualities," Lewis says, "and I love the way you're using emotion as it passes through you. As far as characters, just like people, are made up of different colors, different frequencies, different energies, different rhythms, and emotion has a different way of feeling."

Eventually, things moved all the way to Illinois' Statesville Correctional Center, transformed into Batonga Penitentiary for the flick. Prison officials assured the crew that, were an inmate to take any of them captive, nothing would be given for their safe return. Tommy Lee Jones, who'd done a 180 to the other side of law enforcement in less than twenty-four hours, finishing up a 1993 Oscar-winning turn as a federal marshal in *The Fugitive* to become Batonga's crazed warden in *NBK* the next morning, nearly got into a fight with a prisoner. Lewis, one of the few females present, wasn't permitted to wear tight clothes.

"I knew I was playing in a heightening reality," she says. "But anything I do, whether it's comedy, or drama, really broad or subtle, I always root it in realism, and in something really human. Even though there's a larger-than-life thing, somewhere there's an essence of truth in Mickey and Mallory, in that kind of disturbance, that kind of nihilism, in a way."

Getting ready for the next bit of filming, she and the rest of the crew spent as much as fourteen hours a day in prison, discussing prison life with the staff and residents.

"Your heart would be beating, and it's also because you're in very real danger, because people want to get out of there," she says. "When you're in a prison, with rapists and murderers locked up, there's a palpable energy, because you're dealing with caged rage and chaos, and it's condensed."

Mallory never showed much fear or anxiety, but Lewis wasn't bound by the same rules, talking to men who'd raped, killed, both, or committed other crimes.

"One guy was very sweet, and he asked what it was like on the outside," she recalls. "He was literally looking through me to freedom. That's all he wanted to talk about. This guy was trying to be charming. . . . I hyperventilated. The energy was off the walls."

Outside of filming, she relied on Jimi Hendrix tunes to find her mindset.

"I listened to 'Voodoo Chile' and 'Slight Return,'" Lewis says. "Over and over and over again. I almost hypnotized myself with it. With every bend of Jimi's guitar, he takes you deeper and deeper into a jungle where there's chaos and seduction and the darkest dark and all this unpredictable madness. Before I take off to the location [of filming], I get really in touch with my environment, or just start opening my eyes and absorbing, attracting things that will feed or inform the character. It's all energy based. There's a frustration. I remember driving and listening to VC. Of course, I was doing all the physical fighting. Physically, I was feeling very powerful in a way."

That wouldn't last; she caught pneumonia, and all the smoke in the prison scenes didn't help much.

"I was in prison for fourteen hours a day for weeks, playing a girl who didn't care if she lived or died," she says. "That energy took its toll. You're alert, because you're in a dangerous environment, and you're only slightly protected. I was on alert, and at the end of the day, I was so beat down. I tried to will my way through the end of the film."

As Gale reaches out and grabs the nation's attention during a national interview with Mickey, Scagnetti finally gets alone with his top gal, warning her that he's the only thing left between her and celibacy—Mickey's heading out for good as soon as he's through chatting. Much like she did in the diner and at the gas station, Mallory's seductively responsive.

We all know what's going to happen, but even Scagnetti seems to be allowing his hormones to overcome his rationale. Much like a guy who tosses his life savings at a gorgeous exotic dancer, forgetting that she's going to mock him with her colleagues and forget him as soon as a bouncer throws him out the door, he's too taken, even overtaken with her pseudo-charms.

"It's the feeling of alienation, the feeling that people relate to, on some level," Lewis says. "She's trying to hypnotize him. That's her world, and she's trying to lure him in."

It works, but, as is the case with every man but Mickey, Mallory's dark side comes roaring out, beating the holy hell out of him. There's some debate as to whether Lewis actually broke Sizemore's schnozzle in the ensuing melee; he and Hamsher say yes, she says no. In any case, he's soon laying dazed while a tag team of guards tune her up (ironically, Sizemore and Lewis would have a torrid affair the very next year in Kathryn Bigelow's underrated *Strange Days*!).

"I always felt that I could connect to the deepest, darkest emotions," Lewis says. "We all have them; it's not like I have them more than somebody else. It's just my ability to access them, to exaggerate them, to turn them up, it's a high. It's always been there, since I was a kid, because I had this lethal imagination, good and bad, and in this movie, I got to live in the underbelly of that animal, a real base-level drive, the dark stuff in humanity that I like to tap into."

While his lady is destroying Scagnetti, Mickey's finally lit the fuse that transforms Batonga into the explosion everyone was dreading; his interview sends prisoners everywhere into a full-scale riot, and he's on a trek to find his beloved, Gale's camera crew keeping everything in deadly living color. Surrounded by rioters who weren't just *acting* like prisoners, Lewis, Harrelson, and the rest tried to keep their character composure.

"In a weird way, it was therapeutic for them, because they got to control what normally is out of control," Lewis says. "They got to manifest and fake fights, like kids. Everybody behaved and did their job. It was a riot scene, and nothing happened."

Antonia Chavez (Melinda Renna) calls to her friend and newscasting colleague Wayne Gale in one of the most climactic moments of *Natural Born Killers*.

Back at TV headquarters, a new lady leaps onto the screen. It's one of Gale's colleagues, literally launched straight into action, having to rely much more on off-the-cuff improvisation and showing a hell of a lot more emotion than anchors ever find jammed upon them. He's determined to keep the camera rolling even milliseconds from a fatal shanking, and she's, albeit much less by choice, going to help him.

Fortunately, Melinda Renna had even been there before . . . well, sort of.

"I was an on-air news anchor for an independent television and radio station in Fort Worth, Texas," she recalls. News of an open casting call took her over to Dallas, and Renna was soon before other cameras, tending bar in the midst of the crew that brought Stone his second statuette, for *Born of the Fourth of July*.

"I began working in commercials, industrial films, and films being cast in the area," Renna says. "I never chose the action genre. I auditioned for anything and everything. I think the stars just aligned when I got to do Antonia Chavez. It was a once-in-a-lifetime chance that I recognized only in hindsight."

Her Antonia calls for Gale and his crew, no one really sure what's going on or what will happen. Up until Renna stepped behind Antonia's desk, the *Natural* crew had suffered similar issues. Originally, Antonia had appeared as the everyday anchor—hair bunned back, suit in two pieces, traditional all the way . . . and that's not an adjective that anyone could ever use to describe Stone, or *Killers*.

"We shot about five minutes," Renna says, "and [Stone] said 'No, this isn't what I want.'" Back in wardrobe, Renna was handed a skirt, body suit, and pumps, bra not included. Her toned arms hung bare from her sweater. Clearly, Antonia hadn't had time to spruce up.

"Now we had the feel," Renna says, "an indictment of the media and how far away from journalism we are, the titillation of the captive audience, entertainment and seduction trumping information." Still, after receiving her readings just a few days before shooting, Renna had to react to a blank screen, her mind made to create the riot that hadn't yet been filmed.

"We took about four takes over an hour period," Renna says. "It was wild and wonderful. There was little time to think about preparation or intention. As we all learn, you study and practice and prepare, and then forget it all once you get on set so it doesn't get in your way. But it's there, like muscle memory, like breathing without having to think about breathing. You do your work, then you let go because there is no guarantee you will make the final cut. Luckily the editors found me necessary to the story and pleasing to the eye." Stone felt the same way, giving Renna small parts in his *Nixon* (1995) and *Any Given Sunday* (1999)

As the Knoxes reunite, Gale can't stop blaring out their story, and sappy romantic-comedy-type music fills the air. Even after what they've done and where they are, it almost brings viewers to tears. Even Antonia seems touched, although in a film overfilled with illusion, we'll never really know if that was real or surreal.

But music will come back again, albeit not yet. The Knoxes back together, and Gale off his damned rocker, blasting hell out of attacking guards and everything else that walks, the warden and his not-so-merry men hole up downstairs, ready to gleefully give the Knoxes their just desserts.

It's not to be. A gun to Gale's head—he finally gets to *act*, pretending to be an unwilling hostage—everyone strolls right out, everyone scared to shoot in front of the nation (chances are, such an act today would make someone a hero, at least on YouTube). The inmates attack, there's nowhere to go, and the warden and others are massacred as the inmates celebrate and viewers hear the type of triumphant music that makes one just want to jump up and run a marathon.

Still, it's not the end. There's one more message to send, and for the final time, it comes from the title characters themselves. Knowing that Gale will follow them forever, knowing he'll forever mooch his own fame from them without caring about them, before he stalks them as their own personal Inspector Javert, they stick him right in front of the only place he was ever comfortable, his camera, and blast him to oblivion. Now caught all the way off guard back at the studio, Antonia can't figure out how to react as her friend is gone.

Remember all that superficiality I was ranting about back at the beginning of this profile? From his biggest fans to his loudest detractors, no one has or ever could accuse Oliver Stone of that label, or failing to go beneath the surface of his own subject matter. His fellow crew, his cast, even he felt that all the way through filming (this has to be mentioned—*NBK* knocked *Forrest Gump*, one of the most feel-good movies of the 90s, out of the top box-office spot when it came out; define black irony!).

Perhaps that's why Mickey and Mallory get away at the end (unless someone finds the director's cut, on which they die). Because that would be a forced happy ending, removing the focal point of the film itself. It would have come across as artificial, doing something for no purpose other than to give the audience something to feel good about as they left, taking the easy way out.

NBK was not about two people who manipulated their way through a killing spree, but the effect that said spree had upon them. Perhaps they were even ashamed of what they'd done. They were tired of the death, the destruction, the fame that came with it. For all the people in society today that are famous for no reason other than being famous, maybe they—and Stone—wanted to send a lesson that not only is this not healthy for everyone, it's out and out unhealthy for all. Hurtful. Even dangerous.

"At the end of the day, Oliver Stone was holding a magnifying glass up to the journalism, the state of mainstream media culture, and infuriating them," Lewis says. "He antagonized them. We the actors are the talking heads of the movie."

Perhaps Mickey and Mallory realize and show that they represent the true royally decrepit nature of society today. Their final murder is one of remorse, of a sad message.

Don't follow us. Don't pay attention to us. Most importantly, don't *like* us. We don't want it like we thought we did, and it's not healthy for you. Just leave us alone, let us fade away, and go and fix your own lives, rather than worrying about us. Rather than glorifying the stuff we did, turn your head and mind toward something a bit more meaningful—your job, your family . . . your own life and mark in the world.

Maybe we truly can learn something from society's dark side after all.

Haing Ngor had the worst kind of preparation for his Oscar-winning role in 1984's *Killing Fields*, having lived through the same Cambodian hell he'd act out.

Haing Ngor: *Killing Fields*

RIGHT AFTER THE BRILLIANT and beautiful comedienne Gilda Radner finished her hellish fight with ovarian cancer, a disease that tortured her for years before finally, perhaps mercifully, stealing her at age 42 in 1989, a friend of hers said something along the lines of, "Sometimes, if we have faith, we can take some sort of message or lesson from it, but I'm having a lot of trouble with this one."

I couldn't think of a better way to sum up the tragic life of Dr. Haing Ngor.

The man suffered for years in his Cambodian homeland. While Pol Pot and his Khmer Rouge, Asia's answer to Hitler and the Nazis, turned the country into a giant slave labor camp, killing unthinkable numbers—estimates range between one and three million—Ngor watched his pregnant wife die before his eyes. His father, mother-in-law, and many other family members were murdered or died from the suffering at the hands of these terrorists. Ngor himself was forced through torture that would have caused many, perhaps even most of us, to give up long ago.

But with his health in shambles, his material possessions stolen, his medical practice a thing of the surreal past, Ngor made it to Thailand, and then to America. Somehow, he came out of nowhere to roar past many other performers with decades' more worth of experience to take home an Academy Award. Continuing his career as a virtual afterthought compared to the other charity work he did, spending much of his own money along the way, Ngor was much more than many of us ever dream of.

And then he was murdered by three worthless, piece-of-shit human beings out looking for a drug fix, probably because Ngor refused to part with jewelry containing a photo of his wife.

And we have to sit here and wonder why the hell things like that happen, so damned obscene it's impossible not to get angry just from writing about them. Fortunately, Ngor gave us—not only the moviegoing world, but anyone looking for a role model—enough righteousness to remember him for the right reasons.

Growing up in the Cambodian capital of Phnom Penh, already ravaged by war, Ngor watched both the government and local rebels extort money from civilians by kidnapping them and forcing their families to pay ransom, a fate suffered several times over by both of Ngor's parents. As a young man, Ngor was falsely arrested, his hand jammed into a vice and his body beaten with sticks, all in an attempt to force a "confession" of being a Communist (absolutely nothing compared to what would be forthcoming).

As the nation drifted closer and closer to out-and-out civil war (helped along, in part, by a bombing and troop withdraw by President Nixon that turned the country into chaos) Phnom Penh's population doubled, then grew even larger. Homelessness and lawlessness were rampant. Ngor had heard of the Khmer Rouge, a terrorist Commie group, on its way in to take over, but he was certain that a doctor such as himself would be left alone. But as he spent more and more endless nights helping injured soldiers, as he heard more and more shells and bombs falling in a distance that grew ever closer, as his father's lumber mill was overtaken by the enemy, the pain of reality started to increase.

"It surprises me now," he said, "but most of us pretended that life was almost normal. We made ourselves believe that Phnom Penh was a little island of peace and that it was going to stay that way." But soon, Pol Pot's people overtook the area, forcing the city population into the streets.

As his city emptied, Ngor wondered if he'd ever see his parents, siblings (he had six), or fiancée Huoy again. And he knew his career as a doctor was, for all intents and purposes, finished.

He saw a familiar nurse in the masses.

"Doctor Ngor . . ." she began.

"I am not a doctor anymore," he said. "Call me 'brother.'" In times such as this, it was best to leave one's identity in the yonder.

Eventually, he did find Huoy and the rest of his family; unlike many, they'd made it out of the first line of "vacating." But soon after, everyone would experience the forced labor camp-like atmosphere that the Rouge would soon transform Cambodia into.

Forced into the fields to hoe, and soon out to repair the roads, Ngor watched many of his friends get taken away, never to be seen again. Guards whipped him for not working fast enough. In the span of a few weeks, he and Huoy had gone from first-class lives and top-quality restaurants every night to subsisting on a diet of mice and ants.

His mother committed suicide. Malnutrition, dysentery, skin trouble, and other illnesses came fast and stayed around. Ngor's weight dropped down to about 70 pounds.

"Why are the Gods so blind?" he thought. "Did I do something wrong in a previous life that I have to do this now?"

A month in, he decided that the end was near. Probing for his pulse, Ngor discovered a small, slow motion.

"My heart is slowing down," he said. "In a few more hours it will stop." His father and Huoy sadly tried to convince him to fight on, but there was little they could do.

Then, for the first time in days, the Rouge handed out food to its captives. Huoy, who he'd eventually marry, hurried out and brought back some yams, and fed them to her husband with a spoon.

Ngor's strength returned, and his digestive problems slowed. He had to relearn to walk with a cane. His weight went back to triple digits.

And he was sent right back into the fields. Eventually, he was sent to a prison for stopping work to grab some food—and that's when the Rouge's true nature started to come to light.

Tied to a huge tree with his hands behind his back, Ngor was attacked by red ants.

"The more I struggled, the more they swarmed over me," he said. "I strained against the confinement of the ropes, scratching and moving my feet in a frenzy, unable to move enough."

Eventually, a guard came over—after stopping to rip a fingernail out of a nearby female prisoner. A comrade arrived, and knocked Ngor onto his side. The men demanded that Ngor admit he was a doctor, but having seen his colleagues die for being of the profession, Ngor wouldn't give it up. The first one stepped on the prisoner's wrist, and swung a hatchet down.

"There was an excruciating pain in my little finger," he said. "Automatically, I gasped and stiffened, but no matter how hard I clenched, the pain was there, from the tip of my finger up my arm exploding into my brain."

The two men pushed him back against the tree, then swung the axe at his foot.

"I could see my ankle," he said, "The white bone exposed in the middle of the wound, the flesh red and bleeding around the edges."

Still, his medical mindset kicked back in, and he rubbed his heel in the dirt and coated his ankle wounds to stop the bleeding.

He was left there for another two days without sleep, defecating and urinating on himself. Eventually, after another beating, the guards allowed him to go.

But it still wasn't enough. The rumors about Ngor's medical background began to spread, and soon after, two unfamiliar soldiers showed up to take him back to prison—and torture worse than any horror film in history.

Once again, the men attempted to coerce Ngor's doctorship from him; he flatly insisted that he was a taxi driver.

Something slammed into his ribs.

"I fell over on my side," Ngor says. "Then the other guard kicked me with the hard edge of his rubber-tired sandals. I arched my back in agony." He was quickly covered in bruises, then taken to a nearby field.

Guards put together a makeshift cross, and tied Ngor to it. Then they piled rice hulls at his feet, and used a cigarette to light the mess.

"Please Gods," he prayed, "when I have gone either to hell or paradise, keep me away from the Khmer Rouge. When I am reborn, don't send me near them.... In my next life, let me be happy." He shouted at the guards to shoot him, but such an act was too merciful by Rouge standards.

Smoke burned through his eyes and mouth, and his feet and legs became blistered (hulls can burn for days at a time). He prayed and prayed, and wondered what he had done to deserve this, and who could be so cold as to perform it.

Prisoners around him were taken down and suffocated. For four days and nights, no one ate or drank.

Soon, the guards took him down. But Ngor still wouldn't admit to being a doctor, only pleading with them to kill him. A woman next to him, a pregnant lady, was suffocated and disemboweled.

Then someone dumped a pail of muddy water onto Ngor's face.

"I had never tasted anything so good," he remembered. "I tilted my head back and it filled my mouth and I swallowed again and again."

As their strength began to return, Ngor and the rest of the prisoners—of the seventeen he'd arrived with, only four were alive—were put to work raking and gardening at the prison, feasting on watery rice. For two months, Ngor never knew if he was at his last day, or even hour.

Still, he was released, and back to "freedom," which meant more work outside. But that had to be it, right? How much pain and suffering could one person endure? Surely, life would improve ... wouldn't it?

No. Things actually got worse.

Soon after, Ngor's father was stolen. One more stint in jail resulted in another beating and water torture on a man who was all but desperate to die soon.

"Why did I survive?" he wondered. "To me, the only answer that makes sense is that the Gods willed it. It was not chance, because the mathematical odds against me were too high." Still, he had Huoy to live for—and when the cracks in the Rouge foundation began to show in 1977, caused by infighting and a growing rebellion by the captives, it seemed that things might work out in the end.

Then, in late 1977, they were overjoyed to learn that Huoy was pregnant. The weather dried out in early 1978, and food, scarce as it had been throughout, became even harder to find, with everyone stealing.

Malnourishment hit Huoy hard, and Ngor's desperate searches for food came up empty. One night, about seven months into her pregnancy, Huoy suddenly started feeling sharp pains in her stomach. There was no hospital or equipment, and Ngor couldn't deliver the baby, or everyone would learn that he'd been a doctor all along. A neighboring midwife came over, but, again, no one had anything in the areas of tools or medication.

The contractions continued, lowering everyone's hope that it was false labor. They kept going, and at about 11 p.m., her water broke. But her contractions stopped, and that meant trouble.

Everyone could see the baby's head, but without forceps, it was all but impossible to deliver it. A C-section might have solved everything, but there was no way to perform one.

Ngor ran to Khmer Rouge headquarters, but no one would help him.

Shattered, he returned to Huoy, knowing there was nothing that could be done.

"Save my life," she weakly said. "I'm too tired. I need a spoonful of rice."

He lifted her into his lap, and cradled her.

"Take care of yourself," she said. Then she and the baby died.

For the next few months, Ngor lived in a stupor, full of anger and bitterness, through months he would never remember. There was no energy, only more hope for death.

It was only later that he realized that things were changing around him. Fewer people were being corralled and punished. Violence began to break out between civilians and soldiers, and the soldiers didn't always win.

Then, on April 17, 1979, four years to the day after his nightmare had begun, Vietnamese troops liberated the area, and Phnom Penh was free again. Shortly after, Ngor happened upon a group of people beating a Khmer Rouge member.

Tossing the Hippocratic Oath to the wind, Ngor stepped forward, and the crowds parted.

He kicked the scumbag right between the legs, and the crowd continued to beat the impromptu prisoner. Moments later, someone hacked off the man's head and posted it on a pole for everyone to see.

Ngor made his way to Thailand and worked as a refugee doctor. Then he headed across the water.

"The place I wanted to be was called Los Angeles," he said. "I didn't know where Los Angeles was. I didn't know if it was a state or city, whether it was big or small, on the seacoast or the mountains, hot or cold, whether a lot of Cambodians lived there or only a few." But his niece Sophia (herself a Cambodian escapee) and cousins lived there, and that was enough.

"He was my mother, father, uncle, best friend," Sophia sadly recalls. "Without him, I would have been in an orphanage. I think of him every day. He was so full of passion, whether it was about rebuilding Cambodia and bringing the Khmer Rouge to justice or my grades in school as we both tried to adapt to life in Los Angeles and learn English. He always took care of me. I owe my life to my uncle."

Upon arriving, Ngor took a job as a caseworker, helping his countrymen find jobs, government assistance, and medical treatment across the city. In March 1982, two acquaintances strolled into his office and told him about an upcoming film about Cambodia's plight.

"They tried to get me interested," Ngor said, "but I really wasn't listening. My clients were real people with real problems, and I didn't have time for daydreams." Acting hadn't carried much stardom in his homeland, and the cinema had never been a huge part of his life anyway.

Shortly thereafter, he was invited to a wedding, and ran into a local casting director.

"She asked me to sit for a photograph and give her my name and phone number," he remembered. "But a live band was playing and the guests were dancing the romvong [a popular dance from his homeland]. It had been a long time since I'd danced the romvong, and I told her no." Eventually, however, he gave in, but didn't have much reason to remember the meeting for the next four months.

Then he got a call to come in for a meeting, and reluctantly made his way to Long Beach.

"Okay, Haing," the castmaker said, "if you were with some Americans and you had to convince the Khmer Rouge that the people you were with were *not* Americans, how would you do it?"

The non-actor acted his way through a quick scene. A week later, he came back for another interview, then two more. Each time, there were less and less fellow performers there. He didn't know it at the time, but about 7,000 Cambodians had applied for the film.

On his fourth interview, Ngor met Director Roland Joffe, and told Joffe his life story.

"I talked for an hour," Ngor said. "He watched me with intense blue eyes and listened carefully."

Joffe brought a camera to the next discussion, and Ngor and the casting director acted a scene in which he played a doctor, trying to convince a nurse he loved that she had to leave Cambodia to save her life, but that he had to stay in his homeland.

"Roland Joffe brought the camera in closer and closer, but it didn't make me nervous," Ngor said. "I knew that if I put myself in the situation and believed what I was saying . . . the camera didn't matter."

Finally, the two shared a "farewell," and Ngor had to imagine how he'd force himself to say goodbye.

"You have to leave right now," he said, in character, with broken English. "You have to listen me. Situation now very hard. You foreign people. Khmer Rouge don't like you. For me no problem. I'm Cambodian people." He held her and wept.

Then he realized that he couldn't stop crying. Doing a similar scene in the next audition, the same thing happened.

Three months passed before he heard anything, and then only to get asked whether he could go to Thailand for shooting. Ngor said yes, but nothing was finished.

By then, he'd had time to reconsider his views of the film. He'd thought about losing Huoy and other loved ones. He thought about how many of his countrymen had suffered, and how few outside of Cambodia were aware of any of it; America has never worried much about wars it isn't involved in.

"I had changed my mind," he said. "If I could be in the film . . . I could help tell the story of Cambodia, and that was important because it was a story nobody really knew. Most Americans didn't even know where Cambodia was. Even in L.A., non-Cambodian Asians didn't know what had happened under the Khmer Rouge."

And then he realized, or at least admitted, the real reason he didn't want to enter *The Killing Fields* (1984).

"Ever since coming to the United States, I'd had nightmares," he said. "Huoy died in my arms over and over and over. I saw my father tied to the tree and trying to tell me something, but afraid to speak . . . I felt more alienated than ever, and not sure how much better America was than what I had left behind, because I hadn't really left it behind, and I couldn't enjoy the best of America." He'd lost Huoy, but her story, and those of millions of others, could still be told.

When her uncle left to do the film, recalls Sophia, "I wasn't happy at all, because that meant he would have to leave me again with other people. I was 12 or 13, and I didn't want to be shuffled from family to family again. I couldn't go with him on location, because I needed to stay in school. I cried so much! I didn't speak to him for a couple of days. He explained that we really needed the money, and so I said okay."

Ngor and the rest of the cast headed overseas. But it wasn't until arrival that the acting rookie learned he'd have one of the biggest roles in the film.

Killing Fields is the true story of Sydney Schanberg, a *New York Times* correspondent during the Rouge takeover, and his Cambodian assistant Dith Pran. While Pran looked to Schanberg for lessons on reporting, Schanberg (tough as it was for him to admit it), needed Pran to lead him through Cambodian culture.

As the Communists descended, Pran helped Schanberg escape, but was himself forced into the labor fields. Over the next four years, Schanberg sadly, angrily, and guiltily believed his friend dead.

But when the Vietnamese arrived, Pran escaped, and the pair was reunited in Thailand in 1979.

"I was [Pran] and he was me," Ngor said, "because we were Cambodian men of about the same age and because we had been under the hammer of the same terrible events: the civil war, then the revolution, then the foreign occupation, and finally pouring into the refugee camps and going to America." Though not of the medical field, Pran had spent time in Cambodian hospitals. Like Ngor, he'd been forced into the fields, eaten watery rice, gathered food for his family, and suffered at Rouge hands (though Pran never went to prison, and his family escaped before he got out). To an extent, Ngor had the best source of preparation for his role; on the other side, he also had the absolute worst.

Ngor asked to meet Pran, but Joffe assured him that the two were already similar enough. But there was chemistry there that needed creating.

At the airport, Ngor met an American to help him on the set. The fellow's name was Sam Waterston, and he'd become Schanberg.

Shortly thereafter, Waterston and Ngor went to the Thai-Cambodian border, and Joffe told Waterston to write some stories about the atmosphere. Ngor taught him about Cambodian life and translated for him.

In other words, the two built the same relationship that Pran and Schanberg had enjoyed.

Ngor took Waterston to his familiar hangouts, to clinics, and to a Khmer Rouge camp in Thailand, where soldiers informed Waterston of their desire to head across the border and mix it up with Vietnamese. Reluctantly, Ngor kept his cool.

"I thought of grabbing [the officers] by their shirts and shouting, 'Fools! You want to fight the Vietnamese?'" Ngor said. "'Look around you at the consequences of your fighting—at the orphans, the handicapped, the civilians with no homes!' I thought of grabbing a rifle and spraying them with bullets." (He didn't).

Giving him space to improv his lines (Ngor created the scene when Rouge guards put bags over captives' heads), Joffe asked Ngor to remember something he'd rather not under most circumstances.

"I prepared for the rice field scenes by remembering how I had felt and walked and worked on the front lines," Ngor said. "When I ate watery rice or caught lizards in the movie, I remembered what hunger was like in the countryside." When Pran fought with his wife, Ngor saw himself with Huoy. When Pran begged for the lives of the Americans, Ngor went back to pretending to be a cabbie.

When Pran said goodbye to his fellow journalists, Ngor recalled saying his final farewell to Huoy.

"I dwelt on that sadness until it grew and the feeling took over, and then just before we started filming I reached into my memory and remembered how I felt when she died." Through all seven takes, he hardly stopped weeping.

It wasn't the only time that things got a little too close to reality. During a scene when Pran is beaten, one of the men playing the guards missed Ngor's protective pads with the giant stick, striking skin and bone.

"For a moment, it was too real," Ngor said, "the shock, the pounding of my blood in my ears, knowing I was going to die."

Even after filming, Ngor didn't let anyone, including himself, forget the *Fields* message: he arrived at a cast party dressed in black, from his tunic to his sandals.

"In Khmer Rouge costume," he said. "To remind them that we were doing more than just making a movie."

Back in New York, he ran into Pran and Schanberg at the film premiere.

"[Pran] was gentle and peaceful, not hyperactive like me," Ngor said. "My experiences were worse than his under the Khmer Rouge, but it didn't matter. Meeting him was like discovering a twin. I knew we would be friends for life."

As *Fields* publicity swept the film world, Ngor—who'd been sharing the screen not only with Waterston, but John Malkovitch, Craig T. Nelson, and others—found much of the film's attention focused on him. He took home a few British Academy Awards.

Sophia got to join her uncle and the rest of the cast for a special screening.

"It was tough," she says of seeing it for the first time. "I couldn't talk, my throat was so choked up. I was shocked and angry—I still feel angry sometimes when I think about it. Watching the movie for the first time, I wondered why nobody did anything to help us in Cambodia if there was news coverage of the Khmer Rouge. The movie reminded me of the way Cambodia was ignored by the rest of the world."

Then he learned that he'd be up for a Supporting Actor Oscar—just one more, albeit pretty legitimate reason, to take time off from his caseworking career.

At the 57th edition of the Oscars on March 25, 1985 at the Dorothy Chandler Pavilion, Ngor and his competitors (including Malkovitch, up for *Places in the Heart*) watched the previous year's top Supporting Actress, Linda Hunt, step on stage to read off the nominees.

"When she came to my name," Ngor said, "the television cameras panned around the audience, but couldn't find me because the usher had taken us to the wrong seats."

No matter. When his name was announced moments later, everyone got a good look.

"When I got on the stage," he said, "my mind went blank. The stage lights and TV cameras were on me, but I couldn't think what to say. I had practiced a speech, but couldn't remember a word of it. Even Hollywood movies do not have endings so unlikely. Nobody would believe them if they did."

Still, he continued, "I knew that my best performances were in Cambodia, and the prizes there were much greater."

Many would have considered their journey back from such a debacle and rousing success, and leave it at that. But not Ngor.

Indeed, he continued to act in movies and television, appearing on *Miami Vice*, *Highway to Heaven*, *China Beach*, and other shows. But things went far beyond that; royalties from his 1987 autobiography, *A Cambodian Odyssey*, went to help Cambodians both in America and back home. He worked with several America-based organizations to help those affected by the Khmer Rouge. Many times, he returned to the Thai-Cambodia border to help get a medical center started.

"Acting is only a means to an end," he said. "It gives me the money and the free time to do my real job, which is helping Cambodians."

Someday, he dreamed, the fighting would end in Cambodia. The Vietnamese troops would depart, the Khmer Rouge would leave power, and he and Pran, who died of cancer in 2008, would be able to return.

"With me will be Buddhist monks," he said. "We will hold a ceremony and build a monument for [Huoy] next to the temple on the mountainside. We will pray for Huoy and her mother and my parents and family, and for all those who lost their lives. Then maybe their souls will be at peace, and maybe mine will be too."

Ngor might have been right; chances are, he was. But he never got to see his vision come true.

On Feb 25, 1996, he went out to visit some friends in Long Beach (Ngor lived in the same apartment he'd held since before *Fields*). Upon his return, Ngor was allegedly accosted in his garage by three people. He gave up his Rolex watch, but wouldn't relent on the chain and locket with Huoy's photo. Angered at a refusal of something that could only mean a great deal to one person in the world, one of the men in the group shot Ngor to death.

Immediately afterward, the public feared that the murder had political connections. Could it be Vietnamese sympathizers, upset at Ngor's escape from Cambodia? Might it have been the Rouge, jealous of his success and furious at his film's portrayal of their organization?

As it turned out, things were much simpler and even sadder. Two months after the shooting, three gang members, all age 20 or 21, were charged with the murder. It had been a robbery gone wrong; Ngor had been a random victim in the wrong place at the wrong time.

Once again, that is.

Because of the killers' age, the D.A. decided not to seek the death penalty, a pathetic excuse to prioritize law over justice. On April 16, 1998, the three were convicted of murder and robbery.

It's tough to comprehend Ngor's story—how, why one human being could suffer so much, only to suffer a bit more. Actually, it's not tough at all. It's far beyond impossible. But what we can learn from Ngor goes past being a decent actor. I didn't have the pleasure of knowing this man, but based on what I've read, he didn't seem to want to be remembered as a great actor, or at least, not only that way. This isn't a story of an actor who took a bit of time between movies to help others; it's about a humanitarian who took time off from his work to make a movie and TV show here and there.

Haing Ngor suffered more than most did, and more than any deserve. We shouldn't forget that, and thanks to people like him and the rest of the *Killing Fields* crew, we won't. But while many would have been content with getting out of the darkness, he got all the way out and became a shining light, someone determined never to leave his country, or his unthinkably painful memories behind. That's the man we should never forget. That's the man who was a hero, and always will be.

We shouldn't remember Ngor because of the type of actor he was—at least, not just because of that. We should remember him as the type of person we all should try to be.

Even against Woody Harelson's wackjob Charlie, Myra (Linda Bright Clay) was fighting off the much tougher and realistic evil of cancer in 2012's *Seven Psychopaths*.

Long Nguyen/Linda Bright Clay: *Seven Psychopaths*

HE HAD TO RECREATE one of the most memorably heartbreaking moments millions ever saw, up close and otherwise, and still see today with the click of a Web search. She had to act out a battle that millions of innocent women find themselves forced into every day in every country. Both of them would have to help their characters find some solace in faiths the performers hadn't much explored.

Even in the action genre, which itself can step away from reality for dramatic purpose, even in a film in which surrealism is one of the biggest plot points, neither still had to look too far for the first steps of prepping.

"I would like to remind everyone, including myself," asserts Long Nguyen, "that the biggest break and the best action is our own life. Once we realize that, we can be calm, fully living the time on and off the set—and when we are on the set, this perspective would help our acting become alive, just as the [first assistant director] always called out 'Live on the set' before the director said 'Action!'"

His character wouldn't actually exist in *Seven Psychopaths* (2012), but still managed to help close the film's plot. Linda Bright Clay's lady showed up much earlier and ended up, well, ending early—but just at the right point to ignite the flick's climax.

Still, someone else nearly became Myra, the wife of Christopher Walken's Hans, both of whom looking longingly to their Quaker faith as an extra weapon in Myra's fight with breast cancer. But even playing a member of a faith that lives on the concept of nonviolence, Clay wasn't too enthralled with the ... ahem, aspects that guaranteed *Psychopaths* a hardcore R-rating.

"When you audition," she explains, "you're given sides for your character which are isolated scenes and you don't necessarily get a complete picture of the film. Usually your sides have the scenes before and after yours crossed out, but you read them, hoping to glean valuable info to get more of an understanding of what's going on." She did, and didn't like much of what she saw, not at first.

"What I read in those crossed-out sections was enough to give me second, third, and fourth thoughts about auditioning. There was violence, blood, gore, profanity aplenty. Yes, there was the title, *Seven Psychopaths,* and I shouldn't have expected it to be a fairytale, and yes, Myra's character seemed to be cut from a different cloth, but still, not having any more to go on than what was in those few pages..."

The pages of a different Book, as they have for millions of millennia, helped her find a way down a different path.

"Being a Christian, I knew I needed guidance about what to do," Clay remembers, "and having more than a few days before I had to tape my audition, I prayed about it. When I got peace about auditioning, I proceeded."

A few years before, Nguyen, like most of the film world, had been wowed by Martin McDonagh's work behind the camera and screenwriting pen of 2008's *In Bruges*, the shadily humorous tale of two Irish hitmen and their attempts to hide in the Belgium title town. With Colin Farrell heading up the cast, McDonagh had roared into the American cinematic spotlight with a screenplay that the Oscars chose as one of 2008's finest. Now McDonagh was at it again, with Farrell back up front. Only this time, he was Marty Faranan, a struggling screenwriter—and really, isn't *every* writer such before publication?—looking for the elusive answers in his script. He had a title, and it was good enough for the film itself, but putting some literary meat on the plot's bones, well, that was a longer journey.

Still, he had some help, like from his pal Billy. Along with nine-tenths of his work colleagues, Sam Rockwell's Billy was an actor without a role, or even an audition, forced to team up with Hans for the lucrative nature of dognapping from the local well-off and selling back the canines. Plenty of time to think up some scenarios for the title characters.

Like his imagination of a Vietnamese priest, armed and ready to take revenge on those evil Americans that had killed so many of his brothers and sisters. Or a solider in the Vietcong, the group whose name got blackened worse by America during the war than Isis or Al Queda have lately.

But we don't have to take Billy's words for it. Nguyen got to show us both characters. We see him here in the U.S., prepared for a one-man raid, then taking out some malevolent Americans in battle.

The war scene, short as it was, was one of his toughest, Nguyen recalls, and not only because he got to burn and shoot three enemies in seconds.

To try to inspire the muse of *Seven Psychopaths*, Long Nguyen acted out the infamous 1963 photo of a Buddhist monk's self-immolation suicide.

"It was a challenging terrain, a picturesque creek with tall grass," he says. "The stunt soldiers had to wear elaborated whole body protection [suits] doused with flammable [liquid]. The cameraman, with hand-held [cameras], had to do everything just right. We all held our breath through the take. The sun was going down, and we were able to do it in one take."

But back in reality, things get too personal for Marty, Billy, and Hans. One of the stolen dogs belonged to small-town, high-tempered gangster Charlie Costello, very attached to his beloved Shih Tzu; her dog tags promise those who fail to return her that, "you will fucking die," so subtlety is clearly not important here.

And neither is guts. When Charlie (Woody Harrelson, putting yet another entry in his resume full of playing head cases) finds out Hans' involvement, he goes after the person who can't stand up and kick his ass: because, again, Clay is fighting something sadly stronger than he could ever dream of being.

"I spoke with a friend about certain aspects of having a mastectomy, and consulted with a nurse to get a health practitioner's input," Clay recalls of getting ready. "The first step was to study, and continuously study, the script, to get the facts directly presented to uncover pertinent info about Myra: physical description, attributes, limitations, relationships, other background, info, etc. I looked up things referred to in the script that I wasn't familiar with. I developed a backstory for Myra: her family makeup, how she and Hans met and married. Every film genre has an engine driving the plot: survival, love, revenge, greed, etc. I found my part in the engine was largely moved by love and survival within the complex machinery of this story."

She looked over one of the oldest faiths in religious history, albeit one far less common in this time than during America's foundation.

"I also researched the Quaker religion to have an understanding of their history, views, practices, and relationship with African Americans over a span of eras," Clay explains, "especially as it relates to inter-racial marriage and how that would've affected Hans and Myra." Quakers were some of the strongest and earlier opponents to slavery, and today have a higher population in Africa than any other part of the world.

But violence, even against those who can't fight back, and respect for someone who's got the backbone to laugh in the face of the stronger, unfortunately, are tough to find in the bullies of the world, real and cinematic, the ones all too quick to jump to violence and gunfire to get things fixed. Like Charlie, who unceremoniously executes someone more manly than he. Now her husband and the rest have no choice, or so it seems.

"Unbeknownst to [Myra], she was the reason for Hans' involvement in this particular criminal enterprise," Clay says. "She was both a victim and heroine: weak physically, but strong in character and spirit. Even though she suffered her own doubts, she was a moral lynchpin in the film. As actors, it's important to remember that it's still the 'human' engine that builds and drives the story. Our job is to find our character's truth and live it in every scene."

The trio leads Charlie into the desert, but Hans, still holding to his non-violence faith, slips away before anything happens. Charlie kills Billy and gets arrested, and Hans commits a form of suicide, tricking some crazy gunmen into thinking he's armed, and gunning him down. But as Marty finds his friend's body, there's a tape recorder on Hans, giving him the final piece to the puzzle, the last acts of Nguyen's characters.

He's back as the priest, now in a meeting full of American military alumni, prepared to take everyone out, including himself. But that's dishonorable. It's not what a man of true faith, whatever the type, could ever do and still call himself a representative of the belief. By now, Nguyen had run himself through as many changes as his roles.

"As a 'Boat People' refugee, running from the Communists, the term 'Vietcong' has a nightmarish quality for my younger self," he recalls. "I was brought up in a devout Catholic family, and even joined the seminary from sixth to eighth grade to become a priest. I imagined a few backstories to go with various scenes. I then substitute the characters in my imagined backstories with the people I know, either real or familiar with, through other sources as books or films. Working my 'Sense Memories,' recalling all these childhood memories, I built up a reservoir of images and feelings, trusting them to manifest appropriately with the actions."

In the summer of 1963, less than two years before America went full force into the conflict, a Buddhist monk named Quang Duc, known locally as the Reverend Thich-Quang-Duc, sat down to meditate in the middle of a busy Saigon street, surrounded by his colleagues. Protesting the government's persecution of his brethren, Duc doused himself with gasoline, and, looking like a man at full peace, burned himself to death. Images of the act ran worldwide, and are still considered some of the saddest, albeit most inspirational to those looking through the right eyes. Many may look down on suicide, but others saw this as a man giving himself for something so much more important, more special—his country, and through it, his faith. A young boy living in Saigon at the time, Nguyen found one more model to complete his role.

The Buddhist faith, like many others, preaches a combination of the purity of both the body and the mind, and, for his last role in the flick, he looked for it as well.

"I combined appropriate exercises to help my body state to be more in sync with my mental state," he says. "For example, I would do rapid breathing and squatting before the take, to initiate, or to add to the heightened fear and exhaustion required for a certain scene."

Nguyen recreates Duc's act. Through it, Marty finds the inspiration for the final piece of the *Seven Psychopaths* writing.

"The proxy civil war, the religious conflicts," Nguyen remembers, "all these affected me deeply."

Ólafur Darri Ólafsson and his work in 2012's *The Deep* made cinematic history in Iceland.

Ólafur Darri Ólafsson: *The Deep*

NATURE CAN BE MANKIND'S worst nightmare. When Mother Nature gets an attitude and decides to fire down a hurricane, tsunami, tornado, drought, blizzard, or whatever else, there's not much we mere mortals can do, especially if we happen to get caught outside.

However, acting out such a battle gives us a special kind of one-on-one plight, a rare kind of conflict that gives performers a chance to face one of the most unpredictable enemies around—and carry off a ton of screen time in the process.

Tom Hanks almost won an Oscar for becoming a modern-day Robinson Crusoe in 2000's *Cast Away*. Emile Hirsch damned well should have been nominated for squaring off with the Alaskan wilderness seven years later in *Into the Wild*. Leo DiCaprio grabbed his first statuette in 2015 after making his way through the blizzard-blankented American South of the 1800s in *The Revenant*.

Those are just the performances that we in America are lucky enough to know much of. One who left this land has found similar success a distance away.

Before he'd even gotten to elementary school, Ólafur Darri Ólafsson's family headed from his Connecticut birthplace to his folks' homeland back in Iceland. Throughout the new millennium, he's been on the A-plus acting list in a land of glaciers and volcanoes.

His name first showed up on the Edda Award list (Iceland's Oscar equivalent) in 2006 for helping bang out the screenplay for *Children*, a drama about a dad trying to leave his criminal lifestyle behind. It won him, along with the rest of the writing team, an Edda, and nearly got him a supporting actor win. A year later, his work in *Parents* helped it win the top film award.

In 2011, one year after another supporting acting nom came along, he finally got a main man statuette for the dramedy *Stormland*, playing a teaching revolutionary who tries to lead Iceland out of materialism and into morality by any means necessary.

"One of my teachers in drama school told me that if an actor has a performance in the theater in the evening," Ólafur recalls, "he has started his preparations as soon as he wakes up. I think there is a lot to that. If I have to do a very emotional scene and I'm not quite there, I sometimes put on my headphones and listen to music as a warmup." Warmth would be but a dream in the role that put him up against the negative extremes of weather in 2012's *The Deep*.

On March 11, 1984, two days before Ólafur's eleventh birthday, Gudlaugur Fridthorsson and some friends went fishing off the south coast of Iceland. Then their boat capsized, with Fridthorsson the only one left alive.

He survived for several hours in water just above freezing temperature before making it to land. But the end was still far away; he had to hike through miles of lava-ravaged land (he was near a volcano) before finally finding help.

Finishing up a play alongside Director Baltasar Kormákur Samper at Iceland's National Theater in 2011, Ólafur heard that Samper (himself a six-time Edda winner) was bringing Fridthorsson's story to the screen.

"I told him about my interest and he decided that I would be a good fit," Ólafur remembers. "My prep for the role involved rehearsals and conversations with the director, and then, as we got closer to shooting, a lot of swimming in the ocean." Even in Iceland's summertime, the water's typically about fifty degrees, but that's even warmer than Fridthorsson had had to deal with, and there'd been no director or crew to yell, "Cut!" and save him.

"I don't think I approached this project much differently that I would any other," Ólafur explains. "What makes it different from most of the films I have done is that it is based on a true story, and therefore it requires a certain amount of sensitivity for its subject matter. I think we achieved that: we made a movie based on those events, but in essence it is a fictional movie.

His character's name shortened to Gulli, Ólafur and his crew used an actual sunken boat for filming, then left him on his own for about half an hour's worth of film time—just him, the waves, and some serious discussions with himself, fate, and Someone else.

"I did a lot of open water swimming in the prep, just to get used to how cold it can be," Ólafur remembers. "Of course, when we were shooting, I wore a wetsuit and that really helped with the cold. After having spent weeks, often alone, swimming, it really became a very Zen experience. I would spend my breaks just out there floating in the ocean."

His work worked. So did Samper's. So did, well, *everything* else about *The Deep*. That's why it scored—are you ready?—*sixteen* Edda nominations (no American film has ever scored more than fourteen noms, and only *All About Eve* (1959) and, ironically enough, fellow shipwreck epic *Titanic* (1997) have done that). It won eleven awards—tying *Titanic*, *Ben-Hur* (1959), and *Lord of the Rings: Return of the King* (2003) in the all-time Oscar ranks.

The Deep was also submitted as Iceland's offering for the Best Foreign Language film Oscar nominee, but it wasn't selected; though the country has put up a film for Academy Award selection every year since 1980, *Children of Nature* (1991) is the only one to get to the ceremony, and it fell to Italy's *Mediterraneo*.

Still, you'll never hear Ólafur prattle too much about his work, past, present, or future (he got nominated again the next year for *XL*). But that's not just him; stoicism in the face of trouble, rolling with the punches, persevering against adversity, even far from their control, these are just the trademarks that Iceland tradition instills in its inhabitants. Like when the country's economic and political worlds felt the same effect as Fridthorsson's in 2008, Iceland stayed together and battled back, calling itself recovered by 2012. By contrast, America, for all its patriotic bluster, saw its economy stumble in 2012, and it's still up for debate as to whether we're back, to a great extent. When Gulli steps away from fame and publicity after his arrival back home, that's a true depiction of how Fridthorsson handled things.

No, even after all he's done and will do in the acting world, wherever it may lead (American audiences briefly saw Ólafur in 2014's *A Walk Among the Tombstones*, 2015's *The Last Witch Hunter*, and other films), Ólafur is far from his own favorite conversation subject in any sense. Acting's certainly important to him—but he'd rather show you than tell you.

"I think the best advice would be to do the work," he tells upcomers. "Try different things and remember that you learn as much from your worst experiences as you do from your best. Be generous with other actors: the more you give, the more you will get."

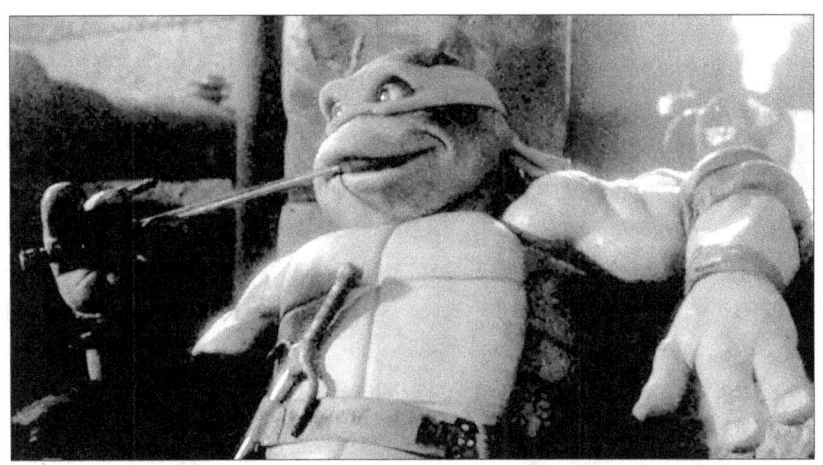

Josh Pais stepped inside a turtle costume and made martial arts madness as Raphael in 1990 for *Teenage Mutant Ninja Turtles*.

Josh Pais/Michelan Sisti/Francois Chau: *Teenage Mutant Ninja Turtles*

JOSH PAIS COULDN'T BELIEVE what he'd just heard, even after hearing it over and over.

"I had him repeat it three times," he remembers of the sales pitch his manager threw that fateful day.

Pais was being asked to become an action hero, one who, with a team of his allies, whomps all the baddies, saves the pretty girl, and watches his mentor fight his arch enemy to the death in a classic climax.

Not too unusual, right? Sort of like the script of several lines of boxes' worth of films in the "Martial Arts" section of any video store, doesn't it?

Now here's the catch that made the pitch so hard to snare; Pais would be doing the job under a 70-pound costume, made up to look like one of nature's most unthreatening animals: a turtle!

"It was completely ridiculous," he says of his original concept of the 1990 live-action *Teenage Mutant Ninja Turtles* flick. Though the acrobatic amphibians had graced the small screen in both cartoon and video game form in the late 1980s, the shot at cinema was the first Pais had heard of them.

Then the relative newcomer to acting (he'd had small roles on *The Cosby Show* and *Murphy Brown*) reconsidered: after all, what could be better at a fast establishment of credibility than to bring a personality to a walking, backflipping, sai-swinging turtle?

"A lot of the audition was finding the physical body of Raphael," Pais says of the squad's unofficial leader (the name's a bit strange, but they're all named after old-time artists). "I had the idea that he was a real street guy. I grew up in the lower east side of New York City, a dangerous neighborhood full of wonderful characters. [As Raphael], I kind of embodied one of those guys: a guy who walks down the street, taking up as much space as possible and trying to dominate the environment by the way that he moves, so that nobody'll mess with him." The red-headband-wearing turtle was something of a dark sheep to the turtle family (raised by mutant rat and sensei Splinter), as his anger caused a huge rift throughout the first part of the film.

An experienced martial artist, Pais grabbed the role and Raphael's tri-pronged blades along with it, and flew off to London to prepare in the most unconventional of manners.

Meanwhile, Michelan Sisti was debating a similar role with his agent.

"We both laughed at the prospect and admitted that neither one of us knew anything about TMNT," he recalls. Still, he came in to read for Raphael's role, and got a call back, told to create his own martial arts scene.

"I returned with my full-tilt-Bozo performance," he says. "The only problem was, the office ... was half the size of the space I had rehearsed in the night before, and when I ended my scene with a big flourish and a roundhouse kick, I put my foot right through the office wall!"

Fortunately, director Steve Barron cracked up.

"He said he thought that any actor who would be that committed to the energy of the scene and character, should be one of his Turtles," Sisti says, "and would I accept the role of Michelangelo! Steve liked the 'quirky' comic quality I had and wanted that in his movie. I took my cues when creating Mikey's physicality from the fun-loving way he was written, the overall style of *TMNT*, and the restrictions of the suit."

"We were body-casted from head to toe, except for straws in our nostrils," Pais remembers with a slight shudder. "They kept us sealed up in plaster for a little longer than was actually necessary, to build the mold for the costume. They wanted to see how we could deal with the pressure of being completely sealed in."

If that sounds tough enough by itself, let's hear Sisti's millimeter-by-millimeter, groan-by-groan description of life in the suits, themselves created by Jim Henson's Creature Shop company.

"My own personal slice of Hell," he quips. "The first suit had all of the largish servo motors and the computer mounted on a large metal plate attached to a backpack harness I wore, and covered by the fiberglass shell on my back. The motors were connected via a thick bundle of bicycle cables to the many mechanisms in the head. This meant that I could not separate my Turtle head from the body. I could take off the head, but I had to hold it on my shoulder or ask for help to support it. Everything, when we were not connected directly by a master cable, was powered by a series of hefty batteries fashioned into a belt or harness to wear."

Putting the suit on alone took over twenty minutes per day, Sisti says.

"Add to all of this, the foam latex body suit," he continues. "The body suit was skin tight, and much thicker than a diving wetsuit. It also acted like a giant sponge that soaked up sweat, making it progressively heavier the longer you wore it. When you put it all together, and sweated the body suit, the first Turtle suit weighed more than 70 pounds! With my Mikey head on, the only way I could see was to look out the two pencil eraser-sized eyeholes behind my orange Mikey bandana, or down through the opened mouth on occasion."

Finally, it was time to deal with the welcome environment of about four months of intense martial arts training back in the states.

"I got to know the physicality of the character," Pais says. "My impulses and my intuitions could take over, and that's how I approach most things, to get to that sense where I can just play. Basically, what I try to do is get to a place where I try to get in the moment, and the way actors get into a moment is having your attention on the information that's in your body and the information in your immediate environment, getting out of your thoughts and into your body. Once you're there, you can really listen to what happens as the scene unfolds."

As filming kicked off, he'd have quite a bit to listen to; lines, scene calls from the director, and the occasional scream for mercy, both on and off the screen.

"From morning to lunch break, we would lose about five pounds, and we would just sweat unbelievably," he says of filming in North Carolina's summer heat. "They'd have to shoot compressed air in our faces between takes. It was incredibly challenging, and periodically, one of us would just freak out, because it would just be so hot. Around the set, there would be smoke to create a visual effect, and it would be hard to breathe. You just felt like you were burning up. Once in a while, you'd hear somebody screaming 'Take the head off!' which would be tough, because the heads were glued on."

However, it was worth the pain, for the time being.

"When we were shooting, the costume was great," he says, "because it helped me to create the physicality of Raphael, to bring his pain and his anger; wearing that suit brought it all to the surface."

And he still worked on making his turtle turn as real as possible.

"The summer before we started shooting, I had been camping on vacation," he says. "I ran into a lot of turtles and studied how they moved. They kind of scoop and push their hands behind them. I studied that and tried to see how I could pass that movement into my hands. I was able to incorporate that into my physicality as a turtle."

Still, while the actual animals can retreat back into their shell if things get crazy nearby, Pais and his creature colleagues weren't as lucky.

"Sometimes we couldn't see at all," he says. "We'd rehearse physical actions while we could see, and then they would seal off our vision, because when camera was close, they didn't want to see our eyes behind the turtle eyes. We just had to work blind." During distance shots, however, the actors could see through slits in their masks.

Like all of the four, Pais has a cameo in the film; while Raphael chases an assailant down a street, he slides over a cab windshield; an inner shot reveals Pais himself as the passenger.

"They had it so I, in a cameo, was responding to me, jumping over the car," he says. "It was fun, me responding to me in a suit!" Sisti got to talk to himself during filming, playing a pizza deliveryman that Michelangelo shortchanges.

Of the four, Pais was the only one to do both his character's physical and voice work (Corey Feldman voiced his teammate Donatello, and Robbie Rist spoke for Michaelangelo).

"I was talking while we were shooting," he says, "but because I was so inside the costume, it was hard to get clear sentences. After the movie was edited, I spent a week in a Los Angeles sound stage, where I did the audio, which is what we hear when we see the movie."

In the end, the turtles and their master, the rat Splinter, vanquished the evil Shredder and his Foot Clan followers, and audiences responded; the flick grossed a then-independent film record $135 million. Still, when plans came up for a sequel, Pais decided to let someone else wield the sai, and Kenn Scott, who'd done stunt work on the first film, became the new Raphael, though Sisti returned.

"I was really happy and honored to do the first movie," says Pais, "but not really interested in having a career in a costume. When the second film came out, I was doing *Law and Order* at the time." He's had a recurring role on the original *Law and Order* since 1990, and has shown up on its counterparts *Criminal Intent* and *Special Victims Unit* several times. He's also been on *The Sopranos*, *Rescue Me*, *Ray Donovan*, and *Sex and the City*, along with small big-screen roles in *Rounders* (1998), *Scream 3* (2000), *Teeth* (2007), *Adventureland* (2009), and other films.

Just one year after the first *TMNT* flick hit the screen, the second rolled along, this one subtitled *The Secret of the Ooze*. It performed respectably at the box office, though far less than the original, and did okay with the critics—notwithstanding Vanilla Ice's infamously execrable "Ninja Rap" concert scene.

Like Pais, original Shredder James Saito bowed out of the second coming of the turtles. For just his second film role—well, third if we count voicing Quick Kick in the 1987 *G.I. Joe* cartoon movie—Francois Chau stepped into comic villainy.

"Like every other actor, I jumped at it," he recalls, "and was lucky enough to be cast. I think Shredder fit me because I'm pretty good at playing the 'bad guy.' Most of the roles I do are usually 'bad guy' roles."

Though a lifelong comic book fan, the Cambodia native had never really gotten into the Turtles' printed adventures—something he was quick to remedy.

"I bought all the comic books and read them as soon as I could," he says. "There wasn't really any time to prepare for the role once I got cast. Things moved pretty quickly."

Playing the character brought more of a challenge than it may have seemed to viewers.

David McCharen, who'd given Shredder his evil-speaker-esque voice in the first film, returned to do the second, so Chau couldn't use his own voice to sound intimidating. Not only that, but because Shredder's eyes are the only visible part of his body, the actor had to appear evil without much facial expression either (however, it wasn't a journey he fought alone—Kevin Nash, whose name would become much more recognizable to fans of professional wrestling only a few years later, played the overgrown "Super-Shredder" near the end of the film).

"I think the camera angles and the editing was what made the character intimidating," Chau says. "The only thing you could see of me was my eyes, so that was where my 'acting' came in, I guess. I just remember having a great experience making the film. I think the TMNT films and cartoons were appealing because they were fresh and new for the comic books when they came out, and the timing was right."

Long before we had any lady Terminators, the *Chameleon* films gave Bobbie Phillips the chance to blend humanity with mechanics.

Bobbie Phillips: *Chameleon* films

PAIN DOESN'T *ALWAYS* HAVE to be paired with suffering. More often than we really consider, it can actually be a bit uplifting.

A stomachache after a large, fulfilling meal. Sore muscles after a workout we gave it all to, or after setting a new personal time record in a recent run.

Yes, aching can be a message from our body to inspire. It's like it's saying to us, "OK, you hit me pretty hard in the nerves, but it was worth it!"

It's a pretty common feeling for those in the action acting land, particularly the ones who toss off their guns, knives, and other "easy" ways to take down the bad guys and square off with fists and kicks filling the air. Putting out all the effort, then later seeing yourself on the screen, everything put together well, knowing that you couldn't have worked harder, it's worth it. It's all worth it. Just like in the world of fitness modeling; of all the people that a magazine could have selected to represent the physicality it preaches, you were chosen to grace the front. You earned the right to be the pages' first impression.

Four times, Bobbie Phillips has felt the honor in the literary sense; that's how often *Muscle & Fitness*, one of America's premier periodicals for those looking to slim down and buff up, has placed her on its cover. Even more commonly, she's seen herself taking a ton of physical labor from the tough worlds of rehearsal and getting it to pay off before the cameras.

Still, it was a hell of journey long before much happened with her career; figuratively, *much* longer than Phillips' cross-nation hop from her South Carolina hometown to Hollywood.

"One never knows exactly how it's going to play out," she remarks. "This goes for life, in general. But in the entertainment business there are so many variables completely out of one's control. It's not always easy, but the key is to do the work and trust in that. Also, to allow yourself to gravitate towards what truly inspires you." Once again, in her case, that typically meant tearing it up (and leaving some left over for her opponents) on the action genre.

As Arnold Schwarzenegger first showed us back in 1991, even a machine called a Terminator can be a good guy. A few years before Kristanna Loken showed the female side of the shape-shifting death machine in *T3*, producers of *Chameleon* (1998) looked to tell a similar story on the small screen.

Quite ironically—well, maybe not so much, considering this is the film world!—Phillips' debut flick had given her a shot at just that sort of role.

"The concern was if I could do all of the martial arts required," she recalls of 1993's *TC 2000*. "This was low budget and they really needed someone who could do their own action." She had a month to convince the crew of such, and martial arts legend Billy Blanks stepped away from his own prep work at becoming the film's male lead to help her out.

"Fortunately, he thought with hard work I was the one for the job," Phillips remembers. "I made a commitment to Billy that I would train every moment that I wasn't filming or sleeping."

In a future we hope never comes true, the movie made Blanks and Phillips into a law enforcement pair, battling a group of local bottom-feeders trying to take over the area. One of them finds a way to Phillips' Zoey, slaughtering her, hoping to scare Blanks' Jason and the rest of the crew into submission.

Calling up memories of both Dr. Frankenstein and the *Terminator* series (which, remember, had only had two go-rounds by this point), the local highers-up turn her into the title form, a part-human, part machine, totally unstoppable force that takes invincibility to a brand new level.

"I had to make choices to differentiate between the two characters," she remembers. "This way, when Zoey would peep through TC2000X, the audience could tell the difference. It was great fun playing dual roles like that!"

But just as what happened to Frank's creator and those that invented the terminators, she eventually goes wrong, and Jason's forced to go into battle with the lady he stood alongside for so long. Off the set, however, he and Phillips kept moving up together.

"When we weren't on set," she remembers, "he had me at the YMCA training in full force. One day, we went right from an all-night shoot directly to the Y and trained for hours. Billy Blanks is a machine! I was so grateful that he took the time and care. I can still hear him in my ear when I was exhausted and ready to give in: 'Keep your spirit up, girl! Let's go!' Somehow, that worked and I did!" Alongside late wrestling legend Roddy Piper (author's note: I tried so hard to interview Piper about his work on the classic 1988 thriller *They Live* before his tragic passing in 2015.) the two worked together again that same year in *Back in Action*.

"A *huge* part of acting is camaraderie and relationships," Phillips says. "Once you do the work and training, it's about connecting in an honest way. It's really nice when you have a comfortable off-screen relationship. I think it can help bring the acting to another level."

Clearly, Phillips had the right background to become *Chameleon*'s title goddess Kam (her 1996 Universe Reader's Choice Award-winning performance for an episode of *The X-Files* helped her credibility as well). But would she actually get the part of the cyborg-ess, created by a dictatorial government to shut down and take out those with the guts to badmouth it? Did she want it badly enough?

"I loved the creative freedom within the context of the character simply because of who she was," Phillips explains. "Kam was genetically enhanced with different animals, which all had different characteristics. But, there was also the training and attempt to control her and her instincts, both human and animal, which created internal and external battles with added complexities. Plus, knowing there would be plenty of action and martial arts immediately appealed to me."

As she had with *TC*, Phillips fired herself into a month-long regiment of the martial arts.

"There was only about a month to prepare," she recalls. "I trained every day with my kung fu instructor, as well as breaking down the screenplay with my acting coach." Like Lokan's future *TX*, Kam could switch forms in a millisecond. Like Arnold's T-800 in *T2*, she unexpectedly develops a parental connection with a young boy who happens to be the child of a movement leader (in this case, it was Eric Lloyd's Ghen, rather than Edward Furlong). Like Arnold in, well, all the *Terminator* films, Kam spent most of her travel time atop a Harley.

"I went to work and amped up my training," Phillips proudly asserts. "I worked with my trainers in Los Angeles and then with the incredible stunt team in Australia. As well, they sent me for specialized training with the police force in Australia. This was all incredible and, many times, surreal. I recall motorcycle training, on a closed course, on my super-cool specialized Harley. Riding along flanked by stunt drivers and thinking to myself: 'Am I dreaming? This is *amazing!*'"

The very next year, she came back to help Kam rescue a group of hostages in a casino (*Chameleon* had originally been intended for a series). In 2000, the pair got back together for *Chameleon: Dark Angel*, in which Kam's forced to fight back her evil brother Kane.

"I recall being quite exhausted and sore pretty much the entire shoot!" Phillips says. "I'm sure we all were. I was fortunate to work with most of the same crew on all three films. Most of them had worked on *The Matrix* as well." Alex Kuzelicki, who stunted on *The Matrix* (1999) and *The Matrix Reloaded* (2003), was Kane.

"It was actually a bit difficult, and maybe a little painful," she admits, "but I knew if I gave it my all that it would probably turn out pretty awesome. I think everyone did a great job on all three, especially on a tight budget and fast shooting schedule. I knew how hard every single person worked and the heart that was put into it."

Including herself, although Phillips doesn't really like discussing *that* part of her work.

"I feel it's highly important to connect with the right people," she explains. "To get respect, one must give respect. Leave ego at the door and work together to lift others up. What you give out really does come back to you. That's how it has worked in my world. I can look back and connect the dots. I see it in my life today. I knocked on many closed doors, but the *right* ones open. Trust your heart. Trust your journey." Whether it's towards actions film or otherwise, she finishes.

"If you love martial arts, then train, work hard, talk to others that inspire you," Phillips says. "If you want to act in action films, study acting and take stunt classes. Go after it. But not just for fame or reward. Those things are fleeting and not sustainable. They don't last. To me, happiness is living an authentic life and following your heart and inspiration."

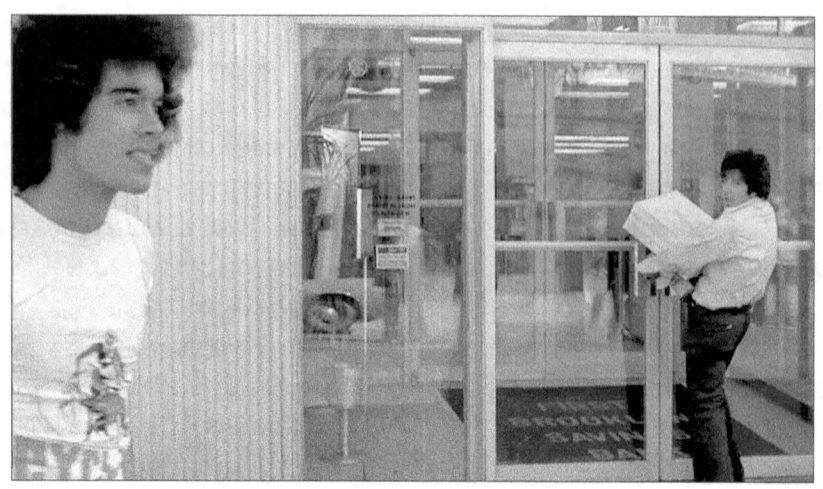

Showing that fifteen seconds (not even minutes!) of fame is too much for too many to resist, Lionel Pina's pizza guy danced before the news cameras in the midst of a hostage situation in *Dog Day Afternoon*.

Lionel Pina: *Dog Day Afternoon*

ONCE IN A WHILE, we should be totally wrong.

A time here, a belief there, it would be nice if our view for the future was off. Many of the greatest prophets have predicted all sorts of things that no one hoped would happen (for example, many have sworn that the world would end on *this day*, but as of this writing, we're still here).

Well, Sidney Lumet never called himself a prophet—most known as such are awarded the title by others—but quite a bit of his work looked toward the direction American culture was heading. *Network* (1976) is probably the prime example, the film brilliantly highlighting the nation's distaste for taste in entertainment, not to mention its short attention span. Four decades later, it's far too easy to find examples of "humor" in America that exercise the gag reflex and have the substance of water spilled on a table, much more so than anyone of way back when, even Lumet, probably ever thought would occur.

However, the story of a newsman named Howard Beale and the tidal wave he inadvertently sent across America (i.e., like our watery enemies, Beale got huge quickly and crashed even faster), Lumet had already taken some of the first steps toward another sad display of Americana that no one wanted to come true. In today's world, the term of paparazzi is often seen as dirtier than most of the seven deadly sins, the entertainment media is considered its own military troop, filling up tabloids with needless information and exploiting people with little to no relevance (well, in the positive sense) to society. And there are those that invite it to do as much—forget that whole "fifteen minutes of fame" thing; some people just want a couple of nanoseconds!

Dog Day Afternoon (1975) showed us that this is nothing new.

A year after grabbing a role in *Law and Disorder*, Lionel Pina learned that the same casting crew was filling up the *Afternoon* cast and went in for a shot. A quick encounter with Lumet landed him a role in the flick. It would take a while to get to his role and he wouldn't stay long, but the character would mean quite a bit.

Things aren't going well for rookie bank heisters Sonny Wortzik and Sal Naturale. What was expected to be an in-and-out job at a Brooklyn bank spins out of control, and the two are forced to take hostages—to their credit, it's without violence so far—then try to decide what exactly one in this unenviable position is supposed to do.

And, just as it would happen today, a crux of humanity forms outside, braving the intense summer heat that gave the film its moniker. Not just the cops trying to get things fixed, but a ton of people with nothing better to do (work? Family? What are they?). Some might hope to see some violence and bloodshed. Others are into cheering for the robbers—think they'd help out the guys if arrests were made? Then there's some, or at least one, looking for a piece of the attention action.

For about three weeks, Pina had been training with a local pizza shop owner, learning the ins and outs of the food that kicked off the delivery business. When Al Pacino's Sonny, much more considerate than most in the captive-holding occupation, calls for a delivery, Pina's guy is too happy to get involved; there's more to this than just a chance at a tip.

It's the lights, the cameras, and the action. As Sonny takes the food back inside, the delivery guy reaches out and steals the spotlight, filling the area with screaming and jumping.

Part of this was Frank Pierson's Oscar-winning script. Some of it came from Pina himself.

"My line 'I'm a fucking star!' was a result of Lumet leading me in an emotional direction and improv," Pina recalls. "It just popped out of my mouth on one take and I didn't know if it worked or not, but Lumet was happy."

He's quickly removed from the scene, and most of us—at the scene and from the screen—probably congratulated ourselves on never having done, or that we'd never do, something like that. But until we've been in his position, we'll never really know if we were right or not. Such an act today might just transform someone into an Internet sensation, maybe more well known than those who star on screens big and small.

"Al Pacino in an interview summed it up for the character," Pina says, "the pizza boy stands for the power the media can have on a real-life event." The film was indeed based on the true story of two men who robbed an area bank three years before, mainly because one's wife needed some green to switch genders all the way to femininity. Chris Sarandon's *Afternoon* work as Sonny's "gal" pal got him an Oscar nomination, and Pacino was nominated too (in a controversial act, John Cazale wasn't nominated for playing Sal).

Three decades later, Pina got a reprisal of sorts, delivering pizzas to a group of bank hostages in Spike Lee's *Inside Man* (2006); Marcia Jean Kurtz, one of Sonny's hostages, played the same role in *Man* as well.

Christian Pitre rained death all over the *Bounty Killer* group in the futuristic 2013 thriller.

Christian Pitre: *Bounty Killer*

SHE MIGHT HAVE BEEN scared with guns pointed at her face, bullets meant for her flying too closely nearby... but Mary wasn't.

She might not have the intestinal fortitude to yank out a gun over half her size and blast the guy trying to give the same to her, or go hand to hand and win without a scratch... but Mary did.

She had to be different than she ever imagined she could be. She had to be death itself. Death Herself.

She had to be the Maxine to the Mad Max we all saw running around *Thunderdome* in 1985, itself just the watershed of post-Apocalyptic action films Hollywood has thrown our way.

Part of breaking into the acting world is acceptance that we'll be other people at times, and this was going to take one actress still trying to break on through to the other side to that extreme. Getting ready for a trip to and through a new world, though hardly an impossible one, and one that's been explored by the film world more than twice, Christian Pitre had to go where several had indeed been before... but she certainly hadn't.

"Mary is extremely independent, raised by gypsies, but has always been her own person, and has decided she wants to join the Bounty Killers and put the world back together," Pitre elucidates. "She's who probably every woman wishes she could be: strong and sexy and independent, and yet there's a vulnerable side that she tends to hide."

The gypsies? They're a group of people that, along with most other common folk of the film, found themselves forced into poverty by the rich folk, the big businesses of the world that crossed human life off their priority list and replaced it with dollar signs.

The Bounty Killer, or Killers? First off, it's the name of the 2013 tale itself, which, like *Sin City* (2005) and *300* (2006), had made its way from graphic novel pages to the big screen. Secondly, the title characters are the final outcasts, destined to bring violent death to all the white-collar crooks that ruined the world, and become nationwide heroes in the bargain.

And Mary? Well, again, that's Mary Death. Perhaps not the most skilled Killer, but certainly the most popular; as those with the advantage of being gorgeous women usually do, she enjoys quite a bit more fame and fortune—and funding; she is, after all, there for the bounties—than her fellow hitmen and women. Having recently broken away from her gypsy homelanders, Mary's now pursuing her former instructor and lover, a man just called Drifter (Matthew Marsden), as the two try to keep from killing each other on their way to a final showdown with the rich assholes looking to wipe them off the face of the already-mudblasted earth, along the way fighting off the gypsies that still want the honor to themselves.

Getting ready for the biggest tryout of her acting career, Pitre reached for Mary's mindset, ready to knife-fight her way through an audition.

"My husband and I broke down the entire scene and who we thought this woman was and then we played with it for hours," Pitre recalls. "The scene called for Mary to pull out a switchblade, so, without thinking it through, we incorporated a knife my husband owned that could simulate a switch blade if I pulled it out the right way. Looking back on it, it probably wasn't the smartest idea we have ever had . . . but Mary Death would have brought a real knife to the audition."

As the *Killer* cast looked on, she went into Death mode, acting out Mary's favorite practice of bestowing her last name upon those unlucky enough to try her.

She whipped out the knife.

"I'm Christian Pitre," she declared, "and I *am* Mary Death. I didn't even flinch."

But blades aren't always available in the heat of combat, where, again, Mary felt right at home. Fists and feet, however, are there if we need them, and need to be just as deadly.

Yet another new world for Pitre.

"After I booked the role, it was time to see if I could even throw a punch!" she says. "I had never done any type of fighting before, but I *had* done choreographed dancing, so it was very easy for me to remember the moves. The biggest character building exercise for me was training to fight *hard* so that I really believed I was as tough as Mary."

There's quite a bit about Mary that we don't see, but we can certainly imagine. Decapitating someone with one swing of her trademark high-heeled boots, taking knockout blows to the face without blinking, blasting one human target after another in a way that would make the world's top snipers jealous and doing it all without the slightest bit of remorse, this is a lifestyle that the character has lived for quite some time and thoroughly enjoyed it. Becoming Mary for one murder (justifiable homicide, more specifically) after another, Pitre felt the character evolving more and more inside her.

"Oddly enough, I gravitated toward the violence more than I thought I would," she says. "I was like, wow, I really love this, beating people up, playing with knives, blowing things up.

"There were times when I knew I would be bleeding after the next stunt, but I also knew that once it was over I would be tougher than I was before and a lot less scared. In my head, if Mary could do it . . . I could do it."

As per usual for this type of flick's plot, Mary and her small group indeed manage to fight and massacre their way all the way through the villainy.

Just as these films have a tendency to end, there's hope for the cinematic inhabitants that the enemy's been vanquished, back at the start of a new battle they have new hope and reason to fight. But from Mary, there's almost a sad streak. Normalcy and enjoyment for her have been mass murder and violence, justified though they may have been. Now that there's no one left to fight and kill . . . what is her purpose? Pitre felt something new for her, and to an extent, to herself. Even after Mary's last kill, the two weren't apart just yet.

"I just thought it was so much fun and I love to see Mary having fun!" she says. "For the first time ever in my career, I watched a movie that I was a lead of and forgot I was in it. It was the best feeling in the world to get lost in the story and characters and enjoy it like anyone else would! I STILL enjoy watching the movie every single time I see it."

Before Pitre got the role, she opened to door to Mary. As camera action commenced, staying in Mary mode gave her the strength inside and outside to become someone else. And it sounds like, somewhere deep down, Mary Death still has her own place in the performer.

Speaking of *Mad Max*'s outings . . .

Few were surprised when a new story of a madman named Max and his adventures in apocalyptic lands wandered down the cinematic road in 2015. Hollywood had been talking about it for years; several projects had stepped into the ominous world of "pre-production," "in development," and every other Hollywood term that's euphemistic for, "Hey, it *might* happen one of these years, if the stars align and the fairies fly together and a triple rainbow stretches through the sky!"

Far before his epic of William Wallace or even the tales of Martin Riggs, a then-barely sparkling star named Mel Gibson headed way down under in every term sense in 1979, his Max

Rockatansky a cop driven over the brink by the murder of his family in war-ravaged Australian lands. *Mad Max* didn't just make an absolute pantload of green and revitalize worldwide interest in Australian flicks; it took the most unthinkable (we hope!) of situations and made it look as possible as unthinkable can be.

Her Vulvalini colleagues watch in awe as their gleeful Keeper of the Seeds (Melissa Jaffer) shows what a lady with an attitude and a really large gun can do in *Mad Max: Fury Road* (2016).

"The main reason for the ongoing popularity of the *Mad Max* series is its plausibility," theorizes Melissa Jaffer. "The bizarre human behavior that is part of that post-apocalyptic time is, to some extent, believable. What lengths will we go to to survive? It's almost imperative that we go further and further into the possibilities."

When Max returned in 1981 and then ventured into Thunderdome four years later, his journey kept setting the supernova standard in the dark future subgenre of action we'd see just about every other month since then. They vary to some degree, of course, but countless tales from around the world have told their own stories of humanity after civilization, and, therein, the *Max* crew's work almost always shows up in one semblance or another.

That's why, when we learned a new chapter of Rockatansky's specific story would be written, it wasn't exactly a plot twist for film fans. Still, we weren't *that* optimistic, not all of us. Even if George Miller, the man behind the camera for the first three flicks, was back again, why fix what wasn't broken? Why even take a chance on messing up something that worked so well? There was a chance that the newness would be an improvement, but why risk it? Film fans can be about as cynical as Max himself became when it comes to messing with our loved ones, so why go back to territory that had been explored? Unwillingly, unwittingly, dangerous, and sometimes even fatally explored, yes, but we'd *been* there!

"Some say that Max is every man," Jaffer claims, "and his experience is our experience, and now at my advanced age, I am inclined to agree—just when life seems to have quieted down, those wheels start screeching again and another potential disaster looms and needs to be dealt with!" To many, *Mad Max: Fury Road* gave off such an aura from the moment its light turned green.

But not too much, and not for long. Enough that tweaking the storyline a bit breathed some fresh life into it—a hell of a risk to be sure (just about everything is so in a remake), but it can work if the right people are there to pull it off. Whatever reluctance anyone might have had towards the new legend was wiped away fast, with box-office blasts and word of mouth teaming up to yell at high volume, racking up nearly $400 million across the globe. The flick scored ten Oscar nominations (second only to *The Revenant*'s twelve), including Best Picture, and brought home six statuettes, the most of the ceremony.

Many attributed *Fury Road*'s new landmark in film history to its willingness to take a new shot. Even with Ellen Ripley and Katniss Everdeen establishing the credibility ranks, many today (too many) are iffy about letting a woman lead the way in action. But Miller and the rest of the *Fury Road* crew felt confident enough to make the new Max (Tom Hardy) almost secondary in his own film, handing Imperator Furiosa the new rebellious lead. Charlize Theron's Furiosa had been good enough to rise above about all the other War Boy scavengers to become warlord Immortan Joe's right-hand lady; now she'd seen enough to turn good, Joe's murderously misogynistic nature inspiring her and the rest of the area ladies to rise up and start their own movement. In a neat twist, Hugh Keays-Byrne, so evil as Toecutter in the first *Max* outing, came back to go at Gibson's successor as Joe.

It's not about feminism; it's about survival. Area men—like, say, Max!—weren't the enemy, or the opponent, even if some sense needed to be beaten into them to show that. Soon, the group reaches a huge tower, a makeshift seminary for a wise regime of women carrying the matriarchal moniker of the Vuvalini.

Nearly two years before, Jaffer and the rest of the valiant Vuvalini tryout squad had been sitting in Miller's office, hoping to make the final *Fury* lineup. Even after being picked and heading down to South Africa's Namibia for filming, the group wasn't certain who would end up as who.

"I had no access to the script before then," recalls Jaffer, who won an Australian Film Award (her Australian homeland's Oscar equivalent) for 1976's *Caddie*. "Everything was highly confidential. However, we were afforded the luxury of several days to workshop the Vuvalini before our shooting began. This time together was invaluable, and, of course, survival emerged as our overriding motivation."

Her Keeper of the Seeds was quite acquainted with the concept, the eldest member of the Vuvalini and mentor of Furiosa. With no real option left (Furiosa's homeland and original target was decimated by the same radiative climate change that had ruined so much of the land), the group heads back to Joe's place, looking to spring some traps and steal some supplies.

Of course, it doesn't work—this is, after all, a *Mad Max* film. Joe and his army are ready; then again, the Vuvalini's looking to prove its own worth. Bullets and knives pierce the air, the women gleefully forcing these dirtbags' bad medication right back down their throats, probably wishing they could do so in suppository form.

Some Boys die. Sadly enough, so do a few ladies. It's about the epitome of cowardice to stab an old gal to death, but chivalry went out with the rest of civilization in this world, and the Keeper falls.

"None of the work was easy to do," remembers Jaffer. "Those scenes involving the use of firearms at close range were a little scary! And the scene in which I was fatally wounded by a chainsaw from above slicing through my neck took some concentration!"

With a knife wound to the lung, it looks like Furiosa's going to perish in battle. But Max is here to revive her with an impromptu operation and blood transfusion, leaving her to lead Joe's former captives as he slips away, on his way to find the next sequel/remake (scheduled, but not out yet at publication time).

Even after Allene Quincy had helped put the film together, *Raze*'s pain got to be too much for her Brenda.

Allene Quincy/Rebecca Marshall: *Raze*

WOULD IT ALL BE worth it?

Calling up things that no acting teacher could ever teach, that could never be learned without all kinds of pain from both the body and the mind, allowing them to go on display in front of millions? Early in a career, taking a shot at something that could certainly be a hell of an asset ... but very easily blast our credibility?

Would it pay off?

Weeks of time, loads of funding, to put together a film full of subject matter that the acting world is still very iffy about, calling into question whether anyone would ever see the flick, let alone take it seriously and recognize, respect how much ground it had truly broken?

Long before *Raze* even reached the filming stages, no one had any idea about the answers. With most of her acting resume peppered with shorts and TV shows, Allene Quincy had taken a huge step toward establishing her "contender-ship" on her own in the business, putting together her own self-named production company. Fresh off Quincy Pictures' first production, she was approached by a producer from her past.

He and others were trying to do something that few had tried and even fewer had succeeded at, a sad reminder of the superficiality of Hollywood inside and out. 2013's *Raze* would be a full-length flick, based on a bunch of fighters in a hand to hand, kick, and headbutt tourney to the death, their prize being far beyond anything they could ever dream of.

In and of itself, that trek might not sound all that innovative. Here came the extreme exception: the competitors would all be women.

As an action fan, that might sound like a great idea, something that we'd really like to watch, even pay a few bucks to check into. But when several figures' worth of one's own dollars are on the line, newness can be a chance not worth taking. The flick had already been in development for a year, and in a blow as hard as any of its characters would land, a top backer had pulled out. Now straws were being grabbed at.

"I read the script and it was pretty gory and badass and all female," Quincy recalls, "so I was like, HELL YES!" Mere weeks later, she'd attached her company to the film to help it get going. Best of all, she'd even snare one of her biggest roles to date as a competitor.

From the physical side of things, Quincy wouldn't have too much trouble. Up to the point of having to bash someone's skull in, it was something she'd enjoy.

"I discovered at age nine that I was physically super strong," she says. "I learned that I could sprint faster than the girls—and boys—I raced in school. I could do pushups and pullups like the boys. I also grew up with three brothers, making me a bit of a scrapper, and, because my family moved around about every year . . . all the neighborhoods we ended up in were mainly inhabited by boys, so I learned to fight pretty early."

A college trip to Japan got her into the martial arts, which eventually switched to kickboxing and even more gym time.

"I started weightlifting in college, and I mean heavy!" Quincy remembers. "I weighed 115 pounds and my ten-rep max on the bench was 165. I even graduated to a one-rep max of 225. It was insane! Weightlifting and martial arts gave me so much confidence."

And none of that rom-com stuff at the movies for her; making her into something of an impossible dream date for most guys, Quincy preferred watching men like Stallone, Schwarzenegger, and anyone else who drew blood and loved it.

But every great action performer has more to offer than the looks and blows rained. To find these characters, something extra was going to come along, something more than difficult to even locate, let along incorporate into new territory.

Right around that time, Director Josh Miller sent out a script to an old colleague. Millions had seen Rebecca Marshall help close out America's top horror franchise of the early 2000s a few years before; after finding herself on the receiving end of agony and ultimately murder in 2010's *Saw 3D*, the series' seventh and (for then) farewell installment, Miller hoped the lady he'd worked with on the short *Escape* back in 2006 could now dish out some suffering.

"Of course I'd wanted to be part of the *Saw* franchise," Marshall recalls. "It was one of the number-one horror franchises of all time. I wasn't a big character, but I liked the choices I had with her. She wasn't a bad person; she just cut a lot of corners to get the job done and ended up suffering for it."

She played Suzanne, a lawyer to one of the flick's main men. Early on in the flick, the killer places her in a grisly reanimation of the "See, Hear, Speak No Evil" display, trapping her in rotating steel frame, inches from spikes just ominously waiting to blast through her eyes and mouth.

Rebecca Marshall took some serious beatings and begged for more as the crazy Phoebe in *Raze*.

Her client has one chance, one endless minute to save her. He's got to lift a pair of weights for a full sixty seconds. Might not sound tough, considering he's quite the mesomorphic type.

But horror movie villains don't play by the rules, as any *Saw* fan can tell you. As he grasps the weights, the fellow's sides are suddenly torpedoed by a pair of rods. He desperately tries to hold on as Suzanne falls into hysterics, and it looks like he just might. But with seconds left, he has to let go, and she horrifyingly dies.

"It was a very emotional day," Marshall remembers of her finale. "I was working sixteen, seventeen hours a day on that film. We shot it in order; we were cracking jokes on that set, and then everyone started dying. I think I was the third to die. They were blaring Yo Yo Ma on the set. It was a very draining day." Nowhere near, however, the role that Miller was offering her in his writeup.

"I read it and called him, and said 'I think you're mistaken,'" Marshall says. "'You said you wanted me to read for Phoebe. She's a sociopath!' I said I couldn't do that role. I was terrified."

Then, however, she came to one of the same realizations that had brought Quincy into battle.

"It was a big role to take on," Marshall says. "Women don't get to play a lot of strong characters, so when a role like this came along, I went for it."

Less than a month before shooting, she came out to play—and things wouldn't have been tougher if she'd been about to step into the Ultimate Fighting Championships for real.

Five days a week, Marshall recalls, "There was an hour of strength conditioning, an hour of boxing, and three hours of fight training. I would cry and keep going, it was so physically exhausting. I lost about thirteen pounds for the role."

Again, though, there was the characters' mindsets for both actresses. Mental illness was rampant in both; to find Phoebe's backstory, Marshall went the scholarly route.

"I did a lot of research on sociopaths and met with psychiatrists," she explains. "When I started out, I thought that sociopaths were like serial killers. Serial killers always say they stem from a bad history: child abuse, sexual abuse, and violence that triggered it. But with sociopaths, it's literally that you're born with a disease where you just don't have an emotional attachment to things. It's easy to manipulate people and use their feelings against that, because a sociopath doesn't have that remorse, those feelings."

Putting together the story of a life she'd act out, Marshall stayed away from personal opinion, at the beginning.

"The first thing I had to do was *not* judge Phoebe," she says. "I had to figure out where she was coming from, why she does the things she does. I proceeded to write a biography and entwine my life into hers. I started from the time she was born, and wrote up to the time of the movie or the show. It helps me as an actor have understanding of this character. I take things that have happened to me in my life that would help me get a better understand of the character. Half of it is real, half of it is fictional. That way, when I go into character, I have an emotional attachment to her."

Quincy also hit the books, learning about schizophrenia. But, sadly, she also had a past that didn't need inventing to utilize.

"I have witnessed the actings out of mental illness in my family [bi-polar]," she says, "and I lost a lover to suicide in 2010. In hindsight, I believe he was bipolar/schizophrenic and I carried a tremendous amount of guilt about not having understood that in the years I was with him. I have since started learning to forgive myself about not seeing the signs through therapy—and I remind myself that professionals were unable to diagnose him properly, either, though I still miss him tremendously."

Early on, we the viewers are a bit mislead. *Raze* kicks off with a couple on an early date, with him trying to convince her that he's actually an OK guy, not like most. It appears to work; her guard goes down far enough to reveal her dream of kickboxing stardom, something she clearly hasn't revealed to many.

Relaxing in the heavenly offerings of a warm bubble bath, she suddenly sees a masked figure above her. Off guard, she's captured and unconscious.

The lady in question just happens to be Rachel Nichols. This is different than her role as James Kirk's gorgeous green alien galpal in *Star Trek* (2009), albeit not as much from going on the physical offensive as Scarlett alongside the rest of the *G.I. Joe* group, also in 2009.

Still, she's a star. An established name in the acting game. So we might expect her to be the heroine here, *Raze*'s protagonist, brawling through it all to take down the evil that kicked things off.

We would be wrong.

Her Jamie finds herself in a dark hallway, no idea what's going on. Then another woman, only slightly more together, appears nearby. The lady calls herself Sabrina, and the two soon reach another room. Jamie's still on the edge of control, pounding doors and walls, calling for someone, anyone to get her out or at least let her know what the hell this is about.

Sabrina knows, although she seems to wish she didn't. Then she could avoid what's coming. She attacks. This is what the gamesmasters want.

With escape suddenly not her top priority, Jamie fights back. None of that catfighting shit here; there's enough punching and kicking going on to know that both these people have been trained in this sort of thing; maybe Jamie was closer to her fighting dreams than she revealed.

It's World War III for a few shocking minutes. Finally, Sabrina grabs the upper hand, sadly bashing Jamie's head into oatmeal.

Then she looks around and calls out. Asking, nearly begging for someone to arrive, to let her go. She's just taken the life of someone she never truly knew, someone who could have been her best friend, could have done some amazing things. But one life had to be lost, and Sabrina had made it someone else's.

Sabrina was Zoe Bell, who'd taken steps for women in action acting long before *Raze*, stunting in *Inglorious Basterds* (2009), both *Kill Bill*s, and *Iron Man 3* (2013), just to name a few. Now she was being asked to strike another blow for her colleagues in a film she'd help produce.

But not alone. Soon Sabrina and the rest of the competitors are herded into another room, the rules of this "game" gleefully explained.

As it turns out, they've already made some serious progress. This tournament began with dozens of competitors, and now the herd has thinned. But it wasn't just the losers who had died, showing perhaps the flick's saddest aspect; winning the fights isn't about money, stardom, or anything else . . . it's about saving the lives of loved ones. Every time someone falls in a fight, they're shortly joined in the afterlife by someone they love.

Cautiously strolling into her first brawl, Phoebe shares her sad tale with her opponent. Nothing personal about this; she's got to win or her mom dies.

She quickly takes down her shorter opponent, but the lady fights back and gets atop her. Still, Phoebe manages to climb back above, and wears her opponent out with punches and axhandles.

Soon enough, the woman's dead. But Phoebe's not done, joyfully pounding her unrecognizable. Even against an opponent she'd never met, this was a personal thing.

Perhaps because she was pretending to beat down someone else, Phoebe growls about hating her mother. Here came some of the toughest parts of Marshall's preparation.

To find this sort of mentality, she explains, "It doesn't have to be what's actually happening, it's just what you can use from your life to bring an emotional effect. She hates her mother. That doesn't mean I hate my mother; it just means I have to go to a place in my life that I felt that way towards something or someone. It's just a form of bringing your emotion to it. It could be like when someone lost their dog as a child: how they felt was a real emotion and it entwines into the character."

In the impromptu class, Phoebe's still egging everyone on. But as things go forward, it's a bit tougher to despise her.

We hear her boast of a criminal past. Taking her pain out on animals. Still, there are also tales of her getting passed around the foster system. What some of the men she'd looked to for protection had done to her.

"Phoebe wasn't always a bad person," Marshall says. "There were things that happened to her that made her the person that she was. She was ostracized from society, an awful upbringing, a horrible life. It doesn't give her an excuse to become what she did, but it's a reason why. So when she gets into this event, it's the first time in her life that she's actually felt accepted by something."

Between her hopes of taking out some more opponents, Phoebe hears some welcome news; whoever wins might just get to be a part of a new society.

"That's why she asks 'Does this mean we get to join your organization?'" Marshall says. "For the first time in her life, she's being accepted into something, as sick and twisted as it is."

Here came one of the film's perfect examples of humor, blacker than an Alaskan midnight and more twisted than a category-five funnel cloud. At the event's helm are Joseph and Elizabeth, a married couple putting on a show for their friends, clearly a long-running event. In roles far from anything else they'd done before, Doug Jones and Sherilyn Fenn showed a hell of a lot more chemistry in a bloody action film than many others of all kinds of genres. Joseph's in charge, explaining things to the group. Elizabeth's taking care of the guests, hopeful that everyone has a nice time. The two obviously have some huge plans for the night, and for many more following. There's some mad love, admiration, even awe of each other. . . .

If not for their delving into death, the two have the type of marriage that many believe only happens in the movies!

One of Phoebe's main targets happens to be the lovely brunette right in front of her: Brenda. The person Quincy had worked so hard to become.

"Brenda [is] a mentally unstable woman who wants to die," Quincy says. "I chose NOT to make her weak: she is broken and vulnerable, but never weak—and she welcomes death. Death is Brenda's escape from the hell that is the arena."

It appears she has another, although much longer plan in her first fight; disregarding her opponent, Brenda futilely tries to dig her way under the walls. Even in this sort of tale, the most common acting techniques kept coming into play for Quincy.

"Improv helped me *a lot* in *Raze*," she says. "At the last minute, I had to improvise my lines because I was told my acting surpassed what was written, so I had to think fast on set. This happens in indies, so you have to be quick. Even the 'dog moves' I did, scratching under the door of the arena at the top of my fight to possibly dig my way out, was improvised because Brenda sees her lover through the door and wants to save him, she literally turns animal."

Perhaps thinking she'll have an easy time of it, the other women attacks. But like the panicked wild creature she looks to be becoming, Brenda destroys her and stomps her into the dirt.

Off the set, the crew tried to lighten the tension with jokes and relaxation. Quincy chose to stay in Brenda mode.

"I made the other actors and crew who were laughing around me into a fantasy," she says. "These jokesters and I were at my former lover's funeral in my mind. Their making jokes and not taking what had happened to him seriously hurts Brenda very, very much, so every time the camera came to me, it was like immediate excruciating pain and waterworks, because Brenda would continue to suffer, even off-camera."

Her suffering would end soon, but not in the way everyone expected. Her mind and body both all but destroyed, Brenda can't find the means to maneuver herself into the room for her next brawl.

Elizabeth is called down for assistance; perhaps one lady can talk sense to another.

Almost maternally, Elizabeth encourages Brenda to find it within to go back to battle. She reminds her that Brenda's family's life is on the line here. It doesn't work.

"In the scenes with Elizabeth and Joseph, Brenda is not seeing *them*," Quincy explains. "Brenda is seeing the parents of her lost love *in* them. It is very hard for her to face them given the tremendous guilt and sadness and blame and anger she is experiencing."

And the anger comes out hard; Brenda suddenly smashes her own head into Elizabeth's, bloodying the hostess' nose. That's an automatic disqualification; Elizabeth takes a henchman's gun and plants it right between Brenda's eyebrows.

Finally, Brenda gets what she always wanted—and all it takes is her brains being splattered across the wall behind her.

"My death was tough to pull off," Quincy says. "I wish I had been able to take more time dying, but I was just more concerned with it working. The contraption was hard to create on our budget and we could only do two takes. It was an air compressor deal linked up to a pipe going out the back of my head. The pipe was filled with spaghetti sauce and meat chunks, and each take was messy as hell, but I was glad it at least looked very real."

The ranks keep dropping. One woman after another suffers her final defeat. In the film's second cameo shocker, Rosario Dawson even steps into the pits for a moment. Unfortunately, she's not as tough here as in *Sin City* (2005) and alongside Bell in *Death Proof* (2007), brutally losing her fight and life.

Phoebe's having a grand old time. Headbutting, punching, kicking . . . giving or taking, this is her heaven. It isn't that she doesn't feel the pain; she certainly does. She simply enjoys it. Still, she gleefully drags an opponent's head slowly down a brick wall until the last blow is struck.

"I don't even like confrontation," Marshall says of reality. "I'm always apologizing for everything. This was creepy."

Suffering even more so than she did as a POW, Sabrina's out with an injury she doesn't have time to recover from. But toppling her will make Phoebe's entire life, so the same taunting techniques she's been using throughout bring Sabrina into battle.

No epic this time; Sabrina pounds away, harder than ever before. Less than two minutes in, Phoebe's about gone, her dazed, bloody face staring up at Sabrina.

But even this was what she appeared to want; Phoebe mockingly blares out one more round of cackling before Sabrina puts her down for good.

"[Phoebe was] the most fun role I've ever played and the hardest role I've ever played," Marshall says. "I cried a lot when I was driving home at night because of the dark weird place I was in. It was exhilarating. It took two weeks to really regroup after the movie."

Sabrina keeps fighting. She appears to let another woman win, only to spring the pair's surprise partnership on those in control. Her colleague is killed, but Sabrina makes it out. In another rarity for woman—well, except for *Kill Bill* (2003)—she gorily slaughters the guards, then Elizabeth and Joseph. She makes her way into the main lobby, only to find a family party (kids included) watching her and the rest of festivities. She makes her way out the front door and bolts across a large bridge, seemingly escaping. But she can't quite get all the way away. . . .

It takes a load of guts to even attempt to open a door in the acting world, and one can hardly do it alone. In *Raze*'s case, more than enough opposition had to be overcome to get it going. Quincy and Bell had to shoot from both producer and performer. Marshall and the rest of the cast had to do some portraying that many would be too intimidated about to even begin. Others had to put up some time and quite a bit of folding green. But the film showed that all audiences need is a chance as well—a shot at enjoying something new.

It worked. Bell, Marshall, Quincy, and the rest got to show that a woman could do a hell of a job pulling off real-life action and violence. Miller showed that such a film could be directed. Audiences showed that they'd pay enough attention to enjoy it. Dark clouds may be said to have a silver lining . . . but sometimes, one can shine through blood and death as well.

She fought because *it was all she knew!* She fought because *she'd do anything for a* *dream*!

Yes, we've heard those before, the standard "heartwarming" one-liners that have been attached to just about every other fighting film since *Rocky*.

It's *based on a true story*! Sure, the other tried, true, and desperate as hell attempt to play on audience's emotions, at least enough to get them to watch.

Bare Knuckles didn't completely shy away from the typical tactics; the 2013 film just went about them a bit differently, both in what the tale showed outright and the story we'd have to look past the screen to learn. The battles we saw Jeanette Roxborough act through represented a battle she's been in for decades, and still fights today; the opponents her Samantha takes on and out personify an opposition without an individual face, name, or figure, but one that still visits all kinds of unthinkable unfair treatment on its innocent victims. It's how the film ended up being something of a pseudo biopic of not just Roxborough herself, but so many others in a fight that, in an ideal world, they'd never have had to start at all.

OK, getting a bit heavy here so early in the profile. Let's lighten things up for a few paragraphs.

"I was *such* an action movie fan!" Roxborough exclaims. "I loved them, and I *always* wanted to be in them!" Athletics and longtime devotion are two pretty strong assets for those looking to wander down that career path, and the Canada native got rolling on both quite early.

After spending a few years in the popular northern pastime of figure skating, Roxborough followed her older brother into the martial arts.

"He joined a karate school, and then he quit," she recalls. "I kept going. I met an amazing teacher, and stuck with it." And she didn't even think about stopping until she reached the third degree level of black belt-(wo)manship and recognition around Earth!

"Karate is quite beautiful," she explains. "It was for the fun of it, and it's so competitive." Along the way, she took the same first steps that carry so many over the starting line to the action cinema, stepping into small-screen stunt work for the short-lived Melissa George venture *Thieves* in 2001.

The next year, well, things exploded to a greater level than the highest kicks she'd ever used to pierce a dojo's atmosphere.

The stunt coordinator on *Thieves*, she remembers, "made a few calls. He told everyone I looked a lot like Yancy." That would be Yancy Butler, herself blending reality and supernatural, the comic books with the television in *Witchblade*.

With the acquisition of the title object, Butler's Sara Pezzini turned into a superhuman machine that made her NYPD colleagues glad she was on their side. Episode after episode, Pezzini effortlessly knocked back evil in every form with just *maybe* a single drop of sweat. Still, when things really got crazy before the cameras, Roxborough became Butler's blade-waving, fist-throwing, no-pain-feeling, even occasionally telekinetic (OK, that part might have been all special effects!) double.

Right around that time, Roxborough stepped in for Denise Richards (alongside Eddie Griffin) in *Undercover Brother* and for Jennifer Love Hewitt (alongside Jackie Chan) in *The Tuxedo*. A few years later, while Bruce Willis got the acting credit and Richard Donner the directing mark for *16 Blocks*, Roxborough landed on the stunt crew.

Right around that time, Eric Etebari gave her a call. He'd been both alongside and against Butler (and, through her, Roxborough) as Ian Nottingham on *Witchblade*. Now he was looking to step behind the cameras for the first full-length time.

"He wanted to add some of my story into a fight script he was working on," Roxborough recalls. Etebari's story would be of young single mom Samantha, stunt doubling through her days and bartending at night, hoping that things would one day get just a bit better for her and the daughter she'd raised as an unmarried lady.

She obviously had the stunt work down to a science. The bar scenes flashed Roxborough back to the beer commercials that had started off her acting career.

And a few years before that, she'd had a daughter. Soon after, the sole parenting aspect had been forced on Roxborough.

But that wasn't all; for the first time, she'd be leading the way through the action film worlds she'd dreamt of for decades.

As Samantha hoped for a few more tips one night, fight promoting washout Sonny Cool (Martin Kove, in a name and role not even in the same galaxy as *Karate Kid* villain John Kreese) drowned his sorrows in flop sweat and booze, ready to fall the rest of the way down and out.

Then, suddenly, the shit hits the fan, with the drinks' help, of course. Your common, everyday barroom brawl breaks out, but Samantha just happens to handle herself as if this is the most natural thing in the world. Since this is, after all, an action flick, the Cool man automatically knows she might just be his new (and maybe only remaining) special shining star, out to shock the local underground and heavily wagered upon field of lady sports fighting.

With a pair of unsteady jobs and a daughter at home—her solider husband Troy, played by Etebari, was killed in action before the story—Samantha's about out of choices. All that sparring Roxborough had done became a years-long prep session for Samantha's work, her in the rings and gyms, injecting Samantha with the same spirit that had taken the actress through so many colors of belt ranks in martial arts.

"She was more of a reluctant fighter, which I could identify with," Roxborough recalls. "A lot of what I saw in her, I already had. I trained a lot in LA. I always had a hard time building muscle." Herself switching from stunt work to acting, Bridgett Riley taught Roxborough some of the boxing skills that had gotten Riley to the physical crew of 2004's Best Picture champ *Million Dollar Baby*.

In character, however, the women's roles changed more than a bit; Riley's Mona is the reigning local champ, and none too ready to give up her throne. Samantha's first fight puts her in a cage with Mona, and it's the veteran that walks out.

"Getting beat up is harder than beating somebody else!" Roxborough claims. "We shot very quickly, so I didn't have any time to recover." The entire film was shot in less than two weeks, with her in every scene.

"When you're doing an intense scene when you're throwing yourself around," she recalls, "and you wake up the next day, bruised and sore from the intensity, you still had to carry on."

Early on, Etebari and the rest of the crew had been cast calling for Samantha's daughter Mila. Just about out of nowhere, someone brought up a young gal named Teya.

Everyone knew the name, but the choice would carry a risk for a big-budget flick with tons of time, let alone one with hardly a few days and a low budget.

At just a few days old, Teya hadn't been eating properly. A barrage of tests found that her cerebellum hadn't developed. Many thought she wouldn't survive, let alone walk. Now Teya had gotten to elementary school, albeit without hearing or much motor coordination.

But there was one reason to believe in her for Mila, a connection to Samantha that a million acting classes wouldn't create.

She was Roxborough's daughter.

Teya Roxborough's scene-stealing performance gave *Bare Knuckles* (2010) a heart that's tough to find in action films.

"It hit me really hard," she remembers of first learning of Teya's condition. "I spent most of my life, and still do, feeling like I'm on the outside looking at a normal life." Teya's therapy had taken the two as far away as a physiotherapist in Chile (Roxborough, of course, learned sign language), and now, after some serious specialized therapy, Teya was taking her first steps.

"Everything about the deaf world is different than the hearing world," Roxborough says. "The bureaucracy surrounding special needs in challenging, but it's been really challenging to work through all the paperwork." Things get very close to reality in the film, with one of Cool's moron tormentors mocking Mila as, "that crippled kid!"

"She didn't really prepare, and she had never been in a movie before," Roxborough recalls. "She's always been very good at living her life 'in the present moment' so she was very natural in a scene... She eventually started getting her scenes in two takes and it was the joke on set. She's been exposed to a film environment since she was a baby so it's normal to her and she doesn't get too excited or nervous about the process."

With someone to work for, Samantha's back in training. In typical action film mode, a bazillion-dollar tournament happens nearby, and Sonny manages to get her a spot.

Surrounded by the type of folk that feel the need to show everyone just how damned well-to-do they truly are, the women go to ring war, the audience cheering them on like they're at an upper-class cockfight. Leaving her karate-earned poise at the outside, Samantha cautiously steps to the ring, and manages to step out, not just conscious, but victorious.

And so does Mona. She's won this before and knows she will again. Her boyfriend, surprisingly something less than a model citizen, is running the event with some others that it's a bit dangerous to owe green to. Mona's actually a decent sort, but if she falls, she'll lose more than money.

It's time for the two to step in one last time. But this isn't the same Samantha that got crushed a few scenes ago. It's the one with a few hundred grand and the stability that she and Mila have never enjoyed just a victory away.

Jeanette Roxborough's Samantha (left) takes home the main event in 2010's *Bare Knuckles*.

The first round's pretty even, but Mona hammers her with a high heel kick midway through the second, and it looks like Samantha might be done.

"Stand up!" Cool says, a pep talk that's almost pleading. "It's your time, baby!" Yeah, that's so far from "Sweep the leg," you can't believe it.

Samantha's saved by the bell, and Mona's back at full strength. It's going to take a miracle for Samantha to come out on top, or at least a hell of a knockout.

Both swing wildly, some hitting, some missing. But Mona suddenly finds herself against the ropes, her energy draining like a waterfall.

A left to her side, and a ref's ten-count later, Samantha scores the upset. With she and Cool in love and money, she and Mila might just be OK.

And just maybe, someday, Roxborough and Teya will be too. Just after wrapping *Knuckles*, the younger lady scored her own commercial debut. Her mom's still stunting, for both Gillian Anderson and Katherine Isabelle on TV's *Hannibal* in 2015, just after working on the *Robocop* flick remake. She's also branching into more acting and writing.

Maybe someday, the story that became the *Knuckles* storyline will have its own Hollywood-level happy ending, even if it has to move a few (hundred) miles north to the Roxboroughs' Canadian homeland.

"She's overcome a lot," Roxborough says. "Exposing my life in that way was a bit of a challenge, and it can be a little hard on the heart. She had a great time, but it was OK. It's extraordinary, the challenges raising a child that is unique, but it's also very rewarding in a lot of ways."

Patrick Reynolds' Mandroid (left) leads the rest of the *Eliminators* (1986) through time and space to take on evil.

Patrick Reynolds: *Eliminators*

NOW STOP ME IF you've read this one....

In the action-film-jammed world of the 1980s, we saw the tale of a young muscleman, gearing up in every sense of the term to play a not-quite-human being, more machine than alive, to do evil's dark work. But no one, he nor us, could have guessed that a decade later, he'd be right in the midst of the political world, so much tougher than the cinema could ever be....

What? Did you just yell to knock it off, and scoot through to the next profile? Think this is the story of a name pronounced *Ah-nuld* and his foray into the first of (it seems!) countless *Terminator* turns?

Incorrect—although Arnie's elsewhere in this tome! This is a whole new bio altogether.

"Most unknown actors would jump at the chance for lead role in a feature film," remarks our subject, "whether it was action or science fiction, a western, or an eighteenth-century period film. In my case, it was a little different."

Like so many others, he'd dreamt of being the next De Mille, Wilder, or Hitchcock from behind the cameras, starting off in elementary school, with a small movie camera and so many dreams. He'd studied film at UCLA and USC.

And, like too many others, things hadn't moved more than a degree past that for Patrick Reynolds. A TV role here and there, some small jobs, but nothing to write his name and put it out there after about a decade on the outside looking into acting, even from the classrooms of many acting schools, the same schools that pushed his classmates (like a fellow named Swayze and a beauty named Pfeiffer) into their own careers.

To be fair, though, Reynolds *had* stepped before the cameras of 1977's *Pumping Iron*, the documentary that somehow managed to take a moniker as mysterious (outside of Austria!) as Schwarzenegger and start making it household!

"I used to see him around the gym in the early 1970s when I was working out as a young bodybuilder," Reynolds recalls with a chuckle. "People thought he wouldn't make it as an actor because he was too muscular. I guess Schwarzenegger got the last laugh."

As the 80s arrived, though, Reynolds started to accept that his name might just be buried too deep in the performing shuffle.

"I had *really* gotten fed up with the movie business," he remembers. "I hated the process of going on cattle calls for the prospect of one or two days of work." In business with his in-laws' bus company with plans to tell his family's tale in a book someday (a dream he'd realize), Reynolds' phone rang.

"My agent called and asked if I wanted to go on one more audition," he says. "Some people I had screen-tested for a year before wanted to see me."

They wanted to see the man. They wanted to see him become something else.

"[My agent said] I'd be playing a robot," Reynolds says. "He'd be metal from the neck down, with one eye. A quarter of his head would be metal." No, again, this was 1985, so it wasn't the sequel to *The Terminator*, itself just a year old; *T2* didn't come about until 1991.

Eliminators creators weren't looking for a machine hidden under skin, as James Cameron had. This Mandroid would be a resurrected solider fallen in battle, equipped, engineered, and improved to do the work of a man who'd make Victor Frankenstein mutter, "Now, someone needs to put a stop to that chap!" There's also a time machine involved here!

Yes, of course that sort of role had launched Arnold's career. But it was just a role. Enjoyable, yes. A challenge, sure. Paying? Perhaps most importantly. But Reynolds was ready to hear the dreaded N-O combination that actors get about ninety-eight percent of the time.

"I went on the audition not really caring if I got the part," he explains. "I wanted it, but I wasn't desperate. I hadn't been working for hours every week with three different coaches, developing my craft. I was able to sit back in the interview and say, 'I'd like this role. Let me know.'" An uncommon approach, certainly not one most performers would admit to, but effective. Less than a day later, he was the Mandroid!

In name, at least. Now Reynolds had to develop it on his own.

"I went back to lifting weights," he says. "I hired a trainer, trained and dieted like an S.O.B., lost twenty-eight pounds. If I did that, Mandroid would have the right look, chiseled cheekbones, the whole thing."

Still, it wasn't just the look; Mandroid had once been a man named John, dead in a plane crash until he was found and turned into an electronic tool to do the deeds of collecting heirlooms from the past by crazed hoarder Abbot Reeves (Ray Dotrice, light-centuries away from playing the title character's pappy in 1984's Best Picture *Amadeus*!).

But Mandroid is a machine, not a man, so it's easy for Reeves to destroy his creation when the job comes to a close. But Reynolds' robot escapes, and, with the help of Denise Crosby's scientist Nora Hunter, heads back to the dangerous waters of South America to hunt his former master's sorry ass down.

"As far as [John's] personality went," Reynolds says, "he had crashed in a plane, been pulled out by henchmen, and his body was basically salvaged. He was put in a robot suit, his memory and mind taken over by chip. He has no self-determination; he's controlled by the chip as he breaks out of the evil scientist's compound. My two cents was him not feeling sorry for himself."

At that point in his life, however, Reynolds had his own sad reasons to do so.

"I worked out my anger at my absentee father with a therapist," he says. His father R.J. hadn't been much in his life before passing when the younger Reynolds was a teenager—and if the name R.J. Reynolds is softly ringing bells in the audience's minds, it should, if not for the right reasons.

Reynolds had also lost his mom, shortly before becoming the robot.

"I had no time to grieve," he says. "I threw myself into the work. All of that helped my performance as Mandroid. In a sense, it was like an early Marvel movie, with this dark, sad character."

Way down south, the group finds Reeves, but it's too late; he's already a new cyborg, ready to jump right back into his time machine and head back to Rome to finish Julius Ceaser's work—just let Brutus, Cassius, and the rest of those assassins try to take *this guy* out!

It almost works; the Mandroid gives his life (his "life") to save his friends, but Reeves gets away. Still, this is one of the few times that brute force overcomes brains—the group destroys the machine, shoving its creator way past ancient times and too far back to even count as B.C., too far from anything to ever return.

It was his last film role to date, but Reynolds started a fight that we only wish had as many happy endings as the film world does. About those political issues back in the opening....

Reynolds' grandfather, also named R.J., had launched the eponymous tobacco company that still sells millions of cigarettes in America every year. Emphysema took R.J. Jr. in 1964.

The younger Reynolds held his tobacco stock until 1979, and smoked until right around the time he made *Eliminators*. In 1986, he spoke to ban cigarette ads with none other than a House Subcommittee.

"The more I learned about what big tobacco companies were up to, the more angry I became," he says. "My life really took a big turn at that point. In my Congressional testimony, I pointed out, 'If the hand that once fed me is the tobacco industry, then that same hand has killed millions of people and will continue to, unless people wake up to the dangers of smoking.' I also said, 'My only memories of my father are of a man lying down and gasping for breath.' There was huge news coverage, and I was thrust into the spotlight. I realized then I had a great platform to speak against smoking, and make a real difference with my life."

Today, Reynolds keeps telling people not to use the products his ancestors profited from. He speaks all over the US and internationally on the topic, urging kids not to start, and encouraging smokers to quit. He informs university audiences about the state of tobacco control, and always closes with his inspiring promise of a coming tobacco-free society.

"My tour of Greece in 2009 proved there's a good chance we'll receive national news coverage," he says. "If I could repeat Greece in China or India, we could get a billion people thinking about smoking, just for a day," he says. "Looks like I've found what I was supposed to do with my life, and there is much I still want to do." Reynolds' website is www.TobaccoFree.org.

"I'll be candid about a pet peeve of mine, when it would be less risky to keep my mouth shut," he says. "For many years, about eighty percent of Big Tobacco's political donations have gone to Republican candidates and PACs, and under Bush (Jr.), we couldn't get a tobacco tax passed in Congress, year after year. Neither could we get long overdue FDA regulation of tobacco. But when Obama took office, we had a 69-cent Federal tobacco tax passed in two weeks, and FDA regulation six months after he first took office. Because of the tax, today there are three million fewer smokers. Smoking just became too expensive for kids and for many adults, too."

Actors in Action

Donny Donowitz (Eli Roth) lived the dream of every fellow Jew in the times of World War II, helping the *Inglorious Basterds* destroy Nazi evil in 2009.

Eli Roth: *Inglorious Basterds*

IT WAS PERSONAL. IT was all *very* personal.

The man was experiencing both the best and the worst of war. The worst because he got to see close up the death and destruction, the darkness that war spreads over man's lands and lives there long after the last victim falls. Buildings had burned and exploded, now hardly even memories. Lives would never see the chance to finish out on their own terms.

But there was also a very bright side. He was the one doing it. He was the one dishing it out to the ones that so much more than deserved it. Victory was in hand, quite literally, in the bat he used to feed it to others, forcefully. With every swing, with every contact, with every blow, he was striking for those who would so have loved to have the bat in their own hands.

He was realizing the dream that many secretly held both throughout and since World War II.

Taking the typical soldier's way out of putting a bullet from hundreds of yards away through the head of a man we never knew or perhaps even saw—the *impersonal* way of combat—just wasn't going to work for this guy. He wanted to look into their scared, pathetic, all too human eyes as they died, watching them silently beg for the mercy they had denied so many of his countrymen, women, and children. And then deny them it.

This wasn't about getting a crack at the evil sonsabitches who had dared to attack him at Pearl Harbor, or those that had backed them up. It wasn't about being quicker on the draw than the guy on the other side of the lines who had a gun too.

It was deeper. These people had literally hurt his people, his family, his friends.

All the senseless pain that his ancestors had been forced through. All the lives that had been stolen. All the suffering that they and millions of others had endured simply because Germany needed someone innocent to blame for getting its ass kicked inside out during World War I.

It was time for some comeuppance. And Eli Roth was going to hand some out—in character and otherwise.

"I guess I've always wanted to take a part and dive into it the way like De Niro dived into *Raging Bull* [1980]," says Roth, behind the camera for *Cabin Fever* (2002) and the first two *Hostel* films (2005/2007), "but I never had a reason to."

Until late 2004, that was. Fresh off the *Kill Bills* of 2003 and 2004, a fellow director named Tarantino, himself looking to foray off into historical fiction, started to write a story about World War II that so many wish could have been the way it really turned out.

Imagine a huge group of Nazis, the Holocaust's evil architects in full force, kicking back like they're on top of the world. And then, just as they're lulled into the most secure of securities, someone (or ones) arrives to dish out punishment written all in capital letters.

No arrests. No wasting time at Nuremberg. No getting a hangman's hands dirty, or serving all that prison food to someone not even good enough for it. They would be the judges, jurors, and gleeful executioners.

They would be the Inglorious Basterds.

All with a Jew leading the way. In Tarantino's dream world, that was just the way things would work out.

For the head henchman of such a group was the Bear Jew, who'd given up a haircutting career in Boston to head across the water to Germany. Let someone else take care of the other Axis powers—this guy would be on a mission to kill those who had killed his.

Still, nothing went too far forward with the project for a few years. But as Roth and Tarantino hung out more and more, Roth discussed his own past in Beantown. Tarantino persuaded him into a small part in the 2007 mini-feature *Death Proof*. Hey . . . this guy could act.

Perhaps spurred on by the torture that the Curse of the Bambino had laid on it for so many years, many in Beantown had taken to carrying bats in their own car, and using them to hit everything but a baseball.

"I said, 'Quentin, did you know I had a baseball bat in my car growing up?'" Roth says. "I mean, that's a real Boston thing. You have a baseball bat and most of the time you use it off the field. . . . Over the years, he had hung out with me enough and heard enough of my Boston stories, and he said, 'Now when I'm writing [Bear Jew Donny] Donowitz I'm starting to hear your voice.' So he hinted that he was thinking about having me do it."

Not too much later, Tarantino asked Roth to combine the spirit of Dr. Frankenstein and his own creation, the strength of the monster with the mindset of the creator.

"I went back to Boston where I'm from," Roth explains, "and I just *was* the character, researched the part, created the backstory and did all the research and talked to World War II veterans."

Of course, it was more than muscle and channeling the spirit of Ted Williams that made the Bear Jew into the icon of intimidation the Basterds needed. It was his mind, his mannerisms that would make him stand all the way up and out.

"What's difficult is getting that look in your eye and making sure that that's real," Roth remembers. "You can't *act* that. You have to really be in a state of psychosis. I knew that people would have to look at this guy and see that rage and that fury and that this guy, there's *no question* this guy comes out and will beat you to death. And that was exhausting and much more draining than I ever anticipated."

Killing Nazis (or "Naatzees," as Brad Pitt's Sgt. Aldo Raine proclaims them) is not so much a matter of enjoyment to Donowitz—taking pleasure in something usually involves having a choice to make. This is about obligation. Doing it not because it's right or fair or just, but because there's simply nothing else to do. There's no Plan B, no other option. These men *have* to pay. They *must* suffer. They *will* feel a semblance of the pointless agony that they jammed through the lives of so many others.

And in order to dish out all the pain the Nazis deserved to feel, Roth had to put himself through it first. Not only the strains and sprains he might have picked up in the gym, putting on 40 pounds of muscle for the role, but the mental agony that can hurt so much more.

Things started on the personal side, and history soon joined in.

"My grandparents got out of Europe," Roth recalls. "Most of their relatives were murdered in the Holocaust, so I grew up with this knowledge, and my parents saying, 'Thank your lucky stars you were born in Boston, 'cause if you were born in Europe, you would've been killed in the concentration camps.'

"So I grew up with this psychotic hatred of the Nazis and just these fantasies of killing them. . . . It was very cathartic, it was extremely personal to do the role." Unused scenes showed Donowitz's past as a Boston barber, discussing his murderous hopes against the Nazis, then having the local Jewish community autograph a bat in the hopes that their names will one day rest on a Nazi's forehead.

At a Passover Seder, he and Tarantino discussed all those who had taken part in the attempted destruction of an entire people.

"We talked about the Jews, when we were slaves and the Holocaust and, sitting, explaining . . ." Roth says. "This wasn't just Hitler. This was 60 million people. It was the whole world teaming up to exterminate and they were very successfully doing it, so that puts you on the defensive all the time. There's no forgiving that. There's no absolution. You kill every one of those people or they're going to kill you and that's how it is." He'd use Donowitz to get a certain measure of revenge.

Roth went back to the pain of having his heart broken in the past. He thought about getting into some tough fights, and not always coming out on the winning side. He imagined losing a loved one. The tunes of hard rock bands like Guns N' Roses and Iron Maiden kept the blood pumping at high speed and volume.

Then came an incident that scarred him worst of all—well, maybe.

"My girlfriend, as a joke, put Hannah Montana on my iPod mix," Roth says, "and at first I was laughing, I was like, 'What is this? Oh my God.' I couldn't believe she'd done that."

Miley Cyrus inspiring someone pretending to commit slow, brutal murder? It started to happen!

"I was kind of dancing around to the music, thinking, 'Oh my God, am I actually getting into this?'" Roth says. "What if Brad Pitt caught me listening to Hannah Montana? What if Quentin knew I was listening to Hannah Montana? How would I explain that away? And I just went psycho. And that was the song that would take me to my psycho place."

As the Bear Jew started to bear the mindset of his animalistic namesake, Roth kept the tunes in his leering skull.

"When I was beating the guy, I started thinking, 'What if *I* was Hannah Montana?'" he says. "Quentin's like, 'Eli, you ready?' I'm like, 'Oh yeah. Yes, yes sir.' And little do they know that that's why I look so insane, is I'm torturing myself with thoughts of 'How could I actually pull off being a high-school student and a pop star at night as Hannah Montana?'"

It's time to get serious again. Roth and the rest of the Basterds indeed got a rare moment of enjoyment out of his dirty work that was clean in intent, but doing it at all, even as an act, required a mentality that one can never fully appreciate or understand until actually participating. Roth didn't go that far, but it was within sight.

"I knew that no matter what I did, no matter how much muscle I put on, what would really sell it was the look in [Donowitz's] eyes," he says. "You had to look at his face and in his eyes and feel that violence and this pure, murderous rage, that he wants to beat every Nazi to death, and he has to look like a killer. And in order to do that, you have to really, really work yourself up into such a state that you feel like you're capable of doing that, and you have to dredge up the most painful memories of your life, and the most horribly upsetting things, and bring them to the surface as if it happened 10 minutes ago."

As difficult as it had been for Roth to locate and collect these emotions, hanging on to them long enough to stay in Donowitz's mind wasn't much easier. While his colleagues were doing their thing, capturing and interrogating a Nazi officer, Roth spent days inside a nearby cave, slugging a punching bag and working out.

"You have to keep yourself in that state, and there are certain tricks you can do to do that," he says. "I was just back there ... working myself up into this frenzy, thinking about those painful experiences in my life."

Finally, *finally*, it was time. Time to take it out on what both Roth and Donowitz's relatives had been forced through. Time to make someone pay. Time to show why everyone, even the Nazis, had heard of the Bear Jew.

"We got a German who wants to die for his country!" Raine gleefully informs Donowitz of an uncooperative officer. "Oblige him!"

Sounds start to emit from Donowitz's cave. Noises like his infamous bat smacking into a wall. Music starts to play, a much more uplifting tune that one typically hears in war movies. If this were Wrestlemania, fans would be going crazy, just knowing that one of their heroes is about to race out and kick hell from someone who's just begging for it.

"I finally came out and just walloped the guy, just let him have it," Roth says, "but I had no idea how exhausting it was, doing that. Because at the end of the day, even though you know the scene you're shooting is pretend, the stuff you're thinking of is very real. And after you're done shooting, you just want to crawl into a hole and die, you feel so terrible." Over and over, he blasts away, far more brutally than most action heroes (usually, it's the bad guys that cause the most hurt), then basks in the cheers of his own impromptu fans, much like Donowitz's hero Ted Williams did for so many years at Fenway Park. Unconfirmed Internet reports claim that one name carved into the Bear bat is none other than Anne Frank, a young girl who never knew how much her writings would change the world.

It wouldn't be the last time he'd feel as such. As the Basterds' own final solution gets going, as they burst into a theater, looking to take out the Nazis once and for all, be it by the huge guns they've stolen, the bombs strapped to their legs, or an inferno that's been conveniently set by a fellow conspirator that we'll meet in a while, Donowitz and a fellow Basterd roll straight into the balcony. A bat would be nice for the Bear Jew, but it would certainly take too long.

Instead, the putrid heads of Hitler and right-hand-slave Joseph Goebbels explode in a mass of rapid machine-gun fire. The dream of every red-blooded celebrator of Hanukkah, living or dead, is realized. That Donowitz is killed in the subsequent explosion is OK—he never got to come down off the high of realizing his eternal dream.

But the *Basterd* audience didn't see what Roth and the rest went through while putting the scene together—or how much of him Donowitz now controlled.

"In the fire in the theater," he says. "It felt like 2000 degrees Fahrenheit. I had never experienced pain like that. But with thousands of clip reloads and weapon changes, this adrenalin kicked in. I was possessed, on auto-pilot. We've got to do this. If we die doing this shot, we've got to do this!" Finally able to step back out of character, he fainted at Tarantino's call of "Cut!"

Roth had gotten to take his own stint in the director's chair during filming, putting together the Nazi-asskiss propaganda flick *Nation's Pride* that the Final Solution Speakers watch during their last night of existence. His previous ventures into horror direction had won him all kinds of attention, but this was real, more real than before, too real for too many. It was a remake of something that had actually happened.

"This is about the glory of the swastika," Roth recalls, "and it was perfect that he had the Jewish guy do it, because I knew that the more authentic the movie was, the more ridiculous it would make Hitler and Goebbels look. So I was saying, 'More swastikas, more swastikas.'"

However, when the film's audience (or should we say, the "film's audience," as it was during a shoot) felt the *Pride*, Roth got to hear hundreds of extras screaming Nazi praise.

An act it was, but this sort of thing had really happened for decades in Nazi Germany, and far too many still carry the opinion even today. The act hit Roth hard in the home and the digestive system.

Melanie Laurent's Shosanna casts a darkly murderous glare down upon those who'd killed her family, friends, and countrymen (and women) in the climactic battles of *Inglorious Basterds*.

"I know they were in character and we were filming a scene from a movie," he says, "but there was a moment where I looked at Quentin and I said, 'What have I done? . . . Why would you ever make a movie like that?' But then I thought, 'You know what? I would have been a great Nazi propaganda filmmaker.'"

With the exception of 1992's *Reservoir Dogs*, Tarantino's films have always been known for their powerful female characters, both mentally and physically. After Uma Thurman got to take both to the extreme during the *Kill Bill* movies, it was **Melanie Laurent's** turn to do so.

Col. Hans Landa could have saved the entire Nazi party with the help of a bullet. He might have shifted the entire balance of WWII with a single shot. But as he hunts down the Dreyfuss family early in the film, young Shosanna is the only one who manages to escape—and rather than take her down, the man responsible for the deaths of so many other Jews allows this one to go free.

In one action, the previews for both characters are established, and they quickly fade into the background as the title characters take over for a while. Landa's back soon enough, and not much has changed in his ways. Shosanna, on the other hand, has lowered her blood temperature into the single digits.

Like Donowitz, she's looking for payback. Not just revenge, but punishment. After spending some time developing a movie theater into one of Paris' finest, she's got a chance to get back at those who took her family. If not the individuals who actually did the deed, perhaps their higher-ups. With the party picking her theater for the premiere of *Nation's Pride*, designed to let them know just how wonderful they truly are, that chance is finally here—and if it means sacrificing everything she's worked for . . . that's not too big of a paying price.

Like Roth, Laurent had fantasized of getting a true shot at the Nazis long after WWII ended.

"I just made that dream since I was four to just kill Hitler," she recalls. "So it's like an obsession for me, and [Tarantino] just did it. So you're like, 'It's gonna be hard, if I don't get that part I'm going to be so disappointed.'" As you've probably figured out by now, she indeed did.

Acting wouldn't be new territory for Laurent, as she'd been making movies for over a decade and won a Most Promising Actress César (the French's Academy Awards) in 2006 for her work in *Don't Worry, I'm Fine*. But while many in her French homeland were long well aware of this American director's name and work, not many back in *his* land knew much of her.

Though her character hadn't been directly in combat on the outside, Shosanna's mind had gone through as much as a pair of D-Days, and the same stoicism that so many war vets find themselves under the spell of after days of battle end enveloped her, and Laurent. While Pitt and Landa's Christoph Waltz, along with many others, filled their characters with all sorts of charisma, Laurent turned Shosanna into a volcano looking for an excuse to blow.

"I think Shosanna, she's dead inside . . . she's very, very strong . . . especially during that dark, terrible war, because everything was organized," she recalls. "We know now that a lot of SS and huge Nazi were very calm, and during the interrogation they were very, very calm. And they just torture you. I played that character and I was always thinking that—that she was dead."

Getting ready for her role, Laurent changed the reels during a showing at Tarantino's theater in Los Angeles.

"It was an amazing experience," she says. "I just loved that. The experience at the Beverly, it had many, many tensions because nobody knew and I was alone in the projection booth and I was like, 'OK, I can't fuck up.' I really loved to prepare the reel, just to fix the reel with the little glue. You are in your laboratory and you're just so close to movies in a different way."

Like a soldier heading into war, Shosanna methodically builds her plan of attack—she'll clip the film to insert herself taunting the tormentors, just before turning the place into an inferno. Still, not too much compared to what they put millions through during the Holocaust. It's her icy coldness up against unspeakable evil, and beating them at their own horrific game.

Dressing for battle, war paint included, we know she's ready to die for the cause, as long as her enemies do first.

"I think we built Shosanna in a very cold way—I didn't want it to be too much like 'I'm going to do THIS and THIS!'" Laurent says. "I think because of that first scene [her family's murder], she was just dead inside. It was not logical to see her being passionate, even with her crazy ideas. So I really wanted her to be cold, like this clever person you've just met who lives so much in their mind that they can explain something to you and you just go, 'What?' She tells everything she has in her mind. . . . 'We're going to do this and this and this. We're going to burn that freaking cinema with everybody inside.'"

And when she finally hits center stage and takes the offensive side for the first time, all of that anger, pain, frustration that's built up inside Shosanna since that first massacre comes roaring out in hysterical laughter on her own big screen, something that puts herself right up next to the Wicked Witch and Vincent Price on that scale (sadly, her character has already been killed, but she's definitely cheering herself on from the afterlife!).

"I was terrified when I saw [the scene on paper]," Laurent admits. "Honestly, I really didn't know what I would do until [Tarantino] said 'action.' You have two options: You can think about it all the time, be obsessive, try out lots of laughs every day . . . or you can just say, 'Of course it's gonna come out. We will see. And maybe I can use my surprise to discover my own laugh. . . .' I just choose my characters and trust them, and after that, it's about the director taking your hand. [Tarantino] puts you in the middle of a grand *mise-en-scène* and it's easy, actually, because everything is there to help you."

While Roth took some strong jumps both into history and the gym to become the Bear Jew, **Christoph Waltz's** methods were a bit more subtle. Blending evil with coolness—the good kind, rather than the stoic sort—he morphed into one of those whose head Donowitz dreamed of turning into a home run.

Hans Landa may have been monikered "The Jew Hunter," (a name he didn't like) but he only got wild at sporadic times. His brutality often lurked beneath the surface, just venturing out when necessary. And in all fairness, watching the film, you couldn't help but sort of like the guy. He was indeed hunting and killing, but more because he had a job, probably a well-paying job, to do, and also because he was particularly good at it—not, however, because he especially enjoyed it.

Perhaps it was this restraint that enticed Waltz to get ready for his role in a far less emotional manner than Roth or Laurent.

"I'm always very keen to find out what's in the script," he says. "I did read around a little and watched a few documentaries [and Tarantino's films]. But I like to take it all from the source, which is the script."

Actors in Action

Holding the end of World War 2 between his hands, Col. Hans Landa (Oscar-winning Christoph Waltz) offers the Basterds a final chance for all of them to make it out alive.

After two months of learning about the why's of Landa, Waltz felt the character seeping through his mind, throughout the rest of his body.

"You can't avoid it," he explains. "You read it, and the thing starts to ferment in a way, subconsciously, consciously, whatever. So actually, in the literal sense of the word, that is a cultivation. But, I don't aim at cultivation. I just try to find out what is in front of me on the page."

Another trademark of Tarantino's is the blending of character emotion in his film. When it comes to these stories, there's very little black and white; just about everyone is almost completely gray. There's villains that we can't help but like, "good guys" who commit all kinds of violent acts, and many that show that the terms "protagonist" and "hero" don't have to end up together in a film synopsis.

Many praised *Pulp Fiction* (1994) as a masterpiece of character development and exploration, and they were absolutely right. With *Reservoir Dogs*, *Jackie Brown* (1997), even his *Four Rooms* segment (1995), rarely do we ever see someone with just one emotion, one reason for being and doing.

Some called Waltz more of a demonstration of this sort of thing than just about anyone else in Tarantino lore. Perhaps it's because, when it comes to interpretation, this guy is a gold mine for film school debaters. This kind of development asks its analysts to take a few minutes to look beneath the surface and ask a few more questions of why. For example, in his first conversation (just about everything with this guy turns into some kind of interrogation), Waltz compares Germans to hawks on the hunt and Jews to the rats they prey upon.

A cheap bit of anti-Semitism? Well, not to Waltz, or those that thought about this stuff a bit more.

"That really is a clue for the whole part [of Landa]," he explains. "Others apply moral connotations, and derogatory and racist and dangerous connotations, but he, Landa, says, 'I look at the rat. The rat has fantastic qualities, and the Jews have fantastic qualities.' He's in full appreciation of what this whole layer of reality entails. . . . They understand how to survive under terrible circumstances. They still know to survive. [Landa] says that, because he appreciates what immense feats human beings are capable of."

And what of the end, when Landa traps the two main Basterds in a restaurant? He lets Raine know that he'll help the Allies win the war, but only if they help him escape a hero. Is he selfish for not fighting to the death for his nation? Is he punishing those who forced him into a pastime he didn't want or like? Does that entitle him to something? The debates on this need never stop.

Still, film fans wouldn't be satisfied unless he got at least *some* kind of payback, and Tarantino gaily allowed it, with Raine carving a swastika into a terrified Landa's forehead, then proclaiming it, "my masterpiece." A bullet may have disfigured Hitler's head, but this is an OK consolation prize.

"In real life, so many things happen at the same time," Waltz explains. "It's not just one strand of reality that you're operating in, because you would be a robot. We're all human beings. Landa understands all these strands, these fibers, these levels of various realities, and he can jump between them. He can turn quickly around because he's following his own agenda, his own goal."

The goal might have ended up a bit tainted for his character, but not for the man behind him, as Waltz strolled all the way to an Oscar statuette, and finally got to play a good guy—albeit one as violent as Landa—in front of Tarantino in 2012's *Django Unchained* (another Oscar-winning role). The award had helped him realize the goal of almost every performer who's ever stepped before a camera—but it shouldn't be their first.

The *Basterds* Oscar, he says, "I did not see coming, definitely not. I was too busy. I couldn't think of awards. I would advise every beginning actor . . . not to think of awards before starting the job."

The Wrestler (2008) helped turn Mickey Rourke into one of Hollywood's top comeback stories of the new millennium, helped along by real-life squared circle veteran Ernest Miller (right).

Mickey Rourke: *The Wrestler*

BACK IN THE MID-1980S, Mickey Rourke was officially one of "The Men," when it came to movie fans.

Ever since he came of age with Kevin Bacon, Daniel Stern, and others in the 1982 Barry Levinson brainchild *Diner*, the Rourke rocket had launched. He shattered Matt Dillon's tough-guy little brother persona the next year in *Rumble Fish*. He fueled the hormone crazes of teenage boys who snuck into their parents' movie stashes to drown their urges in *9 ½ Weeks* (1986). He turned Lisa Bonet into a dark-hearted sexpot in 1987's *Angel Heart*, notwithstanding their bloody love scene that got famous for all the wrong reasons. He even turned down a chance to star in *Platoon* (1986) which ended up getting Oliver Stone some seriously overdue recognition.

"I woke up that day and, for no reason whatsoever, thought Oliver Stone had pissed me off," Rourke remembers. "Big fucking mistake!"

Indeed, Rourke was on a rock to roll. So why didn't he end up at the top of the A-list when it came to acting? Why was it that, as the 90s rolled out, he was stuck playing second fiddle to Denzel Washington, Matt Damon, and Antonio Banderas?

Well, nearly two decades after Rourke's career pushed the down button on the elevator, no one's quite sure.

"With me, it was never drugs, it was never booze," Rourke said. "It was abandonment issues, issues of shame. Anger and hardness are a shield. They mask other things."

That's why, up until a few years ago, no one even dreamed of Rourke one day reaching the stage of Hollywood's finest—least of all the man himself.

"It's voted for by people from the movie business," he said of the Oscars, "and in the past, I've hacked them all off. I was good at that. It came easy to me. I stupidly said acting wasn't a job for a real man. I threatened producers, raged at directors, forgot my agent's name. I really burned my bridges. And a lot of people have long memories.

"It was all Mickey Rourke's fault. I had a very naive idea about what the acting was going to be. I was not prepared to deal with the politics or the business." But no one can stop talent, even the person who owns it—and over the past few years, that's something that Rourke has re-discovered, along with the audiences who stuck around long enough to give him one more second chance.

To be fair, Rourke never FULLY disappeared from the public eye; he just faded into the background. Ever since his starring role in 1991's *Harley Davidson and the Marlboro Man*—a film Rourke openly admits he did just for the paycheck—he showed up in a few films almost every year.

The problem was, well, people just didn't pay to see them (Quick! Name someone who saw *Exit in Red* (1996), *Thursday* (1998), *Out in 50* (1999), *Animal Factory* (2000), or *Masked and Anonymous* (2003)! Can't do it, can you?). But Rourke kept working his scene-stealing magic, snaring a few minutes of screen-time in moderately successful flicks like *Rainmaker* (1997) and *Man on Fire* (2004). Then, in 2005, his star started shining just a little bit brighter.

How much talent does it take to be given a character whose description runs along the lines of "criminal, drunk, disfigured, murdering, beaten down street thug with a face not even a mother could love," and turn it into one of the year's biggest comeback stories? That's what Rourke did in the 2005 Frank Miller/Robert Rodriguez comic-book-to-cinema creation *Sin City*.

He was Marv, a gravelly-voiced go-go bar mainstay who'd somehow scored with the prettiest lady he'd seen in a while (though Jessica Alba was around to give some competition in that department), then found her dead. Firing out classic one-liners all the while ("I love hitmen. No matter what you do to them, you don't feel bad," and "Worth dying for. Worth killing for. Worth going to hell for. Amen."), Marv somehow gets the entire audience behind him as he, for over half an hour, becomes the film's scene-stealing hero.

So it wasn't all surprising that a few years later, Rourke would take a similar route to even greater stardom. . . .

When it comes to the big screen, professional wrestling has long been a dark sheep. Once in a while, there's a decent enough effort, but for every *Nacho Libre* (2006), there's probably about ten *Ready to Rumble*s (2000), and when it comes to drama (i.e., films that try to pass a non-sport off as realistic athletic competition), forget it: remember the 1989 Hulk Hogan . . . thing *No Holds Barred*? Maybe so, but for all the wrong reasons.

So for an actor whose fortunes finally seemed to be turning around, a commonly unpopular film topic might not be a step in the right direction. Then Rourke heard from a filmmaker named Darren Aronofsky.

"I went to see a couple of his films, and I could tell that he was something really special," said Rourke. Aronofsky's 1998 flick *Pi* brought him a directing victory at the nationally renowned Sundance Film Festival, and his *Requiem for a Dream* was found on quite a few top-10 lists for 2000.

"He reminded me of a Coppola, a renegade that marched to the beat of his own drum," Rourke said. "He had the balls to point his finger at me and tell me what he wanted from me."

What Aronofsky wanted was to do what no filmmaker had ever successfully done before—a pro wrestling-based flick that the general public and the critics would appreciate. A film that would show the dark reality of the business that so many people superficially label fake. A character study of those who are only truly at home where they're between the ropes—perhaps even show why wrestling legends like Ric Flair, Roddy Piper, and Hogan himself stay in the business years after they should have unlaced the boots forever.

"No one's ever made a serious film about wrestling," Aronofsky said, "and I think that is because most people perceive wrestling as a joke, and because it's fake, and they sort of write it off."

With so many people clamoring for success in Hollywood, it's never going to be tough to cast a feature film, let alone a mainstream one. Point is, it doesn't take much to hurt a career, because people sometimes have too many options for favorites to really have time to miss someone who fades away. But Aronofsky could see, in every sense of the word, that there was something about Rourke, and Rourke's career, worth caring about for a little longer.

"No one believed in Mickey Rourke . . ." Aronofsky said. "[They said] He has no value as a commodity. Well, I sat with him and looked into his eyes. His eyes aren't dead. They're alive, yearning, thinking. When you meet him, he has all this armour on him, but that's because inside he's soft as jelly and he has such a big heart. He's an incredible actor and completely in control of his craft."

And though Rourke wasn't a wrestling fan at the time, he could already sense a kinship between himself and Randy "The Ram" Robinson, a former big-time sports-entertainment star now lucky to get an autograph request and $50 a shot doing independent shows in armories.

Rourke saw a man who had had it all, lost most of it, and couldn't tell where it had gone or how it had slipped away. He saw a fellow who had once enjoyed fame and fortune, only to realize that it would only last until there was nothing left for the hangers-on to grab hold of. He read a script of a person who just knew he could make someone proud if he just had one last chance.

It wasn't a biography, but it was pretty damn close.

"We'd found someone who was really more in a state of helplessness at the time than me," Rourke said. "It made me think, 'Oh God, I'm glad I'm not him,' but I *was* him. I could have been him."

Ever meet anyone with the attitude of, "Oh, man, wrestling's, like, SO fake! I don't watch that stuff, because it's not real! Those guys never really get hurt or anything!"? Next time you hear that, tell them to step into a ring for five minutes and see—or agonizingly feel—just how fake it is. That's a journey Rourke had to take.

"I had a preconceived idea of how I thought it was," Rourke said. "I couldn't have been more wrong. I looked at wrestling like, it is a pre-determined outcome. It is choreographed. I thought I could do that in a heartbeat."

Then he got the great-grandpappy of all wake-up calls.

"I got in there with the training sessions—which was about a four-month period. I think after the first two months I had three MRIs. These guys aren't only athletes. They're entertainers and athletic. Somebody that's over 230 pounds picks you up and slams you down, something is going to shake, rattle, and roll."

Getting slammed to the mat a few dozen times, jumping off the top rope, doing the flying legscissors like the world's biggest gymnast . . . everyday life for many pro wrestlers became a new nightmare for the game's oldest rookie.

"It was murder," Rourke said. "I walk around at about 192 pounds, and I had to get up to 228 and put muscle on, not fat. I found this trainer, this Israeli ex-commando, and he made it real serious. He's like, 'You gotta be here at this time. You've gotta eat seven meals a day. You have to run every day.' [Darren] wanted me to put on about 30 pounds of muscle. He wanted his pound of flesh." Bodybuilding legend Lou Ferrigno of *Incredible Hulk* fame helped him buff up.

Inside and out, Aronofsky answered.

"My biggest job was just to push, pull, encourage, inspire, challenge . . . for him to really, really dig deep," said the director. "Just sitting with him, you look into his eyes and, you know, his body is just all this armor, and he wears all these outfits, and it's all about keeping people away from looking in his eyes, because the second you look into his eyes . . . there's so much there."

That's the same thing he sees while looking into the hearts of those that hit the ring for sports entertainment fans everywhere.

"I think people basically roll [wrestling] off saying, 'Oh, it's fake,' and they forget all about it," Aronofsky said. "But what was interesting to me was that whole line between real and fake. What is real? What is fake? The film is very clear that wrestling is staged, but is it fake when you're a 260-pound guy jumping 10 feet onto a concrete floor? Even if you're trying to protect yourself and your opponent, damage is happening to you. Then, you meet these guys who've been wrestling [since] 10 or 20 years ago, and they're just riddled with injury. They are true athletes. It's just they're almost more like stunt men, so there's that line of real and fake."

It's a line that was tap-danced on, crossed, and re-crossed in front of thousands back in March 2008; the film's climactic battle was filmed over two nights during intermission of a Ring of Honor promotion event (the entire flick was filmed in just over a month).

"When we did the wrestling scenes, they were actually having real wrestling events and we'd run in real quick with the cameras," Rourke said. "I had to know my shit; my partner had to know my choreography. We had maybe three takes before the next live bout was going to come on. And then there was the pressure of having to pull it off in front of 3,000 crazy wrestling fanatics."

But beyond realism in the ring, there's a strong camaraderie in any wrestling locker room; it's a group of men and women in the same boat, working together not only to put on a good show that night, but to take the next step from 150-people crowds to those of thousands or millions. In *The Wrestler*'s final battle, there's a nod to the brotherhood that exists between those in sports entertainment.

As Randy heads into the last arena of his career (and possibly even more than that, as he'd suffered a heart attack earlier in the flick), he runs into a fellow matster from yester-decade. The fellow turns around, his face lit up like a set of Christmas lights, and shakes Randy's hand like an old fraternity buddy.

It's tough to believe that only a few minutes later—in both film and real time—the two men will be acting like they're beating each other senseless.

"Being a wrestler, it was easy to get into the role, because it was real," said longtime World Championship Wrestling staple Ernest Miller of becoming the Ayatollah, the New York Yankees to Randy's Boston Red Sox. "The character, the Ayatollah, was a retired wrestler who was big at one time, then decided it was time to move on. He went on and started a new career [car dealership]."

Miller could relate; after four years performing as "The Cat" in WCW, he spent time as both an in-ring competitor and color commentator in World Wrestling Entertainment before retiring in 2004.

"It was easy to translate that to the Ayatollah," Miller said. "He's tough on the screen as a character, but outside of the ring, he has a family and another job and everything."

In a wrestling pay-per-view event, a competitor may have to do a backflip off the top rope, piledrive his opponent's head into the ground, or blast his heel into someone's chin to get a strong crowd reaction. On the big screen, however, everyday moves like bodyslams, headscissors, and a single punch can be enough to get a crowd going. Working with both the change in venue and a newcomer to the ring, Miller sat down to write up the film's main event.

"It was real hard, because [Rourke] had never been in the ring and there were a lot of things that he couldn't do," Miller said. "I had to take charge and make it turn out the best that I could, making him look like a wrestler. He threw some things out, saying 'I want to do this.' I did the best I could to make it a good match, so people would feel that he was a great wrestler and make people feel for him. It wasn't just a match; it was telling a story during a match." That's because, as the match winds down, an inner enemy starts to flare up in Randy, and the ending leaves things truly up to the audience.

"People really give a lot to being a wrestler, to entertaining the crowd. Even for the young guys, wrestling's a story," Miller said. "*The Wrestler* may not be their story, but it's a story. I know guys who are wrestlers, were at the top of their game and making millions of dollars. Twenty years later, they're still working in the same ring, the same city, but for a lot less money and less people, in high school gyms and places like that. It's the story of a wrestler."

But it's much more than that; it's story of man whose demons outside the ring hurt him far worse than any backdrop or steel chair to the back ever would. We see Randy attempting a painful reconciliation with his estranged daughter Stephanie (Evan Rachel Wood, who matches Rourke for talent throughout her too-short appearance) and his desperation for love with Cassidy, an ageless stripper who can't reciprocate (Marisa Tomei nabbed her second Oscar nomination for the role). There's his failed attempts to make it in "everyday" life—the painful supermarket scene in which Randy's loudly recognized by an old fan took us inside the pain of those with one-dimensional lifestyles, and brought back some more bad memories for Rourke.

"I begged [Aronofsky] not to do that scene," Rourke said. "because I think it brought up issues of shame with me, because it was too close to the belt. It's like, here is somebody who used to be somebody and now he is working in a goddamned deli. I remember going for several years to the 7-Eleven to get something in the middle of the night. There'd be a line, seven, eight people. Somebody would go, 'Didn't you used to be in . . .'—I'd go, 'Let me get out of here.'"

But the film finally started Rourke's journey back to where he always deserved to be—on the high list of movie stars. And while his first Academy Award nomination fell short to Sean Penn for *Milk* ("An [Oscar] would mean a great deal," Rourke told Barbara Walters before the ceremony. "It would be tremendous. But in the big picture, you can't eat it, you can't [have sex with] it, and it won't get me into heaven."), he knew he could look back at Randy and know he'd given his best.

"It's been way over ten years since I gave everything to anybody," he says. "It was a good feeling at the end of the day. I'd forgotten what it felt like."

And as nice as it was for Rourke to take home the top acting award at the year's Golden Globes, and many other honors besides, a certain group of people at the film premiere gave him an extra verbal high-five—the only people who really had the right to express such an opinion.

Rourke met some stars that wrestling fans of the 1980s grew up watching. He ran into Ric Flair, who won dozens of titles and is generally seen as the greatest in-ring performer of the past half-century. He was introduced to Brutus Beefcake, who headlined pay-per-views in both the World Wrestling Federation and World Championship Wrestling.

"All these guys, the old wrestlers from the 80s, they all came to the premiere. We were nervous because we wanted their approval," Rourke says.

Flair, Beefcake, and others congratulated him. Then Rourke truly saw the effect that his work had had on another wrestling legend.

It was late legend Rowdy Roddy Piper, one of the most well-known and beloved personalities in wrestling history. Aside from Piper's action in the ring, he's commonly considered the most talented performer to make the jump from the ring to the screen, as his starring role in the 1988 John Carpenter alien flick *They Live* is commonly considered not only the best ring-to-screen performance, but one of the most well-done political allegories in recent film history.

As Rourke met Piper, he saw that the legendary mat man had tears streaming down his face. That's when Rourke finally realized that he'd done something especially special.

"I didn't really care too much about what anybody else thought, except for those guys," he says. "I went oh, my god, there is Nature Boy [Flair], and there's Rowdy, and everybody. They came over and said, 'Hey, brother, you are one of us.' I couldn't have been paid a higher compliment."

As his career keeps rolling back up the mountain it nearly topped before, it's something Rourke hopes to hear again.

"I've had two and a half strikes," he says. "I'm not going back to the hell I was living before—no way."

Jennie Russo went back to the Grindsploitation days and into the world of a vengeful vixen in 2016's *She Kills*.

Jennie Russo: *She Kills*

For CERTAIN TYPES OF films, there's a pretty effective rule to follow: if you're not worried about credibility, kill it dead yourself before the critics have a chance to work their dark magic.

You didn't have time or money to dig up great acting, so go the other way—tell your performers to try hard *not* to do their thing. Special effects? Make them cheesy enough for a season of Green Bay football! Don't be afraid to have a plot and screenplay that toss realism straight out the window and even further! Overdo everything in every regard, to the extent that film reels nearly catch fire and microphone-bearing grips topple into the midst of scenes and everyone keeps going! Entire genres have been built with these tools!

Like the one called grindhouse exploitation, collectively as Grindsploitation, that packed in audiences and racked up ticket sales in the 1960s and 70s! About a half century later, a director named Ron Bonk reached out his bottle to re-catch some lightning.

Back in 2007, he produced *Clay*, the tale of a young man and the serial killer he'd become. It marked the film debut of a lady named Jennie Russo. Now Bonk was looking to go all the way back to the Grind, and wanted familiar company.

"Ron asked me to audition, because he knew what he was looking for with one of the characters," Russo recalls. "He knew I could get into the more serious side."

Seriousness is tough to find in the entire genre, and *She Kills* (2016) was nothing of an exception. Or so we viewers thought.

Yes, when Sadie's fiancée finds his head squashed and intestines ripped out by the unthinkably powerful hand of a gangster, who suddenly goes into hysterics along with his colleagues, the gang-rape they visit on her is tough to appreciate for its horrifics, overshadowed by the ludicrousness of the atmosphere. We couldn't have known why Russo almost had said no to Sadie, and how she'd gotten a sense of her character. That it required quite a bit more than anyone might guess would go into such a persona, or such a film.

"There were moments of, 'Do I really want to get involved with this?'" she admits. "But I think what finally made me realize I definitely do is that Sadie gets her revenge. That part of it just felt very empowering, as campy as it is at times, when she's getting her revenge are just powerful moments."

One of her tormentors-come-victims was a lady who just happened to be in the right cosmetic station at the right moment.

"I was doing hair and makeup for people on the set, and one of the actors wasn't able to make it from Virginia," recalls Martha Zemsta, bad gal Beatrice. "They wanted me to fill in for her spot. I haven't done much acting, but I've done some commercials. I thought it would be fun to try."

Perhaps taking out her frustration over having to go through life named Beatrice, the B-Babe watched her boys visit all kinds of pain and suffering on Russo's angel of purity, her topless sunbathing practice notwithstanding.

"I read the script just as I was about to say my lines, and learned as I went," Zemsta says. "I was surrounded by people that were really good at going from one person, then completely being in a new mindset. It came natural to me." Of course, Sadie gets revenge. But not for a while . . .

A trip to a psychic friend—or was it just seduction of the lesbianic kind?—suddenly turns Sadie into Lady Bruce Lee, whaling those who stole her man. But in the first scene, we see just how personal this is, as she rips off a guy's manhood and beats him nearly unconscious with it, and every man watching can feel his testosterone dropping by the nanosecond.

Yup. This isn't going to get cleaner.

With soothing music egging her on and deranged mime makeup across her face, Sadie, now the campish cousin of Eric Draven, ninja-whups a tormentor in a bar and violates him with a bottle/donkey punch combo, and knifes Beatrice in the bargain. Even so, she still looked back at some training from the legendary Lee Strasberg Theatre and Film Institute and her work with interactive theater.

"Finding comedy there [at the theater] was kickass," she remembers. "The martial arts stuff, I learned as we were going along. In 1970s grindhouse films, the actors trained as they went. Physically, I tried to get in better shape; I had to get myself back to not be huffing and puffing through those scenes, and be comfortable in scenes where I'm going to have my clothes off."

Now, with the eyepatch that was prerequisite attire for grindhouse heroes and heroines for decades, it's off to the main mean man's hideout. With sudden pinpoint gun control marks(wo) manship, martial arts, mind control, and another weapon from way down below, Sadie gorily lowers the male population one by one.

"It was fun to just play a badass," Russo says. "I'm not a badass person in real life, but it's fun to play a person so far from us in real life. I'd never done anything like the fight scenes, and ended up with bruises, but I didn't mind." Finally, she finds the leader, the man who stole so much from her and so many others.

How that one ends couldn't possibly be described in a believable sense on a page like this one. Suffice it to say that it shows how beneficial a regular kegal workout could be.

With *She Kills* about finished, Russo finally revealed the story that had given her the saddest, most unwelcome source of strength to take Sadie's revenge. In 2000, while living in Brooklyn, she heard about the man who'd become known as the Greenpoint Rapist, among other names.

One night, as Russo made her way to her apartment, he struck.

"I was blindfolded," she recalls. "I was tied up and raped and gunpoint." For another year, she and the rest of the area lived in fear that he would strike again. He did.

Not until the summer of 2001 was Carlos Ramos captured. Two years later, he was convicted of two rapes and three attempts (probably a fraction of those he committed). When Ramos was sentenced to thirty-five years in prison, Russo spoke at his hearing.

"I did not tell anyone working on the film," she says. "I didn't want to make them uncomfortable. I didn't want them to feel like they needed to be extra careful. When I got the script, it was not just did I want to do this, but could I? Is this making light of rape, turning it into a joke? What made me want to be a part of this was that she gets her revenge, and I felt like I needed that myself. That was what ended up selling it to me: to draw from my feelings, my emotions. It was sort of a cathartic experience."

There's "pretty ugly."

"Civil war."

And "safe sex." At least in the film world, it's as big an oxymoron as any.

Horror has shown this in the multitude ranks, but action's close behind. You'd think that by now, these characters would have figured out that they might just make it through if they could tone down those hormones until a mere millisecond after the closing credits.

You get laid, you get dead, and usually very violently.

You cannot do it in the sack. You must not, *must not*, from the back. You could not, should not in a car. You will not dance beneath the stars.

Somewhere, elsewhere, nowhere at all. Don't have sex.

In 2016, a group of exploitative grinders decided to spell it all the way out. Their film? The slightly un-subtle *Don't Fuck in the Woods*.

"A very catchy title!" remarks Brandy Mason, echoing the sentiment, for better or worse, of probably *everyone* who even glanced over it. "As soon as I saw that, I was interested."

Many of her first few resume lines, with entries from the big and small screen and even the video game world (she showed up in 2012's horror-filled *Fear Fighter*), have paid the same sort of tribute as Russo and the rest of the *She Kills* clan, including a small piece in 2016's also clear-but-redundantly titled anthology *Grindsploitation*.

"It's raw, it's gritty, and it's based off of things that were groundbreaking stuff back in the 60s and 70s," she explains. "I've always found that kind of stuff interesting."

About a year before film fans were watching where *not* to do it in certain film areas, Mason saw a Facebook acting colleague outline the film's casting calls. One friend request later, Shawn Burkett was telling her all about his directive endeavor.

"I sent him a photo and resume, and he sent me a script," she recalls. "He thought it would come easy to me." Let's not pardon a single pun here.

She'd get things going early on in the film. Wearing those huge thick glasses that always signify some serious intellectualism, Meg shows up at a dark campground, ticked off at her boyfriend for one of the infinite number of reasons that men do wrong without a clue as to how.

"I have watched so many horror films since I was young," Mason claims. "I don't think I've ever seen an episode of *Sesame Street* or *Mr. Rogers*; I was watching horror films, studying different actors and actresses."

With Burkett's help, she'd torn the script apart, putting Meg's lines and mentality inside her mouth and mind, and herself in those ominous woods that so often hide a murderous creature far from humanity.

"You do multiple takes, and you're so into the character that you *are* that character," she says. "It's pretty easy. You just do it over and over and practice it."

And if we've seen anything else concerning a film gal with large . . . glasses, there's a) that simply removing them will automatically up her sex appeal a millionfold, and failing that, that b) within the nerdiness we perceive always lurks a sexual dynamo on the edge of exploding forth. Meg's boyfriend is lucky enough to experience the latter, her anger drowning him in serious passion. Soon, the glasses are all she's wearing.

"Doing sex scenes isn't really that hard," says Mason. "I still get super nervous getting nude, but after a few minutes of that, you're just like, 'Ok.'"

As the two start to get crazy, we know the fellow's going to rate this romp as far past the OK level. But we can't forget the film's title (ever!), and we know that the punishment for breaking its rule will be of the capital kind.

Up wanders the film's Grendel stand-in, driven absolutely nuts by such blatant trespassing and disregard for common public courtesy.

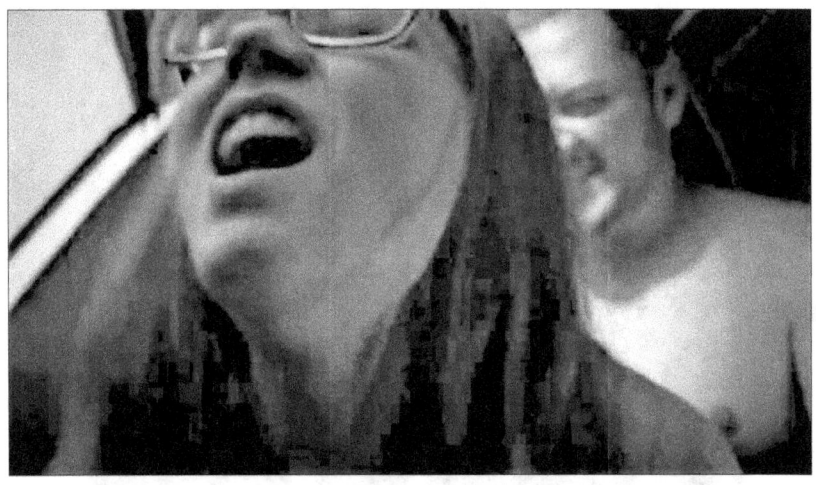

Per usual for the action/horror genre, the erotic adventures of Meg (Brandy Mason) and her boyfriend will soon permanently end for their breaking of the title rule of 2016's *Don't Fuck in the Woods*.

Something splattering across her back (and much more so than if it were the expected fluid!), Meg turns around. There's a hole through her boyfriend, and enough of his DNA is on her to feed a family of vampires.

She rushes out, but just *happens* to trip on something outside. Now there's something upon her, and it's not as entranced by her looks as her guy was. . . .

"If you've had sex before, you can make it believable," Mason says. "But you've never died before, so how can you make that believable? You've been injured and scared, so you use that. If you've ever had a traumatic event, or even had nightmares, you take stuff like that, like when I fell out of a tree when I was a kid. You use that fear and put it into the character."

A group of friends soon follows, including Meg's sister, unaware of the heartbreaking truth. However, they eventually become helpless victims of the obsessiveness of sexuality, and not-so-innocent prey of the creature, soon to be seen as a shorter T-Rex sort of thing (the torment turned real during filming, disrupted by a bee swarm attack).

But of course, one escapes to tell the tale later, and just maybe host *Don't Fuck in the Woods 2: Why Didn't You Listen?*

She was nowhere near big enough to take him on in his familiar pro fighting rings, but Bob Sapp (left, like you had to ask) found an even more dangerous opponent as Stone in *Elektra*, up against Jennifer Garner's title character.

Bob Sapp: *Elektra/Conan the Barbarian*

PEOPLE KEEP WATCHING. THEY keep listening. They keep buying.

And most of all, they keep following.

There's something special about this person, something that makes people want to keep paying attention to him, whatever he does, wherever he goes.

Some people just have *it*. Something that makes them stronger than a magnet when it comes to attraction. We don't always know why, and we really can't. It's just human nature, and in the epitome of unpredictability known as the entertainment world, we just keep seeing it. *Something* makes people want to get behind someone else and follow them around.

In Bob Sapp's case, the line has spread around the globe. It started out in the world of martial arts all over the Orient, then to the music world. Now it's finally starting to follow Sapp back home, here to America.

"There's 196 countries, and I think I've been to 148," Sapp recalls. "The last thing you do when you go overseas is present like you're going to have any problems. In Korea, it's impossible for me to go anywhere. To go four blocks in Japan might take me three or four hours; in Korea, it takes about six to eight!"

Things didn't start out well for the big man from Colorado, and we're not even near his acting career.

He'd *almost* hit it big in the NFL, snaring a spot with Minnesota for two years—playing in all of a single game before being released.

He'd *almost* been something special in the pro wrestling world, training with World Championship Wrestling before—like so many other up-and-comers in the sports entertainment world—losing his shot at stardom when the company dropped in early 2001.

Running out of options, and money, Sapp didn't have time for many more "almosts." Then someone reached across the Pacific Ocean and offered a new shot.

Starting out in one of the sports world's most dangerous games in one's late 20's is all but impossible, but at about six and half feet tall and three bills' worth of pounds, Sapp at least had the physical givings of a mixed martial artist. Searching for its newest phenomenon, Pride, one of Japan's top fighting organizations, hoped Sapp just might be it.

In April 2002, Sapp battered his first opponent straight into a TKO in minutes. Two months later, he did it again to someone else, this time in seconds.

Then something very strange happened.

Sapp's star blasted through Japan with as much force as any mutated lizard ever had. Fans nearly tore the doors off to get into his fights. More tuned into watch on TV than ever before. Even if he wasn't winning—which, admittedly, was more often than he came out ahead—people charged to him, and kept charging.

The endorsement deals poured in like lava. Commercials, interviews, all kinds of deals, appearances everywhere. In a foreign land, the man had become an entertainment entity all his own.

"I did commercials in Japan and Korea, and started to learn the language," Sapp says. "It was hard to remember how to speak English again, I'd been in Japan for so long. It's truly been a blessing in my life. It's been pretty crazy, just from doing sports and entertainment."

In 2003, he moved from Pride over to K-1. "They were worth about $300,000 when I got there," Sapp says. "We reached $8 million in three months. I had to go home once, and they were very, very nervous. I left for a few weeks, and crime went up, and the stock market went down. I went back for a week, and the numbers went back up." He even stepped into the entertainment side of combat, becoming the first black man to win the New Japan heavyweight title and later winning a world title in Korea.

In 2005, an event occurred that nearly shocked the hell out of the sports world. Just after Sapp brought home another K-1 win, he was confronted by a fellow named Mike Tyson. Perhaps still smarting from his planet-shaking loss to Buster Douglas in Tokyo in 1990, Tyson signed with K-1 to hit the mat with Sapp, looking for Japanese redemption.

Unfortunately, citing Tyson's rape conviction and other legal problems, the country refused to grant him a visa. Other proposals came about, but nothing ever happened.

Although sumo wrestling has long been a tradition in the Asian land, men of Sapp's size, rare in America, are just about unheard of in Japan.

"What I do is focus on the similarities, instead of the differences, between America and other countries," Sapp says. "They never really have big guys over there, except the sumo guys. I just sit down and start eating sushi. Americans pass out when they try to eat raw fish, but I am very comfortable eating the Japanese cuisine. You find something new, some similarities, and your whole world changes."

So after all of that, it wasn't much of a surprise for Sapp to roll over into the entertainment business. More endorsement deals came about, then a few small film roles in Japan. Even the music industry came calling.

"I did a lame rap album," Sapp recalls jokingly. "The first 100,000 sold to see if it was good—the second 100,000 sold because it was terrible!"

Finally, it was time to grab a new shot at the American magic. Though he continued to bounce around the globe from one fighting world to another until retiring in April 2014 (time will tell if he follows the fighters' tradition of returning from retiring), Sapp's first film foray came about in 2005.

"I fell into acting from getting popular in Japan," Sapp remembers. "I got popular for doing pro wrestling and fighting, and they started putting me into more and more shows. In acting, you get the ability to make comedy. You learn to get your point across by learning a different language, and using body language. I got to be really good at reading people." After putting on all kinds of shows without speech for years, he'd have to do a similar job in one of his first big roles.

Death has never been much of an inconvenience for superheroes and heroines in the comics and movies, so few were surprised when Elektra showed back up in her own 2005 flick, despite heading six feet down two years before in *Daredevil*. In quite the character shift from General Zod, Terence Stamp became Stick, the blind martial arts master who brings Jennifer Garner's title character back from the dead, giving her a new shot in the "hitwoman" career.

Sapp would be Stone, a henchman of Cary-Hiroyuki Tagawa's crime boss Roshi, looking to eliminate the lady killer. It didn't work; as women in action films have a tendency to do, Elektra managed to somehow come out on top against an opponent whose arms alone probably outweighed her entire body.

"Stone was a big dumb baby," Sapp recalls. "I had to really tell that part. I practiced the role without any speech, doing more and more things with body language and facial expressions."

Just as Americans were about to see him hit the big screen, Sapp discussed his new exploit on Jay Leno's couch. Someone special happened to be watching.

Years after more had gone to see him on the gridiron in *The Waterboy* (1998) than had any other audience for an American football flick, Adam Sandler was putting together another, slightly different story. Different in the sense that it was far from Sandler's typical characters at the time—the man-child act was starting to wear on audiences—but not from sports film history. Decades before, Burt Reynolds had told us the tale of a fellow who loses everything to the dark side of sports, only to find it again in prison.

Sandler may not have had the tough-guy image that Reynolds holds even today, but maybe he could find a new way to travel *The Longest Yard* (2005), and he wanted Sapp's help.

It came down to Sapp going to either extreme on the field. Would he be the big bruiser, the tough guy that he'd tried to be through so many years on the gridiron in real life? Or the weakling, the wimp trapped in an oversized body, the guy whose pitiful attitude can't help but travel all the way over to comic relief?

Just as Richard Kiel had in the original, Sapp took the cowardly way out.

"I knew from fighting that I needed to pick the weakest part," he explains. "I didn't want to be the strongest—nobody's looking at you then."

Not surprisingly, he checked out the original. Shockingly, he also got inspiration from one of Disney's earliest offerings.

"I looked at *Bambi*," Sapp says. "It was heartfelt, and that was what they wanted to see. They wanted to see my eyes tear up a little bit. They put me in a room with a bunch of kids, and I watched how the kids worked and played. I learned from that."

With Reynolds coaching the team he'd played for in the 1974 original—and a cast with Steve Austin, Bill Goldberg, Terry Crews, Brian Bosworth, and otherwise more testosterone than anything since *Con Air*—the film became an exception to the remake rule in Hollywood; while new versions tend to fall short, this one hit hard, bringing in more dough than any other gridiron tale in American history: except, of course, for *The Waterboy*.

"As crazy as the role is, it was the whole crazy USA movie experience," Sapp says. "I had done some movies in Japan, but nothing compared to a Hollywood movie. In HD, in the camera, you can really feel the difference. Japan had taught me patience. I never knew you had to wait so long, waiting for hours and hours. I was happy that Japan taught me that."

In an even bigger rarity, a film about an American sport was a smash in Japan; thanks, at least in a huge part, to the guy who played resident chicken Switowski.

"It was totally incredible," Sapp says. "Sometimes I think, how did I get a chance at Hollywood? I didn't think I'd ever make it!"

A few years later, he came back for another shot at something old. The *Conan the Barbarian* (and *Destroyer*) series had put some fellow named Schwarzenegger on the map decades before. In 2011, a new chapter was added, with Sapp in the game.

He wasn't the title character, although it's certainly interesting to consider how that would have worked out. Jason Momoa was leading the way, with Stephen Lang as Khalar Zym, the warlord looking to destroy Conan and master the art of reincarnation to bring back his dead wife. Sapp played Ukafa, Zym's right-hand man with a sword even more indestructible than Sapp could have ever felt between the ring ropes.

A huge fan of the first *Conan* go-rounds, Sapp set about one of the few forms of combat he had yet to try.

"I was studying stickfighting," he says. "There was a large amount of people that had been there to show me that in Japan. I was practicing with a double-weighted knife."

Then, in the midst of training, his impromptu Japanese homeland was rocked by a tsunami that killed thousands and caused hundreds of billions in damage. Sapp set Ukafa aside for a while to head back to the land where his own sun had risen years before.

"It was a really sad time," he says. "I was asked to come in and smile, brighten them up a little." He performed on a few comedy shows, some of which involved wrestling.

After about a month, he came back to finish *Conan*. When the final cut was called, Sapp went right back to Japan to help out those who'd helped him.

"It was nuts," he recalls. "There were people sleeping in schools, on the ground. There were so many aftershocks. We didn't know what would happen."

All the way back from two careers whose ends came far too soon, Sapp's conquered a few of the toughest tasks in entertainment. Now his new quest continues.

"It's something you look back at," he says, "seeing myself in the movies, where I always wanted to be, it's been great. I love acting. It's crazy, to see everything, in Japan and everywhere where somebody knows me. It really shows the power of the media, it's amazing. It's been a real blessing in my life."

Noodles Aaronson (Scott Schutzman) waves goodbye to his friends, heading off to juvie at about the halfway point of *Once Upon a Time in America*.

Scott Schutzman/Julie Cohen: *Once Upon a Time in America*

OVER THREE DECADES AFTER its emergence in 1984, *Once Upon a Time in America* has never really gotten the recognition, and more importantly, the respect it should. Taking over a decade to put together, one of the world's most well-known directors at the helm, in his unknowingly final work, an exemplary cast; there was no reason the film shouldn't be right up there next to the *Godfather* movies that had already emerged and the Scorsese epics to follow in the ranks of gangster elite.

Until the studios got hold of it.

"The first experience was depressing and devastating," remembers Scott Schutzman of seeing his debut flick for the first time, "as it was for everyone who worked on the movie."

Once Upon a Time in America's distribution company felt that viewers wouldn't be able to appreciate a film of about four hours at a time. Sergio Leone had a bit more faith. Audiences had watched—and appreciated the hell out of!—the films that made him the originator of the whole "spaghetti western" genre. This film took the battles away from six-shooters and saloons and moved them to New York, patrolled by mob men with guns and fists. Leone's first rounds had established a fellow named Eastwood as the quintessential action hero; after passing up the chance to helm 1972's *The Godfather*, he gave a fellow named De Niro a new shot.

Robert was David "Noodles" Aaronson, a gangster nickname not quite as intimidating as The Butcher, The Golden Don, Machine Gun Kelly, certainly not Scarface or even Legs Diamond. Hanging out in the same Manhattan neighborhood that he and the rest of the Jewish gangster crowd put their claws into way back around the anarchic times of Prohibition, Noodles glances through a small hole in a restaurant wall.

And now we're back in the time where America showed the government just how long it would tolerate being forced into sobriety.

When we see Noodles' eyes again, they're a few decades younger. Now they belong to Schutzman.

"I got the movie when I was fourteen," he recalls. "My mother had just died a year before, and I started auditioning for professional roles. My agent called me with a project, saying I had a meeting at a Manhattan hotel." He arrived at a hotel to meet with Leone and Cis Corman, one of the casting world's most underrated names: she'd help find the performers for *Raging Bull* (1980), *Deer Hunter* (1978), *Last Temptation of Christ* (1988), and others.

Others had already been picked.

"I'd been a pro actress since I was about eight," says Julie Cohen, out to become one of Noodles' first gal pals. "My manager sent me on auditions, and when I heard who the director was, I was like 'Oh, *Fistful of Dollars*!' From a spaghetti western to a Jewish gangster movie, it sounded promising."

The Broadway veteran arrived at a Manhattan townhouse, expecting to run into a secretary, or maybe Corman. Instead, Leone stepped out.

"I auditioned while he had breakfast," she says. "He spoke with me through an interpreter. It was playful and fun. He was like Santa Claus. He didn't see anybody else."

It took Schutzman slightly longer.

"I first met with Sergio at the hotel," he says, "and then I didn't hear anything for months. Then I met with Corman and read scenes. Three times a month, I'd go in and read for her. She'd give me directions." Then he found out who was playing the older Noodles.

"When I found out Robert De Niro was going to be the lead," explains Schutzman, "I didn't remember anybody else in the movie. The reason I wanted to be an actor [was] because I wanted to be talked about. I wanted people to think about me. People in Middle America, in their homes, around the dinner tables, what they talked about was Robert De Niro. I thought people's lives revolved around what actors were doing, and I wanted to be the one they were talking about."

As Cohen's journey had begun and ended at a townhouse, Schutzman's spent some time in similar settings.

"It all culminated with an audition at Ruth Gordon's apartment," he remembers (yes, the same Gordon who'd won an Oscar in 1968 for *Rosemary's Baby* and torn it up three years later in *Harold and Maude*). "We had to show up wearing period clothing, costumes that reminded us of 1920. We were there for hours with Sergio." He and the rest of the gangsters-in-puberty, the younger forms of De Niro, James Woods' Max Bercovicz, and everyone else stepped back in time and into street war.

"Corman was coaching me, and her main note was 'Be that! You have to be a mean dirty punk. More violent!'" Schutzman says. "But that wasn't the end." The group morphed up to Montreal.

"Sergio had to have one last little twist in the story," he says. "They told me I was very close to getting the part, but they were doing a final screen test. All the young actors who were being considered, we took photos and tried different costumes to see how we all looked together as a group." But Leone might have had just a few tricks up his clipboard all along, a sort of preparation that no one knew they were receiving. . . .

Schutzman made it through hours of testing facial moles to match De Niro's. He tried on hundreds of hats, as Noodles' head would be covered for much of the film. Finally, the young actor had had about enough.

"I'm a fourteen-year-old little punk," he says, not ashamed. "I went to Sergio and asked him if I had the part." Leone's translator put the words into his language. The director stared nearly through the kid.

"Sergio looked at me for what felt like a minute, but it was probably only about three seconds," Schutzman says. "He squinted at me, and slowly nodded his head up and down.

"They told us we had to film our first scene tomorrow."

After so many months, so much rehearsal, so much line memorization and makeup tricks, the group had all of a day to get the rest of the way into character. If that had been Leone's plan—train the group until the mentality of the times made it into them, perhaps known only to him—it might have just worked.

"We did the scene where we burn down the newsstand," Schutzman says. "It was a very easy film to shoot: my one line in the whole scene was 'Here's your money, sir.'"

Then it was down—way down!—to Brooklyn, telling the early tales of Noodles, Max, and the relationship that turned them into a little Jewish mob to be reckoned with (Rusty Jacobs played the young Max).

"The audition process was so long," Schutzman says, "that as the momentum grew, all I thought about was that character. Once you're on the set of a Leone movie, once you put the costume on, you're there in the moment. Sergio tells you exactly what he wants to do. Often, he would act out the role for you."

One day, Noodles meets his young gal pal Peggy, one of the youngest "friends with benefits" relationships in film history. That was Cohen.

"You take whatever role you are given," she explains. "It's hard to make a living. You don't get to choose your roles until later, and most actors are willing to do anything for a paycheck. I was lucky to get a great part in such a great movie. I started hearing De Niro and James Woods' names, and I thought, 'Holy shit, I'm going to be in a big movie!'" While Schutzman had been moving up through the ranks of potential Noodles-es, she'd been studying Peggy's side scenes. She'd also turned eighteen between getting the role and filming it, which turned out to be legally fortuitous for Peggy's most memorable scenes of her youth.

There's a cop named Whitey, with apparently nothing better to do than harass the young gangsters in the course of their jobs. The boys not-so-affectionately nickname him "Fartface," which seems very diplomatic compared to what most cops get labeled today. But the White man (longtime character actor Richard Foronjy) has a weakness for youth, which is Peggy's secret way of making her own dime.

Julie Cohen began the transition from child to grownup star as Noodles' girlfriend Peggy.

The kids catch Whitey in the act, and Peggy doesn't seem to mind. A few illicit snapshots write Whitey's job's death warrant . . . unless he promises to lay off the kids and put them on the cut.

"It was challenging to do nudity and sexual situations," Cohen remembers. "I had to be bold and brave and just go for it, so I dove in and took a lot of risks. Richie Foronjy was so kind and helpful. I felt very safe and cared for."

Making her way through an awkward scene, Cohen noticed an older gentleman looking over her work.

"I thought it was my dad," she remembers. "Then I realized it was Robert De Niro in old-age makeup. I was really nervous, but he said I looked really beautiful. It meant a lot to me, as a young actress taking a lot of risks."

Peggy might have grabbed Noodles' libido, but his heart belonged to Deborah, a ballerina that first grabbed his attention through a back room wall hole, just as the elder Noodles looked through it early in the flick.

She was a debuting Jennifer Connelly, two years from *Labyrinth* (1986) and nearly two decades from an Oscar for *A Beautiful Mind* (2001).

"I was a horny kid who thought he was all that," Schutzman theorizes. "I had this swagger. It was how Sergio was pushing me. I was pretty obnoxious in real life, and I had a chip on my shoulder the size of Mount Rushmore. Jennifer was from a very well-off Long Island family, and they were a little snooty. Jennifer thought she was all that, because she had been a model and was more established than I was. The casting was kind of perfect; she annoyed me, because she was kind of aloof and snotty, and the sarcasm we had with each other was already built in."

Before anything goes anywhere, however, outside forces intervene in the form of a nearby group of youngsters who want their own control. Fists and bullets fly, Noodles' friend dies, and he puts a knife into an enemy youth and a cop, sending him behind bars for a decade. By the time he's out, he's De Niro.

"That scene was five days of no cameras, just working with professional stuntmen, choreographing the movements." Schutzman remembers. "It's tough to act like you're getting hurt, to have the shit beaten out of you, then to do it over and over and over again. Fatigue set in, not only to be a good actor, but to have incredible stamina, to be good for a long, long time. Sergio didn't like to do one take; he liked to do twenty takes."

Getting much closer to the stoicism that had won him an Oscar for *Godfather 2* (1974) than the psychotic rage that scored another for *Raging Bull* six years later, De Niro made Noodles into the intellectual type, slipping into violence only a few times.

"Sergio showed me how to think on screen, to contemplate on screen," Schutzman says. "Noodles was always the brains of the operation, and that was so not me. I was very impulsive, flying off the handle. De Niro wanted to show another side of himself, so he went for more the internal, levelheaded type of character, except for the rape scenes where he does lose it." One of them is upon the adult Deborah (Elizabeth McGovern), who ends up with Woods' Max—although film conspiracy theorists claim that everything after 1934 in the film was a combination of Noodles' imagination and some outside substances.

If that were the case, Peggy would have ended up as a Manhattan madam, in Amy Ryder mode.

"I only met her a couple of times," Cohen says. "She sang at the same cabaret clubs that I did. She was cast to match me, which was good for my ego." Schutzman says he only met with De Niro a few times as well.

After all the hard work they'd done, the time and effort they'd spent, *Once*'s cast and crew felt they were part of a classic. At least some thanks. Hopefully a little recognition. Just what was coming to them. Only fairness.

Not to have their project mutilated by a group of people convinced that they knew what audiences wanted better than anyone else, a group of folk whose only job was releasing the film, and chose to overstep their boundaries by a mile.

The Ladd Company had established itself over the first part of the decade, giving out 1981's Best Picture *Chariots of Fire* and the sci-fi classic *Blade Runner* the next year. Clearly, they felt they knew how much *Time* America would want.

Even better that those who'd designed it from beginning to final cut.

First off, they went Freddy Krueger on the final cut. Leone had planned his flick to be above to four mark, and been persuaded partway through the lower it. Ladd stepped in and chopped out nearly another hour and a half.

Then they rearranged it. *The Godfather* flicks had shown that flashbacks can be effective, even necessary to the flow of a successful film; Ladd didn't think so, putting things back into the boring world of "linear-ality."

It's probably the first time in history that a 135-minute film can be called superficial, but Ladd managed to make the wrong kind of history.

"They chopped it up like Swiss cheese," Schutzman recalls, "after all the work we had put into it. It wasn't Sergio's movie anymore. It was like an extended trailer for the film."

Critics brought the bad news, railing against the film with more veracity than all of its death and violence put together. Leone and his crew could only watch helplessly as audiences stayed away.

It took months for anyone in America to see Leone's final project—his *own* project. And people loved it. Critics called the redone and certainly improved *Once* one of the top films of the year.

Unfortunately, the film's release and editing kept it from finding a place at the Oscars. Even sadder, Leone wouldn't get to make another film, passing in April 1989 (Eastwood dedicated his 1992 Oscar for directing *Unforgiven* to Leone).

"It was very sad," Schutzman remembers. "With so much expectation, to know you're working on something that's a grand piece of art, and to have it be ruined like that. There are a lot of people whose careers would have been different in movie had been released in full." With Martin Scorsese's help, Leone's family was able to release a 251-minute version of the film to homes in September 2014.

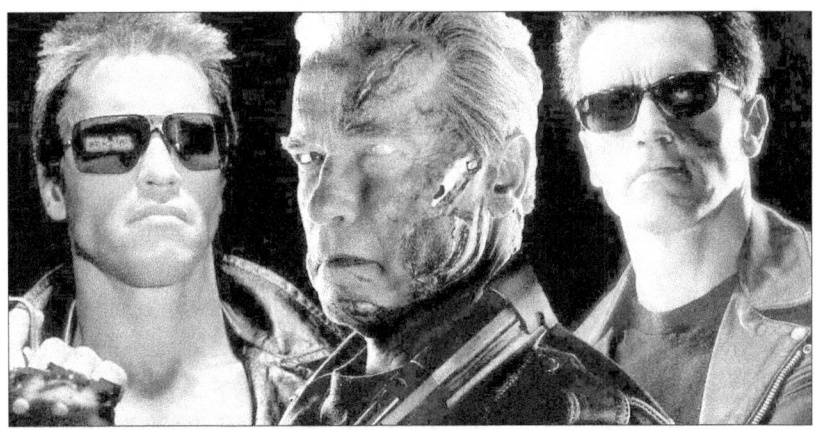

Through three decades and five films, Arnold Schwarzenegger made the *Terminator* series into one of the most legendary in American history.

Arnold Schwarzenegger: *Terminator* films

WHAT EXACTLY MADE ARNOLD Schwarzenegger into the quintessential action star? What made his name and face synonymous with the art of asskicking?

His unusual name, which has been a household moniker for decades? That might have helped his legacy, but name value only lasts for so long, and can die off at high speed if there's a negative connotation attached to it (it's why we feel sorry for people with the last name of Manson or Bundy).

His physique? Impressive to be sure, but there's bodybuilders all over the world.

The fact that he turned a 74-word performance into a symbol of one of Hollywood's top careers? That he, as so few of his colleagues dare to do, had the nerve to express a solid opinion in the cutthroat world of politics, marrying into one of America's most well-known political families, then turning out a career from the other direction (Aside from Maria Shriver, how many other women can claim to be both the niece of a Democratic president and a Republican first lady?). His natural charisma, likeability as a person?

Now we're getting somewhere. And also, maybe we love Arnold (for this profile, I'm sticking with the first name to save typing time) because of the guts he showed.

Not just against the monsters, machines, even Satan himself, and the rest of the enemies he so heroically fought till the director yelled "Cut!" But because it would have been so easy for him to be stereotyped; a deep accent and huge physical stature have ruined, or at least limited, many a career, and early in Arnold's career—before Conan, *Commando* (1985), and anything else—he ran into many of the same obstacles.

"I see agents," he complained to an acting teacher in the early 80s. "They say, 'Your accent is too heavy. You're too big.'"

But even with two strikes against him, Arnold took a big swing at the plate, and hit a homer. He taught actors of the past and future that desire can get a person to the top, and a special type of drive keeps them there. Many have had the talent to succeed in Hollywood, but have made the subconscious choice not to, because it seems too hard, or takes too long. But Arnold simply looked at what he had to work with, and never stopped accentuating the positives.

"I don't care if I ever become an actor," he says. "I'm going to be a star, and everyone is going to know the name Schwarzenegger." He became the fellow often known quite simply as *Ah-nuld*.

His first venture into *Conan*-land in 1982 gave Arnold a personality, a way to develop his screen presence and charisma that none of his first five films had. Then, two years later, he stepped into movie lore as the representative of Skynet, a mechanical race that starts the war to end all humanity.

Call it either a coincidence or an example of lottery-victory-type luck, but O.J. Simpson was *this close* to being signed as the Terminator before Arnold got the role—imagine what a disaster that would have ended up becoming! Whether that's what Director James Cameron (himself still on the outside of filmmaking) actually wanted is unclear, but he didn't seem to see the Austrian muscleman as his personal T-800 killing creation.

That is, until they met for lunch.

"For half an hour," Arnold recalls, "I told [Cameron] how the Terminator should act." Despite showing early interest in the role of heroic Kyle Reese, Arnold wanted to be the killing machine.

Cameron was shocked.

"Well, there goes this 'Blow This Up Over Creative Differences' scenario," he recalls.

Over the next few months, Arnold thought about how to become the inhuman.

"The thing that I learned from my acting teacher . . . was not to act, but to be," he says. "I envisioned the character and what his moves will be."

Since machines *do* instead of *perform*, how to *be* in this case would require something far different than Conan's superhero-hood.

"If this guy really is a machine, he won't blink when he shoots," Arnold pontificates. "When he loads a new magazine into his gun, he won't have to look because a machine will be doing it, a computer. When he kills, there will be absolutely no expression on his face, not joy, not victory, not anything."

But Arnold's preparation for this role had, as is often the case, begun far before he started acting; the stealth-like stoicism he exhibited while roaring to the top of the world's bodybuilding contests is the same one that helps "I'll be back," (he wanted the line to be "I will be back," as the contraction seemed too human and unthreateneing) slip a big toe over the line from dispassionate to fearsome. He furthered this as Conan (both as *the Barbarian* and *Destroyer*), training himself to never even consider blinking while looking death in the eye—a warrior isn't afraid of death; a machine can't be.

And for those who think it might be easy to play without having to show any emotion, much facial expression, or voice alterings . . . well, Arnold found that that's not the case either.

"Because I was playing a machine," he explains, "I had to sound like a tape recorder without giving off human reflections. I could not pause."

Early on, a desperate Reese tries to explain the situation to damsel in distress Sarah Conner (Linda Hamilton, in another star-making performance).

"It doesn't feel pity!" he cries. "Or remorse! Or fear!"

Or anything else, for that matter. When Reese wastes him with a machine gun at a nightclub in their first run-in, Arnold couldn't show pain. He had to blast the hell out of a police station and walk through doors of fire without fear, without surprise, without hesitation. He had to be able to load a gun without looking at it—after all, that's what Terminators are programmed to do, and they can't think for themselves.

Though a stint in the army of his Austrian homeland had taught him to clean and assemble weapons blindfolded, Arnold spent more months training at shooting ranges with every kind of firearm he could locate, studying not only how to use them, but how to act if they were being used around him. Machine guns, rifles, revolvers, even the occasional grenade became commonplace to him (FBI agents showed up on set to guard the film's Uzi). He traveled to Los Angeles' worst areas to get a feel for the area, learning how to brave the dangers of life without so much as glancing from side to side.

Perhaps the best thing about *Terminator* is its simplicity. The storyline of a hero protecting the lady from a much larger, stronger baddie. The dialogue—again, Arnold has just 74 words. The costume: Arnold's leather jacket and sunglasses would become legendary. The simplest ideas often work the best in filmmaking, and very few filmmakers show this as effectively as Cameron, Arnold, and the rest of the crew did.

Film audiences loved it, often cheering more for the machine than for his prey. *Time* called it one of the top 10 films of 1984, and it finished in the same list for box-office success. From then on, it was full-blown good guy mode for the man from Austria, leading the fight against aliens (1987's *Predator*) and evil scientists (1990's *Total Recall*), and even managing to squeeze in a few right crosses in the comedic means (1988's *Twins*, 1990's *Kindergarten Cop*).

So as the last decade of the 1900s rolled toward them, Cameron approached his action colleague with an offer to put together a step back into machinery. At first, Arnold leaned toward becoming a bad guy again for *Terminator 2: Judgment Day* (1991)

"I have to terminate," Arnold maintained when Cameron told him of his self-contradictory role as the protector of Sarah's pre-teenage son John (Ed Furlong), who'd grow up to save the world from the machines. "That's what the audience wants to see: me kicking in the doors, machine-gunning everybody... that's the character."

Cameron won out, with some modifications; Arnold would still get to kick in doors, fire people around like dolls, and even do his NRA audition. But this time, his opponent would be the evil T-1000 (Robert Patrick), one quite a bit more advanced than the T-800 himself (in pre-production, officials had actually considered having Arnold play both roles). Being able to automatically recover from wounds (the special effects for *T2* were simply mind-rocking for the time) and take the shape of people and objects it touches, the evil force made audiences see Arnold, for the first time in his career, as the underdog. He'd also attempt to make a machine more human, trying to make sense of the weird sounds of "Hasta la vista, baby," and other slang-ology.

Arnold spent months preparing for the chase scene where the Terminator chases a mack truck through a drainage canal, whipping his huge shotgun around and firing it with deadly accuracy like this stuff is everyday for him—or it.

"I couldn't wear a glove because it would get stuck in the gun mechanism," he remembers, "and I tore the skin off my hand and fingers practicing a hundred times until I mastered the skill. Then I had to do it while riding the Harley. Then I needed to put the riding and the gun skill together with the acting. It's hard to watch where you're driving and look where the director wants you to look at the same time." After everyone made it through the first film in six weeks, *T2* took eight months to shoot.

Arnold even got to stand on the top of a building, methodically destroying an army of police vehicles. But for one of the only times in his cinematic career, he didn't take a life, even being hilariously forced by John to place his hand in the air and taking a makeshift oath that, "I swear I will not kill anybody."

The film, which by itself sold over half the total amount of tickets at American movie theaters during Independence Day weekend of 1991, turned out to be a landmark, not just for action flicks, but moviemaking in general. The early image of Arnold, right back in his jacket and sunglasses, riding a motorcycle around Los Angeles searching for John will live forever in the minds of film fans.

The plainness of the screenplay and storyline that worked so well in the first film are equally effective; the whole "hero bravely protecting the vulnerable from a powerful enemy" is here to work, and Arnold's new simple lines, "Hasta la vista, baby," and "Trust me," would join "I'll be back," on the list of legendary film quotes. Still, few action films even attempt to touch the human heart the way *T2* did, with an emotional storyline that even dramas and romances rarely get anywhere near.

And perhaps that's what has truly kept the man from falling into the typecasting pitfalls that so many of his action hero contemporaries have: that he not only turned a manufactured killer into a leading "man," but later managed to incorporate a heart into something that wasn't even human.

Sara, who Hamilton—with the help of thrice-a-day physical training for months—developed into a fighting machine in the second flick, has two quotes that truly sum up the effect (much more special than artificial limb regeneration) of both the Terminator and the "man" he was. About midway the film, she watches her son trying to teach his alloyed ally how to be "cool" through the eternal act of high-fiving.

"Watching John with the machine, it was suddenly so clear," she says. "The Terminator wouldn't stop. It would never leave him. It would never hurt him or shout at him or get drunk and hit him or say it was too busy to spend time with him. And it would die to protect him. Of all the would-be fathers that came over the years, this thing, this machine, was the only thing that measured up. In an insane world, it was the sanest choice."

The second comes at the end, after the Terminator saves John from the villainous T-1000, then forces Sarah to help him self-terminate—how many of us ever thought that the cinematic loss of a machine would bring us to tears?

"The unknown future rolls toward us," she muses, sounding sad and uncertain but upbeat. "I face it for the first time with a sense of hope—because if a machine, a Terminator, can learn the value of human life . . . maybe we can too."

It's that sort of thing that set the *Terminator* series apart, that truly made it stand out from all the explosion-based, four-letter-word-dropping, special-effects-dominated action flicks that allow their storylines to get lost in the mix; it had a human story that few could have pulled off. (to be fair, Arnold's third go-round as the machine, 2003's *T3: Rise of the Machines*, was little more than a superficial combination of the first two flicks, as Arnold saved John (now Nick Stahl) from Terminatrix beauty Kristanna Loken, and 2009's Christian Bale mishap *Terminator: Salvation* was an attempt to suck the last few drops of blood out of a rock). *Terminator: Genisys* (2015) turned John Connor into the bad guy and made Sarah Conner into Emilia Clarke's much younger and smaller form, and it was a decent watch, but injecting comedy and lightening things to a PG-13 rating took away some of the emotion established in the first two films.

So let's go back to the beginning—why has *Ah-nuld* remained such a popular force on and off the screen for so long, while so many of his action co-stars have faded? It's a question without a sure answer—ask a few hundred people, and chances are, there might be three figures of thought out, credible answers. But according to someone with quite a bit more credibility in the field than I'll ever have, it might just all go back to there being a little Terminator inside us all.

"I think people root for him," says Cameron, "because there's some little chittering demon down in the back of everyone's mind that would like to be him for about two minutes—to go in and talk to the boss without using the doorknob."

Arnold may be the only performer who can lay claim to appearing in all the *Terminator* films, but only one fellow can boast of showing up as the same *character* three different times. While Arnie played five different robots, Earl Boen had the tough task of showing up three times in just under twenty years—all as Sarah Connor's non-malicious nemesis Dr. Silberman.

The December before filming began on part one, Boen bumped into a pair he'd worked with years before on 1980's *Battle Beyond the Stars*, with none other than the infamous Roger Corman behind the camera.

Dr. Silberman (Earl Boen) can't believe his lying eyes as the T-1000 approaches in *Terminator 2*.

"I saw Gale Anne Heard at a Christmas party," he remembers. "Then James Cameron walked up and said they had worked on a script, and wanted to start shooting [in] January or February." Boen, who'd been acting everywhere since the mid-1970s, asked if there might be a spot for him in the cast. Cameron said maybe.

After the holidays, the two met at Cameron's house, and Boen checked over the script. "I couldn't stop reading, which is unusual," he says. "I told Jim that if he shot this as he'd written it, he'd have a major hit. This thing was relentless, very classically constructed." Cameron asked if he'd want to be the cop doctor, the one who interrogates Kyle Reese about this thing called Skynet and its destruction of humanity.

"My take on [Silberman] was that the guy is very good at what he does," Boen explains, "but after doing it for so long, he was like 'Oh God, another loony at 3 a.m., and I have to get up!'" Hence his scientific diagnosis of Reese to Sarah: "In technical terminology, he's a loon!" Filming took less than two weeks, but Boen could feel the Terminator's power.

"You're on a set, and the crew guys say they smell a monster hit," he says. "It just came out and blew everybody away."

He'd show up on just about every show on TV over the next few years, including some voice work that would start to come in serious handy later on.

Then came another call from his agent, who'd been rung up by Cameron again. Another sit-down discussion occurred—a very quick one.

"He asked if I'd be interested in doing Silberman again," Boen says. "I said, 'Oh yes.'"

Cameron said the new version would be quite a bit deeper (remember, Hollywood trusted him with quite a bit more green than it had the first time), and *much* darker. Silberman's sarcasm would be around again, but less of it.

"You have to be flexible and fly by the seat of your pants based on the moment," he explains, "because if [the director] doesn't like it, you've got to have a B-plan and probably a C-plan. You just try to do exactly what they want, because they've got a clearer idea than you have. You are the script—one hundred percent if you can, and 99.9999 percent if you can't. Don't start rewriting the script."

Well, to a small extent, Cameron allowed him to. Directors are more apt to do that for performers that show up ready to go.

As Silberman, now running the show at Pescadero State Hospital, explains the plight of one of his most infamous "clients," we see Sarah, now looking like she's days away from an Ultimate Fighting Championship ring war.

"How's the knee?" she sarcastically queries, disrupting his pompousness.

When first written, the script just had Silberman explaining that Sarah had stabbed him. He called Cameron aside to ask for a little elaboration.

"I said, 'James, what did she use to stab me? They don't keep knives and forks in psychiatric hospitals,'" Boen explains. "The only thing I could think of is my pen." Hence the doc's line, "She stabbed me in the knee with my pen a few weeks ago."

"It's funnier that way," Boen says. "Little things like that don't really seem to mean anything, but they're funnier if they're specific." He did get some smartassery in as well—remember his snarky, "Model citizen!" mutterance after Sarah attacks?

Later on, Silberman is finally convinced that Sarah's Terminator soothsayings were correct all along. Hampered by an arm that Sarah broke, he's barely able to stand, helped along by an injection of something that must have been pretty strong.

Then the T-1000 walks, literally, through a set of bars. The needlecap falls from Silberman's gaping mouth.

"That was awestruck horror!" he describes. Sarah and the T-800 manage to escape, but the original script had Silberman loaded into a straightjacket and hauled off, blithering the same supposed gibberish that had landed Sarah in the cell to begin with! It wasn't done—and if it had been, the doctor might not have been able to show back up for a cameo in 2003's *Terminator 3*! Boen had dropped the curtain on his own acting career right around then, but the chance to make the third time a charm was too much to resist (video game fans still hear him today, voicing the *World of Warcraft* series and other games).

With Sarah dead, the cops follow Arnold's machine to her grave to grab some weaponry. Katherine Brewster (Claire Danes), destined to become Mrs. Connor, still isn't sure what the hell's going on. Silberman shows up with the cops, but it's déjà vu all over again, and he, now knowing the sad, dark truth, runs off in a panic.

"They made me a decent offer, with the money," Boen says. "They gave me a car and driver, and said I'd only have to work for four or five days. I'd never had that before." He might have been killed in the Judgment Day that occurred at the end of Part Three, or maybe not, assuming *Genisys* averted it.

Then, of course, there's the chance that Sarah *was* right, that Cameron was right, and that Judgment Day is still rolling toward us. As society puts more and more trust in technology, there's more and more chance that humans will give away too much.

"James knows that there are threats there, and they're finding that now," Boen says. "If we're not careful, we're going to make ourselves obsolete. There's little indications all over the place. We don't need many people anymore; we've embraced technology to the point of insanity. We worry that kids aren't making eye contact or personal contact, always on their computers or cell phone, talking like robots. I'm very wary of technology taking over. You've got this killing machine that wants to erase us from the Earth because we're a pain in the tush. That's just my opinion."

Jimmy Conway (Robert De Niro) welcomes Henry Hill and Tommy DeVito (Christopher Serrone, left, and Joseph D'Onofrio) to the gangster fold early in *Goodfellas*.

Christopher Serrone: *Goodfellas*

BASEBALL PLAYER.
   Actress.
   Musician.
   Doctor.
   President of the United States, or even Grand High Ruler of the World.
   Ask some kids what they'd like to be when the perils of adulthood descend, and there are quite a few answers you expect. But children of a few decades before, especially in a few specific areas of Old Glory, had something else to talk about. Fellows like Al Capone might have had to break all the rules and more than a few skulls to get there, but the life that mafia men like him ended up with was all kinds of envious to many.
   Tons of money, gorgeous women at the snap of the fingers, not a single rule or law to follow . . . sounds like Utopia, especially for those too young to really grasp the concept of consequence. So when we hear the first narrated words of *Goodfellas* (1990), listening to film focal point Henry Hill describe his childhood ambition to end up as a member of one of the world's oldest families, we know he's not the only one.
   However, also for Capone and many like him, the lifestyle of luxury—and life itself—didn't last for very long. When it comes to organized crime, what goes up almost always comes straight down, and quite often it doesn't stop until it's even further south than when it started,

like ending in the number on the right side of a tombstone's dash. That's what so many of Hill's colleagues end up finding out, and he himself loses about everything *but* his life. The lifestyle seems like a dream, but every dream ends, and sometimes with a painful wakeup call.

Still, Hill stays above the law for more years than many in the business. The fellow who personifies him before Ray Liotta takes over started out with just as lucky a break.

He'd had a hell of a time in school plays, but Christopher Serrone was getting a bit tired of watching his family members hang onto the performance limelight.

"I had a couple of cousins involved in the industry, models and aspiring actors," remembers the New York native. "I kind of sat back and watched it all." He'd gotten into modeling, but acting didn't seem like the most realistic goal.

After a tough day before a still camera, Serrone was recuperating in his agent's office, waiting for the gentleman to finish out a phone call. It would take some time; the agent was hearing a casting representative's worst nightmare.

A friend was describing a search that had dragged her and her crew across America. Not just there in the Apple, but all the way over to Chicago, and even to Los Angeles. The group was looking for an actor that could hardly hope to stand out—he'd be sharing the screen with some of the biggest names in the business—but would be the prologue performer in a piece that everyone knew would be huge.

The agent asked what she was looking for. Sitting across the table, Serrone watched his agent's eyes start to enlarge.

"She said that wanted someone who was about yea tall, *this* young, with *this* kind of look," Serrone says. "Streetwise, but not too streeting. Kind of Italian, but not overly." He's only half; Serrone's father is from Italy.

The agent somehow knew that the solution was a few feet away. He sent Serrone on his way.

"He looked at me, saw his eyes getting bigger and bigger. Said, 'I thik I'm looking at him. I can send him over right now.'

"At this moment, I'm in my modeling clothing," Serrone remembers. "It's even more than your Sunday best. These clothes are bought by your parents for only wearing on a modeling audition."

They'd become innocent victims; on his way to the tryout, Serrone brutalized his flannel shirt. Channeling the spirit of the legendary novel *The Outsiders*, a virtual Bible for kids his age, he tore a hole in his jeans and doused his hair with gel. With just a little modeling experience, less formal training, and absolutely nothing on the auditioning level, he knew it was all about looking the part.

Just an hour after finding out that the film was even in the planning stages, he was trying out for it. Lines, readalongs; it was a tryout.

"When I left, I didn't feel confident, but then I had nothing to compare it to," he says. "I was kind of bummed out, walking around."

Then his beeper went off (yes, there was a very long part of American history where portable phones weren't the necessities they are today!). Serrone found a pay phone and called back.

"My agent told me that they had loved me," he says. "The first thing I said was thank God, because my mom was going to kill me for messing up the outfit!"

But he was far from *Fella*-ship; the callback process stretched out to over half a year.

"I went back at least twenty times as the pool got smaller and smaller," he says. "I'm twelve years old, I should be worrying about if I did my homework or writing a book report. This was nerve-racking, the first time I ever felt under the gun. My parents did what they could to give me a proper childhood: family first, school first."

As he made one cut after another, Serrone met more and more of the crew. Then one day, he stepped in to meet the man who'd be behind the camera.

"I didn't really know too much about him," he recalls. "Most of his films, I wasn't really allowed to watch due to my age. I'd watched a very, very closely screened version of *Raging Bull*, with a *lot* of fast-forwarding and pausing."

Perhaps sensing his charge's nerves, Martin Scorsese pushed formality aside and asked that Serrone called him Marty. The youngster felt his fear disappear.

"I read the script, and he gave me direction," Serrone says. "Then he gave me a little more. I thought I was screwing up, but then I came to find out that's what directors do to try to get as many ways out of you as they can. He told me he was impressed and shook my hand."

Soon enough, he'd hang out with future co-star Joe D'Onofrio (despite the unusual name, he's not related to longtime character actor Vincent) . . . and a man named De Niro.

"We didn't even read the script that day," Serrone says. "We just talked for about an hour, getting to know each other. It was a positive that I didn't have full scope as to who De Niro was. I consider myself an actor, but that man is like the Super Actor, the God of Acting."

Soon after, Serrone as his family were in church for Good Friday. Back home, his agent had blown up the answering machine with screeched messages.

Deciphered, the result was a bit clearer: Serrone would indeed be the young Henry.

Now it was time to learn about the same history that had made Henry want to get mobbed.

"My dad was born in Queens and there was a strong Italian community there," Serrone says. "He took me around to guys he knew. I listened to stories about guys who were the power in the neighborhood back in the early 50s and 60s. One guy flat out told me how they would wait for stores to close, then clean them out when the [storekeeper] was in the parking lot warming up his car." He also got a handle on Henry's sneakiness, laying low for lone (without the parents!) views of previous mob cinematic masterpieces like *Godfather* and *Scarface*.

While Serrone was being cast, the crew was pursuing a top-lister for the lead. Enveloped in the busy workload that so many upcoming performers hope for, he almost wasn't available. But a few weeks after Hill's younger self was picked, his "current" form came about.

Liotta. Now, Serrone would meet the man he'd pretend to grow up to be.

"I had three occasions to get to know him," Serrone says. "I followed him around all day. We ate lunch and I watching him do his thing. He asked me if there was anything I repeated, like nervous tics. He said I looked like his yearbook picture, so he nicknamed me Yearbook."

Famous for his devotion to continuity, Scorsese spent five figures on contact lenses to turn Serrone's brown pupils to Liotta's crystal blue, all for a few close-ups.

Some scenes, however, required a hell of a lot more than just props. Early on, Henry starts acting out the stories Serrone heard from his old neighbors, sharpening his skills in thievery, vandalism, and even auto arson.

"That's where acting comes in," Serrone says. "A lot of the situations that we're going to encounter in the script, we've never done personally. That being said, you still have to find the truth in it . . . about the cars, I worked until about two in the morning. I did my own stunts, and there was real dynamite in the cars. I was loving life."

Henry starts skipping school to hang out with D'Onofrio's young Tommy DeVito, De Niro's Jimmy Conway, and the rest of the local crew.

Then his dad (Beau Starr) suddenly finds out, and shows his faith in physical discipline.

When he was young, Serrone says, "I had a belt on my butt. If I talked back, I knew I was going to get a belt. My dad never hit me in the face like I was in *Goodfellas*. I had padding on my back during the scene."

But Hill proves his worth, and doesn't even have to get jumped into the gang. There's an awesome scene where Jimmy congratulates his for not ratting anyone out after his arrest, and he's in the crew for life.

Until, of course, his own gets endangered. But by then, Liotta had stepped in.

The next year's Best Picture race ironically pitted De Niro against himself; competing with *Goodfellas* was *Awakenings*, in which he was Oscar nominated for playing a catatonic that Robin Williams' doctor "revives" with huge dopamine levels. Also, there were *Godfather III*, the sequel to the film that notched De Niro his first Oscar nomination and win, and *Ghost*, perhaps the ultimate date movie of the decade.

But everyone knew the race would be down to *Goodfellas* against *Dances with Wolves*. In a decision that still causes all kinds of controversy today, the top two statuettes went to Kevin Costner and the film he starred in and directed.

"*Goodfellas* was completely robbed," Serrone says, "not just because I was affiliated with it. I'm a student of film. Nothing against Kevin Costner, but why Martin didn't get Best Director, I don't know. Politics, perhaps?" His flick did take home a pair of awards, for the screenplay and Joe Pesci's supporting work as the older Tommy.

After becoming Henry, Serrone didn't put much on his acting resume for a few decades. He went back to school. He traveled ("I lived in eight states!"). He became a three-time dad.

"Then somebody called and wanted to cast me in a part," he remembers. "The money was right. The second I said yes, I was bitten by that bug all over again." In 2011, he showed up in the World War II drama *Pathfinder: In the Company of Strangers*, ironically alongside Michael Conner Humphreys, who played Tom Hanks' young form in *Forrest Gump*.

In the midst of my high school years in 1996 Hampton, VA, I was working at a movie theater when *Sleepers* came out. One day, a classmate of mine stopped by to catch it.

Heading out afterward, she stepped toward me—barely. Like had been the case with most people who saw it (including me!), the film had knocked her straight off balance.

She looked up to me, shaken as hell. "Was that written by Stephen King?" she asked.

It wasn't, but you could certainly see the connection. *Sleepers* was certainly scarier than many we'd find in the horror section. Some might say it was even more graphic that King's 1982 prison manuscript *Rita Hayworth and Shawshank Redemption*, which made its way to screens with a shortened title twelve years later.

Joe Perrino portrayed *Sleepers* author and film protagonist Lorenzo Carcaterra in the 1996 flick.

In part, that's probably because of the subject matter; stuff happening to kids hits us harder than seeing adults get abused. It's also because *Sleepers* is said to be a true story—and it almost certainly is, in one way or another.

Not far from the film's Hell's Kitchen setting, a crew member was looking for needle/haystack-level luck on the street. Maybe a potential main star would just . . . happen by.

He did. This stuff doesn't just occur in the movies.

"I was approached on the street by a casting scout who was searching for new faces and asked me to come in for the film," Joe Perrino remembers. "I was not aware of the book at the time."

If inexperienced actors are jargoned "green," Perrino was every shade from money to shamrocks. Nothing there yet, not even a school play. But why not just take a shot anyway (wink wink, nudge nudge, up-and-comers!)?

"I worked with a great on-set acting coach," Perrino says, "and we just focused on putting myself in the imagined circumstances and dealing with them honestly." Fortunately, the performer himself never had been in such a situation. Tragically, many have. Many still do.

According to the 1995 writing that put Lorenzo Carcaterra's name atop bestseller lists, he and some friends took teenage male immaturity down to a new level one hot day in the Kitchen, stealing a vendor's cart to get some free food. But it topples down some steps and into a bywalker, and they end up in juvie (of course, it's called a Home for Boys, like anyone's ever going to be fooled).

It's where we find out just how blurred the line between cop—or guard—and criminal is. It's also where we realize just why so many come out of jail worse than they were going in.

We saw Jason Patric's name and heard his voice for the first part, playing Carcaterra himself, labeled Shakes by his pals. But Perrino, as the writer and protagonist's younger self, might have had a tougher job, and nothing here to do with lack of experience.

"I imagine if someone is going to play a real person," Perrino says, "especially if the person was/is famous, there must be attention paid to getting down the physical characteristics and nuances of that person, while still bringing yourself to the role." Again, we all wish no one would ever have any way to bring themselves to such knowledge.

Shakes and his friends (Brad Renfro, who'd become a sad victim of the dark side of Hollywood, played pal Michael) get turned right into victims of the very ones entrusted to keep safety. Physical abuse? That might be preferred. No, this is much worse.

If *River Wild* (1994) had established Kevin Bacon's ability to play evil, *Sleepers* rammed it home like a jackhammer. He's the leader of a group of guards that do the kind of shit that should warrant an immediate death penalty. That's the kind of stuff that Perrino had to act out.

"Working with such a talented cast and crew made it much easier to deal with such heavy material," he remembers. Some of his toughest scenes came alongside another of the top names in Hollywood history, himself in the midst of some serious repertoire expansion.

People had known Robert De Niro could act for over a decade—being Oscar nominated for *Taxi Driver* (1976), *The Deer Hunter* (1978), and *Cape Fear* (1991), and winning for *Godfather II* (1974) and *Raging Bull* (1980) had been more than enough proof there—as had that *Goodfellas* (1990) tale you just read about! Still, *Awakenings* (1990) notwithstanding, audiences of the time still associated him quite a bit too much with playing, well, crazies. Characters full of pain themselves and/or visiting it on others. Gangsters, or those who could be, in their own minds or in actuality.

A protector? Of children? A *priest*?! Even after two decades of De Niro, that might have seemed unthinkable. But not in *Sleepers*, as the legend—if he hadn't reached that rank by then, he certainly has by now—played Father Bobby, a stickball-skilled man of faith there to mentor the boys from being the next from falling off the path. But as the Home's guards' dirty work starts to take over, the boys fall further and further away, including Shakes.

"The scenes with De Niro were a standout to me," Perrino says. "It was very emotional, and I just recall feeling very connected. I think it might have helped that I was working with one of the best actors to ever have lived."

About halfway through, Perrino, Renfro, and the youths disappear, now in adulthood, with a fellow named Brad Pitt as the elder Michael. It's time for revenge against those who did harm that still destroys some of them.

Per usual, the grownups got all the attention for *Sleepers*, at least before the film came out. Not surprisingly, though, many gave the kids higher marks after its release, Perrino's work called one of the highlights. Ironically, it wasn't until after filming that Perrino made his way through his role model's pages.

Yeah, about that. The film tells you it's true, and Carcaterra (who helped produce the film) and others have as well. Who the hell would be so open about being victimized, we might wonder. But New York's legal system, religious community, and many others then and now still question the film's legitimacy, and Carcaterra's long since gone silent on the matter.

But of course it's a true story. Of course these things happened to too many young inmates, of every age and either gender. Of course they still do today. If nothing else, we can be glad that this sort of crime, once so easy to sweep under the rug, is quick to come into the public eye, what with today's high-speed electronic and media-dominated age. We only hope that this sort of thing might just scare straight a few offending authorities.

"Now that twenty-plus years have gone by," Perrino says, "I feel the film is aging well. It's a really good movie, and I'm so grateful to have been a part of it."

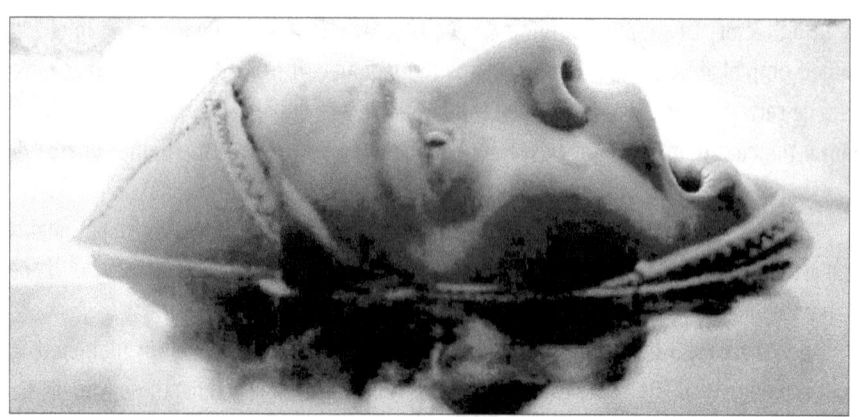

Lauren Mae Shafer's Rachel desperately searched for an escape from
the icy trap imprisoning her for the majority of *The Dark Below* (2015).

Lauren Mae Shafer: *The Dark Below*

MAYBE AUDIENCES JUST WOULDN'T notice. Or, better yet, they would – they'd just be too impressed to care.

"I love a good challenge," asserts Lauren Mae Shafer. "I was told by the director that this would be the most physically demanding role I'd ever attempt. To have a character struggle for her life, and only be able to physicalize that, was so appealing. Sign me up!"

He might have been a serial killer, she his latest prey. Possibly a spousal spat that went tragically far too far. Or both, or neither. Either way, early in 2015's *The Dark Below* (not released until 2017), Shafer's Rachel was choked near to afterlife, her (almost) killer, ahem, escorting her to an icy lake, intending to be the only one walking away.

"Love is cold," he whispers, sounding like an evil wizard from a Disney cartoon or something.

No one spoke again for the entire film. You see, that's what Shafer meant by "only able to physicalize." *Below* would be about 99.999 percent speechless.

Deep breaths, sure. Screams of pain from just about all parties involved, absolutely. But no dialogue.

Not that Rachel would have much of a way to do so, spending a large chunk below sea level. A new kind of sadist, her captor shoves her under the ice with diving gear attached, seemingly hoping to keep her coherent enough to know that she's slowly freezing away.

"We used a lot of different methods," recalls Shafer, who got scuba certified for the part. "It was also interesting getting direction... because our director was not in the water, and we would be underwater for five or ten minutes per take, getting as much footage as we could until I felt good about it or I just needed a break." Crew members signaled directions to her with flashlight Morse code.

"It was also on my acting bucket list to do an underwater scene, so I was able to check that one off," Shafer remembers. Finding the same superhuman endurance so easily and often located in the persona of a typical action victim, Rachel survives hours and hours in the midst of freezing water, her torturer wondering why she just won't give up and die. Like so many have before her.

That's the story starting to unfold in flashback mode. We see where everything began for her and the guy we come to despise as Ben (David Brown). The day they met, the way that almost everyone but her could see what a cretin he was, him having done this before, how their having a daughter made it too late for her to make a clean break, and the horrible things he did to the little girl that she couldn't ignore anymore. Until, again, time ran out there as well, and we ended up here with her in the storyline.

All, again, without anyone doing any verbalizing. We'd see Rachel's pain inside and out, and Ben's near-jubilance at her plight, then his frustration. Rachel's love for her hubby and daughter was clear, but her agony was even more obvious.

Inner dialogue can be tough to performers to convey, but when it's all an actress has, she might put in some more effort to make it scream.

"I thought with a film like this I would miss the spoken word," Shafer says, "but it helped me to get into the head of my character. It made the journey more organic for me. When (Ben) was hurting me both physically and mentally, it made the knife cut a bit deeper. David and I were able to connect on a higher level in the scenes, and it felt amazing."

In hindsight, maybe. Watching the film, certainly, for us the audience and those that had earned the right to be proud to make it. At the time, working in the coldly realistic work of nature's art, everyone just hoped to be able to feel anything long enough for the credits to roll.

"We filmed in the dead of winter in Michigan," claims Shafer, who rode snowmobiles to the set. "A huge snowstorm, 'Snow-maggedon,' was our backdrop. The safety concern there was the cold. We had lots of space heaters, warming tents, blankets, and sleeping bags to warm us."

Barely managing out of the water, Rachel's forced back under the ice – now without her gear or a finger stolen by frostbite – when he draws a gun as long as her. Then she yanks him under the water, and the two battle it out among the waves, screaming sounds we still can't decipher.

The sinister music we just heard now replaced by tunes of triumph, she crawls out, then across the ice. Even when Ben, making the requisite last-gasp that such film villains always summon, follows her out, the song continues, drowning out his scream of pain as she plants a knife into his guts, what little there are.

"I wanted there to be this intense primal gut-wrenching scream that I let out," Shafer remembers. "The character has been through a lot and is absolutely exhausted. It was my last shot of the day and we got one take in; I wanted to keep going, but then I started to lose circulation and couldn't feel my fingers. When I come out of the water into the cold, that is my real body heat coming from my wetsuit."

"That, my friend, is the magic of filmmaking in minus-15 temperatures, and yet I've never had such a blast. The crew was amazing."

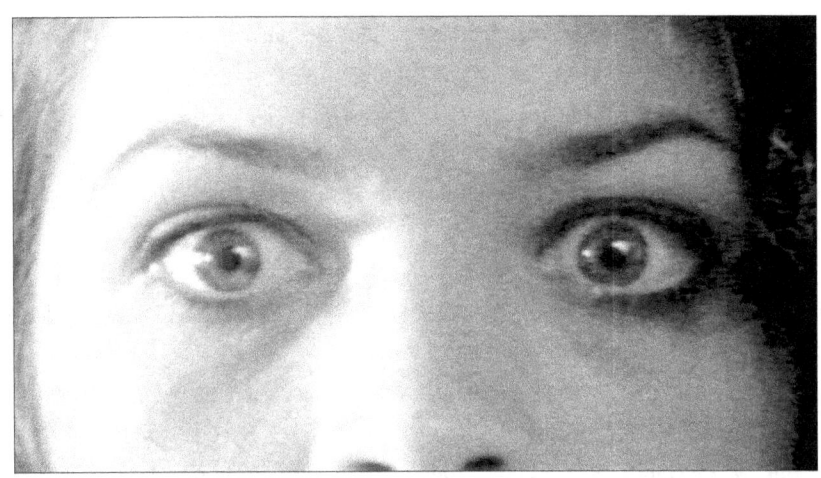

Aleisa Shirley's wide, unfocused eyes showed the pain her Melissa had been through during *Sweet 16* . . . and foreshadowed her handing out some of her own should part 2 ever be made.

Aleisa Shirley: *Sweet 16*

THEY WERE WATCHING HER, just as millions would be in a very near future. They were judging her—not in a malicious or even judgmental way, per se, just hoping she could pick up a pretty heavy load and carry it around throughout filming.

Fair enough. Much of the rest of *Sweet 16*'s (1983) cast and crew had more of a past in the filmmaking business than Aleisa Shirley. Not that that said much; after the first interview, first audition, first callback of her career (if one can give it such a label so early), the Northern California native was leading *16*—yes, it went by the numerics, not the written-out version that other films and songs usually utilize. Other names would be above Shirley's in the billing, as audience familiarity sells tickets, but she'd end up with as much screen time and as any and much more than most in the cast.

Her Melissa was losing friends, and those who wanted to be more than friends with her, by the bloody minute. One after another, someone would get near her, only to wind up dead. But was she *losing* them . . . or was this a certain sort of disposal? Focusing on the mystery behind the murders, rather than the violent deaths themselves, helped *Sweet 16* distinguish itself from the slasher flick genre, but quality is quality no matter the category, and most people hadn't had a chance to decide if Shirley was worth taking a credible chance upon.

Her first day of filming brought Shirley one of the biggest challenges she'd face during filming. One of Melissa's friends had just been slaughtered outside a bar, and Shirley had to chock-fill her with shocked hysterics: tears, screaming, all sorts of frenzy.

"I was so nervous," Shirley remembers. "I walked by the wagons, the trailers, the full crew, knowing I had to cry on cue over and over. I was so nervous doing this really overwhelming thing." As she'd do both before and during filming, Shirley went back to her past; her grandmother had passed just before filming.

The memories worked: Melissa broke down and nearly apart. Take after take, Shirley held up her end of Melissa's bargain and carried it all around. The cast and crew knew they'd taken a big chance, and that it was going to pay off all the way.

Susan Strasberg, as Melissa's mom Joanne, stretched her "maternality" into realism.

"She looked me in the eyes, said, 'I think you got this, kid. Can I get you some hot chocolate?'" Shirley says. "In her eyes, I'd gone from rookie to actress. Oh God, that was awesome. I knew then I wanted to do this for a long time." Strasburg, whose father Lee helped establish Manhattan's Actors Studio, one of the world's most prestigious acting schools, acted on stage and screen for four decades before becoming yet another tragic victim of cancer in early 1999.

Like many gals pounding on the walls of acting's inner circle then and today, Shirley was waiting tables in Los Angeles between acting classes in the early 1980s. On her way to a shift, she stopped to drop off some personals at a production office.

A fellow came to the desk, and the two had a brief chat. Then Shirley had to head off to the uncertain world of special order instructions and hopeful tips.

"I wasn't rude," she says. "I just said I had to go." Shortly thereafter, she got a call.

The man she'd met had been Jim Sotos, who'd directed commercials, videos, shows, and a few movies. *Sweet 16* would be his next project, and, in an impromptu conversation, he'd found his new leader.

"Whatever I said made him think I'd be right for the part," Shirley remembers. "When I got a callback, I was very surprised. Then I found out who all was in it." Along with Strasburg as Joanne, Patrick Macnee was Melissa's dad John, with Bo Hopkins, with a résumé already full of action like *The Getaway* (1972), *American Graffiti* (1973), and *Midnight Express* (1978), would be Sheriff Burke, tossed into action by the local murder rash. A year before, Dana Kimmell had battled supernatural horror in the third *Friday the 13*[th] film; playing Burke's daughter Marci turned her into an adult-oriented Nancy Drew.

"We did a read-through, and that was really helpful for me to get a feel for the characters and how they all relate to each other," says Shirley. "They were all in character, and it helped me to become my character for the role. I was kind of bratty and insecure. It was all a front. I felt like the new girl in town even getting that role, when they'd done so many roles."

In a new town just before one of the most important birthdays in a youngster's life, Melissa can't wait to grow up and drink and sleep all the way around, her hardcore flirtatious ways putting the local guys and girls on notice, in opposite ways of course.

"She was like a big-city girl who had moved to a small town," Shirley says, "and I kind of felt like that, having just moved to LA from Northern California. I had just turned eighteen, and I didn't really understand Hollywood. I didn't know how to navigate it. I had a tough exterior that I felt I had to keep, but inside, it was overwhelming to jump right into Hollywood that quick."

Melissa starts to make friends here and there, obviously more so in the ranks of male persuasion. But there's a problem, and a pretty big one—her dates keep ending up dead. And not naturally or anything; more than one life gets violently stolen. Is Melissa secretly one of the youngest serial killers in film or realistic history, and one of the first females in the ranks (hell, Aileen Wuornos wasn't even around yet!)? Or does she just keep ending up in the wrong place at the wrong time, perhaps followed (stalked!) by someone letting jealousy take over?

"The ending was changed several times," Shirley says. "They had one ending in which I was the killer."

With little time left in the flick, the audience is in a race with the Burkes to nab the murderer. At a campsite one midnight, Melissa finds her latest beau dead . . . again.

She takes off running (in terror or to escape, we're not sure yet), when she's caught by Don Stroud's Billy, himself on the same hot, plasma-stained trail.

"He really got into character," Shirley says. "He grabbed me a little bit too hard, and I cracked a rib. I was wet in a spaghetti dress, and we had to do it over and over." That's when she felt the same rush the opener had sent through her and the rest at the start.

"It hit me," she says. "The whole intensity of what it means to be an actor hit me right between the eyes. I totally got it. I was in the moment, I was the character. It was a huge moment for me as an actress." Regardless of size, the time would come around again.

Billy's soon dead. The sheriff arrives. But he's not there for Melissa—it's her mom.

Long before Melissa arrived, Joanne's twin sister was raped, and died in an institution. Her mom killed her dad to save her daughters. Moving to the new town, a smaller area in which men would have closer access to her daughter, sent Mom back over the edge, taking out anyone who got close.

And ultimately herself. The sheriff's talk-down attempt fails, with Joanne planting the same knife we'd seen used throughout straight through her own heart.

Melissa wanders off, stepping into a nearby apartment building. Her robe falls away, and we see she's holding her own knife.

We focus on her eyes, so wide. So without expression. Without emotion. Nothing on her face has anything to read.

Then we get closer to her irises, near enough to see through to her mind. We hear screams of pain, for mercy. We feel Joanne's shattered mind slipping into her daughter. We can see Melissa carrying on Mom's work. Perhaps someday, *Sweet 16 II: Melissa's Revenge* will tell her tale!

"It was kind of scary and unpredictable," Shirley says of the finale. "In the last part, I kind of went vacant in my mind, and allowed a bit of crazy. I felt like I could go off at any moment, letting myself go a little crazy in my mind. When I heard 'Cut!' I thought, OK, it's safe to come near me now!"

That whole "more screen time than any" would apply to Shirley and Melissa in a couple of ways, and not always positively. She'd be the first thing *16* viewers would see, and they'd see quite a bit. Mere moments in, the camera just happened to catch Melissa relaxing in the ever-present digs of showering, and just *happening* to take her luxuriously enjoyable time in there!

"The shower scene was an unnecessary part of the story," Shirley angrily asserts. "The nudity part wasn't in there when we finished the film, but they told me they wanted more T&A. It was totally unnecessary nudity. I was reluctant, but I did it." Though Shirley was obviously above age, Melissa the character actually being fifteen at this point in the film was something the crew hoped audience would be hormonal enough to gloss over.

That scene's a big reason why Shirley, as of 2017, still hadn't let her daughter see Melissa's story. No matter—the younger gal already had a perfect reason to brag about her mom's acting work. Before Alicia Silverstone became the drop-dead gorgeous face of Aerosmith music videos in the 90s, Shirley showed the Boston band's work to MTV fans in 1988's "Rag Doll" video, a song from the album *Permanent Vacation* the year before. Between flashbacks to the group's stage work in Kentucky, we'd see Shirley's transformation from a hardly innocent schoolgirl into a fashionable party girl across the street of New Orleans.

"My daughter loves to tell everyone I was in an Aerosmith video," Shirley says. "I was always a huge Aerosmith fan, like everyone was. We did 'Rag Doll' in New Orleans, on Bourbon Street. We went crazy at Mardi Gras. It was awesome!"

For a fellow with no lines and just a few moments of screen time in a near-three-hour flick, Geno Silva turned the Skull into one of *Scarface*'s most unforgettable characters.

Geno Silva: *Scarface*

SOME FILMS, IT'S IMPOSSIBLE to watch just once. Some say it should even be illegal. Once in a while, a film comes around the theaters that can't be fully grasped by a single viewing.

The Big Lebowski (1998). *Breakfast Club* (1985). *The Shawshank Redemption* (1994). *Stand By Me* (1986). *The Godfather* (1972). Just about anything two fellows named Tarantino and Scorsese ever put together.

And then there's 1983's *Scarface*. America's desire or even need for gratuitous film violence wasn't full-blown out when it hit the screens back in the 1980s, part of the reason why the story of a man named Montana was badmouthed or outright ignored by many critics and audiences alike when it first came out. But as we as a nation grew more accustomed to action, to seeing violence, to watching aggression as a way of feeding off it, or perhaps relieving our own inner tension, *Scarface* became a perfect embodiment of whiz-bang, one-lining humor. It was a loss of control that we self-servingly take pleasure in seeing people on top have forced upon them, and buildups of bloody violence that go like a volcano, inching toward the final eruption like a car accelerator slowly dropping towards the floor.

Otherwise, it also showed us that it's not only possible to make a film with virtually no redeemable characters, but to get viewers to miss it enough to love the film, to live with characters we couldn't stand, even if we wanted to see more of them. Pretty much everyone in the film ends up chest-deep in drugs and/or violence, and the main character not only goes further in both than anyone else, but is *freaking incestuous*, trying to get with *his own sister*! How in *hell* do we make this work?

Many men found out. Now we'll meet one who took a small part that the film couldn't have survived without.

"My agent told me they were going to do a show called *Scarface*," remembers Geno Silva. "I thought it was about Al Capone." Many probably did at the time; the film's title is the legendary gangster's infamous nickname, and it's about a guy who, like him, rises from blundering mob wannabe to kingpin, only to get caught up in money laundering and tax evasion, among other things.

Oh, but while Capone got to die without violence, Tony Montana didn't have such a luxury, mainly because of the man Silva would end up becoming.

If Silva's name hasn't quite reached out and grabbed the attention of *Scarface* fans reading this just yet, let's hold off for the time being. While his acting career kicked off in front of the camera in the concluding times of the 1970s, another fellow was trying out a new tactic behind one.

In the midst of yardwork on a hot afternoon at his Laurel Canyon home, Silva's phone rang (not cells—they weren't even a pipe dream yet!).

"I was trimming," he recalls, "and my agent called, and said they wanted to see me right now at Warner Brothers." Impressed with his work in a few TV shows, a young filmmaker had a spot for Silva in his new work.

"I said I couldn't go," Silva says. "I was all dirty. I'd go tomorrow." But not having to drop everything at once and haul ass to an audition is a luxury budding actors at any time can't enjoy, so it was off to Hollywood Boulevard for a tryout.

Arriving, Silva noticed several others going for the role, with the director trying to decide who could act like the toughest toughguy with a subtle sense of humor—this was, after all, for a comedy.

At his turn, Silva skipped the looks and the chat. He reached into his pocket and pulled out a push-button knife/comb combo.

"I combed my mustache," he says. "I whipped out my New Mexico talk, and said something silly. I threatened them in the pachuco language." The bit went a while: the crew was wowed, and he'd be Martinez in 1979's *1941* (Silva's parents had married the very day of the infamous bombing).

Note: Pachuco was a Hispanic/Latino American subculture about halfway through the 20th century. Starting out in Texas and eventually moving to Los Angeles, it's typically associated with zoot suit-wearing gangs. Silva had put it to use on both Broadway stages and cinema screens in 1981 with *Zoot Suit*, the story of the Zoot Suit Riots—no, it's not just a tumor-esque song lyric!—of Los Angeles in the times of World War II.

Oh, and the director whose career was slowly becoming a sonic boom? Last name Spielberg.

The two would meet again: in 1997 alone, Silva captained a barge full of overgrown reptiles in *Jurassic Park: The Lost World* and a slave ship in *Amistad* (about as impressive as playing both an MC and hotel manager for David Lynch in 2001's *Mulholland Drive*).

He hit the research books hard to become Ruiz, one of the first captives of the title ship slave rebellion that lead to one of America's first legal battles against slavery.

"When Spielberg casts somebody," Silva says, "he's confident that they are going to bring something to it, be it energy or improv. On virtually every film I've worked with him, it's a collaborative art form. He knows that the actors are going to bring something to the role, and that gives you a lot of confidence."

Do we remember Silva just yet? If not, let's go ahead and jump back a decade and a half, back to the film that, while not right away, eventually found it way past audience loyalty to culthood, even iconic in American culture.

Just as Scorsese's films have shown many times, the mob so often turns men (and the occasional woman) into monster. No loyalty, twenty shades of truth, nothing. Sooner or later, it all comes down to either the almighty dollars, or backstabbing—more often head-shooting!—of others to keep one's own cranium free of bullet holes. Demonstrations that, as untouchable (hey, there's another can't-see-once film title!) as some men may seem, they and we all too often find out just how human they truly are.

Only slightly more established than Spielberg had been at Silva's first meeting with him, Brian De Palma was putting a new spin on the mob mentality that Francis Ford Coppola had established in the 1970s with the first two *Godfather* films. Like Coppola, De Palma had Al Pacino leading the way, but Tony Montana's job description would be about all he and Michael Corleone would have in common. While Michael's persona had been stoic stone-cold evil, Montana would be over the top with speed that could shatter the sound barrier, throwing control of himself and his empire out the window (doing mountains of cocaine can have that effect on someone).

Pacino, Silva says, "was never Al; he was always Tony. From the moment he walked out of his dressing room and on set, he was Tony Montana. You never said 'Hey Al, how are you doing?' He was in character the entire time."

In all fairness, Silva's character had more in common with Coreleone than Montana did. No emotion, no pleasure. Just a fellow who's doing what he's here to do.

With De Palma and script man Oliver Stone helping him along, Silva stepped into The Skull. Tragically, he didn't have to mentally invent a backstory of violence for the character.

"I grew up in the baddest, oldest barrio in New Mexico," he recalls. "We had a higher heroin rate than Harlem, the south side of Chicago, or L.A. I saw one of my best friends get stabbed in the second grade at recess. I got jumped a bunch of times, and I had to learn to fight back. I'm the luckiest man on Earth that I survived and to have a career as an actor."

Early on, Tony, still searching for a foothold in his new venture, heads down to Bolivia with his pal Omar (F. Murray Abraham) to cut a nose powder deal with a mob boss. As is often the case in both film and reality with this sort of thing, everything's going smoothly until Omar steps out, leaving Tony alone with the boss.

That's when the fellow casually quips that Omar's on the take with the law. Moments later, we see an already-beaten-to-hell Omar getting shoved from a chopper by a man in black (clothes, sunglasses, everything). The guy's called The Skull, and a person better suited for contract murder would be tough to find.

"I had originally auditioned to be The Skull's partner," Silva says (the character had been intended for a black performer). "I read for them three or four times." Eventually, he'd get flown to the Big Apple to try out right next to Pacino. It worked.

"He was called The Skull because he wears shades at night," Silva says. "Brian wanted him to look like death. In all the acting I've done, it's the only role I've ever had where I didn't say a word."

Indeed, The Skull's only around for a short while—no speaking, no character development, no hesitation, no doubt in what he does. To learn more about him would detract from the focus of the story; we're supposed to see him as a mob instrument, there to be used to get a tough job done and nothing else.

After crossing the mob boss he'd met earlier, a coked-out Tony has nothing left. With an army of mob men attacking his mansion and killing his own workers and sister—it took fewer people to take out Osama bin Laden—Tony and his little friend are saying hello at high speed, putting away an array of attackers by themselves. But The Skull has found his way upstairs, and blasts Tony to oblivion with his own not-so-little companion as the film ends.

"It took a long, long time to shoot that whole scene," Silva recalls (Pacino was legitimately hurt during filming, pausing everything for a while). "I was very stealthful. When I see the movie again for the thousandth time, I feel like I should have said, 'Say *goodbye* to my little friend!'

"I get asked about that movie all my life," he continues. "People come up to me all the time and say, 'Hey, you're the dude that killed Scarface. You're the dude that killed Tony Montana.' They say they've seen it about twenty times. The best part is that now, thirty-some years later, I might have a residual for *10 fucking grand*!"

Actors in Action

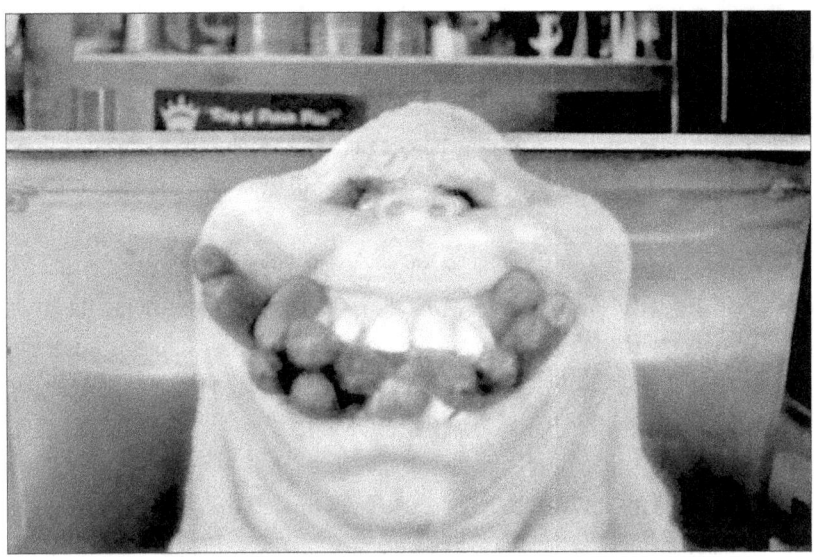

Who could want to capture such a guy? All the Slimer wanted was a good snack of franks in *Ghostbusters* (1984)!

They Who Played the Slimer!

THERE'S A GREAT REASON why the green guy became a full-blown good guy.

From the moment we, along with Bill Murray's Peter Venkman, saw the ghost we'd come to know and love in that legendary hotel hallway scene in 1984, there was something clear about the apparition, but more so than his green covering.

Like his supernatural pal the Stay Puft Marshmallow Man (and, to a larger extent, even Godzilla and King Kong), the Slimer didn't seem to mean much harm. Just give the thing a large room and steady stream of hot dogs and he'd be quiet!

Two years after *Ghostbusters* zapped hell out of the box office, The Real Ghostbusters came to the small, animated screen — and its makers were smart enough to put Slimer on their team, the squad sidekick. In 1988, the show was renamed *Slimer and the Real Ghostbusters*. For a ghost, looks like he made quite the lasting impression on viewers of all screens.

"What I enjoyed about Slimer was the reckless abandon," recalls Robin Shelby. "He did what he wanted, whenever he wanted. He ate what he wanted, went wherever he wanted to go, no matter what. I liked his stick-to-it-iveness and his bravery."

Fresh off a stint on the makeup crew of of *Greystoke: The Legend of Tarzan, Lord of the Apes*, Steven Johnson was handed the chance to take his sculpting talents to the supernatural. Johnson's group had almost won an Oscar (he'd worked alongside Rick Baker as Baker grabbed a 1981 statuette for *An American Werewolf in London*). Without today's technology, Johnson turned to a friend.

"He was trying to break the mold," remembers Mark Bryan Wilson, "and he opened the door."

Wilson was tasked with creating the librarian ghost, she who shocks the first three title characters, and the audience, early on. Days later, Gozer's two Satan-spawned canines were added to his agenda.

"Randy Cook had done the body," he says (Cook would later with three Oscars for his visual effects work in the *Lord of the Rings* series), "but they wanted me to do the horns, the claws, and the other stuff that needed to be sculpted." Someone must have been impressed; over the next few weeks, Wilson's itinerary was stretched to the same type of performance he'd given as one of the zombies who backed up Michael Jackson in 1983's *Thriller*.

Another performer had been originally in the Slimer role, Wilson remembers, "but they came to me and told me it would be more cost-effective to just put the life cast on me. I was thrilled – I had been lobbying intently to be included as a performer. I had seen the designs and I thought it was a really cool character."

He, Johnson, and everyone else glanced over the Slimer's genetics and storyboards, seeing the drawn out version of the tale they'd perform.

"(Slimer) was a John Belushi spin-off character," Wilson recalls (Belushi would almost certainly have been a part of the 1984 flick if not for his tragic death in March 1982). "He was kind of comedic, like something out of a Tex Avery cartoon." Avery helped create future household names like Daffy Duck, Elmer Fudd, and even a walking-upright rabbit named Bugs.

"We talked about where we were going to hide the puppeteers," Wilson explains, "and which suit we were going to use – the one with the closed lips, with a partially opened mouth, or a huge opened mouth."

After working his ectoplasmic self-defense on Venkman (and we thought the ink-bag escape used by our octopus pals was icky!), the green guy's caught in the hotel ballroom, a helpless victim of the deadly sin of gluttony. He escapes one blast after another, but soon gets caught in the three streams they can't cross.

"When he's on the ceiling, that's me inside the rubber suit," Wilson says. "When they were shooting up to the ceiling, I had to imagine electrical bolts hitting my fingertips like I was in a cage of energy." His character's soon snared in a similar box, allowing Venkman to bellow the legendary declaration, "We came, we saw, we kicked its ass!"

But remember, Slimer's only "attack," if one can call it as such, comes in self-defense, not malice. Even when the ghosts escape later on, his top priority is making life hell for hot dog vendors. He's even the last thing we see; as the 'Busters drive off, he comes straight at the audience before the end credits.

Aided by a quick re-release in 1985, *Ghostbusters* became the decade's top humorous moneymaker. On a break from her upcoming acting career, a California high-schooler became one of its million-plus ticketbuyers.

"I fell in love with it, just like the world did," Shelby recalls. "It was classic comedy." A veteran of child's and musical theater, Shelby snared the same sort of Slimer shot that Wilson had as the second round of *Ghostbusters* brawls came around in 1989, one year after the cartoon kicked off.

Surrounded by some seriously groundbreaking special effects, the title character of 1988's *Willow* (Warwick Davis) scurries across a bridge. As if the murderous trolls after him aren't enough to worry about, there's a two-headed hydra in the water below.

A hungry such critter doesn't discriminate between good and evil, and one of the trolls becomes its lunch as Willow escapes.

Shelby had been the meal. The appearance (calling it a cameo would be too generous) was enough to convince the *Ghostbusters II* crew that she deserved a tryout.

"They didn't even tell me what it was for," she recalls. "I went in and spent an hour auditioning with the head of special effects. They put me in some scenarios, like 'you're eating, and you hear somebody coming to your right. You're freaked out, and you go back to eating.' They test your physicality, and being the right size (she's 4'11") showed them I would have a lot of fun doing the role."

With the 'Busters rolling toward a battle with a reincarnated magician from centuries before (kind of like an older, meaner Rasputin), their little brother-type pal Louis Tully (Rick Moranis) happens to run into a familiar face – only to us, as he didn't meet the Slimer in 1984 – back at the ghost's diet-destroying ways, sending both away in panic.

In other words, we saw Shelby giving the special-effects laden version of the performance she'd used to wow the crew into giving her the role to start with.

"I was excited, happy, and scared to death," she remembers. "(Slimer) was a beloved character, and obviously you don't want to screw that up."

Rather than reviewing the first 'Busters flick, she'd looked to channel a different kind of spirit, heading back to the work Belushi had done to put *Saturday Night Live* on the TV map as one of the sketch show's first members back in the 1970s.

"There was a manic, crazy, reckless abandonment that he had," she says. "I also made sure I was in shape, rollerblading, running, making sure I could do whatever they wanted."

She'd spend nearly an hour getting into Slimer's suit – arms, body, tights underneath, and a huge head – then stay there for up to fifteen hours a day, doing her thing before a blue screen.

"I pushed myself to the point where they were talking to me and I wasn't responding," she remembers. "That was the hardest part, with the weight of the costume, with so many motors and wires and tubes. Even with puppeteers doing the eyebrows and the cheeks, it was very heavy."

With his pals losing their museum battle with the bad guy, Louis straps on his own proton pack and heads to action. In true movie luck, Slimer just happens to be riding by in a conveniently placed bus to give him a lift.

Rumors of a third *Ghostbusters* film started rolling around in the 1990s, one project after another lurching forward and ending before Harold Ramis' sad passing in Feb. 2014 ruined any full reunion hopes. Instead, an all-gal cast took over in 2016, the three remaining 'Busters showing up for cameos (including Ramis, to an extent, as his Egon Spengler became an office statue a character walks by early on).

The Christmas before, a special Tweet had landed in Shelby's inbox.

"I was screaming," she remembers. "My husband thought something had gone horribly wrong. I had to hold my tongue (about the film) for months."

Not surprisingly, things get tough for the 'Buster babes – and guess who they run into taking advantage of an abandoned hot dog cart?

Again, it's about escape over attacking for him, managing to steal the gals' car and, telekinetically gassing the pedal, drive off. Later on, he and some pals drive by, including his new gal pal; in true Ms. Pac Man mode, she's expressing her feminity with a hair bow.

He'd played a singer early on, and now Adam Ray was voicing the green ghost. His girlfriend? That was Shelby.

"In *Ghostbusters II*, I spent fifteen-hour days in a very heavy, hot costume with some amazing people," she remembers (the Christmas Tweet had been an invitation to the role from director Paul Feig). "In 2016, I spent one day in an air-conditioned recording booth with some amazing people. It was so much fun to voice a character. I made hysterical laughing noises and screaming. People would have called police if they'd heard me in the recording booth."

Perhaps more than any other single figure in the *Star Wars* universe, Darth Vader would come to signify the series' true iconic meanings to the world of cinema.

Star Wars' Darth Vader(s)

AS WE STEPPED INTO theaters in the summer of 1977, we knew that we'd be learning the story of a man named Skywalker—just not the one we expected.

As the first *Star Wars* installment rolled into theaters, millions of viewers, who would push the film to the all-time top of the box office ranks (twice!), got to know a man named Luke, a young man on a distant planet, content to live his life on a farm with his aunt and uncle. But he's suddenly pushed into battle, into the next chapter of the eternal war between the good Jedi and evil Empire, and through luck (good and bad) and newfound skill, he becomes the everyman underdog that saves the galaxy—for now. . . .

Darth Vader? He was there too, and he was terrifying from the start. From the moment the doors on the Death Star opened, Vader jammed a dark spot into our memories without so much as moving. And as he strolled into a meeting of shocked-stoic Empire crew, he didn't speak—but the machine-assisted breathing that methodically blasted from his helmet drifted off the screen and found its chilling way straight down our spines. Then his voice, robotic but still somehow evil, rolled out on its own, almost as if it was daring us not to listen.

Who was he? What was he? What did he want, and what would he do to get it? We wouldn't get these questions answered much early on—other than finding out that he had killed (hypothetically, as it turned out) Luke's dad, and now was willing to go to the ends of the galaxy to find Luke for some unclear reason—but the end of the second *Star Wars* flick shocked us in a way few films have before or since, and the third one pushed Vader further into the dark limelight than anyone else from the series. By the time the prequels came around a few decades later, Luke wasn't around just yet—we wanted to know more about his daddy.

As time passed, Darth Vader would become a symbol stretching far beyond the eight *Star Wars* films, the countless cartoons and novels made about the series, and anything else. He'd also go past an image of American pop culture that managed to make its way around the globe. Vader's form has been commercialized to high heaven for everyone from children of all ages every Halloween to advertisements, cartoons both political and strip-based, and everywhere else. Many people know more about him than about their neighbors.

But even beyond that, Vader, or at least the fellow inside the costume, personified something even greater. Through him, Anakin Skywalker, in all sorts of living colors, showed us firsthand the battle between good and evil, from both the inside and outside. We learned about the causes of the battle, from self and society. We saw war's effects over a period of time, the reasons that the inherently good can become evil. The thing that terrified us through five full series chapters and 99-hundreths of another became emblematic of hope, a final triumph of good over evil, of love over hate.

"I had lots of Darth this and Darth that, and Dark Lord of the Sith," series creator George Lucas recalled of putting the storyline together, a process he began while script scribbling in 1972. "The early name was Dark Water (a worse name than Luke's original moniker of Dirk Starkiller? Reader, judge it for yourselves!).

"Darth is a version of dark," Lucas explained, "and Vader is a variation of father. So he's basically Dark Father." The Anakin part came from Lucas' friend, British filmmaker Ken Annakin.

Little by little, details about Vader's physical being started to creep in. His all-black look, his six-foot-plus height, his flowing cape in a manner of midnight-black royalty . . . and his legendary mask.

But it wouldn't take them nearly as long to find someone to get inside it all.

"I didn't have to do anything," says British weightlifting champ David Prowse of snaring the role (he was in the Mr. Universe competitions, which would elevate a fellow named Schwarzenegger toward icon-hood). "In fact, they offered me two parts." Given a toss-up between oversized Wookie Chewbacca and the Darkest of Dark Lords, he took the bad guy, leaving Peter Mayhew to get furry.

"George Lucas asked me why I wanted to play the villain," explains Prowse, who'd had a small role in 1971's *A Clockwork Orange* (he was Mr. Alexander's bodyguard) and been Frankenstein's monster in a few films. "I said, 'Because he'll be remembered.'"

Still, after being set inside his sixty-five-pound, "absolutely sweltering," costume, Prowse didn't get much guidance in making the original "Man in Black" show that his heart was the color of his outfit.

"At the outset of it," he says, "I had to make Darth Vader as imposing as possible. So in the end, I decided, as big as I am [6'7"], I have to get everybody on the run.... That was the thing that defined the whole character: the walk. Obviously I had to act the part and create it as expressively as possible because everybody else had to react to me. But because there was no expression in the face or anything else, it was all done with the body."

Still, in all fairness to Prowse, his Welsh accent didn't translate very well through Vader's mask, and Lucas decided to hand the voice work to someone else, a fact Prowse only found out from audience seats. The crew had originally thought about Orson Welles for the voice work—then found someone else.

"The technique about recording that voice was to keep it within very strict boundaries of inflection," explains James Earl Jones, who taped all of the character's lines in less than three hours. "There was no way to enlighten the voice with awareness. In fact, my job was to keep awareness out of Darth Vader's voice—take all humanity out of it . . . good, effective dialogue will evoke in the viewer or listener all kinds of wonderful things that come from the viewer's mind."

When Luke and his new buddy Han Solo (Harrison Ford—hey, whatever happened to him, anyway?) blasted away Vader's beloved Death Star and sent him spiraling out of control (but not dying—Lucas was too smart for that) at the end, everyone knew that Vader and his empire would be back for more. But no one knew what secrets would follow.

When the Empire struck back, Vader's mask suddenly became the disfigured face of the *Star Wars* franchise. All over the film's pre-production materials and armed with a new spaceship the size of Pittsburgh, Vader was back, and he was slightly less than perky.

As tough as it is for anything to stay secretive today, what with Twitter, Facebook, blogs, up-to-the-second tabloid news, and everything else, Lucas went to the ends of the earth and every galaxy outward to hide Vader's paternal secret. Prowse and other cast members were given false dialogue for their scenes to hide the revelation, leaving everyone—cast, audiences, EVERYONE (except Lucas and a handful)—still believing that Vader had killed Daddy Skywalker in the most horrifyingly literal of mannerisms.

Filming the tornado-esque twist, Prowse actually told Luke, "Obi-Wan killed your father." He himself didn't know about the twist until actually watching the film for the first time.

But even then, no one's certain about Vader's credibility. Is he lying to coldly mock Luke? Even Jones, while doing the dialogue, didn't believe his own words. After all, exactly when did Vader discover that Luke was his son? This was a big change that only the closest lookers might have noticed in the 1997 re-release of *Empire*: in the original, Emperor Palpatine tells him Luke's name, and Vader doesn't react, indicating that he knew far more than he was letting on. In the updated version, however, Palpatine actually calls the youngster "the offspring of Anakin Skywalker." Vader's shocked—well, as shocked as Vader ever got—and questions how such a thing could even be true. Needless to say, even after we got the full story in 2005's *Revenge of the Sith*, this thing is a gold mine for *Star Wars* novelists, cartoonists, and conspiracy hunters galore.

After Prowse and Alec Guinness acted out Vader's killing of Obi-Wan as their own stuntmen (two weeks of rehearsal went into that scene), Bob Anderson took over the lightsaber work for the Skywalker-Skywalker clashes in *Empire* and, eventually *Return of the Jedi* in 1983. A national fencing coach for decades and veteran of screen swordplay instruction, Anderson found Vader's costume even more constraining than Prowse had.

"I'm six foot one, and I had three inches on my helmet and two inches on my boots," says Anderson, wearing an oversized costume to make up for his size difference to Prowse. "I had a couple of cloaks on, and the helmet was the icing on the cake. Quite often, I was fighting with Mark Hamill and I could only see his feet, so I was doing it virtually blindfolded."

Anderson, Prowse, Jones, and someone to be heard from shortly were the last group of Vaders in 1983 in *Jedi*. A decade and a half later, the series started again, as Lucas handed Vader and Kenobi the spotlight once again in *The Phantom Menace* (1999).

With Kenobi in younger form as Ewan McGregor, he and fellow Jedi knight Qui-Gon Jinn (Liam Neeson), in the midst of straightening out another galactic battle, rescue Queen Amidala (Natalie Portman) from Naboo and land on Tatooine to get their ship repaired. That's where they run into a lovely lady named Shimi and her son Anakin, equipped with a gift for mechanics and, according to Qui-Gon's Spiderman-esque senses, an abundance of midi-chlorians in his bloodstream.

Could this kid really be the chosen one, the one spoken of in a prophecy that could help balance the force and destroy the evil in the world? Anakin's victory in a pod race makes a final impression on the group, and he goes off with them, back to the battle grounds.

But there's already quite a bit of ominous-ness here, and it's subtle, but important. Anakin has spent his entire life—yes, it's been short, but he loved it—in a safe place. Now he's away from his mother, away from the only home he's ever known, and heading off to an uncertain and potentially fatal spot.

On an off note, isn't it amazing that a certain subtlety didn't get more attention here? Anakin didn't have his own father, which even Shimi can't explain, and no one picked up on that as an Immaculate jab? Well, anyway . . .

"When you do a character, you always put so much of yourself into it," explains Pernilla August, the lady behind Shimi and an award-winning actress in her native Sweden. "In a way, it's my thoughts, but she's not very close to me, or like me. But since I have three kids by myself, I can relate to her. She's down-to-earth like me, so yes, in some ways, I guess she is like me. . . . One thing that made me nervous was my accent, and I remember when doing the screen test, I was asking George Lucas how I should deal with it. I was worried about it. He said, 'Don't worry. You're coming from a Swedish galaxy somewhere.' That made me feel much more relaxed."

Actors in Action

The search for Anakin, however, was anything but relaxing. From 1995 to 1997, roughly 3000 child actors tried out, as searching took the crew across Scotland, Ireland, down through Canada, and back to the U.S. Early on, a fellow named Jake Lloyd, who'd snared a recurring role on *ER* (1996) and played Arnold Schwarzenegger's son in 1996's *Jingle All the Way*, popped up in the search. However, it wouldn't be until the summer of '97 that he'd cross the Skywalker finish line.

"When I was six, I was Darth Vader for Halloween," Lloyd recalls. "[Anakin] is a lot like me. I love doing mechanics; he is one mechanical kid. I like to build stuff, he likes to build stuff. I just act like myself." It's the youngster that builds that golden guy C3PO, which entitles him to some serious credit or blame, depending on how we look at it.

On Coruscant, an eager Qui-Gon informs the Jedi Senate of his new find, but their response isn't what he'd hoped for. Namely, it's his emotions, and Yoda, whose soothsayings rank right up there with Socrates in some minds, defines the character present and future.

"Fear is the path to the dark side," he pontificates. "Fear leads to anger. Anger leads to hate. Hate leads to suffering." Far away from the only home and stability he'd ever known, fear was Anakin's abundance. In a nutshell, the Sith could have been crushed and the Jedi triumphed without the last (or first, depending on perspective) three films had the council simply been a bit more optimistic toward a young boy.

As the Rebels destroy the Federation ship, some dark seeds for the future films are sown. First, the mortally wounded Qui-Gon instructs Kenobi to turn Anakin into a Jedi knight. That's fine, but then we see Emperor Palpatine congratulating Amidala on her victory—and letting her know that Anakin will always be in his sights. As we'd start to find out in 2002's *Attack of the Clones*, this guy's intentions were everything but honorable.

With Lloyd too young to play the adult Anakin, it was back on the casting trail to find the man who'd take the first steps toward the Darth dude. Once again, about 1500 applications arrived, and over 400 interviews were conducted.

In May 2000, less than two months before filming was to begin, a struggling Canadian actor met with the crew, and headed home, hoping against hope. Like Qui-Gon had before, Lucas sensed something special in the young man. He wanted someone with a strong sense of humor, but had the negative side that lurks inside us all just hanging out beneath the surface, like swimming a foot underwater in a murky pond.

"I chose Hayden, who had more of a dark side," Lucas says, "knowing I would have to play up his lighter, more naïve side at the beginning of this movie, then gradually let his darker side out."

Hayden Christensen had won the acting lottery.

"I've no idea," he said of how he stood out from so many. "I contemplated that for about a week after I got the part and I couldn't figure it out, so I stopped thinking about it. I guess I look

Actors in Action

a little bit like [Lloyd] . . . The whole time I was auditioning for the film I never once felt like it was feasible I'd get the role. And when they told me it was complete disbelief—it was just a shock to the system. I was on cloud nine for about a week then I got down and started doing my work and trying to figure out the character."

Checking out the first four *Star Wars* flicks, Christensen looked for a piece of himself.

"I'm going to try to bring some of the sensibility that [Lloyd] brought to the role," he says, "and some of the feeling that [Sebastian Shaw, who'll arrive shortly] brought to it. But for the most part, I'm going to create my own Anakin."

Early on in *Clones*, he and Kenobi save Amidala from an assassination attempt, and Kenobi heads to another planet, leaving the two alone.

Anakin declares his love, but Amidala (whose interesting hairstyle in this film would call up memories of her daughter) recalls one of the darkest sides of being a Jedi: the forbidding of marriage. Tormented by both this and thoughts of his long-lost mother, Anakin heads back to his home planet, only to find that she has been sold, kidnapped, and abused.

As helpful as Lloyd had made Anakin, his older self comes off more as a rich kid who was spoiled his entire life, only to see his family go bankrupt and have to go live with a poor uncle. Obi-Wan's teachings are almost seen as restrictions, and Anakin tells anyone willing to listen just how wonderful he is with the lightsaber. Yoda talked about fear leading to anger and anger to hate, but egotism might have been slipped in there somewhere.

Still, it's the ever-dangerous combo of love and fury that drive Anakin towards, though not quite over the edge. Unable to save his mother from a group of Tuskans, he slaughters the entire group (justifiable, but violent as all hell). Remember, it's Padmé's safety that becomes the final precipice pusher. Count Dooku, himself a former Jedi, lops Anakin's arm off near the end, which Anakin would do to his own kin in *Empire*. Back on Coriscant, the Jedi Council vows to launch a new war against the Sith, while Anakin and Amidala are secretly married.

"George came up to me on the set one day during my first *Star Wars* and said something that I never fully understood until after we were done filming," Christensen says. "He said, 'As an actor, you have to think of yourself as a ditch digger.' . . . What he was implying was that on his movie, I needed to think of myself as a ditch digger, because it wasn't the proper arena for actual creative expression. This was his thing. It was all very thought-out in his head, and I needed to show up to make his wants a reality. And so really, what he was saying to me, was: 'Don't let this experience discourage you from what acting can really be about, because that's not what this is.' I just wish I would've figured that out a little sooner."

For the final *Star Wars* episode, fans clamored for the first conclusion. While the first two, both box-office smashes, hadn't been full-blown impressive to critics, no one was going to worry about that for the final flick. This was the final answer to a question that had been asked for a quarter century. The story had ended, the mystery had been solved, and the heroes had won, but this was a mystery whose lost piece was still missing. How had Anakin taken the final steps into the dark side? What had made him finally turn evil?

We see in his eyes the darkness that will soon overtake Anakin Skywalker (Hayden Christensen) up until the very end of *Return of the Jedi!*

It turned out to be one of the most welcome and still dangerous elements of humanity: love itself. Love can be the most beautiful aspect of the human world, but it has caused many to commit unthinkable acts that can end in all sorts of tragedy. Love for one's country, love for one's faith, love of another person—perhaps unrequited—has pushed people to ends that no one, including them, have ever thought possible.

"Evil isn't just pure evil. A lot of times it comes from good," Christensen says. "The transition to the dark side is what I was wanting to do from the get-go, and I wasn't sure why I was being asked to pull back, but now I understand that it had to take place at very specific times in the film."

Escaping from another battle, Anakin learns that he'll be a father soon. But Kenobi and the rest of the Jedi are suspicious of Palpatine, the closest thing to a father figure that Anakin ever had, and Skywalker doesn't know who to trust.

With horrifying visions of Amidala dying in childbirth, Anakin is convinced that the only way to save his true love is to go to the Dark Side and obtain the unlimited power it seems to provide. Now Darth Vader, he's blacker than midnight.

He's in his first battle with Kenobi, and Obi-Wan wins this one, slicing off the former Chosen One's legs and arm and dropping him next to a river of lava, causing burns that nearly remove all of Anakin's skin. But just in time, he's shoved into a new black suit of armor and breathing machines to save his life.

Putting on the Vader costume, Christensen says, "was thrilling. It was something I'd been looking forward to since I found out I got the part, hoping I'd get to don the dark helm. And I hope that my performance as Vader doesn't feel disjointed, that it has a linear connection, so that when people watch the original trilogy, they see my face under the mask."

Amidala dies in childbirth, and her passing sends the new Vader straight over the edge. His son and daughter are placed on separate planets to keep them safe, and the saga re-ends.

Let's finish up by hearing from the shortest-roled Vader—but, according to many, the most important.

Like many across the country and around the world, **Sebastian Shaw** had been all but blown away by the first two galactic battles.

"I was absolutely amazed at the brilliant techniques," he recalled, "which, in many ways, were revolutionary, something quite new. . . . When my chance came to be *in* one, I was delighted, especially when the scene turned out to be such a very momentous moment in the sequence of movies."

His scene would take all of one day to shoot, and fill up less than five minutes of screen time, totaling less than a hundred words. But no *Star Wars* fan would ever come close to forgetting it.

Sebastian Shaw became the Skywalker that finally stood back up to darkness in the closing moments of *Return of the Jedi.*

Before they could, however, the *Jedi* cast went farther than the ends of the galaxy to keep it a secret; for over a year after filming, Shaw couldn't discuss his role with anyone, with friends and family on the list of forbidden.

"I think many people, even some of them who had to do with the administration, didn't really know, until they saw the finished project," said the longtime British actor, who died in 1994. "Everybody concerned—director, producers—were watching that scene, all the time, with hawk-like eyes, because it was so important."

As Ewoks and Rebels battle the dark forces on the Death Star, Luke makes one more valiant effort to save his daddy from darkness. The Emperor's having none of that, and Luke and Vader square off once again. Luke wins the fight, but can't kill Vader, as this would allow his own darkness to take the upper hand. Realizing the young man's strength, the Emperor blasts Luke with Force Lightning, and it appears that Vader's going to let it happen.

But when it seems too late, the good that Vader—or Anakin—had suppressed for so long lurches back to light just in time, as the Dark One hurls the Emperor over the side of the ship, to his death.

Mortally wounded in his son's arms, Vader asks Luke to remove his helmet, and Shaw gets his moment.

"I wore the Darth Vader mask and costume, and played the whole scene through from the moment he sank down," Shaw says. "The scene was so beautifully written that we never altered the dialogue at all. It was just as it was written, and it played quite beautifully."

But his last moment wouldn't be as painful; as the Rebels celebrate their victory back on Endor, Luke cremates his father. Glancing over, he notices the spirits of Kenobi, Yoda, and his dad (Christensen was dubbed in for Shaw when the new versions were released).

"George Lucas actually directed me, in my final bit," said Shaw, "Alec Guinness and I were all happy and beaming in that kind of shimmering *Star Wars* heaven. I look like me in that scene; I haven't got any of that makeup on. When we were filming that sequence, I didn't know why we were doing it. I thought it was for publicity or something. George just said, 'Look happy, smile.'"

"People thought that it was all about Luke," Lucas said in 1995, years away from the prequels' premiere, "but it's not and never was. It's about Darth Vader."

Jones returned as Vader's voice in *Rogue One* near the end of 2016. This time, two men were on the inside of the man in black in the film that showed us exactly what went down between *Sith* and *New Hope*, like how the rebellion first began and what a contractor's nightmare the Death Star was to build.

In an element only slightly less restrictive than the one he rode to national kickboxing stardom back in his Welsh homeland, Spencer Wilding helped Vader use his trusty mind control and lightsaber to whale hell out of a group of rebels, just seconds too late to keep Leia and her pals from escaping (just think; if a few fewer fighters had been there, the story never would have taken off, would it?).

"We studied the movements of Darth Vader," Wilding recalls of getting ready. "We had a trainer who got it bang on. We wanted to keep 'Darth Vader.'" He split scenes with Daniel Naprous, who, like Wilding, appeared on *Game of Thrones* and in the *Harry Potter* series.

Decades after Vader's death, in both real life and film chronology, his influence lived on. In America and around the world, we felt it far from the theaters. We'll continue to do so until the end of time. Still, after seeing his end and then his beginning in the pair of trilogies, many thought the *Star Wars* saga would invent someone new to personify the dark side when the Empire's First Order struck back in 2015.

As *Wars* returned with *The Force Returns* in 2015, the Order just kept trying to make the New Republic old again, even after decades of spreading death and destruction all over the universe (a number that sounds pretty rough until we remember future WWII England and France squaring off for over a century in the 1300s and 1400s, and Chile spending nearly three centuries trying to pull itself away from Spain, a battle won in 1825).

Kylo Ren (Adam Driver) carried on a sad family tradition, bringing evil back to the Skywalker/Solo clan in 2015's *The Force Returns.*

"We have such short memories of huge events and mass genocide, and then we forget about it," observes former Marine **Adam Driver** of the common human race. "Finding these people, a lot of things have changed, but the circumstances are the same." The people in question? Only Han, Leia, Chewbacca, and the rest, now hanging out at Starkiller Base (what a wonderful self-reference!) with the rest of the Republic, hoping that Luke gets rid of his agoraphobia on some other planet and comes back to help out.

But where Luke and Leia had battled back against an older generation of Skywalker films before, now the family's younger side was against them. Personifying the power-starved immaturity that had driven Anakin to evil, Leia and Han's son Kylo Ren had set the war in motion by turning against Uncle Luke, and now followed in Grandpa's footsteps all the way to the Dark Side, commanding the same Stormtroopers so anxious to do Vader's bidding.

Ren, Driver explains, "feels that [Vader] was actually onto something, even though in Vader's final moments where he kind of relents. That even could be interpreted as just a moment. Not to taint an entire life, or career, of doing good work. For [Ren], it's just a moment."

Like Prowse and Anderson, much of Driver's early work came from under a costume and mask. "You really have to rely on the power of thought," he says. "That doesn't mean you can check out in any way. You still have to convey everything physically and trust that thinking is enough." Ren's look had been the end result of tons of trials and errors from the attire crew before filming.

"The costume really says a lot about [Ren] before he says anything," Driver says. "[Ren's] helmet is unpolished and unfinished. It's not refined. It's shiny in parts and reflects back what it sees. These are all metaphors that you can't really play, but it's good information. His lightsaber, you got the sense that it was homemade, and it could spontaneously combust at any minute. It didn't really seem like it was really reliable."

But it was, in one of the saddest moments of the entire saga. In a reversal from *Jedi*, Han asks, implores his boy to come back from the darkness. It looks like it might work. It looks like we might have the happy ending.

Then, of course, we realize that this series has to last at least two more films. Han's got to go the same way Ben Kenobi did back in *A New Hope*. Ren impales him with the saber, completing the violent act that his grandfather never could.

"We discovered Darth Vader first as someone who's very in control and controlled and didn't seem to waver whatsoever in his mission," says Driver, who found Ren's mindset by yelling out his lungs before filming. "That kind of dedication is something my character admires and wants to emulate. . . . [I tried to] not think of him as being bad, or evil, or a villain. Something that was more three-dimensional. He's more dangerous and unpredictable, and morally justified in doing what he thinks his right."

In times of trouble, Americans have always had a habit of turning to the movies for a few brief periods of inspiration, or maybe just a much-needed break from reality. When the Great Depression slammed our economy nearly a century ago, the fledgling film world became one of the few bright spots both for the spenders and the makers of money. As America's finances went from a concern to a near-panic as the 2010s began, we still spent more dough on *Avatar* (2009) than any other cinematic creation in history—until the *Force* awakened six years later, of course. No matter how rough life is in the real world, we always spare a bit of time and a few bucks to hit the movies.

The 1970s were the same, as films represented the reality of the political and inner turmoil engulfing America at the time. With inflation, the oil crisis, the war in Vietnam, Watergate, and every other black spot shining all over the United States—and, as is usually the case, much of the world—movies fit right in. *Jaws* became the all-time new box-office champ. Films like 1974's creations *Earthquake* and *Towering Inferno* may have had happy endings, but they were real. These natural disasters could happen at any time. They showed the sad reality that America was stuck in for the too long time being. In order to get to the uplifting endings that these films handed us, we had to wade through tons of fear and tragedy for the hours beforehand, and, again, we could encounter similar problems as soon as we left the theater.

But just as they always have been and will be, films were there for us. And shortly after the first edition of a club fighter from Philadelphia that gave us all a reason to believe again, another series would reach down and find the wide-eyed, naïve child that so many of us had been forced to force to the back, and took the entire film industry, especially the sci-fi aspect, to a place far, far away—and beyond any before.

No one who ever hit it big in Hollywood did so without taking a few huge chances, and a young man with galaxy-sized dreams was about to be the next one. He'd been working on the storyline for years, and he was flat-out tired of sitting around talking and thinking about seeing it come true. Hanging out with fellow filmmaking greenhorn Brian De Palma, George Lucas searched for a few people who could make his vision a reality.

The story itself wasn't much new: a young man without much experience at the whole social life thing is suddenly pulled into a whole new world, with death and destruction unlike any he's ever seen before. Learning that there's a woman in need of saving and led by a new mentor with a bit more experience in these things, he finds a new strength in battling evil and doing what's right just because it's right. When his role model leaves before the war's won, his sense of decency is derailed, but it's still up to him and the lady to push this fight to the finish line. And spurred on by her love and a desire to prove himself with some serious and never-before-felt self-confidence, just as all seems lost in the final battle, he emerges from near fatality to save the day, win everyone's heart, and live happily ever after.

In storyline terms, it was the same tale that had been only slightly modified in westerns and other action films for decades. It was the settings that would grab everyone's attention like a Death Star tractor beam.

Rather than the O.K. Corral, it would be on planets that existed only in one man's mind. Instead of a gang fight in a bar's back alley somewhere, this one would rage across entire galaxies. There would be no fists or six-shooters; weaponry here consisted of flying fighters and explosive lasers.

Now it was up to Lucas and crew to find the ones that could make it happen. As De Palma filled the cast for his terrifying *Carrie* (1976), Lucas met one potential Luke Skywalker and Princess Leia after another.

A fellow named Tommy Lee Jones stepped in for Skywalker. Kurt Russell's name came up. John Travolta arrived, and De Palma handed him a role in his flick. Then came a youngster who'd had a recurring role on the small screen in *The Texas Wheelers* (1974).

Not even he was sure what to expect. Mark Hamill had gotten a call from his agent, who told him only that the role was a farmboy.

"To show you how much I knew about the film," he remembers, "I started practicing a Midwestern accent." At the interview, he talked about his upbringing; Hamill had moved around a bit, living in Japan for awhile.

"We had two male characters," explains Lucas, "so I wanted the farm boy to be shorter than Han Solo. I also made a decision in the casting to lower the age considerably from what I'd had in mind, because I'd wanted to make a move about kids for kids, though, in a way, it's an adult kid's movie."

Hamill finished up, said thanks, and stepped out. On the female side, it appeared that Jodie Foster, fresh off her Oscar-nominated turn in *Taxi Driver* (1976), was in the lead, standing out among hundreds of others at the tryouts.

The princess, Lucas explains, "is a very sophisticated, urbanized ruler. She's a politician, she's accomplished, she's graduated and got her PhD at 18. I had to find an actress who could be young and still play with a lot of authority."

Carrie Fisher might have gotten a head start in Hollywood, being the daughter of longtime performers Debbie Reynolds and Eddie Fisher, but she didn't find herself too anxious to follow in their footsteps—yet.

"I didn't want to be an actress," she recalls. "I had watched what show business did to both my parents, which was bring them up, celebrate them, and then at about 40 for my mom, and earlier for my dad, it was over." Still, she'd been studying acting in England, and was back around Old Glory's shores for Christmas break when the most unexpected of presents arrived.

"When I saw the script [for *Star Wars*]," Fisher remembers, "I never figured they would hire me because I'm this short, sort of plump little thing. The script said Leia was this beautiful princess—she's just beautiful. I was desperate to do it because it was the best script I had ever seen; it was a fairytale."

Like Hamill, she gave it her all, and, also like him, had long since learned that performers should never set their expectations (if not their hopes and dreams) too high. Christmas came and went, and the second round of calls was made. Hamill and Fisher were lucky enough to be there when the phones started ringing.

Like Fisher, Hamill had been struck by the script, albeit for slightly less enamoring reasons. "Four pages of dialogue," he says of the next rehearsal. "There was one great line . . . and it was the hardest piece of dialogue I'd ever memorized. I came about half an hour early to the test, memorizing this line the way you memorize, 'she sells sea shells by the seashore.'"

The line? "We can't turn back. Fear is their greatest defense. I doubt if the actual security there is any greater than it was on Aquilae or Sullust. What there is, is most likely directed toward a large-scale assault."

"Who talks like that?" Hamill asks. "But you're selling it."

Faced with the task of becoming a person from another world, yet still very much like an Earthling, Fisher tried to go where she'd never been before.

"Leia was unconscious a lot, and I wanted to be unconscious," she says. "I have an affinity for unconsciousness. I thought I could play that very well. But I also wanted to be involved in all of it, with Wookies, with the monsters in the cantina. I would come out of the bathroom and say, 'General Kenobi!' My family thought I was crazy, because the dialogue was, 'A battle station with enough firepower to destroy an entire system.'"

Back to the rehearsals, back to tryouts, and back to uncertainty went the two.

"They taped a rehearsal and they taped another one," Fisher says, "and there was very little direction, and I thought, 'There is no way that I have it. . . . I'm not going to get to have lunch with monsters.'"

In late January, Hamill was having lunch with his agent, and listening to her read off a list of pending business issues. In the midst, she mentioned that he'd gotten the *Star Wars* role.

"I said, 'Wait a minute! Back up!'" he says. Elsewhere, Fisher roared out of a building in excitement after hearing that she'd become Leia.

Star Wars begins with the story of a pair of separate worlds. Luke Skywalker's living with his aunt and uncle on Tatooine, hanging out with them and a wise old fellow from around the dusty neighborhood named Ben Kenobi. Luke seems to bear a passing wonderment about his mother and father, but not really—his fledgling pilot career and those robots are giving him enough to worry about.

One of the first scenes filmed (in England) in March 1976 was Luke's purchase of C3PO and R2-D2, surrounded by a group of local kids hired to dress up as Jawas. When Luke chases down a runaway R2, Hamill originally made Luke go off on C3PO. Lucas told him to downplay Skywalker's emotions (once, R2's remote control malfunctioned and he ended up on the nearby *Jesus of Nazareth* set).

Working with non-humans like R2 and C3PO, Hamill says, was "like the ultimate test as far as using your imagination. Even bluescreen is about trying to imagine flying through space or imagining your reaction to an explosion of a ship."

So in the Skywalker neck of the galactic woods, everybody's happy and content. But not too many worlds away, the skies aren't so friendly. . . .

After trying out over two dozen hairdo types, Fisher and the rest of the crew had finally decided on a pair of earmuff-type buns for Leia, inspired by images of lady Native Americans and Mexican General Pancho Villa's female companions.

"I was a little afraid of it," says Fisher of the legendary 'do (she also lost ten pounds for the role). "I still am a little afraid of how I am going to look in it. I'd be running down a hallway and my hairdo would start falling apart. I didn't like having my breasts taped in. In space, they don't bounce. Princesses don't do that, so they taped me."

Luke and Leia (Mark Hamill and Carrie Fisher) took sibling rivalry to whole new levels and back again through the *Star Wars* series.

It's the most non-civil of wars between the evil Imperial Empire and a group of ragtag rebels on the right side of the law. With the help of superior weaponry and organization, the bad guys are gaining the upper hand in this fight, and the true knockout punch might be the destruction of the rebel base—if only they could find it.

They've been to the planet Alderaan and nabbed Leia from her homeland, but she's holding steady; she didn't get this high on the governmental scale so fast by being a nice yes-woman.

"The character was someone who was feisty, but I felt myself to be a bit of that too," Fisher says. "It would have been unlikely that I would have been cast as a shrinking violet."

Still, with the life of her family, friends, and the rest of Alderaan looking down the barrel of a Death Star death ray, she admits that her rebel pals are on the not-so-distant orb of Dantooine. But as is almost always the case, the Empire is shown to be men far from their word, and Alderaan is slaughtered anyway.

"When they blew up my planet, I was looking at a board with a guy doing this," Fisher says, waving her hand in the air.

But the princess may still have the upper hand after all; the Empire finds Dantooine abandoned, and throws Leia in jail, with her sentence soon to be commuted downwards.

Meanwhile, Luke and Ben have run into Han Solo and his oversized furry friend Chewbacca hanging out at the local watering hole, and gotten themselves caught up in the battle to join the rebel fleet. The first signs of Luke's Force-full abilities are coming out, as Ben's teaching him about using it aboard Han's Millennium Falcon.

And by now, the secret is out about old Ben; his moniker's actually Obi-Wan, and he was the man who ran things in a former time.

"At first, I felt very much like you do when you go before the principal, but then I thought I should be more myself, because that's what he's like," the then-inexperienced Hamill says of working with the more practiced performer, in and out of character. "So we loosened up to the point where I could just sit next to him and not say anything for an hour while they were setting up.... Two or three times, he would say, 'May I suggest something?' And gosh, I wish he would do that all the time, because he was always right. He would say, 'Stop and think of what you're saying. Are you *talking* about going or are you *going*?'"

As Luke's Forces start to swirl, the Falcon's caught in a tractor beam and hauled into the Death Star. Here's where they first learn a man titled Vader and his Kenobi connection.

The group splits up, with the veteran looking to shut down the Star's power and the trio hunting for the princess.

In the prison scene for Vader's torture, Fisher had to make herself scared.

"I was in a little box of a room, so I used the idea of claustrophobia to make it scary," she says. "But it was hard to be afraid of Darth Vader. They called him 'Darth Farmer' because David Prowse had this thick Welsh accent, and he couldn't remember the lines—I guess I could have been afraid of that."

The rescue works, and the group finds its way back to the Falcon. But just as they arrive, Vader and Kenobi are in the midst of their final lightsaber war, and the Man in Black appears to win, slicing through a disappearing (but grinning) Kenobi. A late addition to the storyline itself, Kenobi was originally supposed to escape the Star. Realizing this would render the character with nothing to do afterward, Lucas rewrote the script to have Kenobi die, only to reappear when anyone needed some extra guidance.

Back on the Rebel Base, actually located on a moon of the planet Yavin, the Death Star's only weakness, a six-foot-wide exhaust port, is revealed. With Han on the run after revealing a weakness for the color green and a yellow streak up his back, Luke's ready to prove himself to everyone, including Kenobi's voice in his mind.

As the Star nears, the Rebels start living up to their name, but Vader and others get to taking them out, and soon Luke is one of the only ones left. With the Dark Lord and a colleague on his tail, it looks like Luke's going to run out of time. But Han shows back up and blasts the Imperial fighter, sending Vader spinning out of control. Now with the Force truly with him, Luke hits the ultimate Star shot, and he and Han race away as the evil ship suffers the same fate it laid on Alderaan.

If the storyline had ended right there, everything would have seemed full circle, and had the film bombed at the box office, that would had to have been enough. But *Star Wars* took the rare step from production to phenomenon, as ticket and merchandise sales like never before rolled through their respective markets. It even scored 10 Oscar nominations (including Best Picture) and nabbed seven statuettes.

While many film fans would be entertained so many times over, the film eventually pushed others to fulfill their own filmmaking fantasies. When it came out, a fellow named James Cameron was driving trucks; the Wars sparked an inspiration in him that would help engineer the *Alien* and *Terminator* franchises and box-office bonanzas about a sinking ocean liner and blue-skinned aliens. It made Spielberg nervous about releasing his own sci-fi film, although genre fans would be glad he overcame it when they saw *Close Encounters of the Third Kind* (1977). Peter Jackson, who had to wait until December before the film arrived in his native New Zealand, checked it out several times and later piggybacked on its special effects techniques to bring the long-overdue *Lord of the Rings* box-office and award-snaring smash trilogy to the big screen.

"If you were to take *Star Wars* out of film history for a moment, and therefore all the technology that was generated by *Star Wars*," Jackson says, "you would just be seeing a whole different landscape of entertainment over the last thirty years. Nowhere near as exciting. We'd all be in cinemas with terribly scratchy optical soundtracks watching celluloid disintegrate before our eyes."

As the 1970s ended, the next chapter kicked off, and many still call it the best of the three—or the eight, depending on how we look at it here in early 2017. As *Empire Strikes Back* starts, the *Wars* group is still on the run and end up on the snowy grounds of Hoth (actually Norway). Leia and Han roar off in the Falcon, but Vader's got them soon, and whatever humanity he ever possessed is in the far aftermath.

"The dialogue for our screen test was even more complicated than that in *Star Wars*," Fisher recalls. "The sentences were *so* long. You didn't know what you were talking about, so finally you have to ask, 'George, in my motivation for this scene, you must tell me, what *is* a Bantha? What is the species of Bantha? What am I actually saying?' You just have to give it up and trust that you mean what you're saying. So I went and read after all that English training and was able to get the dialogue out of my mouth." **Note: Banthas are the elephant-like, huge-horned creatures that roam the deserts of Tatooine.**

With Kenobi still leading him from the great beyond, Luke lands on the jungle-like land of Dagobah, where a small, green creature with a not-so-tight grip on the English language takes the pilot under his wing, or at least one of his huge ears, and through some serious Jedi Knight training.

June 25, 1979, marked quite the full day for Hamill; after he and his wife welcomed their new son in the wee hours of the morning, he'd intended to sleep in for the day. But around noon, he got a call asking to come in and jump around before a screen, helping Luke leap from his snowspeeder just before a walker's ominous foot crushes it into rubble.

"It's so funny to have something that personal going on and then have to come in and do a movie. It seems so absurd. Here I am standing in front of a bluescreen with fake snow and just jumping and landing on my face. For this I went to acting school?"

Still, he continues, "I actually found training for the role kind of fun. Before I came over [to Norway], I spent four months learning karate, fencing, kendo, and bodybuilding, because I do a lot of strenuous stunts on the bog planet."

Let's go ahead and play devil's advocate with this and acknowledge a glaring plot hole in the trilogy; after we spend the first film and half of another hearing about how Jedi Knight training requires a lifetime of dedication and devotion, something only a select few are lucky enough to even start, we see Luke complete nearly the entire course in a few days (yes, Yoda does caution that he's not done, but says he's OK in *Return of the Jedi*).

"Even though it [was] difficult and aggravating at times," Hamill says of shooting in the very-far-off-spot, "when the moment actually comes when they're filming, there's that moment when you're really there in your mind, believing it—that's the most fun, when it all becomes real to you. I can't get over that. They give you the outfit, guns, and hardware—it's like being a kid again." Considering the film's final plot twist, that's an interesting choice of words.

Soon, Luke races to his friends' rescue, and he and Vader come lightsaber to lightsaber for the first time.

"The most frightening thing I had to do," he says, "was to back away from Darth Vader along a plank nine inches wide, 30 feet above the ground, with two wind machines going full blast . . . I'd say this is an eight-weeks-in-the-hospital type of fall."

Finally, it was time for the scene in which Vader tries to shine some darkness into Luke's heart, and reveals the secret that, odds are, made Nostradamus wake up and spin in his grave. Here's where he drops the atomic parental bomb.

"At the time we filmed *Star Wars*, I had no idea that Darth Vader was my father," Hamill admits. "I don't think Alec Guinness did either, because in the scene where I ask him who my father was [in *Star Wars*], he hesitated."

By the end of *Empire*, everyone knew that Lucas would try to make the third time a charm with *Star Wars*; nothing was going to end with Han frozen in carbonite! So as *Return of the Jedi* opened on May 25, 1983 (six years to the day after *A New Hope*), it's back to Tatooine, where Jabba the Hutt—truly a villain that you couldn't help but want to hang out with sometime—has the man named Solo prisoner, with Leia enslaved, though many of *Jedi*'s hormone-crazed teenage fanbase was too busy admiring her in that gorgeous skimpy gold outfit to worry too much about her plight.

As he always had a tendency to do, R2-D2 shows up and saves the day, and everyone makes it out OK. Now equipped with both the knowledge of his twin sister's true identity and an alliance with a bunch of miniature gorillas—Ewoks, for those not in the realization—on Endor, Luke leaves to face Big Daddy for the final time. Meanwhile, Leia, Solo, and the rest of the gang set about destroying the shield protecting the new Death Star.

In *Empire*, Fisher says, Leia was, "not exactly helpless or victimized, but the sort of girl who might lose her passport—or the spacecraft." But as *Jedi* came about, "I always felt that Leia had a strength which was more based on anger than a strength that was power. Her strength came from bitterness about wanting to eliminate evil from the universe. All the characters are more developed in *Jedi*. It was interesting . . . because I was much more feminine this time. [In earlier films] I feel like I am under orders and I keep saying the lines like, 'You came in that thing?' And I was insulting people."

Meanwhile, Luke gives in to Vader, but not to the Darkness. Inspired by his son's courage and a long-gone sense of paternity, Vader finally comes back the right way.

"With *Jedi*, I was a bit disappointed," Hamill admits, "because I said 'Gee, it's all so pat and tied up neatly in a bunch.' George explained to me, 'Remember, this is meant to be a film for children.' And it is a fairytale and fairytales are very neatly tied up. Even though it appealed to the child in all of us, I realized he was right, that you have to remain true to your original intent, and it was for really young people."

That's young in years and young at heart, and for more than a few generations; two decades after the films' releases, those who had enjoyed them as children got to watch it alongside their own kids, as the trilogy came back out. In the spring of 1997, after watching the first film at home on the small screen for so long, fans headed back to the theater and spent almost another $200 million. After knocking Spielberg from the top of the box-office ranks by getting past *Jaws*, *Star Wars* shoved another of his films into second place, as *Star Wars* passed *E.T.* for the all-time record (Cameron's *Titanic* and *Avatar* have since slipped above it, only to be overtaken by *Force Awakens*). *Empire* and *Jedi* combined for nearly $100 million in their re-releases, pushing the trilogy total past a billion American dollars.

Just after the first edition came out, Fisher made it a habit of driving by theaters to check out the long lines. Time and time again, she could never believe her eyes.

"I only get a sense of *Star Wars*' importance when a child recognizes me and becomes speechless," she says. "Kids don't think I'm from this planet. Very little children even believe Princess Leia is a real human being who lives in outer space."

"It seems as if *Star Wars* is the life and breath of my existence," Hamill says. "For the most part, I've really been moved by it. The fans are very loyal, and concerned with what I'm doing. I can't help but appreciate their reaction, since I didn't have any of that when I started out."

But the *Star Wars* saga will never truly end, with the new films, books, TV shows, and the like constantly adding their own take to the saga. For her part, Fisher didn't see Leia following in the future political footsteps of her mother (referring to Amidala, not Reynolds).

"I think she would become more of a combination of solider and a human being," she guesses of the princess's future, "and a woman. I think that she would lessen her involvement, it almost seems like a very young thing to participate in a war . . . Leia must be a little too old for war. She would take more of a ruling-space desk job. I would like to see her relax a bit and just take a leisurely space ride when she wasn't being chased by another spaceship."

Hamill saw Luke following in the footsteps of his original mentor. "I think Luke would be someone who's very much like Obi-Wan was in the first film," he says. "I think he's out meditating and becoming more Dalai Lama-like in his pursuit of The Force. And it puts the whole notion of male/female relationships into perspective where, yes that's very nice to marry and have a family and procreate and so forth, but in the greater scheme of things, he's selfless."

To cast the hairiest member of his new flick, Lucas wasn't looking for much.

Chewbacca and Han Solo would form one of the most unlikely and beloved teams in action film history.

His actor needed to be willing to wear a long, thick costume, and grunt for a few hours at a time. He needed to be able to show fear in a non-human sort of way — how, exactly, do a Wookie's emotions work, anyway?

Oh… he also had to be about seven feet tall. Kosher as the bagel/lox combo, right?

Acting, Peter Mayhew admits, "was the last thing I wanted to do. But it's like wandering down a corridor and you've got two doors at the end of the corridor. You don't know what's behind one of them, and you know what's behind the other. Do you take a chance? And that's what I did."

Mayhew stepped into the director's office and sat down to wait. A few minutes later, Lucas came in.

The actor stood up. The director looked up – way up.

"I stand 7'4"," Mayhew says. "That's big, even by George's standards."

Lucas turned to one of the film's producer.

"I think we found him," he said. Chewbacca had been located.

"That, basically, was the interview," Mayhew recalls. "Within an hour, we talked about what we were doing, how the costume is going to work, and what the character was like. Within two weeks, the costume had been made, and we were shooting on our first set." He was becoming Han Solo's right-hand animal, his copilot and amigo on the Millennium Falcon.

"There was a possibility of playing him two different ways," Mayhew says. "The first was big and nasty. The other was still big, but curious, and that was the way that George wanted this character to be played. He wanted Chewie to be a lovable character. We had to develop the character as inquisitive but still protective. We decided to make him a teddy bear."

And that took a different kind of acting than many actors ever get (or take) the chance to give a shot, he continues.

"Chewie doesn't speak," Mayhew explains, "so you have to play him as a mime artist. Therefore, you have to have the awareness, when you're with other people, that you don't stand there for too long in the same place."

Fortunately, he had a bit of extra help in developing the Wookie Language.

"That was a brown bear that they found in San Diego," Mayhew says of the creature's "voice." "They recorded it when it was happy, when it was sad, when it was hungry and when it was full. That way, you've got all four emotions."

Even as Star Wars became a landmark in cinema history, not everything was easy for the Grand High Wookie.

"(The costume) was bloody hot most of the time," Mayhew says. "Of course, when we filmed Empire in Norway, I was the only one who stayed warm. I could have made a fortune renting out that costume.

"Your character builds and builds and builds, and fans know exactly what you're talking about," Mayhew says. "It's relatively easy because you just know out of instinct, 'This is right, that's what he would do, that's not what he would do.'" At the height of his fame, Chewy was getting thousands of fan letters every week.

"There was never any thought of his having a human voice," Mayhew says. "He's got every other human feeling, but he can't talk. There is, however, a definite language in those barks and growls – aggressive, inquisitive, or passionate… well, passionate is probably not the right word."

Like other actors who have become creatures (hey, it can be a fun trade, just like anything else!), Mayhew had to find some humanity in the non-human, to take something with characteristics out of this species – and, in this case, twenty light-years out of this world – and use them to make a lovable character. It's why, by the time the Jedi returned, Chewy was one of the series' most lovable characters, and still is today (it's easy to believe that many people watched Revenge of the Sith to see how their favorite Wookie came about – the creature's costume even had to be re-made, Mayhew points out, because he'd have been younger at the time the story took place).

"Once that mask goes on," he says, "I can sit down, be talking to people waiting to go on, they put the mask on and Chewie just comes alive. It's crazy, I know, and it happens on every movie. And with the 20-year gap between Jedi and Revenge of the Sith, I'd worn the costume a couple of times, but when we went back and made the new costume it was just a question of, 'OK, here we go again.' And the character was there. I didn't have to do anything."

It doesn't take much to win the hearts of acting fans. All one needs is to portray someone who does what's right, no matter what it takes. A person they can count on, as their co-stars can. Maybe that's why Lucas chose to kept Chewie going through all the end credits – because he realized that fans would always take to their giant friend.

"Chewy is just a great big teddy bear," Mayhew says. "He is loyal to his friends and he will rip apart anyone who threatens his friends… He's a weird character, but he's a unique character at the same time. Because when you allow droids and robots to do what they want to do, who's gonna stop the wookie?"

Darth Vader might get the majority of attention when it comes to the bad guys of *Star Wars*, and rightfully so, but we shouldn't forget that he was never the top face on the totem pole when it came to Imperial evil. When he was becoming Vader's boss Emperor Palpatine in *New Hope* through *Jedi*, Ian McDiarmid had a task only slightly easier than a lightsaber battle.

"It only slowly dawned on me that if Vader was really the worst creature, the most evil, the darkest, the blackest villain in movie history, I was worse than him," Ian McDiarmid says. "And I'm still slowly coming to terms with that, actually. I think my relationship with Satan is closer than I ever imagined it to be—as a character I hasten to add." Not only that, but he'd have to do it all himself—Vader had one (well, more than one) man doing his physical work, and another in the voice area. McDiarmid carried the full load all the way.

As with Anakin and the man he became, viewers first saw the Emperor at his worst; not until the prequels would anyone get to learn of his remotely human side. Like Vader, Palpatine wasn't always a bad guy—only letting power overcome his sense of right against wrong.

"I didn't know how evil he was going to be," says McDiarmid of getting to know the character the first time around (first time meaning the filming of the *Star Wars* films of the 70s and 80s). "I knew he was going to be pretty evil until I got the script. And I also didn't know that he would have fighting skills, which I had to acquire fairly quickly. I imagined that his power was in his fingers and in his head. Little did I know that he was the fastest lightsaberist in the universe."

After a quick meeting with Lucas won him the role the first time around, McDiarmid went bad three times over, ending with Vader finally turning back to good and saving his son from the Emperor.

It's tough to believe that Emperor Palpatine (Ian McDiarmid) was ever on the side of good as we saw his *Star Wars* dirty work.

"I had some time to get to know this character," McDiarmid says. "I thought, 'Well, he comes from the bowels of the earth. He looks like an old toad.' And before I knew it, I was making the voice . . . It just came out and George, as usual, heard it and within about 10 seconds liked it, fortunately. And I've been stuck with it happily ever since."

Over a decade after his character's death, McDiarmid stepped into a hotel room to hang out with his filmmaking friend.

"[Lucas] said, 'What would you like to drink?' I said, 'I think I'll take a sparkling mineral water.' And he said, 'Oh by the way, do you know anyone who wants to play an emperor?' I said, 'Oh, funny you should say that.' He said, 'Great, you can give the water back.' And that was that once again . . . he did say that the character would be on the sidelines in movies one and two and move into the middle with number three. But I didn't realize he would move in with quite such a bang."

"Bang" is quite the understatement; Palpatine seems pretty harmless at first, persuading Queen Amidala to help him snare the chancellor position of the Galactic Republic, which she does as an afterthought, thinking the position's little more than a paper spot. When someone tries to assassinate her as *Attack of the Clones* (2002) kicks off, he sends Obi-Wan and their collective protégé Anakin to protect her. But his lust for power flares; as the evil droids attack, the Republic gives him emergency powers to call the clones into battle. Meanwhile, Count Dooku starts murmuring about the evil Darth Sidious, secretly running things in the Republic.

And as would be the case with the first young Skywalker, Palpatine's darkness comes straight to light in *Revenge of the Sith*. As Anakin struggles with own inner conflict, taking the typical young adult identity crisis to a whole new level, Palpatine reveals himself as the dark Darth Sidious and convinces Anakin that everyone's out to get him—and just as Mace Windu realizes what's going on and nearly burns Palpatine's face off into ashes, Skywalker takes his last step into evil, showing his final true alliance.

"[Lucas] said, 'You should think of your eyes—Ian's eyes, Palpatine's eyes—as his: Sidious' contact lenses.' In other words, my face was his mask, which is an extremely interesting thing to say to an actor. I knew that in Episode III . . . that this face would have to burst through my own mask. So in a sense I couldn't wait. . . . And it would be my sort of Dr. Jekyll/Mr. Hyde moment, my Dorian Gray moment, when outer good is subverted by inner evil."

He even got to square off with Yoda in the closing moments—as things had gone with Alec Guinness when the elder Obi-Wan had battled Vader in the first film, McDiarmid gave it all he had with some reasonably limited physicality, and got things done fast.

"Fighting Yoda was a joy," McDiarmid says, "and I then got to experience the full beauty of CGI. In other words, actors in battle with invisible people. . . . Then I sensed, in fact, George asked for it in a very polite way, he wanted a few sort of improvised strokes. So basically I did a rap to thin air at the end of the choreographed sequence and then collapsed with exhaustion and hysterical laughter on the floor.

"He was a politician and he turned out to be an evil monster," McDiarmid says of the Emperor. "That's not too difficult a story to follow, either in *Star Wars* or if you happen to be looking at the front of any newspaper in practically any country. If you come from England, various people come to mind. And if you come from the United States, you're not short of candidates there either."

As quick as so many were to hastily draw some comparisons between *Star Wars* and the

Nazi regime, McDiarmid could see some signs of another dictorial-esque government start to emerge through Palpatine and the character's actions.

"Many other layers emerge," he says, "and the one that interests me most, perhaps not unnaturally as I play the character, is the chart of the rise of evil, of fascism, if you like. And it's very carefully plotted in the film, not just through my character but through organizations like the Trade Federation. I bet some of you . . . have not found the Trade Federation fascinating. This may change when you watch the films in sequence because you'll see how my character was manipulating quietly, steadily, patiently—the key word—all the time."

But long before Anakin became Vader and while the Emperor was still in the Senate, another villain had to terrify us and send Qui-Gon Jinn to the same fate that Vader would send Kenobi soon after.

Like his Vader predecessor, *Phantom Menace* bad guy Darth Maul was a combination of two performers; while Ray Park was showing off the skills that won him international karate fame, Peter Serafinowicz underwent the same task that James Earl Jones had stepped into decades before.

After three vocal tryouts, Serafinowicz stepped before the puppeteer himself: Lucas.

"I was trying to exude this coolness, but I kept tripping over things—inside I was nearly having a heart attack," recalls Serafinowicz, who appeared in *Shaun of the Dead* (2004), *Grindhouse* (2007), and his own self-titled satirical talk show. "I did my impression of Darth Vader for him and he laughed."

Like Jones, he did the full voice work in a single day. That doesn't sound tough when we consider that Maul only speaks four lines (the most memorable of which being simply, "Yes, my master."), but there was quite a bit to cram into each one: evil, intensity . . . maybe even a bit of seductive hypnotism.

Serafinowicz looked back at previous *Star Wars* characters for help, like Grand Moff Tarkin, who Peter Cushing brought to life.

Who's this handsome devil? Why, it's Darth Maul (Ray Park), looking to demonstrate his last name on any who dared diddle with the Empire!

"I was thinking of the legacy of the Star Wars films and these English baddies," he explains.

Behind the red and black makeup and spiked hairdo, Park took a few steps back towards childhood, and added a few flips and jump-kicks along the way.

Star Wars, recalls the Glasgow native, "was the first film I saw when my family moved to London. I was only seven and my dad took me to see it. I remember being completely blown away when Obi Wan pulled out his lightsaber in the bar. I begged my dad to buy me one, and eventually he did. It was one of those old white plastic tubes with a light bulb in it. I used to love having play fights with my younger brother in the street—but I would always have to be Han Solo, because he was the cool one who got the girl!"

It wasn't the only memory he'd revisit; like so many young men of the time did, Park strolled into martial arts after watching Bruce Lee tear things—and people—apart on the screen. Before he was old enough to drive, he'd scored a black belt, and international titles would follow.

As the "first" *Star Wars* came about, Park saw a shot at the miracle.

"Before I got the role," he explains, "I saw pictures of Darth Maul on the storyboards, and I knew that was me." Wowing the crew with kicks, punches, and others moves at speeds unseen since Lee himself, Park got to become the new Man in Black (and Red!).

"I gave 3000 percent in order to get that part, and when I got it, I was over the moon," Park recalls. "I knew what I could do with that character. It came naturally to me in how I would play it on the physical level."

It was that physicality that critics didn't like about Maul, saying it made him less intimidating than Vader, who could scare holy hell out of anyone just by the way he walked and breathed. But that's not a fair comparison; first of all, Park wasn't trying to be like Vader, but made Maul his (or their) own man. This wasn't a time for impersonation. Second of all, Maul's full-body agility and ninja-esque fighting skills gave him a set of weaponry that Vader didn't have. Vader might have been more frightening at first; his mystique just made us feel like he was looking straight through us and into our souls, and that we couldn't see the eyes he was using just dropped the degree level a few more digits. Maul might have had to prove, or display, just what a tough guy he was, but that doesn't mean he wasn't more intimidating, only that he had to show us, whereas Vader could convince us without so much as speaking. Besides, again, Parks wasn't trying to become another Vader—Maul was an individual, not a copy.

"I had always thought George Lucas was God, and had loads of respect for him," Park says. "It was really nerve-racking knowing I would be working with loads of big stars."

But that didn't mean that he, castmate Ewan McGregor, and the rest of the Jedi knights couldn't act like the children who'd once felt the magic of *Star Wars*.

"The fight scenes were funny, because we used to muck about and make the noises of the lightsabers," Park recalls. "We just couldn't help it! We were doing something we used to watch when we were kids—and it was absolutely great.... Some days the fighting was so fiery our lightsabers ended up completely bent, and I remember after one big scene George Lucas came out and said 'Great, but we have to slow these guys down somehow... they're moving too quickly for the camera!'"

You could say (or I could just write) that Jabba the Hutt personifies the teamwork, the effort that made the *Star Wars* saga legendary. You could also label him the victim of technological innovation, proof that computers aren't always so damned helpful.

When we met Jabba in *Jedi* (not acknowledging his cameo in the 1997 rerelease of the first film), we were scared. We were angry, as he'd enslaved our (dreamed-of) girlfriend, and was now going to make Leia's boyfriend Rancor chow.

Still, flaws aside, we couldn't help to think (certainly never out loud) that Jabba was actually pretty cool. Laid back sort, quite financially secure, fine tastes in fine women... yeah, except for that pet of his and his willingness to diversify its diet, we might want to hang out with the Hutt sometime.

Today, decades later, I'm still getting diagnosed with just about every psychiatric disorder for feeling this way by *Star Wars* fans from hither to thither (like my series fanatic wife, who can't possibly comprehend how anyone could think that huge ugly slug was cool!). And yes, Leia's beauty aside, you feel a little guilty for ogling a lady in an outfit she's forced to wear.

The pair wouldn't win any beauty contests, but Jabba the Hutt and Boba Fett made a hell of a mob squad, making Princess Leia into Tatooine's loveliest captive in *Return of the Jedi* in 1983.

See, almost two decades after the Hutt hitman's first showing, we met Jabba again. But we really weren't that impressed when he cameoed in the *New Hope* re-release of 1997. As he and Han Solo discussed a financial debate, Jabba just didn't look too effective, even if CGI was still in its infancy at that time. The self-confidence he'd all but oozed in *Jedi* (and he'd oozed *quite* a bit in *Jedi*!) was gone. He was nothing special now. If his *New Hope* appearance had been left in the first 1977 film, it would have undercut the hell out of his *Jedi* showup.

Even for an overgrown slug, that didn't work for us. Many *Star Wars* fans will tell you that CGI stole a sense of traditionalism from the *Star Wars* fraternity—and after the technological blitzkrieg that all but overrode the plot of *Attack of the Clones*, it's tough to argue.

See, Jabba just deserved better, and now those that made him such a strong part not just of the film, but the entire *Star Wars* series, will explain just how they managed to make it for him.

One challenge after another to even attempt to meet the deadline. One hour after another added to their workload. A group of folk so hard at work, getting larger as the task grew along with it.

Making and operating Jabba the Hutt was some of the greatest fun any of them would ever have.

He hadn't started with much. Stuart Freeborn, leader of the squad behind the legendary makeup of both Yoda and Chewbacca, had handed John Coppinger the Hutt moniker and a miniaturized maquette (small-scale model, intended as a jumping-off point for a larger, more polished one). Now he expected Coppinger to take these two items, add his imagination, and come out with something that would help *Return of the Jedi* personify the whole "third's a charm" cliché. Jabba the Hutt could potentially end up as one of the biggest artificially created characters in film history. Essentially, Coppinger had to make a slug on steroids seems villainous to an audience already terrified by Vader, the Emperor, and others.

"We discussed the name, Jabba the Hutt," he remembers, "and decided George Lucas could have named him and the Ewoks for the Jabberwock in *Alice Through the Looking-Glass*." For physical guidance, they also looked to Frank Herbert's 1981 best-selling sci-fi novel *God Emperor of Dune*, the story of the title character morphed into a half man/half obscenely huge sandworm.

Fresh off working on Jim Henson's *Dark Crystal* (1982) and model-building at the nearby Natural History Museum of London, Coppinger considered his options.

First off, he couldn't do it alone. This was going to be a task that even Jedi Knights couldn't do without assistance. Building Jabba would be a quest slightly simpler than swimming the Pacific; operating him would be even tougher.

"It was immediately obvious that one performer wouldn't be able to span his arms," Coppinger recalls, "so we tested the concept of a two-person 'cockpit' for arm, jaw, and head movements, and external controls for his features. Knowing his main dimensions and volumes, I could then sculpt Jabba in clay while the team built up and Tom McLaughlin began experiments with the chemistry of foam latex." On a quest larger than any in the world of film had ever taken, the two put together some methods they could only hope would work.

"No one had made such large foam pieces before," Coppinger recalls, "and Tom had to find ways to cast foam in fibreglass molds, rather than heavy plaster, allow the foam to be injected under pressure and extend the gel time so the foam wouldn't collapse before it was cooked." While Coppinger and McLaughlin became the Drs. Frankenstein to Jabba, Jez Harris and Bob Keen looked to link radio control for the Hutt's eyes and heart-melting smile.

"This was a radical idea," Coppinger says, "but the two people inside would have plenty to do, operating the jaw, head, and arms, so the number of operators began to increase." Pint-sized Mike Edmonds, recruited to join the Ewok tribe, squeezed himself into Jabba's not-quite-proportionate gut to operate the long tail that curled around Jabba's throne, letting everyone on Tatooine know that this guy had been running the show for centuries, and he was going to stay there as long as he wanted.

"We began devising the mechanism for the tail," Coppinger says, "and Mike Osborne made a woven net of nylon line that would support the foam and allow it to stretch and flex. Mike also suggested a win-win solution for the belly: a large, softly inflated latex balloon that gave the illusion of weight while being extremely light and moveable." Preparation stretched on and on, and everyone hoped it wouldn't blindly crash into the first day of filming.

"I reverse-sculpted inside the fiberglass molds to shape and establish the depth of the foam at different parts of his body," explains Coppinger. "These secondary molds were also used to make a supporting, internal skeleton or shell that the foam would fit onto, with cut-aways for cable or radio-operated paddles to move his face or allow his body to flex." Jabba's jaw and eye mechanics were installed, a new tail was built for Jabba's kicked-back bedroom and sail barge sets. Trampoline springs were added to help the creation raise and float around, and a spring-supported tube allowed Jabba's head to gyrate. As more people joined the Jabba squad, he was finally painted up mere days before filming began.

Still, there needed to be more to Jabba than just looks; his personality had enabled him to roll to the top of Tatooine's organized crime ranks, and one needed to be quite intimidating to scare a gal as gutsy as Leia.

"We had his lines and the story, so it was fairly obvious he was a tyrant," Coppinger says, "but we felt there should be a more complex, even slightly benign, darkly humorous quality to his dictatorship." Giving Jabba large, round eyes would come too close to cartoonish, so Coppinger went with round pupils in larger, oval shapes.

"Each morning, I would go onto the empty set, change out Jabba's eye batteries, and test the radio rig from a distance," remembers Coppinger. "Every time the monster 'woke up,' it made me jump. Maybe I'd been working too many hours!" Someone else came on board to operate the Hutt's mouth, brows, even his nostrils, upping the Jabba operation squad to eight.

By this point, director Richard Marquand didn't always know with whom he was chatting if Jabba had some issues—and he certainly would.

"On the first day we realised that Richard Marquand should address his requests directly to Jabba, rather than talk to any one of the crew," Coppinger says. "We were all on the radio loop, and it was up to us to work out the coordination that would make Jabba believable as a character." With hardly any rehearsal time, Jabba's jobbers hung out within and out to elevate their creation to legend.

"The inside performers only had small black and white monitors, fed from a video camera near the main camera to orientate their movements and Jabba's reactions to the rest of the cast," Coppinger says. "It was a question of learning intuitively, especially for the eyes: triangulating from a corner, out of shot, to make sure Jabba was looking at the person he was talking to, plus getting the right expression, was absorbing to say the least!"

Certain that things will work out in his favor as they always have, even if he has to bend the hell out of righteousness to do so, Jabba giggles as Luke is tossed into the pit of Jabba's favourite pet Rancor, nearly smirking down at the upcoming Jedi knight, who's about to unleash all kinds of hell.

As Jabba glaringly grins down at Luke, "even with everything 'maximum down,' we couldn't quite get a steep enough angle," Coppinger admits. David Tomblin, one of Marquand's directing assistants, suggested pushing Jabba from behind, and it was up to the editors to convince us that the creature had moved all on his own.

"One of the best compliments we ever got," says Coppinger, "was when [Tomblin] barged through us on set, with a backward thumb stab to Jabba, saying 'You did a good job on that thing!'"

As Leia, her brother, and everyone else finally get some final revenge on Jabba, he falls at the hands of the smallest, yet most justified avenger.

"The chain Leia wrapped round [Jabba's] throat tore the foam latex at every take, and we had to make high speed repairs with glue, paint, and hair driers," Coppinger says. Teamwork came around for the shot as well, as a Mike Quinn crouched behind Jabba's belly bulged out the Hutt's eyes, then sank them back in as the Hutt man finally passed.

"The guide track for the music had drilled into our heads on set and generated a very surreal atmosphere," Coppinger exclaims, "alongside the smell of bee smoke, the perfume of latex, and the demands of operating Jabba! All in all, we felt we'd gotten away with it and made Jabba live as a convincing character."

In films, hard work and morality almost always translate into positive effects; it certainly had in *A New Hope*, but not in *Empire*, which ended with the villains in the lead. Coppinger and his colleagues had done as much as anyone else on the sets of *Star Wars* before and after, but the audience would determine the final outcome. Would Jabba be as terrifyingly cool as Marquand, Coppinger, and the rest would hope, or would crowds say, "What the hell? Was that thing supposed to be scary or something?"

If you don't know the answer to that, you probably quit reading this profile after the first few sentences anyway.

"I never expected to be talking about it more than thirty years later," Coppinger admits, "but I do remember thinking, as I left the empty stage for the last time, 'Whatever else happens in my life, I will know I've been on a *Star Wars* set!'"

A long, long time ago (well, decades at least), in a country far, far away (several *hours* by plane, at least from America), Prowse was joined in his South London gym by a fellow named Jeremy Bulloch. A Leicestershire native, Bulloch was looking to transition from child star to grownup performer, and some improvements in the mesomorphic department might help transform boyishness to manliness.

Decades later, the pair would gaze glaringly into each other's eyes yet again, their faces covered in ominous masks, Han Solo's tormented carbon form looming sadly in the background.

A scientific experiment gone terrifyingly right, for his (its) creators on Kamino, Boba Fett was a clone on attack almost from birth, ready to go Jedi preying for the right price. Much more studious for his instructor than Anakin ever was for Kenobi, Fett watched his master Jango bounty hunt through the wars until he became him, then went so far as to evolve, out to destroy the rebellion that threatened his Empire's peaceful galaxy.

Like Vader, it was Fett's skills that earned him quite a bit of respect (certainly not admiration!) from those on both sides of the rebellion. Boba got some serious higher-up reverence from both the Darth man, who put him in charge of moving the Solo iceberg to Tatooine, and a Hutt named Jabba, who gave him a mercenary-ship at the main squid's palace.

Add up the respect he got (hell, *stole*) from guys who could have had him killed in a moment, the skill and smarts that he had with his work, and our ability to continue to decide for ourselves just what the hell was under that costume—as we did with Vader until the last moments of *Return of the Jedi*—and there's a mansion's laundry list of reasons why Fett's name became a force upon itself in the *Star Wars* fraternity, enough that he got a backstory when the prequels arrived!

OK, yes, we'd actually seen the guy under Fett's armor, but the Internet wasn't around to beat the connection into the ground when *Empire* came out. As Leia warns her brother of Vader's trap, she's suddenly snared by an Imperial officer.

He was Lieutenant Sheckil. He was Bulloch. Bulloch was also Fett. Character to character in one film and two degrees!

Between film roles, Bulloch had switched to stages for a time, London audiences watching him at the legendary West End Theatre. His half-brother Robert Watts asked if he'd mind doing some double-timing in the flick Watts was producing on association.

"I was working in the theater," Bulloch recalls, "so I was surprised that [the *Empire* crew] was happy for me to leave in good time to get to the set every day." As he became Fett on the set, the crew became the hunter's first group of fanatical followers.

He switched from chasing Jedi rebels to superspies over the next few years, as Bulloch played Smithers, the sidekick to Q, James Bond's weapons man in *For Your Eyes Only* (1981) and 1983's *Octopussy* (Bulloch had walked by the cameras for *The Spy Who Loved Me* in 1977). But unlike with the end of *A New Hope*, the world knew from the end of *Empire* that another chapter would follow, and it came in 1983, the Jedi returning for the revenge that they were too moral to actually call "revenge."

"I was thrilled to be asked as the films were becoming such a success," Bulloch recalls (Watts also helped produce *Jedi*). "I used the same technique, which is just 'the less I did, the more cool the character appears.'"

Moments away from becoming the Sarlaac's next meal, Luke suddenly mentally yanks a lightsaber into his hand and goes all over the offensive. With Leia strangling the surprised Hutt, Han's unfrozen, but blind, inadvertently knocking Fett down the Sarlaac's gullet.

"I did not really expect to end up in the Sarlaac Pit quite so soon," Bulloch sadly admits. "Jabba's palace was one of the most memorable scenes I appeared in, with all the amazing characters."

Even with little time on screen, although on the side of the Empire, fans still went unexpectedly nuts for the Fett man. Lucas and the rest of the crew noticed, and they sure as hell remembered. The new prequels took *Wars* fans back in time, and one such landing spot would become Boba's backstory.

Attack of the Clones showed the young Boba (now Daniel Logan) developing under Temura Morrison's Jango. The older Fett *just* misses assassinating Padmé, then loses his head to Mace Windu, sending his protégé to the dark side long before Anakin went there. Ironically, though Jason Wingreen (who sadly passed away on Christmas Day 2015) had voiced Boba in the original *Empire*, his voice was replaced by Morrison's when the film came out on DVD in 2001.

Two decades later, in the midst of an Italian vacation, Bulloch got another call for a similar reason as the one way back when from Watts, one he first figured too slick to be true.

The person *claimed* to be Rick McCallum, Watts' producing colleague on the remastered *Star Wars* films. He *said* he'd like Bulloch to show up for a quickie in *Revenge of the Sith*. Bulloch wasn't sure.

"At first I thought it was a friend having a joke with me," he admitted. "Then I realized it really *was* Rick, so I gladly accepted."

As the clones, similar to the one Fett would become, turned against their Jedi masters, the Sundered Heart ship carried Leia, Yoda, and Kenobi to Coruscant. Jeremoch Colton, who'd been flying on Alderaan for generations, did his job at least one more time, ready to retire to the less (or at least, differently!) stressful world of teaching.

Sadly, if one follows the story, his new career and his life, along with so many others, tragically ended with Alderaan's destruction in *A New Hope*.

"It was a pretty easy role to do, playing a pilot," Bulloch says, "rather different from Boba."

Certainly so, but there's something else that hasn't changed—and, no matter how many more conventions Bulloch attends, no matter how many *Wars* fans he meets, it never will.

Even three decades after first becoming Fett, Bulloch still sees lines of admirers, ready to meet and thank their favorite role player. Many of them, some too young to even remember *Sith*'s release, let along *Jedi*'s, still proudly wear the attire that hid Fett's face and quest from the rebellion.

"I am still getting invited to events all over the world," Bulloch states, "and even the little ones I see at conventions are dressed up as Boba Fett and all the other characters. *Star Wars* has appealed to so many people, both young and old, as it is a fairytale story of good over evil with some great characters thrown in.

"Long live *Star Wars*!"

Carrie Fisher, who passed away during the writing of this book, will live forever in the hearts, minds, and memories of film fans (*Star Wars* fans and otherwise) forever.

Sad Epilogue . . .

Of course we were shocked and heartbroken when Han's own son took his life. Not that it was unexpected; something like that sort of had to happen to set the new *Star Wars* series in motion, and give us someone to hate and fear for the duration. Still, you can't help but feel something when a character you've watched, come almost to even *know* for forty years dies a sad, painful death, well, it still upsets you a little.

But it was, still, just a movie. Solo was a character, a creation, a persona played by a man who'd still get up the next morning, rolling toward our next chance to see him on the screen. Sad, certainly, but without the extra burden of reality.

On Dec. 27, 2016, we couldn't say that.

A few days earlier, word had blasted across the world of Fisher suffering a heart attack during a cross-continental plane ride. We hoped, we prayed, we sent all kinds of wishes. We wished that realism would go the same way the Rebellion had for the female face of *Star Wars*.

It didn't happen. No post-credits scene, no sequel to this one. Less than two weeks after *Rogue One* hit American screens, we lost Fisher forever (she'd finished filming *Star Wars: Episode VIII*, which hadn't been released when this book was finished). And when her mom Debbie Reynolds died the very next day, we didn't have the first damned clue how to react. It's not even possible to do so.

Will memories be enough? They'll have to be. We already knew that *Star Wars*, no matter how many new chapters are written to its saga, would never be forgotten. But when we suddenly realize that the past is all we'll have left, it's trying to fill heartbreak with hope.

That's ironic, isn't it? But maybe that can be our first step. In the closing moments of *Rogue One*, a rebel fleet manages to escape the Death Star with some secret plans to exploit its vulnerability, the same one that Jedi forces, led by Leia's bro, would use to destroy it. In her only line of the film, Leia explained just what the plans meant to the resistance: "Hope!"

It certainly was a new hope, and not just in titular form. Hope got the *Wars* rebellion started. It knocked back the Empire when it struck back. It reawakened the force. *Star Wars* sent it across a nation in high need when it first appeared in 1977.

Fisher's work turned Leia into an icon of film feminism, of Americana itself. Her work gave us hope. It sustained the right side in a battle than lasted for decades in sci-fi cinema.

Now it will let her live forever in history.

Aaron Smolinski showed that even the Man of Steel was once a boy early in *Superman* (1978).

The First Men of *Superman*

MOST CHILDREN OF TODAY and forever past and present love to brag just what a Superman their father is. He may not wear tights or capes or fly, but, man . . . when youngsters look up and see the man they call dad, they just know he'll be their hero forever.

Aaron Smolinski's kids are followers of the rule.

"They tell people all the time, 'My dad is *Superman!*'" he says. "People laugh, because every kid thinks so about their dad." If those gigglers only knew. . . .

Nearly half a century after the Man (cap intentional) who personified the term of superhero made it into comic book panels, and a quarter-century after George Reeves took him to the big screen in 1951's *Superman and the Mole Men*, Richard Donner decided it was time to tell a Super tale again in 1978.

Not surprisingly, he'd have his choice in the casting sense.

"I was in Calgary," Smolinski recalls. "They had a big casting call, and my parents took my brother, who was three years older than me, and me in to audition. They were casting a nine-year-old, a six-year-old, and a three-year-old. We got picked because we looked similar to Christopher Reeve at that age.

"I was a kid who was always the center of attention," he continues. "Donner was incredible. I felt really comfortable around him. I got to talk to him on a walkie-talkie, which was fun. I did everything he asked me to do—almost." Yes, even at three, he got to do a bit of negotiating.

We'd seen Marlon Brando's amazing work as Superman's pappy Jor-El (can you believe

Apocalypse Now came the very next year?) save him from the ill-fated land of Krypton by launching him to Earth, crash-landing in the small Kansas town of Smallville.

Then Jonathan and Martha Kent happen by, and can't believe their eyes.

"I get asked a lot, 'How did they get you to crawl out of the spaceship naked?'" Smolinski says. "I didn't want to do it, because I was shy. They gave me a snow globe, and that didn't work. They asked me what I wanted. For a pack of Juicy Fruit, I walked out naked!" The truck-lifting scene where we, and the Kents, see the Super kid's powers in effect was pretty tough as well.

"I had to stand on my tiptoes with my hands in the air for a long time," Smolinski says. "That was one of the most difficult." Still, he wouldn't get to the meet the title performer, not just yet.

Christopher Reeve became the man who fought for truth, justice, and the American way. Battling for better health care and assistance for the disabled after his paralyzing accident nearly two decades later, he did the same work in a different setting.

But before Reeve fastened a huge "S" across his chest, draped the iconic dark curl across his forehead, and added a ton of muscles to his already strapping 6'4" form to become the adult Kal-el (son of Krypton icon Jor-el), he thought about what Superman really represented—to legions of comic book fans, to a generation of television aficionados, and to Reeve himself, who hadn't grown up as a Superman fan.

"Truth and justice seemed relatively easy to understand," remembers Reeve, who snared a role that, according to cinema lore, Robert Redford, Sylvester Stallone, Jon Voight, Paul Newman, a guy named Schwarzenegger, and even Clint Eastwood (?!) had been in the running for, "but what about 'the American way'? What does that mean? Isn't it dangerous or at least counterproductive to imply that the American way is somehow better than others?"

As filming for the flick kicked off in London, Reeve approached Director Richard Donner about the slogan (Steven Spielberg had wanted to direct until the 1975 explosion that was *Jaws* pushed him on to bigger things). Donner, forehead-deep in technical problems and other such issues that seem to always crop up at the last minute—tragically, a stuntman was killed during filming—told Reeve to think a bit more about it on his own.

Not that Reeve himself had things easy in the mind-exploring state; he had to figure out how to become the comic book world's most recognizable face—and body.

"I was physically imposing," Reeve said, "so I played against that, making [Superman] as casual as possible."

He also addressed a glaring hole that's been about the worst-kept secret in comic strip superhero history, something that many have wondered, but few have discussed publically; how in *hell* does no one ever realize that Superman is Clark Kent? He doesn't change hardly anything about his physical appearance when morphing back into the common man (at least Batman, the Flash, and most of their colleagues had the intellect to wear masks!); the only difference between the two is their clothing. Same height, same hair, same build, same voice—how can a simple pair of horn-rimmed glasses throw so many off for so long?

"I remembered seeing George Reeves on TV in the fifties and wondering why Lois Lane didn't immediately recognize Clark Kent as Superman," Reeve said of Reeves, whose typecasting as Superman irreparably (and unfairly) harmed his acting career, concluding in one of Hollywood's most infamous suicides (to be fair, Reeves' death, the story of which was told by Ben Affleck in the main role of 2006's *Hollywoodland*, has been a gold mine for conspiracy theorists).

"Right away, I saw a great opportunity," Reeve said. "I would attempt to create more of a contrast between the two characters. The screenwriters . . . had provided a basis for playing Superman in an understated, offhand way. If the special effects could be truly convincing, then it would not be necessary to strike unnatural, 'macho' poses and attitudes."

A young Clark Kent (Jeff East) realizes the source of his power and his life's work early in the film.

Unlike the heroes of cinematic yester-decade, Superman didn't carry an aura of unemotional invincibility, an unstoppable hero that his helpless, shrinking violet of a victim desperately needed to escape. Under Reeve, Superman became a hero, but also with an edge of humanity; Kent became a quiet introvert, someone who nearly faded into the woodwork. Reeve based his work on Cary Grant's role in the 1938 film *Bringing Up Baby*, in which Grant plays a lovable nebbish paleontologist who needs tough-girl Katherine Hepburn to bail him out.

"Of course, I couldn't *be* Cary Grant," Reeve said, "but there was nothing to prevent me from stealing from him."

But Superman doesn't steal—that's not the American way (unless politics are involved, of course). So when Reeve spent time with Jeff East, who'd play the younger version of the Man of Steel—he who outruns trains for fun and kicks footballs through the ionosphere—the two weren't trying to *take* each other's personalities . . . more like *borrowing*.

"Chris wanted to get to know me, since I was playing him at fifteen and eighteen," says East. "We spent a lot of time together. We played a lot of games of chess."

East had gotten a call from Donner after his performance in *The Hazing*, the 1977 suspense-comedy about a fraternity who tries to cover up a brother's accidental death.

"He'd seen me in *Tom Sawyer*," says East, who played literary icon Huckleberry Finn in both 1973's *Sawyer* and in a title role the next year, "but he didn't know I'd grown up."

Expecting to go for the role as Lois and Clark's lackey Jimmy Olson, East walked into the office. Then he found out he was wanted for the main man.

"I said, 'I'm not going to put on a cape!'" East says. "Then I read the script, and I loved it." The next day, he was on a plane to England, the first of many locations the film would visit: eight film crews trekked across England, Canada, New York, and other locations for the year-long shoot.

"I was on the film from April 1977 to the summer of 1978," East says. "Once they put me in hair, makeup, and put a nose on me, I felt the character. I'd always been a huge fan of Superman. I read tons of comic books."

Like Reeve, he hung out with Donner for some guidance.

"He said that he didn't want me to be Superman," East remembers. "He wanted me to be myself in Clark. He wanted me to show the frustration of Clark. Clark just wanted to be human."

Of course, the fellow didn't mind stepping into superhero mode once in a while, as East's most memorable scene came from showing a passing train exactly what high speed could be.

"They had me on these wires," East remembers of the production. "They lifted me off the ground, and I spent a week practicing running to make it look like I was running in the air. I tore all my thigh muscles and got shin splints."

It might have been a bit too late, but he was finally lowered.

"They had me running with my toes just barely touching the ground," he says. "It looked more real."

And as the scene came to an end, reality almost stepped in a bit too close. Remember, this was the late 1970s, and digitized special effects and blue screens weren't even a pipe dream. The train wasn't artificially created—unlike in the comic books, the makeshift Superman wouldn't do too well in a collision.

"I was swaying [in the wires]," says East, "and I went through the lens in the camera. I went too far and swung almost into the train." Just in time, Gene Hackman's brother Richard, a stuntman on the film, grabbed him.

"He had to pull me out of the way," East says. "Today, they would do it on a computer with a screen."

Like Hepburn, and in contrast to many of her predecessors, Lois Lane was turned by Margo Kidder into a tough, outspoken woman, with just enough of a vulnerable heart to be swept off her feet by a man in a cape. When she asks Superman's identity, he simply responds, "A friend."

"I felt that that was the key to the part," Reeve said. "I tried to downplay being a hero and emphasize being a friend. . . . I tried to work on a stutter a little bit, and tried to create some difference between [Kent and Superman]."

"I went in wearing cowboy boots and a cowboy hat," Kidder recalls of her tryout, "which horrified Christopher. I remember being quite nervous, looking over at Superman, who was the skinniest, dorkiest thing I'd ever seen and going, 'That's Superman?!' I said to myself, 'You really want this part, and the key to it is, look like you really love this stranger, and so that was what I gave myself. She's in love with Superman, so she behaves one way with him, in a little girl-ish, sort of flustered, cooey way. [With Clark], she was more ballsy, kind of toughed him off." She and Reeve were strapped together for over a dozen hours a day at times, filming the flying scenes.

Superman (Christopher Reeve) barrels towards his next objective to show just how justified and truthful the American Way is.

"I let the costume do much of the work," said Reeve, who went through about twenty-five outfits during filming. "This film would be far beyond anything that had been done before, in terms of special effects. I was thinking, 'Don't do too much. Don't pose.' I could underplay the part. Don't come across larger than life."

Still, the man who masqueraded as Kent was far from physically casual, so Reeve set about widening his frame, always athletic but never muscular—until then.

"I told my driver to take me to the gym even if I said I wanted to go home," said Reeve, who trained with bodybuilder David Prowse (Darth Vader in the *Star Wars* trilogy) to get ready for the role, enduring daily four-hour workout sessions for months to gain over thirty pounds of muscle. "Once I was there, there was nothing to do but change into my workout clothes and start lifting weights."

Two films later, as the *Superman III* (1983) villains started to take over the weather, Kent wanders down a street, only to notice a driver trapped inside a flooding car. With no phone booths nearby, he's forced to commandeer an instant-photo spot. Stepping out, he hands the photos to a young fan.

Jack O'Halloran played silent evil with Superman's opponent Non in the first two *Superman* films.

That was Smolinski.

"I finally met him," remembers the former kid. "My hand disappeared into his because it was so big." Two decades later, he'd play a solider next to Henry Cavill, who personified the Man of Steel in *Man of Steel* (2013).

"When I met Henry, it felt like Chris to me," Smolinski says. "He was very sweet, very kind, a nice, good-hearted person."

On the other end of the *Superman* spectrum stood Jack O'Halloran—and not only because he and Reeve would be squaring off both in *Superman* and its first sequel.

Unlike Reeve, O'Halloran had been in shape for quite some time; he'd been a world-renowned heavyweight boxer for nearly a decade. That was important for *Superman*; the Philadelphia native was to play Non, the childlike mesomorph who couldn't speak, forcing O'Halloran, in just his fourth film role, to act with only (or perhaps "only") his physical attributes.

But while he may not have had Reeve's acting expertise, O'Halloran had learned from one of the best, much earlier on.

As he prepared to begin filming 1975's *Farewell, My Lovely*, O'Halloran met acting legend Robert Mitchum on the set. O'Halloran played the intellectually challenged Moose Malloy, who'd just gotten out of jail and hired Mitchum's private investigator Phillip Marlowe to find Malloy's old girlfriend, who'd quit writing to him while Malloy was in the crossbar hotel.

Mitchum asked O'Halloran if he'd gone over the script.

"I said yeah," O'Halloran recalls. "I said, 'I read it back to front. I know my role, your role, everyone's role.'"

"Good," Mitchum said. "Now throw it in the trash, and don't let me catch you doing what thousands of people in this town think is acting."

A bit taken aback, O'Halloran listened.

"Just be yourself," advised Mitchum, who churned out over 100 films in his half-century career (including both the original *Cape Fear* in 1962 and its 1991 remake). "Put yourself into that character and do it like you would do it yourself."

O'Halloran did—and never stopped.

"I found that it worked extremely well," he says. "[Mitchum] guided me pretty well. I learned that I was never afraid of the camera. When that red light comes on, all the guys behind the camera work for you. The camera likes certain people. It finds you."

After turning down chances to appear in *The Thomas Crown Affair* (1968) and *The Great White Hope* (1970) with his friend Steve McQueen during O'Halloran's boxing career, he decided to step in front of the camera after stepping out of the ring for the last time in 1974.

"Knowing the timing in your head for delivering lines and pacing yourself," he says, "sports prepared you for confronting that. Acting is something that you either have or you don't. I don't think it's something that someone can really teach you. Some people are just naturally born at it and do well. I really enjoy acting, but it doesn't obsess me. I can walk in front of a camera and do what I have to do, and then walk away."

Only a few years into his career, O'Halloran was ready to take on one of America's greatest heroes.

"I wanted to do a character that didn't speak," says O'Halloran, inspired in part by Jackie Gleason's critically acclaimed turn as a mute in 1962's *Gigot*. "When I read *Superman*, there were three villains, and one had to relate to the children. Someone had to be there for the young, and be a child-like brute; the idea of doing that, I enjoyed. I learned how to work my eyes and get my superpowers to work, conducting myself like a child but still having brute strength. It was kind of a neat idea."

Right away, he put Mitchum's teachings to work.

"I analyzed the character, and did what I would do if I was walking down the street as Non," says O'Halloran, who jokes that many people he met in public were shocked that he could actually speak.

"I'm amazed how many people come to me and write to me that as much as I scare the shit out of them, they love the character because of his childlike manners. They definitely got that."

Just as with *Lovely*, he was in the presence of Hollywood greatness, with Marlon Brando as Superman's father Jor-El, and Gene Hackman as the treacherous Lex Luthor.

"Every time I worked on a picture," says O'Halloran, "I saw different stars doing things differently. They were respectful of everybody, they showed up on time, and they loved their craft.

"Hackman knows every square inch of the stage; he's a technician. Brando took the time to say hello to every person on the crew, and when he left he said good night to everyone. He didn't whine or bitch or moan, he did what he came to do. I learned from people like that." Of course, we can't forget Terence Stamp, who played Non's boss General Zod, heading to Earth from Superman's homeland of Krypton to square off with the fellow who was Kal-El. Stamp, who'd been nominated for an Oscar for 1962's *Billy Budd*, kicked off a career resurgence in *Star Wars: Phantom Menace* (1999) with his role as Chancellor Valorum, then followed it up with roles in *Yes Man* (2008), *Get Smart* (2008), *Wanted* (2008), and other box-office hits of the next few years.

Superman became one of the few to refuse to kneel before Zod (Terence Stamp) in *Superman*.

"There are certain films that change your life," Stamp recalls of Zod's arrival. "I hadn't worked for about ten years when I got the *Superman* offer and I was very nervous because it was apparent that they just wanted like an ugly and I had the feeling that they were going to just like me ugly and dress me ugly and give me ugly stuff to say."

It turned out that he was exactly right—and that was a good thing here.

"You shouldn't really have doubts about it," a friend told him, "because for loads of kids, *Superman* movies will be the first movie they ever go to see. And by the time they grow up, there'll be more people who want to be like Zod than Superman. So you really shouldn't worry about it. You should just be as ugly and as horrible as you can be."

The friend was dead-on; Zod and his crew (which would get a new addition, who we'll learn of shortly) became one of the most notorious groups of comedic-violence ruffians in recent memory, thrilling children of all ages throughout.

The film roared past the $130 million gross mark in the U.S. alone, putting it in the then-top 10 grossing films of all time. A sequel was all but certain, and Donner didn't waste time, shooting, O'Halloran estimates, "86 percent of the movie . . . it had 24 minutes of Brando." The defeated Zod and Non had been imprisoned in Krypton's Phantom Zone, but the explosion of the nuclear missile in space—launched by Luthor and redirected by Superman—had freed them. Now it was time for a rematch, and the bad guys brought a reinforcement as gorgeous as she was dangerous.

If Sarah Douglas had acted on her anger, she might never have become Ursa.

Not that she didn't have reason; she'd been called in to discuss filming of the *Superman* sequel eight different times, only to have them cancelled, postponed, etc. The ninth time, they were making her wait, and the British babe was ticked.

"Little did I know that the role called for that stroke of meanness!" Douglas understates. That's why all it would take would be a high-kick demonstration, a quick interview, and a trip into the wires to catapult her into villainy.

"The main test was putting me on wires and seeing if I could fly," she says. "It seemed that some actresses actually were very nervous of heights! I loved them and the rest is history."

Unfortunately, Donner was fired due to differences with the film's producers, and Richard Lester was brought in to finish, and re-shoot, a bit of the film. O'Halloran was one of many that almost quit.

"A lot of us were going to walk away," he says. "What happened with the Donner situation was ludicrous. The politics that went on there was bullshit. If you look at the Donner cut and the other part, it's two different movies." A cut of the Donner production was released on DVD in 2006.

"[Lester] came back and re-shot certain things," O'Halloran says. "He re-worked everything and put in a lot of humor. It's sad that Richard never had the chance to finish his project."

Douglas, on the other hand, didn't seem to mind redoing a few shots and sequences.

"It was actually, probably, the best experience an actor can have, to re-shoot something," she says, "a completely different concept [with a] completely different director. [Donner's] a lot looser. He's an actor's director; he's very good with the actors. But I think, for me, I learned a great deal from [Lester]."

The three villains, cursed with an absolute distaste of humanity, arrive on Earth and enlist Luthor's help to battle Superman—Ursa personifies their hatred perhaps stronger than any of her colleagues, destroying an astronaut and later launching a bus at the hero.

Sarah Douglas's Ursa was the bad alongside the goodness of *Superman* heroine Lois Lane (Margot Kidder).

"There was a fraction of settlement as the bus was hoisted up by the chain on the crane," Douglas says. "I have said that I felt it, but as I had superpowers for that split second I was in character, I kept my arms extended, holding up the bus instead of relaxing my arms. Consequently, I have a very bad shoulder still from tearing everything around it at the time!" Not surprisingly, Superman manages to vanquish his victims and continue his fight for others, with Lois' fist sending Ursa spiraling down an abyss.

The film also passed the nine-figure mark, but it would be the last hurrah for the man in red and blue, at least until 2006's *Superman Returns* did well at the box office. Lester directed the critically panned *Superman III* in 1983, and Sidney Lurie did the 1987 box-office bust *Superman IV: The Quest for Peace*. O'Halloran, who was gone for good after part two, labels the last two films "pieces of shit," and even Reeve admitted, "The less said about *Superman IV*, the better."

As advice for upcoming actors, O'Halloran calls back to one last lesson from Mitchum.

"I asked him what it meant to be a star," O'Halloran says, "and he said, 'Let me tell you something. It's a word called 'presence.' The presence that you leave on the screen is what people want to see again. It's important that they enjoy what you're doing, because you're making a presence on the screen.'

"I think I did that with everything I ever did. It's a tough business, being at the right place at the right time, putting your presence on the screen. Some people are persistent as hell, and then they find a niche in movies and make a lot of them."

Actors in Action

Over the past few decades, Superman the character has elevated past a comic strip drawing, past a TV or film character, all the way to basically a symbol of Americana itself. Of course we know he's "just" an image, an epitomic figment, but for some, just believing we could be like him in some way is enough. The waving flag, the apple pie, the firecrackers . . . and Superman. For generations, millions of people around the globe have felt his inspirational pride, some without ever opening a comic book. When he died in the strips in that infamous battle with Doomsday in early 1993, America did everything but go into a national period of mourning.

Unfortunately, comic book heroines haven't really reached such a level of admiration. Just about anyone can *recognize* Jean Grey, the Invisible Woman, Catwoman, the She-Hulk, and whoever else, but we still don't take too many of them seriously past the entertainment level.

Which brings us to our next subject and her many quests. Supergirl has been next to her Kryptonian cousin on the books since 1959, and has proven just as tough and smart as the man also known as Clark. Her Kara has fought tons of battles and come out OK, vanquishing legions of enemies eight times her size, and yet, she's still the dark sheep of the Kal-El family.

Why? Personally, I always thought it had to do with the "Girl" aspect. He's a man, she's a girl—*just* a girl, right? Just like Batgirl constantly got shoved aside by Batman and Robin, in the books and the movies, putting the "girl" label on a superheroine lowers her importance and impact. Granted, "Superwoman" takes a bit longer to say and sounds sort of awkward, but we've got to get *something* done here.

Think about this—the superheroine who's plotted her own path the furthest has probably been Wonder Woman. That's *Woman*! If DC comics had started her out as Wonder *Girl* in late 1941, would she still be around? Probably not. But we've still gotten to read about her in the comics for generations. We loved watching Lynda Carter tear it up as the Amazon Princess on small screens from 1975 to 1979. Today, many see the lady from Themyscira as a symbol of strength and justice, and, of course, feminism—which isn't to disregard the regard she all but forcibly extracts from loads of men (like certain authors!).

There's hope for the comic gals to step out of the inked panels and screens big and small and inspire those lucky enough to check them out, to become icons not only of the Marvel and DC universes, but the U.S. and humanity as a whole. As long as there are people willing to give them a way to do so, there's always a chance that we might just wise up and start responding a bit more.

Gal Gadot got a new shot at resurrecting Wonder Woman's fame and grabbed it like a Lasso of Truth, her cameo standing all the way out of 2016's incredibly disappointing *Batman vs. Superman*, then absolutely rocking the Woman's own film the next year, one of the most overdue events in action flick history.

By then, someone else had handed another special lady her own inspirational opportunity.

OK, so there's probably no chance that it actually went this way. But let's pontificate and have some fun.

Imagine the casting crew of *Supergirl* out on a search for their leading lady, and just happening to prospect straight through a *Glee* go-round! A high school-based musical show spawning a lass of supremacy? Why not?

Who could they choose? Leading gal Rachel Berry? Too small to be a superhero. Kitty, the brat who came to care? Same thing.

Brittany? So lovably ditzy that it's tough to imagine villains wanting to whomp her.

Tina? Mercedes? Quinn? Eternal spitfire Santana? Now we're talking!

There was also Marley. In just two seasons on the show, the young lady's battle with bulimia had pushed the show into more dramatic territory than it usually ventured into. But she'd torn it up as the lead in the club's production of *Grease*, and written "All or Nothing," the tune that helped cement the New Direction squad's regional victory to close out the show's fourth season.

Of course, it just *had* to have been something else that *must* have convinced the *Supergirl* group that Melissa Benoist should be their lady of the blue and red-caped crime-fighting persuasion. Throughout Benoist's first go-round as Marley, Superhero Club fever had swept McKinley High, and many Gleesters had become a part of it, creating their own colleagues of the X-Men, Justice League, and everyone else out to save the world.

As the "Dynamic Duets" tale kicked off in November 2012, Kitty finally talked Marley into accessing her *wild* side! And as the pair teamed up for Bonnie Tyler's "Holding out for a Hero," Marley, adorned in a costume that sort of blended Supergirl and Wonder Woman, had stood back and felt the most super of powers, Kitty's whip fanning into her a sense of inner strength we'd never seen before in Marley.

Yeah, that power, that confidence, that's certainly what convinced everyone that Benoist could find enough superhuman strength to carry an entire series, right?

Yeah, probably not. Considering that it was over *three years* later that *Supergirl* premiered, almost definitely not. But it sure makes for a good piece of drama, right? Benoist's representatives kept me from getting the whole story straight from her, but it really doesn't matter how she became Kara Zor-El, Kara Danvers, and Supergirl all in one show, just that she did—and that she had an agenda in mind well past acting.

"I just want all women to feel like they could be Kara and Superwoman as well," Benoist says. "That goes for anybody. It doesn't matter what sex. It doesn't matter if it's women or men I inspire, I just want to inspire people in general to realize their strengths and their potential, and that you can do the things that you feel like are impossible to accomplish."

Not much of a comic book fan beforehand, Benoist poured herself all over DC Comics' *New 52* line, the DC Universe's rebirth in 2011 that restarted dozens of new series, including, of course, Supergirl. Not surprisingly, she also beat hell out of the gym; boxing, strength training, everything to show everyone that we'd get a hell of a lot more than we saw when it came to her gal.

"I like to think that there's just a part of me that grew up in a way that prepared me for this role," she explains. "I come from this matriarchal family where I didn't have many boy cousins. It was all girls running around, and my mom had only sisters and I had mostly sisters. So we just had this really strong, feminine family, and were really all go-getters. I think that rubbed onto me and helped in facing this role and creating Supergirl."

Just a few weeks into the series, Benoist got a special form of guidance from someone who, not *that* long ago, had been there and tried it out.

Before Kara had come to Earth, her cousin Clark (Tyler Hoechlin) had been there awhile, figuring out just why he was the only one around with all this speed and strength. But he'd run into the Danvers, a brilliant pair of scientists who, per usual for sci-fi productions, just happened to be living nearby, and are ready and able to help him out. When Kara finally showed, they'd taken her in as well, hence her eventual name.

Jeremiah Danvers was Dean Cain, who'd played the super man himself on the *Lois and Clark* TV show back in the 1990s. Helen Slater was Jeremiah's wife Eliza.

Yes, the same Helen Slater who'd been in the title seat in *Supergirl*'s big-screen jaunt of 1984.

"I auditioned with a homemade cape and skirt," recalls Slater, who slipped by then-apprentice performers like Brooke Shields and Demi Moore to become the first Kara. "I had done dance classes, and that fitted [what the crew wanted]."

Unlike her young cousin Kal-El, sent to Earth as his homeland blew, Kara roars to this planet in search of the Omegahedron, an ominous object that just might restore power to her inner-space land of Argo City. But wannabe witch Selena grabs it first, and, as comic book/film villains so often do, looks to take over the world (and we thought Faye Dunaway had been evil back in 1976's *Network*!) before Kara's superpowers win the day.

"I had to go through four months of just bodybuilding," remembers Slater. For four months, five days a week, she ran, swam, lifted, did as much and probably more than Reeve had.

"Eating a high protein diet, lifting weights, running, trampolining, and learning how to navigate the wires to make me fly," she recalls of Kara's fitness regime.

On Leap Year Day 2016, the story of "Solitude" told of a troublemaker named Indigo, looking to use the World Wide Web for blackmail-ish purposes. But one wouldn't need a superheroine to solve that problem.

No, the Web isn't just Indigo's weapon; it's her transportation system. And she's not here for green; her hacks cause a sudden traffic pileup. And she's not even close to human, taking on a blue form like Mystique from *X-Men*, minus the special effects. And she's not really "just" Indigo; that's just the alias for Brainiac 8, a form that tried to wipe out all of Krypton and now looks to ply the trade on Earth. She's actually an ally of the new version of Non, but unlike O'Halloran in the films, Chris Vance got to actually speak his intelligent mind.

Indigo came back—even from death—a few times for the rest of the season until falling to Kara and friends in the first season finale. Just as had been the case with Slater back at the start, Indigo's blueness hid an inside aspect.

Since the fall of 2001, *Smallville* had told a different story of Clark Kent on the small screen, with Tom Welling in the lead. As season seven began just before Halloween of 2007, the soon-to-be-Superman was shocked when a gal who could match his strength arrived in his small Kansas town.

Then he learned that this blonde bombshell was none other than his cousin, the second Supergirl herself, after Slater. Nearly a decade before Benoist had her turn, Laura Vandervoort had gone full-blown heroic (the same season, Slater cameoed on *Smallville* as Superman's mommy Lara).

Like Slater before and Benoist after, Vandervoort had made her body talk through physicality, although she'd had a bit more prep at the ready when the role came calling.

"I started martial arts when I was about seven," recalls Vandervoort, who, also like Benoist, jumped into comic books getting ready to become a part of one of her favorite shows. "When I was nineteen, I had my second-degree black belt [in karate]. Then I had to stop, because I was working a lot and going to school."

Helen Slater (left) started the *Supergirl* tradition on the big screen in 1984, and Laura Vandervoort (center) brought Superman's cousin to *Smallville* in 2010. Five years later, Melissa Benoist (right) headed up the superheroine's own show.

She'd go to battle with her cousin, sometimes by his side and elsewhere in the lead, against Lex Luthor, Brainiac (who even possessed her in one episode), and others over the next few years, her final appearance coming in the series' second-to-last episode of "Prophecy" in 2011.

In case we haven't guessed, yes, Vandervoort was Indigo.

"Supergirl needed to be real physical," she explains. "There was a lot of hand-to-hand combat. I did about 85 percent of my own stunts."

In one more wink-wink nod to the series' history, although probably not the last, Teri Hatcher, who'd been the Lois Lane to Cain's Clark Kent, became the rancidly evil Rhea, out to destroy Kara and the rest of Earth as *Supergirl*'s second season ended. But Kara, of course, vanquished her as well, and we couldn't wait to see what the rest of the show, however long it lasts, had in store for her, for Benoist, and the people she hoped Supergirl would continue to inspire—gender, age, race, and everything else irrelevant.

"As long as Kara and Supergirl are enjoying themselves," Benoist says, "and finding the joy in being a hero and the joy in using her powers . . . that everything stems from that. I always keep in mind her bravery, her hope, her positivity and her strength. I think it will be hard for girls not to look up to that."

The characters of 1999's *Arlington Road* never knew that Jenni Tooley's gal's innocence was an expression of terroristic glee.

Jenni Tooley: *Arlington Road*

*A*RLINGTON *R*OAD (1999). It's a film absolutely drowning in irony.

Irony in that, just one year removed from becoming a hero to laid-back everymen everywhere in *The Big Lebowski*, Jeff Bridges was on top of his action-packed game of intensity, in the midst of a terrorist plot to carry on the work of Timmy McVeigh and Teddy Kaczynski.

Irony because, a few years after spending two decades in prison for a crime he didn't commit in *The Shawshank Redemption* (1994), Tim Robbins became a mass murderer who gets away with his deeds.

And, in the sad side of irony, realizing that not nearly enough people took the time to appreciate one of the most underrated action films of the decade. Notwithstanding *Silence of the Lambs* (1991), films that have the villain win are always a tough sell to audiences.

They're hunks of double-iced cake, however, to then-up-and-comers like Jenni Tooley. Early on in a performer's career, any mark is attractive to make, even if her character does so in an innocent's blood.

"As a young actor, I would have taken pretty much any role offered to me in the legitimate film industry," recalls Tooley, struggling in the South way back then after making her screen debut in *Bottle Rocket* (1996). "I was living in Dallas, and in Texas, most actors take whatever roles that they can find because there are so few available." Not that roles are exactly rolling in anywhere else in America, but the prep certainly remains the same.

Everything you can do, and then even more. Even without experience, showing up to show that no hands need holding here; you came with a purpose, forming a character that you can justify because it made sense to you. The character herself might not be what the cast and crew are looking for, but you'll show yourself as just the kind of person they want. By this time, Tooley had felt the power of performing, but wasn't sure she liked the rush.

"Trying to be what I thought everyone wanted me to be left me empty and miserable," she admits. "Depending on this business to feed my spirit and creativity did not work for me. That sense of desperation: looking around at everyone else in the room, sizing myself up, trying to figure out what I did wrong, why I didn't get the part, schmoozing in an inauthentic way, all of these things killed my self-esteem. They also killed what was awesome about me." It was up to her to find it again. To show it again—to herself, and to others. Starting with the tryout holders down the *Road*.

With Tooley, they didn't quit looking until happening on, "my uniqueness, the things that people can't put their finger on. They just know why they want me on their project because there is something about me." Whatever they saw was enough.

"I had actually gone in for a different role," she admits. "I took a chance at that audition and wore a belt made of bottle caps and a necklace fashioned out of a watch: I went a little more as myself than as a khaki pants and denim short version of me. There was something about me that they liked." Quite a bit, it turned out.

She was asked to . . . *tie her hair into a ponytail*! She said . . . *yes!*

Her character would be known not even as Jane Doe, but as 'Ponytail Girl' even into the credits. It was a title whose nonchalant nature would be the bold-printed definition of misleading.

Tooley's passion for performing had shown just the type of subject matter devotion that casting crews adore. The students of Bridges' Michael Faraday's college history class, on the other hand, felt quite differently at times.

Bringing personal experiences into the classroom is nothing new, and often quite helpful, as it can show students a teacher's individual connection to the subject matter; students who see that it's not just a job might be a bit more apt to pay closer attention, to want to hear more. But there's limits to this sort of thing. Field-tripping a class to the site of an FBI action can give them some serious insight into the issue, but Faraday's links to the place and past went a bit far. Needlessly far. Far enough that they could see that this wasn't about the syllabus for him, but about, perhaps . . . an agenda?

It was the site in which his wife had been killed in an operation gone tragically wrong. The trip, along with Faraday's near-obsessive description of it, we could see how this could rub students the wrong way—especially one in particular.

"It was still early in my career, and my life," recalls Tooley, "so I did a lot of winging it. I didn't have any formal training. I would basically memorize lines and stay really focused, to watch what was going on and listen. My character was bound up in that ponytail." She's one of Faraday's most devoted students, one of the few that seems to feed off his intensity to the point that she's feeling it herself.

She is.

Arriving in town from St. Louis, the site of a recent bombing tragedy, Robbins' Oliver Lang and his wife Cheryl (Joan Cusack, also tough to comprehend in a pitch-black role; her brother John wasn't so mean even as a hitman in 1997's *Grosse Pointe Blank*!) appear to be there to befriend Faraday and his son.

Then suspicions arise. Becoming the impromptu detective that action protagonists so often suddenly morph into, Faraday finds that it's all a set up; the Langs did the bombing, and they're part of an organization out to take down the government, seeing the innocents who have been and will be killed in the same lens as America saw the victims of Hiroshima and Nagasaki. They kill Faraday's girlfriend, and are all too willing and ready to make his son the next small piece of collateral damage.

Like I wrote, this isn't a lone wolf sort of thing; their group planned this out long ago. Their target was fixated on well in advance, starting out with a true inside woman. Robbins helped Tooley find her.

"We basically created a relationship and quick backstory in just a few minutes," she remembers. "He did, really." As the two sat in a parking garage waiting to hear their call to action and glory, Robbins shouted to her.

"He called across to me, 'Is this your first film?'" she says. "I said, 'My biggest film.' He yelled, 'Are you freaking out?!' And they called action right there.

"I created a backstory about how I had lost my boyfriend at Copper Creek," Tooley continues, referring to the battle that killed Faraday's wife, "so it was all about vengeance for me. I was so excited because the character showed up all throughout the movie."

Unfortunately, audiences would never see one of her toughest scenes.

"There was a pivotal scene in which Jeff Bridges' character has a revelation in the classroom," she explains, "where he realizes that I was connected to the terrorists and that I had been in his class all along. It was a great take: the camera spinning around the room, Jeff doing a great job acting that moment of terror. I thought, 'This is it! I have finally gotten a supporting role in a Hollywood movie where I can't be cut!'"

The scene was cut. But we'd still have a tough reason to remember Tooley's ponytail gal.

Faraday's son is stolen, and he's off on a chase to find the youngster, Lang taunting him all along, goading him towards FBI headquarters. We see Faraday crash into a wall, and Lang's "teammates" getting ready, including Tooley's person. A panicked Faraday rushes toward his car, peering into the trunk, his horrified image one of the most memorable of Bridges' career. Lang walks out onto a rooftop across town, needing to see it with his own eyes.

Here's where audiences know that the happy ending we all expected, the one we knew was coming, isn't going to happen. This one can't be saved.

They'd planted a bomb in Faraday's car. He didn't know. He became an unknowing, certainly unwilling dirty worker.

And mass murderer. The bomb kills him, his friends, and nearly two hundred others, even more than McVeigh did in reality. And everyone will always blame Faraday, his name posted and whispered around the world right next to every other mass murderer in history. With the help of someone special, of course.

"All I know is what he told me in his office one day after class," the ponytailed one tells a reporter in the film's final minutes (the Langs are already looking to their next assignment). "He said, 'Sweetheart, one day, those men are going to pay. One day, those men are going to burn.'" Her dark smarminess might easily be written off as relief that a horrible murderer is dead. We, however, know just the real source of her pleasure in pain.

"We were in the middle of shooting another scene when they decided to start grabbing the newscast monologues," Tooley remembers. "They pulled me out of the scene we were doing, changed my clothes, popped a backpack on my back, and I did the monologue a couple of times, all in about ten minutes. That was pretty hard because I wasn't in the headspace for that final scene, and although I had memorized the monologue, I didn't have time to go over it before we did it."

This time, though, what she didn't do worked quite well.

"When I went to see the film," she remembers, "I heard some women talking after the movie and saying 'Who was that girl at the end with the ponytail?' What a great lesson in letting go!"

It would have been very easy for Richard Linklater to let go. It would have been overly simple for the rest of *Boyhood* (2014) to give up throughout the decade it took to make the film, or at least cut a corner or two.

Depicting a character's evolution inside and out is about commonplace in films. Grabbing several actors to play the character isn't so much the easy way out; it's typically seen as the only option. Who would ever wait over ten years to stich a film all the way together?

Linklater did. Ellar Coltrane did, playing Mason Evans Jr., who we'd literally see move from kindergarten almost to adulthood during filming (Linklater's daughter Lorelei was Mason's sister Samantha). Patricia Arquette did, playing Mason's mom Olivia all the way to an Oscar.

Ethan Hawke was Mason's dad, Mason Sr. He and Olivia don't get along too well, sending them apart and him into the arms and heart of Annie. Tooley was Annie.

"No matter what genre I am working in, I start with the character's insides," Tooley says.

"Why are they the way they are? Then I move to their outsides: how does who they are affect how they are, how they move, how they dress? If I have control over wardrobe or hair, then I usually hook onto some wardrobe piece or hairstyle that helps me internalize them."

For one of the first times in her career, Tooley didn't mind asking for help. She and a coach worked their way through a tryout not unlike something found on Lifetime Television.

"Richard also asked questions about my life," Tooley says, "which I answered honestly rather than blowing smoke. I had spent a lot of time while living in New York trying to be someone else and coming up miserable, so when I moved to Austin I committed myself to just being me. It paid off. For Annie, I used a fear of abandonment and a desire to please everyone."

It worked, as she'd be Mason's Mrs. for three years of *Boyhood*.

"*Boyhood* was basically unscripted," she says. "[Filming] year eight, there were some scripted scenes, some scenes we wrote together, and some that were improvised. Then in year nine and ten, I had nothing to work from: no synopsis or script. I showed up, listened, shared my opinion, and followed direction. If I hadn't had the body of that character in place, I would have had nothing to rely on."

Her work helped Hawke earn his own Oscar nomination. It's the same techniques that got her started back as She Who Wielded The Ponytail. It carries on for Tooley.

"Taking care of myself and being comfortable in my own skin has gotten me more work than anything else," she says. "I can walk into an audition today and enjoy myself. I will ask myself, how can I be of service to the director, or the writer, or the person reading with me today? Maybe all I was there to do that day was give the writer a new way to hear a line, or make the exhausted casting director laugh. Treating each audition as an end in itself allows me to get something out of the experience and move along. Living a full life that includes acting professionally, but is not limited to that, has made me a better actor and a happier person."

The faith of José Henríquez (Marco Treviño, right) helped his Chilean mining countrymen, like Darío Segovia (Juan Pablo Raba, left) through an unthinkably difficult time in 2015's *The 33*.

Marco Treviño: *The 33*

SOMETIMES, WE DON'T NEED Hollywood for a happy ending. Once in a while, certainly not often enough, reality and humanity team up to remind us that all the inspiration we need is right here alongside us.

In October 2010, the world got a welcome display. After almost ten weeks trapped underground in a mine in northern Chile, thirty-three men emerged, one after exhausted one, from far too far down below, and celebrations broke out across the planet.

Five years later, we saw their story up close and dramatized in *The 33*.

"The story of the thirty-three is about human beings and hope," explains Marco Treviño. "It was global news and I thought it would be a transcendent film. I saw in *The 33* story a great chance to help tell a story about a group of miners who reach their complete material detachment after facing their imminent death and losing any contact with the rest of the world."

Over a hundred years old, with a record of trouble, the San Jose mine in Copiapó had already claimed several lives in the past. The fellows who made their way through it in August 2010 just hoped to find some copper and head home.

Then the nightmare began. Weakened by age, along with one of history's largest earthquakes and the lingering damage from a tsunami just months before, the mine collapsed, trapping the title characters far underground. Many thought they'd never be found alive, if at all. Trapped with hardly any food, electricity, clean air, or anything at all, no way could anyone last long down there.

But no one counted on how strong the human spirit can become if it's pushed far enough. Just over two weeks later, a note made its way to the surface letting everyone know that they were still there and still determined. That's when everything hit high speed. Rescue efforts, vigils, messages sent back and forth and up and down. Still, no one up on the surface had any real way of knowing what was up down there.

The 33 gave us a chance to see it. Antonio Banderas became involuntary leader Mario Sepúlveda (nicknamed Super Mario, nyuck nyuck), with Lou Diamond Phillips as foreman Luis Urzúa. After three decades of acting elsewhere, Treviño made his Hollywood (and English language) debut as José Henríquez, a man of faith who kept his colleagues' minds focused and spirits up by turning the mine into an impromptu cathedral—contrary to popular belief, Henríquez was not a pastor in the true sense of the title, just a hardcore Christian.

"I embraced the role because it was a great chance for me," Treviño explains. "Fortunately, José Henríquez helped me to reconcile myself with religion."

Treviño looked over some interviews Henríquez gave, and watched some videos of him addressing fellow parishioners.

"I looked for his grounds, motives, and reasons," he remembers. "Avoiding making a bad copy, a caricature of him, I left aside the physical matters. I believe if you can think and feel as the character, you will move and act naturally and consequently."

As the weeks go by, the miners' plight moves closer and closer to impossibility, as words and news, often drenched in hopelessness, starts to spread. First across Chile, then the continent, and finally Earth itself. But as one rescue attempt another falls short, hope and prayer may not be enough.

But that doesn't stop Henríquez, who, like many down there, finds himself victimized by breathing issues and lack of privacy. Over and over, he can only put his head down and look to above, imploring not to be forsaken.

Others join him. During their captivity, more and more pray along with him. "I think the most effective scene was the one in which Darío (Juan Pablo Raba) and José talk about God and forgiveness," Treviño says.

On Oct. 12, 2010, a new rescue operation was launched towards the men. After weeks of possibilities, trials, errors, and everything else, one fellow at a time was, agonizingly slowly, lifted straight toward the surface. As over a billion watched on TV and the 'Net, and those in attendance, including President Sebastián Piñera, sang the Chilean national anthem, one after another emerged. The attempt, which could have given way at any time, lasted twenty-four endless hours. Henríquez was one of the last up.

Aside from a few small medical issues, the men were fine, and the world would forever have a memory of a group of people who came together and came out heroes. After the rescue, Henríquez returned to the mine for one more thanks to a special Someone.

"It was impressive to watch the special effects on the final cut," Treviño says. "It was really fun! And I feel satisfied with our performances."

Zero-Wolf (Raoul Trujillo) was a drill sergeant centuries before the term was coined in 2006's *Apocalypto*.

Raoul Trujillo: *Apocalypto*

THE CONVERSATION DIDN'T TAKE long.

Mel Gibson sat down to chat with Raoul Trujillo, and told the actor he'd been very impressed with Trujillo's performance as both an actor and choreographer in the 2005 drama *The New World*, about the clash between English settlers and Native Americans.

Then Gibson mentioned his own new flick, *Apocalypto* (2006). He wanted Trujillo to become Zero-Wolf.

"Mel and [I] talked, and he already knew that he was going to hire me," says Trujillo. "As soon as we sat down and talked, he was like, 'Yes, you're Zero-Wolf.' Of course, I had no idea who Zero-Wolf was. I hadn't even read a script. He said I had an edge about me that came off, and that was what he was really interested in. I was hoping that Zero-Wolf was going to be a good character, but when I read the script, that's when I realized, 'Wow! This is going to a tough character to get into.'"

Zero-Wolf was the leader of a group of Mayan mercenaries who launch an armed attack on a group of sleeping villagers, including Jaguar Paw (Rudy Youngblood) and the rest of the film's main characters. As the shocked victims watch their loved ones slaughtered, their children orphaned, their parents killed, they're taken into captivity, on the way to a sacrifice that the frightfully nearby Mayan city leaders hope will appease their gods.

"Mel was very clear with me from the first meeting, because I hadn't read a script yet," Trujillo says. "People were going to think Zero-Wolf was the bad guy, but he's not. One of his warriors, Middle Eye, is really the evil one. [Zero-Wolf] is just doing his job, like a war general. He just does what he's told, and believes that what he does is right. But I never saw him as an evil character; I saw him as a real powerful dude. That's what interested me about the character; that he wasn't so black-and-white evil. Yes, he had layers, but he had a humanity about him; it was just a misplaced humanity."

For people like Zero-Wolf, what matters is getting the job done, winning. It's not about killing, pillaging, or humiliating just for the hell of it (viewers saw him refrain from doing so throughout the flick); it's only about getting in, getting done, and getting out, and the few that don't return are collateral damage and nothing to get upset about, because there's no greater honor for a warrior than to die in battle.

Like a lot of military combat leaders, those below him might have wanted to beat him senseless at times, but they knew that when the time came for action, he was going to be there doing his job, and for reasons that were difficult for even them to understand, they couldn't wait to be there with him.

"When we got to Mexico, we had a month to train and get into shape, with total immersion into the Mayan language," says Trujillo, who had learned Native American languages for *New World* and many more films; he's also fluent in German, French, and Spanish.

"Every single day for an hour, we'd go over our lines," he says. "We learned the alphabet. Once we'd memorized our lines, we found the meaning behind what we were saying. It's not any more difficult to learn Mayan than other languages.

"[It] was very helpful: working out non-gym style; lifting other actors, instead of weights, endless running, trying more acrobatic stuff, jumping off one another, etc," he says. "That process and immersion into Mayan helped me get into the cultural and historical aspect of the character. Mel used me to do a whole boot camp with the warriors to get them into the physical shape and non-European manner of movement required for pre-Columbian people to carry themselves . . . wipe out any sense of the modern pedestrian habits. My work as a dancer and choreographer was utilized."

But the physical aspect of nonstop plodding was something else on a different scale.

"As soon as I put all of that armor, prosthetic nose shaped like a beak, tattoos, and leather on, I completely became this character. I was like, 'Oh my God, is this an animal or a man?' There's no work required, other than to [put the costume on and become Zero-Wolf]." Zero-Wolf looked as if his great-great-great-grand-uncle's second cousin was a vulture.

"How do you prepare for something like that?" Trujillo asks. "That's the kind of thing that creeps into your nightmares, and you wake up going, 'Wow, where did THAT come from?'"

Throughout shooting, he was in makeup for between five and eight hours a day. His head was constantly shaved. He was tattooed. Hairpieces were attached.

"Getting into character was a transformation that went on every single day," he says. "Raoul had ceased to exist; I had *become* Zero-Wolf each day."

After the attack, the headhunters bring their captivity across a scorching mountain, a rough river, and some sweltering plains. Then they meet one of the film's most memorable characters, a surreal little girl who speaks of a jaguar, who will "scratch you out, end your world . . . and lead you to your end. Day will be like night."

His character wasn't in that scene, but Trujillo checked it out.

"The oracle scene was more for the warriors to bear witness to, understand the prophecy, and feel the fear," he says. "The most amazing thing for me was watching Mel direct the two little girls. He directed one girl, who was less shy and little more capable, but didn't have the look [Mel wanted for the close up]. The other girl did the talking, and sharp-eyed viewers might notice that her haircut is slightly different when seen from behind. These girls probably had even less work than Trujillo to prepare; they lived in the same type of village that was attacked early in the film.

"To watch [Gibson] work with girls from little Mayan villages that had never seen a movie and didn't have television," Trujillo says, "the father in him came out. It showed me he knew how to work with children. He brought what he needed out of them. That was astounding to me to watch; it's the mark of a very talented director."

Eventually, her words come true; after watching some of his friends be sacrificed, Jaguar Paw is given the sacrificial rite—with a man above him about to plunge a knife into his chest and hundreds on the ground cheering, few movie heroes have found themselves in a more hopeless position.

Then we see the oracle's prophesy; an eclipse turns the bright afternoon to late night, and the gods appear pleased. Zero-Wolf, seemingly a bit upset about not getting to see his hard-earned cargo utilized, is told to dispose of them.

The men are taken to a long field with a jungle at the end. Zero-Wolf sends his son Cut Rock (Ricardo Mendoza, in his acting debut) to the other end to be the "finisher." If the captives make it to the other end of the field and past Rock, they're free—or so they think.

A few take off, only to be cut down by arrows, rocks, and Rock—and we can see the pride rising through Zero-Wolf, again not killing just for the sake of killing.

"That was a very important scene for me," says Trujillo. "Zero-Wolf was war-weary; he had seen it all. But this was his son. There had to be a moment where he actually had to feel the loss."

That is the moment. As Jaguar Paw takes his turn in the dark game, he gets an arrow through the lower stomach. He goes down, and Cut Rock comes over to make his next kill.

Standing back at the starting point, Zero-Wolf and his colleagues can't help but laugh at the fallen prey. Cut Rock stands up and walks around, and he must be ready to celebrate.

Then he collapses.

In the distance, Zero-Wolf's face raffles through a multitude of emotions we've never seen there before: shock, fear, maybe even terror. For the first time in the film, things are out of his control.

He takes off running faster than we've seen all movie. Reaching Cut Rock's body, he sees Paw's arrow through his son's neck, with blood spurting out and things fading fast.

Zero-Wolf calmly assures his youngster that his pain is about to cease, and it does. Then Zero-Wolf's face takes on a whole new display—control is a thing of the past, on the inside and outside, and this isn't just business anymore.

"I wanted to do a scene where I almost break down, but immediately recover," Trujillo says. "That was my moment to give that character that wee bit of humanity, so the audience could see that this was a transformation. Before, he was just doing his job, pure and simple. But now he snapped, and it became personal. I needed that moment so the audience could feel that Zero-Wolf wasn't just sadistic and inhumane; now it was something bigger. From that point on, that's what I tried to keep that character filled with . . . personal revenge."

The chase is on, and the divinations keep coming. As Zero-Wolf leads his men after Jaguar Paw, the men start to fall. A panther and poisonous snake take care of two, and one goes kamikaze-ing over a waterfall.

Jaguar Paw kills two of them, and soon he and Zero-Wolf have their own face-to-face. Apparently unarmed, Jaguar Paw's luck might have run out. As Zero-Wolf charges, he can't wait for justice for his son.

Then, just as a boar did in the film's opening sequence, he trips a trapping wire. Suddenly, a wall of spikes swings toward, and, just as with the boar, through him. As a tired, satisfied smile makes its way across Jaguar Paw's mouth, Zero-Wolf reaches for him one more time, then breathes his last.

"This is no longer the seasoned warrior who knows better and uses his instincts and skill," Trujillo says. "He becomes an emotional, battle-weary man taking all the risks that he never took before—and look what it got him: it got him killed."

"That was pretty nuts," he says of the death scene. "It took three days to film. They put me on a bicycle seat attached to the gate and did a series of different shots with me and then a stunt double attached to a rope running full tilt until the rope stopped before the swing gate . . . very dangerous indeed, but as safe as it could be to make it real. You gotta love making movies."

About a decade later, the work of Trujillo, Youngblood, and Gibson would help another performer in a similar situation.

"Since [*Apocalypto*], I had always dreamt of playing a character similar to that," remembers

James Rolleston. "I also loved the idea of playing a Maori warrior and telling a Maori story and being able to represent my culture, so when this opportunity came about, I pounced at it with both hands. I chose to play Hongi on *The Dead Lands* because I have always thoroughly enjoyed action films and films that balance excitement, action, and laughter well."

Like Youngblood, Rolleston would be a young man out for revenge in the 2014 film, his Maori tribe attacked by some friendship-feigning invaders who steal his dad's head as a trophy. Accompanied by a mysterious stranger—the pseudo-monster who gave the title area its name, making trespassing a capital offense—and inspired by spiritual messages from his grandma, Hongi, like Jaguar Paw, is a man against an army.

A decade after *Apocalypto*, James Rolleston sent his Hongi on a similar tale of vengeance in 2014's *The Dead Lands*.

Growing up in the small New Zealand land of Opotiki, Rolleston had been around all kinds of cultural offerings from the Maori, who first emigrated from Polynesia in the late 1200s.

"Growing up, doing Kapa Haka [a cultural dance] in early primary school days," he recalls, "[then] through to high school and going to many Maori Tangi [days-long funeral rites], I was always surrounded by the traditional ways of Maori and the culture. That helped a lot with preparing for this character." He roared through a crash course in the tribal speakings of Te Reo Maori, an official New Zealand language for three decades, and other non-traditional tradition education.

Of course, the physical part of becoming Hongi would have terrified any gym class.

Along with the whole *Dead Lands* cast, Rolleston went through, "a six-week boot camp that consisted of clean eating, training daily to get fit and strong for both our characters and the long physically demanding days during filming, and also choreographing for the fighting scenes, which some days, were long and tiring."

It certainly paid off, him making Hongi into a fighting machine, brawling his way through the enemy all the way to its leader. But there's no greater honor that the martyrdom that comes from being a warrior fallen in battle, and Hongi spares his enemy's life to leave him to a fast-forgotten death, whenever it may occur.

The mental tenacity, the physical work, it had all been just about backbreaking in every sense of the word, and all been worth it for Rolleston and the rest of the cast, whose film became their country's submission to America's Oscars for Best Foreign Film (it wasn't chosen). Difficulty aside, there had been "Cut!" calls, reshoots, a time to go home for the day and plan for tomorrow. Years later, reality would take a stronger, darker step for Rolleston, one without any kind of script or structure.

On July 26, 2016, in his Opotiki homeland, Rolleston's car smashed into a bridge. "I was crushed from the waist down and suffered multiple fractures to the right side of my pelvis and broke both of my legs," he remembers. "I also suffered a traumatic brain injury which has affected my speech, decision making, coordination, and personality characteristics."

Forget the war and hiking techniques he'd learned for Hongi; now he had to re-learn how to walk, speak, and even think straight again. Now, nearly a year later, he's making it back, one accomplishment at a time—and film fans around the world are behind him.

"It's all getting better by the day," he says in late March 2017. "I've been doing a lot of therapies such as physio, speech and language therapy, and occupational therapy. I'm slowly getting back into things and finding my feet again. I keep making improvements, so I don't see why I won't get back to 100 percent."

This became the kiss of death for *Watchman* star Ursula Zandt (Apollonia Vanova) and her lady friend early in the 2009 film.

Apollonia Vanova: *Watchmen*

GUARANTEEING RIGHT NOW——YOU WILL *never* find a stronger piece of action acting advice than what you're about to read.

A million books by a million writers with a million times my experience and knowledge wouldn't come up with this gem. Socrates, Newton, Tesla, da Vinci, and all the other most brilliant minds in world history could have a three-week expedition to a secluded land and not figure this one.

Ready to get knocked for a loop and then back around? Here you go.

"The film business, especially the action film genre," muses *Watchmen* star Apollonia Vanova, "where special effects, car chases, shooting and fighting take precedence over the narrative and the complexity of the character . . . *is very much like a one-night stand. Do it while you're young and don't do it for too long!*"

There is nothing else that can even remotely touch that. But I'm still going to fill in the rest of this profile. . . .

It's a common stereotype, even a stigma, to go straight to the ending that comic books (or *graphic novels*, as they now prefer, much like yesterday's housewives are today's *domestic engineers*), the films that spring from them, and those that enjoy both should be labeled superficial, with all the thickness of the book's pages themselves.

Not much to any of it, right? A superhero secretly does good, a villain and probably some minions come close to taking it all over, and the superhero, on a huge public scale, manages to somehow overcome it all, defeat them, and probably score the love of a pretty lady in the bargain.

Yeah, that's how things typically have gone for such flicks, yesterday and today. But films like 2009's *Watchmen* went quite a bit deeper—in the sense that, had the film been an archeological dig, the Earth's core would have been reached and burned straight through.

The flick's major standout was character development, showing that even comic heroes have their immoral sides. Few films of any genre take as much time to show as many sides of their main men and women as this flick did, and we learned enough about each of the title characters to fill a book as long as this one. The lines between good and evil are shown to exist in all of them, and even they don't always know which side of said markings they stand upon. Even fighting for the greater good, none of the title characters always go the right way, even in their own minds, and it's why, in the film's imagined world, we as a public are starting to see the imperfection behind the heroism. It's also why the heroes are just about done busting their asses to save ours.

It's something that we see, in the darkest and saddest of forms, before the opening credits are even through rolling.

After finding a sudden, violent start to her crime-fighting career while avenging her sister's death in Nazi Austria, Ursula Zandt charged to America, crusading against the child sex traffic industry, shadowing her prey in the physical form of her gun-mastering persona—The Silhouette.

But it wasn't enough for some people. It never would be. Because for all her wonderful, selfless deeds, there was something else about Silhouette, or rather the lady she was, that would never allow her to live all the way up to others, in too many eyes back then and still too many here in the 2010s.

Years in the gym had gotten the former fitness competitor in shape enough to resemble a superhero, but, "I had never read a comic book in my life," Vanova admits. However, "I already had the Silhouette haircut, I stayed in shape and I had the dance background that enabled me to dip my partner as I leaned in for the kiss. This doesn't happen often, but I knew I had the role the moment I walked in the door and saw their eyes light up."

It would be that kiss that would shorten the character's life.

Remember that flaw we just mentioned? It wasn't that she was secretly evil or a naturally cold person. Ursula just had a habit that, in so many uber-hypocritical eyes, overcame her good work.

She loved women.

The superheroine steps through Times Square as everyone celebrates the end of World War 2. One cheering nurse just "happens" to bump into her and become entranced by her beauty.

The Lady in Black takes the Lady in White in her arms and locks her in one of the film's most loving embraces. Their version is *quite* a bit more remarkable than the actual legendary Times Square solider-nurse kiss photo.

"The kiss was filmed outside on set, with a huge crowd of people throwing ribbons and celebrating victory," Vanova recalls. "It was not in a building in front of a green screen."

"Usually when you have an audition, you prepare scenes and read opposite another actor and you *act*," explains Leah Gibson, the not-quite-impromptu partner, "but in this case, we were informed that we'd be coming in and kissing another girl, but you handle it professionally if that's what the part is."

Stepping into the room, she and the rest of the "tryers" met their kiss-in stand-ins.

"There was this lovely woman, and we came in and we had to re-enact the kiss in the audition," Gibson recalls.

But their moment of public love would be a fatal undoing. As Bob Dylan reminds us that, indeed, "times, they are a-changin'," things fall apart for the heroes. One is killed, another whisked to an institution. Then Ursula and her lover are found shot to death, anti-lesbian graffiti staining the walls with their blood, their last moments spent in a clinch together in bed.

"We talked it out and played around with different physical expressions," Gibson says, "how the lovers would have been found. It's important to be able to tell as much of a story as you can about how the lovers, even in this gruesome setting, died in each other's arms."

Moments into the film, the audience is well aware that this isn't someone's typical comic-to-screen creation.

Putting a new spin on such a genre hadn't been easy for Zack Snyder (not to mention dramatically rewriting history in 2006 with *300*!). In 2013, he embarked on a new task: retelling a specific story, one that had jumped from book to screens small and large many times before. It was the tale of a young man from a foreign land who didn't understand why everyone in his new home was surprised at his X-ray vision, super strength, and ability to fly.

Man of Steel was the new tale of a household name and face called Superman. Snyder's man behind the cape and chest-adorned S was Henry Cavill, with Michael Shannon as General Zod, out to create an army of genetically superior beings that will make Earth into the metropolitan Metropolis that Krypton didn't have the chance to become.

Just as these enemies often do (including the Terence Stamp version of Zod, who had Ursa back in the first two *Superman* movies of 1978 and 1980), Zod convinced a few gorgeous women to follow in his quest. Remembering Vanova's work for him in the past, Snyder gave her a shot at Kryptonian beauty Nadira. For her tryout, Vanova looked back to another lady's legendary-in-the-making action work.

"I was asked to prepare the monologue of [Daryl Hannah's] Elle Driver of *Kill Bill II*, and that was very exciting," she recalls. "The audition is the one place where I experience the most artistic freedom. To get into the [Nadira] role, I just had to ensure I stayed fit so that my weight wouldn't fluctuate during the costume fittings. The costumes were truly spectacular!"

Will she, as Sarah Douglas did as Ursa, find a way to resurrection to battle Superman again? Is there another comic book for her to bring to cinema? Might she one day do what far too few women have gotten the chance to do, and carry off a superhero film with herself doing all the work? Just maybe . . .

"I did not choose action films specifically," she says. "Action films chose me—partly because of my accent, my athletic background, and my appearance. But if one is to be typecast, being a villain or action hero is the ideal character to play. Those types of roles are like vicarious vessels for what most of us wish we could do, without consequence. That is a very powerful feeling to experience."

It took her thousands of years and some reincarnations, but Nefertiti (Rachel Weisz, bottom) managed to come out atop Anck Su Namun (Patricia Velasquez) in 2001's *The Mummy Returns*.

Patricia Velasquez: *The Mummy* films

THERE WAS JUST ONE explanation for Anck Su Namun—all of her good qualities must have been on the outside.

In the BC-age past or just a few decades ago, the woman was out for money, for blood, and, as even those who loved her sadly found out, all for herself.

We didn't see her much in *The Mummy* (1999), but more than enough to jam the film's plot accelerator straight to the ground. Thousands of years ago, strong performance in the concubine trade could win women everything but official royalty, and Namun was doing quite well, winning the libido (if not the whole heart) of the Pharaoh of cinematic times.

Still, even those in the sex trade have a heart of their own, and hers had been stolen by the priest Imhotep (Arnold Vosloo), who himself had forgotten his clerical values to embark on an affair.

It was quite a switch from the lady behind Namun. After nearly winning the 1989 Miss

Venezuela pageant, Patricia Velasquez had modeled all over America, including a few issues of *Sports Illustrated*'s swimsuit edition. As the 90s ended, a new career was rolling for her.

"It was destiny!" asserts the Namun portrayer Patricia Velasquez. "I went to meet the casting director, and they called me that night to offer me the part. I had no idea what it was, no idea it was so big."

At first, it's easy to see Namun and Imhotep as victims. Found out by the Pharaoh, she dies by her own hand, while he flees, hoping to use his resurrective powers later.

It doesn't work, and he's sealed away forever. But when a group of treasure hunters unwittingly bring him back a few millennia later, Imhotep might just get one more chance.

Preparing to become Namun, Velasquez explains, "was mainly the study of the culture and language that didn't exist at the time. I studied with some teachers at UCLA and mainly on the Internet and a lot of mythology."

Her name has been blackened by the Islamic terrorists that so much of the world battles today, but the Egyptian goddess Isis has been worshipped since ancient times, a symbol of maternity and wifehood. She became Velasquez's inspiration to create Namun.

Resurrected in 1926, Imhotep looks for a new shot at life, seeing the lives he'll have to take in the process as a sort of collateral damage. But when he can't get his love back alive, his last gasp of sanity slips away, and it's everything but hell on earth until the same techniques that brought him back send him below again.

Two years later (eight in "film time"), a lovely—again, only in the physical sense—rich gal named Meela Nais led a cult to resurrect Imhotep and basically own all of Egypt in *The Mummy Returns* (2001). We'd jumped to present time (to an extent, as the film happened in 1933), but Meela had more than a bit in common with Namun. The looks, the voice, and, most importantly, the attitude: ready to rob, pillage, and kill the innocent and even her friends to get what she wanted.

The character was about the same, and the actress was identical: Velasquez was now her girl's reincarnation.

"Since I had already done the work for the first role," she explains, "then for Meela I had a much more modern approach, like an independent woman who wanted to get her power back from something. I was able to play a lot and my need for winning was life or death."

One of her toughest scenes came early, as her group captures Rick's brother Jonathan, looking for information about some of Imhotep's treasures. Snakes are terrifying enough when we see one slither by; imagine having such a creature tossed into your face, just so *ready* to clamp down and spit some venom through your veins!

Cooler than an arctic winter—being naturally coldhearted can help us there—Meela wields her living lethal weapon like the two have a kinship, and they probably do. But it showed Velasquez's acting talent in all kinds of subtle ways.

"I have a phobia of snakes," she admits. "I was amazed when I saw the film."

Meela's cult steals Evelyn O'Connell (Rachel Weisz), and eventually Evelen's son, who Meela takes extra pleasure in tormenting. Maybe she's still pissed at Evelyn, because there's more than meets the present life there; Eve's the most recent coming of Nefertiti, the daughter of the Pharaoh who Namun betrayed, leading to both her and Imhotep's death.

"When you scream in Egyptian, they didn't scream, 'AHHHH!'" she says. "Instead, they said, 'JJJJJJ!'" The director wasn't sure why I was screaming that way and after I few takes, he said, 'No, let's do it like we scream now.' We all laughed."

We see a battle that the pair fought in ancient times, with Namun coming out on top. Back in the present, Meela gets the drop and the plunge on Evelyn, fatally planting a knife through her stomach.

"We prepared for two months and it really came out so beautiful," Velasquez says of the brawl. "We treated it like a dance choreography."

But the same powers that brought back Imhotep resurrect Evelyn, and now she wants a rematch: this time it's going all the way to death. Both have their ancestors' strength within, along with some sai blades, and there's no one around to put a stop to this.

Up to now, we might just have a *little* bit of sympathy for Namun. A tad. After all, she truly loved Imhotep, and sacrificed herself for him. He had taken out others to resurrect her. We'd have to look pretty hard, but we might find just a touch of compassion for the two.

Then the film nears its end. He's hanging from a ledge, a ton of demonic souls below, aching for their next meal. He cries out for her to help, and she's just close enough nearby to offer it.

But she doesn't. She runs away. We almost see his heart shatter, sending tears to his eyes. With everything for naught and nothing left, he lets go, ending his struggle forever, perhaps a sad form of redemption for all he caused.

She won't be so lucky. Moments later, she stumbles into a pit full of scorpions, her body giving them a field day for stinging and smothering.

"When you play the role of the evil," Velsaquez says, "[it] is not that you play the bad. It's just that you make choices that people might not agree with. But you can't judge the character and you have to fight for your goal. In my case, it was my love for the mummy."

As the rest of his friends from *The Fast and the Furious* said goodbye to Brian O'Connor in the closing moments of *Furious 7* in 2015, millions of fans of the series bid a tearful farewell to Paul Walker, tragically killed two years before.

Paul Walker: *The Fast and Furious/Hours*

THE EMOTION THEY FELT inside, the tears they wiped away, we felt them too. It's a point that we rarely reach in the action genre; hell, we hardly ever get there in films in general.

Brian O'Connor's friends sat together on a beach, finally getting the chance to kick back after yet another adrenalin-jammed, vehicular-slaughtering battle. They'd been through it more times than any other group in American action history. Now Brian was leaving, saying goodbye to head off into marriage and fatherhood. Better for him, certainly, but not for them.

And, just as it had for all of (*The Fast and*) *Furious 7*, the feelings came over to us in the audience. We'd been feeling it throughout the 2015 film. It was getting a little stronger.

Two years before, which seemed like minutes if you thought too hard, Paul Walker had been stolen from them, from all those who cared for him, and from millions of fans around the world. Just weeks after that heartbreaking afternoon in Nov. 2013, we'd gotten a stronger piece of proof of Walker's ability as a performer than ever before. But we'd never get to thank him for it.

Throughout the seventh round of *Furious* action, we'd wondered how the film would handle the tragedy. Would O'Connor have a heroic death, sacrificing himself to save his friends, passing in the arms of a loved one while passing on a profound proverb, in full dramatic tradition?

Or would our last memories of him be exactly what we all wished Walker would have been there to do? Tough to be sure, but we all hoped so much that the film would try.

It did. We saw *Furious* centerpiece Dom Toretto (Vin Diesel) head off to drown his sadness in a drive, a welcome switch from the high-speed action he'd been through for over a decade of series action.

Not this time. Walker was gone, but his magic wasn't. With the help of special effects joint Weta Digital (co-owned by none other than a director named Peter Jackson), and Walker's brothers Caleb and Cody standing in, we saw that O'Connor wasn't letting his friend get away, pulling up beside him, casting the same smile of confidence he always did, riding behind his best friend one more time.

We felt it too. We felt ourselves finally saying goodbye in that special way that the film world allows. Even if Dom asserts near the end, "It's never goodbye. You'll always be with me. You'll always be my brother." Even in the clips we'd just seen of O'Connor's antics through the first *Furious* feats, we saw the impact he made on so many. We felt the impact Walker made on us. The *Furious* gang was a brotherhood on and off the screen. Its fans felt the same way.

"What we're doing is pretty cool, but let's make sure we're having fun doing it," Walker once said. "And it's important to me that people feel appreciated because that's when you get the best in people. Give people ownership, give them the pat on the back, give them the kudos they deserve." His fans had been doing that for years, and they'll never stop.

This being a book about action acting, of course we must acknowledge Walker's *Furious* work. I'm sure he was very proud of it, and he had every right to be. No other action series in American film history has had so many editions (a number that will probably have reached eight by the time you read this), and he's a big reason for that. Brian O'Connor showed up as much as any other character in *Furious* except for Diesel's Dom Toretto: six editions, the exception being 2006's *Tokyo Drift*. He'd set out as an undercover cop looking to infiltrate some street racing thieves, only to find the livelihood that Dom, his sister Mia (Jordana Brewster), and all the rest had created too strong to resist.

The journey had taken him to Miami and then to Spain, in and out of the FBI, and back into Mia's arms, and, finally, in the seventh flick, back to Los Angeles for one more run.

"I think I've had enough successes to where the journey is more important to me now," Walker said. "There's no guarantee, no matter what. We get one run in life." Even before the seventh flick was through, he'd already announced plans to be in part eight.

"I think early on in life I knew that if I just live by my heart, I'm good," he claimed. "I think the same probably goes with most people . . . I think most people would find that if they can just get to that place, the rest is just noise."

Before he became O'Connor for the final time, someone had walked up to Walker with a different kind of chance. Not just to headline a film. Basically, to be the film. To be all audiences would see for about three-fourths of the movie, and still manage to keep them entertained. The dream and nightmare of just about everyone who has ever been in the business.

The screenplay had been written, the money raised, and crew brought together, everything. Now all those behind *Hours* (2013) were sending Walker a message. He'd earned their trust, their confidence that he could be the one to carry the acting burden in their film, to push them over the finish line they could finally see.

Pulling this one off could be his final ascension to the tops of Hollywood ranks. Bombing it could destroy his career.

"I read [the script] and I was really intimidated," he admitted. "I was like, 'Well, it's kind of sink or swim time, buddy. If you want to do this one, let's really go and see what you can do.' It was really just an opportunity for me to test myself. To be able to sit back and go, 'Hey, look. When you apply yourself, you can relax, when you have something you can really sink your teeth into.' So it's cool." Was he convincing us or himself?

There was nothing that could be controlled here. No happy ending. No ending, period, even years afterward. Everyone is at nature's mercy. If a tornado, a tsunami, an earthquake comes through, there's nothing we can do but be ready. And for millions in the south in August 2005, that wasn't enough.

When Hurricane Katrina crashed through Louisiana, there were no special effects and no one to yell cut. Millions were left homeless. Nearly two thousand died. For weeks, the legendary city of New Orleans and nearby areas lived under water that it seemed would never recede. We can see remnants of the storm even today. We'll never forget it.

As we watched *Hours* (sadly, not nearly enough have, a situation that still has time to be repaired), we only wished it wasn't based on far too many true stories. Too many tragedies. But in the persona of its protagonist, we saw the embodiment of the spirit that so many demonstrated across the area. What turned New Orleans into much more than a Mardi Gras symbol—a reminder of just how far people can go and what they can do, what strength a man can happen upon in a whole new reality, even one full of fear, uncertainty, even danger.

We saw Nolan Hayes go through what should only happen in the movies, and knew that that wasn't the case. We might be a strong as he was. We just hoped we'd never have to try.

Just as New Orleans' most unwelcome visitor shows up, Richardson's wife goes into labor, over a month early.

She dies, leaving a baby he names Abigail, just like her. But as the storm keeps hitting, everything and everyone at the hospital is gone.

No doctors. No nurses. No visitors. No electricity. Since Abigail was born too soon to breathe on her own, no way to save her.

Except him. There's a battery-powered generator there, but it needs to be cranked by hand—every three minutes.

But this is the movies, right? Surely, someone will swoop in for the rescue, just like it always happened with O'Connor's *Furious* friends . . . right?

"I overanalyze shit," Walker admitted, "but so long as I can keep my heart clear and I just listen to what my heart tells me, it never fails. My intuition is good, my instincts are good, my judge of character. It's important to me to be living right and living right is being surrounded by the people I love, loving the people that I love, being surrounded by my friends."

Hours pass. They stretch into days. Food, water, everything's gone. The battery power's dropping, and he's got to crank it more and more. He can hardly take a breath, let alone rest.

A helicopter lands next door, but an idiot shoots at it, forcing it to leave. He finds a radio in an ambulance, but the return call doesn't come in time. Then some morons break in, looking to steal some drugs, and he's forced to blast them away when they get too close to his treasure.

It's looking more and more like she won't make it. Hell, it's looking like he may not either. At this point, how many of us would have stopped trying, or even caring, long ago?

But in these moments, Nolan becomes a form of reality that needs to step off the movies a bit more often. With far too many kids who have no clue what it means to even have a dad these days—trust me, teachers know this sort of thing—we have one willing to do everything that's right, and then a little more.

"The thing that was amazing is that I never realized it," Walker said, "just portraying a role, the body, the spirit doesn't know any difference between what I'm practicing or pretending compared to reality. My victory, my journey in that, even though it was something that was induced, I was forcing myself into it. My spirit didn't know that it wasn't real. The thing that was amazing is at the end of the journey, because we shot it in sequence, at the end of it, that victory, achieving what Nolan achieved, that was my victory."

Victory? How can it even be possible, even in a world of drama? Like enough hasn't gone horribly wrong for him, Nolan accidentally breaks the ventilator's handle.

He tries to go for mouth-to-mouth, but it's risky enough for anyone to do that on a child, let alone a days-old baby. But no matter—there's nothing left in him. Even in the movies, not all battles can be won. Perhaps *Hours* will put us straight in the sad but true tale of yet another innocent who lost everything.

"There was nobody there to throw me off my game path," Walker said. "It was like, 'I know where this starts, I know where this ends, and this is what I've gotta do.' It just effected me a lot more than I thought it was going to." He's not the only one.

Maybe that's another personal issue for those of us who were lucky enough to see it. Maybe we looked at Nolan and wondered if, certainly hoped, we could do what he did. That we could go so far for someone we'd helped give life to, to help her continue it. We could dream of being close to the father he was.

As private as any public figure could be during his career, so much was learned about Walker after it was too late, and America got another blow to the heart when we found out (many for the first time) that there was a daughter he wouldn't be around to see make a success of her own. It reminds us that the people we see on the screen aren't all that far from those in any other profession. There are people that knew them better, than loved them more, and that will miss them in ways we never could.

"My daughter is fourteen years old and I want to take God-given opportunities and I want to maximize," said Walker. "I want her to see [*Hours*]. She was there for the premiere and she's proud. She's excited. And she's proudest, I think, for the same reason why I wanted to be a part of it. It's truthful, it's pure."

Being a dad himself might have made *Hours* especially tough for Walker. Maybe not. Actually, hopefully not—it's not like a guy in this position would have needed any further pressure. But to us on the outside, it certainly makes his work more real, even if only now in hindsight. It shows us one more example of how great he was, and we'll have to be content with what we have. As fans of acting, it's got to be enough. Still, there's a select group who will forever get a special sense of inspiration from Nolan, his plight, and the happy ending that finally comes.

Even in the midst of one of American's history's biggest tragedies, Walker's Nolan Richardson demonstrated the spirit that we wish lived in fathers around the world to save his newborn daughter in 2013's *Hours*.

Those of us still looking forward to fatherhood—like a certain author is, just as he makes his way through this profile—got something extra special from the work. One more example of just how talented Walker was, of course, but a special hope that we could ever find Nolan's strength. That we'd be willing to go so far, to try so hard, for someone so new. That our devotion to those we'd been lucky enough to give life to would be so strong from the moment we saw her, and that's all the time it would take.

Oh, did I mention that, yes, there *does* come an ending worth waiting for?

Nolan's only real companion over the past few hours has been his new four-legged stray friend named Sherlock. With the strength and kindness that's so easy to find in dogs, Sherlock's found his own way to survive. And just as Nolan looks to be through, some paramedics show up, and Sherlock finds them.

Just in time for Nolan—but after two days of suffering, Abigail may already be gone. Her dad's lifted onto a gurney . . . and we hear the most welcome sound that can reach a new parent's ears.

She's crying. It means she's breathing. She's alive. As the film's final scene starts, she's placed on his chest, and it's all been worth it and so much more. Her eyes aren't even open yet, but she's reaching out to grab his beard and feel his face, like she already knows who he is.

And as memorable of the rest of Walker's work—which went *much* further than just the *Furious* films—ever was, this might be the strongest individual image of his too-short career. Hardly able to find the strength to cry, he sobs, he holds her, kisses her, this just the first in his lifetime of always being there for his little lady.

When my daughter—looks like she'll be named Kennedy—arrives for my wife and I in the summer of 2017, I hope I can be like him.

"My victory in that movie was my victory in real life," Walker said of *Hours*. "What I've found is the heart, the soul, whatever you want to call it, it doesn't differentiate. If you really live the experience making a movie, it's the same as living it in real life, as crazy as it sounds."

Hours, "paralleled my life, so much of what was going on with that ventilator and what it represented to me really: the juggling of life and trying to figure out who you are in it, what this represents and what that represents. Sometimes the blessing can be deemed as a curse. Sometimes the hurdles aren't really hurdles at all. They're welcome challenges, tests. Then you come out the end being on top."

Rooster Cogburn gave John Wayne the Oscar he'd been missing for his career, and Kim Darby's Mattie was one of many other reasons that *True Grit* shined through in 1969.

John Wayne: *Sands of Iwo Jima/True Grit*

WE AS AMERICANS HAVE always been a nation of hero-worshipers, making celebrities out of people who haven't really earned the title. While police officers who put their lives on the line for poverty wages, doctors who save those that they've never met and that forget them instantly, and teachers that go to the ends of the earth to educate our next generation, get little or no thanks for their work, we like to look up to those we have every right to stare in the eye.

In a land where people can land million-dollar deals for nothing more than the ability to walk past the camera of a reality show, while millions of others pray that their next meal won't be too far away, we just to, well, *like* others simply because we see them on TV and on the screen.

Through a pessimist's eyes, John Wayne might have personified this. He turned down service in World War II, yet made millions acting like those that had been in the real thing. He couldn't stand horses, yet his cowboy persona is a household image. He may have personified one of the first true action heroes in American film history, but that's all it was: a performance. While thousands of men and women lost their lives to keep America safe, Wayne spent his war time on the sets of Hollywood, shouting about how great America was, while at the same time doing little to turn his words into action.

But that's not how most people look at Wayne. It's not how we should examine the legacy he left. The power of Wayne's persona is just as, and probably more important than the reality. Intentionally or otherwise, the people that he became ended up just as inspirational as many real folk. And if these ideas, these characters, gave Americans a way and a reason to feel good, to believe in themselves, then maybe it didn't really matter what was true and what was performed when it came to Wayne and his work.

"Wayne never was an actor," explained Henry Hathaway, who directed Wayne in *True Grit* (1969), *The Shepherd of the Hills* (1941), and *The Sons of Katie Elder* (1965), "and because he wasn't an actor, he had to do everything real. There wasn't anything in Duke that would allow him to pretend he was something. He couldn't be French, he couldn't have an accent, he couldn't be Olivier. Whatever the actor was called to do in the script, he did it. It wasn't a question of acting; it was a question of reality."

The line between fantasy and reality propelled Wayne to the top of box office lists for longer than nearly everyone else in Hollywood history; from 1949 to 1975, he was one of America's top ten money-making stars, finishing first or second in seven of those years. Audiences used his films to pay their own tribute to those who'd died in WWII. Eventually, films like *The Alamo* (1960) and others helped inspire America to stand up to Communism during the Cold War (which, obviously, we went full overboard with during the McCarthy era, which Wayne supported). They even brought a dramatic (read: only sort of realistic) view of the Vietnam War, which by that point, wasn't sitting quite right with Old Glory.

For someone who appeared in over 150 films, Wayne's career wasn't memorable as a whole; few people could name twenty of them. But he became a legend in Hollywood for giving America a reason to cheer and a path to hope, through his characters if not himself. As flawed as any and even more so than some, Wayne's roles showed us the good that's in so many.

It's why George Wallace offered him a Vice Presidential spot on the third-party American ticket in 1968 (Wayne turned it down to go promote *True Grit*). It's why Congress minted Wayne a special Congressional medal less than two months before his death in June 1979. It's why, even today, upcoming soldiers join the marines with the image of Sgt. Stryker of *Sands of Iwo Jima* (1949) in their hearts and minds. It's why the reissues of his films on DVD still sell like crazy, with fans oftentimes buying several versions of the same flick.

And while his outspokenness and political views cost him some friends and roles, Wayne's patriotism came through when we were reaching out for any kind of hope in a situation that we never dreamed was even remotely possible. Back in his last decade, Wayne made a record of monologues and poems letting everyone know what a great land this was; after the Sept. 11 attacks, it became a new bestseller. In one form or another, America needed people like John Wayne.

"When I started, I knew I was no actor," Wayne said, "and I went to work on this Wayne thing. It was as deliberate a projection as you'll ever see. I figured I needed a gimmick, so I dreamed up the drawl, the squint, and a way of moving meant to suggest that I wasn't looking for trouble, but would just as soon throw a bottle at your head as not."

For such a tough-sounding, long-lasting nickname, Wayne's "Duke" moniker's beginnings were innocent enough: Wayne's original name of Marion won him the rights to endless teasing as a Southern California youth, until a pleasantly fateful day in 1918. Noticing young Marion walking past their station, a group of firemen spotted the family canine, an Airedale named Duke that followed him to school and slept at the station until he returned. The men started calling Marion "Duke," and he grabbed and ran with the nickname, starting countless conversations for the rest of his life with, "Just call me Duke."

By the time his first Oscar-nominated role and elevation towards legend came about, American audiences were used to the Duke; fifteen of his films had been released in 1935 and 1936 alone. *Sands of Iwo Jima* was hardly his first war picture; he'd been doing them for years. But the story of a drill sergeant and the reluctant youths he turns into soldiers would be one of the first forays into a story based not on the actions of the Army, Air Force, or Navy, but the Marines (many will tell you that, 1987's *Full Metal Jacket* notwithstanding, this is still the military's most cinematically underrated group).

Filming at Camp Pendleton, near San Diego, Wayne got into character by chatting for hours with the marines there. He watched one of the toughest officers on base turn the boys into men and the men into soldiers. Many actual marines played marines in the film, and the men immortalized in the image of marines raising the flag on Suribachi were located to recreate it for the film.

As heroic as Stryker was, he had an aura of humanity that many of Wayne's former and future characters lacked, in part because he gives his life, shockingly gunned down by a sniper just after remarking to his troops on how good it is to be on the dangerous beach. But even in Hollywood, war accomplishes little without the loss of decent human life on all sides, and *Iwo Jima* showed us as much.

The film helped secure the Duke legend and garnered Wayne his first Oscar nomination; he wouldn't even get picked again until *True Grit*, angering those who felt he should have gone up for 1949's *She Wore a Yellow Ribbon* and other performances.

Wayne kept up his image the best way he could: by showing and re-showing it to American audiences, who kept paying to see it. On a field, on a ranch, in combat, he decided not to fix what wasn't broken, and viewers kept coming—and while this isn't the most pleasant truth, the box-office results of a career typically matter more than critics.

In the late 1960s, with his career on the downswing (from a critical standpoint, not really a ticket-selling one), Wayne's heroic fervor didn't have the same effect it had earlier on. While audiences had rooted for him all the way through *Sands of Iwo Jima* and other war-based films, American sentiment was starting to turn against Vietnam, and when Wayne championed the war's cause in 1968's *The Green Berets*, the press was all too willing to look past his strong acting performance and blast him for supporting a war his country was no longer sure it wanted (to be fair, the public felt otherwise, as the film was a box-office hit).

Then Henry Hathaway sent him a copy of Charles Portis' novel *True Grit*, and Wayne did everything but a backflip (decades earlier, he'd probably have done several). He put in a high-speed, uber-priced bid for the book, but an official at Paramount had already secured the rights. Disappointed, Wayne called the fellow, and heard a snicker.

Then he told Wayne what he already knew: that he'd be the perfect person to play Rooster Cogburn, the battle-hardened one-eyed marshal who reluctantly took prisoners, preferring to blast them instead.

"Rooster was the kind of marshal the screen had never seen before," Wayne said. "An old sloppy-looking, hard-drinking, disreputable one-eyed son-of-a-gun who'd been around long enough to know that you don't mess around with outlaws, but you use every trick in the book, fair or foul, to bring them to justice." Cogburn knew more than the criminals themselves, and it's a sure bet that his colleagues in law enforcement thanked their lucky stars he'd stayed on their side, because the character came across as the world's smartest potential criminal.

"Here was a guy with an eye patch who's survived because he knew you couldn't give an outlaw a chance. You had to use fair means and foul to bring the outlaw to justice. But he always did it for the greater good, if you will." Ironically, Wayne at first refused to wear Rooster's eye patch.

Best of all, Hathaway explained, Cogburn was past the point of impressing others in the physical sense: attire and diet were dirty words to this guy.

"This was like telling my dad that he did not have to pay that year's federal taxes," recalls Wayne's daughter, Aissa.

Cogburn was the best lawman of the times and places, and teenage Mattie Ross knew it well, enlisting the reluctant gunman to snare revenge on the fellow that drunkenly killed her daddy.

"As someone who'd been trying to fend off a considerable spread since middle age," Wayne gleefully remembered, "I was delighted to be able to forget all that and just eat as much as I wanted. I did try to persuade Henry to let me lose the eye patch [he felt the fans wouldn't like it], but he said, 'You wear that eye patch and give me the performance I want from you and you might even win an Oscar.'"

Still, Wayne knew that it was getting tougher and tougher for audiences to take his action-hero persona seriously; now in his early 60s and having lost a lung to cancer (millions of cigarettes tend to have that effect), Wayne himself wasn't looking for a good fist-to-fist brawl with too many outlaws, acted out or otherwise. Riding horses everywhere and breathing in the mountainous lands of Colorado during filming would be difficult enough. While Wayne's passion for the role was just as high and perhaps even outrising that of which he'd shown for previous roles, he'd have to go further within to find Rooster—action would be behind acting in this one.

Fortunately, there was enough there left over.

Rooster, Wayne explained, "feels the same way about life that I do. He doesn't believe in pampering wrongdoers, which certainly fits into the category of my thinking. He doesn't believe in accommodation; neither do I." Whereas many of the characters he'd played had been something of Western supermen, impervious not only to enemies' bullets but the overindulgences of tobacco, alcohol, and kindness of others, Rooster, like Wayne, was starting to realize his own sense of vulnerability. He lets alcohol get the better of him a few times, and winds up acting not just out of duty, but admiration for Mattie—perhaps she's the one who's truly showing grit in this.

"It's sure as hell my first decent role in 20 years," Wayne said, in probably a bit of an overstatement, "and my first chance to play a character role instead of John Wayne. Ordinarily they just stand me there and run everybody up against me." He called the scene where he and Mattie stay up late and Cogburn starts recalling his life, including his divorce, one of the best scenes of his career.

For the first time in two decades, Wayne's name came back up on the Oscar nomination list (he hadn't been nominated for appearing in *The Quiet Man*, 1952's Best Picture), and the 1969 Best Actor race would be one of the most competitive in Academy Award history: Wayne was up against Jon Voight and Dustin Hoffman from the Best Picture-winning *Midnight Cowboy*, as well as household names Peter O'Toole and Richard Burton.

In one of the biggest coincidences in Oscar history, it would be Barbra Streisand, known as one of Hollywood's most outspoken liberals, who'd call the man who represented the town's conservative voice up to the podium to grab his overdue statue.

"If I'd known what I know now," said a tearful Wayne after a standing ovation, "I'd have put a patch on my eye 35 years ago." When he returned to Arizona for the shooting of *Rio Lobo* (1970) the next morning, the full cast and crew, including the horse, was wearing Rooster's signature patches (one of Wayne's final public appearances was at the Oscar ceremony in April 1979; he died two months later).

He would reprise the role in 1974's *Rooster Cogburn* alongside Katharine Hepburn, and the film managed a respectable box-office take, but plans for a second sequel were dismissed.

"I've played the kind of man I'd like to have been," Wayne once said. Perhaps Rooster brought more truth to the saying than any of his other characters.

In a world where celebrities who express any kind of opinion beyond their favorite color are immediately deemed outspoken and controversial, where terms like "bigot," "insensitive," "closed- and narrow-minded," and the like are tossed around like fodder, Wayne never minded being offensive to some, as long as he was honest. While he always personally made sure never to vilify or even downgrade Native Americans in his movies, he asserted that the land's new settlers had done nothing wrong in inhabiting their former land ("There were great numbers of people who needed new land, and the Indians were selfishly trying to keep it for themselves."). Wayne made statements about blacks that would kill a career dead in the water—or at least cause a trip to sensitivity training—today ("I believe in white supremacy until the blacks are educated to a point of responsibility." "I'm tired of hearing the words 'black American.' I don't go around saying 'I'm a white American.'... The black guy should say, 'I'm an American' or 'I'm an Englishman' or whatever free country they are lucky to live in, and they should say, 'I'm going to show you what I can do,' instead of saying, 'Treat us better because we're browbeaten and downtrodden.'").

However, just as we as a nation are uber-selective as to who we cheer for and who we don't pay to see, at least in the entertainment world, there are some that we look up to for speaking their minds, brutal though their honesty may be, and perhaps Wayne's personas added to this as well. The Duke's characters never gave a good goddamn about political correctness or what others thought of them, and maybe that's why we let Wayne get away with these statements (if he was around to make them today, who knows what our reaction would be?). The Duke fought the good fight on the screen, and often used tactics more underhanded than the villains he was up against; Wayne's outspokenness was exactly what we'd expect from such a person.

John Wayne may never have wanted to be a hero himself, but he certainly knew how to play one. Likewise, when America wanted or needed a new hero at a tough time—or a few tough times, as Wayne's Hollywood star shined throughout three wars—we kept turning back to the Duke. Without today's up-to-the-millisecond cable TV and Internet coverage of goings-on across the globe, we had to be content with watching someone acting out the things that we *hoped* were going on elsewhere, someone who dramatized the type of person that we wanted representing us throughout the world. If Wayne himself wasn't the consummate American, his characters were, and that was enough.

Because, once again, a myth can be powerful and meaningful too.

"Wayne's greatest achievement may have been creating John Wayne," Charlton Heston once said. "The character he played, the character he invented, was the American persona of the man who is hard and believes in doing right, and will do it against all the odds."

Many critics called, if not exactly hailed, *True Grit* as one of the first "feminine Westerns," a term that's wide open when it comes to debate. Suffice it to say that women hadn't gotten much exposure when it comes to Westerns, and whether they have here in the 2010s is a matter of debate.

Incorporating a lady into Western toughness was basically undiscovered territory back when *True Grit* came out; the fact that said lady would be a teenager (well, playing one) made it even tougher. Finding someone who'd been alive for a shorter period of time than Wayne had been acting that could stand up to him—not to mention Robert Duvall, although no one at the time knew how far he'd go—made things even more difficult.

Mia Farrow accepted the role, then changed her mind. Wayne's own daughter Aissa, who'd appeared in some of his earlier films, almost snared the part. Sally Field was even discussed. But Kim Darby's appearance on a TV show won her the young lady lead.

"The thing that I worked off of was that [Mattie] was someone who is tenacious and who will not give up," Darby says. "Even though people think of me as frail and vulnerable, I am very tenacious and I won't give up." Actually in her 20s when *Grit* got going, Darby was recovering from childbirth complications early on in filming, not to mention getting started on a divorce.

Many stories abound about Darby and Wayne not getting along on the set, and all or none of them may be true—decades later, it just doesn't matter anymore. One day during filming, Wayne was taking a photo with Clint Eastwood, Goldie Hawn, and others outside the studio. Noticing Darby sitting nearby, Wayne brought her into the photo.

Wayne, Darby recalls, "was great to work with. He was so professional. He was there before anybody else."

Back to the "feminine Western" comment, *True Grit* was not only one of the first westerns with a strong female lead, but also broke tradition with the lack of relationships—in the amorous sense—between Mattie and the male characters, as well as her farewell to him at the end, when she states she'll never be wed.

"You have to remember that [Mattie] was fourteen," Darby says, "and through those kinds of eyes that was never a part of what was she was doing. . . . She had to do what she had to do. She knew she would have some fight on her hands and she did. She had to fight everybody and continuously. The end part of that is a tribute to [Rooster] from a girl that has had to have vulnerability about her. That character doesn't work unless there is not any vulnerability there. Then she just becomes tough and one-dimensional. That is her way of saying 'This is how much I care for you and this is how much you have done for me.'"

Forty years later, the Coen brothers brought the story of *True Grit* back to the screen, with Jeff Bridges playing Rooster's role. A new Mattie, however, would take a search that eventually encompassed thousands of young women.

Alongside two Oscar winners and a nominee in front of the camera (Bridges, Matt Damon, and Josh Brolin) and with two more victors behind it in the Coens, not to mention the legacy the first film left for them all, standing out would be a load of Jupiter's proportions. But with the everything-to-gain attitude that most upcoming performers use as a board to stardom, Hailee Steinfeld stepped into Mattie's garb before tryouts even began.

Literally—to the audition, she wore an outfit from the character's era that her mother had put together.

That, along with her actual performance of a few scenes from the script, pushed Hailee over the cut: as the "Mattie Pool" got smaller and smaller in the early part of 2010. Down to the final few, Hailee was told that she'd hear something in about five months.

"Every day was waiting, waiting by the phone," she recalls. "It was pure agony. Those five weeks felt like five years. . . . Every time the phone rang, I got so excited. I never wanted to pick it up."

Then one evening, Hailee was in her room, playing on a computer. At 7:02 p.m., the phone rang again. Downstairs, her mother went to answer it.

"She said, 'Hi, David,'" Hailee remembers. "That's my manager's name. Then she lost him on the phone, and she had to call him back."

Hailee Steinfeld's Mattie carried off the new *True Grit* in 2010, scoring her an Oscar nomination and helping the flick get picked as one of the year's finest.

Then her mom shouted for Mattie (yes, that was intentional!) to come down and grab the receiver. Hailee heard the magic words.

"My heart was beating out of my chest," she says. "I was jumping up and down, I was so excited. . . . After I got the job, I looked back at those five weeks and realized how much fun I'd had."

Having already watched the original flick, Hailee knew what to expect from an acting standpoint. The physical aspect, however, needed some help. She spent a few weeks training in horseback riding . . . and learned to fire a gun.

"My dad took me to a shooting range with a friend of ours who's a cop," Hailee says. "He's an LAPD officer, and he taught me how to do it. Having that experience, that kick from a real gun, prepped me for exactly what I needed to think, because with blanks, you have no kick, so I knew exactly how to play it out."

On the plane to filming, Hailee read through Portis' book. Though the audition had already helped her prepare for the time's typical way of verbal communication, this would be a bit more diverse.

Think about this—in a chat with a group of friends, how many of us could go five minutes without using a contraction? How easy is it? It's to the point now where we look at people funny if they say things like, "I cannot go tonight," or "I will be there soon."

Just as Darby had, Hailee would be speaking English for her role—but that didn't mean it was quite the language she was used to.

"The dialogue was a big challenge," she says. "It's almost like American Shakespeare; it's very song like. It just kind of flows. It felt natural after I got on set."

Away from the camera, however, today's language kept rearing its not-always-lovely head.

"Everyone was cursing a lot," she says. Turning to a disciplinary tactic much older than herself, Hailee set up a "Curse Jar." Most curse words cost only a dollar an utterance; the dreaded F-word caused a donation of the Lincoln bill. At the end of filming, the money was donated to an Alzheimer's awareness organization.

After carrying the first few scenes nearly by herself, Hailee's Mattie, equipped with Pippi Longstocking-type brunette pigtails, recruits Rooster to play his revengeful game. Showing the stoicism of someone who's probably seen violence and even death beforehand, Mattie and her new gang never take a backward step until the man who killed her dad is dead. Just as Darby did, Hailee didn't let her young performer ever seem childish; his death brings her closure, but not celebration. It's a job that needed doing, and once it's been done, she's headed back toward home, ready for another task in a life full of them.

"Mattie's journey and the things she goes through, it's amazing," Hailee says. "Some of the stuff, a 14-year-old girl would never be able to handle, but the way she does just turns everything around. During the audition process and filming the film, I was on my own journey along with this character and I learned so much about her." For three and a half months, everyone was back in the Old West (or Central, as the film takes place in Texas).

Just as Thanksgiving neared, Hailee finally got to examine her own work.

After seeing it, she remembers, "I was so overwhelmed. I started crying after seeing it, realizing that the three and a half months of my life were all right there. From the day I got home to the minute I arrived to go see it, I was wondering, 'How is this going to look put together with that? How is this going to look with the music?' [The film] was along the lines of what I was thinking, but 10 times greater." The Academy Awards would agree; the filmed yanked in 10 Oscar nominations, including Best Picture and acting nods for Hailee and Bridges (*Grit* didn't win any statuettes).

Stepping across the red carpet for a premier in Los Angeles, Hailee met Mattie's original trendsetter: Darby.

"It was very surreal that she was right there," Hailee says. "She's the most amazing woman. She was so sweet. She told me how happy she was with the film, which really meant a lot to me [Darby had predicted Hailee's Oscar nomination]. She looked me in the eye, and said 'God bless you, please make the right decisions and choose the right things.'"

So which of the characters truly exemplifies the film's title? Cogburn, for his unshakable duty to his work, whatever and wherever it was about? Mattie, an adult trapped in a child's body and a young girl trapped in a man's world? Or someone else?

"True grit, to me," says Hailee, about to, if not purposely, give a strong look at those looking to make it in her line of work, "would mean perseverance, never retreating, always taking a step forward and follow through. If you get knocked down, you get right back up, and I think everybody demonstrates some of that in the film."

Through four *Alien* films, Sigourney Weaver turned Ellen Ripley into a heroine not just for action film fans, but for feminism in totality, showing that a lady could hold her own and even be the one to save all others.

Sigourney Weaver: *Alien* films

"IN SPACE, NO ONE can hear you scream."

If there's ever in film history—not just action or sci-fi film history—been a better tagline for a film, it's yet to be remembered. Perhaps 1978's *Jaws II*'s "Just when you thought it was safe to go back in the water," comes close, but if the first shark flick had bombed, we never would have gotten to read it (or quote and spoof it endlessly). "Be afraid. Be very afraid," from *The Fly* (1986) was great too, but it's been spoofed too many times to carry its original impact.

No, the grandpappy of all original attention-snarers in print advertising has to be *Alien*'s introduction. That line, along with the poster's simple-but-sinister-to-the-damned-extreme image of a small, hatching alien egg, glowing from huge darkness, would have dropped the temperature of a sauna 40 degrees when late-70s filmgoers started seeing it on the walls of theaters.

But *Alien* (1979) was about so much more than just a terrifying tagline, or even the horror genre itself. It became about launching one legendary career before the camera, and the first of a few more from out behind it. Not to mention a franchise that's been rolling ever since.

Now let's meet one of the few women to personify an entire film series—and not just an action/sci-fi franchise, either.

At the beginning of just about every action film, realistic or otherwise, there's typically a frightened introvert, just there to take orders and hopefully get the hell out alive. Of course, spurred on by the horrors of battle, the necessities of war, and a set of guts that even he (yes, it's usually a guy, just not here) didn't even know was slowly growing inside, that person typically evolves into a—mentally—hardened leader who usually ends up leading a depleted troop to safety.

Alien was no exception. But this time, the war being fought wasn't depicted on the battlefields of the Civil War or World War II (Vietnam wasn't a popular flick subject yet). This time, the job would be done in another world against an enemy with weaponry far from machine guns and bombers.

That, and the whole "lady action hero" thing wasn't the badge of honor so many carry today; it wasn't looked down upon so much as seen as impossible. Princess Leia had already shown us that women could handle themselves in gunplay, but, unlike borderline midget Carrie Fisher, it was legitimate to imagine strapping six-footer Sigourney Weaver squaring off in fisticuff action and coming out on top.

But still, a lady who might actually do a bit of rescuing, rather than hanging out in the bounds of distress? Someone who could dish out the gunfire right next to a man, and even get the chance to boss him around? Even many of those who'd marched and protested for women's rights throughout the 1970s might have had some difficulty with that one.

Including the producers—when *Alien* still existed only on the pages of a treatment, Ripley was a guy. Until, of course, the unusual actress with the unusual name (Susan is her original name; Sigourney, Slavic for gypsy, was taken from a character in *The Great Gatsby*) showed up. Incidentally, Meryl Streep had been considered for the role. It's interesting to think about how that would have turned out.

"All the characters and relationships in the film were written very loosely and the casting people were trying to choose actors who would bring an individuality to the roles," Weaver says. "As a matter of fact, after I read the script I came back and they said, 'Well, what do you think?' And I told them I felt that the human relationships all seemed very bleak. I thought it was best to put all my cards on the table because if they really wanted a *Charlie's Angels*-type, I knew it wouldn't be right for me. But they were the first to admit that it was going to take a lot of development and close working together."

Weaver's screen test started out with a chase scene through the corridors, then one when she seduced the ship captain, complete with a topless shot—as gorgeous a sight as that would have been, it would have kicked the hell out of *Alien*'s novelty.

"I was afraid I was going to be stuck in an office with a potted plant, screaming as if it were the Alien," exclaims a surprised Weaver. Less than two weeks later, shooting was on, with both guns and cameras.

"She went from someone who sort of believed that the world was a certain way," Weaver explains of her cinematic counterpart, "to someone who couldn't believe in anything anymore, and went from a thinking person to an instinctive animal. There were lots of progressions in the character that I just thought would be very interesting to play."

When she and the rest of the Nostromo crew first show up in *Alien*, they're heading back to Earth after a job done far from home. When an SOS call comes from another planet, the group gets ready for another mission. But when they reach the ship, there's an unwelcome surprise. Actually, there's a few thousand, in the form of large eggs.

Too curious for his own good, a crew member gets just a bit too close, and, like a trick by Satan's magician, out pops a creature with a strange and sudden attraction to his face.

With everyone back aboard the ship, Ripley's low on the chain of command, behind—in rank, and probably in chivalric resolve as well—a captain and some other officers (perhaps fearing that Weaver's height would make Ripley too imposing, the film did a great job not showing her standing next to shorter crew people; when she goes into action, Weaver's typically alone on the screen). There's a fellow officer named Ash who keeps overriding everything she says, and the fuse is burning down—fast.

"I felt that [Ripley] was a young ensign type who really went by the book," Weaver says, "and the movie was a journey for her, going from the book to pure instinct. Like Ripley, I was working by the seat of my pants."

The effected crew member appears OK, and everyone celebrates with a dinner, on their way home. But then, in one of the most legendary horrific scenes in history, a strange creature suddenly, and quite bloodily, pops right out of his chest, and the battle begins. It's disgusting on so many levels; aside from the gore, the forced impregnation and consequences of the officer's birthing are just screaming entendres about rape.

Now on the hunt to capture the escaped critter—now full-grown and looking like a lobster on steroids—Ripley and Ash have their final showdown, and Ash's head is conveniently bashed off, revealing him to be an android. Here's where we find out that the mission was forced kamikazeness: the company who sent them wanted an alien brought back for study, and if the humans died, well, that was just too collaterally damaged bad.

"It wasn't scary to make because I was playing someone so brave—not myself!" Weaver says. "I think Ripley doesn't get afraid the way most people do. She's one of those people that goes, 'All right, let's try Plan A. All right, that didn't work, let's try Plan B.'"

Plan B (actually, it might have been at least E or F by this point) involves the crew's new leader leading everyone into a new pod, leaving the ship to explode and take the critter out with it. The enemy manages to take out the rest of Ripley's human colleagues and then stow away aboard the pod. But Ripley uses the engines to burn the hell out of it one more time, and she, along with the crew's pet cat—which escaped, as animals in scary flicks so often do—go back to non-eternal rest for the last flight home.

"To try to run through CO_2, which takes up all the oxygen, through corridor after corridor, day after day, was just exhausting," Weaver says, "and I was bruised. But you don't think about that while you're in the middle of it. Not until you get home, see the bruises and think, 'Oh God, what's happened to me?'"

If anyone behind or before the cameras had been iffy about having a lady rule the action roost before *Alien* came out, the box-office aftereffects put those concerns to rest, as the film brought in almost $80 million in America alone, and director Ridley Scott kept hitting the box office hard with *Thelma and Louise* (1991) and *Hannibal* (2001), both of which took another look at female empowerment, and scored a 2000 Best Picture with *Gladiator*.

After sitting back and letting the men do the majority of the heavy lifting and killing for the majority of the first flick, Ripley and Weaver had finally gone out with guns and flamethrowers blazing in the finale.

Then, as the war on drugs (and, too late, AIDS) broke out across America in the 1980s, action cinema followed suit, as Sylvester Stallone sent both Rocky Balboa and John Rambo into combat. Clint Eastwood gave "Dirty" Harry Callahan another shot, and Charles Bronson went *Missing in Action*, all before the decade was half over—and let's not forget the debuts of the *Terminator*, *Lethal Weapon*, and *Die Hard* franchises.

Getting ready for her film's sequel in 1986, Weaver knew that she'd have to turn Ripley into a leader from the get-go, and kick a few more asses—human and otherwise—in the bargain (getting to be the first woman to make a million dollars for one role was probably an honor she didn't mind much either). Whereas Scott's flick had had Ripley as a bit cautious, at least at first, James Cameron's flick brought home the action.

"What I thought was so exciting was the story [of *Aliens*]," she explains, "the story of this woman who survives this horrific experience in space, comes back fifty years later, tries to warn society about this evil, is dismissed, marginalized and is sent back out not being told the truth to fight this thing again. The structure of this story is so amazing."

But first, it's one tragedy after another, as Ripley obtains her own sad backstory. First, we find that she's been hypersleeping around space for over half a century, and her new world is a far different place. Second, and much, much worse, the daughter that was only a child when her first mission began, grew up without her—and died of cancer (glossed over is the fact that no one, including Ripley, even mentions the girl's father). Note: as important as this storyline seems in hindsight, it was actually left out of the original version; we had to wait for a "Special Edition" of *Aliens* to find out that Ripley's protective nature of a co-star we'll meet in a moment had much more meaning than original viewers knew.

"For Ripley to be able to think about something else instead of what was happening to her was a great joy for me," Weaver says.

Alien was about creating an atmosphere of terror; *Aliens* was a goddamned roller coaster from hell. There would be no running from the enemy this time; no hiding. This was about finding the prey, searching it out, and making it pay for having the nerve to exist in our world, even if we were in theirs!

Deemed unfit for battle at a service station, Ripley is stuck in construction work. But the now-colonized planet from whence she escaped has lost contact with a few of its residents, and she's asked (well, as close to asking as military bosses ever get) to lead an expedition to find out what happened.

This isn't to capture aliens, or use them for study. It's to terminate with extreme prejudice (so they say). Hoping to escape from the memories that have tormented her since her first round, Ripley finally agrees.

With her and Sgt. Apone (Al Matthews, himself a former military sergeant) in charge, the group sets off for Ripley's former workplace. At first, they're the only ones approaching this with any seriousness; gun-trained and pumped to high heaven, these soldiers are ready to get it on, regardless of who happens to be on the other side. This is about the thrill of battle for many of them; they know that they may get hurt or killed, and they don't seem to mind—as long as, of course, they get to take down a few sonsabitches on the other side in the process.

"There is a certain amount of sexism in the film," Weaver explains. "The guys had pinups everywhere, and being a woman officer, I get a certain amount of guff from the guys. I think it's a very important element to show the workplace as a real place. The *Alien* movies are not up-in-the-clouds science fiction. They're not cerebral. They're very down and dirty and about survival, and about who people are. You find out who people are very quickly when you all have to face a common enemy, and it's true that Ripley didn't react to a lot of this sexism; she kept her cool, and I think that was something that was good for women to see. She didn't whine, she didn't complain. She did her job, and tried to save other people."

Stumbling into a lab, the group gets the first interactions with the creatures, finding some facehuggers, miniature but alive, in test tubes. Then one of them hears something hidden under the table.

It's one of their own. It's the lone survivor of the family that had been lost. It's a scared little girl named Rebecca Jordan. *Aliens* film lore would come to remember her as Newt.

Aliens had taken her family (another scene that we inexplicably had to wait until the director's cut to see), and now she was on her own—until Ripley showed up, and found a new side of herself: the maternal, nurturing part she thought her daughter's death had stolen forever.

But all's far, far from OK. As the group heads down to the basement, they find a colonist, alive but "impregnated." An alien bursts from her chest, and one of the marines quickly burns it to death.

Her flames would be hardly a matchstick compared to the inferno that erupts next. Concealed in and around the walls, the creature's colleagues declare war. One marine after another, including Apone, is attacked and killed by the camouflaged ones. The only one with any semblance of control, Ripley rides in to rescue her colleagues, but only a few are left alive.

As if that wasn't enough, an alien sneaks on board their escape ship, takes out the pilot, and causes it to crash as well, leaving them stranded. But with someone new to look after, Ripley takes the young girl back to the station for a nap.

Shortly, the locals are back on the attack, and Newt leads everyone through the air shafts (her name comes from her ability to navigate them). Some marines take out both the creatures and themselves with a grenade blast, but Newt's knocked through the shaft to a level below.

Standing in a pool of water, she glances around, desperately hoping that someone will find a way to her. Then an alien lunges out of the water behind her, and it's arguably the most chilling moment of the series.

Ripley becomes a hero once again, but it's nothing compared to the battle she'll be fighting in a moment. One wrong step later, she and Newt are in the Queen's lair, surrounded by a mother nurturing dozens of future predators (not those that Arnold Schwarzenegger would battle in theaters the next year, though they'd be squaring with the aliens almost two decades later in the *Alien vs. Predator* movies).

For one of the first times all series, Ripley's emotions get the best of her. Perhaps looking into the future and seeing what danger these creatures possess, her natural intensity completely dwarfs that coming from the firearms in her arms, as she blasts the holy hell out of anything that could even move. As the Queen screams in horror—to an extent, audiences might feel some semblance of sympathy for a mother watching her children be slaughtered—Ripley wipes out nearly her entire litter, raging her way through one weapon's worth of ammunition after another.

"I had to shoot bullets, flamethrower, bazooka," recalls Weaver, a staunch gun-control advocate who prepared for the scenes at a shooting range. "That was hard for me."

The group makes it back to the landing dock, and the battles appear over. But no scary flick is complete without one more scare, and the Alien Queen shows back up one more time, ready to give Ripley a taste of her own medicine. The human took out the alien's offspring; now the creature's going for the closest person Ripley has to a child. Just like Grendel, this momma's meaner than her offspring ever was, and this time it's personal on both sides.

As it closes in on Newt, Ripley steps forward, back in the power loader we saw her maneuvering around earlier (though it's tame compared to some of the stuff the marines were spouting earlier, her "Get away from her, you *bitch!*" became a signature line for the series). Once again, it's a battle to the finish: revenge is on both gals' minds, but Ripley's still got someone alive to fight for.

Demonstrating that it does indeed take a real woman to take out a real woman, the two battle into an air shaft, and Ripley manages to get it open. But as the Queen tries to take the human out with her, Ripley manages to overcome the vacuum of space—not the first time this film has stretched the limits of realism—and escape, leaving her opponent lost in space with no time left to start again.

"Pretty amazing," Weaver says of her brawl with the top invading lady. "I had a guy in that power loader behind me; in front of me, I had the Queen Alien being controlled by all kinds of puppeteers. We had so many people running so many different parts of the set and the world. And it was just an explosion of all the great collaboration you get on a big movie, where everything has to be so in-sync in order to do it perfectly. It was a ballet with these two creatures, and we shot it in about three days. We didn't have CGI. It's all real, it's all worked out. I practiced in that power loader every lunch hour for months ahead of time. It was a culmination of a lot people's hard work."

We'll meet some of those other people in a few moments, but for now, let's check out the rest of Weaver's work as Ripley. *Aliens'* smash of the box office and Oscars for sound and visual effects (Weaver went up for Best Actress, unusual for a sci-fi film) all but guaranteed there would be another kick at the outer space can, although it wouldn't show for a few years.

Though he got a great deal of deserved credit for helping one of the most powerful women in entertainment history get some of her first glamorous exposures, directing several of Madonna's MTV videos, David Fincher tends to make his films sad and gloomy to the extreme, with *Se7en* (1995) as perhaps his personal watershed. 1992's *Alien3* started much the same, as the escaped ship crashes into a prison colony, killing Newt dead and leaving Ripley alone once again. Later scenes of the little girl's autopsy and funeral reemphasize Ripley's pain, and we can certainly feel it.

Eventually, the prisoners start violently dying, and she realizes that the ship carried an unwelcome traveler. Not only that, but there's no weapons on this lost planet, leaving everyone to face this thing only with what they have.

And if that weren't bad enough, she eventually finds one of its offspring inside of her. Even if no one else does, Ripley knows she can't make it out alive—and, in the epitome of irony, basically tells everyone that she'll only help them if someone promises to take her out in the finale. She even comes closer to death than ever before, in the scene where the alien traps the weeping Ripley against a wall, only to leave her alone, knowing that she's carrying its next generation.

Alien3 is often called a misfire in the series, commonly the consensus when someone tries to take something in a new direction. But it was just different—and to film audiences, different too often means bad. Rather than action, violence, and the uplifting message of victory in the end, the film's more a venture through darkness, both physically and mentally. It's about making the best of horrible circumstances, something that prisoners face every moment. It's more introspective, rather than action all the way like *Aliens* was.

There's also a ton of religious imagery in this flick; Ripley, the first woman so many of these men have seen in over a decade, is seen as both a messiah and the soothsayer of the end of the world, the dame of the Apocalypse.

Having said that, the film gave Weaver a chance to show more of Ripley's personality than before. Her bald head and baggy, androgynous dress notwithstanding, Ripley, if not for the first time, then the bluntest, makes some overtures towards the prison doctor, goading him towards a sexual encounter. After decades without getting laid, the woman reveals herself to be only human in that regard.

Sex without love is often looked down upon as a female quality—we all but expect it from men!—and it's even stranger when Ripley explores the possibility of such gratification, partly because she never really has before, and partly because millions had seen Weaver get comically turned into a sex-crazed demon (literally, as she's possessed at the time) in 1984's *Ghostbusters*. For the first time, Weaver got to give Ripley a real sense of caring, or of being, in the adult relationship sense, simply acknowledging what many like to deny: that some women truly do enjoy sex for the purpose of having it, are capable of doing it without many strings attached, and shouldn't be badmouthed for this sort of thing.

Eventually, the prisoners rally around Ripley; like the marines of yester-film, they trust someone who's seen this stuff before, and killing this outer space thing will score them some serious bragging rights amongst their colleagues. Their ranks get depleted—the warp-speed chase scenes in the maze are a strong highlight of this film—but eventually the creature gets destroyed again, being doused in hot lead, then with water sprinklers, causing it to, in the tradition of *Jaws* (1975), explode.

Still, Ripley sticks to her final vow, knowing that her death is necessary to keep her passenger and the company that wants to exploit it, from polluting the world. In a scene filmed on Good Friday of 1991, she plummets down into the furnace. As she falls, the alien inside bursts from her chest, and she grasps it, firmly but almost lovingly; for better or worse, they're going down and out together.

In all fairness, Ripley's final fall should have meant so much more than it did, but after millions had seen the same ending in *Terminator 2* the previous summer, the effect was severely lessened. If *Alien3* didn't have its predecessors around to be compared to, it probably would have gotten higher marks. It's hardly a bad film, though the changes made from the first two hurt its impact. But only in America, and only at first: the flick did very well overseas upon release, and many gave it enough of a second look on home video that it ended up doing pretty well.

Weaver's final—well, it appears, here in 2017—spin on the Ripley character came in 1997, and here she got to take her main lady in all kinds of new directions. Because she wasn't Ripley herself—she was Ripley *it*self. As in, a clone of the heroine, created after a great deal of trial and error to harvest an embryo of the creature that lived within its "mother" when she died. Whereas *Alien3* was loaded with religious undertones, this one becomes an updated twist on Frankenstein.

"I was stunned," Weaver says of the fourth level of the storyline, "because one of the reasons I died was to really liberate the series from Ripley. Because I didn't want her to become like a figure of fun that no one ever listened to, waking up in one situation worse than the next."

Alien: Resurrection went hundreds of years into the future, and finds a new and extremely improved Ripley, giving Weaver the ability to toss reality right out the window into space. Her super strength and 200-plus IQ made her so much more than human, removing a constraint that Weaver had carried for the first three films.

"I wasn't playing Ripley anymore," Weaver says. "I was playing a new and improved Ripley. It was as if somebody had put super-octane gas inside of her." That's not entirely hyperbole; the clone's acidic blood burns straight through the floor of the ship, much like that of the creatures she's there to protect everyone from. Weaver had kept notes from the first few films—just in case—on developing and evolving Ripley's persona, and she got to open them one more time. She also got to step a bit further into both their pasts; the Ripley clone notices several failed previous versions of herself, some of which were based on younger photos of the actress.

Still, though she tosses men across the room with one good whack, and flicks in a half-court basketball shot one-handed over the shoulder (Weaver called actually making the shot one of the highlights of her life), the underwater scenes were a bit tough for the actress. Unlike her colleagues, Weaver hadn't been able to participate in previous dive training. Making her way all the way across the 150-foot set, Weaver's nerves kept getting the better of her until divers showed her the way. The scene, the first one filmed, got the hardest stuff out of the way early for the cast—Weaver might have been scared, but an inhuman Ripley never would have been.

"She had changed," she explains of Ripley. "She wasn't this naïve young innocent anymore, who believed that the rules of the book were what you needed to know. In each one, I got to play a completely different set of circumstances. In each one, she becomes more and more of a renegade, until the last one, when she is part alien." Indeed, as aliens breed and take over the ship, they still embrace—literally and figuratively—Ripley as their own, she who gave them life.

Just as everyone left alive escapes, it's found that—you'll never believe this!—an alien . . . *has snuck aboard and stowed away*! Ripley maternally soothes the clone, then flicks her blood onto a porthole, dissolving it and sucking the baby alien outside. Horrified, she watches it slowly die.

Though far less vocally, Ripley begins to feel the pain she put the Queen through two films ago. Finally, she's back where she hadn't been for four films and hundreds of years: Earth.

Viewers' minds will always go straight to Ripley when they think of Weaver's career, and that's fair, but superficial—aside from the four *Aliens* flicks and 2009's *Avatar*, science fiction and horror have actually made up the extreme minority of her acting resume, including two Oscar nominations in the same year, for 1988's *Gorillas in the Mist* and *Working Girl* (she didn't win either).

Even today, over three decades after we met Ellen Ripley, people still call her "manly" or "androgynous," or some other ludicrous description, showing that too many viewers of film still clung desperately to the thought that a woman couldn't possibly have more important things on her mind than finding a man and then waiting around for him to rescue her from the bad guys. Ripley wasn't thinking about men, wifehood, that sort of thing, so that made her different and strange, as though women are just obligated to spend their time dreaming of walking down the aisle and then cleaning houses.

"I feel like Ripley is all of us," Weaver says. "I don't feel like she's an action hero. She is called to reach down and find the resources to fight in every way possible. To me it's about all of us. There's a Ripley in all of us. I think that's why people love the movie and the series. She's not a special person, she's an every-person, and we are put into these circumstances where we have to protect others and not give up."

Now let's meet a few of the other *Aliens* lasses. . . .

Until literally the moment filming began, someone else fully expected to take the call to "Action!" as *Alien*'s lead lady.

"I'd auditioned in America, then gone to Europe and auditioned over there for Ripley," explains Veronica Cartwright. "Back in America, I called my agent and asked if I was playing Ripley, and he'd said yes."

Then she learned she'd actually be Lambert. Cartwright charged back through the script, yanking out as much as she could of the lady behind the *Nostromo*'s controls.

"She seemed a bit weepy, but I refused to make her that," Cartwright claims. "We used her as a reflection of what the audience was feeling. She was incredibly sensible. She knew that there was a problem, and that we needed to get the hell out of there." They're on some joint called Zeta II Reticuli, and there's nothing good this far from home. Even when the crew happens upon a foreign creature whose chest has blasted out, she's the only one who wants to go.

It's not until Kane (John Hurt) finds a creature suddenly plastered to his face that others agree as to the discrediting of this theory.

The ship still docked, Kane seems OK. Then comes the infamous chestbuster scene.

"We were all upstairs in our dressing rooms for four hours," Cartwright recalls. "We knew something was going to come out of John's chest, but didn't know what."

At one last dinner before departure, Kane starts to lose it, convulsing and groaning. Then the creature suddenly blasts itself from his body, and film history was made.

"I leaned right into a blood jet, and it hit me square in the face," Cartwright claims. "The cameras caught each one of us, so we only had to film the scene once."

She lived longer than any man in *Alien* (1979), but Lambert (Veronica Cartwright) became the title character's final victim.

With the creature mesomorphing to giant size, crew members start to fall. Lambert's right on the edge, and Ripley's not far from it. Desperately grabbing up some equipment, Lambert's caught alone and unarmed with the title character, now appearing to show some sadistic pride in its violent deeds.

"It was easy to get into the emotionality of it," Cartwright says. "We lived on the ship for months. You had to go through the corridors and through the engine room to get off the set. It was very claustrophobic."

Ripley rushes in, but it's too late. It's just her and the alien now. After the film's most memorable moment was finished in minutes, it's final death took five days to put together.

Lambert had obtained some frightening inspiration from the most unlikely spots.

"When I was about nineteen, all the lights off and I was coming downstairs," she remembers. "My husband stepped out of a closet. It totally made me freak out, That's what that scene was: when (the alien) comes out, the movements were so slow and deliberate, I let myself go with the emotion."

Like Ripley, the Vasquez character in the film had originally been written for a man. A rather large man, probably with unkempt facial hair, tattoos, and pockmarks best obtained from physically removed pimples and an occasional bar brawl.

But when Jenette Goldstein, one of about 3000 people to try out for a part in the first sequel, showed up, the crew must have seen something special—although, in all honesty, it's unclear as to what, at least at first.

With a look on her face and thoughts in her mind not entirely unlike eroticism, Vasquez (Jenette Goldstein) put her alien-killing energy into some high-class chinup action early in *Aliens*.

Believing that the flick had been about illegal aliens of a different kind (i.e., those in America without a permit), Goldstein appeared in high heels and full makeup, her hair styled like a champ. Surrounded by auditioners in fatigues and other combat regalia, she might have stood out for the wrong reasons.

"I had seen *Alien*, but I had no idea this was a sequel," Goldstein recalls. "It had been so long ago, it didn't even occur to me. I thought it was about actual aliens . . . immigrants to a country. I was wondering why they wanted Americans. I figured the movie was about lots of different immigrants to England."

However, like female military members of the past and present, Goldstein had already been making her mark in a different kind of "man's" world: she'd been a longtime weightlifter. Perhaps seeing her ability to get physical if the situation pushed her a millimeter, producers kept her around.

"You're an actress, not a bodybuilder?" producers kept asking her.

They told her to come back shortly. This time, Goldstein was ready.

Her army boots were scuffed like she'd just stepped out of combat. Her hair was tied back; no stylist would get near it for a while. She was also showing off the results of years of (not entirely intentional) preparation: from the gym.

Six days a week, between dance classes and stage productions in London (she'd studied acting in California and New York before getting married and continuing her career overseas), Goldstein had found her own secret pastime.

"There was a men's gym with a boxing ring that I passed every day," she remembers. "It was good discipline to have when you're unemployed; you need some sort of a discipline. I needed something that I could do that—if I put in the time and effort—I would get results, which you're not guaranteed as a far as acting. . . . I enjoyed lifting weights, and I got hooked on it. It was something to keep me busy. I didn't see it as a tool to get to work, though my friends used to joke that maybe they'll do a film about an American bodybuilder, or something like that, that it'll pay off. It's funny that it did."

She'd spend an hour a day in makeup to be transformed into Vasquez, including dark contact lenses, But physicality wasn't the only change Goldstein would make, calling on her memories of the southern part of the Golden State to invoke Vasquez's feisty Latina persona.

"I had to do it from memory," she explains. "I didn't have a dialect coach, or the time or money to fly back to Los Angeles." She checked over some material from back in L.A., including discussions by gang members, for the character's dialogue.

Dietrich (Cynthia Dale Scott) found out in a nanosecond and far too soon just how strong the aliens were.

Like her, Cynthia Dale Scott had done a bit of acting trade honing in New York (she won a state drama award in high school) before heading to England for stage and singing work. Also like Goldstein, *Aliens* would mark Scott's first big-screen jaunt.

Originally cast as Ferro, pilot of the ill-fated rescue plane, she was quickly switched over to Cpl. Dietrich, the squadron's medical matron.

"I felt Dietrich was one of the more disciplined characters," Scott says. "She's the only one of the group, except Bishop [the android], of course, who had any quasi scientific background, being the medical tech officer. At the same time, she was still a marine, a trained soldier, and a product of the same rigorous military training and locker room carousing as the rest of the grunts. It was an interesting combination."

Goldstein, ordered to gain some hard weight for the role, had already gotten her own self-imposed sense of the training involved.

"Before the role, [Cameron] asked me how big I could get in four weeks," she says. "I had never tried, so I just ate a lot. I gained ten pounds of, basically, fat over my physique. But I kept training, and I had two years of groundwork underneath."

Not everyone else was so lucky.

For over a month beforehand, Scott and Mark Rolston (Vasquez's buddy Drake), spent five days a week in bodybuilding boot camp.

"We underwent rigorous weight training at the hands of this enormous Yorkshireman stuntman, who proceeded to 'pump us up,'" Scott says. "This hurt, but also contributed to establishing a sense of being a professional soldier who is required to have a daily discipline and whose life and body are not her own!"

One day, Scott was working on a backstory for Dietrich when Cameron asked her what was going on. When he found out, the director looked a bit off-kilter.

"He actually didn't want us to approach the work in that way," she says. "He wanted us to get in the mindset of a marine and act as a group from that position. Evidently he felt the lines would give us all the character development we needed!"

Being lucky—or perhaps unlucky, as they probably felt at times—to have a few military men on set (aside from Matthews, Tip Tipping, who played Crowe, had served in the British Special Forces), the cast became an impromptu troop, in which people become fighting machines and the individual pales in comparison to the team's needs. Marching and saluting were taught, as well as gun work.

"We had full weapons training with pistols, rifles, and flamethrowers, with real flames," Scott says. "We learned to deploy through an unknown territory carrying dummy weapons all day, and if we were caught inadvertently pointing our weapon towards anyone we had to hit the deck and do 10 pushups—just like they do in boot camp. All of this was extremely helpful in getting the physicality of a soldier right and moving with confidence. Jim wanted to make the point that the fighting forces of the future were completely unisex, with no difference between men and women. I had to work on removing any traces of femininity from my movements and bearing." The group also read *Starship Troopers*, the story of another group of futuristic soldiers who head elsewhere in the galaxy to take on other inhabitants (the film version was over a decade away).

It was difficult to tell which of Vasquez's guns were more impressive: the nearly-as-tall-as-her handheld cannons she waved around like toothpicks for the majority of her performance, or the muscular pair hanging from her shoulders that she used to do so. Early on, she goes out of her way to show off her biceps, doing bare-armed chin-ups in front of everyone and getting the chance to zing her collaborator Hudson (Him: "Hey, Vasquez, you ever been mistaken for a man?" Her: "No . . . have you?").

"I wanted Vasquez to seem like she only really lived when she was carrying a gun," says Goldstein, who claims she'd never shot a gun before getting the role. "It became part of her, and everything clicked into being. Then again, that gun was so heavy, there was only a certain way you could walk with it."

With Vasquez eagerly at the head of the troop for most of patrol—Goldstein wrote "Adios" on her gun, signifying what it meant to anyone who stepped in her way—the horde arrives and strolls into an abandoned (so they believe) station.

"Who would you want to take point [lead the way]?" Goldstein asks. "The craziest person, the one who doesn't care about dying, because who else would do something like that? It's never mentioned in the film, but in the characters' background, she and Drake are recruited from juvenile prison, where they're under life sentences . . . [Vasquez] had no one or nothing, so she was the logical choice for point. It made perfect sense to the commander. Who would you put in that suicidal potion? Someone who couldn't care less, and whether it's a man or a woman doesn't really matter."

Soon enough (well, not for Vasquez, who just couldn't wait for battle) the troop descends on a group of alien victims, some trapped in cocoons.

"It was an entire day of shooting nothing but me, with lots of close-ups and fire and changes from the director, who was pretty tough on me," Scott says. "I also had to complete a lot of action and hit my marks and fire a live flamethrower all in one long take, while delivering dialogue over a lot of noise. . . . I didn't find any of the dialogue difficult, but the wide array of actions that we had to accomplish in a tight space with perfect timing was difficult." Locating a former human in the traps of a cocoon, Dietrich is forced to blast holy hell out of her with a flame thrower.

"It was a difficult scene because Jim directed me to physically break her resin and fiber-glass encasement with my bare hands, causing a few scratches," Scott says, "and then [he] said 'Let's go again' for another take. The art department guys freaked out because the encasement, made to stay in one piece, was now shattered!"

But while the Earthlings start the battle, their opponents kick it into the highest gear, dropping in from all sides to tear things up and take humans out. Dietrich is one of the first snatched away.

"I did my own stunt when we shot my demise," she says. "I was standing on a giant seesaw with, again, a live flamethrower, and the stuntman in the alien suit landed on the board behind me and grabbed me, while simultaneously some crew guys pulled down on the seesaw and hurtled us up five or six feet vertically—while I lowered my flamethrower and fired it! The first three or four takes, I fell off."

Vasquez manages to make it through for the time being, but later on, just as the group is about at the escape pad, another attack commences. But a marine is there to kill and to die if necessary, and Vasquez sees this as nearly an obligation.

After blasting an alien back to hell, she's burned severely, but demands that everyone keep moving forward. Hudson comes back to help her—apparently with no hard feelings from their verbal dustup—but the two end up obtaining the greatest honor a marine can take, sacrificing themselves with a grenade to take out a throng of attacking critters.

"I think Vasquez is just so angry that it has finally got to her," Goldstein says. "Rather than being scared, she's pissed off she's about to die."

Like Weaver, Goldstein would act with Cameron again, snaring a small role in 1991's *Terminator 2* as John Connor's foster mother (she even got to become the murderous T-1000 for a scene when she handily impales her husband's head), and then with a small role in 1997's *Titanic*. Scott eventually gave up acting to return to her original love of art.

"I think successful acting in horror or sci-fi requires breaking down the scenario to make it real to yourself first," Scott says. "On *Aliens*, we were fortunate to have extensive sets and interactive monsters to create our reality around us. Nowadays you may be reacting to a green screen. It's basic Acting 101—create a situation in your experience that is truly frightening and feel it. A strong horror performance allows your audience to experience the same emotions in their seats that you are feeling as you contemplate your doom at the hands of [the enemy]."

While Vasquez was in a position to prove herself, if only to herself, the film's other top female star didn't mind asking for a bit of protection.

After all, she was still in single-digit grade school.

Goldstein and Scott may have been venturing onto the big screen for the first time, but they'd spent some time in the theater alongside some quality personnel. Carrie Henn, on the other hand, had never even acted in a school play.

One day, some people showed up on Henn's home U.S. Air Force Base (her dad was in the military), looking for some kids who were comfortable before a camera. Then they left, and she went back to the normal life of a nine-year-old.

Then, one day, the phone rang. She was getting a chance to head to the jolly old land of London, and a shot at film superstardom.

"The children who had acted before," recalls producer Gale Ann Hurd, then married to Cameron, "whenever they delivered a line, they'd smile at the end, and it was so inappropriate for this girl who was suffering from traumatic stress, to smile every time she delivered a line. Carrie had none of that conditioning."

She may have had little to smile about in character as Newt, but, unlike many people much larger and older than her, Henn doesn't sound like the Aliens got too far under her skin before and after filming. In preparation, she recalls, "James Cameron said I had to watch *Alien*. I think I was eight at the time. I was laughing at it."

And what about during filming, with all the scary creatures pretending to try to turn her into a snack? "It wasn't scary," Henn insists. "The crew were always trying to scare me, but they couldn't. I never got scared until I saw the movie—even though I knew what was coming." Co-star Bill Paxton, who sadly passed away just weeks before this book went to press, reportedly apologized to Henn for the marines' far-from-PC language—remember that his greatest line of, "Game over, man! What the fuck are we gonna do now?" came in the little lady's presence.

Carrie Henn's Newt found herself far from home and her hosts' smallest prey in *Aliens* (1986).

True or not about Henn's fear, it was appropriate; Newt is the one who shows everyone else that someone can survive the foreign invaded land without training, weapons, or physical stature, and leads them throughout the base—although she had all the reasons for being afraid in character, certain scenes helped the actress create an inadvertent playgrounds.

"Going down the chute was the coolest thing," Henn says. "It was huge, like a three-story chute. I messed up on purpose so I could get up and go back down again, until James Cameron caught on and told me we had to get going with the scene."

Still, things got a bit difficult at times for the young actress; the scene where Newt sees her dad in a facehugger's grip was the first time Henn had seen one of the critters—her scream is scripted, but the terrified look behind it is real (Henn's brother Chris, who'd helped her audition, plays her brother in the film).

For the scene where Ripley finds Newt inside a cocoon, Cameron himself helped Henn inside to ensure her safety; ironically, Weaver injured her hand getting her "protectee" out of it.

"There was one scene when I'm in my little nest, with all the stuff around me," Henn says. "Cameron would not let my brother or mother anywhere near it, because I had to feel like I had no one. It was amazing how I did feel that way . . . I was upset."

One of her toughest tasks, however, came far from the camera lens—both to protect Henn during the stunts and to unstress Weaver's already-injured back, a lifeless copy of the little girl was created for Ripley to carry around during some of the rough stuff.

"I had to do a full-body cast," Henn says. "They had to do my body and face. When they did my face, I felt very claustrophobic. They put some jelly-type stuff on my face with a mask on the top of it, and straws out of my nose. It was kind of weird and scary, but really cool to see how much this dummy looked like me."

In the late 1970s, a graphic design student took a break from his studies in a London bar (or pub, as they call it over in the jolly 'ol lands). He'd stumbled onto film history.

Who could play the title role in *Alien*? Where could the producers find someone tall and lanky enough to fill the costume, yet sufficiently agile to bend and stretch into its modes of personality?

Peter Mayhew had done a hell of a similar job with Chewbacca a few years before, so the *Alien* crew was obviously thinking of him, along with others with unintentional experience in the arts of being over-heighted. Then a casting agent, kicking back with some ale, glanced around the establishment, and saw just who everyone was looking for.

A native of Nigeria, Bolaji Badejo had been around the globe, doing the student thing in Ethopia and America before heading to Britain. Along the way, he'd raised to just under seven feet tall. Acting hadn't been a dream for the fellow, but why not give something new a try, even if just once?

Scott and the rest of the crew breathed a collective sigh of relief. Now came the tougher part, for both him and them.

Putting together a costume, complete with moving parts and mechanics, that would fit Badejo, monstrous head included. He spent hours at a time inside of it, often bathed in all kinds of liquids, like the KY Jelly that made up the critter's spit.

Badejo got in physical shape with the help of a team of trainers, and got some acting conditioning in miming.

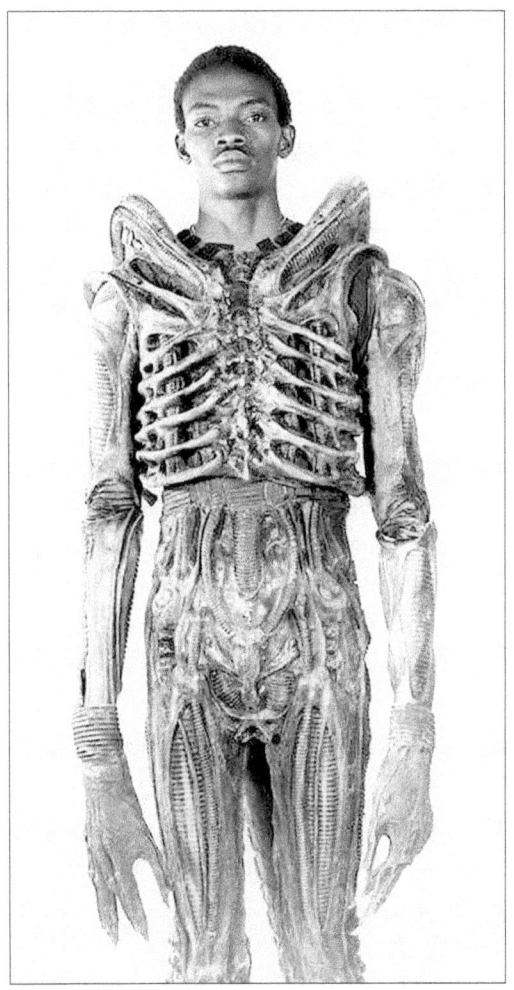

We'd never see his face or hear his voice, but Bolaji Badejo became one of the biggest (literally and figuratively) reasons for *Alien*'s success.

"The idea," Badejo said, "was that the creature was supposed to be graceful as well as vicious, requiring slow, deliberate movements." Horror/action fans might be seeing some parallels with the prep tactics Kevin Peter Hall used to play the *Predator* (1987)—sadly, the two would end up sharing another, much more tragic coincidence.

Like Hall, Badejo couldn't use facial features or his voice. He also had a carry a heavier physical burden than any of Ridley's guns and ammo. "I could barely see what was going on around me," he remembered, "except when I was in a stationary position, while they were filming. Then there were a few holes I could look through. . . . I could only have it on for about 15 or 20 minutes at a time. When I took it off, my head would be soaked."

Unlike Hall, Badejo didn't return for his flick's sequel, nor in any other film, returning to

Nigeria to put his art skills to work. Sadly, the father of two passed away of sickle-cell disease in 1992, one year after Hall died of HIV/AIDS.

"The fact that I played the part of *Alien*," he said, "for me, that's good enough."

And before we step away from *Alien*, let's tribute a previous time one of its stars went at it with those from elsewhere, this time at home on Earth.

Even to those who created it, the original *Invasion of the Body Snatchers* was just a bit too scary.

In the closing moments of the 1956 film, Dr. Miles Bennell (Kevin McCarthy), one of the few unafflicted by the title characters, frantically roars through traffic, desperately warning whoever's in earshot of what's going on, not knowing if it's already too late for those nearby.

"They're here already!" he shouts. Then Bennell points straight at the camera. Right at his viewers.

"*You're next*!"

That's where the flick was supposed to end. But its creators felt that audiences couldn't handle it. So the whole story was tweaked into a flashback, Bennell recounting his tale to a shrink, nearly being taken away before, just in time, everyone realizes how terrifyingly true his words are.

A resident of the nearby Beachwood Canyon suburb at the time, Cartwright had seen the story unfold in front of her, with some of *Snatchers*'s filming going on in her northern Hollywood neighborhood.

"I lived near the big stone arch [seen in the film]," remembers the then-elementary-schooler. "In the grocery store, they have a big picture of everybody running." Seven years later, she'd show up in *The Birds*, her Cathy Brenner barely managing to escape the legendary Hitchcockian flying evil.

Though many labeled it a remake, the film's 1978 reappearance was more of a continuation of the first go-round, she opines. An early scene gives Cartwright's theory a bit more ammo. The new protagonist, now named *Matthew* Bennell and hidden inside Donald Sutherland's body, takes his hopeful new lady Elizabeth (Brooke Adams) to a party.

Suddenly, a fellow who looks familiar, albeit a bit older, jumps onto Matthew's car, screaming that something horrible is coming and everyone's in danger. He makes it away, but out of nowhere comes a parade of people chasing him down the street. Moments later, he's dead, his pursuers standing over him showing emotion that wouldn't collectively cover a dime.

He was McCarthy. Perhaps Miles did make it out two decades before . . . but not this time.

Soon we meet Matthew's friend Jack Bellicec (Jeff Goldblum, in one of his first named roles), proud owner of a local bathhouse with his wife Nancy. That was Cartwright.

"She was really cool," Cartwright says of her character. "You could call her a hippie. She thought things through. She would analyze things. I thought that's what made her interesting: that she lived by her gut feeling more than anything."

Back at the start, we saw a strange race of critters barely escaping their world. Per Earth's luck in the sci-fi/action world, they just *happen* to land here, forming weird-looking pods that collectors just love. Elizabeth had grabbed one, and her boyfriend's emotions suddenly disappeared. Now we start to see the true power of these things—to become anything they touch, and then destroy the original. Soon Jack is gone, as is Leonard Nimoy's psychiatrist Dr. Kibner.

"Nancy knew that something was happening with her husband," Cartwright says. "Then she started realizing that [Kibner] was one of them, and everything builds up. Why can't they come from another planet? What can't they be like monkeys and apes? Nancy was very into thinking things through." She realizes that these things won't catch her if she acts as stoic as them, and manages to escape.

Nancy Bellicec (Veronica Cartwright) terrifyingly realizes that she's one of the last living humans—and maybe not for long—in the shocking ending of 1978's *Invasion of the Body Snatchers*.

But Elizabeth doesn't, and it looks like Matthew won't either. He burns many of the pods, but there's still far too many already in inhuman form.

One morning, we see him at work, looking like he's trying Nancy's technique. He and many other colleagues stroll down a hall, no voices or even eye contact. Walking sadly and alone out into a nearby plaza, he sees Nancy, perhaps his last living colleague.

"[Director] Phillip Kaufman had walked each of us around the block, and talked to us," Cartwright excitedly explains. "He didn't tell us what was going to happen." She, like much of the cast and crew, had no idea how the film would end.

She walks toward Matthew, who doesn't seem the least bit afflicted. Maybe we just don't want to know what we probably can guess.

His jaw suddenly falls, his eyes widen into a macabre sort of attack. A loud and sadly familiar sound erupts from him as he points forward.

It's the call of the pod people—an enemy is approaching.

Yes, he's one of them.

It's one of the most frightening moments in film history, the ending that the first flick didn't have the guts to try. Nancy screams in shock and terror, covering her ears madly. It wasn't all an act—to that moment, Cartwright hadn't learned what had happened to Matthew.

"I didn't expect him to scream at me," she says. "I thought he was one of us, not a pod. I flipped out. I was totally freaked."

But it appears that Nancy did make it out. Sort of.

In 2007, the *Body Snatchers* saga continued, now just called *The Invasion*. In true modern fashion, the lead's a lady now, albeit with the same last moniker. Nicole Kidman's Carol notices that more and more people have started to, well, change. Psychiatrists have a true knack for recognizing this stuff. An early warning comes from her patient Wendy. At least, that's what Cartwright's character was called in the story.

"I was playing the same character," Cartwright says. "Why couldn't she have survived, by dying her hair and melting into the background? All these years later, all of sudden, strange things were happening to people. It was like an homage to Nancy."

With so many stars, so many moons and galaxies, all that unexplored space, just so, so *much* of . . . pretty much everything, it's tough to believe that there's nothing else alive anywhere in the universe. And that's assuming, of course, that this universe is the only one of its kind.

It's weird, but certainly common, how willingly we toss aside the unlikelihood of human/alien interaction with the purchase of a movie ticket. Let's meet a few more folk from this area that have lived, fought, and died with friends and foes from else-planet.

"There is a law of attraction according to which you don't attract what you want," Anamaria Marinca explains of the plight of upcoming performers. "You attract what you are. Sometimes I think that a decision, the choice of a role is an illusion—what if the process is the exact opposite?" About one of her earlier roles, one could express a very similar and very sad sentiment about a similar subject.

It's about space travel. Even putting aside the cinematic aspect so often found in these films—i.e., us getting attacked by weird-looking creatures—there's always going to be a debate as to why we keep going up there. The *Columbia* and *Challenger* disasters gun these matters straight into the public eye, but other questions, over half a century after Sputnik, can't really be answered. Not only what we want, but exactly what we would do if we obtained it. How much, if anything, is worth it, an ionosphere from Earth? Countless time and ludicrous amounts of money have been spent, people have died, and for what? Maybe it will be worth it someday.

Maybe. If our hopes come true, whatever they may be, the science fiction genre in film will become a hell of a lot more real, fast. Until then, stories like *Europa Report* (2013) will have to keep personifying the post-hyphen label of sci-fi.

And those like Marinca will always get a new shot at decoding the laws of acting attraction.

"Who would say no to a trip to a glacial moon more than 600 million kilometers away?" rhetorically queries the Romania native, who blasted to stardom in her homeland with her award-winning work in 2007's *4 Months, 3 Weeks and 2 Days*, the arthouse drama of two women victimized by Communism's forced pro-life laws.

That same year, American audiences got a glace of Marinca in *Youth Without Youth*, with none but Francis Ford Coppola in the chair.

"I had never played an astronaut before," she asserts, in a statement that would seem a bit off-kilter spoken by anyone but an actress. "The thought of exploring a new world was exciting." Ever meet a person who just *vowed* they were ready to ride the newest roller coaster . . . until they actually had to sit down and strap in? Next to a rocket, that feeling probably multiplies into the trillions.

Rosa Dasque's (Anamaria Marinca) confident grin hid some tension and terror that soon came to the forefront of 2013's *Europa Report*.

After nearly two years in space, sadly losing a member along the way, the *Europa* crew lands on its title target, the smallest of Jupiter's four moons (though almost the size of Earth). The crew sends out several probes through the land's dark ice toward ominous seas, until some even more threatening lights start to radiate back.

Before filming began in Brooklyn, Marinca had studied up in the Big Apple, crashing through the world of space travel and the few that have experienced it.

"I had about two weeks of prep in before the takeoff," she remembers, "readings, discussions, research, and time alone imagining the final frontier. All that space between fact and fiction, Earth and Europa, me and the yet mysterious Rosa Dasque." The young pilot, just as off balance as any other Earthling in a world without gravity and so far from home, tries to keep things together, hanging onto stability by focusing on her video diary and the messages she uses it to send back home.

"Filming with eight cameras simultaneously in a confined space is something to remember," explains Marinca. "Hidden lights controlled by a digital dimmer, hidden mics, the sudden movements of the vessel built on a gimbal, the voice of [Director] Sebastian Cordero coming through speakers, the long takes, it all contributed to a sense of distance, isolation—and danger at times." As the film goes farther and farther, there are more and more of those times to experience.

All through the film, we've heard and seen Embeth Davidtz's Dr. Unger telling us all about the mission in a documentary-esque form, somberly informing that one tragedy after another occurred throughout. But she's still here, and the story keeps moving, subtly foreshadowing that there's something worth waiting for.

One astronaut ventures outside the ship, but falls through the ice, running out of oxygen. The group tries to lift off, but crashes back down, another man dead.

Rosa is one of the few left, but there's no hope for her. The only chance they have is to get a message back home—not for rescue, but for education. They're either going to freeze or asphyxiate.

Her last colleague falls through the ice forever, and now the ship's going down too. Rosa's in the cockpit, stealthily pointing the camera below her. She's terrified, but still fascinated, unable to take her eyes off her impending doom. More ice breaks, fatally cold water rolls in. . . .

"Several moments stayed with me," Marinca says, "[such as] trying to contain my emotion when sending the last message home, [and] the urgency and tension of the final scene. There was an earnest attempt to transform the clichés of the genre."

Unlike *Gravity* (2013), which became a man against-nature war (or *woman*, with Sandra Bullock leading the way), *Europa* is more of a documentary about space exploration that, for only a few moments, draws us into the unthinkable possibility that we might not be alone after all. Still, anything else would have had people calling it a bad ripoff of *Gravity*, or any of the *Alien* films, or anything else that involves us heading to another celestial body and finding something that doesn't want us around.

There's something there, and we see it for a moment. It's like a glowing octopus: beautiful as long as there's something very strong and thick between you and it. There's certainly more to the universe that mere humanity. Unger lets us know just how proud she is of her people, and that something was found. Something was learned. Something will be taught. Other films might have gone for the cheap scare, the sudden jump-freak that ends so many self-filmed flicks of every genre.

Once again, *Europa* brings to mind the question we discussed earlier—even if there is something to find, should it be found at all? They may be more to the solar system that can ever meet our eyes and minds.

But does it do us enough good to keep trying?

For an English teacher, when this sort of thing happens, we've got to take advantage: fast.

"I realized that I had a gift with my memory from [when I was] quite young," recalls Jumayn Hunter, "and one day when I was thirteen, we were covering Shakespeare and I recited most of the piece word for word from memory, having read it some years prior."

That doesn't even happen in teachers' dreams too often—but when it does, we've got a responsibility to jump. Fortunately, his lucky instructor had the wherewithal to do so.

"My teacher recognized this latent talent and took time out to mentor me and explained the philosophy behind the art that I didn't know," Hunter says, "therefore expanding my knowledge and giving me free reign to explore increasingly advanced characters and techniques in acting."

And how far he'd go with that! Up against those from out of this world.

"The appeal and allure of the acting world became a reality when I decided to give it a shot and put myself out there," he recalls. "It was my belief that, to live a life worth living, I would have to not only overcome any fears or doubts about myself, but develop my future in such a way to find pride and spiritual wealth inwardly, to lead by example; and that example would be to always break my own limitations."

Action, horror, sci-fi films and the performers they employ aren't often bound by limitations physical or otherwise realistic. So when he, like most of the cast, got a screen shot for the first time with *Attack the Block* (2011), Hunter saw a chance to set himself a true example.

"Action films always appealed to me because the fusion of body and mind being used on so many levels is particularly demanding, and I always like to be challenged," says the young performer. "Plus, as an extra bonus, I've always loved the gadgets and the toys, even the training process of action films." By then, he'd already put his body through martial arts and horseback riding and his mind through philosophy and a boatload of other education, but this was clearly something new.

"In my spare time, I like to study sociology and anthropology, as I believe it helps give me a broader knowledge of the world as a whole," he explains. "Ergo, some roles require me to go and immerse myself in a certain social group, lifestyle, or community and get a truly first-person, hands-on account of certain aspects of life in a very anthropological type of way. I personally like to do both and a few more. For Hi-Hatz, I'd say it was the combination of the two that really brought the character together."

With acting preparation, it's always better to go too far than not enough, to do too much instead of too little. Still, how does one really prepare for a role like Hi-Hatz? A gang leader and drug dealer, the president of his own personally created underworld, one determined to stay the king of the castle.

It's a tough job, in reality or in the portrayal sense. But as *Attack the Block* (2011) began to personify its title, even an experienced man of the streets might not know what to do. Then again, he would be taking on *aliens*!

"Being able to experiment helped a lot," Hunter recalls. "I have my own techniques that I like to help me enhance my character-building experience. I enjoy breaking down a character and getting into their shoes, almost literally. It can be a challenge at times, but it's all worth it in the end." He'd be glad *not* to be in Hi-Hatz's shoes, but it would take some time.

Fresh off the self-imposed high of mugging a helpless gal, a group of street trash suddenly gets a new opponent in some part-dog, part-gorilla thing, full of hair and horrible teeth and lacking eyes. They come out on top, but, per usual for such folk, decide not to leave well enough alone, taking the carcass to their boss: Hi-Hatz himself, it's not entirely clear the origins of the nickname, considering he only wears the requisite baseball cap of the trade.

Hi-Hatz (Jumayn Hunter) doesn't quite realize what he'll soon be up against in *Attack the Block* (2011).

By the way, one of those pseudo-gangmen, Moses, was played by fellow youngster John Boyega; four years later, he'd go to war with different kinds of outer-space life forms as Finn in some little-known tale about an awakening force or something!

"I'd had a chance to read the script," Hunter remembers, "and almost instantly, I decided Hi-Hatz would be a great character to play because of the diversity of emotion and the journey he goes through. When I had a chance to sit down with the director, Joe [Cornish, in his directorial debut], we covered some ideas I had of taking the character to a deeper place and expanding some of the ideas that were already on paper."

The critter might just be the group's newfound finding of fame and fortune, but it's got friends. Two can play the whole gang warfare game, even if we're talking about two separate galaxy clans. Soon everyone's out for blood of the other species.

Hi-Hatz, however, is too ticked about his car getting smashed up to care much about this impromptu war of the worlds!

"I thought Hi-Hatz would be a great character to experiment with and to polish some techniques I'd been experimenting with up until then," Hunter says. "The freedom to play with ideas and be supported in doing so just added to the fact that the writing for the character was particularly interesting for me. The writing and the journey are usually my driving forces when deciding whether or not to take on a role, and then I always think to myself, how can I expand this? How can I make it better and what can I add to leave my signature? How deep can I go?"

Now with him and the visitors to contend with, things aren't looking good for the group. Even while some of Hi-Hatz's main men become meals and targets, he's all about revenge.

"There were scenes that stood out for their particular difficulty and how much we pushed," Hunter says. "If I had to isolate one, it would be the ensemble scene in the garages when the boys crash into Hi-Hatz's car and he kills the first alien. Because most of the cast was on set and there were so many technical things going on simultaneously, it was a delicate time as it was easy to get overwhelmed and sometimes challenging to keep focused, but the scene was also one of my favorites to do." But just when it looks like Hi-Hatz wil indeed have his vengeance on Moses, a group of aliens just can't contain their desire to test his nutritional value.

And acting out all that anger and violence in this type of atmosphere just handed Hunter and the rest of the *Block* crew a whole new set of challenges, he continues.

"Each scene has its own little place in my heart. Even the ones I'm not featured in, guaranteed I'd be standing behind the camera, making jokes. The director would cut and we would all fall about, crying with laughter."

That's the sort of thing that allowed a rookie director and a group of performers whose then-combined work wouldn't fill a single-page resume to turn *Block* into the cult film it's become since, though Boyega's recent success hasn't hurt much either.

"The teamwork is astounding," Hunter says, "getting through the physical taxation on the body yet maintaining control, doing grueling hours yet having to be acutely alert at all times, having the same vision that the director has for the end product, and making that vision come to life with only a green screen and imagination is a feat in itself that I think is worthy of high praise. Action movies definitely aren't for the faint of heart, but they are so much fun."

Fun is just one thing that got Hunter into the business. It's also one of the many reasons he intends to stay there.

"The difficulty, the dedication and the discipline are the things that drive me to excel and push myself further and further," he hopes, "but more so, the freedom to enjoy living, moving, art. As an art form, it is amazing to watch people at work or to work with them in a profession that is so dynamic and so open to new and exciting ideas. To take part in the preparation and to become somewhat of a muse or driving force in a scene takes a deep understanding of something beyond the horizon of conventional method. In this, I find an infinite beauty that can't be compared."

In the midst of watching a porno, have you ever . . .

Got you now, don't I? Bet you want to finish this! There's *quite* a few ways to end that sentence, aren't there?

OK, here goes: in the midst of watching a porno, have you ever . . . wondered if the performers you're seeing wanted to make it to the acting mainstream, or still do?

Most probably did. Many hoped for it, but few even made the effort, and almost no one succeeded.

But some have. After spending much of the 80s in films that, ahem, have their own secluded section at the video store, Traci Lords stepped over to the more legit (well, that might be up for debate) side of performing.

Her mind turned to brilliant evil by the title characters in 1993's *Tommyknockers,* Nancy Voss (Traci Lords) preps to use her new self-created weapon for destruction.

The story behind all that has already been written: by Lords herself, in her 2003 autobiography *Underneath it All*. Let's focus on a film that showed the usual side of alien-human interaction in the movies.

Yes, when aliens decide to visit *us*, well, it tends not to go all that well for the Earthlings.

No, we're not in *E.T.* (1982) territory here. This is *Independence Day* (1996). This is *Invasion of the Body Snatchers* (1956, 1978). This is *Signs* (2002), the *Predator* (1987, 1990) films, and most others —even *Mars Attacks* (1996)!

In most of those films, however, the aliens basically show up and nuke the hell out of us on their own. *The Tommyknockers* (1993), though, had them reaching inside our minds and kicking off self-destruction at high speed. Six years after millions had read the tale, a smaller group would get to act it out.

And the name under the title was all Lords needed to go for being one of them (of course, many triers-out probably felt the same way!).

"When Stephen King asks you to be in one of his films, you say yes!" asserts Lord, who already had about a dozen (non-explicit!) roles in her resume by then. "I was a fan of Stephen King. I still am."

Passersby wouldn't remember, or hardly notice the Maine town of Haven. It's not all that different from another few (hundred thousand) burgs up and down both coasts.

Not that there isn't any scandal; while his wife Becka (Allyce Beasley) is out putting her life on the line walking cop beats, Cliff De Young's postman Joe Paulson is just concerned with trysting with his co-worker Nancy Voss.

"For the role of Nancy Voss," Lords says, "she was a fluffy, ditzy blonde. She was the mailman's assistant. It was magical lipstick, it was nonsense, and delightful to do."

As novelist Bobbi Anderson (Marg Helgenberger) and her poet boyfriend Jim Gardner (Jimmy Smits) start to dig up a huge object hidden in the woods, things start happening across Haven. The residents seem smarter, inventing all kinds of crazy stuff, like a letter sorter that makes Nancy's job much easier. But this is a Stephen King story, so the changes can't all be good. Everyone's health starts to go as well: missing teeth, tumors.

And sleep disorders, which bothered both Lords and the lady she played.

"I had *terrible* insomnia," she remembers. "It's a rather intimidating situation when Stephen King says to you, 'Want me to read you a bedtime story?'"

But regardless of Lords' acting past, her present prep methods ended up right about next to most of her colleagues in acting.

"I read through things, read through them, and read through them," she explains. "I'm one of those actresses that, once I get to the set, I know every word in the script. It's just the way I am. If I can figure out how the character walks, which I usually can, just by the words, I'll just get a hit on it. I'll break it down—what do I want, what happens, what is the journey of this person?"

Her lover gets toasted by one of his wife's creations about halfway through—typical for a King film, the obituary list is much shorter in the movie than the book—but Nancy, like most Haven-ites, is too into her own newfound mentality to worry about him (two decades later, King's

The Colorado Kid would return to the town and the small screen, converted to the 2010-2015 show *Haven*). Now there's actually a bit of control in her life, more to Nancy than we can see.

Like that lipstick creation Lords mentioned a few words ago. It helps her turn a few unsuspecting cops into dust.

With just about everyone in town moving near zombie territory—although, as *not* in the book, most make it out alive—Bobbi and Jim finally finish uncovering the object: an alien spaceship littered with some of the title characters. There's also Bobbi's dog, a missing boy, and his grandfather Ev (E.G. Marshall), all comatose and being drained of their life force by the ship.

One of the few afflicted left with any wherewithal, Nancy follows Bobbi and Jim, intending to insure they don't leave.

"The best directors that I work with cast the person who just *is* it, whatever that energy is," explains Lords. John Power, who died during the writing of this book, was behind the *Tommyknockers* cameras. "They leave you alone to let you bring *that*, and then it's just like conducting. They push things along, and they're gentle."

But someone else wouldn't be—as Nancy steps a bit too close to the grandpa, he wakes all the way up and chokes her out, enabling Bobbi, his grandson, and her dog to escape. Perhaps Marshall was atoning for the dirtbag he played while acting out King's words back in 1982's *Creepshow*!

Jim's mind flies the ship away, then blows him, and it, right to bits. But unlike in the book ending, where everyone dies and the world is still in danger, we get to see a happy ending.

"You give up the parts of how I am going to look, am I going to be pretty, am I going to be OK?" Lords says, "Once you let go of all of that, which is incredibly difficult to do, those are the moments when you're at your best."

As so many women have over the past few decades, Alexandra (Dreya Weber) showed *A Marine Story*'s cast that ladies in the Armed Forces can go straight past equality to supremacy in 2010.

Dreya Weber: *A Marine Story*

How little we could ever understand.

For decades, even after fighting over civil rights for gender and racial issues, one set of discrimination was still perfectly OK. Since America had a military protecting it way back when we went to battle with the British, the greatest solider could be tossed out over an accusation as fallacious as McCarthyism.

When the whole "Don't ask, don't tell" thing went into effect in the early 90s, few (at least, those on the outside looking into the military) saw it as anything but a political issue. "Big deal, right?" we thought. "Now you can be gay in the military, as long as you don't tell anyone."

But for many, it came far too late. Too late for those who had already given so much and lost even more, just because of something that's really nobody's concern.

Here's an aspect of military life of which the cinemas haven't shown much. As "Don't ask," came back into the public eye in the first years of the Obama administration, a story made its own way to the screens.

Looking to portray a character who'd seen her own life ruined, at least at first, by the mindset the military held for too long, Dreya Weber found her emotional anchor in a book about those who'd experienced it for real.

"It was about twenty people who had served," she recalls. "Former service members who had given up their lives, lost their careers, lost their pensions, lost everything, were publically humiliated. It was a series of horror stories."

"But every one of them said their time in the military was the best experience of their lives, and if they had a choice, they would do it all over again, no matter what had happened. That was so overwhelming to me."

Weber herself had never served in the military, but she probably could have—in the physical sense, she had things well in hand for *A Marine Story* (2010).

"Acting and physicality, they've always run parallel to each other," remembers Weber, daughter of a baseball player and an actress. "When I was a competitive gymnast, I was performing in plays and musicals." Along with gymnastics, and becoming one of Mexico's top high school hurdlers in her teenage years, Weber spent most of her athletic time in the air (although the gymnast practices would come back into play in her acting life).

She flew from trapezes in circuses around the world, and spent years training others in the discipline.

"From gymnastics, you already have the strength foundation, the freedom of being in the air," she remembers. "My spirit went crazy. I had a good amount of gymnastics injuries that were very frustrating, and I was introduced to this new world when it didn't matter if my ankle was destroyed, because I spent all this time in the air."

And not just on the trapeze; aerial silks became her next conquest. That's the work where performers climb up some specially made fabric, then wrap themselves up in it, spiral up and down in it, and swing around and around from it. It quite often appears to audiences that these people have found a way around the laws of gravity for the time being.

"It was an overwhelming way to learn," she recalls. "When I trained, I felt the generous spirit of the community of aerialists spreading knowledge. I'd take notes, imagine doing it in slow motion, then go back to the apparatus." In 2002, millions got a look at Weber, and others at her work; she did the silks at the Salt Lake City Olympics and choreographed the aerial numbers for a lady named Cher and those that performed in her *Living Proof* farewell (at least for now!) tour.

"I was brought into the pop world, given this opportunity because I was good at managing the technical parameters," she says. "The marriage of technical and aerial artistry in that realm was amazing. I was teaching aerialists who had never danced before and dancers who had never done aerials before, and showing them what was needed. We were able to make it work with the very fine-tuned animal that a successful tour is, hundreds of people building a show in a different city every night. It was a skill set that I couldn't have known at the time I was building it, for a very remarkable opportunity." That would be her acting career; let's finally go back to that.

It started out with a few small TV and film roles over the end of the last millennium and start of the new one, in the official sense, per se.

"I wanted to be an actor because I grew to love language really early on," she remembers.

"My mom read Shakespeare with me, and I ran lines with her for her auditions. I started to grow a real imaginative garden from stories that had been written on pages that you could just inhabit, being able to step into worlds larger and more different than ones you could imagine at a young age, to pull words from a page and then inhabit them from the script you were given. I could access emotions that I couldn't have imagined, and that was mind-blowing to me."

While she was touring with Cher, Weber and her then-husband Ned Farr started writing up the tale of a gymnast who'd seen her career hobbled by injury, not recovering in time to recapture her glory in a sport whose participants are often considered too old once they hit the quarter-century mark. Per usual in the indy film world, however, they spent years trying to find enough financial supports to bring the film to pass.

"Independent filmmaking is when you scrape together the money yourself," she says, "not when you cast somebody, whether they're right or wrong for the role, in order to get a guarantee from some distributor to pick it up and give you fifty grand. It is brutally tough. In the making of *The Gymnast*, we used any asset we could find, within a realm that wouldn't mean a line item on a budget, and we found Addie, an amazing woman who could do aerials and had tremendous acting skills."

Weber's past had already given her all kinds of preparation for protagonist Jane, a gymnast whose career, and nearly life, had been ruined by injury, now in a nowhere career and unsatisfying marriage. As luck often has it in Hollywood, she happens to meet new performer Serena, played by Addie Yungmee, who'd herself been a concert dancer.

But it's not your typical "underdogs win!" feel-good Disney-type piece. As the impromptu team works more and more, the bond they feel awakens some feelings in Jane, feelings that had probably always existed, but had been held beneath the surface. It's not just platonic here; it's a different kind of love story, a sort that shows that finding love isn't always a friendly journey, even if it's right.

"What is the spark of love?" Weber wonders. "What is love? Does it have to be defined by gender? Working on the screenplay brought incredible wealth." And not just in the monetary sense; the film became a symbol throughout the gay community, praising the *Gymnast* crew for telling a story that probably comes true more often than most of the public wants to admit.

A similar tale arrived in 2010, the same year that Weber choreographed some aerial work for singing sensation Pink, including the performer's performance at the 2010 Grammys (Weber had also worked with Madonna, Katy Perry, Taylor Swift, and others).

It was the *Marine* saga, the one we mentioned back at the start.

"We wanted to do a film with a female role model, to make a positive statement for the LGBT community," Weber says. Before and just after his 2008 election, President Obama discussed getting rid of "Don't ask," but, as we all know, little moves quickly in the political world. Meanwhile, Weber, Farr, and others got busy telling the truth.

Marine starts out as many in the genre do; a marine makes it home from service in Iraq, only to find how little there is for her. Living alone in a little town, she's left it all behind—not really the fighting and death, but the brother and sisterhood that becomes "personhood" in the Marine Corps.

"Marines don't play," she says. "Once a Marine, always a Marine, in and out of uniform. The pride of that branch is very powerful. I knew if I could carry it off, those serving now, men and women, straight or gay, would say yes to me. That was a challenge that I really liked." Making the main person a lady made the film an unusual step, as, even after female marines have served for a century, America still has trouble taking it seriously.

And not just in reality. Early on, Weber's Alexandra finds herself challenged by some drink-fueled morons in a bar, prompting an impromptu arm-wrestling contest (she wins without straining) and demonstration of her hand-to-hand combat skills.

"I love the fight in the bar," she remembers. "That scene was such a thrill. That scene was just about the confidence of strength."

Eventually, she learns of local youngster Saffron (Paris Pickard), who's been led down the wrong path by drugs and the wrong crowd. It's up to Alexandra to show her that a woman from a small town can make it in a tough world.

"I was excited because [Saffron] wasn't your typical female character," Pickard says of her persona. "It was all about working with the director to build a life for Saffron that had depth and being able to relate emotionally with her through my own experiences. I liked that she was strong and had a soft side for her family." That may be, but they'd suddenly disappeared, and she, as many do and have in such a horrible situation, was looking for guidance without worrying about which path it took.

Weber found the military mindset in a friend that had headed up Cher's security squad during *Proof*.

"I learned that he was training some dancers in self-defense, and I took advantage of it when I could," she says. "I explained that the character would need to be believable, a small, but fierce woman. It needed to be believable to take on men and win: survive." For about six months, the two trained Weber to become Alexandra.

"It was all about changing my mind about the way I look at the world, which was that I'm relatively safe," she explains. "He wanted me to consider that as a soldier that you can never assume you're safe, that everything is a weapon and everyone is a potential threat. When you go into any room, you need to consider the direction you face, consider where you put yourself, consider where you don't want to be standing if there's danger. You never fight if you don't have to, but if you're going to hit someone, you hit them hard enough that they don't get back up." Like many in the military, that's the type of mindset that people can't leave behind when they leave the service, a big reason why crime, addiction, and self-harm have befallen so many after discharge.

Especially if they're forced out—by injury, or for political bullshit. We didn't know it yet, but Alexandra had fallen into the second category (the film came out in 2010, but it's set years before—as in, while a certain pathetic ban was still going strong).

"The goal was to be able to do a couple pull-ups," remembers Pickard, "and be able to ensure the shooting process, which involved running up and down hills and biking in hundred-plus degree weather. I spent time doing pushups in the sauna and doing cardio . . . being able to get into the physical stuff helped me to not think about 'acting' quite so much and I think that helped my performance." She, Weber, and some trainers went through some infamously wrenching P90X treatment to buff up and out.

Things seems to be going well for Saffron and Alexandra for a while. But, per usual for those back home, some conniving jerk tries to reach out a steal some of Alexandra's accomplishment, sneaking around (flashback alert!) with a camera to catch her taking time with another lady, in something that never had any business going public. For too long, that's all it took to wipe the longest list of accomplishments and rewards clean, even in the dirtiest of manners.

Alexandra had become just another victim, and it had followed her home to be victimized by a small town's small-mindedness. Now it came time for Weber to find the tribute, to acting out paying a price that had bankrupted so many who'd given much more than those who'd put out both the anti-gay rules and the "Don't ask," pathetic compromise.

"I found out more and more details about the sacrifices made by closeted LGBT service members," she says. "The story opened itself up, and the need to tell it became very important, so we were too emotionally committed. We took the money *The Gymnast* was making, and used it for *A Marine Story*."

It's all falling apart for the character. Her career gone, her public image crushed, her protégé lost faith in her. Decades from now, this sort of bigotry will seem as senseless as gender and racial issues. The only person Alexandra can really rely on is herself. But the Marine's belief that even if it's difficult, even if it's thankless, even if it's dangerous, what's right is always right is still inside her, and saving Saffron from those who held her down from the start is just that. Even if it takes her own life or safety. . . .

Weber and Alexandra still had their own duty; to do what a Marine should, and to pay tribute to those that had. Perhaps, just maybe, the decision-makers might just see the film and learn stories like it, and see just how hurtful and needless every act of military inequality has ever been.

"The whole thing completely changed my mind about military service and why people serve," Weber says. "I don't like our policy of 'We have the biggest stick, so we can swing it in arguably immoral ways,' the idea that politicians can use our military for their own idiot purposes."

It wasn't about those that give the orders and steal the credit—like the politicians who, usually, couldn't be bothered to serve a single day. It's not like the war films that end with the main people celebrating and trying to pass off some happy ending crap that never happens in war. No glory, no prestige, nothing about any of that.

A Marine Story was, in part, for closeted service members with the guts to say, "'I believe that this idea of democracy is worth sacrificing my life for,'" Weber says. "Not having a personal life, not able to be married, not being able to visit my loved ones in the hospital. 'I'm giving up my life for the idea that this country holds, even if it doesn't include me in the finale.' I can't say enough about how proud I am of this film."

Maybe the *Story* made a huge difference, maybe not. Perhaps (check that, almost definitely) there's always going to be some discrimination, legal or otherwise, behind the military scenes. But there's one thing that's no longer open for debate: one year after the film was released, Obama and those with him took out the "Don't ask" issue. The words, "I'm gay," are no longer grounds to destroy the lives of those who serve their nation.

What will happen? Will this discriminatory policy end up as shameful a period as all the other biogoted laws in our history? It's been a "baby steps first" process, just like so many race and gender issues, but it may someday have its own finish line. And if it does, one reason why will be tales like *A Marine Story*, which showed us those who've been needlessly hurt, and offer an opportunity to say the thanks that so, *so many*, will always deserve.

Epilogue

"You're not going to make it. Come on, go try something more stable."

"No chance, there, dude (or dudette). Too many people ahead of you. How are you going to stand out? Not worth it."

"You live too far away."

"You don't have enough experience."

"You shouldn't try this because . . . (fill in your own answer)."

You know who has heard all of these and far too many more? *Everyone who has ever made it in the acting business*!

They've all heard it from all kinds of people, well intentioned and otherwise, and it didn't stop them. Bothered them, depressed them, pissed them off, probably. But it didn't stop them.

That's why you know their names and recognize them today. It's why, when you see them headlining a new movie, or even just appearing in one, you're excited, but not surprised. Why not get others to feel that way about you?

It might take a long time, or you might get lucky right off the bat, an instant lottery-level victory. Acting is a mixed bag like that. You never know when you'll get a break, or how, or from whom. It's about trying, and then trying again. And again. And then some more.

If you look at the back cover jacket of this book, and others I've written, you'll notice that I'm a movie freak in all kinds of regards. But I'm not an actor myself. Sure, I've dreamt about it, like most people do, but I never took the shot.

But you can. Hopefully, through my words, you've found some entertainment, and maybe a bit of inspiration. I didn't go for it. Not because I didn't want to, but because I found some things I was better at. Like the years as a reporter that launched my writing career, or the near-decade I've spent teaching others to read, write, and research just a bit better.

Does that make me a wannabe? A failure? Maybe in some regards. But I write these books, yes, because I want to entertain, to instruct. But also to inspire others to do what I didn't (couldn't, shouldn't, wouldn't, call it whatever you wish). If my words help launch a career or two, the realization of someone else's hopes and dreams, I'll be OK with that. That's what teachers do all day, every day.

And here in the spring of 2017, I have one more special reason to feel that way.

This past May, I became a father for the first time. My wife and I can't wait to spend the next few decades helping our wonderful daughter Kennedy make her dreams come true. Will she be an actress? Will she ever want to read her dad's writings? I don't know—I hope so!

But I'm going to end this book with the same message that teachers like me send their students every day, and now I ask of you. I'll be hoping all of this for someone else, for a very, very long time.

In your hopes, your dreams, your goals, don't make them like mine. Don't pick up all my habits. Don't be all that much like me at all.

Be so much better.

References

ABC News. (2015, Dec. 10). 'Star Wars: The Force Awakens' Cast on Training for Roles. *YouTube*. Retrieved on Nov. 19, 2016, from https://www.youtube.com/watch?v=s0CU6EGiJ64

Abrams, Natalie. (2015, July 2). Supergirl. *Entertainment Weekly*. Retrieved on June, 1, 2017, from http://ew.com/article/2015/07/02/supergirl-melissa-benoist-cbs-interview/

Actor Christoph Waltz for 'Inglorious Basterds.' (2012, Feb. 15). *Charlie Rose*. Retrieved on October 11, 2012, from http://www.charlierose.com/view/interview/10864

Adamo, Susan. (1982, December). Mark Hamill. *Starlog*. 65. 18-22.

afi. (2009, Aug. 24). Sigourney Weaver On Ellen Ripley From The ALIEN Films. *Youtube*. Retrieved on Jan. 2, 2012, from http://www.youtube.com/watch?feature=fvwp&v=zev0m1Gmw0g&NR=1

Alexander, John. Phone interview. Jan. 16, 2017.

Alien 3 DVD

Alien: Resurrection – One Step Beyond DVD

Alien Saga DVD

Alonso, Maria Conchita. E-mail interview. March 8, 2017.

Andrews, Nigel. (1996). *True Myths: The Life and Times of Arnold Schwarzenegger*. Carol Publishing Group: Secaucus, NJ.

ANJ. (2009, July 11). Helen Slater Interview. Comic Box Commentary. Retrieved on June 1, 2017, from http://comicboxcommentary.blogspot.com/2009/07/helen-slater-interview.html

Ansen, David and Setoodeh Ramin. Feb. 2, 2009. Inside The Actor's Studio. *Newsweek*. 54-63.

Anson, Jasper. (2012). Eli Roth Interview. *Ask Men*. Retrieved on October 11, 2012, from http://www.askmen.com/celebs/interview_300/334_eli-roth-interview.html

Aronofsky, Darren. (2008). *The Wrestler*. DVD. Wild Bunch.

Baganov, Vitali. Phone interview. May 10, 2016.

Bako, Brigitte. Phone interview. Nov. 18, 2014.

Balfour, Brad. (2005, February 2005). Hilary Swank: Hitting a Million. *Pop Entertainment*. Retrieved on January 19, 2010, from http://www.popentertainment.com/swank.htm

Barbara Walters Special, ABC. Feb 21, 2009.

Barclay, James. (n.d.). Robert Powell: How portraying Christ changed his life. *Powellisimo Robert Powell Site*. Retrieved on December 28, 2010, from http://powellisimo.free.fr/index.html

Barron, Dana. Phone interview. Aug. 24, 2016.

Bdkreviewsdotcom. (2010, Dec. 21). Hailee Steinfeld Interview for TRUE GRIT. *Youtube*. Retrieved on Aug. 12, 2011, from http://www.youtube.com/watch?v=GoL7mTvcldc

Bennett, Tara. (2015, Oct. 22). Supergirl producers and star Melissa Benoist reveal how their heroine stands apart. *Syfy Wire*. Retrieved on June, 1, 2017, from http://www.blastr.com/2015-10-22/supergirl-producers-and-star-melissa-benoist-reveal-how-their-heroine-stands-apart

Benoist, Melissa. (2016, Feb. 5). Melissa Benoist: What Playing Supergirl Means to Me. *Time Inc.* Retrieved on June, 1, 2017, from http://motto.time.com/4208202/melissa-benoist-supergirl/

Best Supporting Actor Christoph Waltz Press Room Quotes. (2010, March 10). *BuzzSugar*.Retrieved on October 11, 2012, from http://www.buzzsugar.com/Best-Supporting-Actor-Christoph-Waltz-Press-Room-Quotes-2010-03-07-220400-7662972

Blair, Macon. E-mail interview. Oct. 22, 2016.

Blythe, Janus. Q+A session at Virginia Beach horror film convention. July 22, 2016.

Boen, Earl. Phone interview. Aug. 21, 2016.

Bogdanovich, Peter. (2004). *Who The Hell's In It*. Alfred A. Knopf: New York.

Bolling, Tiffany. E-mail interview. Feb. 1, 2017.

Boorman, Imogen. E-mail interview. Jan. 14, 2017.

Bounty Killers DVD

Bray, Tony. The R. Lee Ermey Interview with Tony Bray.*TV Guide*. Retrieved on Nov. 18, 2011, from http://www.space-2063.de/finfo24.htm

Breznahan, Kevin. Phone interview. Aug. 26, 2016.

Brown, Todd (2008, Feb. 2). Splice's Creature Speaks! *TwitchFilm*. Retrieved on Nov. 29, 2010, from http://twitchfilm.com/interviews/2008/02/splices-creature-speaks-an-interview-with-delphine-chaneac.php

Buchanan, Kyle. (2009, August 19). Mélanie Laurent on Tarantino's Inglourious Basterds: 'To Survive On That Set, You Learn Fast!' *Movieline*. Retrieved on October 11, 2012, from http://movieline.com/2009/08/19/inglourious-basterds-melanie-laurent/

Bulloch, Jeremy. E-mail interview. March 14, 2017

Burn, Natalie. E-mail interview. Sept. 15, 2016.

C., Ximena Gallardo. & Smith, C. Jason (2004).*Alien Woman: The Making of Ellen Ripley*. Continuum: New York.

Calderon, Corina. E-mail interview. August 4, 2016.

Cartwright, Veronica. Phone interview. June 14, 2017.

Chau, Francois. E-mail interview. Dec. 21, 2009.

Chandler, Charlotte. (2005). *It's Only A Movie*. Simon and Schuster: New York.

Chanoine, Alain. Phone interview. Jan. 21, 2017.

Chewie Interview. (2004). *Toazted*. Retrieved on July 4, 2010, from http://www.toazted.com/playinterview/577/Chewie-Interview-24.html

Chiarella, Chris. (2004, Oct. 1). Mark Hamill Interview. *Home Theater*. Retrieved on September 23, 2011, http://www.hometheater.com/news/100104hamill/

Christoph Waltz: Dancing with Tarantino. (2009, August 18). *Hollywood and Fine*. Retrieved on October 11, 2012, from http://hollywoodandfine.com/interviews/christoph-waltz-dancing-with-tarantino/

Christoph Waltz Interview "Inglorious Basterds." (2012). *Film Annex*. Retrieved on October 11, 2012, from http://www.filmannex.com/movie/christoph-waltz-interview-inglourious-basterds/17123

Ciafalio, Carl. Phone, E-mail interview. Oct. 18, 2009.

Clark, Krystal. (2015, January 22). Helen Slater Reveals How She Became the First Supergirl, talks CBS Reboot. *Syfy Wire*. Retrieved on June, 1, 2017, from http://www.blastr.com/2015-1-22/exclusive-helen-slater-reveals-how-she-became-1st-supergirl-talks-cbs-reboot

Clay, Linda Bright. E-mail interview. Oct. 15, 2015.

Cohen, Julie. Phone interview. May 3, 2016.

Colceri, Tim. Phone interview. May 7, 2014.

Coppinger, John. E-mail interview. March 19, 2017.

Crawford, Daz. E-mail interview. Aug. 23, 2016.

Cullotta, Frank. Phone interview. July 16, 2016.

Darren Aronofsky On 'The Wrestler' (2009, April 17). *NPR*. Retrieved on Nov. 29, 2010, from http://www.npr.org/templates/story/story.php?storyId=103205984

Darth Maul: The Voice. (2009). *The Darth Maul Estrogen Brigade*. Retrieved on October 5, 2011, from http://www.dmeb2.org/cast/voice.html

The Darth Maul Estrogen Brigade. (2009). Retrieved on October 5, 2011, from http://www.dmeb2.com/media/sounds/Forcecast_CJ_073008_Ray_Park.mp3

Davis, Ronald L. (1998). *Duke: The Life and Image of John Wayne*. University of Oklahoma Press: Norman, OK.

Davis, Susan Bluestein. (1997). *After Midnight*. Pocket Books: New York.

Dent, Catherine. Phone interview. March 29, 2017.

Dorment, Richard. (2009, August 7). Eli Roth Interview. *Esquire*. Retrieved on October 11, 2012, from http://www.esquire.com/the-side/qa/eli-roth-interview-080709

Drake, Larry. Q+A session at Scares That Care horror movie convention, Williamsburg, VA, July 25, 2015.

Duffy, Thomas. Phone interview. Aug. 27, 2016.

East, Jeff. Phone interview. April 8, 2011.

Ebert, Roger. (1974, April 7). Charles Bronson. *Roger Ebert*. Retrieved on August 26, 2016, from http://www.rogerebert.com/interviews/charles-bronson-its-just-that-i-dont-like-to-talk-very-much

Ebert, Roger. (2011). Interview with John Wayne. *Roger Ebert*. Retrieved on Aug. 8, 2011, from http://rogerebert.suntimes.com/apps/pbcs.dll/article?AID=/19690629/PEOPLE/906290301

Elman, Mali. (2009, August 19). Interview: Christoph Waltz for Inglourious Basterds. *Screen Crave*. Retrieved on October 11, 2012, from http://screencrave.com/2009-08-19/interview-christoph-waltz-for-inglourious-basterds/

Elliott, Brennan. Phone interview. July 21, 2009.

Eric Harris & Dylan Klebold. (2017, July 5). *A Columbine Site*. Retrieved on July 7, 2017, from http://www.acolumbinesite.com

Esteban, Samantha. Phone interview. April 25, 2014.

Eyman, Scott. (2014). *John Wayne: The Life and Legend*. Simon & Schuster.

Fagen, Herb. (2009). *Duke: We're Glad We Knew You*. Citadel Press: New York.

Fairchild, Krisha. E-mail interview. Feb. 2, 2016.

Feinberg, Scott. (2011, Jan. 20). Interview With Hailee Steinfeld, A True-ly Great Young Actress. *Scott Feinberg*. Retrieved on Aug. 12, 2011, from http://scottfeinberg.com/haileesteinfeld

Farris, Lorraine. Phone interview, July 3, 2013.

Field, Chelsea. Phone interview. March 27, 2015.

Fierman, Hannah. Phone interview. June 25, 2017.

Finochio, Stephanie. E-mail interview. Jan. 9, 2017.

Fisher, Carrie. (2016). *The Princess Diarist*. Blue Rider Press: New York.

Flick Mojo (2010, Aug. 25). Interview With Splice Actress Delphine Chaneac. *Daily Motion*. Retrieved on Nov. 29, 2010, from http://www.dailymotion.com/video/xdkhsi_flickmojo-interview-with-splice-act_news

Florino, Rick. (2010, June 1). Interview: Adrien Brody & Delphine Chaneac of "Splice." *Artist Direct*. Retrieved on Nov. 29, 2010, from http://www.artistdirect.com/nad/news/article/0,,6930863,00.html

Frieman, Barry. (2010, Feb. 15). "Exclusive 2005 Cult TV Superhero Celebration Superhero Expo Coverage." *Superman Homepage*. Retrieved on July 19, 2010, from http://www.supermanhomepage.com/movies/movies.php?topic=interview-expo-sarah

Gaffey, Aaron. E-mail interview. Oct. 27, 2016.

Garrett, Hank. Phone interview. Aug. 26, 2016.

Gibson, Leah. Phone interview. Feb. 6, 2015.

Gilbert, Lewis. (2000). *Moonraker*. DVD. United Artists.

Gilchirst, Todd. (2005, November 5). Interview: Ian McDiarmid. *IGN Movies*. Retrieved on October 5, 2011, from http://dvd.ign.com/articles/658/658064p2.html

Gower, Carlena. Phone interview. Jan. 4, 2016.

Greenberger, Robert. (1983, June). Carrie Fisher. *Starlog. 71*. 32-36.

Guest, Lance. E-mail interview. May 28, 2015.

Hallenbeck, Bruce C. (Winter 1992/93). Barbarian Queen. *Femme Fatales*. 56-59.

Hamsher, Jane. (1997). *Killer Instinct*. Broadway Books: New York.

Hayden Christensen Interview (2005). Star Wars Universe. Retrieved on September 23, 2011, from http://starsontop.com/starwars/haydeninterview.htm

Hayes, Megan. Phone interview. Aug. 27, 2016.

Hee, Dana. E-mail interviews. Feb. 23/March 3, 2011.

Hilary Swank Interview. (2008, May 5). *Academy of Achievement*. Retrieved on January 19, 2010, from http://www.achievement.org/autodoc/page/swa0int-1

Holland, Tom. E-mail interview. Dec. 10, 2009.

Hollitt, Raye. E-mail interview. March 24, 2011.

Howell, Maria. E-mail interview. Sept. 6, 2016.

Hunter, Jumayn. E-mail interview. January 5, 2017.

IAmRogue. (2012, May 10). EXCLUSIVE VIDEO: Joel Murray and Tara Lynne Barr Talk 'God Bless America.' *YouTube*. Retrieved on Dec. 15, 2012, from http://www.youtube.com/watch?v=6h3zyi5mbCA&feature=fvwp&NR=1

"Inglourious Basterds" Interview: Melanie Laurent. (2012). *Ask Men*. Retrieved on October 11, 2012, from http://www.askmen.com/celebs/interview_300/336_inglourious-basterds-interview-melanie-laurent.html

Interview with Jenette Goldstein, 1987. (2013, April 23). *Strange Shapes*. Retrieved on June 4, 2014, from http://alienseries.wordpress.com/2013/04/22/interview-with-jenette-goldstein-1987/

Interview with Michelan Sisti. (n.d.). Retrieved on Oct. 20, 2010, from http://members.ziggo.nl/rutgergret/sisti%20interview.html

Jackson, Sally. Phone interview. Nov. 18, 2015.

Jaffer, Melissa. E-mail interview. Jan. 24, 2016.

Jecchins, Kieron. E-mail interview. April 12, 2015.

Jones, Brian Jay. (2013). *Jim Henson: The Biography*. Ballentine Books: New York.

Jones, O-Lan. Phone interview. May 26, 2009.

Jones, Sam. Q+A event at Tidewater ComicCon, Virginia Beach, VA. May 21, 2016.

Joyner, Michelle. Phone interview. Sept. 22, 2009.

Juliette Lewis Interview. (2013). *YeahTV*. Retrieved on June 6, 2013, from http://link.brightcove.com/services/player/bcpid2240974179001?bckey=AQ~~%2cAAACCaPOWnk~%2c7OKSlvhXQyv6acfl6R8VeLB1LWZNt9Jy&bctid=2433889513001

Katarina, Anna. Phone interview. June 7, 2016.

Kaye, Don. (2015, Dec. 10). 'Star Wars 7': Adam Driver Talks 'Reckless' Kyloe Ren & Dark Side Intrigue. *Screen Rant*. Retrieved Nov. 25, 2016, from http://screenrant.com/star-wars-7-adam-driver-interview/

Keuck, Andre. Phone interview. June 12, 2017.

Kiel, Richard. (2002). *Making it Big in the Movies*. Reynolds and Hearn, Ltd.: Great Britain.

Kove, Martin. Phone interview. Oct. 13, 2016.

Lana Clarkson. (2007). Retrieved on March 10, 2010, from http://www.lanaclarkson.com/

Lagano, Alicia. Phone interview. March 18, 2017.

Larnick, Eric. (2011, July 17). Sigourney Weaver on the Legacy of 'Aliens' & Her Sequel That Hollywood Won't Make. *Moviefone*. Retrieved on Jan. 2, 2012, from http://blog.moviefone.com/2011/07/17/sigourney-weaver-interview-aliens-25th-anniversary-sequel/

LaurieAnn523. (2012, May 12). God Bless America Interview with Joel Murray and Tara Lynne Barr*Youtube*. Retrieved Dec. 15, 2012, from http://www.youtube.com/watch?v=6YpJvKjZXdg

Le, Hiep Thi. E-mail interview. Oct. 13, 2015.

Leamer, Laurence. (2005). *Fantastic: The Life of Arnold Schwarzenegger*. St. Martin's Press: New York.

Lee, Bruce. (2000). *Bruce Lee: The Celebrated Life of the Golden Dragon*. (Ed. John Little). Tuttle Publishing: Boston.

Leigh, Wendy. (1970). *Arnold*. Congdon and Weed, Inc.: Chicago.

Lindsley, Blake. Phone interview. Oct. 31, 2014.

Little, John. (1996). *The Warrior Within*. Contemporary Books, Inc.: Chicago.

Lords, Traci. Q+A session at horror movie convention in Virginia Beach, VA. July 22, 2016.

Lozzi, Edward. Phone interview. Dec. 2, 2009.

Lozzi, Edward. E-mail interview. March 15, 2010.

Maillet, Robert. E-mail interview. Feb. 9/12, 2010.

Marinca, Anamaria. E-mail interview. March 13, 2017.

Marshall, Peter. E-mail interview. Jan. 25, 2017.

Marshall, Rebecca. Phone interview. Sept. 17, 2014.

Mathieson, Craig. (2012, Nov. 15). Murray shoots to the top of bill. *Sydney Morning Herald*. Retrieved on Dec. 15, 2012, from http://www.smh.com.au/entertainment/movies/murray-shoots-to-the-top-of-bill-20121114-29cdj.html#ixzz2DbhYvTXk

Mattson, Helena. E-mail interview. Aug. 15, 2016.

McArthur, Alex. Phone interview. Aug. 20, 2016.

McGinnis, Graham. Phone interview. Nov. 6, 2016.

Meyers, Richard. (1978, May). The Man Behind the Mask. *Starlog. 13.* 22-25, 44-45

Michaell, Monnae. Phone interview. July 14, 2009.

Miller, Ernest. Phone interview. April 17, 2009.

Miraudo, Simon. (2012, November 15). Interview: Joel Murray (God Bless America). *Quickflix*. Retrieved on Dec. 15, 2012, from http://blog.quickflix.com.au/2012/11/15/interview-joel-murray-god-bless-america/

Modine, Matthew. (2005). *Full Metal Jacket Diary*. Rugged Land: New York City.

Mohamed, Jasmin. (2017, Jan. 1). Rogue One: Darth Vader Actor on How he Prepared for the Sith Lord's 'Presence.' *Screen Rant*. Retrieved on Jan. 11, 2017, from http://screenrant.com/rogue-one-darth-vader-actor-how-he-prepare-for-sith-lords-presence/

Moran, Kent. E-mail interview. Jan. 19, 2017.

MoviesIreland (2011, Feb. 2) 'True Grit' Interview with Hailee Steinfeld. *Youtube*. Retrieved on Aug. 12, 2011, from http://www.youtube.com/watch?v=DYhSCII-hEU&feature=related

Munn, Michael. (2003). *John Wayne: The Man Behind the Myth*. New American Library: New York.

Murray, Rebecca. (2011). Ian McDiarmid on Playing the Most Evil 'Star Wars' Character of the Franchise. *About.com*. Retrieved on October 5, 2011, from http://movies.about.com/od/starwars3/a/star-wars101205.htm

NaturalTalents9. (2010, Dec. 22). Hailee Steinfeld - True Grit Interview. *Youtube*. Retrieved on Aug. 12, 2011, from http://www.youtube.com/watch?v=WC7Q728YqTE

The Nerdery. (2016, May 28). Laura Vandervoort interview at Space City Comic Con 2016. *Youtube*. Retrieved on June, 1, 2017, from https://www.youtube.com/watch?v=KIjDMxL8U8g

Ngor, Haing & Roger Warner. (1987). *A Cambodian Odyssey*. Macmillian Publishing Company: New York.

Nguyen, Long. E-mail interview. Oct. 19, 2015.

O'Halloran, Jack. Phone interview. Dec. 27, 2009.

O'Shea, Daniel. Phone interview. Jan. 26, 2016.

Ólafsson, Ólafur Darri. E-mail interview. Aug. 21, 2016.

Page, Thomas. (2016, March 7). Bolaji Badejo: The Nigerian giant who played 'Alien.' *CNN*. Retrieved on March 8, 2016, from http://www.cnn.com/2016/03/07/africa/bolaji-badejo-alien/?iid=ob_homepage_deskrecommended_pool&iref=obinsite

Paige, Tarah. E-mail interview. Sept. 2, 2016.

Pais, Josh. Phone interview. July 29, 2009.

Papillion Soo Soo. (2004). Retrieved on Nov. 2, 2010, from http://panho.webs.com/

Parfitt, David. (May 27, 2009). Star Wars Weekends: Peter Mayhew/Chewbacca Interview. *DIS Unplugged*. Retrieved July 4, 2010, from http://www.disunplugged.com/2009/05/27/star-wars-weekends-peter-mayhewchewbacca-interview/

PatrickMcD. (2012, May 10). Interview: Joel Murray Takes No Prisoners in 'God Bless America.' *Hollywood Chicago*. Retrieved Dec. 15, 2012, from http://www.hollywoodchicago.com/news/18418/interview-joel-murray-takes-no-prisoners-in-god-bless-america#ixzz2DbkiUuJN

Peecher, John Phillip. (1983). *The Making of Star Wars: Return of the Jedi*. Ballantine Books: New York.

Pelkert, Mark (2013, March 12). Paul Walker Comes to SXSW for 'Hours.' Backstage. Retrieved on Feb. 25, 2017, from http://www.backstage.com/interview/paul-walker-comes-sxsw-hours/

Phillips, Bobbie. E-mail interview. Oct. 17, 2015.

Phipps, Keith. (2009, August 17). Eli Roth. *A.V. Club*. Retrieved on October 11, 2012, fromhttp://www.avclub.com/articles/eli-roth,31811/

Pickard, Paris. E-mail interview. August 17, 2016.

Pileggi, Nicholas. (1995). *Casino*. New York. Simon and Schuster.

Pina, Lionel. E-mail interview. July 14, 2015.

Pitre, Christian. E-mail interview. Nov. 9, 2013.

Priani, Adam. (1987, July). Sebastian Shaw. *Starlog*. 120. 56-57, 96.

Quincy, Allene. E-mail interview. Sept.16, 2014.

Radish, Christina. (2013, Nov. 18). Paul Walker Says 'Fast & Furious 8' Guaranteed. Collider. Retrieved on Feb. 20, 2017, from http://collider.com/fast-furious-7-8-paul-walker-interview/

Rafiq, Fiaz. (2009). *Bruce Lee Conversations*. Midpoint Trade Books: New York.

Ramsey, Anessa. E-mail interview. Feb. 4, 2017.

Rankin, Claire. E-mail interview. Aug. 29, 2016.

Reeve, Christopher. (2002). *Nothing is Impossible*. Random House Publishing Group: New York.

Reeve, Christopher. (1998). *Still Me*. Random House Publishing Group: New York.

Reherman, Lee. Phone interview. March 17, 2011.

Renna, Melinda. E-mail interview. January 5, 2015.

Reynolds, Patrick. Phone interview. May 9, 2016.

Rinzler, J.W. (2007). *The Making of Star Wars*. Ballantine Books: New York.

Rinzler, J.W. (2005). *The Making of Star Wars: Revenge of the Sith*. Del Ray Books: New York.

Roberts, Randy, and James Olson. (1995). *John Wayne: American*. Free Press: New York.

Robinson, Stuart. Phone interview. Aug. 24, 2016.

Rolleston, James. E-mail interview. March 21, 2017.

Romanus, Richard. E-mail interview. March 11, 2016.

"Rourke's Days Of Rage." Oct. 23, 2009. *The Week. 9 (435)*. 10.

Rowland, Hilary. (n.d.). Exclusive Interview with Two-Time Oscar Winner Hilary Swank. *Hilary Magazine*. Retrieved on January 19, 2010, from http://www.hilary.com/celebrity/hilary-swank.html

Rowley, David. (2012, July 11). Interview: Bobcat Goldthwait and Joel Murray for God Bless America. *Eat Sleep Film*. Retrieved Dec. 15, 2012, from http://www.eatsleeplivefilm.com/interview-bobcat-goldthwait-and-joel-murray-for-god-bless-america/

Roxborough, Jeanette. Phone interview. July 14, 2017.

Rubinek, Saul. Phone interview. Sept. 10, 2016.

Russo, Jennie. Phone interview. Nov. 30, 2016.

Sapp, Bob. Phone interview. Oct. 27, 2014.

"Sarah Douglas Interview." (n.d.). *AngelFire.com*. Retrieved on July 19, 2010, from http://www.angelfire.com/ca4/sarahdouglasp2/interview.html

Schlund, Stephanie Leigh. E-mail interview. Sept. 29, 2016.

Schutzman, Scott. Phone interview. April 29, 2016.

Schwarzenegger, Arnold. (2012). *Total Recall: My Unbelievably True Life Story*. Simon & Schuster: New York.

Screen Crave. (2009, August 10). Eli Roth talks 'Inglourious Basterds.' *You Tube*. Retrieved on October 11, 2012, from http://www.youtube.com/watch?v=bhhp3F9z8Cs

Scott, Cynthia Dale. E-mail interview. May 2, 2012.

Serrone, Christopher. Phone interview. Sept. 17, 2014.

Shirley, Alesia. Phone interview. Nov. 30, 2016.

Silva, Geno. Phone interview. Sept. 6/Oct. 18, 2013.

Smith, Nigel. (2012, May 11). Bobcat Goldthwait and Joel Murray Talk 'God Bless America' and Why They Hate (Some) Reality TV. *IndieWire*. Retrieved on Dec. 15, 2012, from http://www.indiewire.com/article/bobcat-goldthwait-and-joel-murray-talk-god-bless-america-and-why-they-hate-some-reality-tv

Smith, Nigel M. (2013, March 19). 'Hours' Star Paul Walker. *IndieWire*. Retrieved on Feb. 25, 2017, from http://www.indiewire.com/2013/03/sxsw-hours-star-paul-walker-on-finally-getting-serious-about-acting-and-driving-vin-diesel-fcking-crazy-40064/

Smolinski, Aaron. Phone interview. Nov. 5, 2016.

Splice Junket Interview - Delphine Chanéac. (n.d.). *Trailer Addict*. Retrieved on Nov. 29, 2010, from http://www.traileraddict.com/trailer/splice/junket-interview-delphine-chaneac

Steptoe, Sonja. (2001, August 13). Down to Earth. *People*. Retrieved on June 3, 2014, from http://www.people.com/people/archive/article/0,,20135092,00.html

Swires, Steve. (1983, August). Mark Hamill: Life After 'Star Wars.' *Starlog*. *73*. 38-41.

Teenage Mutant Ninja Turtles II: The Secret of the Ooze. (n.d.). *Internet Movie Database*. Retrieved on Dec. 21, 2009, from http://pro.imdb.com/title/tt0103060/maindetails

Ten. (2010, Oct. 11). Carrie Fisher Extended Interview. *Youtube*. Retrieved on September 23, 2011, from http://www.youtube.com/watch?v=6a6VS3IjMC4

Thomas, Bruce. (1994). *Bruce Lee: Fighting Spirit*. Frog, Ltd.: Berkley, Calif.

Tibbetts, John C. & Welsh, James M. (1998). *Encyclopedia of Movies into Film*. New York: Facts on File, Inc.

Tijerina, Cecilia. Phone interview. Dec. 9, 2009.

Tom Sizemore Interview. (2013). *YeahTV*. Retrieved on July 10, 2013, from http://link.brightcove.com/services/player/bcpid2240974179001?bckey=AQ~~,AAACCaPOWnk~,7OKSlvhXQyv6acfl6R8VeLB1LWZNt9Jy&bctid=2431036422001

Topel, Fred. (2013, Dec. 9). Exclusive Interview: Paul Walker. Crave. Retrieved on Feb. 20, 2017, from http://www.craveonline.com/site/615173-exclusive-interview-paul-walker/2

Tooley, Jenni. E-mail interview. Sept. 20, 2016.

Treviño, Marco. E-mail interview. May 31, 2016.

Truitt, Brian. (2013, Dec. 1). For Paul Walker, Family was Key to His Legacy. USA Today. Retrieved on Feb. 25, 2017, from http://www.usatoday.com/story/life/movies/2013/12/01/paul-walker-last-interview/3794309/

Trujillo, Raoul. Phone interview. July 27, 2009.

Turton, Kett. Phone interview. July 6, 2017.

Vanova, Apollonia. E-mail interview. Feb. 3, 2015.

Velasquez, Patricia. E-mail interview. Feb. 22, 2017.

Wayne, Aissa. (1991). *John Wayne: My Father*. Random House: New York.

Weber, Dreya. Phone interview. Feb. 13, 2016.

Weintraub, Steve. (2009, August 19). Interview with the Bear Jew (Eli Roth). *Collider*. Retrieved on October 11, 2012, from http://collider.com/exclusive-interview-with-the-bear-jew-eli-roth-inglourious-basterds/5997/

Weldon, Glen. (2013). *Superman: The Unauthorized Biography*. John Wily and Sons, Inc.: Hoboken: New Jersey.

Wigler, Josh. (2009). Chewbacca: The Heeb Interview. *Heeb*. Retrieved July 4, 2010, from http://www.heebmagazine.com/chewbacca-the-_heeb_-interview/

Windham, Ryder, and Peter Vilmur. (2009). *Star Wars: The Complete Vader*. Balantine Books: New York.

Woerner, Meredith. (2015, Dec. 21). Adam Driver of 'Star Wars' reflects on the man behind the mask, Kylo Ren. *Los Angeles Times*. Retrieved Nov. 25, 2016, from http://www.latimes.com/entertainment/hero-complex/la-et-hc-star-wars-adam-driver-20151221-story.html

Worth, Michael. E-mail interview. Aug. 22, 2009.

Index

The 33, 453-5
300, 211-3, 314, 474
Academy Awards (Oscars), 4, 8, 48, 25, 26, 27, 40, 41, 43, 59, 63, 64, 67, 84, 85, 92, 103, 104, 105, 107, 116, 127, 132, 134, 141, 142, 159, 186, 188, 190-1, 192, 194, 195, 196, 218, 222, 228, 230, 251, 264, 265, 277, 282, 290, 294, 298, 300, 311, 312, 317, 342, 344, 345, 347, 351, 365, 367, 368, 380, 382, 396, 411, 415, 440, 449, 451, 452, 461, 475, 476, 477, 478, 479, 481, 482, 484, 491, 494
Aerosmith, 390
Alexander, John, 103-5
Alien films, 67, 145, 485-504, 508
Alive, 24-7
All She Can, 32-4
Alonso, Maria Conchita, 142
American Gladiators, 118-23
An American Werewolf in London, 103, 396
Amistad, 393
Anderson, Bob, 402
Apocalypse Now, 238, 431-2
Apocalypto, 456-60
Arlington Road, 448-451, 452
Arquette, Patricia, 451
Artist, The, 260
Aronofsky, Darren, 348, 349, 351
Attack the Block, 510-2
August, Pernilla, 402
Avatar, 8, 409, 417, 494
Awaken, 28-31
Badejo, Bolaji, 502-4
Baganov, Vitali, 1-3
Baker, Rick, 103, 105, 396
Bako, Brigitte, 4-9
Bale, Christian, 86, 373
Bare Knuckles, 326-31
Barr, Tara Lynne, 258, 261
Barron, Dana, 76-7
Bassett, Angela, 6, 8
Batman movies, 51, 86, 153, 443
Believe in Me, 37-40
Bell, Zoe, 323
Benoist, Melissa, 444-7
Berg, Peter, 225
Berry, Halle, 220-1, 222
Bigelow, Kathryn, 7-8, 278
Blair, Macon, 10-12

Blood of Heroes, The, 168, 169-71
Blue Ruin, 10-12
Bluestein, Susan, 65, 66, 67-8, 69
Blythe, Janus, 13-15
Boen, Earl, 374-6
Bolling, Tiffany, 21-23
Bonnie's Kids, 21-23
Boorman, Imogen, 15-18
Born of the Fourth of July, 193, 235
Bounty Killer, 313-5
Boyhood, 451-2
Boys Don't Cry, 41
Breznahan, Kevin, 24-7
Bridges, Jeff, 116, 448, 449, 450, 451, 481, 484
Brochtrup, Bill, 106, 112-4
Brody, Adrien, 192
Bronson, Charles, 71-9, 488
Bulloch, Jeremy (Boba Fett), 425, 429-31
Bullock, Sandra, 153, 508
Burn, Natalie, 28-31
Buscemi, Steve, 3
Calderon, Corina, 32-4
Cameron, James, 7-8, 333, 370-2, 374-6, 417, 488, 496, 498, 500, 501-2
Cape Fear, 265, 382, 439
Carrey, Jim, 250, 266
Cartwright, Veronica, 494-5, 504-6
Casino, 54-59, 63
Challenger, The, 254-7
Chameleon films, 306-9
Chan, Jackie, 188, 201, 328
Chaneac, Delphine, 44-6
Chanoine, Alain, 47-8
Chau, Francois, 301, 304-5
Chiklis, Michael, 125
Christensen, Hayden, 403-6
Ciarfalio, Carl, 54, 57-60
Clapp, Gordon, 106, 110-12
Clarkson, Lana, 49-53
Clay, Linda Bright, 293-4, 295-6
Cliffhanger, 164-7
Clockwork Orange, A, 241, 400
Clooney, George, 86, 153
Cohen, Julie, 363, 364, 365-7
Colceri, Tim, 241-4, 245
Conan the Barbarian, 362
Craven, Wes, 14

Crawford, Daz, 119, 122
Cullotta, Frank, 54-6
D'Onofrio, Vincent, 6, 170, 233, 235, 238-240
Dangerfield, Rodney, 269-70
Darby, Kim, 475, 481, 483, 484
Dark Below, The, 394-6
Darkman films, 81-3
Davis, Brad, 64-70
Day-Lewis, Daniel, 26
De Niro, Robert, 55, 61, 62-63, 134, 247, 337, 364-7, 377, 379, 380, 382-3
De Palma, Brian, 393, 394, 410, 411
Death of the Incredible Hulk, 168-9
Death Race movies, 146-9
Death Wish, 71-9, 245-6
Deep, The, 298-300
Deepwater Horizon, 224-6
Dent, Catherine, 125, `126-7, 128-9, 130
Departed, The, 63
DiCaprio, Leonardo, 298
Dog Day Afternoon, 310-2
Dogtooth, 92-93
Donner, Richard, 433-4, 436, 441
Don't Fuck in the Woods, 355-7
Douglas, Michael, 259
Douglas, Sarah, 441-2, 465
Downey Jr., Robert, 213, 270
Drake, Larry, 81-3
Driver, Adam, 408-9
Duchovny, David, 5
Duffy, Thomas, 74-6
Dunaway, Faye, 21, 132, 445
Duncan, Michael Clarke, 254, 257
Dust Devil, 98
Dust Up, 115-7
East, Jeff, 435, 436
Eastwood, Clint, 41, 43, 78, 251, 363, 368, 434, 481, 488
Elektra, 358, 360-1
Eliminators, 332-5
Elliott, Brennan, 227, 228-9
Emmy Awards, 65, 68, 73, 76, 81, 106, 107, 111, 119, 125, 229
Enter the Dragon, 200-1
Ermey, R. Lee, 235, 236, 238-40, 242, 243
Escape from New York, 159-60
Esteben, Samantha, 84-7
Europa Report, 506
Expendables 3, The, 29
Extreme Justice, 99

Fairchild, Krisha, 88-91
Farrell, Colin, 294
Farris, Lorraine, 273-4
Fast and the Furious, The (series), 469-70
Fast Times at Ridgemont High, 49-50
Field, Chelsea, 94-99
Fiennes, Ralph, 4-8
Fierman, Hannah, 18-20
Fight Club, 59-60
Finochio, Stephanie, 100-3
Fisher, Carrie, 411, 412-3, 414, 415, 417, 418, 431-32, 486
Flash Gordon, 161-3
Flight 93, 228-30
Ford, Harrison, 189, 190, 191, 192, 401
Foster, Meg, 96, 97
Franz, Dennis, 106-110
Freeman, Morgan, 43
Friedkin, William, 217-8, 219
From Dusk Till Dawn (TV show) 86-7
Fugitive, The, 189-92, 196, 277
Full Metal Jacket, 6, 193, 231-250, 477
G-Spot, 8-9
Gaffey, Aaron, 115-7
Gandolfini, James, 3
Garner, Jennifer, 358, 360
Garrett, Hank, 72, 73-48
Gere, Richard, 66
Ghostbusters movies, 395-8
Gibson, Leah, 464
Gibson, Mel, 29, 219, 315, 317, 456, 458-9
Glee, 444
God Bless America, 258-62
Godfather films, 134, 363, 364, 367, 368, 379, 380, 382, 391, 393
Godot, Gail, 443
Goggins, Walton, 124, 126, 127-8, 129-30
Goldblum, Jeff, 76, 504
Golden Globes, 9, 106, 351
Goldstein, Jenette, 496-7, 499-500
Goodfellas, 54, 55, 56, 61, 63, 377-80
Gorillas in the Mist, 104
Gower, Carlena, 131-4
Green Dragon, 196-7
Greystoke: The Legend of Tarzan, Lord of the Apes, 103
Guest, Lance, 135-7
Guns, Girls, and Gambling, 214-6
Hamburger Hill, 250-3
Hamill, Mark, 411-2, 413, 414, 416, 417-418
Hamsher, Jane, 271, 278

Hanks, Tom, 298, 381
Hannah, Daryl, 30-31, 464
Hardcore, 156-9
Harley Davidson and the Marlboro Man, 97, 347
Harrelson, Woody, 139, 263, 265, 267, 270, 279, 293, 295
Harsh Times, 86
Hawke, Ethan, 26, 84-5, 451-2
Hayes, Megan, 138, 141-2
Heart of America, 176-9
Heaven & Earth, 193-6
Hee, Dana, 150-5
Hellraiser II: Hellbound, 15-18
Henn, Carrie, 500-2
Henstridge, Natasha, 154, 215
Hercules: The Legendary Journeys, 204, 205
Hills Have Eyes, The, 13-15
Hoffman, Dustin, 167, 477
Holland, Tom, 50
Hollitt, Raye, 120, 122-3
Horsemen, The, 79-80
Hours, 470-2, 473-4
Howell, Maria, 139
Hubley, Season, 156-60
Hunger Games movies, 19, 27, 138-142, 170
Hunter, Jumayn, 509-12
Hurt Locker, 8
I Spit on Your Grave, vi-vii
Inglorious Basterds, 323, 336-45
Invasion of the Body Snatchers, 504-6
Jabba the Hutt, 424-7
Jackson, Sally, 274-6
Jaffer, Melissa, 316, 317-8
James Bond movies, 122, 180-3, 249, 430
Jecchins, Kieron, 244-5
Jesse, 100-2
JFK, 194, 265
Jones, James Earl, 401, 402, 407, 421
Jones, O-Lan, 266-9
Jones, Sam, 161-3
Jones, Tommy Lee, 105, 189, 190-1, 196, 277, 411
Joy, Robert, 77
Joyner, Michelle, 164-7
Jurassic Park: The Lost World, 76, 393
Karate Kid, The movies, 185-8, 328
Katarina, Anna, 168-71
Keaton, Camille, vi-vii
Keitel, Harvey, 61
Keuck, Andre, 172-5
Kidder, Margot, 437, 442

Kidman, Nicole, 153, 506
Kidnap, 220-3
Kiel, Richard, 180-4
Kill Bill films, 31, 323, 326, 337, 341, 464
Killing Fields, The, 282, 287-92
Kilmer, Val, 242, 265
King, Stephen, 50, 77, 142, 381, 513
Kiss the Girls, 219
Kove, Martin, 185-188, 328
Krabbe, Jereon, 189-92
Krisha, 88-91, 92
Kubrick, Stanley, 231-2, 233, 234, 235, 236, 237, 238, 239, 241, 242, 243, 245, 246, 247, 248, 249, 271
L.A. Law, 81-2
Lagano, Alicia, 37-40
Last Boy Scout, The, 98
Last Starfighter, The, 135-7
Laurent, Melanie, 341-43
Lawless, Lucy, 203, 204
Lawrence, Jennifer, 26-7, 138
Le, Hiep Thi, 193-7
Lee, Bruce, 150, 198-202, 364, 424
Leick, Hudson, 203-5
Leone, Sergio, 363-4, 365, 368
Lewis, Juliette, 6, 8, 263, 265-272, 275-9, 281
Lindsley, Blake, 206-10
Lloyd, Jake, 402
Longest Yard, The, 361
Lords, Traci, 512-4
Lucas, George, 161, 400, 401, 402, 403, 407, 410, 411, 412, 414, 416, 418, 419, 420, 421, 422, 423, 424, 425, 426, 440
MacFarlane, Seth, 163
Mad Max films, 313, 315-8
Maillet, Robert, 211-3
Malkovitch, John, 290
Margolin, Stuart, 73
Marinca, Anamarie, 506-9
Marine Story, A Marine, 515, 516-20
Marshall, Peter, 79-80
Marshall, Rebecca, 319, 320-2, 324, 326
Mason, Brandy, 356-7
Masters of the Universe, 94-97
Mattson, Helena, 214-6
Mayhew, Peter, 400, 419-20, 502
McArthur, Alex, 217-9
McDiarmid, Ian, 420
McGinn, Chris, 220-3
McGinnis, Graham, 224-6

McQueen, Steve, 131, 132, 133
Mean Streets, 61-3
Men in Black, 104-5
Michaell, Monnae, 227-8, 229-30
Midnight Express, 64-8, 388
Mighty Joe Young, 105
Miller, Ernest, 350-1
Million Dollar Baby, 40-3
Modine, Matthew, 231-8, 241, 242, 243, 248, 249
Moore, Michael, 228
Moore, Roger, 180, 182, 184, 249
Moran, Kent, 254-7
Mortal Kombat movies, 150, 154-5
Mummy films, 466-8
Murray, Bill, 260, 395
Murray, Joel, 258, 260, 262
Natural Born Killers, 209, 260, 263-281
Neeson, Liam, 82-3, 402
Network, 132, 262, 310, 445
Ngor, Haing, 186, 195, 196, 282-92
Nguyen, Long, 293, 294-5, 296-7
Norris, Chuck, 187, 198, 201, 202, 268
NYPD Blue, 68, 106-114, 127, 128
O'Halloran, Jack, 438-40, 441, 442, 445
O'Shea, Daniel, 250-300
Olafsson, Olafur Darri, 298-300
Outbreak, 167
Pacino, Al, 73, 311-2, 393, 394
Paige, Tarah, 34-6
Pais, John, 301-2, 303-4
Papoulia, Angeliki, 92-93
Park, Ray, 421-2
Perrino, Joe, 381-3
Pesci, Joe, 55, 56, 58, 380
Phillips, Bobbie, 306-9
Pina, Lionel, 310-2
Piper, Roddy, 308, 348, 352
Pitre, Christian, 313-5
Pitt, Brad, 59-60, 338-9, 342, 383
Platoon, 193, 209, 235, 250, 252, 346
Predator movies, 145-6, 371, 490, 503, 513
Prowse, David, 400-1, 427, 438
Pulp Fiction, 264, 344
Quaid, Dennis, 66, 153
Quaid, Randy, 66
Quincy, Allene, 319-20, 324-5, 326
Raging Bull, 54, 56, 63, 337, 364, 367, 379, 382
Raimi, Sam, 82-3
Rambo movies, 67, 187, 488

Rampage (1992 film), 217-9
Ramsey, Anessa, 146-9
Reherman, Lee, 119, 121-2, 123
Rankin, Claire, 77-8
Raze, 319-26
Reeve, Christopher, 431, 433-9, 442, 445
Renna, Melinda, 279-80
Reservoir Dogs, 264, 341, 344
Reynolds, Patrick, 332-335
Robbins, Tim, 448, 449
Robinson, Stuart, 74
Rolleston, James, 459-61
Romanus, Richard, 61-3
Roth, Eli, 336-41
Rourke, Mickey, 97, 346-52
Roxborough, Jeannette, 327-331
Rubinek, Saul, 78
Running Man, The, 138, 142-145, 170
Russell, Kurt, 159-60, 162, 190, 411
Russo, Jennie, 353-5, 356
Sands of Iwo Jima, 476, 477, 478
Sapp, Bob, 358-62
Scarface, 50, 274, 379, 391, 393-4
Schindler's List, 5
Schlund, Stephanie Leigh, 139-40
Schutzman, Scott, 363, 364-5, 367, 368
Schwarzenegger, Arnold, 95, 138, 142, 143, 162, 307, 308, 320, 332, 333, 362, 369-374, 376, 400, 403, 434, 490
Scorsese, Martin, 54-6, 59, 61-2, 63, 363, 368, 379, 380, 391, 393
Scott, Cynthia Dale, 497-9, 500
Scott, George C., 157
Serafinowicz, Peter, 421
Serrone, Christopher, 377, 378-81
Seven Psychopaths, 216, 293-7
Shafer, Lauren Mae, 384-6
Shaw, Sebastian, 406-7
She Kills, 353-5, 356
Sherlock Holmes, 211, 212, 213
Shield, The, 124-30
Shirley, Alesia, 387-90
Silence of the Lambs, 220, 222
Silva, Geno, 391-4
Silver Linings Playbook, 27
Sin City, 314, 326, 347
Sisti, Michelan, 301, 302-3
Sizemore, Tom, 8, 272, 274, 278
Slater, Helen, 446, 455

Smolinski, Aaron, 433-4, 438
Soo Soo, Papillon, 248-50
Sopranos, The, 1-3, 110, 125, 304
Species movies, 154, 215
Spielberg, Steven, 50, 393, 415, 417, 434
Splice, 44-6
Stallone, Sylvester, 74, 77, 146, 164, 165-6, 320, 438, 488
Stamp, Terence, 440-1
Star Wars films, 65, 188, 399-432, 438, 440
Starship Troopers, 206-10, 499
Steinfeld, Hailee, 482-4
Stewart, Patrick, 12
Stick It, 34-6
Stone, Oliver, 64, 66, 193-5, 196, 223, 251, 263-5, 267, 269, 270, 271, 272, 273, 275, 279, 280, 281, 346, 394
Strange Days, 4-9, 278
Suicide Squad, 34, 47-8
Supergirl, 444-7
Superman films, 432-43, 464-5
Swank, Hilary, 40-3, 188
Sweet 16, 387-90
Tarantino, Quentin, 77, 86, 264, 337, 338, 340, 341, 342, 343, 344, 345, 391
Taxi Driver, 63, 382, 411
Taylor, Kirk, 245-8
Ted, 163
Teenage Mutant Ninja Turtles, 188, 301-305
Terminator films, ix, 87, 145, 154, 306, 307, 308, 332, 333, 369-76, 415, 486, 488, 492, 500
There Will Be Blood, 26
Theron, Charlize, 105, 317
Tijerina, Cecilia, 50-1
Tommyknockers, The, 512-4
Tooley, Jenni, 448-452
Towering Inferno, The, 131-4, 410
Travolta, John, 66, 411

Training Day, 84-6
Treviño, Marco, 453-5
True Grit (1969), 476, 477-80, 482
True Girt (2010), 481-84
Trujillo, Raoul, 456-9
Turton, Kett, 176-9
United 93, 230
V/H/S, 18-20
Vandervoort, Laura, 446-7
Vanova, Apollonia, 462-5
Velasquez, Patricia, 466-8
Wahlberg, Mark, 163, 225
Walken, Christopher, 249, 293
Walker, Paul, 469-74
Walking Dead, The, 19
Waltz, Christopher, 342, 343-5
Washington, Denzel, 84, 85, 346
Watchmen, 462-5
Waterston, Sam, 289
Wayne, John, 72, 116, 246, 247, 475-81
Weaver, Sigourney, 104, 485-94, 498, 500, 502
Weber, Dreya, 515-20
What's Love Got to do With It?, 6
Wilding, Spencer, 407-8
Williams, Lynn, 120-1
Willis, Bruce, 77, 98, 216, 242, 328
Willow, 397
Winter's Bone, 26-7
Witchblade, 327-8
World Trade Center, 101, 228
Wrestler, The, 346-52
X-Files, The, 5, 308
X-Men, 27, 48, 220, 444, 445
Xena: Warrior Princess, 203-5
Yelchin, Anton, 12
Zemsta, Martha, 354
Zero Day, 172-5, 177

www.ingramcontent.com/pod-product-compliance
Lightning Source LLC
Chambersburg PA
CBHW060311230426
43663CB00009B/1663